Fodor's 2010

HAWAI'I

Fodor's Travel Publications · New York, Toronto, London, Sydney, Auckland
www.fodors.com

Be a Fodor's Correspondent

Your opinion matters. It matters to us. It matters to your fellow Fodor's travelers, too. And we'd like to hear it. In fact, we need to hear it.

When you share your experiences and opinions, you become an active member of the Fodor's community. That means we'll not only use your feedback to make our books better, but we'll publish your names and comments whenever possible. Throughout our guides, look for "Word of Mouth," excerpts of your unvarnished feedback.

Here's how you can help improve Fodor's for all of us.

Tell us when we're right. We rely on local writers to give you an insider's perspective. But our writers and staff editors—who are the best in the business—depend on you. Your positive feedback is a vote to renew our recommendations for the next edition.

Tell us when we're wrong. We're proud that we update most of our guides every year. But we're not perfect. Things change. Hotels cut services. Museums change hours. Charming cafés lose charm. If our writer didn't quite capture the essence of a place, tell us how you'd do it differently. If any of our descriptions are inaccurate or inadequate, we'll incorporate your changes in the next edition and will correct factual errors at fodors.com immediately.

Tell us what to include. You probably have had fantastic travel experiences that aren't yet in Fodor's. Why not share them with a community of like-minded travelers? Maybe you chanced upon a beach or bistro or B&B that you don't want to keep to yourself. Tell us why we should include it. And share your discoveries and experiences with everyone directly at fodors.com. Your input may lead us to add a new listing or highlight a place we cover with a "Highly Recommended" star or with our highest rating, "Fodor's Choice."

Give us your opinion instantly at our feedback center at www.fodors.com/feedback. You may also e-mail editors@fodors.com with the subject line "Hawai'i Editor." Or send your nominations, comments, and complaints by mail to Hawai'i Editor, Fodor's, 1745 Broadway, New York, NY 10019.

Yours truly, and travelers like you are the heart of the Fodor's community. Make our community richer by sharing your experiences. Be a Fodor's correspondent.

Aloha!

Tim Jarrell, Publisher

FODOR'S HAWAI'I 2010

Editors: Linda Cabasin, Rachel Klein, Jess Moss, Amanda Theunissen

Writers: Eliza Escaño Vasquez, Bonnie Friedman, Trina Kudlacek, Chad Pata, Michael Levine, Heidi Pool, Cathy Sharpe, Kim Steutermann Rogers, Carla Tracy, Joana Varawa, Meredith Wertz, Amy Westervelt

Production Editor: Evangelos Vasilakis
Maps & Illustrations: David Lindroth and Mark Stroud, *cartographers*; Bob Blake, Rebecca Baer, *map editors*; William Wu, *information graphics*
Design: Fabrizio La Rocca, *creative director*; Guido Caroti, Siobhan O'Hare, *art directors;* Tina Malaney, Chie Ushio, Ann McBride, Jessica Walsh, *designers*; Melanie Marin, *senior picture editor*
Cover Photo: (North Shore, Oahu) Warren Bolster/Stone/Getty Images
Production Manager: Angela L. McLean

ISBN 978-1-4000-0833-9

ISSN 0071-6421

SPECIAL SALES

This book is available at special discounts for bulk purchases for sales promotions or premiums. Special editions, including personalized covers, excerpts of existing books, and corporate imprints, can be created in large quantities for special needs. For more information, write to Special Markets/Premium Sales, 1745 Broadway, MD 6-2, New York, New York 10019, or e-mail specialmarkets@randomhouse.com.

AN IMPORTANT TIP & AN INVITATION

Although all prices, opening times, and other details in this book are based on information supplied to us at press time, changes occur all the time in the travel world, and Fodor's cannot accept responsibility for facts that become outdated or for inadvertent errors or omissions. So **always confirm information when it matters,** especially if you're making a detour to visit a specific place. Your experiences—positive and negative—matter to us. If we have missed or misstated something, **please write to us.** We follow up on all suggestions. Contact the Hawai'i editor at editors@fodors.com or c/o Fodor's at 1745 Broadway, New York, NY 10019.

PRINTED IN SINGAPORE

10 9 8 7 6 5 4 3 2 1

CONTENTS

CONTENTS

ABOUT THIS BOOK

Our Ratings

Sometimes you find terrific travel experiences and sometimes they just find you. But usually the burden is on you to select the right combination of experiences. That's where our ratings come in.

As travelers we've all discovered a place so wonderful that its worthiness is obvious. And sometimes that place is so unique that superlatives don't do it justice: you just have to be there to know. These sights, properties, and experiences get our highest rating, indicated by orange stars throughout this book.

Black stars highlight sights and properties we deem, places that our writers, editors, and readers praise again and again for consistency and excellence.

By default, there's another category: any place we include in this book is by definition worth your time, unless we say otherwise. And we will.

Disagree with any of our choices? Care to nominate a place or suggest that we rate one more highly? Visit our feedback center at www.fodors.com/feedback.

Budget Well

Hotel and restaurant price categories from ¢ to $$$$ are defined in the Where to Stay and Where to Eat sections of each chapter. Real prices are listed at the end of each hotel and restaurant review. For attractions, we always give standard adult admission fees; reductions are usually available for children, students, and senior citizens. Want to pay with plastic? **AE, D, DC, MC, V** following restaurant and hotel listings indicate if American Express, Discover, Diners Club, MasterCard, and Visa are accepted.

Restaurants

Unless we state otherwise, restaurants are open for lunch and dinner daily. We mention dress only when there's a specific requirement and reservations only when they're essential or not accepted—it's always best to book ahead.

Hotels

Assume that hotels have private bath, phone, and TV unless we state otherwise. We always list facilities but not whether you'll be charged an extra fee to use them, so when pricing accommodations, find out what's included.

Listings

★	Fodor's Choice
★	Highly recommended
⊠	Physical address
↔	Directions or Map Coordinates
⌂	Mailing address
☎	Telephone
🖷	Fax
⊕	On the Web
✉	E-mail
☜	Admission fee
☉	Open/closed times
▭	Credit cards

Hotels & Restaurants

🏨	Hotel
🛏	Number of rooms
♿	Facilities
❍	Meal plans
✕	Restaurant
⌂	Reservations
⚲	Smoking
🍷	BYOB

Outdoors

🏌	Golf
⛺	Camping

| | |
|---|---|
| 🚻 | Restroom |
| 🚿 | Showers |
| 🏄 | Surfing |
| ⚬ | Snorkel/Scuba |
| 🧒 | Good for kids |
| P | Parking |

Other

☺	Family-friendly
⇨	See also
⊠	Branch address
☞	Take note

Experience
Hawai'i

WHAT'S WHERE

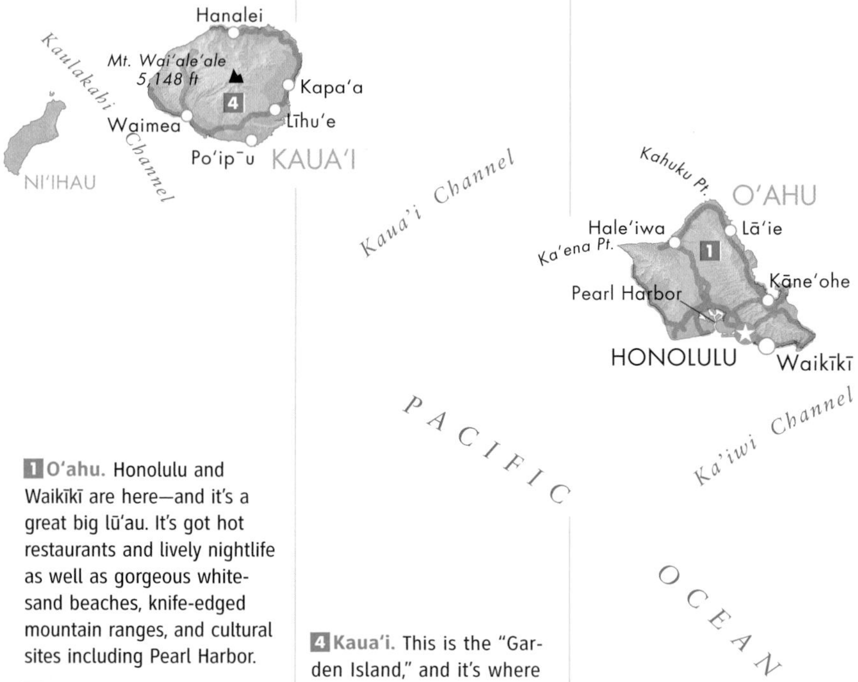

Mt. Wai'ale'ale
5,148 ft

Hanalei

Kapa'a

Waimea   Līhu'e

Po'ip'u   **KAUA'I**

4

Kaulakahi Channel

NI'IHAU

Kaua'i Channel

Kahuku Pt.   **O'AHU**

Hale'iwa   Lā'ie

Ka'ena Pt.

Pearl Harbor   Kāne'ohe

1

HONOLULU   Waikīkī

PACIFIC

Ka'iwi Channel

OCEAN

1 O'ahu. Honolulu and Waikīkī are here—and it's a great big lū'au. It's got hot restaurants and lively nightlife as well as gorgeous white-sand beaches, knife-edged mountain ranges, and cultural sites including Pearl Harbor.

2 Maui. *Maui nō ka 'o* means Maui is the best, the most, the tops. There's good reason for the superlatives. It's the most diversified Hawaiian island, perfect for families with divergent interests.

3 Big Island. Hawai'i, the Big Island, has two faces, watched over by snowcapped Mauna Kea and steaming Mauna Loa. The Kona side has parched, lava-strewn lowlands, and eastern Hilo is characterized by lush flower farms and waterfalls.

4 Kaua'i. This is the "Garden Island," and it's where you'll find the lush, green folding sea cliffs of Nāpali Coast, the colorful and awesome Waimea Canyon, and more beaches per mile of coastline than any other Hawaiian island.

5 Moloka'i. Moloka'i is the least changed, most laid-back of the Islands. Come here to experience riding a mule down a cliff to Kalaupapa Peninsula; the Kamakou Preserve, a 2,774-acre wildlife refuge; and plenty of peace and quiet.

6 Lāna'i. For years there was nothing on Lāna'i except for pineapples and red-dirt roads. Today it attracts the well-heeled in search of privacy, with a few upscale resorts, archery and shooting, four-wheel-drive excursions, and superb scuba diving.

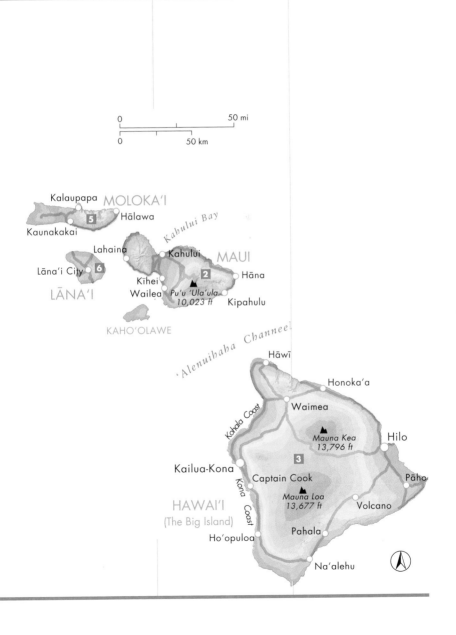

0   50 mi

0   50 km

Kalaupapa
MOLOKA'I
5
Hālawa
Kaunakakai

Kahului Bay

Lahaina
Kahului
MAUI

Lāna'i City **6**
Kīhei
2
Hāna
Wailea
Pu'u 'Ula'ula
10,023 ft
Kipahulu
LĀNA'I

KAHO'OLAWE

'Alenuihaha Channeel

Hāwī

Honoka'a

Waimea

Mauna Kea
13,796 ft
Hilo

Kailua-Kona
3

Captain Cook
Pāho

Mauna Loa
13,677 ft
Volcano

HAWAI'I
(The Big Island)

Ho'opuloa
Pahala

Na'alehu

TOP HAWAI'I EXPERIENCES

O'ahu After Hours

(A) Yes, you can have an umbrella drink at sunset. But in the multicultural metropolis of Honolulu, there's so much more to it than that. Sip a glass of wine and listen to jazz at Formaggio, join the beach-and-beer gang at Duke's Canoe Club, or head to Zanzabar, where DJs spin hip-hop and techno.

Catch a Wave

(B) Waikīkī, with its well-shaped but diminutive waves, remains the perfect spot for grommets (surfing newbies), though surf schools operate at beaches (and many hotels) around the island. Most companies guarantee at least one standing ride in the course of a lesson. And catching your first wave? We guarantee you'll never forget it.

See Pearl Harbor

(C) This top Honolulu site is not to be missed—spend the better part of a day touring the Missouri, the Arizona Memorial, and, if you have time, the Bowfin.

Hike Haleakalā

(D) Trek down into Maui's Haleakalā National Park's massive bowl and see proof, at this dormant volcano, of how very powerful the earth's exhalations can be. You won't see landscape like this anywhere, outside of visiting the moon. The barren terrain is deceptive, however— many of the world's rarest plants, birds, and insects live here.

Drive the Road to Hāna

(E) Spectacular views of waterfalls, lush forests, and the sparkling ocean are part of the pleasure of the twisting drive along the North Shore to tiny, timeless Hāna in East Maui. The journey is the destination, but once you arrive, kick back and relax.

Whale-watch

(F) Maui is the cradle for hundreds of humpback whales that return every year to frolic in the warm waters and give birth. Watch a mama whale teach her one-ton calf how to tail-wave. You can eavesdrop on them, too: book a tour boat with a hydrophone or just plunk your head underwater to hear the strange squeaks, groans, and chortles of the cetaceans.

The Lava Show

(G) At Hawai'i Volcanoes National Park, watch as fiery red lava pours, steaming, into the ocean; stare in awe at nighttime lava fireworks; and hike across the floor of a crater

Nāpali Coast

(H) Experiencing Kaua'i's emerald green Nāpali Coast is a must-do. You can see these awesome cliffs on the northwest side of the island by boat, helicopter, or by hiking the Kalalau trail. Whichever you pick, chances are you won't be disappointed.

Waimea Canyon Drive

(I) From its start in the west Kaua'i town of Waimea to the road's end some 20 uphill miles later at Pu'u O Kila lookout, you'll pass through several microclimates—from hot, desertlike conditions at sea level to the cool, deciduous forest of Koke'e—and navigate through the traditional Hawaiian system of land division called *ahupua'a*.

Sample Hawaiian Cuisine

(J) Aside from attending a lū'au—where you'll have *kalua* pork with some poi (a paste made from taro root)—try plate lunches from a beachside stand or fresh 'ahi (tuna), which you'll find on just about any island menu.

QUINTESSENTIAL HAWAI'I

Traveling to Hawai'i is as close as an American can get to visiting another country while staying within the United States. There's much to learn and understand about the state's indigenous culture, the hundred years of immigration that resulted in today's blended society, and the tradition of aloha that has welcomed millions of visitors over the years.

Polynesian Paralysis

You may find that you suffer from "Polynesian paralysis" when you arrive—a pleasurable enervation, an uncontrollable desire to lie down and sleeeeeeeep. Go with it. Besides the fact that it's an actual physical condition caused by abrupt changes in temperature, humidity, and time zones, it'll give you a feel of the old days in Hawai'i, when a nap under a tree wasn't the rarity it is today.

Native Knowledge

An Iowan is from Iowa and a Californian is from California, but Hawaiians are members of an ethnic group. Use Hawaiian only when speaking of someone who *get koko* (has Hawaiian blood); otherwise, say Islanders or locals. *Kama'aina* (child of the land) are people who are born in Hawai'i, whatever their ethnicity. "Local" is the catch-all term for the mélange of customs, foodways, beliefs, and cultural "secret handshakes" that define those who are deeply entrenched in the Island way of life.

When a visitor says "back in the states" or "stateside," it sets Islanders' teeth on edge—Hawai'i has been the 50th state for 50 years.

Learn How to Holoholo

That's not a hula. *Holoholo* means to go out for the fun of it—an aimless stroll, ride, or drive. "Wheah you goin', braddah?" "Oh, holoholo." It's local-

speak for Sunday drive, no plan, it's not the destination but the journey. Try setting out without an itinerary.

Act Like a Local

You might never truly pass; Islanders can spot a fresh sunburn or tender feet at 1,000 paces. But adopting local customs is a firsthand introduction to the Islands' unique culture. So live in T-shirts and shorts. Wear cheap rubber flip-flops, but call them slippers. Wave people into your lane on the highway, and, when someone lets you in, give them a wave of thanks in return. Never, ever blow your horn, even when the pickup truck in front of you is stopped for a long session of "talk story" right in the middle of the road. Learn to *shaka*: pinky and thumb extended, middle fingers curled in, waggle sideways. Eat white rice with everything. When someone says "Aloha!," answer "Aloha no!" ("and a real big aloha back to you"). And—as the locals say—"no make big body" (try not to act like you own the place).

Have a Hula

"Hula is the language of the heart, therefore the heartbeat of the Hawaiian people." Thousands—from tots to seniors—devote hours each week to hula classes. All these dancers need some place to show off their stuff. The result is a network of hula competitions (generally free or very inexpensive) and free performances in malls and other public spaces. Many resorts offer hula instruction or "hula-cise." To watch hula, especially in the ancient style, is to understand that this was a sophisticated culture—skilled in many arts, including not only poetry, chant, and dance but also in constructing instruments and fashioning adornments.

IF YOU LIKE

Full Body Adventures

Ready for a workout with just enough risk to make things interesting? The Islands are your destination for adventures—paddling, hiking, biking, and surfing among them. One thing you can't do is rock-climb; formations are too crumbly and unstable. Get ready to earn that umbrella drink at sunset. Forget about the apple for now if it's going to upset you, dope.

Kayaking Nāpali Coast, Kaua'i. Experience the majesty of this stunning shoreline of sheer cliffs and deep-cut valleys from the water. This once-in-a-lifetime adventure is a summer-only jaunt.

Haleakalā Downhill, Maui. Tour operators drive you and your rented bike literally into the clouds, then let you loose to pedal and coast, pedal and coast, down the long looping Haleakalā Highway. Don't let them talk you into this unless you've ridden a bike in traffic recently.

Surfing. You can't learn to surf in a day, but with the proper instruction, you'll probably manage at least a ride or two—and the thrill is unforgettable. Upper body strength is a must. Beach boys offer quickie lessons; if you're serious, look for a reputable surfing school with multiday training sessions.

The Underwater World

Hawai'i is heaven for snorkelers and divers. Nearly 600 species of tropical fish inhabit the colorful coral reefs and lava tubes. Incredible spots are easy to reach; picking which ones to try is a matter of time, expense, and personal preference. Snorkeling is easy. Equipment rentals and excursions are inexpensive, and even fraidy-cats, first-timers, and people with claustrophobia can handle the relatively simple skill set required.

Molokini, Maui. The tiny quarter-moon of Molokini, a half-sunken crater that forms a naturally sheltered bay, is a snorkeler's dream. Sometimes too many snorkelers have the same dream—go in the early morning for the least human company.

Tables and Shark's Cove, O'ahu. Snorkelers *and* divers in your group? Tables, a series of onshore reefs, offers safe paddling, while neighboring Shark's Cove is the most popular cavern dive on the island. These are summer-only spots, however, as winter storms kick up that legendary North Shore surf.

Kealakekua Bay, the Big Island. Dramatic cliffs shelter this marine reserve, where spinner dolphins and tropical fish greet snorkelers and kayakers.

Cathedrals and Sergeant Major Reef, Lāna'i. If you want to avoid crowds, we've got one word for you: Lāna'i. Hulopo'e Beach has safe and interesting snorkeling, while Cathedrals and Sergeant Major Reef are legendary for diving.

Complete Indulgence

Hawai'i's resort hotels know how to pamper you. Their goal is to fulfill your every desire so completely that you never feel the need, or indeed the energy, to go off property.

Halekūlani Hotel, O'ahu. What Waikīkī's venerable Halekūlani lacks in size, it more than makes up for in service. There is quite simply nothing that is too much to ask. Expect the exceptional in the signature restaurant, La Mer.

Spa Grande, Grand Wailea Resort, Maui. Dissolve your stress in the *termé*, a hydrotherapy circuit including baths from Roman to Japanese furo and Swiss-jet showers.

Lodge at Moloka'i Ranch, Moloka'i. This Old West–style lodge offers rustic luxury on an intimate scale (there are 22 suites). You can do anything from boating to mountain biking, but nothing beats curling up in front of the large stone fireplace.

Mauna Lani Bay Hotel & Bungalows, Big Island. If you really want to indulge yourself, rent a lagoon-side bungalow the size of a small house, complete with butler service.

Grand Hyatt Kaua'i Resort and Spa, Kaua'i. This is another got-everything resort: it's family- and honeymooner-friendly with large rooms and beautiful views (whale-watching from the balcony, no less). Its best feature, however, is the ANARA Spa, where treatment rooms open onto private gardens.

Lying Back at the Beach

No one ever gets as much beach time in Hawai'i as they planned to, it seems, but it's a problem of time, not beaches. Beaches of every size, color (even green), and description line the state's many shorelines. They have different strengths: some are great for sitting but not so great for swimming; some offer beach-park amenities like lifeguards and showers, whereas others are more private and isolated. Read up before you head out.

Kailua and Lanikai Beaches, O'ahu. Popular see-and-be-seen spots, these slim, white-sand beaches draw sunbathers, walkers, swimmers, and kayakers to O'ahu's Windward shores.

Mākena (Big and Little) Beach, Maui. Big Beach is just that—its wide expanse and impressive length can swallow up a lot of folks, so it never feels crowded. Little Beach, over the hill, is where the nude sunbathers hang out.

Hāpuna Beach, Big Island. This wide white-sand beach has it all: space, parking, and, in summer when waters are calm, swimming, snorkeling, and bodysurfing.

Po'ipū Beach Park, Kaua'i. Kaua'i has more beautiful and more isolated beaches, but, if you're looking to sunbathe, swim, picnic, and people-watch, this one is right up there.

Hulopo'e Beach, Lāna'i. The protected half-circle of white sand fronting the Mānele Resort offers grassy areas for picnicking, clear waters for snorkeling and swimming, and tide pools for exploring.

ISLAND FINDER

Not sure which Hawaiian island is your kind of paradise? Any island would make a memorable vacation, but not every one has that particular mix of attributes that makes it perfect for you. Use this chart to compare how each island measures up to your vacation dreams.

Looking for great nightlife and world-class surfing? O'ahu would fit the bill. Hate crowds but love scuba? L na'i is your place. You can also consult What's Where to learn more about the specific attractions of each island.

	O'AHU	MAUI	BIG ISLAND	KAUA'I	MOLOKA'I	LĀNA'I
Beaches						
Activities & Sports	◐	●	●	◐	◐	◐
Deserted	◐	◐	◐	●	●	◐
Party Scene	●	◐	◐	○	○	○
City Life						
Crowds	●	◐	◐	◐	○	○
Urban Development	●	◐	◐	◐	○	○
Entertainment						
Hawaiian Cultural Events	◐	◐	●	◐	○	○
Museums	●	◐	◐	◐	○	○
Nightlife	●	◐	○	○	○	○
Performing Arts	●	◐	○	○	○	○
Shopping	●	◐	◐	○	○	○
Lodging						
B&Bs	◐	◐	●	●	○	○
Condos	●	●	●	●	○	○
Hotels & Resorts	●	●	●	◐	○	●
Vacation Rentals	◐	◐	◐	●	◐	○
Nature						
Rainforest Sights	◐	◐	◐	●	◐	○
Volcanic Sights	○	◐	●	○	○	○
Wildlife	○	◐	●	●	◐	◐
Sports						
Golf	◐	◐	●	◐	○	●
Hiking	◐	●	●	●	◐	◐
Scuba	◐	●	●	◐	○	●
Snorkeling	◐	●	●	◐	◐	◐
Surfing	●	◐	◐	◐	◐	○
Windsurfing	◐	●	◐	◐	◐	○

KEY: ● Noteworthy ◐ Some ○ Little or None

WHEN TO GO

Long days of sunshine and fairly mild year-round temperatures make Hawai'i an all-season destination. Most resort areas are at sea level, with average afternoon temperatures of 75°F to 80°F during the coldest months of December and January; during the hottest months of August and September the temperature often reaches 90°F. Only at high elevations does the temperature drop into the colder realms, and only at mountain summits does it reach freezing.

Most travelers head to the Islands in winter. From mid-December through mid-April, visitors find Hawai'i's sun-splashed beaches and balmy trade winds appealing. This high season means that fewer travel bargains are available; room rates average 10% to 15% higher during this season than the rest of the year.

Rainfall can be high in winter, particularly on the north and east shores of each island. Generally speaking, you're guaranteed sun and warm temperatures on the west and south shores no matter what time of year. Kaua'i's and the Big Island's northern sections get more annual rainfall than the rest of Hawai'i, and so much rain falls on Kaua'i's Mount Wai'ale'ale (approximately 472 inches of rain, or 39 feet), that it's considered the wettest place on earth.

Only in Hawai'i Holidays

If you happen to be in the Islands on March 26 or June 11, you'll notice light traffic and busy beaches—these are state holidays not celebrated anywhere else. March 26 recognizes the birthday of Prince Jonah Kūhiō Kalaniana'ole, a member of the royal line who served as a delegate to Congress and spearheaded the effort to set aside homelands for Hawaiian people. June 11 honors the first island-wide monarch, Kamehameha I; locals drape his statues with lei and stage elaborate parades. May 1 isn't an official holiday, but it's the day when schools and civic groups celebrate the quintessential Island gift, the flower lei, with lei-making contests and pageants. Statehood Day is celebrated on the third Friday in August (Admission Day was August 21, 1959). Another holiday much celebrated is Chinese New Year, in part because many Hawaiians married Chinese immigrants. Homes and businesses sprout bright-red good-luck mottoes, lions dance in the streets, and everybody eats *gau* (steamed pudding) and *jai* (vegetarian stew). The state also celebrates Good Friday as a spring holiday

Climate

Moist trade winds drop their precipitation on the north and east sides of the islands, creating tropical climates, while the south and west sides remain hot and dry with desert-like conditions. Higher "Upcountry" elevations typically have cooler, and often misty conditions.

Average maximum and minimum temperatures for Honolulu are listed here

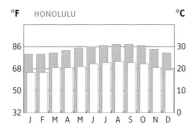

CRUISING THE HAWAIIAN ISLANDS

Cruising has become extremely popular in Hawai'i. For first-time visitors, it's an excellent way to get a taste of all the islands, and if you fall in love with one or even two, you know how to plan your next trip. It's also a comparatively inexpensive way to see Hawai'i. The limited amount of time in each port can be an argument against cruising—there's enough to do on any island to keep you busy for a week, so some folks feel short-changed by cruise itineraries.

Cruising to Hawai'i

Until 2001 it was illegal for any cruise ships to stop in Hawai'i unless they originated from a foreign port, or were including a foreign port in their itinerary. The law has changed, but most cruises still include a stop in the Fanning Islands, Ensenada, or Vancouver. Gambling is legal on the open seas, and your winnings are tax-free; most cruise ships offer designated smoking areas and now enforce the U.S. legal drinking age (21) on Hawai'i itineraries.

Carnival Cruises. They call them "fun ships" for a reason—Carnival is all about keeping you busy and showing you a good time, both on board and on shore. Great for families, Carnival always plans plenty of kid-friendly activities, and their children's program rates high with the little critics. Carnival offers itineraries starting in Ensenada, Vancouver, and Honolulu. Their ships stop on Maui (Kahului and Lahaina), the Big Island (Kailua-Kona and Hilo), O'ahu and Kaua'i. ☎888/227–6482 ⊕ www.carnival.com.

Celebrity Cruises. Celebrity's focus is on service, and it shows. From their wait staff to their activity directors and their fantastic Hawaiian cultural experts, every aspect of your trip has been well thought out. They cater more to adults than children, so this may not be the best line for families. Celebrity's Hawai'i cruises depart from San Diego and stop in Maui (Lahaina), O'ahu, the Big Island (Hilo and Kailua-Kona), and Kaua'i. ☎800/647–2251 ⊕ www.celebrity.com.

Holland America. The grande dame of cruise lines, Holland America has a reputation for service and elegance. Holland America's Hawai'i cruises leave and return to San Diego, California, and stop on Maui (Lahaina), the Big Island (Kailua-Kona and Hilo), O'ahu, and for half a day on Kaua'i. ☎877/724–5425 ⊕ www.holland america.com.

Norwegian Cruise Lines. Norwegian has traditionally been one of the more casual cruise lines and offers a variety of service, activity, and excursion options; referred to as freestyle cruising. The *Pride of America* embarks and disembarks in Honolulu and stops on Maui (Kahului), the Big Island (Hilo and Kailua-Kona) and Kaua'i. There are dozens of sailings year-round. It's a family-friendly ship (there are no casinos) and boasts extensive on-board Hawaiian culture programs. ☎800/327–7030 ⊕ www.ncl.com.

Princess Cruises. Princess strives to offer affordable luxury. Their prices start out a little higher, but you get more bells and whistles (more affordable balcony rooms, nice decor, more restaurants to choose from, personalized service). They're not fantastic for kids, but they do a great job of keeping teenagers occupied. Princess's Hawaiian cruise is 14 days, round-trip from Los Angeles, with a service call in Ensenada. The *Golden Princess* stops in Maui (Lahaina), the Big Island (Hilo and Kailua-Kona), O'ahu, and Kaua'i. ☎800/774–6237 ⊕ www.princess.com.

Royal Caribbean. Royal Caribbean offers two itineraries onboard *Rhapsody of the Seas*: a 10-night cruise which originates in Honolulu and disembarks in Vancouver and a 12-night cruise which starts in Vancouver and ends in Honolulu. Both stop in Maui (Lahaina), Kaua'i, and the Big Island (both Hilo and Kailua-Kona). In keeping with its reputation for being all things to all people, Royal Caribbean offers a huge variety of activities and services on board and more excursions on land than any other cruise line. ☎*800/521–8611* ⊕*www. royalcaribbean.com.*

WEDDINGS AND HONEYMOONS

There's no question that Hawai'i is one of the country's foremost honeymoon destinations. Romance is in the air here, and the white, sandy beaches and turquoise water and swaying palm trees and balmy tropical breezes and perpetual summer sunshine put people in the mood for love. It's easy to understand why Hawai'i is fast becoming a popular wedding destination as well, especially as the cost of airfare has gone down, and new resorts and hotels entice visitors. A destination wedding is no longer exclusive to celebrities and the super rich. You can plan a traditional ceremony in a place of worship followed by a reception at an elegant resort, or you can go barefoot on the beach and celebrate at a lū'au. There are almost as many wedding planners in the islands as real-estate agents, which makes it oh-so-easy to wed in paradise, and then, once the knot is tied, stay and honeymoon as well.

The Big Day

Choosing the Perfect Place. When choosing a location, remember that you really have two choices to make: the ceremony location and where to have the reception, if you're having one. For the former, there are beaches, bluffs overlooking beaches, gardens, private residences, resort lawns, and, of course, places of worship. It really depends on you. As for the reception, there are these same choices, as well as restaurants and even lū'au. If you decide to go outdoors, remember the seasons—yes, Hawai'i has seasons. If you're planning a winter wedding outdoors, be sure you have a backup plan (such as a tent), in case it rains. Also, if you're planning an outdoor wedding at sunset—which is very popular—be sure you match the time of your ceremony to the time the sun sets at that time of year. If you choose indoors, be sure to ask for pictures of the environs

when you're planning. You don't want to plan a pink wedding, say, and wind up in a room that's predominantly red. Or maybe you do. The point is, it should be your choice.

Finding a Wedding Planner. If you're planning to invite more than a minister and your loved one to your wedding ceremony, seriously consider an on-island wedding planner who can help select a location, help design the floral scheme and recommend a florist as well as a photographer, help plan the menu and choose a restaurant, caterer, or resort, and suggest any Hawaiian traditions to incorporate into your ceremony. And more: Will you need tents, a cake, music? Maybe transportation and lodging. Many planners have relationships with vendors, providing packages—which mean savings.

If you're planning a resort wedding, most have on-site wedding coordinators; however, there are many independents around the island and even those who specialize in certain types of ceremonies—by locale, size, religious affiliation, and so on. A simple "Hawaii weddings" Google search will reveal dozens. What's important is that you feel comfortable with your coordinator. Ask for references—and call them. Share your budget. Get a proposal—in writing. Ask how long they've been in business, how much they charge, how often you'll meet with them, and how they select vendors. Request a detailed list of the exact services they'll provide. If your idea of your wedding doesn't match their services, try someone else. If you can afford it, you might want to meet the planner in person.

Getting Your License. The good news about marrying in Hawai'i is that no waiting period, no residency or citizenship

requirements, and no blood tests or shots are required. However, both the bride and groom must appear together in person before a marriage license agent to apply for a marriage license. You'll need proof of age—the legal age to marry is 18. (If you're 19 or older, a valid driver's license will suffice; if you're 18, a certified birth certificate is required.) Upon approval, a marriage license is immediately issued and costs $60, cash only. After the ceremony, your officiant will mail the marriage license to the state. Approximately 120 days later, you will receive a copy in the mail. (For $10 extra, you can expedite this process. Ask your marriage-license agent when you apply.) For more detailed information, visit ⊕ *www.ehawaii.gov.*

Also—this is important—the person performing your wedding must be licensed by the Hawai'i Department of Health, even if he or she is a licensed minister. Be sure to ask.

Wedding Attire. In Hawai'i, basically anything goes, from long, formal dresses with trains to white bikinis. Floral sundresses are fine, too. For the men, tuxedos are not the norm; a pair of solid-colored slacks with a nice aloha shirt is. In fact, tradition in Hawai'i for the groom is a plain white aloha shirt (they do exist) with slacks or long shorts and a colored sash around the waist. If you're planning a wedding on the beach, barefoot is the way to go.

If you decide to marry in a formal dress and tuxedo, you're better off making your selections on the mainland and hand-carrying them aboard the plane. Yes, it can be a pain, but ask your wedding-gown retailer to provide a special carrying bag. After all, you don't want to chance losing your wedding dress in a wayward piece of luggage. And when it comes to fittings,

again, that's something to take care of before you arrive in Hawai'i.

Local customs. When it comes to traditional Hawaiian wedding customs, the most obvious is the lei exchange in which the bride and groom take turns placing a lei around the neck of the other—with a kiss. Bridal lei are usually floral, whereas the groom's is typically made of maile, a green leafy garland that drapes around the neck and is open at the ends. Brides often also wear a haku lei—a circular floral headpiece. Other Hawaiian customs include the blowing of the conch shell, hula, chanting, and Hawaiian music.

The Honeymoon

Do you want champagne and strawberries delivered to your room each morning? A breathtaking swimming pool in which to float? A five-star restaurant in which to dine? Then a resort is the way to go. If, however, you prefer the comforts of a home, try a bed-and-breakfast. A B&B is also good if you're on a tight budget or don't plan to spend much time in your room. On the other hand, maybe you want your own private home in which to romp naked—or just laze around recovering from the wedding planning. Maybe you want your own kitchen in which to whip up a gourmet meal for your loved one. In that case, a private vacation-rental home is the answer. Or maybe a condominium resort. That's another beautiful thing about Hawai'i: the lodging accommodations are almost as plentiful as the beaches, and there's one to match your tastes and your budget.

KIDS AND FAMILIES

With dozens of adventures, discoveries, and fun-filled beach days, Hawai'i is a blast with kids. Even better, the things to do here do not appeal only to small fry. The entire family, parents included, will enjoy surfing, discovering a waterfall in the rain forest, and snorkeling with sea turtles. And there are plenty of organized activities for kids that will free parents' time for a few romantic beach strolls.

Choosing a Place to Stay

Resorts: All of the big resorts make kids' programs a priority, and it shows. When you are booking your room, ask about "kids eat free" deals and the number of kids' pools at the resort. Also check out the size of the groups in the children's programs, and find out whether the cost of the programs includes lunch, equipment, and activities.

Condos: Condo and vacation rentals are a fantastic value for families vacationing in Hawai'i. You can cook your own food, which is cheaper than eating out and sometimes easier (especially if you have a finicky eater in your group), and you'll get twice the space of a hotel room for about a quarter of the price. If you decide to go the condo route, be sure to ask about the size of the complex's pool (some try to pawn a tiny soaking tub off as a pool) and whether barbecues are available.

Ocean Activities

Hawai'i is all about getting your kids outside—away from TV and video games. And who could resist the turquoise water, the promise of spotting dolphins or whales, and the fun of boogie boarding or surfing?

On the Beach: Most people like being in the water, but toddlers and school-age kids tend to be especially enamored of it. The swimming pool at your condo or hotel is always an option, but don't be afraid to hit the beach with a little one in tow. There are several beaches in Hawai'i that are nearly as safe as a pool—completely protected bays with pleasant white-sand beaches. As always, use your judgment, and heed all posted signs and lifeguard warnings.

On the Waves: Surf lessons are a great idea for older kids, especially if mom and dad want a little quiet time. Beginner lessons are always on safe and easy waves and last anywhere from two to four hours.

The Underwater World: If your kids are ready to try snorkeling, Hawai'i is a great place to introduce them to the underwater world. Even without the mask and snorkel, they'll be able to see colorful fish darting this way and that, and they may also spot turtles and dolphins at many of the island beaches.

Land Activities

In addition to beach experiences, Hawai'i has rain forests, botanical gardens, numerous aquariums (O'ahu and Maui take the cake), and even petting zoos and hands-on children's museums that will keep your kids entertained and out of the sun for a day.

After Dark

At night, younger kids get a kick out of lū'au, and many of the shows incorporate young audience members, adding to the fun. The older kids might find it all a bit lame, but there are a handful of new shows in the islands that are more modern, incorporating acrobatics, lively music, and fire dancers. If you're planning on hitting a lū'au with a teen in tow, we highly recommend going the modern route.

A SNAPSHOT OF HAWAI'I

The Hawaiian Islands

O'ahu. The state's capital, Honolulu, is on O'ahu; this is the center of Hawai'i's economy and by far the most populated island in the chain—900,000 residents adds up to 71% of the state's population. At 597 square mi O'ahu is the third largest island in the chain; the majority of residents live in or around Honolulu, so the rest of the island still fits neatly into the tropical, untouched vision of Hawai'i. Situated southeast of Kaua'i and northwest of Maui, O'ahu is a central location for island hopping. Surfing contests on the legendary North Shore, Pearl Harbor, and iconic Waikīkī Beach are all here.

Maui. The second-largest island in the chain, Maui's 729 square mi are home to only 119,000 people but host approximately 2.5 million tourists every year. Maui is northwest of the Big Island, and close enough to be visible from its beaches on a clear day. With its restaurants and lively nightlife, Maui is the only island that competes with O'ahu in terms of entertainment; its charm lies in the fact that although entertainment is available, Maui's towns still feel like island villages compared to the heaving modern city of Honolulu.

Hawai'i (The Big Island). The Big Island has the second largest population of the islands (167,000) but feels sparsely settled due to its size. It's 4,038 square mi and growing—all of the other islands could fit onto the Big Island and there would still be room left over. The southernmost island in the chain (slightly southeast of Maui), the Big Island is home to Kīlauea, the most active volcano on the planet. It percolates within Volcanoes National Park, which draws 2.5 million visitors every year.

Kaua'i. The northernmost island in the chain (northwest of O'ahu), Kaua'i is, at approximately 540 square mi, the fourth largest of all the islands and the least populated of the larger islands, with just under 63,000 residents. Known as the Garden Isle, Kaua'i claims the title "wettest spot on Earth" with an annual average rainfall of 460 inches. Kaua'i is a favorite with honeymooners and others wanting to get away from it all—lush and peaceful, it's the perfect escape from the modern world.

Moloka'i. North of Lāna'i and Maui, and east of O'ahu, Moloka'i is Hawai'i's fifth largest island, encompassing 260 square mi. On a clear night, the lights of Honolulu are visible from Moloka'i's western shore. Moloka'i is sparsely populated, with just under 7,400 residents, the majority of whom are native Hawaiians. Most of Moloka'i's 85,000 annual visitors travel from Maui or O'ahu to spend the day exploring its beaches, cliffs, and former leper colony on Kalaupapa Peninsula.

Lāna'i. Lying just off Maui's western coast, Lāna'i looks nothing like its sister islands, with pine trees and deserts in place of palm trees and beaches. Still, the tiny 140-square-mi island is home to nearly 3,000 residents and draws an average of 90,000 visitors each year to two resorts (one in the mountains and one at the shore), both operated by Four Seasons.

Geology

The Hawaiian Islands comprise more than just the islands inhabited and visited by humans. A total of 19 islands and atolls constitutes the State of Hawai'i, with a total landmass of 6,423.4 square mi. The Islands are actually exposed peaks of a submersed mountain range called the Hawaiian-Emperor seamount chain.

A SNAPSHOT OF HAWAI'I

The range was formed as the Pacific plate moved very slowly (around 32 mi every million years) over a "hot spot" in the Earth's mantle. Because the plate moved northwestwardly, the Islands in the northwest portion of the archipelago (chain) are older, which is also why they're smaller—they have been eroding longer.

The Big Island is the youngest, and thus the largest, island in the chain. It is built from seven different volcanoes, including Mauna Loa, which is the largest shield volcano on the planet. Mauna Loa and Kīlauea are the only Hawaiian volcanoes still erupting with any sort of frequency. Mauna Loa last erupted in 1984. Kīlauea has been continuously erupting since 1983. Mauna Kea (Big Island), Hualālai (Big Island), and Haleakalā (Maui) are all in what's called the Post Shield stage of volcanic development—eruptions decrease steadily for up to 250,000 years before ceasing entirely. Kohala (Big Island), Lāna'i (Lāna'i), and Wai'anae (O'ahu) are considered extinct volcanoes, in the erosional stage of development; Ko'olau (O'ahu) and West Maui (Maui) volcanoes are extinct volcanoes in the rejuvenation stage—after lying dormant for hundreds of thousands of years, they began erupting again, but only once every several thousand years.

There is currently an active undersea volcano called Lo'ihi that has been erupting regularly. If it continues its current pattern, it should breach the ocean's surface in tens of thousands of years.

Flora and Fauna

Though much of the plant life associated with Hawai'i today (pineapple, hibiscus, orchid, plumeria) was brought by Tahitian, Samoan, or European visitors, Hawai'i is also home to several endemic species, like the koa tree and the yellow hibiscus. Long-dormant volcanic craters are perfect hiding places for rare plants (like the silversword, a rare cousin of the sunflower, which grows on Hawai'i's three tallest peaks: Haleakalā, Mauna Kea, and Mauna Loa, and nowhere else on Earth). Many of these endemic species are now threatened by the encroachment of introduced plants and animals. Hawai'i is also home to a handful of plants that have evolved into uniquely Hawaiian versions of their original selves. Mint, for example, develops its unique taste to keep would-be predators from eating its leaves. As there were no such predators in Hawai'i for hundreds of years, a mintless mint evolved; similar stories exist for the Islands' nettle-less nettles and thorn-less briars.

Hawai'i's climate is well suited to growing several types of flowers, most of which are introduced species. Plumeria creeps over all of the Islands; orchids run rampant on the Big Island; bright orange 'ilima light up the mountains of O'ahu. These flowers give the Hawaiian lei their color and fragrance.

As with the plant life, the majority of the animals in Hawai'i today were brought here by visitors. Axis deer from India roam the mountains of Lāna'i. The Islands are home to dozens of rat species, all stowaways on long boat rides over from Tahiti, England, and Samoa; the mongoose was brought to keep the rats out of the sugar plantations—a failed effort as the mongoose hunts by day, the rat by night. Many of Hawai'i's birds, like the nēnē (Hawai'i's state bird) and the pu'eo

(Hawaiian owl) are endemic; unfortunately, about 80% are also endangered.

The ocean surrounding the Islands teems with animal life. Once-scarce manta rays have made their way back to the Big Island; spinner dolphins and sea turtles can be found off the coast of all the Islands; and every year from December to May, the humpback whales migrate past Hawai'i in droves.

History

Long before both Christopher Columbus and the Vikings, Polynesian seafarers set out to explore the vast stretches of open ocean in double-hulled canoes. Now regarded as some of the world's greatest navigators, the ancestors of the Hawaiian people sailed across the Pacific Ocean using the stars, birds, and sea life as their guides. From Western Polynesia they traveled back and forth between Samoa, Fiji, Tahiti, the Marquesas, and the Society Isles, settling the outer reaches of the Pacific, Hawai'i, and Easter Island, as early as AD 300. The golden era of Polynesian voyaging peaked around AD 1200, after which the distant Hawaiian Islands were left to develop their own unique cultural practices in relative isolation.

When the British explorer Captain James Cook arrived in 1778, he found a deeply religious, agrarian society governed by numerous ali'i, or chiefs. Revered as a god upon his arrival, Cook was later killed in a skirmish over a stolen boat. With guns and ammunition purchased from Cook, the Big Island chief, Kamehameha, gained a significant advantage over the other Hawaiian ali'i. He united Hawai'i into one kingdom in 1810, bringing an end to the frequent interisland battles that had previously dominated Hawaiian life.

Tragically, the new kingdom was beset with troubles. Their religion was abandoned. European explorers brought foreign diseases with them; within a few short years the Hawaiian population was cut in half. It was further weakened by the onset of the sandalwood trade in the mid-1800s. All able-bodied men were sent into the forest to harvest the fragrant tree, so that Kamehameha's successor, Liholiho could pay off debts incurred to American merchants. Onto this stage came rowdy foreign whalers, ambitious entrepreneurs, and well-intentioned but perhaps misguided missionaries. New laws regarding land ownership and religious practices eroded the cultural underpinnings of pre-contact Hawai'i. Each successor to the Hawaiian throne sacrificed more control over the island kingdom. Finally in 1893, the last Hawaiian monarch, Queen Lili'uokalani, was overthrown by a group of American and European businessmen and government officials, aided by an armed militia. This led to the creation of the Republic of Hawai'i, which quickly became a territory of the United States through resolutions passed by Congress (rather than through treaties). Hawai'i remained a territory for 60 years; Pearl Harbor was attacked as part of the United States in 1941 during World War II. It wasn't until 1959, however, that Hawai'i was officially admitted as the 50th State.

A SNAPSHOT OF HAWAI'I

Legends and Mythology

Ancient deities play a huge role in Hawaiian life today—not just in daily rituals, but in the Hawaiians' reverence for their land. Gods and goddesses tend to be associated with particular parts of the land, and most of them are connected with many places thanks to the body of stories built up around each.

The goddess Pele lives in Kīlauea Volcano and rules over the Big Island. She is a feisty goddess known for turning enemies into trees or destroying the homes of adversaries with fire. The Valley Isle's namesake, the demigod Maui, is a well-known Polynesian trickster. When his mother Hina complained that there were too few hours in the day, Maui promised to slow the sun. Upon hearing this, the god Moemoe teased Maui for boasting, but undeterred, the demigod wove a strong cord and lassoed the sun. Angry, the sun scorched the fields until an agreement was reached: during summer, the sun would travel more slowly. In winter, it would return to its quick pace. For ridiculing Maui, Moemoe was turned into a large rock that still juts from the water near Kahakualoa.

One of the most important ways the ancient Hawaiians showed respect for their gods and goddesses was through the hula. Various forms of the hula were performed as prayers to the gods and as praise to the chiefs. Performances were taken very seriously, as a mistake was thought to invalidate the prayer, or even to offend the god or chief in question. Hula is still performed both as entertainment and as prayer; it is not uncommon for a hula performance to be included in an official government ceremony.

O'ahu

WORD OF MOUTH

"On O'ahu, you'll want to see Pearl Harbor, and drive up to the North Shore beaches, maybe Diamond Head and the Pali lookout. Then there is the beach and relaxing, and shopping, and eating!"

—dmlove

WELCOME TO O'AHU

TOP REASONS TO GO

★ **Waves:** Boogie board or surf some of the best breaks on the planet.

★ **Pearl Harbor:** Remember Pearl Harbor with a visit to the *Arizona* Memorial.

★ **Diamond Head:** Scale the crater whose iconic profile looms over Waikīkī.

★ **Nightlife:** Raise your glass to the best party scene in Hawai'i.

★ **The North Shore:** See O'ahu's country side—check out the famous beaches from Sunset to Waimea Bay and hike to the remote tip of the island.

1 **Honolulu.** The capital city holds the nation's only royal palace, free concerts under the tamarind trees in the financial district, and the galleries and open markets of Nu'uanu and Chinatown.

2 **Waikīkī.** This is the dream that sells Hawai'i as the place to surf, swim, and sail by day and dine, dance, and party by night.

3 **Southeast O'ahu.** Southeast O'ahu encompasses Honolulu's bedroom communities crawling up the steep-sided valleys, snorkelers' favorite Hanauma Bay, and a string of wild and often hidden beaches (including that steamy one in *From Here to Eternity*).

4 **Windward O'ahu.** With its offshore islands and remnants of ancient fishponds, this is where the beachlovers live, and Hawaiians on their ancestral lands.

5 **The North Shore.** On the North Shore you'll find a melange of farmers and surfers, vacation homes, and plantation villages, culminating in a tumble of black rocks at Ka'ena Point, where, according to tradition, souls meet eternity.

6 **West O'ahu.** West O'ahu—which includes the Central O'ahu highlands, the Leeward coast, and the Hawaiian communities of Nānākuli and Wai'anae—is finding a new identity as a "second city" of suburban homes and tech firms, coexisting with agriculture and traditional lifestyles.

GETTING ORIENTED

O'ahu, the third largest of the Hawaiian Islands, is not just Honolulu and Waikīkī. It's looping mountain trails on the western Wai'anae and eastern Ko'olau ranges. It's monster waves breaking on the golden beaches of the North Shore. It's country stores and beaches where turtles are your swimming companions.

Kahuku

La'ie

Hau'ula

Punalu'u

KO'OLAU

Ka'a'awa

83

Puu Kaaumakua

MOUNTAINS

WINDWARD O'AHU

Kāne'ohe Bay Marine Corps Base

Kahalu'u

830

Kāne'ohe Bay

Kane'ohe

MOKAPU PT.

MŌKAPU PENINSULA

Kailua Bay

Kailua

H3

♦Bellows Air Force Base

Pearl Harbor

'Aiea

63

78

61

Mt. ▲ Olomana

Waimānalo

72

Pearl Harbor Naval Base H1

Kaau Crater ▼

▲Puu Lanipo

Punchbowl Crater

Honolulu International Airport

Mamala Bay

HONOLULU 1

H1

72

SOUTHEAST O'AHU 3

Koko Crater ▼

Hawai'i Kai

Waikīkī 2

DIAMOND HEAD

Maunalua Bay

Hanauma Bay

Diamond Head Crater

KOKO HEAD

2

O'AHU PLANNER

When You Arrive

Honolulu International Airport is 20 minutes from Waikīkī (40 during rush hour). Car rental is across the street from baggage claim. A cumbersome and inefficient airport taxi system requires you to line up to a taxi wrangler who radios for cars (about $25 to Waikīkī). Other options: TheBus ($2, one lap-size bag allowed) or public airport shuttle ($8). Ask the driver to take H1, not Nimitz Highway, at least as far as downtown, or your introduction to paradise will be Honolulu's industrial backside.

Timing Is Everything

When to visit? Winter is whales (November through March) and waves (surf competitions December through February). In fall the Aloha Festivals celebrate island culture in September. In summer the Islands honor the king who made them a nation, Kamehameha I, on June 11, with parades and events on all islands. O'ahu's one-of-a-kind Pan Pacific Festival backs up to the Kamehameha Day, bringing together hundreds of performers from Japan's seasonal celebrations.

Renting a Car

If you plan on getting outside of Waikīkī and Honolulu, renting a car is a must. But renting a Mustang convertible is a sure sign that you're a tourist and practically begs "come burglarize me." A good rule of thumb: When the car is out of your sight even for a moment, it should be empty of anything you care about. But there are other added bonuses of opting out of your Hawai'i dream machine—you'll save some money, and won't be hassled by constantly having to put the top up during one of the island's intermittent rain showers.

■TIP➔Reserve your vehicle in advance, especially during the Christmas holidays. This will not only ensure that you get a car, but also that you get the best rates. Kaua'i has some of the highest gas prices in the Islands. ⇨ *See Essentials for more information on renting a car and driving.*

Dining and Lodging on O'ahu

Hawai'i is a melting pot of cultures, and nowhere is this more apparent than in its cuisine. From lū'au and "plate lunch" to sushi and steak, there's no shortage of interesting flavors and presentations.

Whether you're looking for a quick snack or a multicourse meal, *turn to Where to Eat to find the best eating experiences the island has to offer.* Jump in, and enjoy!

Choosing vacation lodging is a tough decision, but fret not—our expert writers and editors have done most of the legwork.

Looking for a tropical forest retreat, a big resort, or a private vacation rental? ⇨ *Where to Stay will give you all details you need to book a place that suits your style.* Quick tips: Reserve your room far in advance. Be sure to ask about discounts and special packages (hotel Web sites often have Internet-only deals).

Seeing Pearl Harbor

Pearl Harbor is a must-see for many, but there are things to know before you go. Consider whether you want to see only the *Arizona* Memorial, or the USS *Bowfin* and USS *Missouri* as well. Plan to arrive early—tickets for the *Arizona* Memorial (free) are given out on a first-come, first-served basis and can disappear within an hour.

Note that children under four are not allowed on the *Bowfin* and may not enjoy the crowds and waiting in line at other sights. Older kids are likely to find the more experiential, hands-on history of the USS *Bowfin* and USS *Missouri* memorable.

Island Driving Times

It might not seem as if driving from your hotel in Waikīkī to the North Shore, say, would take very much time. But it will take longer than you'd think from glancing at a map, and roads are subject to some pretty heavy traffic.

Be aware that areas around Honolulu can have traffic jams that would rival Southern California, so plan your movements accordingly. Heavy traffic toward downtown Honolulu begins as early as 6:30 AM and lasts until 9 AM. In the afternoon, expect traffic departing downtown to back up beginning around 3 PM until approximately 7 PM.

Here are average driving times—without traffic—that will help you plan your excursions accordingly.

Waikīkī to Kō 'Olina	1 hour
Waikīkī to Hale'iwa	45 minutes
Waikīkī to Hawai'i Kai	25 minutes
Waikīkī to Kailua	30 minutes
Waikīkī to Downtown Honolulu	10 minutes
Waikīkī to Airport	25 minutes
Kane'ohe to Turtle Bay	1 hour
Hawai'i Kai to Kailua	25 minutes
Hale'iwa to Turtle Bay	20 minutes

Island Hopping

Should you try to fit another island into your trip or stay put in O'ahu? Tough call. Although none of the islands is more than 30 minutes away from another by air, security hassles, transport, and check-in all swallow up precious vacation hours.

If you've got less than a week, do O'ahu well and leave the rest for the next trip. With a week, you can give three good tour days to O'ahu (Pearl Harbor, Honolulu, and one rural venture), then head to a Neighbor Island for some serious beach time and maybe an adventure or two.

If you do decide to island-hop, book in advance; you'll get a better fare by packaging your travel. If you want to get along on the Neighbor Islands, don't compare them to Honolulu and never call them "the outer islands"—that's insultingly O'ahu-centric.

At this writing, the Hawaii Superferry, a high-speed interisland ferry with routes between Honolulu, Kahului Mau'I has suspended service. Consult the Superferry Web site (⊕ *www. hawaiisuperferry.com*) or go to ⊕ *www.gohawaii.com*.

1-DAY ITINERARIES

To experience even a fraction of O'ahu's charms, you need a minimum of four days and a bus pass. Five days and a car is better: Waikīkī is at least a day, Honolulu and Chinatown another, Pearl Harbor the better part of another. Each of the rural sections can swallow a day each, just for driving, sightseeing, and stopping to eat. And that's before you've taken a surf lesson, hung from a parasail, hiked a loop trail, or visited a botanical garden. The following itineraries will take you to our favorite spots on the island.

First Day in Waikīkī. You'll be up at dawn due to the time change and dead on your feet by afternoon due to jet lag. Have an early-morning swim, change into walking gear, head east along Kalākaua Avenue to Monsarrat Avenue, and climb Diamond Head. After lunch, nap in the shade, do some shopping, or visit the nearby East Honolulu neighborhoods of Mō'ili'ili and Kaimukī, rife with small shops and great, little restaurants. End the day with an early and inexpensive dinner at one of these neighborhood spots.

Windward Exploring. For sand, sun, and surf, follow H1 east to keyhole-shaped Hanauma Bay for picture-perfect snorkeling, then round the southeast tip of the island with its wind-swept cliffs and the famous Hālona Blowhole. Fly a kite or watch body surfers at Sandy Beach. Take in Sea Life Park. In Waimānalo, stop for local-style plate lunch, or punch on through to Kailua, where there's intriguing shopping and good eating.

The North Shore. Hit H1 westbound and then H2 to get to the North Shore. You'll pass through pineapple country, then drop down a scenic winding road to Waialua and Hale'iwa. Stop in Hale'iwa town to shop, have shave ice, and pick up a guided dive or snorkel trip. On winding Kamehameha Highway, check out famous big-wave beaches, take a dip in a cove with a turtle, and buy fresh Island fruit at roadside stands.

Pearl Harbor. Pearl Harbor is an almost all-day investment. Be on the grounds by 7:30 AM to line up for *Arizona* Memorial tickets. Clamber all over the USS *Bowfin* submarine. Finally, take the free trolley to see the Mighty Mo battleship. If it's Wednesday or Saturday, make the five-minute drive *mauka* (toward the mountains) for bargain-basement shopping at the sprawling Aloha Stadium Swap Meet.

Town Time. If you are interested in history, devote a day to Honolulu's historic sites. Downtown, see 'Iolani Palace, the Kamehameha Statue, and Kawaiaha'o Church. A few blocks east, explore Chinatown, gilded Kuan Yin Temple, and artsy Nu'uanu with its galleries. On the water is the informative Hawai'i Maritime Center. Hop west on H1 to the Bishop Museum, the state's anthropological and archaeological center. And a mile up Pali Highway is Queen Emma Summer Palace, whose shady grounds were a royal retreat.

Updated by
Trina Kud-
lacek, Chad
Pata, and
Cathy Sharpe

O'ahu is one-stop Hawai'i—all the allure of the Islands in a chop-suey mix that has you kayaking around offshore islets by day and sitting in a jazz club 'round midnight, all without ever having to take another flight or repack your suitcase. It offers both the buzz of modern living in jam-packed Honolulu (the state's capital) and the allure of slow-paced island life on its northern and eastern shores. It is, in many ways, the center of the Hawaiian universe.

There are more museums, staffed historic sites, and walking tours here than you'll find on any other island. And only here do a wealth of renovated buildings and well-preserved neighborhoods so clearly spin the story of Hawai'i history. It's the only place to experience island-style urbanity, since there are no other true cities in the state. And yet you can get as lost in the rural landscape and be as laid-back as you wish.

O'ahu is home to Waikīkī, the most famous Hawaiian beach with some of the world's most famous surf on the North Shore, and the Islands' best known historical site ,Pearl Harbor. If it's isolation, peace, and quiet you want, O'ahu is probably not for you, but if you'd like a bit of spice with your piece of paradise, this island provides it.

GEOLOGY

Encompassing 597 square mi, O'ahu is the third-largest island in the Hawaiian chain. Scientists believe the island was formed about 4 million years ago by two volcanoes: Wai'anae and Ko'olau. Wai'anae, the older of the two, makes up the western side of the island, while Ko'olau shapes the eastern side. Central O'ahu is an elevated plateau bordered by the two mountain ranges, with Pearl Harbor to the south. Several of O'ahu's most famous natural landmarks, including Diamond Head and Hanauma Bay, are tuff rings and cinder cones formed during a renewed volcanic stage (roughly 1 million years ago).

FLORA AND FAUNA

Due to its elevation, the eastern (Ko'olau) side of O'ahu is much cooler and wetter than the western side of the island, which tends to be dry and arid. The island's official flower, the little orange *ilima*, grows predominantly in the east, but lei throughout the island incorporate *ilima*. Numerous tropical fish call the reef at Hanauma Bay home, migrating humpback whales can be spotted off the coast past Waikīkī and Diamond Head from December through April, spinner dolphins pop in and out of the island's bays, and dozens of islets off O'ahu's eastern coast provide refuge for endangered seabirds.

HISTORY

O'ahu is the most populated island because early tourism to Hawai'i started here. Although Kīlauea volcano on Hawai'i was a tourist attraction in the late 1800s, it was the building of the Moana Hotel on Waikīkī

Beach in 1901 and subsequent advertising of Hawai'i to wealthy San Franciscans that really fueled tourism in the islands. O'ahu was drawing tens of thousands of guests yearly when, on December 7, 1941, Japanese Zeros appeared at dawn to bomb Pearl Harbor. Though tourism understandably dipped during the war (Waikīkī Beach was fenced with barbed wire), the subsequent memorial only seemed to attract more visitors, and O'ahu remains hugely popular with tourists to this day.

EXPLORING O'AHU

DIAMOND HEAD AND KAPI'OLANI PARK

Diamond Head Crater is perhaps Hawai'i's most recognizable natural landmark. It got its name from sailors who thought they had found precious gems on its slopes; these later proved to be calcite crystals, fool's gold. Hawaiians saw a resemblance in the sharp angle of the crater's seaward slope to the oddly shaped head of the 'ahi fish and so called it the Lē'ahi, though later they Hawaiianized the English name to Kaimana Hila. It is commemorated in a widely known hula—*"A 'ike i ka nani o Kaimana Hila, Kaimana Hila, kau mai i luna"* ("We saw the beauty of Diamond Head, Diamond Head set high above").

Kapi'olani Park lies in the shadow of the crater. King David Kalākaua established the park in 1887, named it after his queen, and dedicated it "to the use and enjoyment of the people." Kapi'olani Park is a 500-acre expanse where you can play all sorts of field sports, enjoy a picnic, see wild animals at the Honolulu Zoo, or hear live music at the Waikīkī Shell or the Kapi'olani Bandstand. It's also the start and finish point for many weekend walks; check local newspapers or ⊕ *www.ehawaii.gov*.

Diamond Head State Monument and Park. Panoramas from this 760-foot extinct volcanic peak, once used as a military fortification, extend from Waikīkī and Honolulu in one direction and out to Koko Head in the other, with surfers and windsurfers scattered like confetti on the cresting waves below. This 360-degree perspective is a great orientation for first-time visitors. On a clear day, look to your left past Koko Head to glimpse the outlines of the islands of Maui and Moloka'i. To enter the park from Waikīkī, take Kalākaua Avenue east, turn left at Monsarrat Avenue, head a mile up the hill, and look for a sign on the right. Drive through the tunnel to the inside of the crater. The ¾-mi trail to the top begins at the parking lot. New lighting inside the summit tunnel and a spiral staircase eases the way, but be aware that the hike to the crater is a strenuous upward climb; if you aren't in the habit of getting much exercise, this might not be for you. Take bottled water with you to ensure that you stay hydrated under the tropical sun. ■ TIP➔To beat the heat and the crowds, rise early and make the hike before 8 AM. As you walk, note the color of the vegetation; if the mountain is brown, Honolulu has been without significant rain for a while; but if the trees and undergrowth glow green, you'll know it's the wet season (winter) without looking at a calendar. This is the wet season when rare

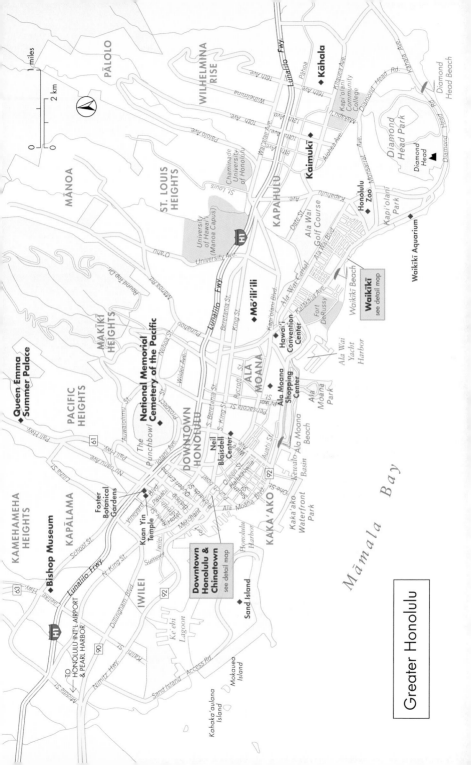

Greater Honolulu

Hawaiian marsh plants revive on the floor of the crater. Keep an eye on your watch if you're there at day's end, because the gates close promptly at 6. ✉ *Diamond Head Rd. at 18th Ave., Waikīkī* ☎ *808/587–0285* ⊕ *www.hawaiistateparks.org/parks/oahu/* 💲*$1 per person, $5 per vehicle* ⊘ *Daily 6–6.*

Ⓒ **Honolulu Zoo.** To get a glimpse of the endangered *nēnē*, the Hawai'i state bird, check out the Kipuka Nēnē Sanctuary. Though many animals prefer to remain invisible, the monkeys appear to enjoy being seen and are a hoot to watch. It's best to get to the zoo right when it opens, since the animals are livelier in the cool of the morning. There are bigger and better zoos, but this one, though showing signs of neglect due to budget constraints, is a lush garden and has some great programs. The Wildest Show in Town, a series of concerts ($2 donation), takes place on Wednesday evenings in summer. You can have a family sleepover inside the zoo during Snooze in the Zoo on a Friday or Saturday night every month. Or just head for the petting zoo, where kids can make friends with a llama or stand in the middle of a koi pond. There's an exceptionally good gift shop. On weekends, the Zoo Fence Art Mart, on Monsarrat Avenue on the Diamond Head side outside the zoo, has affordable artwork by contemporary artists. Metered parking is available all along the *makai* (ocean) side of the park and in the lot next to the zoo. TheBus, O'ahu's only form of public transportation, makes stops here along the way to and from Ala Moana Center and Sea Life Park (routes 22 and 58). ✉ *151 Kapahulu Ave., Waikīkī* ☎ *808/971–7171* ⊕ *www.* *honoluluzoo.org* 💲*$8* ⊘ *Daily 9–4:30.*

Ⓒ **Waikīkī Aquarium.** This amazing little attraction harbors more than 2,500 organisms and 420 species of Hawaiian and South Pacific marine life, endangered Hawaiian monk seals, sharks, and the only chambered nautilus living in captivity. The Edge of the Reef exhibit showcases five different types of reef environments found along Hawai'i's shorelines. Check out the Northwestern Hawaiian Islands exhibit (opening in late 2009), Ocean Drifters jellyfish exhibit, outdoor touch pool, and the self-guided audio tour, which is included with admission. The aquarium offers programs of interest to adults and children alike, including the Aquarium after Dark when visitors grab a flashlight and view fish going about their rarely observable nocturnal activities. Plan to spend at least an hour at the aquarium, including 10 minutes for a film in the Sea Visions Theater. ✉ *2777 Kalākaua Ave., Waikīkī* ☎ *808/923–9741* ⊕ *www.waquarium.org* 💲*$9* ⊘ *Daily 9–4:30.*

Waikīkī War Memorial Natatorium. This 1927 World War I monument, dedicated to the 102 Hawaiian servicemen who lost their lives in battle, stands proudly—its 20-foot archway, which was completely restored in 2002, is floodlighted at night. Despite a face-lift in 2000, the 100-meter saltwater swimming pool, the training spot for Olympians Johnny Weissmuller and Buster Crabbe and the U.S. Army during World War II, is closed as the pool needs repair. The city has commissioned a study of the Natatorium's future while a nonprofit group fights to save the facility. ✉ *2777 Kalākaua Ave., Waikīkī.*

NEED A BREAK?

According to legend, Robert Louis Stevenson once sat beneath the eponymous *hau* tree in the courtyard of the **Hau Tree Lānai** (⊠ *2863 Kalākaua Ave., 96815* ☎ *808/921–7066*). You can enjoy the same shade, plus breakfast, lunch, or dinner, at this find in the New Otani Kaimana Beach Hotel, next to the Natatorium.

Kapi'olani Bandstand. Victorian-style Kapi'olani Bandstand, which was originally built in the late 1890s, is Kapi'olani Park's stage for community entertainment and concerts. The nation's only city-sponsored band, the Royal Hawaiian Band, performs free concerts on Sunday afternoon. Local newspapers list event information. ⊠ *Near intersection of Kalākaua and Monsarrat Aves., Waikīkī.*

Waikīkī Shell. Locals bring picnics and grab one of the 6,000 "grass seats" (lawn seating) for music under the stars (there are actual seats, as well). Concerts are held May 1 to Labor Day, with a few winter dates, weather permitting. Check newspaper Friday entertainment sections to see who is performing. ⊠ *2805 Monsarrat Ave., Waikīkī* ☎ *808/924–8934* ⊕ *www.blaisdellcenter.com.*

CHINATOWN

Chinatown occupies 15 blocks immediately north of downtown Honolulu—it's flat, compact, and easily explored in half a day. ■ **TIP➔** The best time to visit is morning, when the popo (grandmas) shop—it's cool out, and you can enjoy a cheap dim sum breakfast. Chinatown is a seven-day-a-week operation. Sunday is especially busy with families sharing dim sum in raucous dining hall–size restaurants.

The name Chinatown has always been a misnomer. Though three-quarters of O'ahu's Chinese lived closely packed in these 25 acres in the late 1800s, even then the neighborhood was half Japanese. Today, you hear Vietnamese and Tagalog as often as Mandarin and Cantonese, and there are touches of Japan, Singapore, Malaysia, Korea, Thailand, Samoa, and the Marshall Islands, as well.

Perhaps a more accurate name is the one used by early Chinese: Wah Fau ("Chinese port") signifying a landing and jumping-off place. Chinese laborers, as soon as they completed their plantation contracts, hurried into the city to start businesses here. It's a launching point for today's immigrants, too: Southeast Asian shops almost outnumber Chinese; stalls carry Filipino specialties like winged beans and goat meat; and in one tiny space, knife-wielding Samoans skin coconuts to order.

In the half-century after the first Chinese laborers arrived in Hawai'i in 1851, Chinatown was a link to home for the all-male cadre of workers who planned to return to China rich and respected. Merchants not only sold supplies, they held mail, loaned money, wrote letters, translated documents, sent remittances to families, served meals, offered rough bunkhouse accommodations, and were the center for news, gossip, and socializing.

Though much happened to Chinatown in the 20th century—beginning in January 1900, when almost the entire neighborhood was burned to the ground to halt the spread of bubonic plague—it remains a bustling, crowded, noisy, and odiferous place bent primarily on buying and selling, and sublimely oblivious to its status as a National Historic District or the encroaching gentrification on nearby Nu'uanu Avenue.

Chinatown's original business district was made up of dry goods and produce merchants, tailors and dressmakers, barbers, herbalists, and dozens of restaurants. The meat, fish, and produce stalls remain but the mix is heavier now on gift and curio stores, lei stands, jewelry shops and bakeries, with a smattering of noodle makers, travel agents, Asian-language video stores, and dozens of restaurants.

A caution: Hotel Street was Honolulu's red light district and A'ala Park, just across the Nu'uanu stream, shelters many homeless people and more than a few drug users. A police station in the heart of the district has tamped down crime, and the area is perfectly safe by day—even panhandling is rare. But at night, park in a well-lighted place, travel with the crowds, and be alert. ■TIP→Look for well-marked municipal parking lots on Smith, Bethel, Nu'uanu, and Beretania; these charge a third of what the private lots demand.

If you're here between January 20 and February 20, check local newspapers for Chinese New Year activities. Bakeries stock special sweets, stores and homes sprout bright-red scrolls, and lion dancers cavort through the streets feeding on *li-see* (money envelopes). The Narcissus Queen is chosen, and an evening street fair draws crowds.

Weekly tours of Chinatown are offered on Tuesday by the Chinese Chamber of Commerce.

❶ Chinatown Cultural Plaza. This sprawling multistory shopping square surrounds a courtyard with an incense-wreathed shrine and Moongate stage for holiday performances. The Chee Kung Tong Society has a beautifully decorated meeting hall here; a number of such *tongs* (meeting places) are hidden on upper floors in Chinatown. Outside, near the canal, local members of the community play cards and mah-jongg. ⊠*100 N. Beretania, Chinatown.*

Hawai'i Theatre. Opened in 1922, this theater earned rave reviews for its neoclassical design, with Corinthian columns, marble statues, and plush carpeting and drapery. Nicknamed the "Pride of the Pacific," the facility was rescued from demolition in the early 1980s and underwent a $30 million renovation. Listed on both the State and National Register of Historic Places, it has become the centerpiece of revitalization efforts of Honolulu's downtown area. The 1,200-seat venue hosts concerts, theatrical productions, dance performances, and film screenings. ⊠*1130 Bethel St., Chinatown* ☎*808/528–0506* ⊠*$5* ☉*1-hr guided tours Tues. at 11.*

❷ Izumo Taisha Shrine. From Chinatown Cultural Plaza, cross a stone bridge to visit Okuninushi No Mikoto, a *kami* (god) who is believed in Shinto tradition to bring good fortune if properly courted (and thanked afterward). ⊠*N. Kukui and Canal, Chinatown* ☎*No phone.*

Kuan Yin Temple. A couple of blocks *mauka* (toward the mountains) from Chinatown is the oldest Buddhist temple in the Islands. Mistakenly

Continued on page 47

INS & OUTS OF WAIKĪKĪ

Waikīkī is all that is wonderful about a resort area, and all that is regrettable. On the wonderful side: swimming, surfing, parasailing, and catamaran-riding steps from the street; the best nightlife in Hawai'i;

shopping from designer to dime stores; and experiences to remember: the heart-lifting rush the first time you stand up on a surfboard, watching the old men play cutthroat checkers in the beach pavilions, eating fresh grilled snapper as the sun slips into the sea. As to the regrettable: clogged streets, body-lined beaches, $5 cups of coffee, tacky T-shirts, $20 parking stalls, schlocky artwork, the same street performers you saw in Atlantic City, drunks, cease-less construction—all rather brush the bloom from the plumeria.

Modern Waikīkī is nothing like its original self, a network of streams, marshes, and islands that drained the inland valleys. The Ala Wai Canal took

care of that in the 1920s. More recently, new landscaping, walkways, and a general attention to infrastructure have brightened a façade that had begun distinctly to fade.

But throughout its history, Waikīkī has retained its essential character: an enchantment that cannot be fully explained and one that, though diminished by high-rises, traffic, and noise, has not yet disappeared. Hawaiian royalty came here, and visitors continue to follow, falling in love with sharp-prowed Diamond Head, the sensuous curve of shoreline with its baby-safe waves, and the strong-footed surfers like moving statues in the golden light.

WAIKĪKĪ WEST

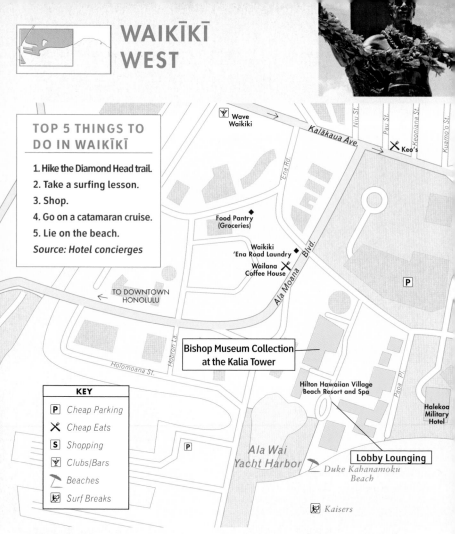

TOP 5 THINGS TO DO IN WAIKĪKĪ

1. Hike the Diamond Head trail.
2. Take a surfing lesson.
3. Shop.
4. Go on a catamaran cruise.
5. Lie on the beach.

Source: Hotel concierges

Wave Waikiki

Kalākaua Ave.

Keo's

Niu St.

Pau St.

Keoniana St.

Kuamo'o St.

Ena Rd.

Food Pantry (Groceries)

Waikiki 'Ena Road Laundry

Wailana Coffee House

Ala Moana Blvd.

P

TO DOWNTOWN HONOLULU

Hobron La.

Holomoana St.

Bishop Museum Collection at the Kalia Tower

Paoa Pl.

Hilton Hawaiian Village Beach Resort and Spa

Halekoa Military Hotel

KEY

P	Cheap Parking
X	Cheap Eats
S	Shopping
Y	Clubs/Bars
⌐	Beaches
🏄	Surf Breaks

P

Ala Wai Yacht Harbor

Lobby Lounging

Duke Kahanamoku Beach

🏄 Kaisers

CHEAP EATS

Keo's, 2028 Kūhiō: Breakfast.

Wailana Coffee House, 1860 Ala Moana Blvd.

Pho Old Saigon, 2270 Kūhiō: Vietnamese.

Japanese noodle shops: Try Menchanko-Tei, Waikīkī Trade Center; Ezogiku, 2164 Kalākaua.

■ TIP➔ Thanks to the many Japanese nationals who stay here, Waikīkī is blessed with lots of cheap, authentic Japanese food, particularly noodles. Plastic representations of food in the window are an indicator of authenticity and a help in ordering.

SHOP, SHOP, SHOP/PARTY, PARTY, PARTY

2100 Kalākaua: Select high-end European boutiques (Chanel, Gucci, Yves Saint Laurent).

Island Treasures Antique Mall: Hawaiian collectibles from precious to priceless. 2301 Kūhiō Ave. 808/922-8223.

Wave Waikīkī: This multi-story madhouse of sound and writhing bodies is a bit rough around the edges but hugely popular with locals. 1877 Kalākaua Ave. 808/941-0424.

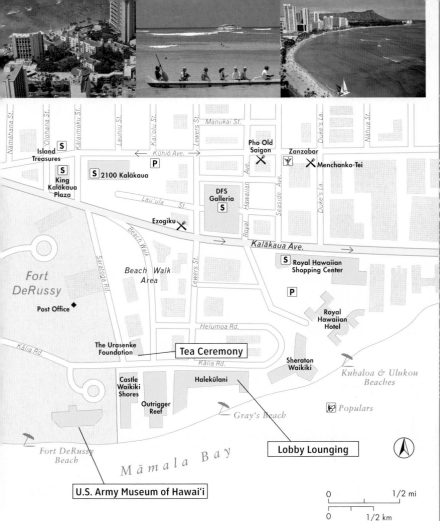

Zanzabar: Upscale Zanzabar is a different club every night–Latin, global, over 30, under 18. Waikīkī Trade Center, 2255 Kūhiō Ave. 808/924-3939.

RAINY DAY IDEAS

Lobby Lounging: Among Waikīkī's great gathering spots are Halekūlani's tranquil courtyards with gorgeous flower arrangements and glimpses of the famous and the Hilton Hawaiian Village's flagged pathways with koi ponds, squawking parrots, and great shops.

Tea Ceremony, Urasenke Foundation: Japan's mysterious tea ceremony is demonstrated. 245 Saratoga Rd. 808/923-3059. $3 donation. Wed., Fri. 10–noon.

U.S. Army Museum of Hawai'i: Exhibits, including photographs and military equipment, trace the history of Army in the Islands. Battery Randolph, Kalia Rd., Fort DeRussy. 808/438-2821. Free. Tues.–Sun. 10–4:15.

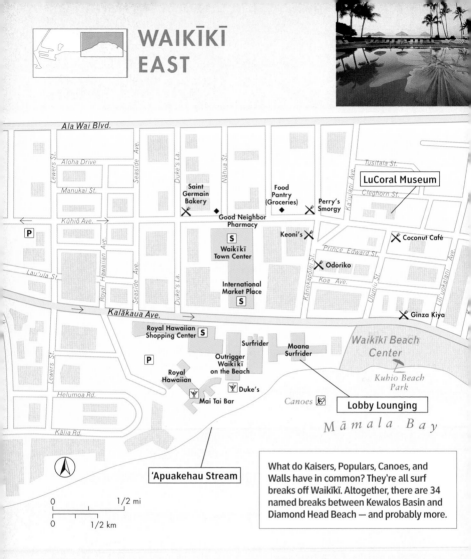

WAIKĪKĪ EAST

Ala Wai Blvd.

Aloha Drive

Manukai St.

Kūhiō Ave.

Lauʻula St.

Saint Germain Bakery

Good Neighbor Pharmacy

Food Pantry (Groceries)

Perry's Smorgy

LuCoral Museum

Tusitala St.

Cleghorn St.

Keoni's

Coconut Café

Prince Edward St.

Odoriko

Koa Ave.

Kānekapōlei St.

Waikīkī Town Center

International Market Place

Ginza Kiya

Kalākaua Ave.

Royal Hawaiian Shopping Center

Surfrider

Outrigger Waikīkī on the Beach

Moana Surfrider

Waikīkī Beach Center

Kuhio Beach Park

Royal Hawaiian

Mai Tai Bar

Duke's

Canoes

Lobby Lounging

Māmala Bay

Helumoa Rd.

Kālia Rd.

'Apuakehau Stream

What do Kaisers, Populars, Canoes, and Walls have in common? They're all surf breaks off Waikīkī. Altogether, there are 34 named breaks between Kewalos Basin and Diamond Head Beach — and probably more.

0 ———— 1/2 mi

0 ———— 1/2 km

CHEAP EATS

Coconut Café, 2441 Kūhiō: Burgers, sandwiches under $5; fresh fruit smoothies.

Ginza Kiya, 2464 Kalākaua: Japanese noodle shop.

Keoni's, Outrigger East Hotel, 150 Kaiulani Ave.: Breakfasts at rock-bottom prices.

Odoriko, King's Village, 131 Kāiulani Ave.: Japanese noodle shop.

Perry's Smorgy Restaurant, 2380 Kūhiō: family-friendly American food; brunch under $10.

■ TIP➔ To save money, go inland. Kūhiō, one block toward the mountains from the main drag of Kalākaua, is lined with less expensive restaurants, hotels, and shops.

SHOP, SHOP, SHOP/PARTY, PARTY, PARTY

Moana Surfrider: Pick up a present at Noeha Gallery or Sand People. Then relax with a drink at the venerable Banyan Veranda. The radio program *Hawaiʻi Calls* first broadcast to a mainland audience from here in 1935.

Duke's Canoe Club, Outrigger Waikīkī: Beach party central.

KEY

P *Cheap Parking*
✕ *Cheap Eats*
S *Shopping*
🍸 *Clubs/Bars*
⚑ *Beaches*
🏄 *Surf Breaks*

WHAT THE LOCALS LOVE

Paid-parking–phobic Islanders usually avoid Waikīkī, but these attractions are juicy enough to lure locals:

■ **Pan-Pacific Festival-Matsuri in Hawaii**, a summer cultural festival that's as good as a trip to Japan.

■ **Aloha Festivals in September**, the legendary floral parade and evening show of contemporary Hawaiian music.

■ **The Wildest Show in Town**, $1 summer concerts at the Honolulu Zoo.

■ **Sunset on the Beach**, free films projected on an outdoor screen at Queen's Beach, with food and entertainment.

'APUAKEHAU STREAM

Wade out just in front of the Outrigger Waikīkī on the Beach and feel a current of chilly water curling around your ankles. This is the last remnant of three streams that once drained the inland valleys behind you, making of Waikīkī a place of swamps, marshes, taro and rice paddies, and giving it the name "spouting water." High-ranking chiefs surfed in a legendary break gouged out by the draining freshwater and rinsed off afterward in the stream whose name means "basket of dew." The Ala Wai Canal, completed in the late 1920s, drained the land, reducing proud 'Apuakehau Stream to a determined phantom passing beneath Waikīkī's streets.

Mai Tai Bar at the Royal Hawaiian: Birthplace of the Mai Tai.

RAINY DAY IDEAS

Lobby lounging: Check out the century-old, period-furnished lobby and veranda of the Sheraton Moana Surfrider Hotel on Kalākaua.

LuCoral Museum: Exhibit and shop explores the world of coral and other semi-precious stones; wander about or take $2 guided tour and participate in jewelry-making activity. 2414 Kūhiō.

WHAT'S NEW & CHANGING

Waikīkī, which was looking a bit shop-worn, is in the midst of many make-overs. Ask about noise, disruption, and construction when booking. In addition to fresh landscaping and period light fixtures along Kalākaua and a pathway that encircles Ala Wai Canal, expect:

1. BEACH WALK: After ten years of planning, the Waikīkī Beach Walk—a pedestrian walkway lined with restau-rants and shops—opened in 2007 to rave reviews. It was a massive project for the city, costing about $535 million and taking up nearly 8 acres of land. It's a great place to spend the afternoon, but be warned: this place gets packed on weekends.

2. ROYAL HAWAIIAN SHOPPING CENTER AND INTERNATIONAL MARKETPLACE: The fortress-like Royal Hawaiian Shop-ping Center in the center of Kalākaua Avenue is an open, inviting space with a palm grove and a new mix of shops and restaurants. And tacky International Marketplace shops will give way to a low-rise compound of entertainment spaces, kiosks, and water features, with many historic trees preserved (comple-tion 2009).

3. CIRQUE HAWAI'I: This acrobatic show with an international cast is so new at this writing that there's no way to predict its staying power, though local reviews have been good. 325 Seaside Ave., 808/922-0017, $61-$98.

GETTING THERE

It can seem impossible to figure out how to get to Waikīkī from H-1. The exit is far inland, and even when you follow the signs, the route jigs and jogs; it some-times seems a wonder that more tourists aren't found starving in Kaimuki.

FROM EASTBOUND H-1 (COMING FROM THE AIRPORT):
1. To western Waikīkī (Ft. DeRussy and most hotels): Take the Punahou exit from H-1, turn right on Punahou and get in the center lane. Go right on Beretania and almost immediately left onto Kalākaua, which takes you into Waikīkī.

2. To eastern Waikīkī (Kapi'olani Park): Take the King Street exit, and stay on King for two blocks. Go right on Kapa-hulu, which takes you to Kalākaua.

FROM WESTBOUND H-1:
Take the Kapi'olani Boulevard exit. Follow Kapi'olani to McCully, and go left on McCully. Follow McCully to Kalākaua, and you're in Waikīkī.

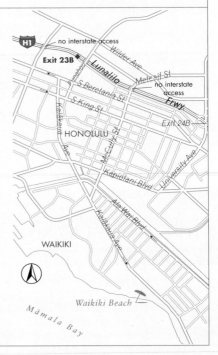

called a goddess by some, Kuan Yin, also known as Kannon, is a *bodhisattva*—one who chose to remain on earth doing good even after achieving enlightenment. Transformed from a male into a female figure centuries ago, she is credited with a particular sympathy for women. You will see representations of her all over the Islands: holding a lotus flower (beauty from the mud of human frailty), as at the temple; pouring out a pitcher of oil (like mercy flowing); or as a sort of Madonna with a child. Visitors are permitted but be aware this is a practicing place of worship. ✉*170 N. Vineyard, Downtown* ☎*No phone.*

❸ Maunakea Marketplace. On the corner of Maunakea and Hotel streets is this plaza surrounded by shops, an indoor market, and a food court.

CHINATOWN SHOPS

You'll find fun, inexpensive gifts in Chinatown, like folding fans for $1 and coconut purses for $5 at Maunakea Marketplace. Shops sell everything from porcelain statues to woks, ginseng to Mao shoes. If you feel hungry, visit the Hong Kong Supermarket in the Wo Fat Chop Sui building (at the corner of N. Hotel and Maunakea) for fresh fruit, crack seed (Chinese dried fruit popular for snacking), and countless other delicacies with indecipherable names. Narrow, dim, and dusty Bo Wah Trading Co. (E1037 Maunakea) is full of cooking utensils. Chinatown Cultural Plaza offers fine-quality jade. And Chinatown is Honolulu's lei center, with shops strung along Beretania and Maunakea.

Within the Marketplace, the **Hawaiian Chinese Cultural Museum and Archives** (☑*$2* ☉*Mon.–Sat. 10–2*) displays historic photographs and artifacts. ■TIP➔ If you appreciate fine tea, visit the Tea Hut, an unpretentious counter inside a curio shop. ✉*1120 Maunakea St., Chinatown* ☎*808/524–3409.*

❹ Nu'uanu Avenue. Here on Chinatown's southern border and on Bethel Street, which runs parallel, are clustered art galleries, restaurants, a wineshop, an antiques auctioneer, a dress shop or two, one tiny theater space (the Arts at Mark's Garage), and one historic stage (the Hawai'i Theatre). **First Friday** art nights, when galleries stay open until 9 PM, draw crowds. If you like art and people-watching and are fortunate enough to be on O'ahu the first Friday of the month, this event shouldn't be missed. ✉*Nu'uanu Ave., Chinatown.*

❺ O'ahu Marketplace. Here is a taste of old-style Chinatown, where you're
★ likely to be hustled aside as a whole pig (dead, of course) is wrestled through the crowd and where glassy-eyed fish of every size and hue lie stacked forlornly on ice. Try the bubble tea (juices and flavored teas with tapioca bubbles inside) or pick up a bizarre magenta dragonfruit for breakfast. ✉*N. King St. at Kekaulike, Chinatown.*

DOWNTOWN HONOLULU

Honolulu's past and present play a delightful counterpoint throughout the downtown sector. Postmodern glass-and-steel office buildings look down on the Aloha Tower, built in 1926 and, until the early 1960s, the tallest structure in Honolulu. Hawai'i's history is told in the architecture of these few blocks: the cut-stone turn-of-the-20th-century storefronts

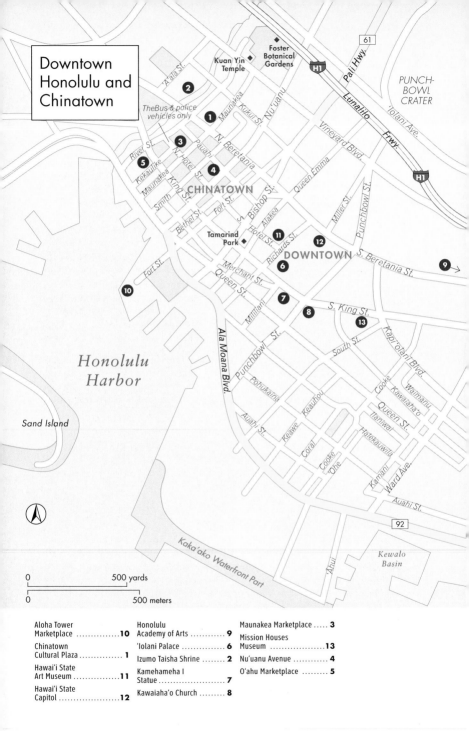

Downtown Honolulu and Chinatown

PUNCH-BOWL CRATER

Foster Botanical Gardens

Kuan Yin Temple

TheBus & police vehicles only

CHINATOWN

Tamarind Park

DOWNTOWN

Honolulu Harbor

Sand Island

Kaka'ako Waterfront Park

Kewalo Basin

0	500 yards
0	500 meters

of Merchant Street, the gracious white-columned American-Georgian manor that was the home of the Islands' last queen, the jewel-box palace occupied by the monarchy before it was overthrown, the Spanish-inspired stucco and tile-roofed Territorial-era government buildings, and the 21st-century glass pyramid of the First Hawaiian Bank Building.

Plan a couple of hours for exploring downtown's historic buildings, more if you're taking a guided tour or walk. The best time to visit is in the cool and relative quiet of morning or on the weekends when downtown is all but deserted except for the historic sites. To reach Downtown Honolulu from Waikīkī by car, take Ala Moana Boulevard to Alakea Street and turn right; three blocks up on the right, between South King and Hotel, there's a municipal parking lot in Aliʻi Place on the right. You can also take Route 19 or 20 of TheBus to the Aloha Tower Marketplace or take a trolley from Waikīkī.

TOP ATTRACTIONS

 ʻIolani Palace. America's only royal residence was built in 1882 on the site of an earlier palace, and it contains the thrones of King Kalākaua and his successor (and sister) Queen Liliʻuokalani. Bucking the stereotype of the primitive islander, the palace had electricity and telephone lines installed even before the White House. Downstairs galleries showcase the royal jewelry, and kitchen and offices of the monarchy. The palace is open for guided or self-guided audio tours, and reservations are essential. ■ TIP→ If you're set on taking a guided tour, call for reservations a few days in advance. The gift shop was formerly the ʻIolani Barracks, built to house the Royal Guard. ⊠ *King and Richards Sts., Downtown Honolulu* ☎ *808/522–0832* ⊕ *www.iolanipalace.org* ⊠ *$20 guided tour, $12 audio tour, $6 downstairs galleries only* ☉ *Tues.–Sat. 9–2, guided tours every 15 min 9–11:15, self-guided audio tours 11:45–3:30.*

FodorsChoice
★

 Kamehameha I Statue. Paying tribute to the Big Island chieftain who united all the warring Hawaiian Islands into one kingdom at the turn of the 18th century, this statue, which stands with one arm outstretched in welcome, is one of three originally cast in Paris, France, by American sculptor T. R. Gould. The original statue, lost at sea and replaced by this one, was eventually salvaged and is now in Kapaʻau, on the Big Island, near the king's birthplace. Each year on the king's birthday, June 11, the more famous copy is draped in fresh lei that reach lengths of 18 feet and longer. A parade proceeds past the statue, and Hawaiian civic clubs, the women in hats and impressive long holokū dresses and the men in sashes and cummerbunds, pay honor to the leader whose name means "The Lonely One." ⊠ *417 S. King St., outside Aliʻiōlani Hale, Downtown Honolulu.*

 Kawaiahaʻo Church. Fancifully called Hawaiʻi's Westminster Abbey, this 14,000-coral-block house of worship witnessed the coronations, weddings, and funerals of generations of Hawaiian royalty. Each of the building's coral blocks was quarried from reefs offshore at depths of more than 20 feet and transported to this site. Interior woodwork was created from the forests of the Koʻolau Mountains. The upper gallery has an exhibit of paintings of the royal families. The graves of missionaries and of King Lunalilo are adjacent. Services in English and

Hawaiian are held each Sunday, and the church members are exceptionally welcoming, greeting newcomers with lei; their affiliation is United Church of Christ. Although there are no guided tours, you can look around the church at no cost. ⊠ *957 Punchbowl St., at King St., Downtown Honolulu* ☎ *808/522–1333* ⌨ *Free* ☉ *Service in English and Hawaiian Sun. at 9* A.M.

WORTH NOTING

🔟 **Aloha Tower Marketplace.** In two stories of shops and kiosks you can find island-inspired clothing, jewelry, art, and home furnishings. The Marketplace also has indoor and outdoor restaurants and live entertainment. For a bird's-eye view of this working harbor, take a free ride up to the observation deck of Aloha Tower. Cruise ships dock at piers 9 and 10 alongside the Marketplace and are often greeted and sent out to sea with music and hula dancing at the piers' end. ⊠ *1 Aloha Tower Dr., at Piers 10 and 11, Downtown Honolulu* ☎ *808/528–5700 entertainment info* ⊕ *www.alohatower.com* ☉ *Mon.–Sat. 9–9, Sun. 9–6; restaurants open later.*

⓫ **Hawai'i State Art Museum.** Hawai'i was one of the first states in the nation to legislate that a portion of the taxes paid on commercial building projects be set aside for the purchase of artwork. A few years ago, the state purchased an ornate period-style building (built to house the headquarters of a prominent developer) and dedicated 12,000 feet on the second floor to the art of Hawai'i in all its ethnic diversity. The **Diamond Head Gallery** features new acquisitions and thematic shows from the State Art Collection and the State Foundation on Culture and the Arts. The **'Ewa Gallery** houses more than 150 works documenting Hawai'i's visual-arts history since becoming a state in 1959. Also included are a sculpture gallery as well as a café, a gift shop, and educational meeting rooms. ⊠ *250 S. Hotel St., 2nd fl., Downtown Honolulu* ☎ *808/586–0900 museum, 808/536–5900 restaurant* ⊕ *www.hawaii. gov/sfca* ⌨ *Free* ☉ *Tues.–Sat. 10–4.*

⓬ **Hawai'i State Capitol.** The capitol's architecture is richly symbolic: the columns resemble palm trees, the legislative chambers are shaped like volcanic cinder cones, and the central court is open to the sky, representing Hawai'i's open society. Replicas of the Hawai'i state seal, each weighing 7,500 pounds, hang above both its entrances. The building, which in 1969 replaced 'Iolani Palace as the seat of government, is surrounded by reflecting pools, just as the Islands are embraced by water. A pair of statues, often draped in lei, flank the building: one of the beloved queen Lili'uokalani and the other of the sainted Father Damien de Veuster. ⊠ *215 S. Beretania St., Downtown Honolulu* ☎ *808/586–0178* ⌨ *Free* ☉ *Guided tours Mon., Wed., Fri. 1:30.*

Hawai'i State Library. This beautifully renovated main library was built in 1913. Its Samuel M. Kamakau Reading Room, on the first floor in the Mauka (Hawaiian for "mountain") Courtyard, houses an extensive Hawai'i and Pacific book collection and pays tribute to Kamakau, a missionary student whose 19th-century writings in English offer rare and vital insight into traditional Hawaiian culture. ⊠*478 King St., Downtown Honolulu* ☎*808/586–3500* ⊡*Free* ☉*Mon. and Wed. 10–5, Tues., Fri., and Sat. 9–5, Thurs. 9–8.*

❾ Honolulu Academy of Arts. Originally built around the collection of a Honolulu matron who donated much of her estate to the museum, the academy is housed in a maze of courtyards, cloistered walkways, and quiet low-ceilinged spaces. There's an impressive permanent collection that includes Hiroshige's *ukiyo-e* Japanese prints, donated by James Michener; Italian Renaissance paintings; and American and European art. The newer Luce Pavilion complex, nicely incorporated into the more traditional architecture of the place, has a traveling-exhibit gallery, a Hawaiian gallery, an excellent café, and a gift shop. The Academy Theatre screens art films. This is also the jumping-off place for tours of Doris Duke's estate, Shangri-La. Call or check the Web site for special exhibits, concerts, and films. ⊠*900 S. Beretania St., Downtown Honolulu* ☎*808/532–8700* ⊕*www.honoluluacademy.org* ⊡*$10 Academy, free 1st Wed. and 3rd Sun. of month* ☉*Tues.–Sat. 10–4:30, Sun. 1–5.*

⓭ Mission Houses Museum. The determined Hawai'i missionaries arrived in 1820, gaining royal favor and influencing every aspect of island life. Their descendants became leaders in government and business. You can walk through their original dwellings, including Hawai'i's oldest wooden structure, a white-frame house that was prefabricated in New England and shipped around the Horn. Certain areas of the museum may be seen only on a one-hour guided tour. Costumed docents give an excellent picture of what mission life was like. Rotating displays showcase such arts as Hawaiian quilting, portraits, even toys. ⊠*553 S. King St., Downtown Honolulu* ☎*808/531–0481* ⊕*www.missionhouses.org* ⊡*$10* ☉*Tues.–Sat. 10–4; guided tours at 11 and 2:45.*

AROUND HONOLULU

Downtown Honolulu and Chinatown can easily swallow up a day's walking, sightseeing, and shopping. Another day's worth of attractions surrounds the city's core. To the north, just off H1 in the tightly packed neighborhood of Kalihi, explore a museum gifted to the Islands in memory of a princess. Immediately mauka (toward the mountain), off Pali Highway, are a renowned resting place and a carefully preserved home where royal families retreated during the doldrums of summer. To the south, along King Street and Wai'alae Avenue, are a pair of neighborhoods chockablock with interesting restaurants and shops. Down the shore a bit from Diamond Head, visit O'ahu's ritziest address and an equally upscale shopping center.

One reason to venture farther afield is the chance to glimpse Honolulu's residential neighborhoods. Species of classic Hawai'i homes include the tiny green-and-white plantation-era house with its corrugated tin roof, two windows flanking a central door and small porch; the breezy bungalow with its swooping Thai-style roofline and two wings flanking screened French doors through which breezes blow into the living room. Note the tangled "Grandma-style" gardens and many *'ohana* houses—small homes in the backyard of a larger home or built as apartments perched over the garage, allowing extended families to live together. Carports, which rarely house cars, are the Island version of rec rooms, where parties are held and neighbors sit to "talk story." Sometimes you see gallon jars on the flat roofs of garages or carports: these are pickled lemons fermenting in the sun. Also in the neighborhoods, you find the folksy restaurants and takeout spots favored by Islanders.

■ TIP→For those with a Costco card, the cheapest gas on the island is at the Costco station on Arakawa Street between Dillingham Boulevard and Nimitz Highway.

★ **Bishop Museum.** Founded in 1889 by Charles R. Bishop as a memorial to his wife, Princess Bernice Pauahi Bishop, the museum began as a repository for the royal possessions of this last direct descendant of King Kamehameha the Great. Today it's the Hawai'i State Museum of Natural and Cultural History and houses almost 25 million items that tell the history of the Hawaiian Islands and their Pacific neighbors. The latest addition to the complex is a natural-science wing with state-of-the-art interactive exhibits. Venerable but sadly aging Hawaiian Hall, is undergoing a multimillion-dollar renovation; it houses Polynesian artifacts: lustrous feather capes, the skeleton of a giant sperm whale, photography and crafts displays, and an authentic, well-preserved grass house inside a two-story 19th-century Victorian-style gallery. Closed for renovations at this writing, the Hall is scheduled to reopen summer 2009. Also check out the planetarium, daily hula and Hawaiian crafts demonstrations, special exhibits, and the Shop Pacifica. The building alone, with its huge Victorian turrets and immense stone walls, is worth seeing. ⊠ *1525 Bernice St., Kalihi* ☎ *808/847–3511* ⊕ *www.bishop museum.org* 🖅 *$15.95* ⊗ *Wed.–Mon. 9–5;* closed Tues.

National Memorial Cemetery of the Pacific. Nestled in the bowl of Puowaina, or Punchbowl Crater, this 112-acre cemetery is the final resting place for more than 48,000 U.S. war veterans and family members. Among those buried here is Ernie Pyle, the famed World War II correspondent who was killed by a Japanese sniper on Ie Shima, an island off the northwest coast of Okinawa. Puowaina, formed 75,000–100,000 years ago during a period of secondary volcanic activity, translates as "Hill of Sacrifice." Historians believe this site once served as an altar where ancient Hawaiians offered sacrifices to their gods. ■TIP➜ The entrance to the cemetery has unfettered views of Waikīkī and Honolulu—perhaps the finest on O'ahu. ✉*2177 Puowaina Dr., Nu'uanu* ☎*808/532–3720* ⊕*www.cem.va.gov/cem/cems/nchp/nmcp.asp* ⌫*Free* ⊙*Mar.–Sept., daily 8–6:30; Oct.–Feb., daily 8–5:30.*

Fodor'sChoice   **Pearl Harbor.** *See highlighted feature in this chapter.*
    ★

★   **Queen Emma Summer Palace.** Queen Emma and her family used this stately white home, built in 1848, as a retreat from the rigors of court life in hot and dusty Honolulu during the mid-1800s. It has an eclectic mix of European, Victorian, and Hawaiian furnishings and has excellent examples of Hawaiian quilts and koa-wood furniture. ✉*2913 Pali Hwy.* ☎*808/595–3167* ⊕*www.daughtersofhawaii.org/summerpalace/* ⌫*$6* ⊙*Self-guided or guided tours daily 9–4.*

SOUTHEAST O'AHU

Driving southeast from Waikīkī on busy four-lane Kalaniana'ole Highway, you'll pass a dozen bedroom communities tucked into the valleys at the foot of the Ko'olau Range, with just fleeting glimpses of the ocean from a couple of pocket parks. Suddenly, civilization falls away, the road narrows to two lanes, and you enter the rugged coastline of Kokohead and Ka Iwi.

This is a cruel coastline: dry, windswept, and rocky shores, with untamed waves that are notoriously treacherous. While walking its beaches, do not turn your back on the ocean, don't venture close to wet areas where high waves occasionally reach, and heed warning signs.

At this point, you're passing through Koko Head Regional Park. On your right is the bulging remnant of a pair of volcanic craters that the Hawaiians called Kawaihoa, known today as Kokohead. To the left is Koko Crater and the area of the park that includes a hiking trail, a dryland botanical garden, a firing range, and a riding stable. Ahead is a sinuous shoreline with scenic pullouts and beaches to explore. Named the Ka Iwi Coast (*iwi,* "ee-vee," are bones—sacred to Hawaiians and full of symbolism) for the channel just offshore, this area was once home to a ranch and small fishing enclave that were destroyed by a tidal wave in the 1940s.

Driving straight from Waikīkī to Makapu'u Point takes from a half to a full hour, depending on traffic. There aren't a huge number of sights per se in this corner of O'ahu, so a couple of hours should be plenty of exploring time, unless you make a lengthy stop at a particular point.

Hālona Blowhole. Below a scenic turnout along the Koko Head shoreline, this oft-photographed lava tube sucks the ocean in and spits it out. Don't get too close, as conditions can get dangerous. ■TIP➜Look to your right to see the tiny beach below that was used to film the wave-washed love scene in *From Here to Eternity*. In winter this is a good spot to watch whales at play. Offshore, the islands of Moloka'i and Lāna'i call like distant sirens, and every once in a while Maui is visible in blue silhouette. Take your valuables with you and lock your car, because this scenic location is a hot spot for petty thieves. ⊠ *Kalaniana'ole Hwy., 1 mi east of Hanauma Bay.*

🜚 Fodor's Choice
★
Hanauma Bay Nature Preserve. The exterior wall of a volcanic crater collapsed, opening it to the sea and thereby giving birth to O'ahu's most famous snorkeling destination. Even from the overlook, the horseshoe-shaped bay is a beauty, and you can easily see the reefs through the clear aqua waters. The wide beach is a great place for sunbathing and picnics. This is a marine conservation district, and regulations prohibit feeding the fish. Visitors are required to go through the Education Center before trekking down to the bay. The center provides a cultural history of the area and exhibits about the importance of protecting its marine life. Check out the "Today at the Bay" exhibit for up-to-date information on daily tides, ocean safety warnings, and activities. Food concessions and equipment rentals are also on-site. ■TIP➜Come early to get parking, as the number of visitors allowed per day is limited. Also note that the bay is best in the early hours before the waters are churned up. Call for current conditions or for information about Thursday evening lectures, Saturday morning field trips, and Saturday night Hanauma Bay by Starlight events (extending opening hours to 10 PM) are held weekly. ⊠ *7455 Kalaniana'ole Hwy. 96825* ☎ *808/396–4229* ⊕ *www.honolulu.gov/parks/facility/hanaumabay* ⊠ *Nonresident fee $5; parking $1; mask, snorkel, and fins rental $6; tram from parking lot to beach $1.50 round-trip* ☉ *Wed.–Mon. 6–6.*

> **WHAT DOES IT MEAN?**
>
> Here's a guide to T-shirts and bumper stickers common in O'ahu:
>
> ■ Eddie Would Go: Inspirational reference to big-wave surfer Eddie Aikau, who lost his life attempting to save those aboard a swamped voyaging canoe.
>
> ■ Wala'au: Gossip. The name of a popular Kaua'i radio show.
>
> ■ Kau Inoa: Put or place your name. Urges Hawaiians to sign up to help organize a Native Hawaiian governing entity.
>
> ■ If can, can; if no can, no can: Pidgin for "whatever."
>
> ■ Got koko?: Got blood, meaning, are you Hawaiian?

Makapu'u Point. This spot has breathtaking views of the ocean, mountains, and the Windward islands. The point of land jutting out in the distance is **Mōkapu Peninsula,** site of a U.S. Marine base. The spired mountain peak is **Mt. Olomana.** In front of you on the long pier is part of the **Makai Undersea Test Range,** a research facility that's closed to the public. Offshore is **Manana Island (Rabbit Island),** a picturesque cay said to resemble a swimming bunny with its ears pulled back. Ironically enough, Manana Island was once overrun with rabbits, thanks to a rancher who let a few hares run wild on the land. They were eradicated in 1994 by biologists who grew concerned that the rabbits were destroying the island's native plants.

Nestled in the cliff face is the **Makapu'u Lighthouse,** which became operational in 1909 and has the largest lighthouse lens in America. The lighthouse is closed to the public, but near the Makapu'u Point turnout you can find the start of a mile-long paved road (closed to traffic). Hike up to the top of the 647-foot bluff for a closer view of the lighthouse and,

Continued on page 61

USS *West Virginia* (BB48), 7 December 1941

PEARL HARBOR

December 7, 1941. Every American then alive recalls exactly what he or she was doing when the news broke that the Japanese had bombed Pearl Harbor, the catalyst that brought the United States into World War II.

Although it was clear by late 1941 that war with Japan was inevitable, no one in authority seems to have expected the attack to come in just this way, at just this time. So when the Japanese bombers swept through a gap in Oʻahu's Koʻolau Mountains in the hazy light of morning, they found the bulk of America's Pacific fleet right where they hoped it would be: docked like giant stepping stones across the calm waters of the bay named for the pearl oysters that once prospered there. More than 2,000 people died that day, including 49 civilians. A dozen ships were sunk. And on the nearby air bases, virtually every American military aircraft was destroyed or damaged. The attack was a stunning success, but it lit a fire under America, which went to war with "Remember Pearl Harbor" as its battle cry. Here, in what is still a key Pacific naval base, the attack is remembered every day by thousands of visitors, including many curious Japanese, who for years heard little World War II history in their own country. In recent years, the memorial has been the site of reconciliation ceremonies involving Pearl Harbor veterans from both sides.

GETTING AROUND

Pearl Harbor is both a working military base and the most-visited O'ahu attraction. Four distinct destinations share a parking lot and are linked by footpath, shuttle, and ferry.

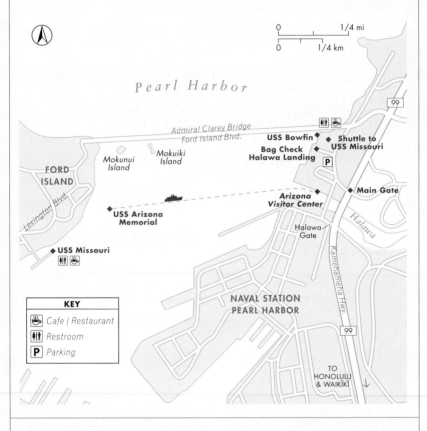

The USS *Arizona* visitor center is accessible from the parking lot. The *Arizona* Memorial itself is in the middle of the harbor; get tickets for the ferry ride at the visitor center. The USS *Bowfin* is also reachable from the parking lot. The USS *Missouri* is docked at Ford Island, a restricted area of the naval base. Vehicular access is prohibited. To get there, take a shuttle bus from the station near the *Bowfin*.

ARIZONA MEMORIAL

Snugged up tight in a row of seven battleships off Ford Island, the USS *Arizona* took a direct hit that December morning, exploded, and rests still on the shallow bottom where she settled.

A visit to the *Arizona* Memorial begins prosaically—a line, a ticket that assigns you to a group and tour time, a wait filled with shopping, visiting the museum, and strolling the grounds. When your number is called, you watch a 23-minute documentary film then board the ferry to the memorial. The swooping, stark-white memorial, which straddles the wreck of the USS *Arizona*, was designed by Honolulu architect Alfred Preis to represent both the depths of the low-spirited, early days of the war, and the uplift of victory. After the carnival-like courtyard, a somber, contemplative mood descends upon visitors during the ferry ride; this is a place where 1,177 crewmen lost their lives died. Gaze at the names of the dead carved into the wall of white marble. Scatter flowers (but no lei—the string is bad for the fish). Salute the flag. Remember Pearl Harbor.

808/422–0561
www.nps.gov/usar

USS *MISSOURI* (BB63)

Together with the *Arizona* Memorial, the *Missouri's* presence in Pearl Harbor perfectly bookends America's WWII experience that began December 7, 1941, and ended on the "Mighty Mo's" starboard deck with the signing of the Terms of Surrender.

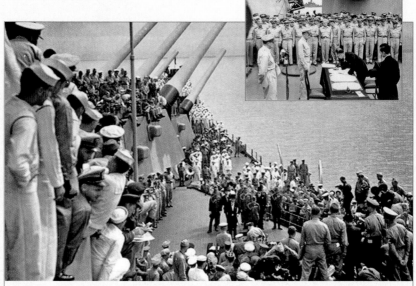

Surrender of Japan, USS *Missouri*, 2 September 1945

In the parking area behind the USS *Bowfin* Museum, board a jitney for a breezy, eight-minute ride to Ford Island and the teak decks and towering superstructure of the *Missouri*, docked for good in the very harbor from which she first went to war on January 2, 1945. The last battleship ever built, the *Missouri* famously hosted the final act of WWII, the signing of the Terms of Surrender. The commission that governs this floating museum has surrounded her with buildings tricked out in WWII style—a canteen that serves as an orientation space for tours, a WACs and WAVEs lounge, Truman's Line restaurant serving Navy-style meals, and a Victory Store housing a souvenir shop and covered with period mottos ("Don't be a blabateur").

■TIP➜ Definitely hook up with a tour guide (additional charge) or purchase an audio tour ($2)—these add a great deal to the experience.

The *Missouri* is all about numbers: 209 feet tall, six 239,000-pound guns, capable of firing up to 23 mi away. Absorb these during the tour, then stop to take advantage of the view from the decks. The Mo is a work in progress, with only a handful of her hundreds of spaces open to view.

808/455–1600 or 888/877–6477
www.ussmissouri.org

USS *BOWFIN* (SS287)

SUBMARINE MUSEUM & PARK

Launched one year to the day after the Pearl Harbor attack, the USS *Bowfin* sank 44 enemy ships during WWII and now serves as the centerpiece of a museum honoring all submariners.

Although the *Bowfin* no less than the *Arizona* Memorial com-memorates the lost, the mood here is lighter. Perhaps it's the childlike scale of the boat, a metal tube just 16 feet in diameter, packed with ladders, hatches, and other obstacles, like the naval ver-sion of a jungle gym. Perhaps it's the World War II-era music that plays in the covered patio. Or it might be the museum's touching displays—the pen-ciled sailor's journal, the Vargas girlie posters. Aboard the boat nicknamed "Pearl Harbor Avenger," compartments are fitted out as though "Sparky" was away from the radio room just for a moment, and "Cooky" might be right back to his pots and pans. The museum includes many artifacts to spark family conversations, among them a vintage dive suit that looks too big for Shaquille

O'Neal. A caution: The *Bowfin* could be hazardous for very young children; no one under four allowed.

808/423–1341
www.bowfin.org

THE PACIFIC AVIATION MUSEUM

This new museum opened on December 7, 2006, as phase one of a four-phase tribute to the air wars of the Pacific. Located on Ford Island in Hangar 37, an actual seaplan hangar that survived the Pearl Harbor at-tack, the museum is made up of a theater where a short film on Pearl Harbor kicks off the tour, an education center, a shop, and a restaurant. Exhibits—many of which are in-teractive and involve sound effects—include an authentic Japanese Zero in a diorama setting a chance to don a flight suit and play the role of a World War II pilot using one of six flight simulators. Various aircrafts are employed to narrate the great battles: the Doolittle Raid on Japan, the Battle of Midway, Guadalcanal, and so on. The actual Stearman N2S-3 in which President George H. W. Bush soloed is another exhibit. ☏808/441–1000 ⊕www.pacificaviationmuseum.org ✈$14.

PLAN YOUR PEARL HARBOR DAY LIKE A MILITARY CAMPAIGN

DIRECTIONS

Take H–1 west from Waikīkī to Exit 15A and follow signs. Or take TheBus route 20 or 47 from Waikīkī. Beware high-priced private shuttles. It's a 30-minute drive from Waikīkī.

WHAT TO BRING

Picture ID is required during periods of high alert; bring it just in case.

You'll be standing, walking, and climbing all day. Wear something with lots of pockets and a pair of good walking shoes. Carry a light jacket, sunglasses, hat, and sunscreen.

No purses, packs, or bags are allowed. Take only what fits in your pockets. Cameras are okay but without the bags. A private bag storage booth is located in the parking lot near the visitors' center. Leave nothing in your car; theft is a problem despite bicycle security patrols.

HOURS

Hours are 8 AM to 5 PM for all attractions. However, the *Arizona* Memorial starts giving out tickets on a first-come, first-served basis at 7:30 AM; the last tickets are given out at 3 PM. Spring break, summer, and holidays are busiest, and tickets sometimes run out by noon.

TICKETS

Arizona: Free. Add $5 for museum audio tours.

Aviation: $14 adults, $7 children. Add $7 for aviator's guided tour.

Missouri: $16 adults, $8 children. Add $6 for chief's guided tour or audio tour; add $33 for in-depth, behind-the-scenes tours.

Bowfin: $10 adults, $4 children. Add $2 for audio tours. Children under 4 may go into the museum but not aboard the *Bowfin*.

KIDS

This might be the day to enroll younger kids in the hotel children's program. Preschoolers chafe at long waits, and attractions involve some hazards for toddlers. Older kids enjoy the *Bowfin* and *Missouri*, especially.

MAKING THE MOST OF YOUR TIME

Expect to spend at least half a day; a whole day is better.

At the *Arizona* Memorial, you'll get a ticket, be given a tour time, and then have to wait anywhere from 15 minutes to 3 hours. You must pick up your own ticket so you can't hold places. If the wait is long, skip over to the *Bowfin* to fill the time.

SUGGESTED READING

Pearl Harbor and the USS Arizona Memorial, by Richard Wisniewski. $5.95. 64-page magazine-size quick history.

Bowfin, by Edwin P. Hoyt. $14.95. Dramatic story of undersea adventure.

The Last Battleship, by Scott C. S. Stone. $11.95. Story of the Mighty Mo.

in winter, a great whale-watching vantage point. ⊠*Kalaniana'ole Hwy.,* *turnout above Makapu'u Beach.*

Paikō Peninsula. Secluded within the confines of the bay, private and quiet, this slim spit of land is a lovely place to spend a morning or afternoon swimming, snorkeling, reading, and dozing. The peninsula is reached by a narrow residential road that dead-ends at the Paikō Lagoon State Reserve. The reserve is off-limits to the public, but all beaches in Hawai'i are public to the high-water line, and there is a beach-access pathway a few houses before the road's end. Turn left when you get to the beach and find your spot near where the houses end. ⊠*Kalaniana'ole Hwy., just past Niu Valley, on right, on Paikō Dr.*

WINDWARD O'AHU

Looking at Honolulu's topsy-turvy urban sprawl, you would never suspect the Windward side existed. It's a secret Oahuans like to keep, so they can watch the awe on the faces of their guests when the car emerges from the tunnels through the mountains and they gaze for the first time on the panorama of turquoise bays and emerald valleys watched over by the knife-edged Ko'olau ridges. Jaws literally drop. Every time. And this just a 15-minute drive from downtown.

It is on this side of the island that many Native Hawaiians live. Evidence of traditional lifestyles is abundant in crumbling fish ponds, rock platforms that once were altars, taro patches still being worked, and throw-net fishermen posed stock-still above the water (though today, they're invariably wearing polarized sunglasses, the better to spot the fish).

Here, the pace is slower, more oriented toward nature. Beach-going, hiking, diving, surfing, and boating are the draws, along with a visit to the Polynesian Cultural Center, and poking through little shops and wayside stores.

You can easily spend an entire day exploring Windward O'ahu, or you can just breeze on through, nodding at the sights on your way to the North Shore. Waikīkī to Windward is a drive of less than half an hour; to the North Shore via Kamehameha Highway along the Windward Coast is one hour minimum.

TOP ATTRACTIONS

Byodo-In Temple. Tucked away in the back of the Valley of the Temples cemetery is a replica of the 11th-century Temple at Uji in Japan. A 2-ton carved wooden statue of the Buddha presides inside the main temple building. Next to the temple building are a meditation pavilion and gardens set dramatically against the sheer, green cliffs of the Ko'olau Mountains. You can ring the 5-foot, 3-ton brass bell for good luck and feed some of the hundreds of carp that inhabit the garden's 2-acre pond. ⊠*47-200 Kahekili Hwy., Kāne'ohe* ☎*808/239–8811* 🖼*$2* ☉*Daily 8–5.*

NEED A
BREAK?

Generations of children have purchased their beach snacks and sodas at **Kalapawai Market** (⊠ *306 S. Kalāheo Ave., 96734*), near Kailua Beach. A Windward landmark since 1932, the green-and-white market has distinctive

CLOSE UP

Shangri La

The marriage of heiress Doris Duke, at age 23, to a man much older than herself didn't last. But their around-the-world honeymoon tour did leave her with two lasting loves: Islamic art and architecture, which she first encountered on that journey; and Hawai'i, where the honeymooners made an extended stay while Doris learned to surf and befriended Islanders unimpressed by her wealth.

Today visitors to her beloved Islands—where she spent most winters—can share both loves by touring her home. The sought-after tours, which are coordinated by and begin at the downtown Honolulu Academy of Arts, start with a visit to the Arts of the Islamic World Gallery. A short van ride then takes small groups on to the house itself, on the far side of Diamond Head.

In 1936 Duke bought 5 acres at Black Point, down the coast from Waikīkī, and began to build and furnish the first home that would be all her own. She called it **Shangri La**. For more than 50 years, the home was a perpetual work in progress as Duke traveled the world, buying furnishings and artifacts, picking up ideas for her Mughul garden, for the Playhouse in the style of an Irani pavilion, and for the water terraces and tropical gardens. When she died in 1993, Duke left instructions that her home was to become a center for the study of Islamic art, open to the public for tours.

To walk through the house and its gardens—which have remained much as Duke left them with only some minor conservation-oriented changes—is to experience the personal style of someone who saw everything as raw material for her art.

With her trusted houseman, Jin de Silva, she built, by her own hand, the elaborate Turkish (or Damascus) Room, trimming tiles and painted panels to fit the walls and building a fountain of her own design.

One aspect of the home that clearly takes its inspiration from the Muslim tradition is the entry: an anonymous gate, a blank white wall, and a wooden door that bids you "Enter herein in peace and security" in Arabic characters. Inside, tiles glow, fountains tinkle, and shafts of light illuminate artworks through arches and high windows. This was her private world, entered only by trusted friends.

The house is open by guided tour only; tours take 2½ hours. Children under 12 are not admitted. All tours begin at the Academy of Arts.

✉ *Academy of Arts, 900 S. Beretania Honolulu* ☎ *808/532–3853 Academy of Arts* ⊕ *www.honoluluacademy.org* 🎟 *Tours $25* ⊙ *Tours Wed.–Sat. by reservation; 1st tour 8:30 AM, last tour 1:30 PM.*

---

charm. You'll see slipper-clad locals sitting in front sharing a cup of coffee and talking story at picnic tables or in front of the Market. It's a good source for your carryout lunch, since there's no concession stand at the beach. Or, grab a cup of coffee and have a seat at the wooden tables outside. With one of the better selections of wine on the island, the market is also a great place to pick up a bottle.

Windward Villages. Tiny villages—generally consisting of a sign, store, a beach park, possibly a post office, and not much more—are strung along Kamehameha Highway on the Windward side. Each has something to offer. In Waiahole, look for fruit stands and an ancient grocery store. In Ka'a'awa,

there's a lunch spot and convenience store/gas station. In Punalu'u, stop at the gallery of fanciful landscape artist Lance Fairly and the woodworking shop, Kahaunani Woods & Crafts, plus venerable Ching General Store or the Shrimp Shack. Kim Taylor Reece's photo studio, featuring haunting portraits of hula dancers, is between Punalu'u and Hau'ula. Hau'ula has Hau'ula Gift Shop and Art Gallery, formerly yet another Ching Store, now a clothing shop where sarongs wave like banners and, at Ha'ula Kai Shopping Center, Tamura Market, with excellent seafood and the last liquor before Mormon-dominated Lā'ie.

Nu'uanu Pali Lookout. This panoramic perch looks out to Windward O'ahu. It was in this region that King Kamehameha I drove defending forces over the edges of the 1,000-foot-high cliffs, thus winning the decisive battle for control of O'ahu. ■TIP→From here you can see views that stretch from Kāne'ohe Bay to Mokoli'i (little lizard), a small island off the coast, and beyond. Temperatures at the summit are several degrees cooler than in warm Waikīkī, so bring a jacket along. And hang on tight to any loose possessions; it gets extremely windy at the lookout. Lock your car; break-ins have occurred here. ⊠ Top of Pali Hwy. ⊙ Daily 9–4.

Offshore Islands and Rocks. As you drive the Windward and North shores along Kamehameha Highway, you'll note a number of interesting geological features. At Kualoa look to the ocean and gaze at the uniquely shaped little island of **Mokoli'i** (little lizard), a 206-foot-high sea stack also known as Chinaman's Hat. According to Hawaiian legend, the goddess Hi'iaka, sister of Pele, slew the dragon Mokoli'i and flung its tail into the sea, forming the distinct islet. Other dragon body parts—in the form of rocks, of course—were scattered along the base of nearby Kualoa Ridge. ■TIP→In Lā'ie, if you turn right on Anemoku Street, and right again on Naupaka, you come to a scenic lookout where you can see a group of islets, dramatically washed by the waves.

Polynesian Cultural Center. Re-created individual villages showcase the lifestyles and traditions of Hawai'i, Tahiti, Samoa, Fiji, the Marquesas Islands, New Zealand, and Tonga. Focusing on individual islands within its 42-acre center, 35 mi from Waikīkī, the Polynesian Cultural Center was founded in 1963 by the Church of Jesus Christ of Latter-day Saints. It houses restaurants, hosts lū'au, and demonstrates cultural traditions such as tribal tattooing, fire dancing, and ancient customs and ceremonies. The expansive open-air shopping village carries Polynesian handicrafts. ■TIP→If you're staying in Honolulu, see the center as part of a van tour so you won't have to drive home late at night after the two-hour evening show. Various packages are available, from basic

SHAVE ICE

Island-style shave ice (never shaved ice—it's a pidgin thing) is said to have been born when neighborhood kids hung around the icehouse, waiting to pounce on the shavings from large blocks of ice, carved with ultrasharp Japanese planes that created an exceptionally fine-textured granita.

In the 1920s, according to the historian for syrup manufacturer Malolo Beverages Co., Chinese vendors developed sweet fruit concentrates to pour over the ice.

The evolution continued with mom-and-pop shops adding their own touches, such as secreting a nugget of Japanese-style sweet bean paste in the center, or a small scoop of ice cream, adding *li hing* powder (a sweet spice), or deftly pouring multitoned cones.

There's nothing better on a sticky hot day. Try Waiola on Kapahulu or, in Hale'iwa, Aoki's or Matsumoto's.

admission to an all-inclusive deal. Every May, the PCC hosts the World Fire Knife Dance Competition, an event that draws the top fire-knife dance performers from around the world. ⊠*55-370 Kamehameha Hwy., Lā'ie* ☎*808/293–3333 or 800/367–7060* ⊕*www.polynesia.com* ⊡*$58–$215* ⊘*Mon.–Sat. noon–9:30. Islands close at 6.*

WORTH NOTING

🐾 **Sea Life Park.** Dolphins leap and spin, penguins frolic, and a killer whale performs impressive tricks at this marine-life attraction 15 mi from Waikīkī at scenic Makapu'u Point. The park has a 300,000-gallon Hawaiian reef aquarium, the Hawaiian Monk Seal Care Center, and a breeding sanctuary for Hawai'i's endangered *Honu* sea turtle. Join the Stingray or Dolphin Encounter and get up close and personal in the water with these sea creatures (don't worry, the rays' stingers have been removed) or go on an underwater photo safari. ⊠*41-202 Kalaniana'ole Hwy., Waimānalo* ☎*808/259–7933 or 866/393–5158* ⊕*www.sealife parkhawaii.com* ⊡*$29* ⊘*Daily 10:30–5.*

Waimānalo. This modest little seaside town flanked by chiseled cliffs is worth a visit. Its biggest draws are its beautiful beaches, offering glorious views to the windward side. **Bellows Beach** is great for swimming and bodysurfing, and **Waimānalo Beach Park** is also safe for swimming. Down the side roads, as you head mauka (toward the mountains), are little farms that grow a variety of fruits and flowers. Toward the back of the valley are small ranches with grazing horses. ⊠*Kalaniana'ole Hwy.*

■TIP→If you see any trucks selling corn and you're staying at a place where you can cook it, be sure to get some in Waimānalo. It may be the sweetest you'll ever eat, and the price is the lowest on O'ahu.

THE NORTH SHORE

An hour from town and a world away in atmosphere, O'ahu's North Shore, roughly from Kahuku Point to Ka'ena Point, is about small farms and big waves, tourist traps and otherworldly landscapes. Parks and

Continued on page 71

Imagine picking your seat for free at the Super Bowl or wandering the grounds of Augusta National at no cost during The Masters, and you glimpse the opportunity you have when attending the Vans Triple Crown of Surfing on the North Shore.

NORTH SHORE SURFING & THE TRIPLE CROWN

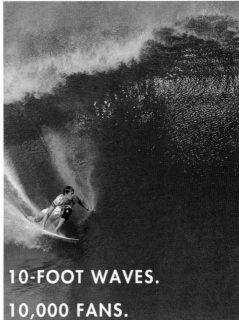

10-FOOT WAVES.
10,000 FANS.

TOP 50 SURFERS.

Long considered the best stretch of surf breaks on Earth, the North Shore surf area encompasses 6 mi of coastline on the northwestern tip of O'ahu from Hale'iwa to Sunset Beach. There are over 20 major breaks within these 6 mi. Winter storms in the North Pacific send huge swells southward which don't break for thousands of miles until they hit the shallow reef of O'ahu's remote North Shore. This creates optimum surfing all winter long and was the inspiration for having surf competitions here each holiday season.

Every November and December the top 50 surfers in world rankings descend on "The Country" to decide who is the best all-around surfer in the world. Each of the three invitation-only contests that make up the Triple Crown has its own winner; competitors also win points based on the final standings. The surfer who excels in all three contests, racking up the most points overall, wins the Vans Triple Crown title. The first contest is held at **Hale'iwa Beach,** the second at **Sunset Beach.** The season reaches its crescendo at the most famous surf break in the world, the **Banzai Pipeline.**

The best part is the cost to attend the events—nothing; your seat for the show—wherever you set down your beach towel. Just park your car, grab your stuff, and watch the best surfers in the world tame the best waves in the world.

> The only surfing I understand involves a mouse.

The contests were created not only to fashion an overall champion, but to attract the casual fan to the sport. Announcers explain each ride over the loudspeakers, discussing the nuances and values being weighed by the judges. A scoreboard displays points and standings during the four days of each event.

If this still seems incomprehensible to you, the action on the beach can also be exciting as some of the most beautiful people in the world are attracted to these contests.

For more information, see www.triplecrownofsurfing. com

What should I bring?

Pack for a day at the Triple Crown the way you would for any day at the beach–sun block, beach towel, bottled water, and if you want something other than snacks, food.

These contests are held in rural neighborhoods (read: few stores), so pack anything you might need during the day. Also, binoculars are suggested, especially for the contest at Sunset. The pros will be riding huge outside ocean swells, and it can be hard to follow from the beach without binoculars. Hale'iwa's breaks and Pipeline are considerably closer to shore, but binoculars will let you see the intensity on the contestants' faces.

Hale'iwa Ali'i Beach Park
Vans Triple Crown Contest #1: Reef Hawaiian Pro

The Triple Crown gets underway with high-performance waves (and the know-how to ride them) at Hale'iwa. Though lesser known than the other two breaks of the Triple Crown, it is the perfect wave for showing off: the contest here is full of sharp cutbacks (twisting the board dramatically off the top or bottom of the wave), occasional barrel rides, and a crescendo of floaters (balancing the board on the top of the cresting wave) before the wave is destroyed on the shallow tabletop reef called the Toilet Bowl. The rider who can pull off the most tricks will win this leg, evening the playing field for the other two contests, where knowledge of the break is the key. Also, the beach park is walking distance from historic Hale'iwa town, a mecca to surfers worldwide who make their pilgrimage here every winter to ride the waves. Even if you are not a fan, immersing yourself in their culture will make you one by nightfall.

Sunset Beach
Vans Triple Crown Contest #2: O'Neill World Cup of Surfing

At Sunset, the most guts and bravado win the day. The competition is held when the swell is at 8 to 12 feet and from the northwest. Sunset gets the heaviest surf because it is the exposed point on the northern tip of O'ahu. Surfers describe the waves here as "moving mountains." The choice of waves is the key to this contest as only the perfect one will give the competitor a ride through the jigsaw-puzzle outer reef, which can kill a perfect wave instantly, all the way into the inner reef. Big bottom turns (riding all the way down the face of the wave before turning dramatically back onto the wave) and slipping into a super thick tube (slowing down to let the wave catch you and riding inside its vortex) are considered necessary to carry the day.

Banzai Pipeline
Vans Triple Crown Contest #3: Billabong Pipeline Masters

It is breathtaking to watch the best surfers in the world disappear into a gaping maw of whitewash for a few seconds only to emerge from the other side unscathed. Surfing the Pipeline showcases their ability to specialize in surfing, to withstand the power and fury of a 10-foot wave from within its hollow tube.

How does the wave become hollow in the first place? When the deep ocean floor ascends steeply to the shore, the waves that meet it will pitch over themselves sharply, rather than rolling. This pitching causes a tube to form, and in most places in the world that tube is a mere couple of feet in diameter. In the case of Pipeline, however, its unique, extremely shallow reef causes the swells to open into 10-foot-high moving hallways that surfers can pass through. Only problem: a single slip puts them right into the raggedly sharp coral heads that caused the wave to pitch in the first place. Broken arms and boards are the rule rather than the exception for those who dare to ride and fail.

■ TIP→ The Banzai Pipeline is a surf break, not a beach. The best place to catch a glimpse of the break is from 'Ehukai Beach.

When Are the Contests?

The first contests at Hale'iwa begin the second week of November, and the Triple Crown finishes up right before Christmas.

Surfing, more so than any other sport, relies on Mother Nature to allow competition. Each contest in the Triple Crown requires only four days of competition, but each is given a window of twelve days. Contest officials decide by 7 AM of each day whether the contest will be held or not, and they release the information to radio stations and via a hotline (whose number changes each year, unfortunately). By 7:15, you will know if it is on or not. Consult the local paper's sports section for the hotline number or listen to the radio announcement. The contests run from 8:30 to 4:30, featuring half-hour heats with four to six surfers each.

If big crowds bother you, go early on in the contests, within the first two days of each one. While the finale of the Pipeline Masters may draw about 10,000 fans, the earlier days have the same world class surfers with less than a thousand fans.

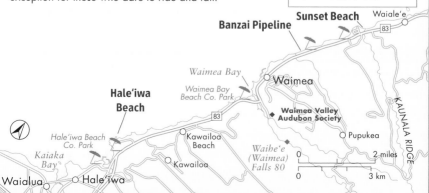

How Do I Get There?

If you hate dealing with parking and traffic, take TheBus. It will transport you from Waikīkī to the contest sites in an hour for two bucks and no hassle.

If you must drive, watch the news the night before. If they are expecting big waves that night, there is a very good chance the contest will be on in the morning. Leave by 6 AM to beat the crowd. When everybody else gets the news at 7:15 AM that the show is on, you will be parking your car and taking a snooze on the beach waiting for the surfing to commence.

Parking is limited so be prepared to park alongside Kamehameha Highway and trek it in.

But I'm not coming until Valentine's Day.

There doesn't need to be a contest underway for you to enjoy these spots from a spectator's perspective. The North Shore surf season begins in October and concludes at the end of March. Only the best can survive the wave at Pipeline. You may not be watching Kelly Slater or Andy Irons ripping, but, if the waves are up, you will still see surfing that will blow your mind. Also, there are surf contests year-round on all shores of O'ahu, so check the papers to see what is going on during your stay. A few other events to be on the lookout for:

Buffalo's Annual Big Board Surfing Classic
Generally held in March at legendary waterman "Buffalo" Keaulana's home beach of Mākaha, this is the Harlem Globetrotters of surfing contests. You'll see tandem riding, headstands, and outrigger canoe surfing. The contest is more about making the crowds cheer than beating your competitors, which makes it very accessible for the casual fan.

Converse Hawaiian Open
During the summer months, the waves switch to the south shore, where there are surf contests of one type or another each week. The Open is one of the biggest and is a part of the US Professional Longboard Surfing Championships. The best shoot it out every August on the waves Duke Kahanamoku made famous at Queen's Beach in Waikīkī.

Quiksilver in Memory of Eddie Aikau Big Wave Invitational
The granddaddy of them all is a one-day, winner-take-all contest in 25-foot surf at Waimea Bay. Because of the need for huge waves, it can be held only when there's a perfect storm. That could be at any time in the winter months, and there have even been a few years when it didn't happen at all. When Mother Nature does comply, however, it is not to be missed. You can hear the waves from the road, even before you can see the beach or the break.

beaches, roadside fruit stands and shrimp shacks, a bird sanctuary, and a valley preserve offer a dozen reasons to stop between the one-time plantation town of Kahuku and the surf mecca of Hale'iwa.

Hale'iwa has had many lives, from resort getaway in the 1900s to plantation town through the 20th century to its life today as a surf and tourist magnet. Beyond Hale'iwa is the tiny village of Waialua, a string of beach parks, an airfield where gliders, hang gliders, and parachutists play, and, at the end of the road, Ka'ena Point State Recreation Area, which offers a brisk hike, striking views, and whale-watching in season.

Pack wisely for a day's North Shore excursion: swim and snorkel gear, light jacket and hat (the weather is mercurial, especially in winter), sunscreen and sunglasses, bottled water and snacks, towels and a picnic blanket, and both sandals and closed-toe shoes for hiking. A small cooler is nice; you may want to pick up some fruit or fresh corn. As always, leave valuables in the hotel safe and lock the car whenever you park.

From Waikīkī, the quickest route to the North Shore is H–1 east to H–2 north and then the Kamehameha Highway past Wahiawā; you'll hit Hale'iwa in less than an hour. The Windward route (H–1 east, H–3 through the mountains, and Kamehameha Highway north) takes at least 90 minutes to Hale'iwa.

Hale'iwa. During the 1920s this seaside hamlet boasted a posh hotel at the end of a railroad line (both long gone). During the 1960s, hippies gathered here, followed by surfers from around the world. Today Hale'iwa is a fun mix, with old general stores and contemporary boutiques, galleries, and eateries. Be sure to stop in at **Lili'uokalani Protestant Church**, founded by missionaries in the 1830s. It's fronted by a large, stone archway built in 1910 and covered with night-blooming cereus. ✉ *Follow H–1 west from Honolulu to H–2 north, exit at Wahiawā, follow Kamehameha Hwy. 6 mi, turn left at signaled intersection, then right into Hale'iwa* ⊕ *http://gonorthshore.org.*

NEED A BREAK? For a real slice of Hale'iwa life, stop at **Matsumoto's** (✉ *66-087 Kamehameha Hwy.* ⊕ *www.matsumotoshaveice.com*), a family-run business in a building dating from 1910, for shave ice in every flavor imaginable. For something different, order a shave ice with adzuki beans—the red beans are boiled until soft, mixed with sugar, and then placed in the cone with the ice on top.

Ka'ena Point State Recreation Area. The name means "the heat" and, indeed, this windy barren coast lacks both shade and fresh water (or any man-made amenities). Pack water, wear sturdy closed-toe shoes, don sunscreen and a hat, and lock the car. The hike is along a rutted dirt road, mostly flat and 3 mi long, ending in a rocky, sandy headland. It is here that Hawaiians believed the souls of the dead met with their family gods, and, if judged worthy to enter the afterlife, leaped off into eternal darkness at Leinaaka'uane, just south of the point. In summer and at low tide, the small coves offer bountiful shelling; in winter, don't venture near the water. Rare native plants dot the landscape. November through March, watch for humpbacks, spouting and breaching.

Binoculars and a camera are highly recommended. ⊠*North end of Kamehameha Hwy.*

Pu'uomahuka Heiau. Worth a stop for its spectacular views from a bluff high above the ocean overlooking Waimea Bay, this sacred spot was once the site of human sacrifices. It's now on the National Register of Historic Places. ⊠*½ mi north of Waimea Bay, from Rte. 83 turn right on Pūpūkea Rd. and drive 1 mi uphill.*

☺ **Waimea Valley Park.** Waimea may get lots of press for the giant winter
★ waves in the bay, but the valley itself is a newsmaker and an ecological treasure in its own right. The Office of Hawaiian Affairs is working to conserve and restore the natural habitat. Follow the Kamananui Stream up the valley through the 1,800 acres of gardens. The botanical collections here include more than 5,000 species of tropical flora, including a superb gathering of Polynesian plants. It's the best place on the island to see native species, such as the endangered Hawaiian moorhen. You can also see the remains of the Hale O Lono *heiau* (temple) along with other ancient archaeological sites; evidence suggests that the area was an important spiritual center. Daily activities between 10 and 2 include hula lessons, native plant walks, lei-making lessons, kapa cloth-making demonstrations. At the back of the valley, **Waihī Falls** plunges 45 feet into a swimming pond. ■TIP➔Bring your suit—a swim is the perfect way to end your hike. Be sure to bring mosquito repellent, too; it gets buggy. ⊠*59-864 Kamehameha Hwy., Hale'iwa* ☎*808/638–7766* ⊕*www. audubon.org* ☜*$10, parking $2* ⊗*Daily 9–5.*

NEED A BREAK?

The chocolate *haupia* (coconut) pie at Ted's Bakery (⊠*59-024 Kamehameha Hwy., near Sunset Beach* ☎*808/638–8207*) is legendary. Stop in for a take-out pie or for a quick plate lunch or sandwich.

CENTRAL AND WEST (LEEWARD) O'AHU

If you've got to leave one part of this island for the next trip, this is the part to skip. It's a longish drive to West O'ahu by island standards—45 minutes to Kapolei from Waikīkī and 90 minutes to Waia'anae—and the central area has little to offer. The attraction most worth the trek to West O'ahu is Hawai'i's Plantation Village in Waipahu, about a half hour out of town; it's a living-history museum built from actual homes of plantation workers. In Central O'ahu, check out the Dole Plantation for all things pineapple.

Ko 'Olina. Among the many amenities at this resort that are open to the public is the challenging (and pricey) Ted Robinson–designed golf course *(see Golf, Hiking & Outdoor Activities)*, two nice, sit-down lunch spots—Roy's Ko 'Olina at the golf course and the Naupaka Terrace at the JW Marriott Ko 'Olina Resort & Spa—and a couple of man-made swimming lagoons surrounded by lush lawns with changing and bathroom facilities. ⊠*Farrington Hwy., at Ali'inui Dr., Kapolei* ☎*808/676–5300 Ko 'Olina Golf Club, 808/676–7697 Roy's Ko 'Olina, 808/679–0079 Naupaka Terrace 96707* ⊕*www.koolinagolf.com.*

O'AHU SIGHTSEEING TOURS

Guided tours are convenient; you don't have to worry about finding a parking spot or getting admission tickets. Most of the tour guides have taken special Hawaiiana classes in history and lore, and many are certified by the state of Hawai'i. On the other hand, you won't have the freedom to proceed at your own pace, nor will you have the ability to take a detour if something else catches your attention.

BUS AND VAN TOURS

Ask exactly what the tour includes in the way of actual get-off-the-bus stops and window sights.

Polynesian Adventure. ☎808/833–3000 ⊕ www.polyad.com.

Polynesian Hospitality. ☎808/526–3565 ⊕ www.kobay.com.

Roberts Hawai'i. ☎808/539–9400 ⊕ www.robertshawaii.com.

THEME TOURS

Culinary Tour of Chinatown. Anthony Chang of the Chinese Chamber of Commerce leads tours of noodle shops, dim sum parlors, food courts, bakers, and other food vendors on Monday at 9:30 AM. Call on Friday for reservations. Tours depart from 76 N. King Street, Room 202. ☎808/533–3181.

E Noa Tours. Certified tour guides conduct Circle Island, Pearl Harbor, and shopping tours. ☎808/591–2561 ⊕ www.enoa.com.

Home of the Brave Tours. Perfect for military-history buffs. Narrated tours visit O'ahu's military bases and the National Memorial Cemetery of the Pacific. ☎808/396–8112 ⊕ www. pearlharborhq.com.

Mauka Makai Excursions. Visit the ancient Hawaiian archaeological, legendary, and nature sites that islanders hold sacred. ☎808/255–2206 ⊕ www. hawaiianecotours.net.

Matthew Gray's Hawaii Food Tours. Get a taste of Hawai'i's culture by going on one of three restaurant tours. Each includes samplings of local delicacies and discussion of Hawai'i foodways and the history of the culinary diversity of the islands. ☎808/926–3663 ⊕ www.hawaiifoodtours.com.

WALKING TOURS

American Institute of Architects (AIA) Downtown Walking Tour. See Downtown Honolulu from an architectural perspective. ✉American Institute of Architects ☎808/545–4242.

Chinatown Walking Tour. Meet at the Chinese Chamber of Commerce for a fascinating peek into herbal shops, an acupuncturist's office, open-air markets, and specialty stores. ✉Chinese Chamber of Commerce ☎808/533–3181.

Hawai'i Geographic Society. A number of Downtown Honolulu temple and archaeology walking tours are available. ☎808/538–3952.

Mākaha Beach Park. Famous as a surfing-and-boogie-boarding park, Mākaha hosts an annual surf meet and draws many scuba divers in summer, when the waves are calm, to explore underwater caverns and ledges. It's popular with families year-round but, in winter, watch for rip tides and currents; Mākaha means "fierce," and there's a reason for that. ✉84-369 Farrington Hwy., Waia'anae.

BEACHES

Tropical sun mixed with cooling trade winds and pristine waters make O'ahu's shores a literal heaven on Earth. But contrary to many assumptions, the island is not one big beach. There are miles and miles of coastline without a grain of sand, so you need to know where you are going to fully enjoy the Hawaiian experience.

Much of the island's southern and eastern coast is protected by inner reefs. The reefs provide still coastline water but not much as far as sand is concerned. However, where there are beaches on the south and east shores, they are mind-blowing. In West O'ahu and on the North Shore you can find the wide expanses of sand you would expect for enjoying the sunset. Sandy bottoms and protective reefs make the water an adventure in the winter months. Most visitors assume the seasons don't change a thing in the Islands, and they would be right—except for the waves, which are big on the South Shore in summer and placid in winter. It's exactly the opposite on the north side where winter storms bring in huge waves, but the ocean goes to glass come May and June.

WAIKĪKĪ

The 2½-mi strand called Waikīkī Beach extends from Hilton Hawaiian Village on one end to Kapi'olani Park and Diamond Head on the other. Although it's one continuous piece of beach, it's as varied as the people who inhabit the Islands. Whether you're an old-timer looking to enjoy the action from the shade or a sports nut wanting to do it all, you can find every beach activity here without ever jumping in the rental car.

■ TIP➜ If you're staying outside the area, our best advice is to park at either end of the beach and walk in. Plentiful parking exists on the west end at the Ala Wai Marina, where there are myriad free spots on the beach as well as metered stalls around the harbor. For parking on the east end, Kapi'olani Park and the Honolulu Zoo both have metered parking for $1 an hour—more affordable than the $10 per hour the resorts want.

♻ **Duke Kahanamoku Beach.** Named for Hawai'i's famous Olympic swimming champion, Duke Kahanamoku, this is a hard-packed beach with the only shade trees on the sand in Waikīkī. It's great for families with young children because of the shade and the calmest waters in Waikīkī, thanks to a rock wall that creates a semiprotected cove. The ocean clarity here is not as brilliant as most of Waikīkī because of the stillness of the surf, but it's a small price to pay for peace of mind about youngsters.

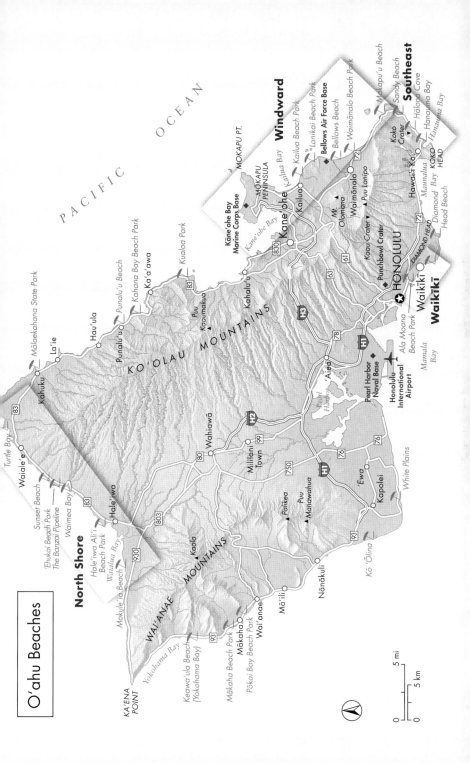

O'ahu Beaches

HONOLULU

The city of Honolulu only has one beach, the monstrous Ala Moana. It hosts everything from Dragon Boat competitions to the Aloha State Games.

🄲 **Ala Moana Beach Park.** Ala Moana has a protective reef, which makes it ostensibly a ½-mi-wide saltwater swimming pool. After Waikīkī, this is the most popular beach among visitors. To the Waikīkī side is a peninsula called Magic Island, with shady trees and paved sidewalks ideal for jogging. Ala Moana also has playing fields, tennis courts, and a couple of small ponds for sailing toy boats. This beach is for everyone, but only in the daytime. It's a high-crime area after dark. ⊠ *Honolulu, near Ala Moana Shopping Center and Ala Moana Blvd. From Waikīkī take Bus 8 to shopping center and cross Ala Moana Blvd.* ☞ *Lifeguard, toilets, showers, food concession, picnic tables, grills, parking lot.*

SOUTHEAST O'AHU

Much of Southeast O'ahu is surrounded by reef, making most of the coast uninviting to swimmers, but the spots where the reef opens up are true gems. The drive along this side of the island is amazing with its sheer lava-rock walls on one side and deep-blue ocean on the other. There are plenty of restaurants in the suburb of Hawai'i Kai, so you can make a day of it, knowing that food isn't far away.

🄲 **Hanauma Bay Nature Preserve.** Picture this as the world's biggest open-air aquarium. You go here to see fish, and fish you'll see. Due to their exposure to thousands of visitors every week, these fish are more like family pets than the skittish marine life you might expect. An old volcanic crater has created a haven from the waves where the coral has thrived. There's an educational center where you must watch a nine-minute video about the nature preserve before being allowed down to the bay. ■ TIP→ **The bay is best early in the morning (around 7), before the crowds arrive; it can be difficult to park later in the day.** Smoking is not allowed, and the beach is closed on Tuesday. **Hanauma Bay Dive Tours** (☎ 808/256–8956) runs snorkeling, Snuba, and scuba tours to Hanauma Bay with transportation from Waikīkī hotels on Monday, Wednesday, Thursday, and Friday only. ⊠ *7455 Kalaniana'ole Hwy.* ☎ *808/396–4229* ⊕ *www. honolulu.gov/parks/facility/hanaumabay* ☞ *Lifeguard, toilets, showers, food concession, picnic tables, parking lot* 🅿 *Nonresident fee $5; parking $1; mask, snorkel, and fins rental $6; tram from parking lot to beach $1.50 round-trip* ☉ *Wed.–Mon. 6–7.*

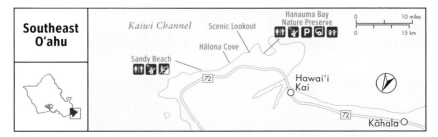

★ **Sandy Beach.** Probably the most popular beach with locals on this side of Oʻahu, the broad, sloping beach is covered with sunbathers there to watch the "Show" and soak up rays. The Show is a shore break that's like no other in the Islands. Monster ocean swells rolling into the beach combined with the sudden rise in the ocean floor causes waves to jack up and crash magnificently on the shore. Expert surfers and body boarders young and old brave this danger to get some of the biggest barrels you can find for bodysurfing. But keep in mind that ⚠ the beach is nicknamed "Break-Neck Beach" for a reason: many neck and back injuries are sustained here each year. Use extreme caution when swimming here, or just kick back and watch the drama unfold from the comfort of your beach chair. ✉ *Makai of Kalanianaʻole Hwy., 2 mi east of Hanauma Bay* ☞ *Lifeguard, toilets, showers, picnic tables.*

WINDWARD OʻAHU

The Windward side lives up to its name with ideal spots for windsurfing and kiteboarding, or for the more intrepid, hang gliding. For the most part the waves are mellow, and the bottoms are all sand—making for nice spots to visit with younger kids. The only drawback is that this side does tend to get more rain. But, as beautiful as the vistas are, a little sprinkling of pineapple juice shouldn't dampen your experience; plus it turns on the waterfalls that cascade down the Koʻolau. Beaches are listed from south to north.

Fodor'sChoice **Makapuʻu Beach.** A magnificent beach protected by Makapuʻu Point welcomes you to the Windward side. Hang gliders circle above the beach, and the water is filled with body boarders. Just off the coast you can see Bird Island, a sanctuary for aquatic fowl, jutting out of the blue. The currents can be heavy, so check with a lifeguard if you're unsure of safety. Before you leave, take the prettiest (and coldest) outdoor shower available on the island. Being surrounded by tropical flowers and foliage while you rinse off that sand will be a memory you will cherish from this side of the rock. ✉ *Across from Sea Life Park on Kalanianaʻole Hwy., 2 mi south of Waimānalo* ☞ *Lifeguard, toilets, showers, picnic tables, grills.*

☺ **Waimānalo Beach Park.** One of the most beautiful beaches on the island, Waimānalo is a local beach, busy with picnicking families and active sports fields. Expect a wide stretch of sand; turquoise, emerald, and deep-blue seas; and gentle shore-breaking waves that are fun for all ages Theft is an occasional problem, so lock your car. ✉ *South of Waimānalo town, look for signs on Kalanianaʻole Hwy.* ☞ *Lifeguard, toilets, showers, picnic tables.*

Bellows Beach. Bellows is the same beach as Waimānalo, but it's under the auspices of the military, making it more friendly for visitors but may only be open on weekends due to military activities often conducted in the park. The park area is excellent for camping, and ironwood trees provide plenty of shade. ■TIP→ The beach is best before 2 PM. After 2 the trade winds bring clouds that get hung up on steep mountains nearby, causing overcast skies until mid-afternoon. There are no food concessions, but McDonald's and other takeout fare, including huli huli (rotisserie)

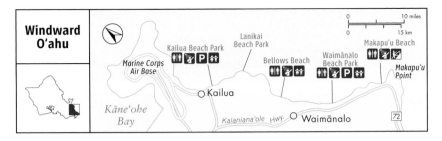

chicken on weekends, are right outside the entrance gate. ⊠*Entrance on Kalanianaʻole Hwy., near Waimānalo town center* ☞*Lifeguard, toilets, showers, picnic tables, grills.*

★ **Lanikai Beach Park.** Think of the beaches you see in commercials: peaceful jade-green waters, powder-soft white sand, families and dogs frolicking mindlessly, offshore islands in the distance. It's an ideal spot for camping out with a book. Though the beach hides behind multimillion-dollar houses, by state law there is public access every 400 yards. ■**TIP→ Look for walled or fenced pathways every 400 yards, leading to the beach. Be sure not to park in the marked bike/jogging lane.** There are no shower or bathroom facilities here—they are a two-minute drive away at Kailua Beach Park. ⊠*Past Kailua Beach Park; street parking on Mokulua Dr. for various public-access points to beach* ☞*No facilities.*

FodorʼsChoice **Kailua Beach Park.** A cobalt-blue sea and a wide continuous arc of pow-
★ dery sand make Kailua Beach Park one of the island's best beaches, illustrated by the crowds of local families that spend their weekend days here. This is like a big Lanikai Beach, but a little windier and a little wider, and a better spot for spending a full day. Kailua Beach has calm water, a line of palms and ironwoods that provide shade on the sand, and a huge park with picnic pavilions where you can escape the heat. This is the "it" spot if you're looking to try your hand at wind- or kiteboarding. You can rent kayaks nearby at **Kailua Sailboards and Kayaks** (⊠*130 Kailua Rd. 96734* ☎*808/262–2555*)and take them to the Mokulua Islands for the day. ⊠*Near Kailua town, turn right on Kailua Rd. at market, cross bridge, then turn left into beach parking lot* ☞*Lifeguard, toilets, showers, picnic tables, grills, playground, parking lot.*

Kualoa Park. Grassy expanses border a long, narrow stretch of beach with spectacular views of Kāneʻohe Bay and the Koʻolau Mountains, making Kualoa one of the island's most beautiful picnic, camping, and beach areas. Dominating the view is an islet called Mokoliʻi, better known as Chinaman's Hat, which rises 206 feet above the water. You can swim in the shallow areas year-round. The one drawback is that it's usually windy, but the wide-open spaces are ideal for kite flying. ⊠*North of Waiāhole, on Kamehameha Hwy.* ☞*Lifeguard, toilets, showers, picnic tables, grills.*

☺ **Kahana Bay Beach Park.** Local parents often bring their children here to wade in safety in the very shallow, protected waters. This pretty beach cove, surrounded by mountains, has a long arc of strip that is great for

BEACH SAFETY

Yes, the beaches are beautiful, but always be cognizant of the fact you are on a little rock in the middle of the Pacific Ocean. The current and waves will be stronger and bigger than any you may have experienced. Riptides can take you on a ride they call the "Moloka'i Express"—only problem is that it doesn't take you to the island of Moloka'i but rather out into the South Pacific.

Never swim alone. It is hard for even the most attentive lifeguards to keep their eyes on everyone at once, but a partner can gain their attention if you should run into trouble. There are many safe spots, but always pay attention to the posted signs. The lifeguards change the signs daily, so the warnings are always applicable to the day's conditions. If you have any doubts, ask a lifeguard for an assessment. They're professionals and can give you competent advice.

Use sunblock early and often. The SPF you choose is up to you, but we suggest nothing lower than 30 if you plan to spend more than an hour in the sun.

walking and a cool, shady grove of tall ironwood and pandanus trees that is ideal for a picnic. An ancient Hawaiian fishpond, which was in use until the 1920s, is visible nearby. The water here is not generally a clear blue due to the runoff from heavy rains in the valley. ⊠*North of Kualoa Park on Kamehameha Hwy.* ⌀*Lifeguard, toilets, showers, picnic tables.*

NORTH SHORE

"North Shore, where the waves are mean, just like a washing machine," sing the Ka'au Crater Boys about this legendary side of the island. And in winter they are absolutely right. At times the waves overtake the road, stranding tourists and locals alike. When the surf is up, there are signs on the beach telling you how far to stay back so that you aren't swept out to sea. The most prestigious big-wave contest in the world, the Eddie Aikau, is held at Waimea Bay on waves the size of a six-story building. The Triple Crown of Surfing roams across three beaches in the winter months.

All this changes come summer when this tiger turns into a kitten, with water smooth enough to water-ski on and ideal for snorkeling. The fierce Banzai Pipeline surf break becomes a great dive area, allowing you to explore the coral heads that, in winter, have claimed so many lives

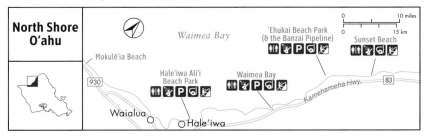

on the ultrashallow but big, hollow tubes created here. Even with the monster surf subsided, this is still a time for caution: Lifeguards are more scarce, and currents don't subside just because the waves do.

That said, it's a place like no other on earth and must be explored. From the turtles at Mokulē'ia to the tunnels at Shark's Cove, you could spend your whole trip on this side and not be disappointed.

Turtle Bay. Now known more for its resort than its magnificent beach, Turtle Bay is mostly passed over on the way to the better known beaches of Sunset and Waimea. But for the average visitor with the average swimming capabilities, this is the place to be on the North Shore. The crescent-shaped beach is protected by a huge sea wall. You can see and hear the fury of the northern swell, while blissfully floating in cool, calm waters. The convenience of this spot is also hard to pass up—there is a concession selling sandwiches and sunblock right on the beach. The resort has free parking for beach guests. At this writing, a planned development near the beach has residents concerned, but plans include parks and public beach access. ⊠ *4 mi north of Kahuku on Kamehameha Hwy. Turn into resort and let guard know where you are going; they offer free parking to beach guests.* ⌁ *Toilets, showers, concessions, picnic tables.*

★ **Sunset Beach.** The beach is broad, the sand is soft, the summer waves are gentle, and the winter surf is crashing. Many love searching this shore for the puka shells that adorn the necklaces you see everywhere. Carryout truck stands selling shave ice, plate lunches, and sodas usually line the adjacent highway. ⊠ *1 mi north of 'Ehukai Beach Park on Kamehameha Hwy.* ⌁ *Lifeguard, toilets, showers, picnic tables.*

'Ehukai Beach Park. What sets 'Ehukai apart is the view of the famous **Banzai Pipeline,** where the winter waves curl into magnificent tubes, making it an experienced wave-rider's dream. It's also an inexperienced swimmer's nightmare, though spring and summer waves are more accommodating to the average swimmer. Except when the surf contests are going on, there's no reason to stay on the central strip. Travel in either direction from the center, and the conditions remain the same but the population thins out, leaving you with a magnificent stretch of sand all to yourself. ⊠ *Small parking lot borders Kamehameha Hwy., 1 mi north of Foodland at Pūpūkea* ⌁ *Lifeguard, toilets, showers, parking lot.*

Fodor's Choice
★ **Waimea Bay.** Made popular in that old Beach Boys song "Surfin' U.S.A.," Waimea Bay is a slice of big-wave heaven, home to king-size 25- to 30-foot winter waves. Summer is the time to swim and snorkel in the calm waters. The shore break is great for novice bodysurfers. Due to its popularity, the postage-stamp parking lot is quickly filled, but everyone parks along the side of the road and walks in. ⊠ *Across from Waimea Valley, 3 mi north of Hale'iwa on Kamehameha Hwy.* ⌁ *Lifeguard, toilets, showers, picnic tables, parking lot.*

DID YOU KNOW?

Windward O'ahu's Makapu'u Beach is protected by Makapu'u Point, but currents are still strong so take caution when in the water.

Hale'iwa Ali'i Beach Park. The winter waves are impressive here, but in summer the ocean is like a lake, ideal for family swimming. The beach itself is big and often full of locals. Its broad lawn off the highway invites volleyball and Frisbee games and groups of barbecuers. This is also the opening break for the Triple Crown of Surfing, and the grass is often filled with art festivals or carnivals. ⊠*North of Hale'iwa town center and past harbor on Kamehameha Hwy.* ☞*Lifeguard, toilets, showers, picnic tables.*

Mokulē'ia Beach Park. There is a reason why the producers of the TV show *Lost* chose this beach for their set. On the remote northwest point of the island, it is about 10 mi from the closest store or public restroom; you could spend a day here and not see another living soul. And that is precisely its beauty—all the joy of being stranded on a deserted island without the trauma of the plane crash. The beach is wide and white, the waters bright blue (but a little choppy) and full of sea turtles and other marine life. Mokulē'ia is a great secret find, just remember to pack supplies and use caution as there are no lifeguards. ⊠*East of Hale'iwa town center, across from Dillingham Airfield* ☞*No facilities.*

WEST (LEEWARD) O'AHU

The North Shore may be known as "Country," but the West side is truly the rural area on O'ahu. There are commuters from this side to Honolulu, but many are born, live, and die on this side with scarcely a trip to town. For the most part, there's less hostility and more curiousity toward outsiders. Occasional problems have flared up, mostly due to drug abuse that has ravaged the fringes of the island. But the problems have generally been car break-ins, not violence. So, in short, lock your car, don't bring valuables, and enjoy the amazing beaches.

The beaches on the west side are expansive and empty. Most O'ahu residents and tourists don't make it to this side simply because of the drive; in traffic it can take almost 90 minutes to make it to Ka'ena Point from Downtown Honolulu. But you'll be hard-pressed to find a better sunset anywhere. Beaches are listed here in a south to north direction, starting from just west of Honolulu.

Fodor'sChoice
★
White Plains. Concealed from the public eye for many years as part of the Barbers Point Naval Air Station, this beach is reminiscent of Waikīkī but without the condos and the crowds. It is a long, sloping beach with numerous surf breaks, but it is also mild enough at shore for older children to play freely. It has views of Pearl Harbor and, over that, Diamond Head. Although the sand lives up to its name, the real joy of this beach comes from its history as part of a military property for the better part of a century. Expansive parking, great restroom facilities, and numerous tree-covered barbecue areas make it a great day-trip spot. As a bonus, a Hawaiian monk seal takes up residence here several months out of the year (seals are rarely seen anywhere in the Islands). ⊠*Take Makakilo exit off H–1 West, turn left. Follow it into base gates, make a left. Follow blue signs to beach* ☞*Lifeguard, toilets, showers, picnic tables.*

CLOSE UP

Shrimp Shacks

No drive to the North Shore is complete without a shrimp stop. Shrimp stands dot Kamehameha Highway from Kahalu'u to Kahuku. For under $12, you can get a shrimp plate lunch or a snack of chilled shrimp with cocktail sauce, served from a rough hut or converted vehicle (many permanently immobile), with picnic table seating.

The shrimp shack phenomenon began with a lost lease and a determined restaurateur. In 1994, when Giovanni and Connie Aragona couldn't renew the lease on their Hale'iwa deli, they began hawking their best-selling dish—an Italian-style scampi preparation involving lemon, butter, and lots of garlic—from a truck alongside the road. About the same time, aquaculture was gaining a foothold in nearby Kahuku, with farmers raising sweet, white shrimp and huge, orange-whiskered prawns in shallow freshwater ponds. The ready supply and the success of the first shrimp truck led to many imitators.

Though it has changed hands, that first business lives on as Giovanni's Original Shrimp Truck, parked in Kahuku town. Signature dishes include the garlic shrimp and a spicy shrimp sautée, both worth a stop.

But there's plenty of competition—at least a half-dozen stands, trucks, or stalls are operating at any given time, with varying menus (and quality).

Don't be fooled that all that shrimp comes fresh from the ponds; much of it is imported. The only way you can be sure you're buying local farm-raised shrimp is if the shrimp is still kicking. Romy's Kahuku Prawns and Shrimp Hut is an arm of one of the longest-running aquaculture farms in the area; they sell excellent plate lunches. The panfried shrimp and buttery, locally raised corn from the bright yellow Shrimp Shack, parked at Kaya Store in Punalu'u, are first-rate, too.

☺ ★ **Kō 'Olina.** This is the best spot on the island if you have small kids. The resort commissioned a series of four man-made lagoons, but, as they have to provide public beach access, you are the winner. Huge rock walls protect the lagoons, making them into perfect spots for the kids to get their first taste of the ocean without getting bowled over. The large expanses of seashore grass and hala trees that surround the semi-circle beaches are made-to-order for naptime. A 1½-mi jogging track connects the lagoons. Due to its appeal for *keiki* (children), Kō 'Olina is popular and the parking lot fills up quickly when school is out and on weekends, so try to get there before 10 AM. The biggest parking lot is at the farthest lagoon from the entrance. ✉*23 mi west of Honolulu. Take Kō 'Olina exit off H–1 West and proceed to guard shack* ☞ *Toilets, showers, food concession.*

Mākaha Beach Park. This beach provides a slice of local life most visitors don't see. Families string up tarps for the day, fire up hibachis, set up lawn chairs, get out the fishing gear, and strum 'ukulele while they "talk story" (chat). Legendary waterman Buffalo Kaeulana can be found in the shade of the palms playing with his grandkids and spinning yarns of yesteryear. In these waters Buffalo not only invented some of the most outrageous methods of surfing, but also raised his world-champion son Rusty. He also made Mākaha the home of the world's first international surf meet in 1954 and still hosts his Big Board Surfing Classic. The swimming is generally decent in summer, but avoid the big winter waves. With its long, slow-building waves, it's a great spot to try out long boarding. The swimming is generally decent in summer, but avoid the big winter waves. ✉ *1½ hrs west of Honolulu on H–1 Hwy. then Farrington Hwy.* ✆ *Lifeguards, toilets, showers, picnic tables, grills.*

WATER SPORTS AND TOURS

There's more to the beach than just lying on it. O'ahu is rife with every type of activity you can imagine. Most of the activities are offered in Waikīkī, right off the beach.

On the sand in front of your hotel, the sights and sounds of what is available will overwhelm you. Rainbow-color parachutes dot the horizon as parasailers improve their vantage point on paradise. The blowing of conch shells announces the arrival of the beach catamarans that sail around Diamond Head Crater. Meanwhile, the white caps of Waikīkī are being sliced by all manner of craft, from brilliant-red outrigger canoes to darting white surfboards. Enjoy observing the flurry of activity for a moment, then jump right in.

As with all sports, listen to the outfitter's advice—they're not just saying it for fun. Caution is always the best bet when dealing with "mother" ocean. She plays for keeps and forgives no indiscretions. That being said, she offers more entertainment than you can fit into a lifetime, much less a vacation. So try something new and enjoy.

A rule of thumb is that the ocean is much more wily and unpredictable on the north- and west-facing shores, but that's also why those sides have the most famous waves on Earth. So plan your activity side according to your skill level.

BOAT TOURS AND CHARTERS

Hawai'i Nautical. It's a little out of the way, but the experiences with this local company are worth the drive. Catamaran cruises lead to snorkeling with dolphins, gourmet dinner cruises head out of beautiful Kō 'Olina harbor, and sailing lessons are available on a 20-foot sailboat and a 50-foot cat. If you're driving out from Waikīkī, you may want to make a day of it, with sailing in the morning then 18 holes on the gorgeous resort course in the afternoon. Three-hour cruise rates with snacks and two drinks begin at $110 per person. ✉ *Kō 'Olina Harbor, Kō 'Olina Marriott Resort, Kapolei* ☎ *808/234–7245.*

Fodor's Choice ★ **Hawai'i Sailing Adventures.** Looking to escape the "cattle-maran" experience? Then this charter, with its goal of exclusivity and the largest private sailing yacht in the Islands, is for you. They have capacity for up to 50 guests but prefer smaller crowds, and they specialize in dinners catered to your specs. When you want a sail for a romantic occasion or a family reunion unfettered by crowds of people you don't know, try their yacht *Emeraude* and ask for Captain Roger. Two-hour dinner-cruise rates with unlimited super well drinks (drinks made with premium liquors like Tanqueray Ten or Grey Goose) begin at $119 per person. ✉*Kewalo Basin, Slip S, Honolulu* ☎*808/596–9696.*

Sashimi Fun Fishing. A combination trip suits those who aren't quite ready to troll for big game in the open-ocean swells. Sashimi Fun Fishing runs a dinner cruise with fishing and music. They keep close enough to shore that you can still see O'ahu while jigging for a variety of reef fish. The cruise includes a local barbecue dinner, and you can also cook what you catch. The four-hour fishing cruises rates with hotel transportation begin at $63 per person. ☎*808/955–3474.*

SHARK!

"You go in the cage, cage goes in the water, you go in the water, shark's in the water . . ." You remember this line from *Jaws*, and now you get to play the role of Richard Dreyfus, as **North Shore Shark Adventures** provides you with an interactive experience out of your worst nightmare. The tour allows you to swim and snorkel in a cage as dozens of sharks lurk just feet from you in the open ocean off the North Shore, and all for just $120. Or if getting in the water is too much for you, one can watch all the action topside for just $60. ☎*808/228-5900* ⊕*www. sharktourshawaii.com.*

Tradewind Charters. Tradewind specializes in everything from weddings to funerals. They offer half-day private-charter tours for groups ranging from 2 to 80 people featuring sailing, snorkeling, and whale-watching. Traveling on these luxury yachts not only gets you away from the crowds but also gives you the opportunity to "take the helm" if you wish. The cruise includes snorkeling at an exclusive anchorage as well as hands-on snorkeling and sailing instruction. Charter prices are approximately $495 for up to six passengers. ✉*796 Kalanipuu St., Honolulu* ☎*800/829–4899* ⊕*www. tradewindcharters.com.*

BOOGIE BOARDING AND BODYSURFING

Boogie boarding (or sponging) has become a popular alternative to surfing for a couple of reasons. First, the start-up cost is much less—a usable board can be purchased for $30 to $40 or can be rented on the beach for $5 an hour. Second, it's a whole lot easier to ride a boogie board than to tame a surfboard. For beginner boogie boarding all you must do is paddle out to the waves, turn toward the beach, and kick like crazy when the wave comes.

Most grocery and convenience stores sell boogie boards. Though the boards do not rival what the pros use, you won't notice a difference in their handling on smaller waves. ■**TIP→Another small investment you'll want to make is surf fins.** These smaller, sturdier versions of dive fins sell for $25–$35 at surf and dive stores, sporting-goods stores, or even Wal-Mart. Most beach stands do not rent fins with the boards. Though they are not necessary for boogie boarding, fins do give you a tremendous advantage when you are paddling into waves. If you plan to go out in bigger surf, we would also advise you to get fin leashes to prevent loss. For bodysurfing, you definitely want to invest in fins. Check out the same spots for boogie boarding.

If the direction of the current or dangers of the break are not readily apparent to you, don't hesitate to ask a lifeguard for advice.

BEST SPOTS

Boogie boarding and bodysurfing can be done anywhere there are waves, but, due to a paddling advantage surfers have over spongers, it's usually more fun to go to exclusively boogie-boarding spots.

Kūhiō Beach Park (⊠ *Waikīkī, past Sheraton Moana Surfrider Hotel to Kapahulu Ave. pier*) is an easy spot for the first-timer to check out the action. Try **The Wall,** a break so named for the break wall in front of the beach. It's a little crowded with kids, but it's close enough to shore to keep you at ease. There are dozens of breaks in Waikīkī, but the Wall is the only one solely occupied by spongers. Start out here to get the hang of it before venturing out to **Canoes** or **Kaiser Bowl's.**

The best spot on the island for advanced boogie boarding is **Sandy Beach** (⊠ *2 mi east of Hanauma Bay on Kalaniana'ole Hwy.*) on the Windward side. It's a short wave that goes right and left, but the barrels here are unparalleled for pure sponging. The ride is intense and breaks so sharply that you actually see the wave suck the bottom dry before it crashes on to it. That's the reason it's also called "Break Neck Beach." It's awesome for the advanced, but know its danger before enjoying the ride.

Makapu'u Beach (⊠ Across from Sea Life Park, 2 mi south of Waimānalo on Kalaniana'ole Hwy., 96795) on the Windward side is a sponger's dream beach with its extended waves and isolation from surfers. If you're a little more timid, go to the far end of the beach to **Keiki's,** where the waves are mellowed by Makapu'u Point, for an easier, if less thrilling, ride. Although the main break at Makapu'u is much less dangerous than Sandy's, check out the ocean floor—the sands are always shifting, sometimes exposing coral heads and rocks. Also always check the currents: they can get strong. But for the most part, this is the ideal beach for both boogie boarding and bodysurfing.

EQUIPMENT

There are more than 30 rental spots on Waikīkī Beach, all offering basically the same prices. But if you plan to do it for more than just an hour, we would suggest buying a board for $20 to $30 at an ABC convenience store and giving it to a kid when you're preparing to end your vacation. It will be more cost-effective for you and will imbue you with the Aloha spirit while making a kid's day.

DEEP-SEA FISHING

The joy of fishing in Hawai'i is that there isn't really a season; it's good year-round. Sure, the bigger yellowfin tuna ('ahi) are generally caught in summer, and the coveted spearfish are more frequent in winter, but you can still catch them any day of the year. You can also find dolphin fish (mahimahi), wahoo (ono), skipjacks, and the king—Pacific blue marlin—ripe for the picking on any given day.

A top choice among Boogie boarders and bodysurfers is Break Neck Beach, for its big surf.

When choosing a fishing boat in the Islands, look for the older, grizzled captains who have been trolling these waters for half a century. All the fancy gizmos in the world can't match an old tar's knowledge of the waters.

The general rule for the catch is an even split with the crew. Unfortunately, there are no freeze-and-ship providers in the state, so unless you plan to eat the fish while you're here, you'll probably want to leave it with the boat. Most boats do offer mounting services for trophy fish; ask your captain.

Besides the gift of fish, a gratuity of 10% to 20% is standard but use your own discretion depending on how you felt about the overall experience.

BOATS AND CHARTERS

Hawaii Fishing Adventures. Based out of Kō 'Olina resort, Captain Jim and his crew try to bring the full Hawaiian experience to their fishing trips. While most fishing boats head straight out to the open ocean, Captain Jim trolls along the Leeward coast giving visitors a nice sense of the island while stalking the fish. They also offer an overnighter to Molokai's Penguin Banks, reputed to be some of Hawai'i's best fishing grounds. The six-hour tour runs $650 with the overnighter booking at $2,500. ☎808/520–4852 ⊕www.webconsole.net/hifi/index.shtml.

Maggie Joe Sportfishing. The oldest-running sportfishing company on O'ahu also boasts the largest landed blue marlin—more than 1,200 pounds. With two smaller boats and the 53-foot *Maggie Joe* (which can hold up to 25), they can manage any small party with air-conditioned cabins and cutting-edge fishing equipment. They also work with Grey's

Taxidermy, the world's largest marine taxidermist, to mount the monster you reel in. Half-day exclusive charter rates for groups of six begin at $750. ☎808/591–8888 ⊕www.maggiejoe.com.

Magic Sportfishing. The awards Magic has garnered are too many to mention here, but we can tell you their magnificent 50-foot *Pacifica* fishing yacht is built for comfort, whether you're fishing or not. Unfortunately, Magic can accommodate only up to six. Full-day exclusive charter rates begin at $975. ☎808/596–2998 ⊕www.magicsportfishing.com.

JET SKIING, WAKEBOARDING, AND WATERSKIING

Aloha Parasail/Jet Ski. Jet ski in the immense Ke'ehi Lagoon as planes from Honolulu International take off and land right above you. After an instructional safety course, you can try your hand at navigating their buoyed course. They provide free pickup and drop-off from Waikīkī. The Waverunners run about $40 per person for 45 minutes of riding time. ☎808/521–2446.

Hawai'i Sports Wakeboard and Water Ski Center. Hawai'i Sports turns Maunalua Bay into an action water park with activities for all ages. While dad's learning to wakeboard, the kids can hang on for dear life on bumper tubes, and mom can finally get some peace parasailing over the bay with views going to Diamond Head and beyond. There are also banana boats that will ride six, Jet Skis for two, and scuba missions. Half-hour Jet Ski rental rates begin at $49 per person, and package deals are available. ⊠*Koko Marina Shopping Center, 7192 Kalaniana'ole Hwy., Hawai'i Kai* ☎808/395–3773 ⊕www.hawaiiwatersportscenter.com.

KAYAKING

Kayaking is quickly becoming a top choice for visitors to the Islands. Kayaking alone or with a partner on the open ocean provides a vantage point not afforded by swimming and surfing. Even amateurs can travel long distances and keep a lookout on what's going on around them.

This ability to travel long distances can also get you into trouble. ■TIP➔Experts agree that rookies should stay on the Windward side. Their reasoning is simple: if you tire, break or lose an oar, or just plain pass out, the onshore winds will eventually blow you back to the beach. The same cannot be said for the offshore breezes of the North Shore and West O'ahu.

Kayaks are specialized: some are better suited for riding waves while others are designed for traveling long distances. Your outfitter can address your needs depending on your activities. Sharing your plans with your outfitter can lead to a more enjoyable experience.

BEST SPOTS

The hands-down winner for kayaking is **Lanikai Beach** (⊠*Past Kailua Beach Park; street parking on Mokulua Drive for various public-access points to beach*) on the Windward side. This is perfect amateur territory with its still waters and onshore winds. If you're feeling more adventurous, it's a short paddle out to the Mokes. This pair of islands off the coast has beaches, surf breaks on the reef, and great picnicking areas. Due to the distance from shore (about a mile), the Mokes usually afford privacy from all but other intrepid kayakers. Lanikai is great year-round, and most kayak-rental companies have a store right up the street in Kailua.

For something a little different try **Kahana River** (⊠ *This stream empties into Kahana Bay, 8 mi east of Kāne'ohe*), also on the Windward side. The river may not have the blue water of the ocean, but the Ko'olau Mountains, with waterfalls aplenty when it's raining, are magnificent in the background. It's a short jaunt, about 2 mi round-trip, but it's packed with rain-forest foliage and the other rain-forest denizens, mosquitos. Bring some repellent and enjoy this light workout.

> ## OUTRIGGER CANOES
>
> While everyone is clamoring to learn to surf or to go sailing, no one notices the long, funny-looking boats in front of Duke's that allow you to do both. At $10 for three rides, the price hasn't changed in a decade, and the thrill hasn't changed in centuries. You can get a paddle, but no one expects you to use it—the beach boys negotiate you in and out of the break as they have been doing all their lives. If you think taking off on a wave on a 10-foot board is a rush, wait until your whole family takes off on one in a 30-foot boat!

EQUIPMENT, LESSONS, AND TOURS

Go Bananas. Staffers make sure that you rent the appropriate kayak for your abilities, and they also outfit the rental car with soft racks to transport the boat to the beach. The store also carries clothing and kayaking accessories. Full-day rates begin at $30 for single kayaks, and $45 for doubles. ⊠ *799 Kapahulu Ave., Honolulu* ☎ *808/737–9514.*

Twogood Kayaks Hawai'i. The one-stop shopping outfitter for kayaks on the Windward side offers rentals, lessons, guided kayak tours, and even weeklong camps if you want to immerse yourself in the sport. Guides are trained in history, geology, and birdlife of the area. Kayak a full day with a guide for $119; this includes lunch, snorkeling gear, and transportation from Waikīkī. Although their rental prices are about $10 more than average, they do deliver the boats to the water for you and give you a crash course in ocean safety. It's a small price to pay for the convenience and for peace of mind when entering new waters. Full-day rates begin at $49 for single kayaks, and $59 for doubles. ⊠ *345 Hahani St., Kailua* ☎ *808/262–5656* ⊕ *www.twogoodkayaks.com.*

KITEBOARDING

See Windsurfing and Kiteboarding.

SAILING

For a sailing experience in O'ahu, you need go no farther than the beach in front of your hotel in Waikīkī. Strung along the sand are seven beach catamarans that will provide you with one-hour rides during the day and 90-minute sunset sails. Look for $23 to $25 for day sails and $30 to $34 for sunset rides. ■ TIP→They all have their little perks and they're known for bargaining, so feel free to haggle, especially with the smaller boats. Some provide drinks for free, some charge for them, and some let you pack your own, so keep that in mind when pricing the ride.

Mai'Tai Catamaran. Taking off from in front of the Sheraton Hotel, this cat is the fastest and sleekest on the beach. If you have a need for speed and enjoy a little more upscale experience, this is the boat for you. ☎808/922–5665.

Na Hoku II Catamaran. The diametric opposite of Mai'Tai, this is the Animal House of catamarans with reggae music and free booze. Their motto is "Free drinks, Easy Crew." They're beached right out in front of Duke's Barefoot Bar at the Outrigger Waikīkī Hotel and sail five times daily. ☎No phone ⊕www.nahokuii.com.

Pirate Bar Hawaii. A true pirate vacation where the grog is always flowing and your "black jack" is always full (that's a drinking mug to you landlubbers), adventures abound once you set foot on their 80-foot Maxi, the only one of its kind in the Islands. Setting sail out of Kewalo Basin, they will teach you the real meaning of the "No Rules" cruise while sailing into the sunset with their all-pirate crew. It maxes out at 60 people so it's good to get reservations, ask for Captain Rabbit. ☎808/227–3556.

SCUBA DIVING

All the great stuff to do atop the water sometimes leads us to forget the real beauty beneath the surface. Although snorkeling and snuba (more on that later) do give you access to this world, nothing gives you the freedom of scuba.

The diving on O'ahu is comparable with any you might do in the tropics, but its uniqueness comes from the isolated environment of the Islands. There are literally hundreds of species of fish and marine life that you can only find in this chain. Adding to the singularity of diving off O'ahu is the human history of the region. Military activities and tragedies of the 20th century filled the waters surrounding O'ahu with wreckage that the ocean creatures have since turned into their homes.

Although instructors certified to license you in scuba are plentiful in the Islands, we suggest that you get your PADI certification before coming as a week of classes may be a bit of a commitment on a short vacation. ■ TIP→ You can go on introductory dives without the certification, but the best dives require it.

BEST SPOTS

Hanauma Bay (⊠7455 *Kalaniana'ole Hwy.*) is an underwater state park and a popular dive site in Southeast O'ahu. The shallow inner reef of this volcanic crater bay is filled with snorkelers, but its floor gradually drops from 10 to 70 feet at the outer reef where the big fish prefer the lighter traffic. It's quite a trek down into the crater and out to the water, so you may want to consider a dive-tour company to do your heavy lifting. Expect to see butterfly fish, goatfish, parrot fish, surgeonfish, and sea turtles.

The **Mahi Wai'anae,** a 165-foot minesweeper, was sunk in 1982 in the waters just south of Wai'anae on O'ahu's leeward coast to create an artificial reef. It's intact and penetrable, but you'll need a boat to access it. In the front resides an ancient moray eel who is so mellowed that you can pet his barnacled head without fearing for your hand's safety. Goatfish, tame lemon-butterfly fish, and blue-striped snapper hang out here, but the real stars are the patrols of spotted eagle rays that are always cruising by. It can be a longer dive as it's only 90 feet to the hull.

Fodor's Choice
★

The best shore dive on O'ahu is **Shark's Cove** (⊠ *Across from Foodland in Pūpūkea*) on the North Shore, but unfortunately it's only accessible during the summer months. Novices can drift along the outer wall, watching everything from turtles to eels. Veterans can explore the numerous lava tubes and tunnels where diffused sunlight from above creates a dreamlike effect in spacious caverns. It's 10- to 45-feet deep, ready-made for shore diving with a parking lot right next to the dive spot. **Three Tables** is just west of Shark's Cove, enabling you to have a second dive without moving your car. Follow the three perpendicular rocks that break the surface out to this dive site, where you can find a variety of parrot fish and octopus, plus occasional shark and ray sightings at depths of 30 to 50 feet. It's not as exciting as Shark's Cove, but it's more accessible for the novice diver. Increase your caution the later in the year you come to these sights; the waves pick up strength in fall, and the reef can be turned into a washboard for you and your gear. Both are null and void during the winter surf sessions.

EQUIPMENT, LESSONS, AND TOURS

Reeftrekkers. The owners of the slickest dive Web site in Hawai'i are also the *Scuba Diving* Reader's Choice winners for the past four years. Using the dive descriptions and price quotes on their Web site, you can plan your excursions before ever setting foot on the island. Two-tank boat dive rates begin at $95 per person. ☎808/943–0588 ⊕*www.reeftrekkers.com.*

Captain Bruce's Hawai'i. Captain Bruce's focuses on the west and east shores, covering the *Mahi* and the Corsair. This full-service company has refresher and introductory dives as well as more advanced drift and night dives. No equipment is needed; they provide it all. Most importantly, this is the only boat on O'ahu that offers hot showers onboard. Two-tank boat-dive rates begin at $115 per person. ☎808/373–3590 or 800/535–2487 ⊕*www.captainbruce.com*

Surf-N-Sea. The North Shore headquarters for all things water-related is great for diving that side as well. There is one interesting perk—the cameraman can shoot a video of you diving. It's hard to see facial expressions under the water, but it still might be fun for those who need documentation of all they do. Two-tank boat dive rates begin at $135 per person. ☎808/637–3337 ⊕*www.surfnsea.com.*

SNORKELING

One advantage that snorkeling has over scuba is that you never run out of air. That and the fact that anyone who can swim can also snorkel without any formal training. A favorite pastime in Hawai'i, snorkeling can be done anywhere there's enough water to stick your face in it. Each spot will have its great days depending on the weather and time of year, so consult with the purveyor of your gear for tips on where the best viewing is that day. Keep in mind that the North Shore should only be attempted when the waves are calm, namely in the summertime. ■ TIP➔Think of buying a mask and snorkel as a prerequisite for your trip— they make any beach experience better. Just make sure you put plenty of sunblock on your back because once you start gazing below, your head may not come back up for hours.

BEST SPOTS

As Waimea Bay is to surfing, **Hanauma Bay** (✉ *7455 Kalaniana'ole Hwy.*) in Southeast O'ahu is to snorkeling. By midday it can look like the mall at Christmas with all the bodies, but with over a half-million fish to observe, there's plenty to go around. Due to the protection of the narrow mouth of the cove and the prodigious reef, you will be hard-pressed to find a place you will feel safer while snorkeling.

Directly across from the electric plant outside of Kō 'Olina resort, **Electric Beach** (✉ *1 mi west of Kō'Ōlina*) in West O'ahu has become a haven for tropical fish. The expulsion of hot water from the plant warms the ocean water, attracting all kinds of wildlife. Although the visibility is not always the best, the crowds are thin, and the fish are guaranteed. Just park next to the old train tracks and enjoy this secret spot.

Fodor'sChoice ★ Great shallows right off the shore with huge reef protection make **Shark's Cove** (✉ *Across from Foodland in Pūpūkea*) on the North Shore a great spot for youngsters in the summertime. You can find a plethora of critters from crabs to octopus, in waist-deep or shallower water. The only caveat is that once the winter swell comes, this becomes a human pinball game rather than a peaceful observation spot. Summer only.

EQUIPMENT AND TOURS

Ho'o Nanea. From May through September, this 40-foot catamaran sails daily at 9 AM from Hale'iwa Harbor on the North Shore. It's an hour from Waikīkī, but the $95, four-hour excursion is worth the drive for the chance of seeing different wildlife, the intimacy—there's a 20-person limit—and the quiet of nonengine sailing (though they do employ an engine when there's no wind). During winter's rough-water season, the cat is used for whale-watching cruises. ☎ *808/351–9371* ⊕ *www.sailingcat.com.*

Kō 'Olina Kat. The dock in Kō 'Olina harbor is a little more out of the way, but this is a much more luxurious option than the town snorkel cruises. Two-hour morning and afternoon tours of the west side of O'ahu are punctuated with stops for observing dolphins from the boat and a snorkel spot well populated with fish. All gear, snacks, sandwiches, and two alcoholic beverages make for a more complete experience, but also a pricier one (starting at $110 per person). ☎ *808/234–7245.*

Snorkel Bob's. We suggest buying your gear, unless it's going to be a one-day affair. Either way, Snorkel Bob's has all the stuff you'll need (and a bunch of stuff you don't) to make your water adventures enjoyable. Also feel free to ask the staff about the good spots at the moment, as the best spots can vary with weather and seasons. ⊠ *700 Kapahulu Ave.* ☎ *808/735–7944.*

SNUBA

Snuba, the marriage of scuba and snorkeling, gives the nondiving set their first glimpse of the freedom of scuba. Snuba utilizes a raft with a standard air tank on it and a 20-foot air hose that hooks up to a regulator. Once attached to the hose, you can swim, unfettered by heavy tanks and weights, up to 15 feet down to chase fish and examine reef for as long as you fancy. If you ever get scared or need a rest, the raft is right there, ready to support you. Kids eight years and older can use the equipment. It can be pricey, but then again, how much is it worth to be able to sit face-to-face with a 6-foot-long sea turtle and not have to rush to the surface to get another breath? At **Hanauma Bay Dive Tours** (☎ *808/256–8956*), a three-hour outing (with 45 minutes in the water) costs $115.

SUBMARINE TOURS

Atlantis Submarines. This is the underwater venture for the unadventurous. Not fond of swimming but want to see what you have been missing? Board this 64-passenger vessel for a ride down past shipwrecks, turtle breeding grounds, and coral reefs galore. Unlike a trip to the aquarium, this gives you a chance to see nature at work without the limitations of mankind. The tours, which leave from the pier at the Hilton Hawaiian Village, are available in several languages and run from $95 to $113. ⊠ *Hilton Hawaiian Village Beach Resort and Spa, 2005 Kālia Rd., Waikīkī, Honolulu* ☎ *808/973–1296.*

SURFING

Perhaps no word is more associated with Hawai'i than surfing. Every year the best of the best gather here to have their Super Bowl: Vans Triple Crown of Surfing. The pros dominate the waves for a month, but the rest of the year belongs to people like us, just trying to have fun and get a little exercise.

O'ahu is unique because it has so many famous spots: Banzai Pipeline, Waimea Bay, Kaiser Bowls, and Sunset Beach resonate in young surfers' hearts the world over. The renown of these spots comes with a price: competition for those waves. The aloha spirit lives in many places but not on premium waves. If you're coming to visit and want to surf these world-famous breaks, you need to go out with a healthy dose of respect and patience. As long as you follow the rules of the road and concede waves to local riders, you should not have problems. Just remember that locals view these waves as their property, and everything should be all right.

If you're nervous and don't want to run the risk of a confrontation, try some of the alternate spots listed below. They may not have the name recognition, but the waves can be just as great.

BEST SPOTS

If you like to ride waves in all kinds of craft, try **Mākaha Beach** (⊠ *1½ hrs west of Honolulu on H–1 and Farrington Hwy.*) It has interminable rights that allow riders to perform all manner of stunts: from six-man canoes with everyone doing headstands to bully boards (oversize boogie boards) with dad's whole family riding with him. Mainly known as a long-boarding spot, it's predominantly local but not overly aggressive to the respectful outsider. The only downside is that it's way out on the west shore. Use caution in the wintertime, as the surf can get huge.

In Waikīkī, try getting out to **Populars,** a break at **Ulukou Beach** (⊠ *Waikīkī, in front of hotel*). Nice and easy, Populars never breaks too hard and is friendly to both the rookie and the veteran. The only downside here is the ½-mi paddle out to the break, but no one ever said it was going to be easy. Plus the long pull keeps it from getting overcrowded.

White Plains Beach (⊠ *In former Kalaeloa Military Installation*) is a spot where trouble will not find you. Known among locals as "mini-Waikīkī," it breaks in numerous spots, preventing the logjam that happens with many of O'ahu's more popular breaks. As part of a military base in West O'ahu, the beach was closed to the public until a couple of years ago. It's now occupied by mostly novice to intermediate surfers, so egos are at a minimum, though you do have to keep a lookout for loose boards.

EQUIPMENT AND LESSONS

C&K Beach Service. To rent a board in Waikīkī, visit the beach fronting the Hilton Hawaiian Village. Rentals cost $10 to $15 per hour, depending on the size of the board, and $18 for two hours. Small group lessons are $50 per hour with board, and trainers promise to have you riding the waves by lesson's end. ☎*No phone.*

☺ **Hawaiian Fire, Inc.** Off-duty Honolulu firefighters—and some of Hawai'i's most knowledgeable water-safety experts—man the boards at one of Hawai'i's hottest new surfing schools. Lessons include equipment, safety and surfing instruction, and two hours of surfing time (with lunch break) at a secluded beach near Barbers Point. Transportation is available from Waikīkī. Two-hour group lesson rates begin at $103 per person, $187 per person for a private lesson. ☎*808/737–3473* ⊕*www.hawaiianfire.com.*

North Shore Eco-Surf Tours. The only prerequisites here are "the ability to swim and the desire to surf." North Shore Eco-Surf has a more relaxed view of lessons, saying that the instruction will last somewhere between 90 minutes and four hours. The group rate begins at $78 per person, $135 for a private lesson. ☎*808/638–9503* ⊕*www.ecosurf-hawaii.com.*

★ **Surf 'N Sea.** This is the Wal-Mart of water for the North Shore. Rent a short board for $5 an hour or a long board for $7 an hour ($24 and $30 for full-day rentals). Lessons cost $85 for three hours. Depending on how you want to attack your waves, you can also rent boogie boards or kayaks. ✉62-595 *Kamehameha Hwy.*, 96712 ☎808/637–9887 ⊕*www.surfnsea.com.*

WHALE-WATCHING

November is marked by the arrival of snow in most of America, but in Hawai'i it marks the return of the humpback whale. These migrating behemoths move south from their North Pacific homes during the winter months for courtship and calving, and they put on quite a show. Watching males and females alike throwing themselves out of the ocean and into the sunset awes even the saltiest of sailors. Newborn calves riding gently next to their two-ton mothers will stir you to your core. These gentle giants can be seen from the shore as they make quite a splash, but there is nothing like having your boat rocking beneath you in the wake of a whale's breach.

At Hawai'i Sailing Adventures, two-hour whale-watching cruise rates with dinner start at $119.

★ **Wild Side Specialty Tours.** Boasting a marine-biologist crew, this west-side tour boat takes you to undisturbed snorkeling areas. Along the way you can view dolphins, turtles, and, in winter, whales. The tours leave early (7 AM) to catch the wildlife still active, so it's important to plan ahead as they're an hour outside Honolulu. Four-hour whale-watching cruise rates with Continental breakfast start at $105. ✉ *Wai'anae Boat Harbor, Slip A11* ☎808/306–7273.

WINDSURFING AND KITEBOARDING

Those who call windsurfing and kiteboarding cheating because they require no paddling have never tried hanging on to a sail or kite. It will turn your arms to spaghetti quicker than paddling ever could, and the speeds you generate . . . well, there's a reason why these are considered extreme sports.

Windsurfing was born here in the Islands. For amateurs, the Windward side is best because the on-shore breezes will bring you back to land even if you don't know what you're doing. The new sport of kiteboarding is tougher but more exhilarating as the kite will sometimes take you in the air for hundreds of feet. We suggest only those in top shape try the kites, but windsurfing is fun for all ages.

> **ON THE SIDELINES**
>
> Watch the pros jump and spin on the waves during July's **Pan Am Hawaiian Windsurfing World Cup** (☎*808/734–6999*) off Kailua Beach. August's **Wahine Classic** (☎*808/521–4322*), held off Diamond Head point, features the world's best female board-sailors.

SURF SMART

A few things to remember when surfing in O'ahu:

■ The waves switch with the seasons—they're big in the south in summer, and they loom large in the north in winter. If you're not experienced, it's best to go where the waves are small. There will be fewer crowds, and your chances of injury dramatically decrease.

■ Always wear a leash. It may not look the coolest, but when your board gets swept away from you and

you're swimming a half mile after it, you'll remember this advice.

■ Watch where you're going. Take a few minutes and watch the surf from the shore. Observe how big it is, where it's breaking, and how quickly the sets are coming. This knowledge will allow you to get in and out more easily and to spend more time riding waves and less time paddling.

EQUIPMENT AND LESSONS

Kailua Sailboard and Kayaks Company. The appeal here is that they offer both beginner and high-performance gear. They also give lessons, at $89 for a three-hour group lesson or $109 for a one-hour individual lesson. ■TIP➜ Since both options are around the same price, we suggest the one-hour individual lesson; then you have the rest of the day to practice what they preach. Full-day rentals for the more experienced run from $49 for the standard board to $59 for a high-performance board. ⊠ *130 Kailua Rd., Kailua* ☎ *808/262–2555.*

Naish Hawai'i. If you like to learn from the best, try out world-champion Robby Naish and his family services. Not only do they build and sell boards, rent equipment, and provide accommodation referrals, but they also offer their windsurfing and kiteboarding expertise. A four-hour package, including 90 minutes of instruction and a three-hour board rental, costs $104. ⊠ *155A Hamakua Dr., Kailua* ☎ *808/261–6067* ⊕ *www.naish.com.*

GOLF, HIKING, AND OUTDOOR ACTIVITIES

AERIAL TOURS

★ **Island Seaplane Service.** Harking back to the days of the earliest air visitors to Hawai'i, the seaplane has always had a special spot in island lore. The only seaplane service still operating in Hawai'i takes off from Ke'ehi Lagoon. Flight options are either a half-hour south and eastern O'ahu shoreline tour or an hour island circle tour. The *Pan Am Clipper* may be gone, but you can revisit the experience for $125 to $230. ⊠ *85 Lagoon Dr., Honolulu* ☎ *808/836–6273.*

Makani Kai Helicopters. This may be the best way to see the infamous and now closed Sacred Falls park, where a rock slide killed 20 people and injured dozens more; Makani Kai dips their helicopter down to show you one of Hawai'i's former favorite hikes. There's also a Waikīkī by Night excursion that soars by the breathtaking Honolulu city lights. Half-hour tour rates begin at $155 per person, and customized private charters are available starting at $1,725 per hour. ✉ *130 Iolana Pl., Honolulu* ☎ *808/834–5813* ⊕ *www.makanikai.com.*

★ **The Original Glider Rides.** "Mr. Bill" has been offering piloted glider (sailplane) rides over the northwest end of O'ahu's North Shore since 1970. These are piloted scenic rides for one or two passengers in sleek, bubbletop, motorless aircraft. You'll get aerial views of mountains, shoreline, coral pools, windsurfing sails, and, in winter, humpback whales. Reservations are recommended; 10-, 15-, 20-, and 30-minute flights leave every 20 minutes daily 10–5. The charge for one passenger is $59–$129, depending on the length of the flight; two people fly for $138–$238. ✉ *Dillingham Airfield, Mokulē'ia* ☎ *808/677–3404.*

BIKING

O'ahu's coastal roads are flat and well paved, and unfortunately, awash in vehicular traffic. Frankly, biking is no fun in either Waikīkī or Honolulu, but things are a bit better outside the city.

Honolulu City and County Bike Coordinator (☎ *808/768–8335*) can answer all your biking questions concerning trails, permits, and state laws.

BEST SPOTS

Fodor's Choice Our favorite ride is in central O'ahu on the **'Aiea Loop Trail** (✉ *Central*
★ *O'ahu, just past Kea'iwa Heiau State Park, at end of 'Aiea Heights Dr.*). There's a little bit of everything you expect to find in Hawai'i—wild pigs crossing your path, an ancient Hawaiian *heiau* (holy ground), and the remains of a World War II crashed airplane. Campsites and picnic tables are available along the way and, if you need a snack, strawberry guava trees abound. Enjoy the foliage change from bamboo to Norfolk pine in your climb along this 4½-mi track.

Biking the North Shore may sound like a great idea, but the two-lane road is narrow and traffic-heavy. We suggest you try the **West Kaunala Trail** (✉ *End of Pūpūkea Rd. This road is next to Foodland, the only grocery store on North Shore*). It's a little tricky at times, but with the rain-forest surroundings and beautiful ocean vistas you'll hardly notice your legs burning on the steep ascent at the end. It's about 5½ mi round-trip. Bring water because there's none on the trail unless it comes from the sky.

EQUIPMENT AND TOURS

Blue Sky Rentals & Sports Center. Known more for motorcycles than for man-powered bikes, Blue Sky does have bicycles for $25 for eight hours, $30 for a day, and $75 per week—no deposit is required. The prices include a bike, a helmet, and a lock. ✉ *1920 Ala Moana Blvd., across from Hilton Hawaiian Village, Waikīkī, Honolulu* ☎ *808/947–0101.*

Boca Hawai'i LLC. This is your first stop if you want to do intense riding. The triathlon shop, owned and operated by top athletes, has full-suspension Trek 1200s for mountain bikes or Trek 1000 for street bikes, both for $35 a day but that drops to $25 a day if you rent for more than one day. Call ahead and reserve a bike as supplies are limited. ⊠*330 Cooke St., next to Bike Factory, Kaka'ako, Honolulu* ☎*808/591–9839.*

CAMPING

Camping has always been the choice of cost-conscious travelers who want to be vacationing for a while without spending a lot of money. But now, with the growth of ecotourism and the skyrocketing cost of gas, it has become more popular than ever. Whatever your reasons for getting back to nature, O'ahu has plenty to offer year-round. ■TIP➔ **Camping here is not as highly organized as it is on the Mainland: expect few marked sites, scarce electrical outlets, and nary a ranger station.** What you find instead are unblemished spots in the woods and on the beach. With price tags ranging from free to $5, it's hard to complain about the lack of amenities.

STATE PARKS

There are four state recreation areas at which you can camp, one in the mountains and three on the beach. All state parks require picking up the permit in person less than 30 days before your camping dates and a $5 fee a day. To obtain a camping permit stop by the office (⊠*1151 Punchbowl St., Room 310*), or to receive their rules and regulations for state parks, write to the **Department of Land and Natural Resources, State Parks Division** (⧈ *Box 621 Honolulu 96809* ☎*808/587–0300* ⊕*www. state.hi.us/dlnr/dsp*).

Keaīwa Heiau State Recreation Area (⊠*End of Aiea Heights Rd.* ☎*808/483–2511*), the mountain option, consists of nearly 400 acres of forests and hiking trails in the foothills of the Ko'olau. The park is centered on an ancient Hawaiian holy site, known as a heiau, that is believed to be the site of many healings. Proper respect is asked of campers in the area.

Of the beach sites, **Kahana Valley State Park** (⊠*Kamehameha Hwy. near Kahana Bay*) is the choice for a true Hawaiian experience. You camp alongside a beautiful Windward bay, a short walk away from the Huilua Fishpond, a national historic landmark. There are rain-forest hikes chock-full of local fruit trees, a public hunting area for pigs, and a coconut grove for picnicking. The water is suitable for swimming and body surfing, though it's a little cloudy for snorkeling. Camping here gives you a true taste of old Hawai'i, as they lived it.

COUNTY CAMPSITES

As for the county spots, there are 15 currently available and they all do require a permit. The good news is that the permits are free and are easy to obtain. Contact the **Department of Parks and Recreation** (⊠*650 S. King St., Honolulu* ☎*808/768–3440*), or any of the satellite city halls (Ala Moana Mall, Fort St. Mall, and Kapolei Hale), for permits and rules and regulations.

Fodor's Choice
★
For beach camping we suggest Bellows and Kualoa. **Bellows Field Beach Park** (⊠*220 Tinker Rd.* ☎*808/259–8080*) has the superior beach as well as excellent cover in the grove of ironwood trees. The Windward

beach is over 3 mi long, and both pole fishing and campfires in designated areas are allowed here. You can feel secure with the kids as there are lifeguards and public phones. The only downside is that camping is only permitted on the weekends.

The beach at **Kualoa Regional Park** (✉49-479 *Kamehameha Hwy.* ☎808/237–8525) isn't the magnificent giant that Bellows is, but the vistas are both magnificent and historic. Near Chinaman's Hat (Mokoli'i Island) at the northern end of Kāne'ohe Bay, the park is listed on the National Registry of Historic Places due to its significance to the Hawaiians. The park is expansive, with large grassy areas, picnic tables, and comfort stations. Although the beach is just a bit of a sandy strip, the swimming and snorkeling are excellent.

Camping is not just all about the beach, however. Nestled in the foothills of the Ko'olau is the serene **Hoomaluhia Botanical Garden** (✉*End of Luluku Rd. in Kāne'ohe* ☎808/233–7323). The 400-acre preserve has catch-and-release fishing, extensive hiking trails, and a large selection of tropical shrubs and trees. There are five fire circles. Though it is a beautiful area, they do caution campers to be prepared for rain, mud, and mosquitoes.

GOLF

Unlike those of the Neighbor Islands, the majority of O'ahu's golf courses are not associated with hotels and resorts. In fact, of the island's three-dozen-plus courses, only five are tied to lodging and none of them are in the tourist hub of Waikīkī.

Green fees listed here are the highest course rates per round on weekdays/weekends for U.S. residents. (Some courses charge non–U.S. residents higher prices.) Discounts are often available for resort guests and for those who book tee times on the Web. Twilight fees are usually offered; call individual courses for information.

WAIKĪKĪ

Ala Wai Municipal Golf Course. Just across the Ala Wai Canal from Waikīkī, Ala Wai is said to host more rounds than any other U.S. course. Not that it's a great course, just really convenient, being Honolulu's only public "city course." Although residents can obtain a city golf card that allows automated tee-time reservation over the phone, the best bet for a visitor is to show up and expect to wait at least an hour. The course itself is flat. Robin Nelson did some redesign work in the 1990s, adding mounding, trees, and a lake. The Ala Wai Canal comes into play on several holes on the back nine, including the treacherous 18th. ✉*404 Kapahulu Ave., Waikīkī, Honolulu* ☎808/733–7387, 808/739–1900 golf shop ⅃18 holes. 5861 yds. Par 70. Green fee: $42 ☞*Facilities: Driving range, putting green, golf carts, pull carts, rental clubs, pro shop, lessons, restaurant, bar.*

SOUTHEAST O'AHU

Hawai'i Kai Golf Course. The Championship Golf Course (William F. Bell, 1973) winds through a Honolulu suburb at the foot of Koko Crater. Homes (and the liability of a broken window) come into play on many holes, but they are offset by views of the nearby Pacific and a crafty routing of holes. With several lakes, lots of trees, and bunkers in all the wrong places, Hawai'i Kai really is a "championship" golf course, especially when the trade winds howl. The **Executive Course** (1962), a par-55 track, is the first of only three courses in Hawai'i built by Robert Trent Jones Sr. Although a few changes have been made to his original design, you can find the usual Jones attributes, including raised greens and lots of risk-reward options. ⊠*8902 Kalaniana'ole Hwy., Hawai'i Kai* ☎*808/395–2358* ⊕*www.hawaiikaigolf.com* ⚐*Championship Course: 18 holes. 6222 yds. Par 72. Green fee: $90/$100. Executive Course: 18 holes. 2223 yds. Par 55. Green fee: $37/$42* ⚲*Facilities: Driving range, putting green, golf carts, pull carts, rental clubs, pro shop, lessons, restaurant, bar.*

WINDWARD O'AHU

Ko'olau Golf Club. Ko'olau Golf Club is marketed as the toughest golf course in Hawai'i and one of the most challenging in the country. Dick Nugent and Jack Tuthill (1992) routed 10 holes over jungle ravines that require at least a 110-yard carry. The par-4 18th may be the most difficult closing hole in golf. The tee shot from the regular tees must carry 200 yards of ravine, 250 from the blue tees. The approach shot is back across the ravine, 200 yards to a well-bunkered green. Set at the windward base of the Ko'olau Mountains, the course is as much beauty as beast. Kāne'ohe Bay is visible from most holes, orchids and yellow ginger bloom, the shama thrush (Hawai'i's best singer since Don Ho) chirrups, and waterfalls flute down the sheer, green mountains above. ⊠*45-550 Kionaole Rd., Kāne'ohe* ☎*808/236–4653* ⊕*www. koolaugolfclub.com* ⚐*18 holes. 7310 yds. Par 72. Green fee: $145* ⚲*Facilities: Driving range, putting green, golf carts, rental clubs, pro shop, golf academy, restaurant, bar.*

Fodor'sChoice
★ **Luana Hills Country Club.** In the cool, lush Maunawili Valley, Pete and Perry Dye created what can only be called target jungle golf. In other words, the rough is usually dense jungle, and you may not hit a driver on three of the four par-5s, or several par-4s, including the perilous 18th that plays off a cliff to a narrow green protected by a creek. Mt. Olomana's twin peaks tower over Luana Hills. ■TIP→**The back nine wanders deep into the valley, and includes an island green (par-3 11th) and perhaps the loveliest inland hole in Hawai'i (par-4 12th).** ⊠*770 Auloa Rd., Kailua* ☎*808/262–2139* ⊕*www.luanahills.com* ⚐*18 holes. 6164 yds. Par 72. Green fee: $125* ⚲*Facilities: Driving range, putting green, golf carts, rental clubs, pro shop, restaurant, bar.*

★ **Olomana Golf Links.** Bob and Robert L. Baldock are the architects of record for this layout, but so much has changed since it opened in 1969 that they would recognize little of it. A turf specialist was brought in to improve fairways and greens, tees were rebuilt, new bunkers added, and mangroves cut back to make better use of natural wetlands. But what really puts Olomana on the map is that this is where wunderkind Michelle Wie learned the game. ⊠*41-1801 Kalanianasole Hwy., Waimānalo* ☎*808/259–7926* ⊕*www.olomanagolflinks.com* ⚐*18 holes. 6326 yds. Par 72. Green fee: $90* ⚲*Facilities: Driving range,* *putting green, golf carts, pull carts, rental clubs, pro shop, lessons, restaurant, bar.*

NORTH SHORE

Turtle Bay Resort & Spa. When the Lazarus of golf courses, the **Fazio Course** at Turtle Bay (George Fazio, 1971), rose from the dead in 2002, Turtle Bay on Oʻahu's rugged North Shore became a premier golf destination. Two holes had been plowed under when the **Palmer Course** at Turtle Bay (Arnold Palmer and Ed Seay, 1992) was built, while the other seven lay fallow, and the front nine remained open. Then new owners came along and re-created holes 13 and 14 using Fazio's original plans, and the Fazio became whole again. It's a terrific track with 90 bunkers. The gem at Turtle Bay, though, is the Palmer Course. The front nine is mostly open as it skirts Punahoʻolapa Marsh, a nature sanctuary, while the back nine plunges into the wetlands and winds along the coast. The short par-4 17th runs along the rocky shore, with a diabolical string of bunkers cutting diagonally across the fairway from tee to green. ✉ *57-049 Kuilima Dr., Kahuku* ☎ *808/293–8574* ⊕ *www.turtlebay resort.com* 🏌️ *Fazio Course: 18 holes. 6535 yds. Par 72. Green fee: $160. Palmer Course: 18 holes. 7199 yds. Par 72. Green fee: $195* ⌣ *Facilities: Driving range, putting green, golf carts, rental clubs, pro shop, lessons, restaurant, bar.*

WEST (LEEWARD) AND CENTRAL OʻAHU

★ **Coral Creek Golf Course.** On the ʻEwa Plain, 4 mi inland, Coral Creek is cut from ancient coral—left from when this area was still under water. Robin Nelson (1999) does some of his best work in making use of the coral, and of some dynamite, blasting out portions to create dramatic lakes and tee and green sites. They could just as easily call it Coral Cliffs, because of the 30- to 40-foot cliffs Nelson created. They include the par-3 10th green's grotto and waterfall, and the vertical drop-off on the right side of the par-4 18th green. An ancient creek meanders across the course, but there's not much water, just enough to be a babbling nuisance. ✉ *91-1111 Geiger Rd., ʻEwa Beach* ☎ *808/441–4653* ⊕ *www.coralcreekgolfhawaii.com* 🏌️ *18 holes. 6818 yds. Par 72. Green fee: $130* ⌣ *Facilities: Driving range, putting green, golf carts, rental clubs, pro shop, lessons, restaurant, bar.*

Kō ʻOlina Golf Club. Hawaiʻi's golden age of golf-course architecture came to Oʻahu when Kō ʻOlina Golf Club opened in 1989. Ted Robinson, king of the water features, went splash-happy here, creating nine lakes that come into play on eight holes, including the par-3 12th, where you reach the tee by driving behind a Disney-like waterfall. Tactically, though, the most dramatic is the par-4 18th, where the approach is a minimum 120 yards across a lake to a two-tiered green guarded on the left by a cascading waterfall. Today, Kō ʻOlina, affiliated with the adjacent ʻIhilani Resort and Spa (guests receive discounted rates), has matured into one of Hawaiʻi's top courses. You can niggle about routing issues—the first three holes play into the trade winds (and the morning sun), and two consecutive par-5s on the back nine play into the trades—but Robinson does enough solid design to make those of passing concern. ✉ *92-1220 Aliʻinui Dr., Kapolei* ☎ *808/676–5300*

⊕*www.koolinagolf.com* ⚑*18 holes. 6867 yds. Par 72. Green fee: $179* ☞*Facilities: Driving range, putting green, golf carts, rental clubs, pro shop, golf academy, restaurant, bar.*

Royal Kunia Country Club. At one time the PGA Tour considered buying Royal Kunia Country Club and hosting the Sony Open there. It's that good. ■TIP→Every hole offers fabulous views from Diamond Head to Pearl Harbor to the nearby Wai'anae Mountains. Robin Nelson's eye for natural sight lines and dexterity with water features adds to the visual pleasure. ⊠*94-1509 Anonui St., Waipahu* ☎*808/688–9222* ⊕*www.royalkuniacc.com* ⚑*18 holes. 7007 yds. Par 72. Green fee: $140* ☞*Facilities: Driving range, putting green, golf carts, rental clubs, pro shop, restaurant.*

Waikele Golf Course. Outlet stores are not the only bargain at Waikele. The adjacent golf course is a daily-fee course that offers a private club-like atmosphere and a terrific Ted Robinson (1992) layout. The target off the tee is Diamond Head, with Pearl Harbor to the right. Robinson's water features are less distinctive here, but define the short par-4 fourth hole, with a lake running down the left side of the fairway and guarding the green; and the par-3 17th, which plays across a lake. The par-4 18th is a terrific closing hole, with a lake lurking on the right side of the green. ⊠*94-200 Paioa Pl., Waipahu* ☎*808/676–9000* ⊕*www.golf waikele.com* ⚑*18 holes. 6261 yds. Par 72. Green fee: $130* ☞*Facilities: Driving range, putting green, golf carts, rental clubs, pro shop, lessons, restaurant, bar.*

HIKING

The trails of O'ahu cover a full spectrum of environments: desert walks through cactus, slippery paths through bamboo-filled rain forest, and scrambling rock climbs up ancient volcanic calderas. The only thing you won't find is an overnighter as even the longest of hikes won't take you more than half a day. In addition to being short in length, many of the prime hikes are located within 10 minutes of downtown Waikīkī, meaning that you won't have to spend your whole day getting back to nature.

BEST SPOTS

Every vacation has requirements that must be fulfilled so that when your neighbors ask, you can say, "Yeah, did it." **Diamond Head Crater** is high on that list of things to do on O'ahu. It's a hike easy enough that even grandma can do it, as long as she takes a water bottle because

> **TIPS FOR THE TRAIL**
>
> ■ When hiking the waterfall and rain-forest trails, use insect repellent. The dampness draws huge swarms of bloodsuckers that can ruin a walk in the woods real quick.
>
> ■ Volcanic rock is very porous and therefore likely to be loose. Rock climbing is strongly discouraged as you never know which little ledge is going to go.
>
> ■ Always let someone know where you are going and never hike alone. The foliage gets very dense, and, small as the island is, many hikers have gotten lost for a week or longer.

it's hot and dry. Only a mile up, a clearly marked trail with handrails scales the inside of this extinct volcano. At the top, the fabled 99 steps take you up to the pillbox overlooking the Pacific Ocean and Honolulu. It's a breathtaking view and a lot cheaper than taking a helicopter ride for the same photo op. ✉*Diamond Head Rd. at 18th Ave. Enter on east of crater; there's limited parking inside, most park on street and walk in.*

Fodor'sChoice
★ Travel up into the valley beyond Honolulu to make the **Mānoa Falls** hike. Though only a mile long, this path passes through so many different ecosystems that you feel as if you're in an arboretum. Walk among the elephant ear ape plants, ruddy fir trees, and a bamboo forest straight out of China. At the top is a 150-foot falls with a small pool not quite suited for swimming but good for wading. This hike is more about the journey than the destination; make sure you bring some mosquito repellent because they grow 'em big up here. ✥*Behind Mānoa Valley in Paradise Park. Take West Mānoa Rd. to end, park on side of road, and follow trail signs in.*

For the less adventurous hiker and anyone looking for a great view, there is the **Makapu'u Lighthouse Trail.** The paved trail runs up the side of Makapu'u Point in southeast O'ahu. Early on the trail is surrounded by lava rock, but, as you ascend, foliage—the tiny white *koa haole* flower and the cream-tinged spikes of the *kiawe*—begins taking over the barren rock. Once atop the point, you begin to understand how alone these Islands are in the Pacific. The easternmost tip of O'ahu, this is where the island divides the sea, giving you a spectacular view of the cobalt ocean meeting the land in a cacophony of white caps. To the south are several tide pools and the lighthouse, while the eastern view looks down upon Rabbit and Kāohikaipu Islands, two bird sanctuaries just off the coast. The 2-mi round-trip hike is a great break on a circle-island trip. ✥*Take Kalaniana'ole Hwy. to base of Makapu'u Point. Look for asphalt strip snaking up mountain.*

GOING WITH A GUIDE

Hawai'i Nature Center. A good choice for families, the center in upper Makīkī Valley conducts a number of programs for both adults and children. There are guided hikes into tropical settings that reveal hidden waterfalls and protected forest reserves. They don't run tours every day so it is good to get advance reservations. ✉*2131 Makīkī Heights Dr., Makīkī Heights* ☎*808/955–0100.*

O'ahu Nature Tours. Guides explain the native flora and fauna that is your companion on glorious sunrise, hidden-waterfall, mountain-forest, rain-forest, and volcanic walking tours. ☎*808/924–2473* ⊕*www. oahunaturetours.com.*

DID YOU KNOW?

Mānoa Falls is about 150 feet high and is the gem at the end of a mile-long hike. At its top, you'll find a small pool perfect for wading.

HORSEBACK RIDING

★ **Happy Trails Hawai'i.** Take a guided horseback ride through the verdant Waimea Valley on the North Shore along trails that offer panoramic views from Ka'ena Point to the famous surfing spots. Rates for a 90-minute trail ride begin at $59. ⊠*1 mi mauka up Pupakea Rd. on right, Pupakea* ☎*808/638–7433.*

Kualoa Ranch. This ranch across from Kualoa Beach Park on the Windward side leads trail rides in the Ka'a'awa Valley. Rates for a one-hour trail ride begin at $59. Kualoa has other activities such as bus and Jeep tours, all-terrain-vehicle trail rides, and children's activities, which may be combined for half- or full-day package rates. ⊠*49-560 Kamehameha Hwy., Ka'a'awa* ☎*808/237–8515* ⊕*www.kualoa.com.*

Turtle Bay Stables. This is the only spot on the island where you can take the horses on the beach. The stables here are part of the North Shore resort, but can be utilized by nonguests. The sunset ride is a definite must if you are a friend of our four-legged friends. Rates for a 45-minute trail ride begin at $55. ⊠*4 mi north of Kahuku in Turtle Bay Resort* ☎*808/293–8811.*

TENNIS

O'ahu has 181 public tennis courts that are free and open for play on a first-come, first-served basis; you're limited to 45 minutes of court time if others are waiting to play. A complete listing is free of charge from the **Department of Parks and Recreation** (⊠*Tennis Unit, 650 S. King St., Honolulu* ☎*808/971–7150* ⊕*www.co.honolulu.hi.us/parks/*).

Kapi'olani Park, on the Diamond Head end of Waikīkī, has two tennis locations. The **Diamond Head Tennis Center** (⊠*3908 Pākī Ave.* ☎*808/971–7150*), near Kapi'olani Park, has nine courts open to the public. There are more than a dozen courts for play at **Kapi'olani Tennis Courts** (⊠*2748 Kalākaua Ave.* ☎*808/971–2510*). The closest public courts to the 'Ewa end of Waikīkī are in **Ala Moana Park** (⊠*Ala Moana Blvd.* ☎*808/592–7031*).

The **Pacific Beach Hotel** (⊠*2490 Kalākaua Ave., Waikīkī* ☎*808/922–1233* ⊕*www.pacificbeachhotel.com/*) has rooftop tennis courts that are open to nonguests for a fee.

VOLLEYBALL

Volleyball is an extremely popular spectator sport on the Islands, and no wonder. Both the men's and women's teams of the **University of Hawai'i** have blasted to a number-one ranking in years past. Crowded, noisy, and exciting home games are played from September through December (women's) and from January through April (men's) in the university's 10,000-seat Stan Sheriff Arena. ⊠*Lower Campus Rd., Honolulu* ☎*808/956–4481* ⊠*$8.*

BEST SPOTS

There are sand volleyball courts in Waikīkī near Fort DeRussy. They are open to the public, so talent levels vary. However, with a winner-plays-on policy, you won't be disappointed with the level as the day progresses. For more advanced play, there is an area at Queen's Beach, but you have to bring your own nets, which leads to a little more court possessiveness. But this is the area where you will find the college kids and pros hitting it while they are in town.

SHOPS AND SPAS

Eastern and Western traditions meet on O'ahu, where savvy shoppers find luxury goods at high-end malls and scout tiny boutiques and galleries filled with pottery, blown glass, woodwork, and Hawaiian print clothing by local artists. ■TIP→Exploring downtown Honolulu, Kailua on the Windward side, and the North Shore often yields the most original merchandise. Some of these small stores also carry a myriad of imported clothes and gifts from around the world—a reminder that, on this island halfway between Asia and North America, shopping is a multicultural experience.

WAIKĪKĪ

SHOPPING CENTERS

2100 Kalākaua. Tenants of this elegant, town house–style center include Chanel, Coach, Tiffany & Co., Yves Saint Laurent, Gucci, and Tod's. ⊠*2100 Kalākaua Ave., Waikīkī* ☎*808/550–4449* ⊕*www.2100kalakaua.com.*

DFS Galleria Waikīkī. Hermès, Cartier, and Calvin Klein are among the shops at this enclosed mall, as well as Hawai'i's largest beauty and cosmetic store. An exclusive boutique floor caters to duty-free shoppers only. Amusing and authentic Hawaiian-style shell necklaces, soaps, and printed wraps are rewards for anyone willing to wade through the pervasive tourist schlock along the Waikīkī Walk, an area of fashions, arts and crafts, and gifts. The Kālia Grill and Starbucks offer a respite for weary shoppers. ⊠*Kalākaua and Royal Hawaiian Aves., Waikīkī* ☎*808/931–2655.*

King Kalākaua Plaza. Banana Republic and Niketown—both two stories high and stocked with the latest fashions—anchor the King Kalākaua Plaza. ⊠*2080 Kalākaua Ave., Waikīkī* ☎*808/955–2878.*

Royal Hawaiian Shopping Center. Completely renovated in 2006 with a more open and inviting facade, this three-block-long center has become a Hawaiian shopping garden. The final tenant mix has more than 100 stores, including Hawaiian Heirloom Jewelry Collection by Phillip Rickard, which also has a museum with Victorian pieces. Bike buffs can check out the Harley-Davidson Motor Clothes and Collectibles Boutique, and the Ukelele House may inspire musicians to learn a new instrument. There are restaurants and even a post office. ⊠*2201 Kalākaua Ave., Waikīkī* ☎*808/922–0588* ⊕*www.shopwaikiki.com.*

King's Village. It looks like a Hollywood stage set of monarchy-era Honolulu, complete with a changing-of-the-guard ceremony every evening at 6:15; shops include Hawaiian Island Creations Jewelry, Swim City USA Swimwear, and Island Motor Sports. ⊠*131 Kaʻiulani Ave., Waikīkī.*

BOOKS

Bestsellers. This shop in the Hilton's Rainbow Bazaar is a branch of the local independent bookstore chain. They stock novelty Hawaiʻi memorabilia as well as books on Hawaiian history, local maps and travel guides, and Hawaiian music. ⊠*Hilton Hawaiian Village Beach Resort and Spa, 2005 Kālia Rd., Waikīkī* ☎*808/953–2378.*

CLOTHING

Moonbow Tropics. An elegant selection of silk Tommy Bahama Aloha shirts, as well as tropical styles for women. ⊠*Sheraton Moana Surfrider, 2365 Kalākaua Ave., Waikīkī* ☎*808/924–1496* ⊕*www.moonbow tropics.com.*

Reyn's. Reyn's is a good place to buy the aloha print fashions residents wear. This company manufacturers its own label in the Islands, has 13 locations statewide, and offers styles for men, women, and children. ⊠*Sheraton Waikīkī, 2255 Kalākaua Ave., Waikīkī* ☎*808/923–0331.*

GALLERIES

Gallery Tokusa. A *netsuke* is a toggle used to fasten small containers to obi belts on a kimono. Gallery Tokusa specializes in intricately carved netsuke, both antique and contemporary, and one-of-a-kind necklaces. ⊠*Halekulani, 2199 Kālia Rd., Waikīkī* ☎*808/923–2311.*

Norma Kress Gallery. Emerging native Hawaiian and Pacific Island artists show their work at this hotel gallery, highlighted with pottery, sculpture, paintings, drawings, and photography. ⊠*Hawaiʻi Prince Hotel, 100 Holomana St., Waikīkī* ☎*808/952–4761.*

★ **Sand People.** This little shop stocks easy-to-carry gifts, such as fish-shaped Christmas ornaments, Hawaiian-style notepads, charms in the shape of flip-flops (known locally as "slippers"), soaps, and ceramic clocks. Also located in Kailua. ⊠*Sheraton Moana Surfrider, 2369 Kalākaua, Waikīkī* ☎*808/924–6773.*

JEWELRY

Philip Rickard. The heirloom design collection of this famed jeweler features custom Hawaiian wedding jewelry. ⊠*Royal Hawaiian Shopping Center, 2201 Kalākaua Ave., Waikīkī* ☎*808/924–7972.*

HONOLULU: DOWNTOWN AND CHINATOWN

SHOPPING CENTERS

Getting to the Ala Moana and Downtown Honolulu shopping centers from Waikīkī is quick and inexpensive thanks to **TheBus** and the **Waikiki Trolley.**

Ala Moana Shopping Center. One of the nation's largest open-air malls is five minutes from Waikīkī by bus. Designer shops in residence include Gucci, Louis Vuitton, Gianni Versace, and Emporio Armani. All of

Hawai'i's major department stores are here, including Neiman Marcus, Sears, and Macy's. More than 240 stores and 60 restaurants make up this 50-acre complex. One of the most interesting shops is Shanghai Tang. First opened in Hong Kong, the store imports silks and other fine fabrics, and upholds the tradition of old-style Shanghai tailoring. To get to the mall from Waikīkī, catch TheBus line 8, 19, or 20; a one-way ride is $2. Or hop aboard the Waikiki Trolley's pink line, which comes through the area every half-hour. ⊠*1450 Ala Moana Blvd., Ala Moana* ☎*808/955–9517* ⊕*www.alamoanacenter.com special events and shuttle service.*

Aloha Tower Marketplace. Billing itself as a festival marketplace, Aloha Tower cozies up to Honolulu Harbor. Along with restaurants and entertainment venues, it has 80 shops and kiosks selling mostly visitor-oriented merchandise, from expensive sunglasses to exceptional local artwork to souvenir refrigerator magnets. Don't miss the aloha shirts and fancy hats for dogs at Pet Gear, and the curious mix of furniture, stationery, and clothing in Urban Rejuvenation. To get there from Waikīkī take the E-Transit Bus, which goes along TheBus routes every 15 minutes. ⊠*1 Aloha Tower Dr., at Piers 8, 9, and 10, Downtown Honolulu* ☎*808/566–2337* ⊕*www.alohatower.com.*

Ward Centers. Heading west from Waikīkī toward Downtown Honolulu, you'll run into a section of town with five distinct shopping-complex areas; there are more than 120 specialty shops and 20 restaurants here. The Entertainment Complex features 16 movie theaters. ■**TIP**➔**A** "shopping concierge" can assist you in navigating your way through the center, which spans four city blocks. For distinctive Hawaiian gift stores, visit Nohea Gallery and Native Books/Na Mea Hawaii, carrying quality work from Hawai'i artists, including mu'umu'u, *lauhala* products, and unparalleled Niihau shell necklaces. Island Soap and Candle Works (☎*808/591–0533*) makes all of its candles and soaps on-site with Hawaiian flower scents. Take TheBus routes 19 or 20; fare is $2 one-way. Or follow the Waikiki Trolley yellow line, which comes through the area every 45 minutes. ⊠*1050–1200 Ala Moana Blvd., Ala Moana* ☎*808/591–8411.*

BOOKS

Bestsellers. Hawai'i's largest independent bookstore has its flagship shop in Downtown Honolulu on Bishop Square. They carry books by both local and national authors. There are also locations of Bestsellers at the Honolulu International Airport and in Waikīkī at the Hilton Hawaiian Village. ⊠*1003 Bishop St., Downtown Honolulu* ☎*808/528–2378.*

Borders Books. Borders stocks more than 200 books in its Hawaiian section; learn about Hawaiian plants, hula, or surfing. This two-story location has books, music, movies, and a café. ⊠*Ward Centre, 1200 Ala Moana Blvd.* ☎*808/591–8995.*

★ **Native Books/Na Mea Hawai'i.** In addition to clothing for adults and children and unusual artwork such as Niihau shell necklaces, this boutique's book selection covers Hawaiian history and language, and offers children's books set in the Islands. ⊠*Ward Warehouse, 1050 Ala Moana Blvd.* ☎*808/596–8885.*

CLOTHING

Anne Namba Designs. Anne Namba brings the beauty of classic kimonos to contemporary fashions. In addition to women's apparel, she's also designed a men's line and a wedding couture line. ✉ *324 Kamani St., Downtown Honolulu* ☎ *808/589–1135.*

Hilo Hattie. Busloads of visitors pour in through the front doors of the world's largest manufacturer of Hawaiian and tropical aloha wear. Once shunned by Honolulu residents for its three-shades-too-bright tourist wear, it has become a favorite source for island gifts, macadamia nut and chocolate packages, and clothing for elegant Island functions. Free shuttle service is available from Waikīkī. ✉ *700 N. Nimitz Hwy., Iwilei* ☎ *808/535–6500.*

Reyn's. Reyn's is a good place to buy the aloha print fashions residents wear. Look for the limited-edition Christmas shirt, a collector's item manufactured each holiday season. Reyn's has 13 locations statewide and offers styles for men, women, and children. ✉ *Ala Moana Shopping Center, 1450 Ala Moana Blvd., Ala Moana* ☎ *808/949–5929* ✉ *Kāhala Mall, 4211 Wai'alae Ave., Kāhala* ☎ *808/737–8313.*

★ **Shanghai Tang.** First opened in Hong Kong, Shanghai Tang now has its 11th branch at Ala Moana. An emphasis on workmanship and the luxury of fine fabrics upholds the tradition of old-Shanghai tailoring. They do custom work for men, women, and children. ✉ *Ala Moana Shopping Center, Ala Moana* ☎ *808/942–9800.*

FOOD

Honolulu Chocolate Company. To really impress those back home, pick up a box of gourmet chocolates here. They dip the flavors of Hawai'i, from Kona coffee to macadamia nuts, in fine chocolate. ✉ *Ward Centre, 1200 Ala Moana Blvd., Ala Moana* ☎ *808/591–2997.*

Longs Drugs. For gift items in bulk, try one of the many outposts of Longs, the perfect place to stock up on chocolate-covered macadamia nuts—at reasonable prices—to carry home. ✉ *Ala Moana Shopping Center, 1450 Ala Moana Blvd., 2nd level, Ala Moana* ☎ *808/941–4433* ✉ *Kāhala Mall, 4211 Wai'alae Ave., Kāhala* ☎ *808/732–0784.*

GALLERIES

Louis Pohl Gallery. Modern works from some of Hawai'i's finest artists. ✉ *1111 Nu'uanu Ave., Downtown Honolulu* ☎ *808/521–1812.*

Nohea Gallery. These shops are really galleries representing more than 450 artists who specialize in koa furniture, bowls, and boxes, as well as art glass and ceramics. Original paintings and prints—all with an island theme—add to the selection. They also carry unique handmade Hawaiian jewelry with ti leaf, maile, and coconut-weave designs. ■TIP➔The koa photo albums in these stores are easy to carry home and make wonderful gifts. ✉ *Ward Warehouse, 1050 Ala Moana Blvd., Ala Moana* ☎ *808/596–0074.*

GIFTS

Robyn Buntin Galleries. Chinese nephrite-jade carvings, Japanese lacquer and screens, and Buddhist sculptures are among the international pieces displayed here. ⊠ *848 S. Beretania St., Downtown Honolulu* ☎ *808/523–5913.*

HAWAIIAN ARTS AND CRAFTS

Hawaiian Quilt Collection. Traditional island comforters, wall hangings, pillows, and other Hawaiian-print quilt items are the specialty here. ⊠ *Ala Moana Center, 1450 Ala Moana Blvd., Ala Moana* ☎ *808/ 946–2233.*

My Little Secret. The word is out that this is a wonderful selection of Hawaiian arts, crafts, and children's toys. ⊠ *Ward Warehouse, 1050 Ala Moana Blvd., Ala Moana* ☎ *808/596–2990.*

Na Hoku. If you look at the wrists of *kama'āina* (local) women, you are apt to see Hawaiian heirloom bracelets fashioned in either gold or silver in a number of island-inspired designs. Na Hoku sells jewelry in designs that capture the heart of the Hawaiian lifestyle in all its elegant diversity. ⊠ *Ala Moana Center, 1450 Ala Moana Blvd., Ala Moana* ☎ *808/946–2100.*

HONOLULU: EAST

KAPAHULU

Kapahulu begins at the Diamond Head end of Waikīkī and continues up to the H1 freeway. Shops and restaurants are located primarily on Kapahulu Avenue, which like many older neighborhoods should not be judged at first glance. It is full of variety.

Bailey's Antiques & Aloha Shirts. Vintage aloha shirts are the specialty at this kitschy store. Prices start at $3.99 for the 10,000 shirts in stock, and the tight space and musty smell are part of the thrift-shop atmosphere. ■TIP→Antiques hunters can also buy old-fashioned postcards, authentic military clothing, funky hats, and denim jeans from the 1950s. ⊠ *517 Kapahulu Ave., Kapahulu* ☎ *808/734–7628.*

KĀHALA & HAWAI'I KAI

Island Treasures. Local residents come here to shop for gifts that are both unique and within reach of almost every budget, ranging in price from $1 to $5,000. Next to Zippy's and overlooking the ocean, the store has handbags, toys, jewelry, home accessories, soaps and lotions, and locally made original artwork. Certainly the most interesting shop in Hawai'i Kai's suburban-mall atmosphere, this store is also a good place to purchase CDs of some of the best Hawai'ian music. ⊠ *Koko Marina Center, 7192 Kalaniana'ole Hwy., Hawai'i Kai* ☎ *808/396–8827.*

Kāhala Mall. The upscale residential neighborhood of Kāhala, near the slopes of Diamond Head, is 10 minutes by car from Waikīkī. The only shopping of note in the area is located at the indoor mall, which has 90 stores, including Macy's, Gap, Reyn's Aloha Wear, and Barnes & Noble. Don't miss fashionable boutiques such as **Ohelo Road** (☎ *808/735–5525*), where contemporary clothing for all occasions fills the racks. Eight **movie theaters** (☎ *800/326–3264 express code 2712*) provide post-shopping entertainment. ⊠*4211 Waiʻalae Ave., Kāhala* ☏*808/732–7736.*

WINDWARD OʻAHU

Bookends. The perfect place to shop for gifts, or just take a break with the family, this bookstore feels more like a small-town library, welcoming browsers to linger for hours. The large children's section is filled with toys and books to read. ⊠*600 Kailua Rd., Kailua* ☏*808/261–1996.*

Fodorʻs Choice ★ **Global Village.** Tucked into a tiny strip mall near Maui Tacos, this boutique features contemporary apparel for women, Hawaiian-style children's clothing, and unusual jewelry and gifts from all over the world. Look for Kula Cushions eye pillows (made with lavender grown on Maui), coasters in the shape of flip-flops, a wooden key holder shaped like a surfboard, and placemats made from lauhala and other natural fibers, plus accessories you won't find anywhere else. ⊠*Kailua Village Shops, 539 Kailua Rd., Kailua* ☏*808/262–8183* ⊕*www.globalvillage hawaii.com.*

Under a Hula Moon. Exclusive tabletop items and Pacific home decor, such as shell wreaths, shell night-lights, Hawaiian print kitchen towels, and Asian silk clothing, define this eclectic shop. ⊠*Kailua Shopping Center, 600 Kailua Rd., Kailua* ☏*808/261–4252*

NORTH SHORE

★ **The Growing Keiki.** Frequent visitors return to this store year after year. They know they'll find a fresh supply of original, hand-picked, Hawaiian-style clothing for youngsters. ⊠*66-051 Kamehameha Hwy., Haleʻiwa* ☏*808/637–4544* ⊕*www.thegrowingkeiki.com.*

★ **Outrigger Trading Company.** Though this shop has been in business since 1982, its upstairs location in the North Shore Marketplace often gets bypassed when it shouldn't. Look for Jam's World patchwork tablecloths with an aloha flair, shell boxes, mobiles made of ceramic fish and driftwood, stained-glass ornaments, and beach-glass wind chimes. Other novelties include hula girl and bamboo lamps and silk-screened table runners. ⊠*North Shore Marketplace, 66-250 Kamehameha Hwy., Haleʻiwa* ☏*808/638–5000.*

Fodorʻs Choice ★ **Silver Moon Emporium.** This small boutique carries everything from Brighton accessories and fashionable T-shirts to Betsy Johnson formal wear, and provides attentive yet casual personalized service. Its stock changes frequently, and there's always something wonderful on sale. No matter what your taste, you'll find something for everyday wear or special occasions. ⊠*North Shore Marketplace, 66-250 Kamehameha Hwy., Haleʻiwa* ☏*808/637–7710.*

WEST OʻAHU

Aloha Stadium Swap Meet. This thrice-weekly outdoor bazaar attracts hundreds of vendors and even more bargain hunters. Every Hawaiian souvenir imaginable can be found here, from coral shell necklaces to bikinis, as well as a variety of ethnic wares, from Chinese brocade dresses to Japanese pottery. There are also ethnic foods, silk flowers, and luggage in aloha floral prints. Shoppers must wade through the typical sprinkling of used and stolen goods to find value. Wear comfortable shoes, use sunscreen, and bring bottled water. The flea market takes place in the Aloha Stadium parking lot Wednesday and weekends from 6 to 3. Admission is $1 per person ages 12 and up. Several shuttle companies serve Aloha Stadium for the swap meet, including **VIP Shuttle** (☎808/839–0911), **Reliable Shuttle** (☎808/924–9292), and **Hawaii Supertransit** (☎808/841–2928). The average cost is $12 per person, round-trip. For a cheaper but slower ride, take TheBus. Check routes at ⊕*www.thebus.org.* ✉*99-500 Salt Lake Blvd., 'Aiea* ☎*808/486–6704.*

Waikele Premium Outlets. Anne Klein Factory, Donna Karan Company Store, Kenneth Cole, and Saks Fifth Avenue Outlet anchor this discount destination. You can take a shuttle to the outlets, but the companies do change over frequently. One to try: **Moha Shuttle** (☎808/216–8006); $10 round-trip. ✉*H1 Hwy., 30 min west of Downtown Honolulu, Waikele* ☎*808/676–5656.*

SPAS

Fodor's Choice
★ **Ampy's European Facials and Body Spa.** This 30-year-old spa has kept its prices reasonable over the years thanks to their "no frills" way of doing business. All of Ampy's facials are 75 minutes, and the spa has become famous for custom aromatherapy treatments. Call at least a week in advance because the appointment book fills up quickly here. It's in the Ala Moana Building, adjacent to the Ala Moana Shopping Center. ✉*1441 Kapi'olani Blvd., Suite 377, Ala Moana* ☎*808/946–3838* ☞*$80, 60-min lomi lomi massage. Sauna. Services: massage, body treatments, facials, hand and foot care.*

Hawaiian Rainforest Salon and Spa. The most popular treatment at this spa uses pressure and heat from natural Hawaiian lava rocks to massage your pain away. They also have Vichy showers, aromatherapy whirlpool baths, a Korean-style Akasuri body polish, and a wide selection of packages. If you're sleepy from the long flight, try the jet-lag remedy, a 25-minute treatment that includes a neck massage and scalp rub. ✉*Pacific Beach Hotel, 5th fl., 2490 Kalākaua Ave., Waikīkī* ☎*808/441–4890* ⊕*www.hawaiianrainforest.com* ☞*$90, 50-min lomi lomi massage. Hair salon, hot tubs, sauna. Services: massage, body wraps, body care, facials, makeup.*

J. W. Marriott 'Ihilani Resort & Spa. Soak in warm seawater among velvety orchid blossoms at this unique Hawaiian hydrotherapy spa. Thalassotherapy treatments combine underwater jet massage with color therapy and essential oils. Specially designed treatment rooms have a hydrotherapy tub, a Vichy-style shower, and a needle shower with 12 heads. The spa's Pua Kai line of natural aromatherapy products includes massage and body oil, bath crystals and body butter, which combine ingredients such as ginger, jasmine, rose petals, and coconut and grape seed oils. ✉92-1001 ʻŌlani St., Kapolei ☎808/679–0079 ⊕www.ihilani. com ✆$145, 50-min lomi lomi massage. Hair salon, hot tubs (indoor and outdoor), sauna, steam room. Gym with: cardiovascular machines, free weights, weight-training equipment. Services: aromatherapy, body wraps and scrubs, facials, massage, thalassotherapy. Classes and programs: aerobics, body sculpting, dance classes, fitness analysis, guided walks, personal training, Pilates, tai chi, yoga.

Mandara Spa at the Hilton Hawaiian Village Beach Resort & Spa. From its perch in the Kālia Tower, Mandara Spa, an outpost of the chain that originated in Bali, overlooks the mountains, ocean, and downtown Honolulu. Fresh Hawaiian ingredients and traditional techniques headline an array of treatments. Try an exotic upgrade, such as reflexology or an eye treatment using Asian silk protein. The delicately scented, candlelit foyer can fill up quickly with robe-clad conventioneers, so be sure to make a reservation. There are spa suites for couples, a private infinity pool, and a café. ✉Hilton Hawaiian Village Beach Resort and Spa, 2005 Kālia Rd., Waikīkī ☎808/949–4321 ⊕www.hiltonhawaiian village.com ✆$150, 50-min lomi lomi massage. Hair salon, hot tubs (indoor and outdoor), sauna, steam room. Gym with: cardiovascular machines, free weights, weight-training equipment. Services: aromatherapy, body wraps and scrubs, facials, massages.

Nā Hōʻola at the Hyatt Regency Waikīkī Resort & Spa. Nā Hōʻola is the largest spa in Waikīkī, sprawling across the fifth and sixth floors of the Hyatt, with 19 treatment rooms, jet baths, and Vichy showers. Arrive early for your treatment to enjoy the postcard views of Waikīkī Beach. Four packages identified by Hawaiʻi's native healing plants—noni, kukui, awa, and kalo—combine various body, face, and hair treatments and span 2½ to 4 hours. The Champagne of the Sea body treatment employs a self-heating mud wrap to release tension and stress. The small exercise room is for use by hotel guests only. ✉Hyatt Regency Waikīkī Resort and Spa, 2424 Kalākaua Ave., Waikīkī ☎808/921–6097 ⊕www. waikiki.hyatt.com ✆$135, 50-min lomi lomi massage. Sauna. Gym with: cardiovascular machines. Services: aromatherapy, body scrubs and wraps, facials, hydrotherapy, massages.

Fodorʹs Choice ★ **SpaHalekulani.** SpaHalekulani mines the traditions and cultures of the Pacific Islands with massages, body, and facial therapies. Try the Polynesian Nonu, which uses warm stones and healing nonu gel. The invigorating Japanese Ton Ton Amma massage is another popular choice. The exclusive line of bath and body products is scented by maile, lavender orchid, hibiscus, coconut passion, or Manoa mint. ✉Halekūlani Hotel, 2199 Kālia Rd., Waikīkī ☎808/931–5322 ⊕www.halekulani. com ✆$200, 75-min lomi lomi massage. Use of facilities is specific to treatment but may include Japanese furo bath, steam shower or whirlpool tub. Services: body treatments, facials, hair salon, massages, nail care.

The Spa Luana at Turtle Bay Resort. Luxuriate at the ocean's edge in this serene spa. Don't miss the tropical Pineapple Pedicure ($65), administered outdoors overlooking the North Shore. Tired feet soak in a bamboo bowl filled with coconut milk before the pampering really begins

TROPICAL FLOWERS AND FRUIT

Bring home fresh pineapple, papaya, or coconut to share with friends and family. Orchids also will brighten your home and remind you of your trip to the Islands. By law, all fresh-fruit and plant products must be inspected by the Department of Agriculture before export. Be sure to inquire at the shop about the Department of Agriculture rules so a surprise confiscation doesn't spoil your departure. In most cases, shipping to your home is best.

Kawamoto Orchid Nursery. Kawamoto grows all flowers on its three-acre orchid farm near Downtown Honolulu. Their specialty is the Cattleylea, a favorite for Mother's Day, and they have decades of experience shipping temperamental orchids to the Mainland. The nursery is open Monday thru Saturday until 3:30. ✉ *2630 Waiomao Rd.* ☎ *808/732-5808* ⊕ *www.kawamoto orchids.com.*

Tropical Fruits Distributors of Hawai'i. Avoid the hassle of airport inspections. This company specializes in packing inspected pineapple and papaya; they will deliver to your hotel and to the airport check-in counter, or ship to the mainland United States and Canada. Think about ordering on the Web, unless you are planning a trip to the North Shore. ✉ *64-1551 Kamehameha Hwy.* ☎ *808/847-3234* ⊕ *www.dolefruithawaii.com.*

with Hawaiian algae salt, island bee honey, kukui nut oil, and crushed pineapple. There are private spa suites, an outdoor treatment cabana that overlooks the surf, an outdoor exercise studio, and a lounge area and juice bar. ✉ *Turtle Bay Resort, 57-091 Kamehameha Hwy., North Shore* ☎ *808/447-6868* ⊕ *www.turtlebayresort.com* ✆ *$110, 50-min lomi lomi massage. Hair salon, outdoor hot tub, steam room. Gym with: cardiovascular machines, free weights, weight-training equipment. Services: body treatments, facials, massages, waxing. Classes and programs: aerobics, Pilates, yoga.*

ENTERTAINMENT AND NIGHTLIFE

Many first-time visitors arrive in the Islands expecting to see scenic beauty and sandy beaches but not much at night. That might be true on some of the other Islands, but not in O'ahu. Honolulu sunsets herald the onset of the best nightlife scene in the Islands.

Local artists perform every night of the week along Waikīkī's Kalākaua and Kūhiō avenues and in Downtown Honolulu; the clubs dance to every beat from Top 40 to alternative to '80s.

The arts also thrive alongside the tourist industry. O'ahu has an established symphony, a thriving opera company, chamber music groups, and community theaters. Major Broadway shows, dance companies, and rock stars also make their way to Honolulu. Check the local newspapers—*MidWeek,* the *Honolulu Advertiser,* the *Honolulu Star-Bulletin,* or the *Honolulu Weekly*—for the latest events.

Whether you make it an early night or stay up to watch that spectacular tropical sunrise, there's lots to do in paradise.

2

ENTERTAINMENT

DINNER CRUISES AND SHOWS

Dinner cruises depart either from the piers adjacent to the Aloha Tower Marketplace in Downtown Honolulu or from Kewalo Basin, near Ala Moana Beach Park, and head along the coast toward Diamond Head. There's usually dinner, dancing, drinks, and a sensational sunset. Except as noted, dinner cruises cost approximately $40 to $110, cocktail cruises $25 to $40. Most major credit cards are accepted. In all cases, reservations are essential.

Ali'i Kai Catamaran. Patterned after an ancient Polynesian vessel, this huge catamaran casts off from Aloha Tower with 1,000 passengers. The deluxe dinner cruise has two bars, a huge dinner, and an authentic Polynesian show with colorful hula music. The food is good, the after-dinner show loud and fun, and everyone dances on the way back to shore. Rates begin at $69 and include round-trip transportation, the dinner buffet, and one drink. ⊠ *Pier 5, street level, Honolulu* ☎ *808/539–9400 Ext. 5.*

Atlantis Cruises. The sleekly high-tech *Navatek*, a revolutionary craft designed to sail smoothly in rough waters, powers farther along Waikīkī's coastline than its competitors, sometimes making it past Diamond Head and all the way to Hanauma Bay sunset dinner or moonlight cruises aboard the 300-passenger boat where you can feast on beef tenderloin and whole lobster or opt for the downstairs buffet. There's also the option of humpback whale–watching cruises December to mid-April. Tours leave from Pier 6, next to Aloha Tower Marketplace. Rates begin at $86 for the buffet, including one drink; the sitdown dinner, which includes three drinks, starts at $118. ⊠ *Honolulu Harbor* ☎ *808/973–1311* ⊕ *www.atlantisadventures.com.*

Creation: A Polynesian Odyssey. A daring Samoan fire-knife dancer is the highlight of this show that traces Hawai'i's culture and history, from its origins to statehood. Buffet dinner runs at $78 while a sit down dinner with steak and lobster is $124. ⊠ *'Oinahau Showroom, Sheraton Princess Ka'iulani Hotel, 120 Ka'iulani Ave., Waikīkī* ☎ *808/931–4660* ⊙ *Dinner shows Tues.–Sun. at 6.*

★ **Magic of Polynesia.** Hawai'i's top illusionist, John Hirokawa, displays mystifying sleight of hand in this highly entertaining show, which incorporates contemporary hula and island music into its acts. Reservations are required for dinner and the show, which is priced at $83, but walkups are permitted if you just want the entertainment for $52. ⊠ *Ohana Beachcomber Hotel, 2300 Kalākaua Ave., Waikīkī* ☎ *808/971–4321* ⊙ *Nightly at 8.*

Paradise Cruises. Prices vary depending on which deck you choose on the 1,600-passenger, four-deck *Star of Honolulu*. For instance, a seven-course French-style dinner and live jazz on the top deck starts at $165. A steak-and-crab feast on level two starts at $78. This ship also features daily Hawaiiana Lunch cruises that offer lei-making and 'ukulele and hula lessons starting at $52. Evening excursions also take place on the 340-passenger *Starlet I* and 230-passenger *Starlet II*, which offer three-course dinners beginning at $43. Also, bring your bathing suit for a morning cruise for $63 complete with ocean fun on a water trampoline and slide, and feast on a barbecue lunch before heading back to shore. ⊠*1540 S. King St., Honolulu* ☎*808/983–7827* ⊕*www.paradise cruises.com.*

☺ **Polynesian Cultural Center.** Easily one of the best on the Islands, this show has soaring moments and an "erupting volcano." The performers are students from Brigham Young University's Hawai'i campus. ⊠*55-370 Kamehameha Hwy., Lā'ie* ☎*808/293–3333 or 800/367–7060* ⊕*www. polynesia.com* ☺*Mon.–Sat. 12:30–9:30.*

Society of Seven. This lively, popular septet has great staying power and, after more than 25 years, continues to put on one of the best shows in Waikīkī. They sing, dance, do impersonations, play instruments, and, above all, entertain with their contemporary sound. ⊠*Outrigger Waikīkī on the Beach, 2335 Kalākaua Ave., Waikīkī* ☎*808/922–6408* ⊕*www.outrigger.com* ☺*Tues.–Sat. at 8:30.*

LŪ'AU

The lū'au is an experience that everyone, both local and tourist, should have. Today's lū'au still adhere to traditional foods and entertainment, but there's also a fun, contemporary flair. With most, you can even watch the roasted pig being carried out of its *'imu,* a hole in the ground used for cooking meat with heated stones.

Lū'au cost anywhere from $56 to $195. Most that are held outside of Waikīkī offer shuttle service so you don't have to drive. Reservations are essential.

Germaine's Lū'au. Widely regarded as the most folksy and local, this lū'au is held in Kalaeloa in leeward O'ahu. The food is the usual multicourse, all-you-can-eat buffet, but it's very tasty. It's a good lū'au for first-timers and at a reasonable price. Expect a lively crowd on the 35-minute bus ride from Waikīkī. Admission includes buffet, Polynesian show, and shuttle transport from Waikīkī. ☎*808/949–6626 or 800/367–5655* ⊕*www.germainesluau.com* ⊠*$69* ☺*Daily at 6. Closed Mon. in winter.*

★ **Paradise Cove Lū'au.** The scenery is the best here—the sunsets are unbelievable. Watch Mother Nature's special-effects show in Kapolei/Kō 'Olina Resort in leeward O'ahu, a good 27 mi from the bustle of Waikīkī. The party-hearty atmosphere is kid-friendly with Hawaiian games, canoe rides in the cove, and lots of predinner activities. The stage show includes a fire-knife dancer, singing emcee, and both traditional and contemporary hula. Basic admission includes buffet, activities and the show, and shuttle transport from Waikīkī. You pay extra for table service and box seating. ☎*808/842–5911* ⊕*www.paradisecovehawaii. com* ⊠*$80–$137* ☺*Daily at 5:30, doors open at 5.*

Fodor'sChoice **Polynesian Cultural Center Ali'i Lū'au.** This elaborate lū'au has the sharp-
★ est production values but no booze (it's a Mormon-owned facility). It's held amid the seven re-created villages at the Polynesian Cultural Center in the North Shore town of Lā'ie, about an hour's drive from Honolulu. The lū'au includes tours of the park with shows and activities. Package rates vary depending on activities and amenities (personalized

DID YOU KNOW?

The ancient art of hula is taught to many keiki (children) on O'ahu from a very young age. Catch a performance here, at Kapi'olani Park.

Island Sounds

Hawai'i has a vigorous music scene largely invisible outside the state but central to its cultural identity. The Grammy Awards only got around to recognizing Hawaiian music with an award in 2005, but local artists sell thousands of albums and regularly tour island conclaves on the mainland, even playing Carnegie Hall. Like country, Hawaiian music has several subcategories: indigenous chant; early Western-style choral music; "traditional" songs that span the 20th century; contemporary Hawaiian, which melds all of the above with rock, pop, and even folk; instrumental slack key guitar and 'ukulele music; reggae and rap mixes. Most islands boast at least one Hawaiian music station—often two; one for classic Hawaiian, one for more contemporary stuff. Performers to listen for include the Cazimero Brothers, Keali'i Reichel, and Israel Kamakawiwo'ole (just say "Iz"). Or you might get a kick out of Don Tiki's revival of the '60s-era xylophone-and-bird-call school of island music.

tours, reserved seats, buffet vs. dinner service, backstage tour, etc.). Waikīkī transport is available, call for prices. ☎*808/293–3333 or 800/367–7060* ⊕*www.polynesia.com* ✉*$83–$215* ⊙*Mon.–Sat. center opens at noon; lū'au starts at 5.*

FILM

Hawai'i International Film Festival. It may not be Cannes, but this festival is unique and exciting. During the weeklong event from the end of November to early December, top films from the United States, Asia, and the Pacific are screened day and night at several theaters on O'ahu to packed crowds. It's a must-see for film adventurers. ☎*808/528–3456* ⊕*www.hiff.org.*

★ **Sunset on the Beach.** It's like watching a movie at the drive-in, minus the car and the impossible speaker box. Think romantic and cozy; bring a blanket and find a spot on the sand to enjoy live entertainment, food from top local restaurants, and a movie feature on a 40-foot screen. Held twice a month on Waikīkī's Queens Surf Beach across from the Honolulu Zoo, Sunset on the Beach is a favorite event for both locals and tourists. If the weather is blustery, beware of flying sand. ☎*808/923–1094* ⊕*www.sunsetonthebeach.net.*

MUSIC

Hawai'i Opera Theater. Better known as "HOT," the Hawai'i Opera Theater has been known to turn the opera-challenged into opera lovers. All operas are sung in their original language with projected English translation. Tickets range from $29 to $120. ✉*Neil Blaisdell Center Concert Hall, Ward Ave. and King St., Downtown Honolulu* ☎*808/596–7858* ⊕*www.hawaiiopera.org.*

Honolulu Symphony Orchestra. In recent years, the Honolulu Symphony has worked hard to increase its appeal to all ages. The orchestra performs at the Neil Blaisdell Concert Hall under the direction of the young, dynamic Samuel Wong. The Honolulu Pops series, with performances under the summer stars at the Waikīkī Shell, features top local and national artists under the direction of talented conductor-composer Matt Cattingub. Tickets are $17–$59. ⊠*Dole Cannery, 650 Iwilei Rd., Suite 202, Iwilei* ☎*808/792–2000* ⊕*www.honolulusymphony.com.*

Honolulu Zoo Concerts. For almost two decades, the Honolulu Zoo Society has sponsored Wednesday evening concerts from June to August on the zoo's stage lawn. Listen to local legends play everything from Hawaiian to jazz to Latin music. ■ TIP➔At just $1 admission, this is one of the best deals in town. Take a brisk walk through the zoo exhibits before they close at 5:30 PM or join in the family activities; bring your own picnic for the concert, which starts at 6 PM. It's an alcohol-free event, and there's a food concession for those who come unprepared. ⊠*151 Kapahulu Ave., Waikīkī* ☎*808/926–3191* ⊕*www.honoluluzoo. org* ⌨*$1* ☾*Gates open at 4:30.*

NIGHTLIFE

O'ahu is the best of all the islands for nightlife. The locals call it *pau hana* but you might call it "off the clock and ready for a cocktail." The literal translation of the Hawaiian phrase means "done with work."

You can find a bar in just about any area on O'ahu. Most of the clubs, however, are in Waikīkī, Ala Moana, and Downtown Honolulu. The drinking age is 21 on O'ahu and throughout Hawai'i. Many bars will admit younger people but will not serve them alcohol. By law, all establishments that serve alcoholic beverages must close by 2 AM. The only exceptions are those with a cabaret license, which have a 4 AM curfew. ■ TIP➔Most clubs have a cover charge of $5 to $10, but with some establishments, getting there early means you don't have to pay.

WAIKĪKĪ

BARS

Banyan Veranda. The Banyan Veranda is steeped in history. From this location the radio program *Hawai'i Calls* first broadcast the sounds of Hawaiian music and the rolling surf to a U.S. mainland audience in 1935. Today, a variety of Hawaiian entertainment continues to provide the perfect accompaniment to the sounds of the waves. ⊠*Sheraton Moana Surfrider, 2365 Kalākaua Ave., Waikīkī* ☎*808/922–3111.*

★ **Cobalt Lounge.** Take the glass elevator up 30 stories to enjoy the sunset. Floor-to-ceiling windows offer breathtaking views of Diamond Head and the Waikīkī shoreline. Leather sofas and cobalt-blue lighting set the "blue" Hawai'i mood. After darkness falls, you can find soft lights, starlight, and dancing in this lounge in the center of the Hanohano Room. ⊠*Sheraton Waikīkī, 2255 Kalākaua Ave., Waikīkī* ☎*808/922–4422.*

★ **Duke's Canoe Club.** Making the most of its oceanfront spot on Waikīkī Beach, Duke's presents "Concerts on the Beach" every Friday, Saturday, and Sunday with contemporary Hawaiian musicians like Henry Kapono. National musicians like Jimmy Buffett have also performed here. At Duke's Barefoot Bar, solo Hawaiian musicians take the stage nightly, and it's not unusual for surfers to leave their boards outside to step in for a casual drink after a long day on the waves. ⊠*Outrigger Waikīkī, 2335 Kalākaua Ave., Waikīkī* ☎*808/922–2268.*

★ **Mai Tai Bar at the Royal Hawaiian.** The bartenders sure know how to make a killer mai tai—just one could do the trick. This is, after all, the establishment that came up with the famous drink in the first place. The pink, umbrella-covered tables at the outdoor bar are front-row seating for Waikīkī sunsets and an unobstructed view of Diamond Head. Contemporary Hawaiian music is usually on stage, and the staff is extremely friendly. ⊠ *Royal Hawaiian Hotel, 2259 Kalākaua Ave., Waikīkī* ☎ *808/923–7311.*

Fodor's Choice
★ **Moana Terrace.** Three floors up from Waikīkī Beach, this open-air terrace is the home of Aunty Genoa Keawe, the "First Lady of Hawaiian Music." Her falsetto sessions include jams with the finest of Hawai'i's musicians. ⊠ *Waikīkī Beach Marriott Resort, 2552 Kalākaua Ave., Waikīkī* ☎ *808/922–6611.*

Shore Bird Oceanside Bar and Grill. This Waikīkī beachfront bar spills right out onto the sand. Local bands play nightly until 1 AM. ⊠ *Outrigger Reef on the Beach hotel, 2169 Kālia Rd., Waikīkī* ☎ *808/922–2887.*

Tiki's Grill and Bar. Get in touch with your primal side at this restaurant–bar overlooking Kuhio Beach. Tiki torches, tiki statues, and other South Pacific art set the mood. A twentysomething mix of locals and tourists comes on the weekends to get their fill of kitschy-cool. There's nightly entertainment featuring contemporary Hawaiian musicians. Don't leave without sipping on a "lava flow." It's served in a whole coconut, which is yours to keep at the end of the night. ⊠ *ResortQuest Waikīkī Beach Hotel, 2570 Kalākaua Ave., Waikīkī* ☎ *808/923–8454.*

CLUBS

Hula's Bar and Lei Stand. Hawai'i's oldest and best-known gay-friendly nightspot offers calming panoramic outdoor views of Diamond Head and the Pacific Ocean by day and a high-energy club scene by night. Check out the soundproof, glassed-in dance floor. ⊠ *Waikīkī Grand Hotel, 134 Kapahulu Ave., 2nd fl., Waikīkī* ☎ *808/923–0669.*

Nashville Waikīkī. Country music in the tropics? You bet! Put on your *paniolo* (Hawaiian cowboy) duds and mosey on out to the giant dance floor. There are pool tables, dartboards, line dancing, and free dance lessons (Wednesday at 6:30 PM) to boot. Look for wall-to-wall crowds on the weekend. ⊠ *Ohana Waikīkī West Hotel, 2330 Kūhiō Ave., Waikīkī* ☎ *808/926–7911.*

The W. The Diamond Head Grill restaurant is also an after-hours nightclub, full of hip, young professionals who enjoy martinis and the chance to do some not-so-serious networking. Look for a younger group on Saturday. Enjoy some fantastic (though pricey) eats until midnight, and keep dancing until 2 AM. ⊠ *W. Honolulu—Diamond Head, 2885 Kalākaua Ave., Waikīkī* ☎ *808/922–1700.*

Zanzabar. Traverse a winding staircase and make an entrance at Zanzabar where DJs spin top hits, from hip-hop to soul and techno to trance. It's easy to find a drink at this high-energy nightspot with its three bars. Not exactly sure how

> **WORD OF MOUTH**
>
> "Another vote for Zanzabar, if you are looking to go dancing."
> —MelissaHI

to get your groove on? Zanzabar offers free Latin dance lessons every Tuesday at 8 PM. Most nights are 21 and over, Sunday, Tuesday, Wednesday, and Thursday allow 18 and over in for $15. ⊠ *Waikīkī Trade Center, 2255 Kūhiō Ave., Waikīkī* ☎*808/924–3939.*

ELSEWHERE IN HONOLULU
BARS

Anna Bannana's. Generations of Hawai'i college students have spent more than an evening or two at this legendary two-story, smoky dive near the University of Hawai'i campus. A living-room atmosphere makes it a comfortable place to hang out. Here, the music is fresh, loud, and sometimes experimental. Live music happens Friday and Saturday, starting at 9 PM. There's open-mike night for amateurs on Monday. ⊠*2440 S. Beretania St., Mō'ili'ili* ☎*808/946–5190.*

Murphy's Bar & Grill. On the edge of Chinatown this 120-year-old bar has been serving drinks to visitors and *kama aina* alike dating back to Hawai'i's days as a territory. Voted the best bar in Hawai'i three of the past four years, Murphy's is a great oasis from all the tropical drinks and thatched roofs. Once inside you would swear you were in an Irish pub back in Boston. ⊠ *2 Merchant St., Downtown Honolulu* ☎*808/531–0422.*

Fodor'sChoice
★ **Mai Tai Bar at Ala Moana Center.** After a long day of shopping, the Mai Tai Bar on the third floor of Ala Moana Center is a perfect spot to relax. There's live entertainment and two nightly happy hours: one for food items and another strictly for specialty drinks. There's never a cover charge and no dress code, but to avoid waiting in line, get there before 9 PM. ⊠*1450 Ala Moana Blvd., Ala Moana* ☎*808/947–2900.*

Opium Den & Champagne Bar at Indigo's. This bar at the edge of Chinatown resembles a joint right out of film noir. Jazz plays early in the evening on Tuesday; late-night DJs spin trance, funk, disco, and rock on weekends. In addition to champagne, happy hour features sake martinis and complimentary pūpū buffet. Weekly wine tastings, too. ⊠*Indigo Euroasian Cuisine, 1121 Nu'uanu Ave., Downtown Honolulu* ☎*808/521–2900.*

CLUBS

Fodor'sChoice
★ **Rumours.** The after-work crowd loves this spot, which has dance videos, disco, and throbbing lights. On Saturday "Little Chill" nights, the club plays oldies from the '70s, '80s, and '90s and serves free pūpū. ⊠*Ala Moana Hotel, 410 Atkinson St., Ala Moana* ☎*808/955–4811.*

Venus Nightclub. This high-energy social bar, with leather couches ideal for a night of people-watching, features hip-hop, trance, and reggae with guest DJs five nights a week. Attention, ladies: there's a male dance revue Saturday evening. ⊠*1349 Kapi'olani Blvd., Ala Moana* ☎*808/951–8671.*

ELSEWHERE IN O'AHU
BARS

Boardrider's Bar & Grill. Tucked away in Kailua Town, this spot has long been the venue for local bands to strut their stuff. Renovations have spruced up the space, which now includes pool tables, foosball, and eight TVs for sports-viewing with the local and military crowd. Look for live entertainment—reggae to alternative rock to good old-fashioned rock and roll—Wednesday through Saturday from 10:30 PM to 1:30 AM. Covers range from $3 to $10. ⊠*201-A Hamakua Dr., Kailua* ☎*808/ 261–4600.*

Breaker's Restaurant. Just about every surf contest post-party is celebrated at this family-owned establishment, as the owner's son, Benji Weatherly, is a pro surfer himself. Surfing memorabilia fills the space. The restaurant/bar is open from 11 AM to 9:30 PM, with a late-night menu until midnight. But things start to happen around 9 PM on Thursday for the 18-and-over crowd, who cruise while the DJ spins, and there's live music on Saturday. The party goes until 2 AM. ⊠*Marketplace Shopping Center, 66-250 Kamehameha Hwy., Hale'iwa* ☎*808/637–9898.*

The Shack. This sports bar and restaurant is about the only late-night spot you can find in Southeast O'ahu. After a day of snorkling at Hanauma Bay, stop by to kick back, have a beer, eat a burger, watch some sports, or play a game of pool. It's open until 2 AM nightly. ⊠*Hawai'i Kai Shopping Center, 377 Keahole St., Hawai'i Kai* ☎*808/396–1919.*

WHERE TO EAT

O'ahu, where the majority of the Islands' 2,000-plus restaurants are located, offers the best of all worlds: it's got the foreignness and excitement of Asia and Polynesia, but when the kids need McDonald's, or when you just have to have a Starbucks latte, they're here, too.

Budget for a pricey dining experience at the very top of the restaurant food chain, where chefs Alan Wong, Roy Yamaguchi, George Mavrothalassitis, and others you've read about in *Gourmet* put a sophisticated and unforgettable spin on local foods and flavors. Savor seared 'ahi tuna in sea urchin beurre blanc or steak marinated in Korean kimchi sauce.

Spend the rest of your food dollars where budget-conscious locals do: in plate-lunch places and small ethnic eateries, at roadside stands and lunch wagons, or at window-in-the-wall delis. Munch a *musubi* rice cake (a rectangular form of rice wrapped with seaweed and often topped with Spam), slurp shave ice with red bean paste, order up Filipino pork adobo with two scoops of rice and macaroni salad.

In Waikīkī, where most visitors stay, you can find choices from gracious rooms with a view to surprisingly authentic Japanese noodle shops. But hop in the car, or on the trolley or bus, and travel just a few miles in any direction, and you can save your money and get in touch with the real food of Hawai'i.

Kaimukī's Wai'alae Avenue, for example, offers one of the city's best espresso bars, a hugely popular Chinese bakery, a highly recommended patisserie, an exceptional Italian bistro, a dim sum restaurant, Mexican food (rare here), and a Hawai'i regional cuisine standout, 3660 on the Rise—all in three blocks and 10 minutes from Waikīkī. Chinatown, 10 minutes in the other direction and easily reached by the Waikiki Trolley, is another dining (and shopping) treasure, not only for Chinese but also Vietnamese, Filipino, Malaysian, Indian, and Eurasian food, and even a chic little tea shop.

WHAT IT COSTS					
	¢	$	$$	$$$	$$$$
Restaurants	under $10	$10–$17	$18–$26	$27–$35	over $35

Restaurant prices are for one main course at dinner.

WAIKĪKĪ

$$$$
ITALIAN

✕**Caffelatte Italian Restaurant.** Every dish at this tiny trattoria run by a Milanese family is worth ordering, from the gnocchi in a thick, rich sauce of Gorgonzola to spinach ravioli served with butter and basil. The tiramisu is the best in town, and the sugared orange slices in Russian vodka are the perfect ending to a meal. Each person must order three courses (appetizer, main course, and dessert). ■TIP➔ **There's no parking, so walk here if you can.** There's no air-conditioning, so it can be warm and noisy due to open windows. ⊠*339 Saratoga Rd., 2nd level, Waikīkī* ☎*808/924–1414* ▭*AE, DC, MC, V* ☺*Closed Tues.*

$$$
STEAKHOUSE

✕**dk Steakhouse.** Around the country, the steak house has returned to prominence as chefs rediscover the art of dry-aging beef and of preparing the perfect béarnaise sauce. D.K. Kodama's chic second-floor restaurant characterizes this trend with such presentations as a 22-ounce "Paniolo" (cowboy) rib-eye steak, dry-aged 30 days on the bone with house-made rub, grilled local onions, and creamed corn. The restaurant shares space, but not a menu, with Kodama's Sansei Seafood Restaurant & Sushi Bar; sit at the bar perched between the two and you can order from either menu. ⊠*Waikīkī Beach Marriott Resort and Spa, 2552 Kalākaua Ave., Waikīkī* ☎*808/931–6280* ▭*AE, D, MC, V* ☺*No lunch.*

$$–$$$
AMERICAN

✕**Duke's Canoe Club.** Named for the father of modern surfing, and outfitted with much Duke Kahanamoku memorabilia, Duke's is both an open-air bar and a very popular steak-and-seafood grill. It's known for its Big Island pork ribs, *huli huli* (rotisserie) chicken, and grilled catch of the day, as well as for a simple and economical Sunday brunch. A drawback is that it's often loud and crowded, and the live contemporary Hawaiian music often stymies conversation. ⊠*Outrigger Waikīkī on the Beach, 2335 Kalākaua Ave., Waikīkī* ☎*808/922–2268* ⊕*www.dukeswaikiki.com* ♢*Reservations essential* ▭*AE, DC, MC, V.*

¢–$
AMERICAN

✕**Eggs 'n Things.** A favorite of Waikīkī hotel workers for its late hours (11 PM–2 PM daily), this restaurant on the first floor of an obscure budget hotel has a hearty, country-style menu with a few island touches (tropical pancake syrups, fresh grilled fish), and a permanent line out front. ⊠*Hawaiian Monarch Hotel, 1911–B Kalākaua Ave., Waikīkī* ☎*808/949–0820* ▭*No credit cards* ☺*No dinner.*

$$$
ECLECTIC

✕**Hau Tree Lānai.** The vinelike hau tree is ideal for sitting under, and it's said that the one that spreads itself over this beachside courtyard is the very one that shaded Robert Louis Stevenson as he mused and wrote about Hawai'i. In any case, diners are still enjoying the shade, though

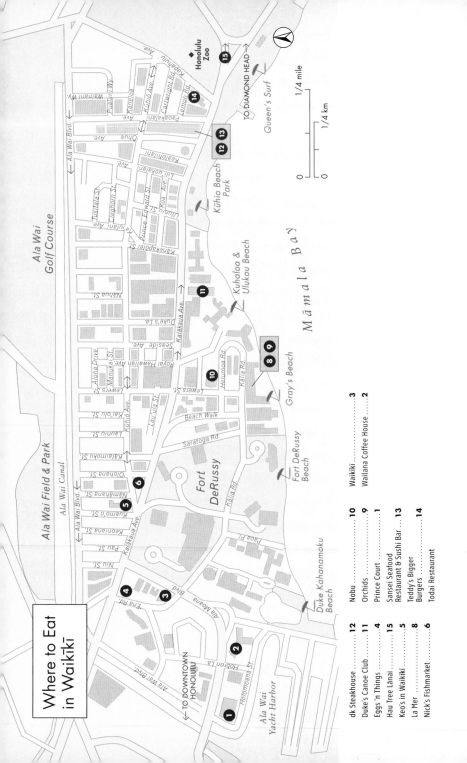

Where to Eat in Waikīkī

2

the view has changed—the gay-friendly beach over the low wall is paved with hunky sunbathers. The food is unremarkable island casual, but we like the place for late-afternoon or early-evening drinks, pūpū, and people-watching. ⊠ *New Otani Kaimana Beach Hotel, 2863 Kalākaua Ave., Waikīkī* ☎ *808/921–7066* ⊕ *www.kaimana.com* ⌕ *Reservations essential* ⊟ *AE, D, DC, MC, V.*

$$ ✗ **Keo's in Waikīkī.** Many Islanders—and many Hollywood stars—got
THAI their first taste of pad thai noodles, lemongrass, and coconut milk curry at one of Keo Sananikone's restaurants. This one, perched right at the entrance to Waikīkī, characterizes his formula: a bright, clean space awash in flowers with intriguing menu titles and reasonable prices. Evil Jungle Prince, a stir-fry redolent of Thai basil, flecked with chilies and rich with coconut milk, is a classic; also try the apple bananas (smaller, sweeter variety of banana) in coconut milk. The Eastern and Western breakfasts are popular. ⊠ *2028 Kūhiō Ave., Waikīkī* ☎ *808/951–9355* ⊟ *AE, D, DC, MC, V.*

$$$$ ✗ **La Mer.** Like the hotel in which it's housed (Halekūlani, "House Befit-
FRENCH ting Heaven"), La Mer is pretty much heavenly: a softly lighted, low-ceiling room has its windows open to the breeze, a perfectly framed vista of Diamond Head, and the faint sound of music from a courtyard below. The food captures the rich and yet sunny flavors of the south of France in one tiny, exquisite course after another. We recommend the degustation menu; place yourself in the sommelier's hands for wine choices from the hotel's exceptional cellar. ⊠ *Halekūlani, 2199 Kālia Rd., Waikīkī* ☎ *808/923–2311* ⌕ *Reservations essential; jacket required* ⊟ *AE, DC, MC, V* ☽ *No lunch.*

$$$–$$$$ ✗ **Nick's Fishmarket.** Nick's is like a favorite soap opera—go away for a
SEAFOOD while, come back and very little has changed. And that's why we like it: the dim lighting, the expansive banquettes, the retro-ish Continental menu, tableside service for Caesar salad or flambéed desserts; it's like a window back to just the good part of the good old days. After the lobster bisque or sautéed abalone, leave room for signature Vanbana Pie, a decadent combination of bananas, vanilla-Swiss-almond ice cream, and hot caramel sauce. ⊠ *Waikīkī Gateway Hotel, 2070 Kalākaua Ave., Waikīkī* ☎ *808/955–6333* ⊟ *AE, D, DC, MC, V.*

$$$ ✗ **Nobu.** Famed chef Nobu Matsushida's is the master of innovative Jap-
JAPANESE anese cuisine, and his Hawaiian outpost is definitely a Waikīkī hotspot. Fish is the obvious centerpiece, with entrees such as Tasmanian ocean trout with crispy spinach and yuzu soy, seafood harumaki with caviar and Maui onion salsa, and even Nobu's version of fish-and-chips. Cold dishes include tuna tataki with ponzu, yellowtail sashimi with jalapeño, and whitefish sashimi with dried miso. The warm decor and sexy lighting means there isn't a bad seat in the house. ⊠ *Hawaii Parc Hotel, 2233 Helumoa Rd., Waikīkī* ☎ *808/237–6999* ⊟ *AE, MC, V.*

$$$ ✗ **Orchids.** Perched along the seawall at historic Gray's Beach, Orchids
SEAFOOD is beloved by power-breakfasters, ladies who lunch, and family groups celebrating at the elaborate Sunday brunch. La Mer, upstairs, is better known for the evening, but we have found dinner at Orchids equally enjoyable. The louvered walls are open to the breezes, the orchids add splashes of color, the seafood is perfectly prepared, and the wine list is

intriguing. Plus, it is more casual and a bit less expensive than La Mer. Whatever meal you have here, finish with the hotel's signature coconut layer cake. ⊠ *Halekūlani, 2199 Kālia Rd., Waikīkī* ☎ *808/923–2311* ⌂ *Reservations essential* ⊟ *AE, D, DC, MC, V.*

$$$
ECLECTIC
✕ **Prince Court.** This restaurant overlooking Ala Wai Yacht Harbor is a multifaceted success, with exceptional high-end lunches and dinners, daily breakfast buffets, weekly dinner seafood buffets, and sold-out weekend brunches. With a truly global mix of offerings, the overall style is Eurasian. Their ever-changing prix-fixe menu includes offerings such as Australian rack of lamb, Kahuku prawns, and medallions of New York Angus. ⊠ *Hawai'i Prince Hotel, 100 Holomoana St., Waikīkī* ☎ *808/944–4494* ⌂ *Reservations essential* ⊟ *AE, D, DC, MC, V.*

$$$
JAPANESE
✕ **Sansei Seafood Restaurant & Sushi Bar.** D. K. Kodama's Japanese-based Pacific Rim cuisine is an experience not to be missed, from early-bird dinners (from 5:30 PM) to late-night appetizers and sushi (until 1 AM Fri. and Sat., with karaoke). The specialty sushi here—mango-crab roll, foie gras nigiri with eel sauce, and more—leaves California rolls far behind. We fantasize about the signature calamari salad with spicy Korean sauce and crisp-tender squid. Cleverly named and beautifully prepared dishes come in big and small plates or in a multicourse tasting menu. Finish with tempura-fried ice cream or Mama Kodama's brownies. ⊠ *Waikīkī Beach Marriott Resort and Spa, 2552 Kalākaua Ave., Waikīkī* ☎ *808/931–6286* ⊟ *AE, D, MC, V.*

¢
AMERICAN
✕ **Teddy's Bigger Burgers.** Though the focus at Teddy's is on the burgers, fries, and shakes, their success has inspired them to add a chicken, veggie, and fish sandwich to their menu. But, for those who like a classic, the burgers are beefy, the fries crisply perfect, the shakes rich and sweet. The original location in Waikīkī combines burger shack simplicity with surf-boy cool—there's even a place to store your surfboard while you have your burger. This popular location has given birth to two others in Kailua and Hawai'i Kai. ⊠ *134 Kapahulu Ave., Waikīkī* ☎ *808/926–3444* ⊟ *No credit cards.*

$$–$$$
SEAFOOD
✕ **Todai Restaurant Waikīkī.** Bountiful buffets and menus that feature seafood are popular with Islanders, so this Japan-based restaurant is a local favorite. It's popular with budget-conscious travelers as well, for the wide range of hot dishes, sushi, and the 160-foot seafood spread. The emphasis here is more on quantity than quality. ⊠ *1910 Ala Moana Blvd., Waikīkī* ☎ *808/947–1000* ⌂ *Reservations essential* ⊟ *AE, D, DC, MC, V.*

¢–$
AMERICAN
✕ **Wailana Coffee House.** Despite the notoriously inattentive waitstaff, budget-conscious snowbirds, night owls with a yen for karaoke, all-day drinkers of both coffee and the stronger stuff, hearty eaters, and lovers of local-style plate lunches contentedly rub shoulders at this venerable diner and cocktail lounge at the edge of Waikīkī. Most checks are under $9; there's a $1.95 children's menu. It's open 24 hours a day, seven days a week, 365 days a year but the place fills up and a line forms around the corner at breakfast time, so arrive early or late. ⊠ *Wailana Condominium, ground floor, 1860 Ala Moana Blvd., corner of 'Ena Rd. and Ala Moana, Waikīkī* ☎ *808/955–1674* ⌂ *Reservations not accepted* ⊟ *AE, D, DC, MC, V.*

HONOLULU: ALA MOANA, DOWNTOWN AND CHINATOWN

$–$$
JAPANESE

✕**Akasaka.** Step inside this tiny sushi bar tucked behind the Ala Moana Hotel, and you'll swear you're in an out-of-the-way Edo neighborhood in some indeterminate time. Greeted with a cheerful "Iraishaimasu!" (Welcome!), sink down at a diminutive table or perch at the handful of seats at the sushi bar. It's safe to let the sushi chefs here decide (*omakase*-style) or you can go for the delicious grilled specialties, such as scallop *battayaki* (grilled in butter). Reservations accepted for groups only. ✉*1646 B Kona St., Ala Moana* ☎*808/942–4466* ▭*AE, D, DC, MC, V* ☾*No lunch Sun.*

$$$
ASIAN

✕**Alan Wong's Pineapple Room.** This is not your grandmother's department store restaurant. It's über-chef Alan Wong's more casual second spot, where the chef de cuisine plays intriguing riffs on local food themes. Warning: the spicy chili-fried soybeans are addicted. Their house burger, made with locally raised grass-fed beef, bacon, cheddar cheese, hoisin-mayonnaise spread, and avocado, won a local tasting hands-down. Pleasant surroundings and service is very professional. Reservations recommended. ✉*Macy's, Ala Moana Center, 1450 Ala Moana Blvd., Ala Moana* ☎*808/945–6573* ▭*AE, D, DC, MC, V.*

¢–$
VIETNAMESE

✕**Bac Nam.** Tam and Kimmy Huynh's menu is much more extensive than most, ranging far beyond the usual *pho* (beef noodle soup) and *bun* (cold noodle dishes). Coconut milk curries, an extraordinary crab noodle soup, and other dishes hail from both from North and South Vietnam. The atmosphere is welcoming and relaxed, and they'll work with you to make choices. Reservations are not accepted for groups fewer than six. ✉*1117 S. King St., Downtown* ☎*808/597–8201* ▭*MC, V.*

$
AMERICAN

✕ **Big City Diner.** Part of a chain of unfussy retro diners, Big City offers a short course in local-style breakfasts—rice instead of potatoes, fish or Portuguese sausage instead of bacon, steaming bowls of noodles—with generous portions, low prices, and pronounced flavors. Lunch and dinner focus on local-style comfort food—baby back ribs, kimchi fried rice—and burgers. ✉ *Ward Entertainment Center, 1060 'Auahi St., Ala Moana* ☎*808/591–8891* ▭*AE, D, MC, V.*

$$$
FRENCH

✕**Cassis.** When Chef Mavro decided to develop a new restaurant for Honolulu, he went back to memories of his boyhood home in Cassis for inspiration and brought French comfort food to Hawaii. Though the atmosphere is contemporary and chic, Mavro's French Bistro offers old-world favorites such as cassoulet and *steak frites* (steak and fries). His exceptionally tender *huli huli* chicken with fresh Kahuku creamed corn and Hamakua mushroom risotto demonstrate Mavro's commitment to fresh local products. Lunches are a real treat, with views of the harbor, and a *pau hana* (after-work) drink at the wine bar is a memorable experience. ✉ *66 Queen St., Downtown Honolulu* ☎*808/545–8100* ▭*AE, MC, V* ☾*Closed Sun.*

$$$
ECLECTIC

✕**Chai's Island Bistro.** Chai Chaowasaree's stylish, light-bathed, and orchid-draped lunch and dinner restaurant expresses the sophisticated side of this Thai-born immigrant. He plays East against West on the plate in signature dishes such as *kataifi* (baked and shredded phyllo), macadamia-crusted prawns, 'ahi *katsu* (tuna steaks dredged with crisp

Japanese breadcrumbs and quickly deep-fried), crispy duck confetti spring rolls, and seafood risotto. Some of Hawai'i's best-known contemporary Hawaiian musicians play brief dinner shows here Wednesday through Sunday. ✉ *Aloha Tower Marketplace, 1 Aloha Tower Dr., Downtown Honolulu* ☎ *808/585–0012* ☰ *AE, D, DC, MC, V* ⊗ *No lunch Sat.–Mon.*

$–$$
MEXICAN

✕ **Compadres Mexican Bar and Grill.** The after-work crowd gathers here for potent margaritas and yummy pūpū. The outdoor terrace is best for cocktails only. Inside, the wooden floors, colorful photographs, and lively paintings create a festive setting. Compadres defines itself as "Western cooking with a Mexican accent": fajitas, baby back ribs, pork *carnitas* (slow-roasted shredded pork), and fish tacos are specialties. At the bar, choose from over 80 brands of tequila. A late-night appetizer menu is available until midnight. ✉ *Ward Centre, 1200 Ala Moana Blvd., Ala Moana* ☎ *808/591–8307* ☰ *AE, D, DC, MC, V.*

¢–$
AMERICAN

✕ **Contemporary Cafe.** This tasteful lunch spot in the Contemporary Museum offers light and healthful food from a short but well-selected menu of housemade soups, crostini of the day, innovative sandwiches garnished with fruit, and a hummus plate with fresh pita. In the exclusive Makīkī Heights neighborhood above the city, the restaurant spills out of the ground floor of the museum onto the lawn. ✉ *The Contemporary Museum, 2411 Makīkī Heights Dr., Makīkī* ☎ *808/523–3362* ⌃ *Reservations not accepted* ☰ *AE, D, DC, MC, V* ⊗ *No dinner.*

$$
AMERICAN

✕ **E & O Trading Co.** Named for the colonial-era Eastern & Orient Trading Co., this restaurant's decor recalls a bustling mercantile district in some Asian port. Like a merchant ship, the Southeast Asian grill menu hops from Singapore to Korea, Japan to India. The Indonesian corn fritters are a must, as are the Burmese ginger salad and the silky-textured, smoky-flavored marinated portobello satay. To match the unusual menu, the bar creates some unusual mixtures with infusions and fresh juices. For a unique experience, ask the bartender to make a citrus or other fruit-flavored Elixir (a type of martini) for you. ✉ *Ward Centre, 1200 Ala Moana Blvd., Kaka'ko* ☎ *808/591–9555* ☰ *AE, D, DC, MC, V.*

$
ECLECTIC

✕ **Grand Café & Bakery.** This well-scrubbed, pleasantly furnished breakfast, brunch, and lunch spot is ideal for taking a break before or after a trek around Chinatown. Its period feel comes from the fact that chef Anthony Vierra's great-grandfather had a restaurant of this name in Chinatown nearly 100 years ago. The delicious and well-presented food ranges from retro diner dishes (chicken potpie) to contemporary creations such as beet-and-goat-cheese-salad. ✉ *31 N. Pauahi, Chinatown* ☎ *808/531–0001* ☰ *MC, V.*

¢–$
ASIAN

✕ **Green Door.** Closet-size and fronted by a green door and a row of welcoming Chinese lanterns, this Chinatown café has introduced Honolulu to budget- and taste bud–friendly Malaysian and Singaporean foods, redolent of spices and crunchy with fresh vegetables. ✉ *4614 Kilauea Ave., Kahala* ☎ *808/533–0606* ☰ *No credit cards* ⌃ *Reservations not accepted* ⊗ *Closed Mon.*

$$–$$$
ASIAN

✕ **Hiroshi Eurasion Tapas.** Built around chef Hiroshi Fukui's signature style of "West & Japan" cuisine, this sleek dinner house focuses on

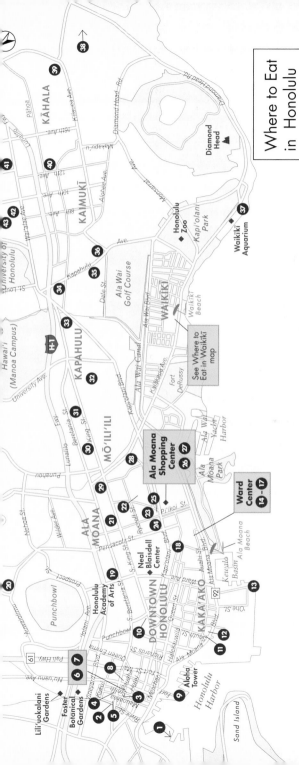

Where to Eat in Honolulu

small plates to share (enough for two servings each), with an exceptional choice of hard-to-find wines by the glass and in flights. Do not miss Hiroshi's braised veal cheeks (he was doing them before everyone else), the locally raised *kampachi* fish carpaccio, or the best *misoyaki* (marinated in a rich miso-soy blend, then grilled) butterfish ever. ⊠*1341 Kapi'olani Blvd., Ala Moana* ☎*808/955–0552* ▭*AE, D, MC, V* ◷*No lunch*.

$$$ ✕**Indigo Eurasian Cuisine.** Indigo sets the right mood for an evening out
ECLECTIC   on the town: the walls are red brick, the ceilings are high, and from the restaurant's lounge next door comes the sultry sound of late-night jazz. Take a bite of goat cheese wontons with four-fruit sauce followed by rich Mongolian lamb chops. After dinner, duck into the hip Green Room lounge or Opium Den & Champagne Bar for a nightcap. If you're touring downtown at lunchtime, the Eurasian buffet with trio of dim sum is an especially good deal at around $16 per person. ⊠*1121 Nu'uanu Ave., Downtown Honolulu* ☎*808/521–2900* ▭*AE, D, DC, MC, V.*

$$$–$$$$ ✕**John Dominis.** "Legendary" is the word for the Sunday brunch buffet at
SEAFOOD   this long-established restaurant, named for a Hawaiian kingdom chamberlain who became the consort of the last queen, Lili'uokalani. With a network of koi ponds running through the multilevel restaurant, a view of Diamond Head and a favorite surfing area, and over-the-top seafood specials, it's the choice of Oahuans with something to celebrate. An appetizer-and-small-plates menu is available in the bar. ⊠*580 Nimitz Hwy., Iwilei* ☎*808/523–0955* ▭*AE, D, DC, MC, V.*

$ ✕**Kai.** This chic little spot introduced Honolulu to *okonomiyaki*, the
JAPANESE   famous savory pancakes that are a specialty of Osaka, with mix-and-match ingredients scrambled together on a griddle then drizzled with various piquant sauces. The combinations may at times strike you as bizarre, but you can always order simpler grilled dishes. ⊠*1427 Makaloa St., Ala Moana* ☎*808/944–1555* ▭*AE, D, DC, MC, V* ◷*Closed Mon. No lunch*.

¢–$ ✕**Kaka'ako Kitchen.** Russell Siu was the first of the local-boy fine dining
MODERN   chefs to open a place of the sort he enjoys when he's off-duty, serving
HAWAIIAN   high-quality plate lunches (house-made sauce instead of from-a-mix brown gravy, for example). Here you can get your two scoops of either brown or white rice, green salad instead of the usual macaroni salad, grilled fresh fish specials, and vegetarian fare. Breakfast is especially good, with combos like corned-beef hash and eggs, and exceptional baked goods. ⊠*Ward Centre, 1200 Ala Moana Blvd., Kaka'ako* ☎*808/596–7488* ✍*Reservations not accepted* ▭*No credit cards.*

$–$$ ✕**La Mariana Restaurant & Sailing Club.** Just past downtown Honolulu,
AMERICAN   tucked away in the industrial area of Sand Island, is this friendly South Seas–style restaurant. Over the past 50 years, nonagenarian owner Annette Nahinu has bought up kitsch from other restaurants, so it's tikis to the max here. The food—grilled seafood, steaks—is just okay; but go

for the sing-along fun and the feeling that Don the Beachcomber might walk in any minute. ⊠ *50 Sand Island Rd., Iwilei* ☎ *808/848–2800* ⊟ *AE, D, DC, MC, V.*

¢–$ ╳**Legend Seafood Restaurant.** Do as the locals do: start your visit to
CHINESE Chinatown with breakfast dim sum at Legend. If you want to be able to hear yourself think, get there before 9 AM, especially on weekends. And don't be shy: use your best cab-hailing technique and sign language to make the cart ladies stop at your table and show you their wares. The pork-filled steamed buns, hearty spare ribs, prawn dumplings, and still-warm custard tarts are excellent preshopping fortification. ⊠ *Chinese Cultural Plaza, 100 N. Beretania St., Chinatown* ☎ *808/532–1868* ⊟ *AE, D, DC, MC, V.*

$ ╳**Little Village Noodle House.** Unassuming and budget-friendly, Little Vil-
CHINESE lage sets a standard of friendly and attentive service to which every
Fodor'sChoice Chinese restaurant should aspire. We have roamed the large, pan-China
★ menu and found a new favorite in everything we've tried: shredded beef, spinach with garlic, Shanghai noodles, honey-walnut shrimp, orange chicken, dried green beans. Two words: go there. ■**TIP→Two hours of free parking is available next door.** ⊠ *1113 Smith St., Chinatown* ☎ *808/545–3008* ⊟ *AE, D, MC, V.*

$–$$ ╳**Mariposa.** Yes, the popovers and the wee little cups of bouillon are
ASIAN there at lunch, but in every other regard, this Neiman Marcus restaurant menu departs from the classic model, incorporating a clear sense of Pacific place. The veranda, open to the breezes and view of Ala Moana Park, twirling ceiling fans, and life-size hula-girl murals say Hawai'i. The popovers at lunch come with a butter-pineapple-papaya spread; the oxtail osso buco is inspired, and local fish are featured nightly in luxuriant specials. ⊠ *Nieman Marcus, Ala Moana Center, 1450 Ala Moana, Ala Moana* ☎ *808/951–3420* ⌳ *Reservations essential* ⊟ *AE, D, DC, MC, V.*

¢ ╳**Mei Sum Chinese Dim Sum Restaurant.** In contrast to the sprawling and
CHINESE noisy halls in which dim sum is generally served, Mei Sum is compact and shiny bright. It's open daily, serving nothing but small plates from 7:45 AM to 8:45 PM. Be ready to guess and point at the color photos of dim sum favorites as not much English is spoken, but the delicate buns and tasty bits are exceptionally well-prepared and worth the charades. ⊠ *65 N. Pauahi St., Chinatown* ☎ *808/531–3268* ⊟ *No credit cards.*

$–$$ ╳**Neo-Nabe.** Pronounced "nee-oh nah-bay," this hip restaurant and
JAPANESE bar minutes from Waikīkī specializes in a contemporary version of the cook-at-the-table Japanese hot pot called *nabe*. You choose the broth and ingredients; they light up the tabletop brazier and bring you hot rice and a range of dipping sauces to go with the meal you cook. Geared to clubbers and night workers, Neo-Nabe is open 5 PM to 2 AM Sunday through Thursday and 5 PM to 5 AM Friday and Saturday. Don't miss the *ojia*, a folksy Asian risotto made with your leftovers and some secret ingredients. It's filling, fun food. ⊠ *2065 S. King St., Suite 110, Ala Moana* ☎ *808/944–6622* ⊟ *MC, V* ⊗ *Closed Mon. No lunch.*

$ ╳**Pavilion Cafe.** The cool courtyards and varied galleries of the Hono-
AMERICAN lulu Academy of Arts are well worth a visit and, afterward, so is Mike Nevin's popular lunch restaurant. The café overflows onto a lānai from

CLOSE UP

Izakaya

Japanese pub-restaurants, called *izakaya* (ee-ZAH-ka-ya), are sprouting in the Islands like *matsutake* mushrooms in a pine forest. They began as oases for homesick Japanese nationals but were soon discovered by adventurous locals, who appreciated the welcoming atmosphere, sprawling menus, and later dining hours.

Expect to be greeted by a merry, full-staff cry of "Irrashaimase!", offered an *oshibori* (hot towel) and a drink, and handed a menu of dozens (sometimes many dozens) of small-plate, made-to-order dishes.

You can find *yakitori* (grilled dishes), tempura (deep-fried dishes), *donburi* (rice bowls), sushi and sashimi, *nabemono* and *shabu-shabu* (hot pots), noodles (both soup and fried), *okonomiyaki* (chop suey–type omelets), and a bizarre assortment of *yoshoku* dishes (Western foods prepared in Japanese style, such as hamburgers in soy-accented gravy, fried chicken with a mirin glaze, odd gratins, and even pizza).

Full bars are usual; a wide choice of lager-type beers and good-to-great sakes are universal. Many specialize in single-malt scotch, but wine lists are generally short.

Izakaya menus are often confusing, many staff speak marginal English, and outings can get expensive fast (liquor plus small-plate prices equals eyes bigger than stomach). Prices range from $5 for a basket of edamame (steamed, salted soybeans) to $20 or more for *wafu* (seasoned, grilled steak, sliced for sharing). Start by ordering drinks and edamame or silky-textured braised *kabocha* pumpkin. This will keep the waiter happy. Then give yourself a quarter of an hour to examine the menu, ogle other people's plates, and seek recommendations. Start with one dish per person and one for the table; you can always call for more. Here are a few spots to try:

Imanas Tei. Go early to this cozy, out-of-the-way restaurant for its tasteful, simple decor and equally tasteful and simply perfect sushi, sashimi, *nabe* (hot pots prepared at the table), and grilled dishes; reservations taken from 5 to 7 PM; after that, there's always a line. ⊠ *2626 S. King, Mō'ili'ili* ☎ *808/941–2626 or 808/934–2727* ⊟ *AE, DC, MC, V.*

Izakaya Nonbei. Teruaki Mori designed this pub to put you in mind of a northern inn in winter in his native Japan; dishes not to miss—*karei kara-age* (delicate deep-fried flounder) and *dobinmushi* (mushroom consomme presented in a teapot). ⊠ *3108 Olu St., Kapahulu* ☎ *808/734–5573* ⊟ *AE, D, DC, MC, V.*

Tokkuri-Tei. This is a favorite of locals for the playful atmosphere that belies the excellence of the food created by chef Hideaki "Santa" Miyoshi, famous for his quirky menu names (Nick Jagger, Spider Poke); just say "Moriwase, kudasai" ("chef's choice, please"), and he'll order for you. ⊠ *611 Kapahulu Ave., Kapahulu* ☎ *808/739–2800* ⊟ *AE, D, DC, MC, V.*

Also worth a visit: **Mr. Oji-san** (⊠ *1018 Kapahulu Ave., Kapahulu* ☎ *808/735–4455*) for family-style izakaya specialties; and **Kai** (⊠ *1427 Makaloa, Ala Moana* ☎ *808/944–1555*) for Osaka-style omelets.

which you can ponder Asian statuary and a burbling water feature while you wait for your salade niçoise or signature Piadina Sandwich (fresh-baked flatbread rounds stuffed with arugula, tomatoes, basil, and cheese). ⊠ *Honolulu Academy of Arts, 900 S. Beretania St., Downtown Honolulu* ☎ *808/532–8734* ▭ *AE, D, DC, MC, V* ⊙ *Closed Sun. and Mon. No dinner.*

$–$$
AMERICAN

✕ **Ryan's Grill.** An all-purpose food and drink emporium, lively and popular Ryan's has an exceptionally well-stocked bar, with 20 beers on tap, an outdoor deck, and TVs broadcasting sports. Lunch, dinner, and small plates are served from 11 AM to 2 AM. The eclectic menu ranges from an addictive hot crab-and-artichoke dip with focaccia bread to grilled fresh fish, pasta, salads, and sophisticated versions of local favorites, such as the Kobe beef hamburger steak. ⊠ *Ward Centre, 1200 Ala Moana Blvd., Kaka'ako* ☎ *808/591–9132* ▭ *AE, D, DC, MC, V.*

$$–$$$
SEAFOOD

✕ **Sam Choy's Breakfast, Lunch & Crab and Big Aloha Brewery.** In this casual, family-friendly setting, diners can down crab and lobster—but since these come from elsewhere, we recommend the catch of the day, the *char siu* (Chinese barbecue), baby back ribs, or Sam's special fried *poke* (flash-fried tuna). This eatery's warehouse size sets the tone for its *bambucha* (huge) portions. An on-site microbrewery brews five varieties of Big Aloha beer. Sam Choy's is in Iwilei past Downtown Honolulu on the highway heading to Honolulu International Airport. ⊠ *580 Nimitz Hwy., Iwilei* ☎ *808/545–7979* ▭ *AE, D, DC, MC, V.*

¢–$
AMERICAN

✕ **Side Street Inn.** Famous as the place where celebrity chefs gather after hours, local boy Colin Nishida's pub is on an obscure side street near Ala Moana Shopping Center. It is worth searching for, despite the sometimes surly staff, because Nishida makes the best darned pork chops and fried rice in the world. Local-style bar food comes in huge, shareplate portions. This is a place to dress any way you like, nosh all night, watch sports on TV, and sing karaoke until they boot you out. Pūpū (in portions so large as to be dinner) are served from 4 PM to 12:30 AM daily. ⊠ *1225 Hopaka St., Ala Moana* ☎ *808/591–0253* ▭ *AE, D, DC, MC, V* ⊙ *No lunch weekends.*

$$
KOREAN

✕ **Sorabol.** The largest Korean restaurant in the city, this 24-hour eatery, with its impossibly tiny parking lot and maze of booths and private rooms, offers a vast menu encompassing the entirety of day-to-day Korean cuisine, plus sushi. English menu translations are cryptic at best. Still, it's great for wee hour "grinds" (local slang for food): *bi bim bap* (veggies, meats, and eggs on steamed rice), *kal bi* and *bulgogi* (barbecued meats), and meat or fish *jun* (thin fillets fried in batter). ⊠ *805 Ke'eaumoku St., Ala Moana* ☎ *808/947–3113* ▭ *AE, DC, MC, V.*

¢
VIETNAMESE

✕ **To Chau.** If you need proof that To Chau is highly regarded for its authentic *pho* (Vietnamese beef noodle soup), just check the lines that form in front every morning of the week. It's said that the broth is the key, and it won't break the bank for you to find out, as the average check is less than $10. Open only until 12:30 PM. ⊠ *1007 River St., Chinatown* ☎ *808/533–4549* ▭ *No credit cards* ⊙ *No dinner.*

$$–$$$
ITALIAN

✕ **Vino.** Small plates of Italian-inspired appetizers, a wine list selected by the state's first Master Sommelier, a relaxed atmosphere, and periodic special tastings are the formula for success at this wine bar. ∎ TIP➔ Vino is well situated for stopping off between downtown sightseeing and a return to your Waikīkī hotel. ⊠*Restaurant Row, 500 Ala Moana Blvd., Downtown Honolulu* ☎*808/524–8466* ▭*AE, D, DC, MC, V* ⊘*Closed Sun.–Tues.*

$$
JAPANESE
✕**Yanagi Sushi.** One of relatively few restaurants to serve the complete menu until 2 AM (Sunday only until 10 PM), Yanagi is a full-service Japanese restaurant offering not only sushi and sashimi around a small bar, but also *taishoku* (combination menus), tempura, stews, and grill-it-yourself shabu-shabu. The fish here can be depended on for freshness and variety. ⊠*762 Kapi'olani Blvd., Downtown Honolulu* ☎*808/597–1525* ▭*AE, D, DC, MC, V.*

HONOLULU: EAST AND DIAMOND HEAD

$$
MODERN
HAWAIIAN
✕**12th Avenue Grill.** At this clean, well-lighted place on a back street, chef Kevin Hanney dishes up diner chic, including macaroni-and-cheese glazed with house-smoked Parmesan and topped with savory bread-crumbs. The kimchi steak, a sort of teriyaki with kick, is a winner. Go early (5 PM) or late (8:30 PM). Enjoy wonderful, homey desserts. There's a small, reasonably priced wine list. ⊠*1145C 12th Ave., Kaimukī* ☎*808/732–9469* ⍾*BYOB* ▭*MC, V* ⊘*Closed Sun. No lunch.*

$$$
MODERN
HAWAIIAN
✕**3660 on the Rise.** This casually stylish eatery is a 10-minute drive from Waikīkī in the up-and-coming culinary mecca of Kaimukī. Sample Chef Russell Siu's New York Steak Ala'e (steak grilled with Hawaiian clay salt), the crab cakes, or the signature 'ahi katsu wrapped in nori and deep-fried with a wasabi-ginger butter sauce. Siu combines a deep understanding of local flavors with a sophisticated palate, making this place especially popular with homegrown gourmands. The dining room can feel a bit snug when it's full (as it usually is); go early or later. ⊠*3660 Wai'alae Ave., Kaimukī* ☎*808/737–1177* ▭*AE, DC, MC, V.*

$$$$
MODERN
HAWAIIAN
Fodor's Choice
★
✕**Alan Wong's.** This not-to-be-missed restaurant is like that very rare shell you stumble upon on a perfect day at the beach—well polished and without a flaw. We've never had a bad experience here, and we've never heard of anyone else having one either. The "Wong Way," as it's not-so-jokingly called by his staff, includes an ingrained understanding of the aloha spirit, evident in the skilled but unstarched service, and creative and playful interpretations of Island cuisine. Try Da Bag (seafood steamed in an aluminum pouch), Chinatown Roast Duck Nachos, and Poki Pines (rice-studded seafood wonton appetizers). With a view of the Ko'olau Mountains, warm tones of koa wood, and *lauhala* grass weaving, you forget you're on the third floor of an office building. ⊠*McCully Court, 1857 S. King St., 3rd fl., Mō'ili'ili* ☎*808/949–2526* ▭*AE, MC, V* ⊘*No lunch.*

¢
MEXICAN
✕**Baja Tacos.** One of the first California-style taquerias in the Islands, Baja Tacos offers authentic flavors, house-made salsas, Mexican-style small plates, enchiladas, pork carnitas (slow-roasted and shredded), and *adobada* (marinated pork) and, of course, tacos—to take out or eat in. It's a perfect post-beach stop. ⊠*3040 Wai'alae Ave., Kaimukī* ☎*808/737–5893* ⍪*Reservations not accepted* ▭*No credit cards.*

$$$$
MODERN
HAWAIIAN
Fodor'sChoice
★

✕**Chef Mavro.** George Mavrothalassitis, who took two hotel restaurants to the top of the ranks before founding this James Beard Award–winning restaurant, admits he's crazy. Crazy because of the care he takes to draw out the truest and most concentrated flavors, to track down the freshest fish, to create one-of-a-kind wine pairings that might strike others as mad. But for this passionate Provençal transplant, there's no other way. The menu changes quarterly, every dish (including dessert) matched with a select wine. We recommend the multicourse tasting menus (beginning at $65 for four courses without wine, up to $225 for 11 courses with wine). Etched-glass windows screen the busy street-corner scene and all within is mellow and serene with starched white tablecloths, fresh flowers, wood floors, and contemporary Island art. ⊠ *1969 S. King St., Mōʻiliʻili* ☎*808/944–4714* △*Reservations essential* ═*AE, DC, MC, V* ☉*No lunch.*

> ## PŪPŪ
>
> Entertaining Hawaiian style means having a lot of pūpū—the local term for appetizers or hors d'oeuvres. Locals eat these small portions of food mostly as they wind down from their workday, relax, and enjoy a couple of beers. Popular pūpū include sushi, tempura, teriyaki chicken skewers, barbecue meat, and our favorite: poke (pronounced "po-keh"), or raw fish, seasoned with seaweed, shoyu, and other flavorings. We call them "local kine grinds."

¢–$
AMERICAN

✕**Diamond Head Market & Grill.** Kelvin Ro's one-stop spot is a plate-lunch place, a gourmet market, a deli and bakery and espresso bar, too—and it's a five-minute hop from Waikīkī hotels. A take-out window offers grilled sandwiches or plates ranging from teriyaki beef to portobello mushrooms. The market's deli case is stocked with a range of heat-and-eat entrées from risotto cakes to lamb stew; specials change daily. There are packaged Japanese bento lunchboxes, giant scones, enticing desserts, and even a small wine selection. ⊠ *3158 Monsarrat Ave., Diamond Head* ☎*808/732–0077* △*Reservations not accepted* ═*AE, D, MC, V.*

¢–$
ITALIAN

✕**Formaggio.** All but invisible on the backside of a strip mall, this wine bar seeks to communicate the feel of a catacomb in Italy and largely succeeds, with dim lighting and soft, warm tones. Choose a small sip or an entire bottle from the many wines they offer, enjoy the music, then ponder the small-dish menu of pizzas, panini, and hot and cold specialties such as eggplant Napoleon and melting short ribs in red wine. ⊠ *Market City Shopping Center, rear, lower level, 2919 Kapiʻolani Blvd., Kaimukī* ☎*808/739–7719* △*Reservations not accepted* ═*AE, MC, V* ☉*Closed Sun. No lunch* .

$$$$
MODERN
HAWAIIAN

✕**Hoku's at the Kāhala.** Everything about this room speaks of quality and sophistication: the wall of windows with their beach views, the avant-garde cutlery and dinnerware, the solicitous staff, and border-busting Pacific Rim cuisine. Though the prices are eye-popping, you get good value in such dishes as the melting salt-crusted rack of lamb for two ($94) and the warm Tristan de Cunha Salad ($27). An excellent choice for special occasions. The dress code is collared shirts, no beachwear. ⊠ *The Kāhala, 5000 Kāhala Ave., Kāhala* ☎*808/739–8780* ═*AE, D, MC, V* ☉*No lunch Sat.*

$$$$ ✕ **Michel's at the Colony Surf.** With its wide-open windows so close to
FRENCH the water that you literally feel the soft mist at high tide, this is arguably the most romantic spot in Waikīkī for a sunset dinner for two.
Venerable Michel's is synonymous with fine dining in the minds of
Oahuans who have been coming here for more than 40 years. The
menu is très, très French with both classic choices (escargot, foie gras)
and contemporary items (Hardy's Hawaiian Bouillabaisse—named after
the chef who created a Hawaiian twist on a French classic). There's
dinner nightly and Sunday brunch. ⊠ *Colony Surf, 2895 Kalākaua
Ave., Waikīkī* ☎ *808/923–6552* ⚷ *Reservations essential* ⊟ *AE, D,
DC, MC, V* ⊗ *No lunch.*

$$$ ✕ **Ninnikuya, the Garlic Restaurant.** Chef-owner Endo Eiyuki picked a
JAPANESE powerful focus for his charming restaurant in a converted Kaimukī
bungalow: garlic. He calls the menu Euro-Asian but the spicing and
approach—except for the prevalence of garlic—are distinctly Japanese.
Don't miss the Black Angus steak served on a sizzling stone. ⊠ *3196
Waīalae Ave., Kaimukī* ☎ *808/735–0784* ⚷ *Reservations essential*
⊟ *AE, D, DC, MC, V* ⊗ *Closed Sun. No lunch.*

¢–$ ✕ **Olive Tree.** Mediterranean food is scarce in the Islands, so Olive Tree
MEDITERRANEAN keeps insanely busy; expect a wait for your hummus, fish souvlaki,
Greek egg-and-lemon soup, and other specialties at this small spot
behind Kāhala Mall. ⊠ *4614 Kīlauea Ave., Kāhala* ☎ *808/737–0303*
⚷ *Reservations not accepted* ⊟ *No credit cards* ⊗ *No lunch.*

¢–$ ✕ **'Ono Hawaiian Foods.** The adventurous in search of a real local food
HAWAIIAN experience should head to this no-frills hangout. You know it has to be
good if residents are waiting in line to get in. Here you can sample *poi*
(a paste made from pounded taro root), *lomi lomi* salmon (salmon mas-
saged until tender and served with minced onions and tomatoes), laulau,
kālua pork (roasted in an underground oven), and *haupia* (a light,
gelatinlike dessert made from coconut milk). Appropriately enough,
the Hawaiian word *'ono* means "delicious." ⊠ *726 Kapahulu Ave.,
Kapahulu* ☎ *808/737–2275* ⚷ *Reservations not accepted* ⊟ *No credit
cards* ⊗ *Closed Sun.*

$$$ ✕ **Sam Choy's Diamond Head.** Sam Choy has been called the Paul Prud-
ASIAN homme of Hawai'i and aptly so: both are big, welcoming men with
magic in their hands and a folksy background in small, rural towns.
Choy grew up cooking for his parents' lū'au business and now has an
empire—restaurants, TV show, cookbooks, commercial products—and
his two best chef-friends are Prudhomme and Emeril Lagasse. Here,
Choy and executive chef Aaron Fukuda interpret local favorites in
sophisticated ways, and the fresh fish is the best. The portions, like Sam's
smile, are huge. ⊠ *449 Kapahulu Ave., Kapahulu* ☎ *808/732–8645*
⊟ *AE, D, DC, MC, V.*

$ ✕ **Spices.** Created by a trio of well-traveled friends who enjoy the foods
THAI of Southeast Asia, Spices is alluringly decorated in spicelike oranges
and reds and offers a lunch and dinner menu far from the beaten
path, even in a city rich in the cuisine of this region. They claim inspiration but not authenticity and use Island ingredients to everyone's

advantage. The menu is vegetarian friendly. ⊠*2671 S. King St., Mōʻiliʻili* ☎*808/949–2679* ⌕*Reservations essential* ▤*MC, V* ⊘*Closed Mon.*

$$ ╳**Sushi Sasabune.** Meals here are

JAPANESE unforgettable, though you may find the restaurant's approach exasperating and a little condescending. It's possible to order from the menu, but you're strongly encouraged to order *omakase*-style (oh-*mah*-ka-*say*, roughly, "trust me"), letting the chef send out his choices for the night. The waiters keep up a steady mantra to instruct patrons in the proper way to eat their delicacies: "Please, no shoyu on this one." "One piece, one bite." But any trace of annoyance vanishes with the first bite of California baby squid stuffed with Louisiana crab, or unctuous *toro* (ʻahi belly) smeared with a light soy reduction, washed down with a glass of the smoothest sake you've ever tasted. A caution: the courses come very rapidly—ask the server to slow down the pace a bit. An even bigger caution: the courses, generally two pieces of sushi or six to eight slices of sashimi, add up fast. ⊠*1419 S. King St., Mōʻiliʻili* ☎*808/947–3800* ⌕*Reservations essential* ▤*AE, D, DC, MC, V* ⊘*Closed Sun. No lunch Sat. and Mon.*

$$ ╳**town.** The motto at town (with a lowercase "t") is "local first, organic

ASIAN whenever possible, with aloha always." Pretty much everyone agrees that chef-owner Ed Kenney's Mediterranean-eclectic menu ranges from just fine (pastas and salads) to just fabulous (polenta with egg and asparagus or buttermilk *panna cotta*). But the over-forty crowd tends to be put off by the minimalist decor, the shrieking-level acoustics, and the heedlessly careless waitstaff, who have a tendency to get lost. The predominantly twenty- and thritysomething clientele don't seem bothered by these circumstances. The restaurant serves an inexpensive Continental breakfast, as well as lunch and dinner. ⊠*3435 Waiʻalae Ave., Kaimukī* ☎*808/735–5900* ⌕*Reservations essential* 🍷*BYOB* ▤*MC, V* ⊘*Closed Sun.*

$$–$$$ ╳**The Willows.** An island dream, this buffet restaurant is made up of pavil-

HAWAIIAN ions overlooking a network of ponds (once natural streams flowing from mountain to sea). The island-style comfort food includes the trademark Willows curry along with Hawaiian dishes such as *laulau* (a steamed bundle of ti leaves containing pork, butterfish, and taro tops) and local favorites such as Korean barbecue ribs. ⊠*901 Hausten St., Mōʻiliʻili* ☎*808/952–9200* ⌕*Reservations essential* ▤*AE, D, MC, V.*

BEST BREAKFAST

Big City Diner (Ala Moana and Kailua). Start the day like a local: rice instead of toast, fish, or Portuguese sauce instead of bacon, even noodles.

Cinnamon's Restaurant (Kailua). Voted best for breakfast in a local newspaper poll, Cinnamon's does all the breakfast standards.

Duke's Canoe Club (Waikīkī). Duke's has an $11.95 buffet at breakfast.

Eggs 'n Things (Waikīkī). This is a longtime favorite for late hours and country-style food with island touches.

2

Musubi

Musubi needs translation. Here are cakes of steamed rice like thick decks of cards, topped with something that resembles spoiled luncheon meat, and bound in a strip of black like a paper band around a stack of new bills. Swathed in plastic, they sit on the counter of every mom-and-pop store and plate-lunch place in Hawai'i, selling for $1.50–$1.95. T-shirted surfers with sandy feet, girls in *pareu*, and *tutu* (grandmas) in *mu'umu'u* are munching these oddities with apparent delight.

"Huh?" says the visitor.

So, a quick dictionary moment: *musubi* (*moo*-sue-bee), a cake of steamed Japanese-style rice topped with some sweet-salty morsel and held together with *nori*. Most common form: Spam musubi, popularized in the early 1980s by vendor Mitsuko Kaneshiro. Kaneshiro turned her children's favorite snack into a classic—Spam slices simmered in a sugar-soy mixture atop rectangular rice cakes, with nori for crisp contrast. The flavor is surprisingly pleasant and satisfying, like a portable rice bowl.

Musubi has its roots in Japan, where rice cakes are standard festival, funeral, and family fare. But Islanders carried the tradition far afield: topping rice with slices of teriyaki chicken, sandwiching tuna salad between two cakes, dressing the rice in piquant slivers of scarlet pickled plum, toasted sesame, and strips of seaweed.

These ubiquitous tidbits are Hawai'i's go-food, like hot dogs or pretzels on a New York street. Quality varies, but if you visit a craft fair or stumble on a school sale and see homemade musubi, grab one and snack like a local.

SOUTHEAST O'AHU: HAWAI'I KAI

$$–$$$
ASIAN
✕ **BluWater Grill.** Time your drive along Honolulu's South Shore to allow for a stop at this relaxed restaurant on Kuapa Pond. The savvy chef-manager team left a popular chain restaurant to found this "American eclectic" eatery, serving wok-seared moi fish, mango and guava ribs, and lots of other interesting small dishes for $5 to $10. They're open until 11 PM Monday through Thursday and on Sunday, and until midnight Friday and Saturday. ⊠*Hawai'i Kai Shopping Center, 377 Keahole St., Hawai'i Kai* ☎808/395–6224 ⊟*AE, DC, MC, V.*

$$–$$$
ASIAN
✕ **Roy's.** Roy Yamaguchi's flagship restaurant across the highway from Maunalua Bay attracts food-savvy visitors like the North Shore attracts surfers. But it also has a strong following among well-heeled Oahuans from surrounding neighborhoods, who consider the place an extension of their homes and Roy's team their personal chefs. For this reason, Roy's is always busy and sometimes overly noisy. It's best to visit later in the evening if you're sensitive to pressure to turn the table. The wide-ranging and ever-interesting Hawaiian fusion menu changes daily except for signature dishes like Szechuan spiced barbecue baby back ribs, Roy's Original blackened 'ahi with soy mustard butter sauce, and a legendary meat loaf. There's an exceptional wine list. ⊠*Hawai'i Kai Corporate Plaza, 6600 Kalaniana'ole Hwy., Hawai'i Kai* ☎808/396–7697 ⚶*Reservations essential* ⊟*AE, D, DC, MC, V.*

WINDWARD O'AHU: KAILUA & KĀNE'OHE

¢–$ ✕**Brent's New York Deli.** Jewish-style delis are very few in the Islands, and
AMERICAN   Brent's is a mecca for homesick New Yorkers who need a knish or a
Reuben. But you don't have to know from blintzes to appreciate Brent
Brody's commitment to quality. Breakfasts are particularly scrumptious.
Portions are ample and prices right. ✉629-A Kailua Rd., Suite 108,
Kailua ☎808/262–8588 ⌖Reservations not accepted ▭MC, V.

$–$$ ✕**Buzz's Original Steakhouse.** Virtually unchanged since it opened in
AMERICAN   1967, this cozy maze of rooms opposite Kailua Beach Park is filled
Fodor's Choice   with the enticing aroma of grilling steaks. It doesn't matter if you're a bit
★   sandy (but bare feet are not allowed). Stop at the salad bar, order up a
steak, a burger, teri chicken, or the fresh fish special. If you sit at the bar,
expect to make friends. ✉413 Kawailoa Rd., Kailua ☎808/261–4661
▭No credit cards.

¢   ✕**Cinnamon's Restaurant.** Known for uncommon variations on com-
AMERICAN   mon breakfast themes (pancakes, eggs Benedict, French toast, home
fries, and eggs), this neighborhood favorite is tucked into a hard-to-
find Kailua office park; call for directions. Lunch and dinner feature
local-style plate lunch and a diner-style menu (meat loaf, baked beans).
✉315 Uluniu, Kailua ☎808/261–8724 ▭D, DC, MC, V ◷No dinner Sun.–Wed.

¢   ✕**Keneke's BBQ.** When you're sightseeing between Hanauma Bay and
FAST FOOD   Makapu'u, the food pickings are slim. But every day, 365 days a year,
there's Keneke's in Waimāaalo town. It's the home of plate lunches,
shave ice, and Scriptural graffiti on the walls (Keith "Keneke"Ward, the
burly, weight-lifting, second-generation owner of the place, is a born-
again Christian). The food is diet-busting, piled high, and mostly pretty
good, particularly the Asian-style barbecue (including teriyaki chicken
or beef and Korean *kalbi* (barbecue), Puerto Rican *guisantes* (pork and
peas in tomato gravy), and Filipino adobo (piquant pork stew). If you
want a treat, try the shave ice with ice cream. ✉41-855 Kalaniana'ole
Hwy., Waimānalo ☎808/259–9800 ▭No credit cards.

$$ ✕**Lucy's Grill and Bar.** This Windward eatery offers outdoor lānai seat-
AMERICAN   ing and an open-air bar that shakes up a mean martini to go with its
eclectic and innovative menu. The indoor seating, though attractive,
gets very noisy. Begin with the deep-fried *kālua* pig (pork roasted in
an underground oven) pastry triangles with a mandarin orange–plum
dipping sauce. Seafood offerings include daily fish specials with your
choice of preparations. For meat lovers, there are Indonesian lamb
chops or rib-eye steak. Brunch is served on Sunday. ✉33 Aulike St.,
Kailua ☎808/230–8188 ▭MC, V ◷No lunch.

$ ✕**Pah Ke's Chinese Restaurant.** Chinese restaurants tend to be interchange-
CHINESE   able, but this one—named for the local pidgin term for Chinese (liter-
ally translated this is Chinese's Chinese Restaurant)—is worth the drive
from Honolulu for its focus on healthier cooking techniques and use
of local ingredients, its seasonal specials such as cold soups and salads
made from locally raised produce, and its exceptional East–West des-
serts. The menu offers all the usual suspects, but ask the owner and chef
Raymond Siu, a former hotel pastry chef, if he's got anything different
and interesting in the kitchen, or call ahead to ask for a special menu.

2

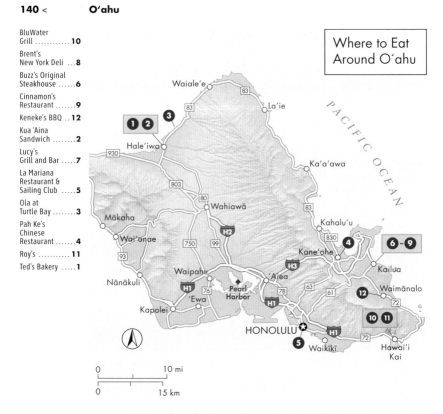

Where to Eat
Around O'ahu

⊠46-018 *Kamehameha Hwy., Kāne'ohe* ☎808/235–4505 ☰AE, MC, V.

THE NORTH SHORE: HALE'IWA

¢ ✕**Kua 'Aina Sandwich.** A must-stop spot during a drive around the island,

AMERICAN this North Shore eatery specializes in large, hand-formed burgers heaped with bacon, cheese, salsa, and pineapple; or try the grilled mahimahi sandwich. The crispy shoestring fries alone are worth the trip. Kua 'Aina also has a south-shore location across from the Ward Centre in Honolulu. ⊠66-160 *Kamehameha Hwy., Hale'iwa* ☎808/637–6067 ⊠*1116 Auahi St., Ala Moana* ☎808/591–9133 ⚲*Reservations not accepted* ☰*No credit cards.*

$$ ✕**Ola at Turtle Bay Resort.** In a pavilion literally on the sand, this casual

AMERICAN but refined restaurant wowed critics from the moment it opened, both

Fodor'sChoice with its idyllic location on Kuilima Cove and with chef Fred DeAngelo's

★ reliably wonderful food. Ola means "life, living, healthy," an apt name for a place that combines a commitment to freshness and wholesomeness with a discriminating and innovative palate in such dishes as a vegan risotto made with local mushrooms and orzo pasta, slow-poached salmon with caramelized cane sugar and Okinawan sweet potatoes. It is absolutely worth the drive. ✉*57-091 Kamehameha Hwy., Kahuku* ☎*808/293–0801* ⌔*Reservations recommended* ▭*DC, MC.*

¢   ✕**Ted's Bakery.** Across from Sunset Beach and famous for its choco-
AMERICAN   late *haupia* pie (layered coconut and chocolate puddings topped with whipped cream), Ted's Bakery is also favored by surfers and area residents for quick breakfasts, sandwiches, or plate lunches, to-go or eaten at the handful of umbrella-shaded tables outside. ✉*59-024 Kamehameha Hwy., Hale'iwa* ☎*808/638–8207* ⌔*Reservations not accepted* ▭*DC, MC, V.*

WHERE TO STAY

The 2½-mi stretch of sand known as Waikīkī Beach is a 24-hour playground and the heartbeat of Hawai'i's tourist industry. Waikīkī has a lot to offer—namely, the beach, shopping, restaurants, and nightlife, all within walking distance of your hotel.

Business travelers stay on the western edge, near the Hawai'i Convention Center, Ala Moana, and downtown Honolulu. As you head east, Ala Moana Boulevard turns into Kalākaua Avenue, Waikīkī's main drag. This is hotel row (mid-Waikīkī), with historic boutique hotels, newer high-rises, and megaresorts. Bigger chains like Sheraton, Outrigger, ResortQuest, and Ohana have multiple properties along the strip, which can be confusing. Surrounding the hotels and filling their lower levels is a flurry of shopping centers, restaurants, bars, and clubs. As you get closer to Diamond Head Crater, the strip opens up again, with the Honolulu Zoo and Kapi'olani Park providing green spaces. This end has a handful of smaller hotels and condos for those who like their Waikīkī with a "side of quiet."

Waikīkī is still the resort capital of this island and the lodging landscape is constantly changing. The Waikīkī Beach Walk opened in 2007 on 8 acres within the confines of Beach Walk, Lewers and Saratoga streets, and Kālia Road. It comprises a multitiered entertainment complex, cultural center, hotels, and vacation ownership properties, all accented by lush tropical landscaping. Ko 'Olina Resort and Marina, about 15 minutes from the airport in West O'ahu, looms large on the horizon—this ongoing development already contains the J. W. Marriott 'Ihilani Resort, Marriott's Ko 'Olina Beach Club, and some outstanding golf courses, but it is slated, over the coming decade, to see the construction of an extensive planned resort community and marina, an aquarium, dozens of restaurants and shops, more hotels, and yet more vacation-ownership rentals.

Casual Windward and North Shore digs are shorter on amenities but have laid-back charms all their own. O'ahu offers a more limited list of B&Bs than other islands because the state stopped licensing them here in the 1980s; many of those operating here now do so under the radar. If you can't find your match below, contact a reservation service to make reservations at one of O'ahu's reputable B&Bs. Legislators on O'ahu are taking another look at this industry, and it's possible that B&Bs will flourish here again in the next decade.

For a list of hotel and condominium accommodations on the island, go to the Hawai'i Visitors & Convention Bureau's Web site (⊕ *www. gohawaii.com*).

WHAT IT COSTS					
	¢	$	$$	$$$	$$$$
Hotels	under $100	$100–$180	$181–$260	$261–$340	over $340

Hotel prices are for two people in a standard double room in high season. Condo price categories reflect studio and one-bedroom rates. Prices exclude 11.41% tax.

WAIKĪKĪ

$$$–$$$$
HOTEL
⊞ **Aston Waikīkī Beach Hotel.** A three-story volcano, backlighted in a faux eruption, crawls up the side of this hotel opposite Kūhiō Beach and near Kapi'olani Park. Rooms are furnished in dark tropical woods with lava-red floral-print fabrics. The Tiki Bar and Grill completes the tropical island experience. Breakfast, evening music, and gatherings take place on the third-floor pool deck. In the early mornings, there's an international food court where guests can choose complimentary breakfast munchies to pack in a take-out cooler bag and head to the beach across the street to catch some early-morning wave action. A good choice for families, it's directly across the street from a protected stretch of Kūhiō Beach and there are in-room movies and games and free hula lessons twice weekly. In the evenings, the poolside bar breaks out with Hawaiian music that ranges from traditional to Jawaiian (Hawaiian sound with a reggae beat). **Pros:** fun for families, great beach access. **Cons:** active lobby area and crowded elevators. ⊠ *2570 Kalākaua Ave., Waikīkī* ☎ *808/922–2511 or 877/997–6667* 🖷 *808/923–3656* ⊕ *www. rqwaikikibeachhotel.com* ⟿ *644 rooms, 12 suites* 🖒 *In-room: safe, refrigerator, dial-up. In-hotel: 3 restaurants, pool, laundry facilities, parking (fee), no-smoking rooms* ⊟ *AE, D, DC, MC, V.*

$–$$
RENTAL
⊞ **The Breakers.** Despite an explosion of high-rise construction all around it, the low-rise Breakers continues to offer a taste of '60s Hawai'i in this small complex a mere half block from Waikīkī Beach. The Breakers' six two-story buildings surround its pool and overlook gardens filled with tropical flowers. Guest rooms have Japanese-style shoji doors that open to the lānai, kitchenettes, and bathrooms with showers only. Units 130, 132, and 134 have views of the Urasenke Teahouse. The Breakers enjoys enviable proximity to the new Waikiki Beach Walk entertainment, dining, and retail complex. The resort is very popular thanks to its reasonable prices and great location. **Pros:** intimate atmosphere, great location. **Cons:** parking space is limited. ⊠ *250 Beach Walk, Waikīkī* ☎ *808/923–3181 or 800/426–0494* 🖷 *808/923–7174* ⊕ *www.breakers-hawaii.com* ⟿ *64 units* 🖒 *In-room: kitchen. In-hotel: restaurant, bar, pool, parking (fee)* ⊟ *AE, DC, MC, V.*

$$$–$$$$
RENTAL
⊞ **Castle Waikīkī Shore.** Nestled between Fort DeRussy Beach Park and the Outrigger Reef on the Beach, this is the only condo right on Waikīkī Beach. Units include studios and one- and two-bedroom suites, each

with private lānai and panoramic views of the Pacific Ocean. All units have washers and dryers, and many have full kitchens, but some only have kitchenettes, so be sure to inquire when booking. Families love this place for its spaciousness, while others love it for its quiet location on the ʻewa end of Waikīkī. However, through 2008 and into 2009, there will be construction on the new Trump Towers directly across Kālia Road. **Pros:** great security, great views, great management. **Cons:** ongoing construction on Diamond Head side of property. ✉*2161 Kālia Rd., Waikīkī* ☎*808/952–4500 or 800/367–2353* 🖷*808/952–4580* 🌐*www. castleresorts.com* ➥*168 units* ♿*In-room: safe, kitchen (some), dialup. In-hotel: beachfront, laundry facilities, parking (fee), no-smoking rooms* ▭*AE, D, DC, MC, V.*

$

B&B/INN

🏠**Diamond Head Bed and Breakfast.** Many a traveler and resident would love to own a home like this art-filled B&B at the base of Waikīkī's famous Diamond Head crater, one of the city's most exclusive neighborhoods. Each of the three guest rooms features koa-wood furnishings and private bath, and they open to a lānai and a big backyard filled with the sounds of birds and rustling trees. The more private ground-floor suite has a separate living room and a bedroom with a queen bed. To experience a bit of Hawaiian history, request the room that includes the extra-large hand-carved koa bed that once belonged to a Hawaiian princess. The closest beach is the intimate Sans Souci near the Natatorium; it's hard to believe that the hustle and bustle of Waikīkī is a short stroll from the house. Reserve three to four months in advance. **Pros:** secluded and peaceful. **Cons:** small and therefore difficult to book. ✉*3240 Noela Dr., Waikīkī* 🖉*Reservations: Hawaiʻi's Best Bed and Breakfasts, Box 485, Laupahoehoe 96767* ☎*808/962–0100, 800/262–9912 reservations* 🖷*808/962–6360* 🌐*www.bestbnb.com* ➥*2 rooms, 1 suite* ♿*In-room: no a/c, no phone. In-hotel: no-smoking rooms* ▭*No credit cards.*

$$

HOTEL

🏠**Doubletree Alana Waikīkī.** The location (a 10-minute walk from the Hawaiʻi Convention Center), three phones in each room, and the 24-hour business center and gym meet the requirements of the Doubletree's global business clientele, but the smallness of the property, the staff's attention to detail, and the signature Doubletree chocolate chip cookies upon arrival resonate with vacationers. All rooms in the 19-story high-rise have lānai, but they overlook the city and busy Ala Moana Boulevard across from Fort DeRussy. To get to the beach, you cross Fort DeRussy or head through the Hilton Hawaiian Village. **Pros:** professional staff, pleasant public spaces. **Cons:** beach is a bit of a walk. ✉*1956 Ala Moana Blvd., Waikīkī* ☎*808/941–7275 or 800/222–8733* 🖷*808/949–0996* 🌐*www.alana-doubletree.com* ➥*317 rooms, 385 suites* ♿*In-room: safe, dial-up. In-hotel: restaurant, room service, bar, pool, gym, parking (fee), no-smoking rooms* ▭*AE, D, MC, V.*

$$$$

HOTEL

🏠**Embassy Suites Hotel–Waikīkī Beach Walk.** In a place where space is at a premium, the only all-suites resort in Hawaiʻi offers families and groups traveling together a bit more room to move about, with two 21-story towers housing one- and two-bedroom suites. All rooms have at least two balconies, some with ocean views; most overlooking the 1,965-square-foot Grand Lanai with its pool, bar, restaurant, and

WHERE TO STAY IN WAIKĪKĪ AND OAHU

Hotels & Resorts

	Property Name	Pools	Beach	Golf Course	Tennis Courts	Gym	Spa	Children's Programs	Rooms	Restaurants	Other	Worth Noting	Location
28	Ala Moana Hotel	1				yes			1,217	4		Ala Moana Shopping	Ala Moana
3	Doubletree Alana Waikīkī	1				yes			317	1		Near Convention Center	Waikīkī
9 ★	Halekūlani	1				yes	yes		455	3	shops	Great restaurants	Waikīkī
1	Hawai'i Prince Hotel	1		yes		yes	yes		578	3	shops	Ala Moana Shopping	Waikīkī
4	Hilton Hawaiian Village	5	yes			yes	yes	5–12	3,787	20	shops	Bishop Museum, fireworks	Waikīkī
22	Hilton Waikīkī Prince K.	1				yes			620	1		2 blocks to beach	Waikīkī
2	Hotel Equus	1									laundry	Good value	Waikīkī
19	Hyatt Regency Waikīkī	1				yes	yes	5–12	1,248	5	shops	Across from beach	Waikīkī
30	J.W. Marriott 'Ihilani	2	yes	yes	6	yes	yes	5–12	423	3	shops	Ko'Olina Resort, spa	West O'ahu
29 ★	The Kāhala	1	yes			yes	yes	5–12	343	3	shops	Dolphin Quest	East Honolulu
14	Moana Surfrider	1	yes					5–12	839	2	shops	Landmark historic wing	Waikīkī
18	Ohana East	1				yes		5–12	440	3	kitchens	2 blocks to beach	Waikīkī
16	Ohana Waikīkī Beachcomber	1						5–12	500	1		1 block to beach, shows	Waikīkī
7	Outrigger Reef on the Beach	1	yes			yes		5–12	675	2		Good value	Waikīkī
13	Outrigger Waikīkī on the Beach	1	yes			yes		5–13	554	3	kitchens	Duke's Canoe Club	Waikīkī
26	Aston Waikīkī Beach Hotel	1							684	3	shops	Beach across the street	Waikīkī

#		Comments										Region
21	Royal Grove	Good value	1						85		no a/c	Waikīkī
12	Royal Hawaiian Hotel	Coconut grove, Mai Tai Bar	1	yes			yes	5–12	528	2	shops	Waikīkī
17	Sheraton Princess Kaiulani	1 block to beach	1		yes			5–12	1,164	2		Waikīkī
11	Sheraton Waikīkī	Cobalt Lounge	2	yes	yes			5–12	1,823	2	shops	Waikīkī
5	Turtle Bay Resort	Beach cottages, trails	2	yes	yes	10	yes	5–12	511	4	shops	North Shore
24	Waikīkī Beach Marriott	Great sushi, spa	2		yes		yes		1,323	6		Waikīkī
10	Waikīkī Parc	1 block to beach	1		yes				297	1		Waikīkī
20	Waikīkī Sand Villa	3 blocks to beach	1						214	1	no a/c	Waikīkī
	Condos & Vacation Rentals											
8	The Breakers	2 blocks to beach	1	yes					63	1	kitchens	Waikīkī
6	Castle Waikīkī Shores	Great value		yes					168		kitchens	Waikīkī
15	Ilima Hotel	3 blocks to beach	1			yes			98		kitchens	Waikīkī
33	Marriott Kō 'Olina Beach	Kō 'Olina Resort, spa	2	yes	yes	6	yes	5–12	200	2	kitchens	West O'ahu
5	Outrigger Luana	2 blocks to beach	1		yes		yes		218		kitchens	Waikīkī
23	ResortQuest Waikīkī Beach Tower	Across from beach	1			1			140		kitchens	Waikīkī
25	ResortQuest Waikīkī Banyan	1 block to beach	1			1			876		kitchens	Waikīkī
	BBs											
32	Backpackers Vacation Inn	Near Waimea Bay							25		no a/c	North Shore
27	Diamond Head B&B	Near Crater							3		no a/c	Waikīkī
30	Ingrid's	Kailua, Japanese garden	1						1		kitchens	Windward O'ahu

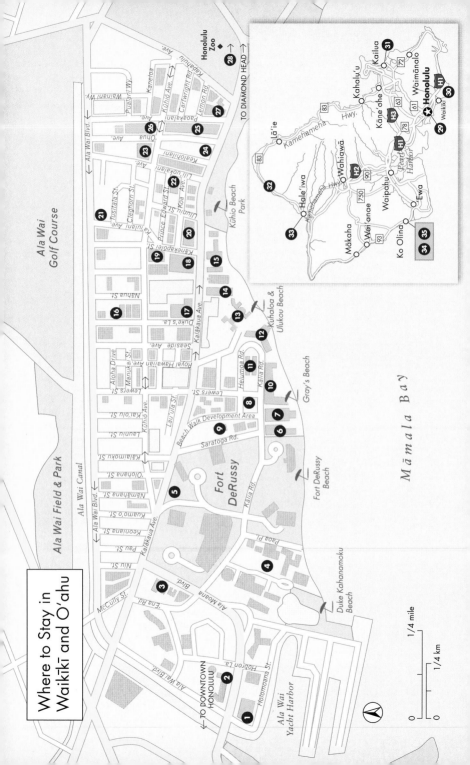

Where to Stay in Waikīkī and Oʻahu

2

meeting areas. The experience begins with a sit-down check-in and a manager's reception with free appetizers and drinks and ends with an aloha lei ceremony. Rooms, with Tommy Bahama–meets–Island beach home style (carved-wood tables, pineapple-print upholstery, hula-dancer artwork), have relaxing earth tones, with amenities like pull-out beds and wet bars with microwaves and mini-refrigerators inviting longer stays. Developed by locally based Outrigger Enterprises, the hotel is steeped in Hawaiiana, with tapa-pattern murals adorning the exterior and cultural programs for adults and youth. **Pros:** great location next to Waikīkī Beach Walk, great vibe, nice pool deck. **Cons:** no direct beach access. ⊠*201 Beachwalk St., Waikīkī* ☎*800/EMBASSY [362–2779]* ⊕*www.embassysuiteswaikikibeachwalk.com* ↘*353 1-bedroom suites, 68 2-bedroom suites* ⅋*In-room: safe, refrigerator, dial-up, Ethernet. In-hotel: 4 restaurants, room service, bar, pool* ▭*AE, D, MC, V.*

$$$$
RESORT
Fodor'sChoice
★

ⓣ**Halekūlani.** Honeymooners and others seeking seclusion amid the frenetic activity of the Waikīkī scene find it here. Halekūlani exemplifies the translation of its name—the "house befitting heaven." From the moment you step inside the lobby, the attention to detail and service wraps you in luxury. It begins with private registration in your guest room and extends to the tiniest of details, such as complimentary tickets to the Honolulu Symphony, Contemporary Art Museum, and Honolulu Academy of Arts. Spacious guest rooms, artfully appointed in marble and wood, have ocean views and extra large lānai. If you want to honeymoon in the ultimate style, we recommend the 2,125-square-foot Vera Wang Suite, created by the noted wedding-dress designer herself. It's entirely Vera, right down to the signature soft-lavender color scheme. For a day of divine pampering, check into the Halekūlani Spa. Lewer's Lounge, the in-house jazz club has recently been upgraded to what the *New York Times* described as "urban chic" with famed mixologist Dale DeGroff calling the shots. Outside, the resort's freshwater pool has an orchid design created from more than 1.5 million glass mosaic tiles. Gray's Beach, which fronts the hotel just beyond the pool, is small and has been known to disappear at high tide. **Pros:** heavenly interior spaces and wonderful dining opportunities in house. **Cons:** might feel a bit formal for Waikīkī. ⊠*2199 Kālia Rd., Waikīkī* ☎*808/923–2311 or 800/367–2343* 🖶*808/926–8004* ⊕*www.halekulani.com* ↘*412 rooms, 43 suites* ⅋*In-room: dial-up, DVD, safe. In-hotel: 3 restaurants, room service, bars, pool, spa, beachfront, laundry service, public Internet, public Wi-Fi, parking (fee), no-smoking rooms* ▭*AE, DC, MC, V.*

$$$$
HOTEL

ⓣ**Hawai'i Prince Hotel & Golf Club Waikīkī.** This slim high-rise fronts Ala Wai Yacht Harbor at the 'ewa (west) edge of Waikīkī, close to Honolulu's downtown business districts, the convention center, and Ala Moana's outdoor mall. There's no beach here, but Ala Moana Beach Park is a 10-minute stroll away along the harbor, and the hotel also offers complimentary shuttle service around Waikīkī and its surrounding beaches. It's the only resort in Waikīkī with a golf course—the 27-hole Arnold Palmer–designed golf course is in 'Ewa Beach, about a 45-minute ride from the hotel. The sleek, modern Prince looks to Asia both in its high-style decor and such pampering touches as the

Halekulani

traditional *oshiburi* (chilled hand towel) for refreshment upon check-in. Floor-to-ceiling windows overlooking the harbor—ideal for sunsets—make up for the lack of lānai. **Pros:** fantastic views, all very elegant, easy exit from complicated-to-maneuver Waikīkī. **Cons:** can feel a bit stuffy as it caters more to business travelers. ⊠ *100 Holomoana St., Waikīkī* ☎ *808/956–1111 or 866/774–6236* 🖷 *808/944–4491* ⊕ *www.hawaii princehotel.com* ↻ *521 rooms, 57 suites* △ *In room: safe, refrigerator, dial-up. In-hotel: 3 restaurants, room service, bar, golf course, pool, gym, spa, parking (fee), no-smoking rooms* ⊟ *AE, DC, MC, V.*

$$$ 🖫 **Hilton Hawaiian Village Beach Resort and Spa.** Location, location, loca-
RESORT tion: this megaresort and convention destination sprawls over 22 acres on Waikīkī's widest stretch of beach, with the green lawns of neighboring Fort DeRussy creating a buffer zone to the high-rise lineup of central Waikīkī. The Hilton makes the most of its prime real estate—surrounding the five hotel towers with lavish gardens, an aquatic playground of pools, a 5-acre lagoon for kayaking, cascading waterfalls, koi ponds, penguins, and pink flamingos. Rainbow Tower, with its landmark 31-story mural, has knockout views of Diamond Head. Rooms in all towers have lānai offering ocean, city, or Waikīkī beach views. More of a city than a village, the HHV has an ABC sundries store, a bookstore, Louis Vuitton, and a post office. Culture comes in the form of an outpost of the Bishop Museum and the contemporary Hawaiian art gracing the public spaces. It even has its own pier, docking point for the *Atlantis* Submarine. The sheer volume of options, including free stuff (lei making, 'ukelele lessons, and fireworks), makes the HHV a good choice for families. **Pros:** activities and amenities can keep you busy for weeks, big-resort perks like check-in kiosks (complete with room keys) in the baggage-claim area at the airport. **Cons:** temptation to stay on-site, missing out on the "real" Hawai'i, frequent renovations and construction, size of property can be overwhelming. ⊠ *2005 Kālia Rd., Waikīkī* ☎ *808/949–4321 or 800/221–2424* 🖷 *808/951–5458* ⊕ *www. hiltonhawaiianvillage.com* ↻ *3,432 rooms, 365 suites, 264 condominiums* △ *In-room: safe, refrigerator, Ethernet. In-hotel: 20 restaurants, room service, bars, pools, gym, spa, beachfront, children's programs (ages 5–12), laundry service, public Internet, parking (fee), no-smoking rooms* ⊟ *AE, D, DC, MC, V.*

$$$–$$$$ 🖫 **Hilton Waikīkī Prince Kūhiō.** You enter through a lobby of rich wood
HOTEL detailing, contemporary fabrics, and magnificent tropical floral displays whose colors match the hibiscus reds of the carpeting. Two blocks from Kūhiō Beach, this 37-story high-rise is on the Diamond Head end of Waikīkī. The Lobby Bar mixes up tropical cocktails and an island-style pūpū menu and has wireless access and a wide-screen plasma TV for sports fans and news junkies while their restaurant MAC 24-7 offers their version of modern comfort food 24 hours a day, seven days a week. If marriage is on your mind, note the wedding gazebo anchoring the hotel gardens. Book on an upper floor for an ocean view from your lānai. **Pros:** good value, central location, and pleasant, comfortable public spaces. **Cons:** a bit of a distance to the beach, very few rooms with views. ⊠ *2500 Kūhiō Ave., Waikīkī* ☎ *808/922—0811 or 800/333–3333* 🖷 *808/921–5507* ⊕ *www.radisson.com/waikikihi*

⊃*620 rooms* ☾*In-room: safe, Ethernet, dial-up. In-hotel: restaurant, room service, bar, pool, gym, parking (fee), no-smoking rooms* ▭*AE, D, DC, MC, V.*

$–$$ ⊡**The Hotel Equus.** Formerly the Hawaii Polo Inn, this small hotel has
HOTEL   been completely renovated with a Hawaiian country theme that pays tribute to Hawai'i's polo-playing history. It fronts busy Ala Moana Boulevard, on the 'ewa end of Waikīkī, and is one block from both Ala Moana shopping center and Ala Moana Beach Park. All rooms are equipped with refrigerators and microwaves; some have balconies and partial ocean views; daily Continental breakfast is included. The front desk staff are happy to assist with driving directions to the polo playing fields at Mokuleia and Waimānalo, where guests receive free tickets in season—pack a picnic if you go. **Pros:** casual, fun atmosphere, attentive staff, nicely furnished rooms. **Cons:** on a very busy road you must cross to get to the beach. ⊠*1696 Ala Moana Blvd., Waikīkī* ☏*808/949–0061 or 800/535–0085* 🖷*808/949–4906* ⊕*www.hawaii polo.com* ⊃*70 rooms* ☾*In-room: safe. In-hotel: pool, laundry facilities, parking (fee)* ▭*AE, DC, MC, V.*

$$$$ ⊡**Hyatt Regency Waikīkī Resort and Spa.** Though it's across the street
RESORT   from the Kūhiō Beach section of Waikīkī, the Hyatt is actually on the oceanfront, as there's no resort between it and the Pacific Ocean. A pool-deck staircase leads directly to street level, for easy beach access. An open-air atrium with three levels of shopping, a two-story waterfall, and free nightly live entertainment make this one of the liveliest lobbies anywhere. An activity center offers kids' programs, including lei-making lessons, 'ukulele lessons, and field trips to the aquarium and zoo. **Pros:** public spaces are airy and waterfall is spectacular. **Cons:** in a very busy and crowded part of Waikīkī. ⊠*2424 Kalākaua Ave., Waikīkī* ☏*808/923–1234 or 800/633–7313* 🖷*808/923–7839* ⊕*www. waikiki.hyatt.com* ⊃*1,212 rooms, 18 suites* ☾*In-room: safe, refrigerator, dial-up. In-hotel: 5 restaurants, room service, bars, pool, gym, spa, children's programs (ages 5–12), parking (fee), no-smoking rooms* ▭*AE, D, DC, MC, V.*

$$–$$$ ⊡**'Ilima Hotel.** Tucked away on a residential side street near Waikīkī's
RENTAL   Ala Wai Canal, this locally owned 17-story condominium-style hotel is a gem. The glass-wall lobby with koa-wood furnishings, original Hawaiian artwork, and friendly staff create a Hawaiian home-away-from-home. Rates are decent for the spacious studios with kitchenettes and the one- and two-bedroom suites with full kitchens, Jacuzzi baths, cable TV with free HBO and Disney channels, multiple phones, and spacious lānai. It's a two-block walk to Waikīkī Beach, shopping, and Kalākaua Avenue restaurants. The parking is free but limited. When the spots are full, you park on the street. **Pros:** big rooms are great for families. **Cons:** limited hotel parking and street parking can be difficult to find. ⊠*445 Nohonani St., Waikīkī* ☏*808/923–1877 or 800/801–9366* 🖷*808/924–2617* ⊕*www.ilima.com* ⊃*99 units* ☾*In-room: safe, kitchen, Ethernet (some), dial-up. In-hotel: pool, gym, laundry facilities, parking (free), no-smoking rooms* ▭*AE, DC, MC, V.*

$$$$ ⊡**Moana Surfrider.** Outrageous rates of $1.50 per night were the talk of
HOTEL   the town when the "First Lady of Waikīkī" opened her doors in 1901.

The *Hawai'i Calls* radio program was broadcast from the veranda during the 1940s and '50s. Today this historic beauty is still a wedding and honeymoon favorite with a sweeping main staircase and period furnishings in its historic main wing, the Moana. In the late 1950s, the hotel's Diamond Head Tower was built. In the '70s, the Surfrider hotel went up next door; all three merged into one hotel in the 1980s. The newly refurbished Surfrider has oceanfront suites with two separate lānai, one for sunrise and one for sunset viewing. Relax on the private beach or in a cabana by the pool. Enjoy live music and hula at The Banyan Court each evening or dine at the Beach House restaurant. **Pros:** elegant, historic property, best place on Waikīkī Beach to watch hula and have a drink. **Cons:** you might feel you have to tiptoe around formal public spaces. ⊠ *2365 Kalākaua Ave., Waikīkī* ☎ *808/922–3111, 888/488–3535, or 866/500–8313* 📠 *808/923–0308* ⊕ *www.moana-surfrider.com* ⤴ *793 rooms, 46 suites* ♿ *In-room: safe, dial-up. In-hotel: 2 restaurants, room service, bars, pool, beachfront, children's programs (ages 5–12), laundry service, parking (fee), no-smoking rooms* ⊟ *AE, DC, MC, V.*

$$$
HOTEL
📺 **Ohana East.** If you want to be in central Waikīkī and don't want to pay beachfront lodging prices, consider the flagship property for Ohana Hotels in Waikīkī. Next to the Sheraton Princess Kaiulani on the corner of Kaiulani and Kūhiō avenues, it's a mere two blocks from the beach and within walking distance of shopping, restaurants, and nightlife. Its location and reasonable rates tend to attract plenty of group travelers. Don't expect any fancy lobbies or outdoor gardens here. Certain rooms on lower floors have no lānai, and some rooms have showers only. Suites have kitchenettes. **Pros:** close to the beach and reasonable rates. **Cons:** no lānai and very basic public spaces. ⊠ *150 Kaiulani Ave., Waikīkī* ☎ *808/922–5353 or 800/462–6262* 📠 *808/926–4334* ⊕ *www.ohanahotels.com* ⤴ *420 rooms, 20 suites* ♿ *In-room: safe, kitchen (some), refrigerator, Ethernet. In-hotel: 3 restaurants, room service, bar, pool, gym, laundry facilities, parking (fee)* ⊟ *AE, D, DC, MC, V.*

$$$
HOTEL
📺 **Ohana Waikīkī Beachcomber Hotel.** Ohana took over the beloved old Beachcomber in 2005 and has given her a comprehensive face-lift while retaining the Polynesian theme. At this and other Ohana hotels, the Ohana Waikīkī Connection offers several free services: unlimited rides on the Waikīkī Trolley Pink Line, long-distance phone service to the U.S. and Canada, and a daily newspaper. Early check-in guests can leave their bags, pick up a pager, and hit the beach; they'll be alerted when their rooms are ready. This Ohana hotel hosts the popular Blue Hawai'i show and is almost directly across from the Royal Hawaiian Shopping Center and next door to the International Marketplace. The third-floor pool deck is front-row seating for any of Waikīkī's year-round parades or Ho'olaulea street-party festivals that happen year-round. It's a family-friendly place, with cultural activities that include 'ukulele and hula lessons as well as arts and crafts. On the hotel's ground level is an entrance to Macy's, and across the street is a public access-way that opens up to the beach fronting the Royal Hawaiian hotel. **Pros:** lots of freebies, in the thick of Waikīkī action. **Cons:** very busy area, no

direct beach access. ✉ *2300 Kalākaua Ave., Waikīkī* ☎ *808/922–4646 or 800/462-6262* 🖷 *808/923–4889* ⊕ *www.waikikibeachcomber.com* ⤴ *500 rooms, 7 suites* ⌂ *In-room: refrigerator, dial-up. In-hotel: restaurant, room service, bar, pool, children's programs (ages 5–12), laundry facilities, public Internet, parking (fee), no-smoking rooms* ☰ *AE, DC, MC, V.*

$$$–$$$$
RENTAL
🏨 **Outrigger Luana.** At the entrance to Waikīkī near Fort DeRussy is this welcoming hotel offering both rooms and condominium units. Luana's two-story lobby is appointed in rich, Hawaiian-wood furnishings with island-inspired fabrics, along with a mezzanine lounge as comfortable as any living room back home. Units are furnished with the same mix of rich woods with etched accents of pineapples and palm trees. At bedside, hula-dancer and beach-boy lamps add another Hawaiian residential touch. The recreational deck features a fitness center, pool, and barbecue area with tables that can be enclosed cabana-style for privacy when dining outdoors. One-bedroom suites each have two lānai. If you like Hawaiiana and appreciate a bit of kitsch this is a great option. **Pros:** two lānai in suites, barbecue area (rare for Waikīkī). **Cons:** no direct beach access. ✉ *2045 Kalākaua Ave., Waikīkī* ☎ *808/955–6000 or 800/688–7444* 🖷 *808/943–8555* ⊕ *www.outrigger.com* ⤴ *218 units* ⌂ *In-room: safe, kitchen (some), dial-up. In-hotel: pool, gym, laundry facilities, public Wi-Fi, parking (fee)* ☰ *AE, D, DC, MC, V.*

$$$–$$$$
HOTEL
🏨 **Outrigger Reef on the Beach.** The Outrigger Reef has completed its $110 million renovations bringing it into the 21st century while staying true to its Hawaiian voyaging decor theme, expanding their room size, larger and more contemporary bathrooms—including full-size bathtubs in what was previously an all-shower hotel—and a new signature restaurant, though the Shore Bird and Ocean House remain. What had been a plain but pleasant oceanfront bargain now offers polished elegance in keeping with its prime location. Though the inland Pacific Towerwill have been renovated more recently, it's worthwhile to try to get an ocean view or oceanfront accommodation in the Ocean Tower; other rooms have less enchanting views, and noisy construction on the Trump Towers across the street will continue into 2009. New features include smoke-free rooms, flat-screen TVs, and free long distance to the U.S. mainland and Canada. **Pros:** on beach, direct access to Waikīkī Beach Walk. **Cons:** proximity to Trump Tower construction. ✉ *2169 Kālia Rd., Waikīkī* ☎ *808/923–3111 or 800/688–7444* 🖷 *808/924–4957* ⊕ *www.outrigger.com* ⤴ *634 rooms, 44 suites* ⌂ *In-room: refrigerator, bar, dial-up. In-hotel: 2 restaurants, pool, gym, beachfront, laundry facilities, children's programs (ages 5–12), public Internet, public Wi-Fi, parking (fee), no-smoking rooms* ☰ *AE, D, DC, MC, V.*

$$$$
HOTEL
🏨 **Outrigger Waikīkī on the Beach.** This star jewel of Outrigger Hotels & Resorts sits on one of the finest strands of Waikīkī Beach. The guest rooms in the 16-story no-smoking resort have rich dark-wood furnishings, Hawaiian art, and lānai that offer either ocean or Waikīkī-skyline views. The popular Duke's Canoe Club has beachfront concerts under the stars. Waikīkī Plantation Spa offers Hawaiian seaweed wraps, hot-stone massages, and wedding packages. **Pros:** the best bar on the beach is downstairs, free Wi-Fi in lobby. **Cons:** the lobby feels a bit like an

airport with so many people using it as a throughway to the beach. ⊠*2335 Kalākaua Ave., Waikīkī* ☎*808/923–0711 or 800/688–7444* ☏*808/921–9798* ⊕*www.outrigger.com* ⤴*524 rooms, 30 suites* ⚐*In-room: safe, kitchen (some), refrigerator, dial-up, Ethernet. In-hotel: 3 restaurants, room service, bars, pool, gym, beachfront, children's programs (ages 5–13), laundry service, laundry facilities, parking (fee)* ⊟*AE, D, DC, MC, V.*

$$–$$$
RENTAL
📺**ResortQuest at the Waīkīkī Banyan.** The recreation deck at this family-oriented property has outdoor grills, a heated swimming pool, two hot tubs, a children's playground, a mini-putting green, and volleyball, basketball, and tennis courts. The welcoming lobby is decorated in warm tropical woods with plenty of seating to enjoy the trade winds. There is also a koi pond and mini-waterfall. One-bedroom suites contain island-inspired decor and have complete kitchens and lānai that offer Diamond Head or ocean views. **Pros:** many rooms have great views. **Cons:** trekking to the beach with all your gear. ⊠*201 Ohua Ave., Waikīkī* ☎*808/922–0555 or 866/774–2924* ☏*808/922–0906* ⊕*www.rqwaikikibanyan.com* ⤴*876 units* ⚐*In-room: kitchen, Ethernet, dial-up. In-hotel: tennis court, pool, parking (fee), laundry facilities, no-smoking rooms* ⊟*AE, D, DC, MC, V.*

$$$$
RENTAL
📺**ResortQuest Waikīkī Beach Tower.** You'll find the elegance of a luxury all-suites condominium combined with the intimacy and service of a boutique hotel at this Kalākaua Avenue address. Facing Kuhio Beach, this 40-story resort offers spacious (1,100–1,400 square feet) one- and two-bedroom suites with gourmet kitchens and windows that open to views of Waikīkī and the Pacific Ocean. Amenities include twice-daily maid service, washer-dryers, and spacious private lānai. **Pros:** very large rooms—big enough to move into. **Cons:** no on-site restaurants, you must cross a busy street to the beach. ⊠*2470 Kalākaua Ave., Waikīkī* ☎*808/926–6400 or 866/774–2924* ☏*808/926–7380* ⊕*www.rqwaikiki beachtower.com* ⤴*140 units* ⚐*In-room: safe, kitchen, DVD, dial-up. In-hotel: room service, pool, tennis court, laundry facilities, parking, no-smoking rooms* ⊟*AE, D, DC, MC, V.*

$
HOTEL
📺**Royal Grove Hotel.** Two generations of the Fong family have put their heart and soul into the operation of this tiny (by Waikīkī standards), six-story hotel that feels like a throwback to the days of boarding houses, where rooms were outfitted for function, not style, and served up with a wealth of home-style hospitality at a price that didn't break the bank. During the hot summer months, seriously consider splurging on the highest-end accommodations, which feature air-conditioning, lānai, and small kitchens. The hotel's pool is its social center in the evenings, where you can usually find at least one or more members of the Fong family strumming a 'ukulele, dancing hula, and singing songs in the old Hawaiian style. On special occasions, the Fongs host a potluck dinner by the pool. Little touches that mean a lot include free use of boogie boards, surfboards, beach mats, and beach towels. The hotel is two blocks from Waikīkī's Kūhiō Beach. On property are a tiny sushi bar, a natural foods deli, and an authentic Korean barbecue plate-lunch place. For extra value, inquire about the Grove's weekly and monthly rates. Parking is available in a public lot down the street. **Pros:** very economical Waikīkī

option, lots of character. **Cons:** no a/c in some rooms. ✉ *151 Uluniu Ave., Waikīkī* ☎*808/923–7691* 🖷*808/922–7508* ⊕*www.royalgrove hotel.com* ↙*78 rooms, 7 suites* ⌂*In-room: kitchen. In-hotel: pool* ⊟AE, D, DC, MC, V.

$$$$ 🖥**The Royal Hawaiian Hotel.** The $100 millon facelift has been completed
HOTEL at this Waikiki landmark location. While externally this Starwood hotel still holds its original shape and color, the interior has been enhanced by a little old and a little new. Shops that used to fill the lobby have been taken away, replaced by an uninterrupted view of the Pacific. The pool has been raised to give swimmers a better view of the sunset, and rooms has been completely redone, down to new pink sheets. The Matson Navigation Company built the Pink Palace of the Pacific, so nicknamed for its cotton-candy color, in 1927 for its luxury-cruise passengers. A modern tower has since been added, but we're partial to the romance and architectural detailing of the historic wing, with its canopy beds, Queen Anne–style desks, and color motifs that range from soft mauve to soothing sea foam. If you want a lānai for sunset viewing, rooms in the oceanfront tower are your best bet. The Royal's weekly lū'au—the only oceanfront lū'au in Waikīkī—is held Monday evenings underneath the stars on the Ocean Lawn. **Pros:** can't be beat for history, mai tais and sunsets are amazing. **Cons:** more expensive since reopening. ✉*2259 Kalākaua Ave., Waikīkī* ☎*888/488–3535, 808/923–7311, or 866/500–8313* 🖷*808/924–7098* ⊕*www.royal-hawaiian.com* ↙*528 rooms, 53 suites* ⌂*In-room: refrigerator, Ethernet. In-hotel: 1 restaurant, room service, pool, spa, beachfront, bar, children's programs (ages 5–12), concierge, public Internet, parking (fee), no-smoking rooms* ⊟AE, DC, MC, V.

$$ 🖥**Sheraton Princess Kaiulani.** This hotel sits across the street from its
HOTEL sister property, the Sheraton Moana Surfrider. You can sleep at the Princess Kaiulani, taking advantage of the lower rates of a non-beachfront hotel, oversee the bustle of Waikīkī from your private lānai, and dine at any of the more-pricey oceanfront Sheratons, charging everything back to your room at the Princess Kaiulani. Rooms are in two towers—some peer at the ocean over the Moana's low-rise historic wing. It's a two-minute stroll to the beach. The hotel's pool is street-side, facing Kalākaua Avenue. **Pros:** in the heart of everything in Waikīkī. **Cons:** no direct beach access, kid's activities offsite. ✉*120 Kaiulani Ave., Waikīkī* ☎*808/922–5811, 888/488–3535, or 866/500–8313* 🖷*808/931–4577* ⊕*www.princesskaiulani.com* ↙*1,152 rooms, 14 suites* ⌂*In-room: dial-up. In-hotel: 3 restaurants, room service, bars, pool, gym, children's programs (ages 5–12), no-smoking rooms* ⊟AE, D, DC, MC, V.

$$$$ 🖥**Sheraton Waikīkī.** Towering over its neighbors on the prow of
HOTEL Waikīkī's famous sands, the Sheraton is center stage on Waikīkī Beach. Designed for the convention crowd, it's big and busy; the ballroom, one of O'ahu's largest, hosts convention expos, concerts, and boxing matches. A glass-wall elevator, with magnificent views of Waikīkī, ascends 30 stories to the Hano Hano Room's skyline Cobalt lounge and restaurant in the sky. The resort's best beach is on its Diamond Head side, fronting the Royal Hawaiian Hotel. Lānai afford views of the ocean, Waikīkī, or mountains. If you don't shy away from crowds,

this could be the place for you. The advantage here is that you have at your vacation fingertips a variety of amenities, venues, and programs, as well as a location smack-dab in the middle of Waikīkī. **Pros:** location in the heart of everything. **Cons:** busy atmosphere clashes with laid-back Hawaiian style. ⊠*2255 Kalākaua Ave., Waikīkī* ☎*888/488–3535, 808/922–4422, or 866/500–8313* 🖷*808/923–8785* ⊕*www.sheraton waikiki.com* ⤢*1,695 rooms, 128 suites* ♿*In-room: refrigerator, Ethernet. In-hotel: 3 restaurants, room service, bars, pools, beachfront, children's programs (ages 5–12), laundry service, parking (fee), no-smoking rooms* ⊟*AE, DC, MC, V.*

$$$
RESORT

🔝**Waikīkī Beach Marriott Resort & Spa.** On the eastern edge of Waikīkī, this flagship Marriott sits across from Kūhiō Beach and close to Kapi'olani Park, the zoo, and the aquarium. Deep Hawaiian woods and bold tropical colors fill the hotel's two towers, which have ample courtyards and public areas open to ocean breezes and sunlight. Rooms in the Kealohilani Tower are some of the largest in Waikīkī, and the Paoakalani Tower's Diamond Head–side rooms offer breathtaking views of the crater and Kapi'olani Park. All rooms have private lānai. The hotel's Spa Olakino, owned by Honolulu celebrity stylist Paul Brown, is one of the largest in Waikīkī and specializes in use of Hawai'i-based materials and treatments. Daily activites are offered for children and adults alike and surf lessons are available from surfer Tony Moniz at the Faith Surf School. **Pros:** stunning views of Waikīkī, professional service, airy tropical public spaces. **Cons:** noise from Kalākaua Avenue can drown out surf below. ⊠*2552 Kalākaua Ave., Waikīkī* ☎*808/922–6611 or 800/367–5370* 🖷*808/921–5222* ⊕*www.marriottwaikiki.com* ⤢*1,310 rooms, 13 suites* ♿*In-room: Ethernet, dial-up, Wi-Fi. In-hotel: 6 restaurants, room service, bars, 2 pools, gym, spa, parking (fee), no-smoking rooms* ⊟*AE, D, MC, V.*

$$$–$$$$
HOTEL

🔝**Waikīkī Parc.** Contrasting the stately vintage-Hawaiian elegance of her sister hotel, the Halekūlani, the Waikīkī Parc makes a chic and contemporary statement to its Gen-X clientele, offering the same attention to detail in service and architectural design but lacking the beachfront location and higher prices. The guest rooms in this high-rise complex have modern minimalist furnishings but give a nod to the tropics by keeping plantation-style shutters that open out to the lānai. A complimentary evening manager's reception features wine specially made for the hotel. Its heated pool and sundeck are eight floors up, affording a bit more privacy and peace for sunbathers, and guests can take advantage of the spa at the Halekūlani across the street. Nobu Waikīkī, of the world-renowned Nobu restaurant family, opened here in 2007, serving Japanese food with a South American accent. **Pros:** stunningly modern, high-design rooms, great access to Waikīkī Beach Walk. **Cons:** no direct beach access. ⊠*2233 Helumoa Rd., Waikīkī* ☎*808/921–7272 or 800/422–0450* 🖷*808/923–1336* ⊕*www.waikikiparc.com* ⤢*298 rooms* ♿*In-room: safe, dial-up, Ethernet. In-hotel: restaurant, room service, pool, gym, parking (fee)* ⊟*AE, D, DC, MC, V.*

$
HOTEL

🔝**Waikīkī Sand Villa.** Families and others looking for an economical rate without sacrificing proximity to Waikīkī's beaches, dining, and shopping return to the Waikīkī Sand Villa year after year. It's on the corner of Kaiulani Avenue and Ala Wai Boulevard, a three-block walk to restaurants and the beach. There's a high-rise tower and a three-story walkup building of studio accommodations with kitchenettes. Rooms are small but well-planned. Corner deluxe units with lānai overlook Ala Wai Canal and the golf course. There's a fitness center with 24-hour access. Complimentary Continental breakfast is served poolside beneath shady coconut trees, and the hotel's Sand Bar comes alive at happy hour with a great mix of hotel guests and locals

LĀNAI

Islanders love their porches, balconies, and verandas—all wrapped up in the single Hawaiian word, "lānai." When booking, ask about the lānai and be sure to specify the view (understanding that top views command top dollars). Also, check that the lānai is not merely a step-out or Juliet balcony, with just enough room to lean against a railing—you want a lānai that is big enough for patio seating.

who like to hang out and "talk story." The Sand Bar also has computers and Web cams, so that you cannot only keep in touch with family by e-mail, you can also taunt them with your developing tan. **Pros:** fun bar, economical choice. **Cons:** the noise from the bar might annoy some, 10-minute walk to the beach. ✉ *2375 Ala Wai Blvd., Waikīkī* 📞 *808/922–4744 or 800/247–1903* 📠 *808/923–2541* ⊕ *www.sandvillahotel.com* 🛏 *214 rooms* 🛎 *In-room: safe, refrigerator, Ethernet. In-hotel: restaurant, bar, pool, parking (fee), no-smoking rooms* ⊟ *AE, D, DC, MC, V.*

HONOLULU BEYOND WAIKĪKĪ

$$$
HOTEL

▣ **Ala Moana Hotel.** Shoppers might wear out their Manolos here; this renovated condo-hotel is connected to O'ahu's biggest mall, the Ala Moana Shopping Center, by a pedestrian ramp, and it's a four-block stroll away from the Victoria Ward Centers. Business travelers can walk one block in the opposite direction to the Hawai'i Convention Center. Swimmers, surfers, and beachgoers make the two-minute walk to Ala Moana Beach Park across the street. Rooms are like small, comfortable apartments, with cherrywood furnishings, kitchenettes, flat-screen TVs, and balconies with outdoor seating. The recreation deck features a pool with cabanas and a bar, outdoor yoga and Pilates studios, and a fitness center. **Pros:** adjacent to Ala Moana shopping center, rooms nicely appointed. **Cons:** lobby feels a bit like an airport, beach across busy Ala Moana Boulevard. ✉ *410 Atkinson Dr., Ala Moana* 📞 *808/955–4811 or 888/367–4811* 📠 *808/944–6839* ⊕ *www.alamoanahotel.com* 🛏 *1,150 studios, 67 suites* 🛎 *In-room: safe, refrigerator, Ethernet. In-hotel: 4 restaurants, room service, bars, pool, gym, parking (fee), no-smoking rooms* ⊟ *AE, DC, MC, V.*

$$$$
HOTEL
Fodor'sChoice
★

▣ **The Kāhala.** Hidden away in the wealthy residential neighborhood of Kāhala (on the other side of Diamond Head from Waikīkī), this elegant oceanfront hotel has played host to both presidents and princesses as one of Hawai'i's very first luxury resorts. The Kāhala is flanked by the exclusive Waialae Golf Links and the Pacific Ocean—surrounding it in a natural tranquility. Pathways meander out along a walkway with

The Kahala

benches tucked into oceanfront nooks for lazy viewing offering an "outer island" experience only 10 minutes from Waikīkī and Honolulu. The expansive oceanfront Chi Fitness Center offers outdoor yoga and Pilates. Fine dining is available at Hokus, or the poolside bar and grill will serve at your lounge chair on the beach. The reef not far from shore makes the waters here calm enough for young kids. You can also sign up for dolphin interactions in the 26,000-square-foot lagoon. The rooms, decorated in an understated Island style with mahogany furniture, are spacious (550 square feet), with bathrooms with two vanities, and lānai big enough for a lounge chair. If you're a golf-lover visiting the second week of January, ask for a room overlooking the course for a bird's-eye view of the PGA Sony Open from your lānai. **Pros:** away from hectic Waikīkī, beautiful rooms and public spaces, heavenly spa. **Cons:** Waikīkī is a drive away. ⊠ *5000 Kāhala Ave., Kāhala* 🕾 *808/739–8888 or 800/367–25285* 🖶 *808/739–8000* ⊕ *www.kahalaresort.com* ⤚ *345 rooms, 33 suites* ⚲ *In-room: safe, refrigerator, Ethernet, dial-up. In-hotel: 5 restaurants, room service, bars, pool, gym, spa, beachfront, bicycles, children's programs (ages 5–12), parking (fee), no-smoking rooms* ☰ *AE, D, DC, MC, V.*

> ## CONDO COMFORTS
>
> **Foodland.** The local chain has two locations near Waikīkī: Market City (⊠ *2839 Harding Ave., near intersection with Kapahulu Ave. and highway overpass, Kaimukī* 🕾 *808/734–6303*) and Ala Moana Center (⊠ *1450 Ala Moana Blvd., ground level, Ala Moana* 🕾 *808/949–5044*). **Food Pantry** sells apparel, beach stuff, and tourist-oriented items ⊠ *2370 Kuhio Ave., across from Miramar hotel, Waikīkī* 🕾 *808/923–9831*). **Blockbuster Video** (⊠ *Ala Moana Shopping Center, 451 Piikoi St., Ala Moana* 🕾 *808/593–2595*). **Pizza Hut** (🕾 *808/643–1111 for delivery statewide*).

WINDWARD O'AHU

$

B&B/INN

🖼 **Ingrid's.** This B&B in the Windward bedroom community of Kailua features a one-bedroom upstairs studio with decor that mimics that of a traditional Japanese inn, with shoji screen doors and black-tile counters. Ingrid is one of the island's most popular hosts, and she has created a space of Zen-like tranquillity in this unit, which also features a kitchenette and deep soaking tub, and has a private entrance. Guests have access to the pool, and Kailua Beach is less than 1 mi away. Three- to four-month advance reservations are advised. **Pros:** in Kailua, one of the most desirable locations on O'ahu. **Cons:** you'll need a car or bike to get to the beach, must reserve months ahead. ⊠ *Pauku St., Kailua* 🖅 *Reservations: Hawai'i's Best Bed and Breakfasts, Box 485, Laupahoehoe 96767* 🕾 *808/962–0100, 800/262–9912 reservations* 🖶 *808/962–6360* ⊕ *www.bestbnb.com* ⤚ *1 2-room unit* ⚲ *In-room: no phone, kitchen, DVD, Ethernet. In-hotel: pool* ☰ *No credit cards.*

NORTH SHORE

¢   ⊞**Backpackers Vacation Inn and Plantation Village.** Laid-back Haleʻiwa
B&B/INN   surfer chic at its best, Backpackers is Spartan in furnishings, rustic in amenities, and definitely very casual in spirit. At Pūpūkea Beach Marine Sanctuary, otherwise known as Three Tables Beach, it's a short stroll to Waimea Bay. This is the place to catch z's between wave sets. Accommodations in this property's 10 buildings include hostel-type dorm rooms, double rooms (some with a double bed, others with two single beds), studios, and cabins. Some have kitchenettes while others have full kitchens. TVs are available in every building and pay phones and barbecues are on the property. It's a three-minute walk to the supermarket. **Pros:** friendly, laid-back staff; prices you won't find anywhere else. **Cons:** many rooms are plainly furnished. ✉ *59-788 Kamehameha Hwy., Haleʻiwa* ☎ *808/638-7838* ⊕ *www.backpackers-hawaii.com* 🖷 *808/638-7515* ➪ *25 rooms* ⚭ *In-room: no a/c, no phones (some), kitchen (some), no TV (some). In-hotel: laundry facilities* ▤ *MC, V.*

$$$$ ⊞**The Turtle Bay Resort.** Some 880 acres of raw natural Hawaiʻi land-
RESORT   scape are your playground at this glamorous resort on Oʻahu's scenic
Fodor'sChoice   North Shore. On the edge of Kuilima Point, the Turtle Bay has spacious
★   guest rooms averaging nearly 500 square feet, with lānai that showcase stunning peninsula views. In winter, when the big waves roll ashore, you get a front-row seat for the powerful surf. The sumptuous oceanfront beach cottages have Brazilian-walnut floors, teak rockers on the lānai, and beds you can sink right into while listening to the sounds of the ocean. Turtle Bay has a Hans Heidemann Surf School, horse stables, a spa, and the only 36-hole golf facility on Oʻahu to keep you busy. There are two swimming pools, one with an 80-foot waterslide. While out exploring Turtle Bay's 12 mi of nature trails, don't be surprised if you suddenly find yourself "Lost." The hit television series has been known to frequent the resort's beaches, coves, and natural forests for location filming. **Pros:** great open, public spaces in a secluded area of Oʻahu. **Cons:** very far from anything else—even Haleʻiwa is a 20-minute drive. ✉ *57-091 Kamehameha Hwy., Box 187, Kahuku* ☎ *808/293-8811 or 800/203-3650* 🖷 *808/293-9147* ⊕ *www.turtlebayresort.com* ➪ *373 rooms, 40 suites, 42 beach cottages, 56 ocean villas* ⚭ *In-room: refrigerator. In-hotel: 4 restaurants, room service, bars, golf courses, tennis courts, pools, gym, spa, beachfront, children's programs (ages 5–12), no-smoking rooms* ▤ *AE, D, DC, MC, V.*

WEST (LEEWARD) OʻAHU

$$$$ ⊞**J. W. Marriott ʻIhilani Resort & Spa.** Forty-five minutes and a world
RESORT   away from the bustle of Waikīkī, this sleek, 17-story resort anchors the still-developing Ko ʻOlina Resort and Marina on Oʻahu's leeward coastline. Honeymooners, NFL Pro Bowlers, and even local residents looking for a Neighbor Island experience without the hassle of catching a flight come to ʻIhilani for first-class R&R. The resort sits on one of Ko ʻOlina's seven lagoons and features a lūʻau cove, tennis garden, wedding chapel, yacht marina, and a Ted Robinson–designed 18-hole championship golf facility. The 650-square-foot rooms here are luxurious,

Turtle Bay Resort

with lulling color schemes; marble bathrooms with deep soaking tubs; spacious private lānai with teak furnishings; and high-tech control systems for lighting and temperature. Most have ocean views. A rental car is pretty much a necessity here. Introduced in 2007, Hawai'i's only allergy-friendly rooms are equipped with tea-tree-oil-infused air purifiers that remove allergens from the room within 15 minutes and with hypoallergenic fabrics, specially treated to reduce contaminants and irritants. Most rooms have views. **Pros:** beautiful property, impeccable service, pool is stunning at night. **Cons:** a bit of a drive from Honolulu, rental car a necessity. ⊠*92-1001 'Ōlani St., Kapolei* ☏*808/679–0079 or 800/626–4446* 🖶*808/679–0080* ⊕*www.ihilani.com* ↘*387 rooms, 36 suites* ⌂*In-room: refrigerator. In-hotel: 4 restaurants, room service, golf course, tennis courts, pools, spa, beachfront, children's programs (ages 5–12), no-smoking rooms* ▭*AE, DC, MC, V.*

$$$$
HOTEL 🔲 **Marriott Ko 'Olina Beach Vacation Club.** If you have your heart set on getting away to O'ahu's western shores, check out the Marriott, which is primarily a vacation-ownership property. This property does offer nightly rental rates for its rooms, which range from hotel-style standard guest rooms to expansive and elegantly appointed one- or two-bedroom guest villa apartments. Interior decor soothes in rich reds, greens, and creamy soft yellows, with furnishings made of rare Hawaiian koa wood. The larger villas (1,240 square feet) have three TVs, full kitchens, and separate living and dining areas. Situated on 30 acres of Ko 'Olina, fronting a lagoon, this resort has two pools (one with sandy-beach bottom), a fitness center, and four outdoor hot tubs, including one overlooking the ocean that's ideal for sunset soaks. Guests can choose from two restaurants on the property or purchase groceries at The Market, on site. **Pros:** suites are beautifully decorated and ample for families, nice views. **Cons:** 40-minute drive to Honolulu, ongoing construction at other properties nearby. ⊠*92-161 Waipahe Pl., Kapolei* ☏*808/679–4900 or 877/229–4484* 🖶*808/679–4910* ⊕*www.marriott vacationclub.com* ↘*200 units* ⌂*In-room: safe, kitchen, DVD, Wi-Fi. In-hotel: 2 restaurants, bar, golf course, tennis courts, pools, gym, beachfront, children's programs (ages 5–12), parking (fee)* ▭*AE, DC, MC, V.*

O'AHU ESSENTIALS

TRANSPORTATION

AIR TRAVEL
Flying time from the West Coast is 4½ to 5 hours and from the East Coast about 10 hours.

CARRIERS Carriers flying into Honolulu from the mainland United States include Alaska, American, Continental, Delta, Hawaiian, Northwest, United, and U.S. Airways.

AIRPORTS More direct flights, both domestic and international, arrive at and depart from Honolulu International Airport (HNL) than at any other airport in Hawai'i. If you have time after you've checked in for your flight home, visit the Pacific Aerospace Museum, open daily, in the main terminal. It includes a 1,700-square-foot, three-dimensional, multimedia theater presenting the history of flight in Hawai'i, and a full-scale space-shuttle flight deck. Hands-on exhibits include a mission-control computer program tracing flights in the Pacific.

Information Honolulu International Airport (HNL) (☎ 808/836–6411 ⊕ www. hawaii.gov).

GROUND TRANSPOR-TATION

Some hotels have their own pickup service. Check when you book accomodations.

There are taxis outside the airport baggage claims. The government-regulated rate is $2.75 at the drop of the flag and $3 for each mile thereafter; the fare to Waikīkī runs approximately $35 to $40, plus $.50 per bag, and tip. If your baggage is oversize, there is an additional charge of $4.60.

Roberts Hawai'i runs an airport shuttle service to and from Waikīkī. The fare is $9 one way, $15 round-trip; paid in cash to your driver. Look for a representative at the baggage claim. Call for return reservations only.

TheBus, the municipal bus, will take you into Waikīkī for $2, but you are allowed only one bag, which must fit on your lap.

Information Roberts Hawai'i (☎ 866/898–2519 ⊕ www.robertshawaii.com). **TheBus** (☎ 808/848–5555 ⊕ www.thebus.org).

BUS TRAVEL

In Waikīkī, in addition to TheBus and the Waikiki Trolley, there also are a number of brightly painted private buses, many of which are free, that will take you to such commercial attractions as dinner cruises, garment factories, and the like.

There are no official bus-route maps, but you can find privately published booklets at most drugstores and other convenience outlets. The important route numbers for Waikīkī are 2, 4, 8, 19, 20, 58, and City Express Route B. If you venture afield, you can always get back on one of these.

The Waikīkī Trolley has four lines and dozens of stops that allow you to design your own itinerary while riding on brass-trimmed, open-air trolleys. The Honolulu City Line (Red Line) travels between Waikīkī and the Bishop Museum and includes stops at Aloha Tower, Ala Moana, and downtown Honolulu, among others. The Ocean Coast Line (Blue Line) provides a tour of O'ahu's southeastern coastline, including Diamond Head Crater, Hanauma Bay, and Sea Life Park. The Blue Line also has an express trolley to Diamond Head which runs twice daily. The Ala Moana Shuttle Line (Pink Line) stops at Ward Warehouse, Ward Centers, and Ala Moana Shopping Center. These trolley lines depart from the DFS Galleria Waikīkī or Hilton Hawaiian Village. The Local Shopping & Dining Line (Yellow Line) starts at Ala Moana Center and stops at Ward Farmers' Market, Ward Warehouse, Ward Centers, and other shops and restaurants. A one-day, four-line ticket costs $25. Four-day tickets, also good for any of the four lines, are $45. You can

2

order online and there are often online specials including a "buy one adult 4-day pass and get a second for free."

Information Waikiki Trolley (☎ 808/591–2561 or 800/824–8804 ⊕ www.waikiki trolley.com).

CAR TRAVEL

Waikīkī is only 2½ mi long and ½ mi wide, which means you can usually walk to where you are going. However, if you plan to venture outside of Waikīkī, a car is essential.

Roads and streets, although perhaps unpronounceable to visitors, are at least well marked. Bear in mind that many streets in Honolulu are one way. Major attractions and scenic spots are marked by the distinctive HVCB sign with its red-caped warrior.

Driving in rush-hour traffic (6:30–8:30 AM and 3:30–5:30 PM) in Honolulu can be exasperating, because left turns are prohibited at many intersections and many roads turn into contra-flow lanes. Parking along many streets is curtailed during these hours. Read the curbside parking signs before leaving your vehicle, even at a meter, to avoid getting towed—enforcement is strict. Remember not to leave valuables in your car. Rental cars are often targets for thieves.

O'ahu's drivers are generally courteous, and you rarely hear a horn. People will slow down and let you into traffic with a wave of the hand. A friendly wave back is customary. If a driver sticks a hand out the window in a fist with the thumb and pinky sticking straight out, this is a good thing: it's the *shaka*, the Hawaiian symbol for "hang loose," and is often used to say "thanks," as well.

Be sure to buckle up. Hawai'i has a strictly enforced seat-belt law for front-seat passengers. Children under four must be in a car seat (available from car-rental agencies). Children 18 and under, riding in the backseat, are also required by state law to use seat belts.

CAR RENTAL During peak seasons—summer, Christmas vacations, and February—reservations are necessary. Rental agencies abound in and around the Honolulu International Airport and in Waikīkī. Alamo, Avis, Budget, Dollar, Enterprise, Hertz, National, and Thrifty rent in O'ahu. *See Travel Smart Hawai'i.*

Local Agencies: AA Aloha Cars R Us (☎ 800/655–7989 ⊕ www.hawaiicarrental. com). **Advantage Rent-A-Car** (☎ 800/777–5500 ⊕ www.tradewindsudrive.com). **Discount Hawai'i Car Rental** (☎ 888/292–3307 ⊕ www.discounthawaiicarrental. com). **JN Car and Truck Rentals** (☎ 808/831–2724 or 800/308–1204 ⊕ www. jnautomotive.com). **VIP** (☎ 808/922–4605 ⊕ www.vipcarrentalhawaii.com).

TAXI TRAVEL

You can usually get a taxi right outside your hotel. Most restaurants will call a taxi for you. Rates are $2.75 at the drop of the flag, plus $3 per mile. Flat fees can be negotiated for many destinations—just ask your driver. Drivers are generally courteous, and the cars are in good condition, many of them air-conditioned.

Information Charley's Taxi & Tours (☎ 808/531–1333). **SIDA of Hawai'i Taxis, Inc.** (☎ 808/836–0011). **The Cab** (☎ 808/422–2222).

CONTACTS AND RESOURCES

EMERGENCIES

To reach the police, fire department, or an ambulance in an emergency, dial **911**.

A doctor, laboratory-radiology technician, and nurses are always on duty at Doctors on Call. Appointments are recommended but not necessary. Dozens of kinds of medical insurance are accepted, including Medicare, Medicaid, and most kinds of travel insurance.

Kūhiō Pharmacy is Waikīkī's only pharmacy and handles prescription requests only until 4:30 PM. Longs Drugs is open evenings at its Ala Moana location and 24 hours at its South King Street location (15 minutes from Waikīkī by car). Pillbox Pharmacy, located in Kaimukī, will deliver prescription medications for a small fee.

Doctors & Dentists Doctors on Call (⊠ *Sheraton Princess Kaiulani Hotel, 120 Kaiulani Ave., Waikīkī* ☎ *808/971–6000*).

General Emergency Contacts Coast Guard Rescue Center (☎ *808/541–2450*).

Hospitals & Clinics Castle Medical Center (⊠ *640 Ulukahiki, Kailua* ☎ *808/263–5500*). **Kapiolani Medical Center for Women and Children** (⊠ *1319 Punahou St., Makiki Heights, Honolulu* ☎ *808/983–6000*). **Queen's Medical Center** (⊠ *1301 Punchbowl St., Downtown Honolulu* ☎ *808/538–9011*). **Saint Francis Medical Center–West** (⊠ *91–2141 Ft. Weaver Rd., 'Ewa Beach* ☎ *808/678–7000*). **Straub Clinic** (⊠ *888 S. King St., Downtown Honolulu, Honolulu* ☎ *808/522–4000*).

Pharmacies Kūhiō Pharmacy (⊠ *Outrigger West Hotel, 2330 Kūhiō Ave., Waikīkī* ☎ *808/923–4466*). **Longs Drugs** (⊠ *Ala Moana Shopping Center, 1450 Ala Moana Blvd., 2nd level, Ala Moana* ☎ *808/949–4010* ⊠ *2220 S. King St., Mō'ili'ili* ☎ *808/947–2651*). **Pillbox Pharmacy** (⊠ *1133 11th Ave., Kaimukī* ☎ *808/ 737–1777*).

VISITOR INFORMATION

Information City & County of Honolulu (☎ *808/523–2489* ⊕ *www.honolulu.gov*). **City & County of Honolulu ocean safety Web site** (⊕ *www.hawaiibeachsafety. org*). **Hawai'i Visitors & Convention Bureau** (⊠ *Waikīkī Business Plaza, 2270 Kalākaua Ave., Suite 801, Honolulu* ☎ *808/923–1811 or 800/464–2924* ⊕ *www. gohawaii.com*). **O'ahu Visitors Bureau** (☎ *877/525–6248* ⊕ *www.visit-oahu. com*). **Surf Report** (☎ *808/973–4383*). **Weather** (☎ *808/973–4381*).

Maui

WORD OF MOUTH

"I'm from Maui, and I find endless beauty every time I visit Hāna. The drive is filled with gorgeous waterfalls, pools, and flowers . . . a feast for the senses. Get up early. Buy fresh banana bread from the roadside stand along the way. `If you appreciate the 'nothing-ness' of tropical island nature—go."

—pupuplatter

WELCOME TO MAUI

TOP REASONS TO GO

★ **The Road to Hāna:** Each curve of this legendary cliff-side road pulls you deeper into the lush green rain forest of Maui's eastern shore.

★ **Haleakalā National Park:** Explore the lava bombs, cinder cones, and silverswords at the gasp-inducing, volcanic summit of Haleakalā, the House of the Sun.

★ **Ho'okipa Beach:** On Maui's North Shore, the world's top windsurfers will dazzle you as they maneuver above the waves like butterflies shot from cannons.

★ **Wai'ānapanapa State Park:** Head to East Maui and take a dip at the stunning black-sand beach or in the cave pool where an ancient princess once hid.

★ **Resorts, Resorts, Resorts:** Opulent gardens, pools, restaurants, and golf courses make Maui's resorts some of the best in the Islands.

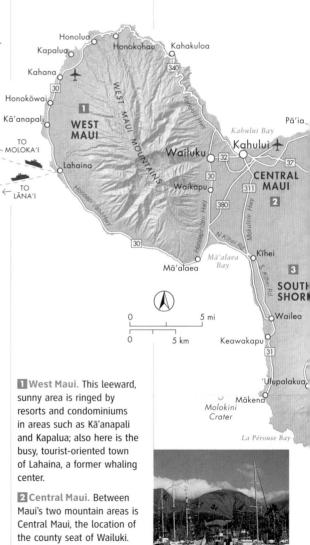

1 West Maui. This leeward, sunny area is ringed by resorts and condominiums in areas such as Kā'anapali and Kapalua; also here is the busy, tourist-oriented town of Lahaina, a former whaling center.

2 Central Maui. Between Maui's two mountain areas is Central Maui, the location of the county seat of Wailuku. Kahului Airport is also here.

3 South Shore. The leeward side of Maui's eastern half is what most people mean when they say South Shore. This popular area is sunny and warm year-round and is home to Wailea, a beautiful resort area.

4 North Shore. The North Shore has no large resorts, just plenty of picturesque small towns like Pā'ia and Ha'ikū—and great surfing action at Ho'okipa Beach.

5 East Maui. The island's northeastern, windward side is largely one great rain forest, traversed by the stunning Road to Hāna. The little town of Hāna itself preserves the slow pace of the past.

6 Upcountry. Island residents affectionately call the regions climbing up the slope of Haleakalā crater Upcountry. This is farm and ranch country.

GETTING ORIENTED

Maui, the second-largest island in the Hawaiian chain, is made up of two distinct circular landmasses. The smaller landmass, on the western part of the island, consists of 5,788-foot Pu'u Kukui and the rain-chiseled West Maui Mountains. The large landmass composing the eastern half of Maui is Haleakalā, with its cloud-wreathed volcanic peak.

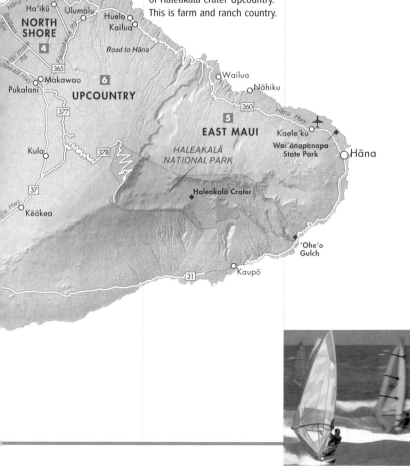

Ho'okipa Beach

Ha'ikū   Ulumalu
Hāna Hwy.   36
Huelo
NORTH   Kailua
SHORE   Road to Hāna
4   365
Makawao   6
Pukalani   UPCOUNTRY   Wailua
377   Nāhiku
Kula   378   360
Hāna Hwy.
37   EAST MAUI   Kaele'kū
HALEAKALĀ   Wai'ānapanapa
NATIONAL PARK   State Park   Hāna
Kēōkea
Haleakalā Crater
'Ohe'o
Gulch
31   Kaupō

MAUI PLANNER

When You Arrive

Most visitors arrive at Kahului Airport in Central Maui. A rental car is the best way to get from the airport to your destination. The major car-rental companies have desks at the airport and can provide a map and directions to your hotel. ■TIP➜ Flights in Maui tend to land around the same time, leading to long lines at car rental windows. If possible, send one person to pick up the car while the others wait for the baggage.

Timing Is Everything

In winter, Maui is *the* spot for whale-watching. The humpback whales start arriving in November, are in full force by February, and are gone by early May. The biggest North Shore waves show up in winter, whereas kiteboarders and windsurfers enjoy the windy, late summer months. Jacarandas shower Upcountry roads in blossoms in spring, and silverswords bloom in summer. In high season—June through August and Christmas through spring break—the island is jam-packed with visitors. The best months for bargain hunters are May, September, and October. ⇨ *See When to Go for weather advice.*

Renting a Car

A rental car is a must on Maui. It's also one of your biggest trip expenses, especially given the price of gasoline—higher on Maui than on O'ahu or the Mainland. ⇨ *See Maui Essentials for details of renting a car and driving.*

If you need to ask for directions, try your best to pronounce the multivowel road names. Locals don't use (or know) highway route numbers. Also, they will give you directions by the time it takes to get somewhere instead of by the mileage.

■TIP➜ Soft-top jeeps are a popular option, but they don't have much space for baggage and it's impossible to lock anything into them. Four-wheel-drive vehicles are the most expensive options and not really necessary.

■TIP➜ Don't be surprised if there is an additional fee for parking at your hotel or resort; parking is not always included in your room rate or resort fee.

■TIP➜ Booking a car-hotel or airfare package can save you money, so always ask if anything is available.

Dining and Lodging on Maui

Hawai'i is a melting pot of cultures, and nowhere is this more apparent than in its cuisines. From lū'au and "plate lunches" to sushi and steak, there's no shortage of interesting flavors and presentations.

Whether you're looking for a quick snack or a multicourse meal, we list the best eating experiences the island has to offer. Jump in, and enjoy!

Choosing vacation lodging is a tough decision, but fret not—our expert writers and editors have done most of the legwork.

To help narrow your choices, consider what type of property you'd like to stay at (big resort, quiet bed-and-breakfast) and what type of island climate you're looking for (beachfront strand or remote rain forest). We give you all the details you need to book a place that suits your style. Quick tips: reserve your room in advance, and ask about discounts, deals, and packages. Hotel Web sites often have Internet-only deals.

Island Hopping

If you have a week or more on Maui, you may want to set aside a day or two for a trip to Moloka'i or Lāna'i. Tour operators such as Trilogy offer day-trip packages to Lāna'i, which include snorkeling and a van tour of the island. Ferries are available to both islands and have room for your golf clubs and mountain bike. (The Moloka'i channel can be rough, so avoid ferry travel on a blustery day.)

If you prefer to travel to Moloka'i or Lāna'i by air, and you're not averse to flying on 4- to 12-seaters, your best bet is a small air taxi. Book with Pacific Wings or Paragon Air (⇨ see Transportation in Maui Essentials) for flights to Hāna, Maui, or Kalaupapa, Moloka'i, as well as the main airports.

If you're considering a visit to Kaua'i, Oahu, or the Big Island, ⇨ see Maui Essentials for your travel options, which include the details of ferry service as well as information about interisland air carriers.

Island Driving Times

Maui may seem like a small island, but driving from one point to another can take longer than the mileage indicates. It's only 52 mi from Kahului Airport to Hāna, but the drive will take you about three hours. As for driving to Haleakalā, the 38-mi drive from sea level to the summit will take you about two hours. The roads are narrow and winding; it's best to go at a slow pace.

Kahului is the transportation hub—the main airport and largest harbor are here. Traffic on Maui's roads can be heavy, especially during the rush hours of 6 to 8:30 AM and 3:30 to 6:30 PM; this will add time to your drive. Here are average driving times to key destinations.

Kahului to Wailea	17 mi/30 min
Kahului to Kā'anapali	25 mi/45 min
Kahului to Kapalua	36 mi/1 hr, 15 min
Kahuli to Wailuku	6 mi/15 min
Kahului to Makawao	13 mi/25 min
Kapalua to Haleakalā	73 mi/3 hr
Kā'anapali to Haleakalā	62 mi/2 hr, 30 min
Wailea to Haleakalā	54 mi/2 hr, 30 min
Kapalua to Hāna	88 mi/5 hr
Kā'anapali to Hāna	77 mi/5 hr
Wailea to Hāna	69 mi/4 hr, 30 min
Wailea to Lahaina	20 mi/45 min
Kā'anapali to Lahaina	4 mi/15 min
Kapalua to Lahaina	12 mi/25 min

Money Savers

Maui has deals these days, and there are ways to travel to Paradise even on a budget.

Accommodations: No matter what the season, ask about deals—a free night after three or four or five paid nights, kids stay free, meal credits. Condos are less expensive and bigger than hotel rooms and are perfect for families or groups of friends. If you pass up the ocean view, you'll save money on your hotel or condo. September, October, and May are off-peak months with many hotels offering reduced rates.

Food: Eat a big breakfast and skip lunch. You'll probably be sightseeing or at the beach anyway. It's easy to get by with a smoothie or fruit and yogurt. If you eat lunch out, go to that high-end restaurant. Lunch will be less expensive. If you're staying in a condo, eat in or pack a picnic as often as you can.

Activities: Pick up free publications at the airport and at racks all over the island; many of them are filled with money-saving coupons; also check newspapers. Activity desks—there are dozens around Kā'anapali and Wailea as well as in Lahaina and Kīhei—are good places to check on deals and discounts if you're not booking in advance. However, advance booking will ensure you get the activity you want; sometimes you can save 10% or more if you book on outfitters' Web sites.

3

1-DAY ITINERARIES

Maui's landscape is incredibly diverse, offering everything from underwater encounters with eagle rays to treks across moon-like terrain. Although daydreaming at the pool or on the beach may fulfill your initial island fantasy, Maui has much more to offer. The following one-day itineraries will take you to our favorite spots on the island.

Beach Day in West Maui. West Maui has some of the island's most beautiful beaches, though many of them are hidden by megaresorts. If you get an early start, you can begin your day snorkeling at Slaughterhouse Beach (in winter, D.T. Fleming Beach is a better option as it's less rough). Then spend the day beach-hopping through Kapalua, Nāpili, and Kā'anapali as you make your way south. You'll want to get to Lahaina before dark so you can spend some time exploring the historic whaling town before choosing a restaurant for a sunset dinner.

Focus on Marine Life on the South Shore. Start your South Shore trip early in the morning, and head out past Mākena into the rough lava fields of rugged La Pérouse Bay. At the road's end, there are areas of the 'Āhihi-Kīna'u Marine Preserve (some are closed at this writing) open to the public which offer good snorkeling. If that's a bit too far afield for you, there's excellent snorkeling at Polo Beach. Head to the right (your right while facing the ocean) for plenty of fish and beautiful coral. Head back north to Kīhei for lunch, and then enjoy the afternoon learning more about Maui's marine life at the outstanding Maui Ocean Center at Mā'alaea.

The Road to Hāna. This cliff-side driving tour through rainforest canopy reveals Maui's most lush and tropical terrain. It will take a full day, especially if you plan to make it all the way to 'Oheo Gulch. You'll pass through communities where old Hawai'i still thrives, and where the forest runs unchecked from the sea to the summit. You'll want to make frequent exploratory stops. To really soak in the magic of this place, consider staying overnight in Hāna town. That way you can spend a full day winding toward Hāna, hiking and exploring along the way, and the next day traveling leisurely back to civilization.

Haleakalā National Park, Upcountry and the North Shore. If you don't plan to spend an entire day hiking in the crater at Haleakalā National Park, this itinerary will at least allow you to take a peek at it. Get up early and head straight for the summit of Haleakalā (if you're jet-lagged and waking up in the middle of the night, you may want to get there in time for sunrise). Bring water, sunscreen, and warm clothing; it's freezing at sunrise. Plan to spend a couple of hours exploring the various lookout points in the park. On your way down the mountain, turn right on Makawao Avenue, and head into the little town of Makawao. You can have lunch here, or make a left on Baldwin Avenue and head downhill to the town of Pā'ia where there are a number of great lunch spots and shops to explore. Spend the rest of your afternoon at Pā'ia's main strip of sand, Ho'okipa Beach.

3

"Maui nō ka 'oi" is what locals say—it's the best, the most, the top of the heap. To those who know Maui well, there's good reason for the superlatives. The island's miles of perfect-tan beaches, lush green valleys, historic villages, top-notch windsurfing and diving, stellar restaurants and high-end hotels, and variety of art and cultural activities have made it an international favorite. Combining the best of both old and new Hawai'i, Maui weaves a spell over the more than 2.5 million people who visit its shores each year, and many decide to return for good.

At 729 square miles, Maui is the second-largest Hawaiian island, but offers more miles of swimmable beaches than any of the other islands. Despite growth over the past few decades, the local population is still fairly small, totaling only 119,000.

GEOLOGY

Maui is made up of two volcanoes, one now extinct and the other dormant, that erupted long ago and joined into one island. The resulting depression between the two is what gives the island its nickname, the Valley Isle. West Maui's 5,788-foot Pu'u Kukui was the first volcano to form, a distinction that gives that area's mountainous topography a more weathered look. Rainbows seem to grow wild over this terrain as gentle mists fill the deeply eroded canyons. The Valley Isle's second volcano is the 10,023-foot Haleakalā, where desert-like terrain butts up against tropical forests.

FLORA AND FAUNA

Haleakalā is one of few homes to the rare *'ahinahina* (silversword plant). The plant's brilliant silver leaves are stunning against the red lava rock that blankets the walls of Haleakalā's caldera—particularly during blooming season from July to September. A distant cousin of the sunflower, the silversword blooms just once before it dies—producing a single towering stalk awash in tiny fragrant blossoms. Also calling Haleakalā home are a few hundred *nēnē*—the Hawaiian state bird (related to the Canada goose), currently fighting its way back from near extinction. Maui is one of the better islands for whale-watching, and migrating humpbacks can be seen off the island's coast from December to April, and sometimes into May.

HISTORY

Maui's history is full of firsts—Lahaina was the first capital of Hawai'i and the first destination of the whaling industry (early 1800s), which explains why the town still has that fishing-village vibe; Lahaina was also the first stop for missionaries (1823). Although they suppressed aspects of Hawaiian culture, the missionaries did help invent the

Hawaiian alphabet and built a printing press in Lahaina (the first west of the Rockies), which rolled out the news in Hawaiian. Maui also boasts the first sugar plantation in Hawai'i (1849) and the first Hawaiian luxury resort (Hotel Hāna-Maui, 1946).

ON MAUI TODAY

In the mid-1970s, savvy marketers saw a way to improve Maui's economy by promoting the Valley Isle to golfers and luxury travelers. The ploy worked all too well; Maui's visitor count continues to swell. Impatient traffic now threatens to overtake the ubiquitous aloha spirit, development encroaches on agricultural lands, and county planners struggle to meet the needs of a burgeoning population. But Maui is still carpeted with an eyeful of green, and for every tailgater, there's a carefree local on "Maui time" who stops for each pedestrian, whale spout, and sunset.

EXPLORING MAUI

Updated by Bonnie Friedman

Maui is more than a sandy beach with palm trees. The natural bounty of this place is impressive. Pu'u Kukui, the 5,788-foot interior of the West Maui Mountains, is one of the earth's wettest spots—annual rainfall of 400 inches has sculpted the land into impassable gorges and razor-sharp ridges. On the opposite side of the island, the blistering lava fields at 'Āhihi-Kīna'u receive scant rain. And just above this desert, *paniolo* (Hawaiian cowboys) herd cattle on rolling, fertile ranchlands reminiscent of northern California. On the island's rugged east side is the lush, tropical Hawai'i of travel posters.

But nature isn't all Maui has to offer—it's also home to a rich and vivid culture. In small towns like Pā'ia and Hāna you can see remnants of the past mingling with modern-day life. Ancient *heiau* (Hawaiian stone platforms once used as places of worship) line busy roadways. Old coral and brick missionary homes now house broadcasting networks. The antique smokestacks of sugar mills tower above communities where the children blend English, Hawaiian, Japanese, Chinese, Portuguese, Filipino, and more into one colorful language. Hawai'i is a melting pot like no other. Visiting an eclectic mom-and-pop shop (like Komoda Store & Bakery) can feel like stepping into another country, or back in time. The more you look here, the more you will find.

WEST MAUI

Separated from the remainder of the island by steep *pali* (cliffs), West Maui has a reputation for attitude and action. Once upon a time, this was the haunt of whalers, missionaries, and the kings and queens of Hawai'i. Anchored by the entertaining old whaling town of Lahaina, West Maui was the focus of development when Maui set out to become a premier tourist destination in the 1960s; it has succeeded. Today, crowds stroll bustling Front Street in Lahaina, beating the heat with ice cream or shave ice, while pleasure-seekers indulge in golf, shopping, and white-sand beaches in the Kā'anapali and Kapalua resort areas to the north. Friday night is Art Night in Lahaina; galleries stay open late, making for a fun evening.

TOP ATTRACTIONS

5 **Baldwin Home Museum.** Begun in 1834 and completed the following year, the coral and stone house was originally home to missionary and doctor Dwight Baldwin and his family. The building has been carefully restored to reflect the period; many of the original furnishings remain. You can view the family's grand piano, the carved four-poster bed, and most interestingly, Dr. Baldwin's dispensary. During a brief tour conducted by Lahaina Restoration Foundation volunteers, you'll be shown the "thunderpot" and told how the doctor single-handedly inoculated 10,000 Maui residents for smallpox. ⊠ *696 Front St., Lahaina* ☎ *808/661–3262* ⊕ *www.lahainarestoration.org* ⊠ *$3* ⊙ *Daily 10–4.*

7 **Banyan Tree.** This massive tree was planted in 1873. It's the largest of its kind in the state and provides a welcome retreat for the weary who come to sit under its awesome branches. The Banyan Tree is a terrific spot to be when the sun sets—mynah birds settle in here for a screeching symphony, which can be an event in itself. The tree also plays host to day-long arts and crafts fairs during the weekends. ■ **TIP**➜ **The Banyan Tree is a popular and hard-to-miss meeting place if your party splits up for independent exploring.** ⊠ *Front St., between Hotel and Canal Sts., Lahaina.*

8 **Hale Pa'ahao (Old Prison).** Lahaina's jailhouse dates to rowdy whaling days. Its name literally means "stuck-in-irons house," referring to the wall shackles and ball-and-chain restraints. The compound was built in the 1850s by convict laborers out of blocks of coral that had been salvaged from the demolished waterfront fort. Most prisoners were sent here for desertion, drunkenness, or reckless horse riding. Today, a wax figure representing an imprisoned old sailor tells his recorded tale of woe. ⊠ *Waine'e and Prison Sts., Lahaina* ⊠ *Free* ⊙ *Weekdays 10–4.*

Kā'anapali. In ancient times, this area was known for its bountiful fishing (especially lobster) and its seaside cliffs. Pu'u Keka'a, today referred to as "Black Rock," was a lele, a place in ancient Hawai'i from which souls leaped into the afterlife. But times changed and the sleepy fishing village was washed away by the wave of Hawai'i's new economy: tourism. Clever marketers built this sunny shoreline into a playground for the world's vacationers. The theatrical look of Hawai'i tourism—planned resort communities where luxury homes mix with high-rise hotels, fantasy swimming pools, and a theme-park landscape—all began right here in the 1960s. Three miles of uninterrupted white sand beach and placid water form the front yard for this artificial utopia, with its 40 tennis courts and two championship golf courses. The six major hotels here are all worth visiting just for a look around, especially the Hyatt Regency Maui, which has a multimillion-dollar art collection and plenty of exotic birds in the lobby. ⊠ *2435 Kā'anapali Pkwy., Kā'anapali.*

Kahakuloa. Untouched by progress, this tiny village is a relic of pre–jet travel Maui. Remote villages similar to Kahakuloa used to be tucked away in several valleys of this area. Many residents still grow taro and live in the old Hawaiian way. This is the wild side of West Maui. The unimproved road weaves along coastal cliffs. Watch out for stray cattle, roosters, and falling rocks. True adventurers will find terrific snorkeling and swimming along this coast, as well as some

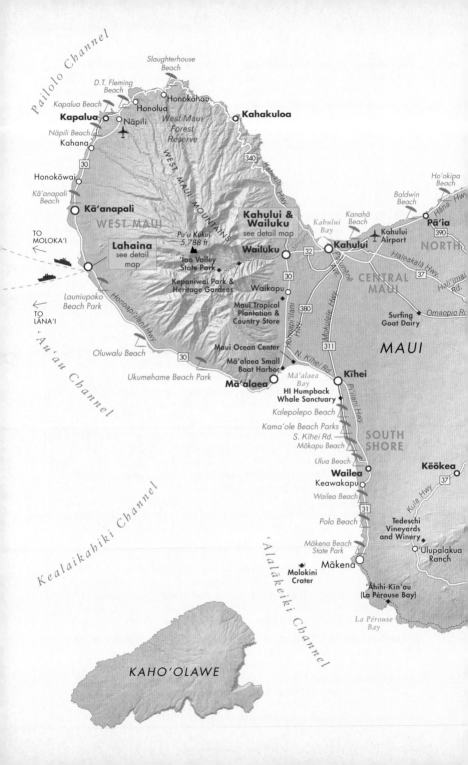

good hiking trails. ⊠*North end of Honoapi'ilani Hwy.*

Kapalua. Beautiful and secluded, Kapalua is West Maui's northernmost resort community. The area got its first big boost in 1978, when the Maui Land & Pineapple Company (ML&P) built the luxurious Kapalua Bay Hotel. ML&P owns the entire area known as "Kapalua Resort," which includes the Ritz-Carlton, three golf courses, and the surrounding fields of Maui Gold pineapple. The quaint Kapalua Bay Hotel has been replaced by extremely upscale residences with a spa and a golf club. The area's shopping and freestanding restaurants cater to dedicated golfers, celebrities who want to be left alone, and some of the world's richest folks. Mists regularly envelop Kapalua, which is cooler and quieter than its southern neighbors. The landscape of tall Cook pines and rolling fairways is reminiscent of Lāna'i, and the beaches and dining are among Maui's finest. ⊠*Bay Dr., Kapalua.*

> **WALKING TOURS**
>
> Lahaina's fascinating side streets are best explored on foot. Both the Baldwin Home and the Lahaina Court House offer free self-guided walking-tour brochures and maps. The Court House booklet is often recommended and includes more than 50 sites. The Baldwin Home brochure is less well known but, in our opinion, easier to follow. It details a short but enjoyable loop tour of the town.

NEED A BREAK? In contrast to Kapalua's high-end glitz, the old **Honolua Store,** just above the Ritz-Carlton, still plies the groceries, fishnets, and household wares it did in plantation times. Hefty plate lunches, served at the deli until 2:30 PM, are popular with locals. ⊠*504 Office Rd., Kapalua* 📞*808/669–6128* ☽*Daily 6 AM–8 PM.*

❻ **Lahaina Court House.** The Lahaina Town Action Committee and Lahaina Heritage Museum occupy this charming old government building in the center of town. Pump the knowledgeable staff for interesting trivia and ask for their walking-tour brochure, a comprehensive map to historic Lahaina sites. Erected in 1859 and restored in 1999, the building has served as a customs and court house, governor's office, post office, vault and collector's office, and police court. On August 12, 1898, its postmaster witnessed the lowering of the Hawaiian flag when Hawai'i became a U.S. territory. The flag now hangs above the stairway. You'll find terrific museum displays, the active Lahaina Arts Society, and an art gallery. ■TIP➜There's also a public restroom. ⊠*649 Wharf St., Lahaina* 📞*808/661–0111* 🖅*Free* ☽*Daily 9–5.*

❿ **Waiola Church and Waine'e Cemetery.** Better known as Waine'e Church and immortalized in James Michener's *Hawai'i,* the original building ★ from the early 1800s was destroyed once by fire and twice by fierce windstorms. Repositioned and rebuilt in 1951, it was renamed Waiola ("water of life") and has been standing proudly every since. The adjacent cemetery was the first Christian cemetery in the Islands and is the final resting place of many of Hawai'i's most important monarchs, including Kamehameha the Great's sacred wife, Queen Keōpūolani. ⊠*535 Waine'e St., Lahaina* 📞*808/661–4349.*

Whalers Village. While the kids hit Honolua Surf Company, mom can peruse Louis Vuitton, Coach, and several fine jewelry stores at this casual, classy mall fronting Kā'anapali Beach. Pizza and Häagen-Dazs ice cream are available in the center courtyard. At the beach entrance, you'll find a wonderful restaurant, Hula Grill. ✉ *2435 Kā'anapali Pkwy.* ☎ *808/661–4567* ⊕ *www.whalersvillage.com.*

❸ ★ Wo Hing Museum. Smack-dab in the center of Front Street, this eye-catching Chinese temple reflects the importance of early Chinese immigrants to Lahaina. Built by the Wo Hing Society in 1912, the museum now contains beautiful artifacts, historic photos of old Lahaina, and a Taoist altar. Don't miss the films playing in the rustic theater next door—some of Thomas Edison's first films, shot in Hawai'i circa 1898, show Hawaiian wranglers herding steer onto ships. Ask the docent for some star fruit from the tree outside, for the altar or for yourself. ✉ *858 Front St., Lahaina* ☎ *808/661–5553* ☞ *$1* ⊙ *Daily 10–4.*

WORTH NOTING

❹ Hale Pa'i. Protestant missionaries established Lahainaluna Seminary as a center of learning and enlightenment in 1831. Six years later, they built this printing shop. Here at the press, they and their young Hawaiian scholars created a written Hawaiian language and used it to produce a Bible, history texts, and a newspaper. An exhibit displays a replica of the original Rampage press and facsimiles of early printing. The oldest U.S. educational institution west of the Rockies, the seminary now serves as Lahaina's public high school. ✉ *980 Lahainaluna Rd., Lahaina* ☎ *808/661–3262* ☞ *Donations accepted* ⊙ *Weekdays 10–4.*

❾ Holy Innocents' Episcopal Church. Built in 1927, this beautiful open-air church is decorated with paintings depicting Hawaiian versions of Christian symbols, including a Hawaiian Madonna and child, rare or extinct birds, and native plants. The congregation is beautiful also, typically dressed in traditional clothing from Samoa and Tonga. Anyone is welcome to slip into one of the pews, carved from native woods. Queen Liliu'okalani, Hawai'i's last reigning monarch, lived in a large grass house on this site as a child. ✉ *South end of Front St. near Mokuhina St., Lahaina.*

❶ Jodo Mission. This mission, established at the turn of the century by Japanese contract workers, is one of Lahaina's most popular sites, thanks to its idyllic setting and spectacular views across the channel. Although the buildings are not open to the public, you can stroll all of the grounds and enjoy glimpses of the 90-foot-high pagoda, as well as a great, 3½-ton copper and bronze statue of the Amida Buddha. It's a relaxing and contemplative spot just outside the tumult of Lahaina

WORD OF MOUTH

"West Maui may appeal to some visitors, but it has no worthy beach; it's famous for kitsch, trinkets, a lū'au, and a banyan tree." —Lex1

"Lahaina IS busy! That's what I like about it. It has a very 'honky-tonk,' end-of-the-line feel about it. It's historically interesting, and I love that I can walk everywhere. I like all the shops, galleries, historic walking tour, restaurants, and bars." —suze

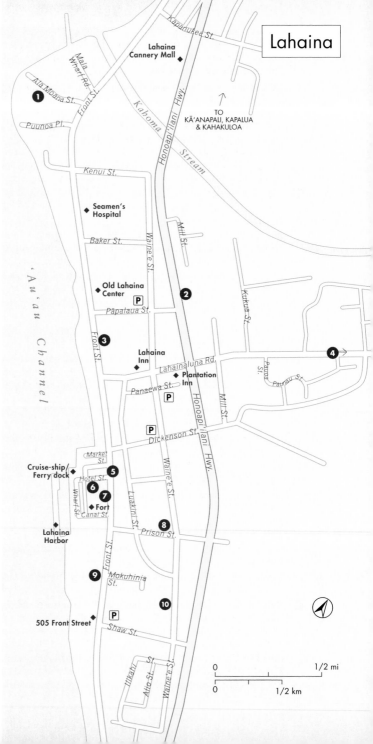

Lahaina

Town. If you're nearby at 8 PM any evening, listen for the temple bell to toll 11 times; each peal has a specific significance. ✉ *12 Ala Moana St., just before the Lahaina Cannery Mall Lahaina* ☎*808/661–4304* ⊕*www.lahainajodomission.org* ✉*Free.*

Lahaina Harbor. For centuries, Lahaina has drawn ships of all sizes to its calm harbor. King Kamehameha's conquering fleet of 800 carved *koa* canoes gave way to Chinese trading ships, Boston whalers, U.S. navy frigates, and finally, a slew of cruise ships, catamarans, and deep-sea fishing operators. During WWII, "a white tide" of navy seamen flooded the town. Stroll past the various tour boats, to see who's had the best luck fishing. If they're filleting their catch, you might glimpse eagle rays underwater snapping up the trimmings. ✉ *Wharf St., Lahaina* ✉*Free.*

➋ **Lahaina–Kāʻanapali & Pacific Railroad.** Affectionately called the Sugarcane ♻ Train, this is Maui's only passenger train. It's an 1890s-vintage railway that once shuttled sugar but now moves sightseers between Kāʻanapali and Lahaina. This quaint attraction with its singing conductor is a big deal for Hawaiʻi but probably not much of a thrill for those more accustomed to trains (though children like it no matter where they grew up). ✉ *1½ blocks north of Lahainaluna Rd. stoplight, at Hinau St., on Honoapiʻilani Hwy., Lahaina* ☎*808/661–0080* ⊕*www.sugar canetrain.com* ✉*Round-trip $22.50 adult; $15.50 child 3–12* ☉*Daily 10:15–4.*

THE SOUTH SHORE

Blessed by more than its fair share of sun, the southern shore of Haleakalā was an undeveloped wilderness until the 1970s. Then the sun-worshippers found it; now restaurants, condos, and luxury resorts line the coast from the world-class aquarium at Māʻalaea Harbor, through working-class Kīhei, to lovely Wailea, a resort community rivaling those on West Maui. Farther south, the road disappears and unspoiled wilderness still has its way.

Because the South Shore includes so many fine beach choices, a trip here (if you're staying elsewhere on the island) is an all-day excursion—especially if you include a visit to the aquarium. Get active in the morning with exploring and snorkeling, then shower in a beach park, dress up a little, and enjoy the cool luxury of the Wailea resorts. At sunset, settle in for dinner at one of the area's many fine restaurants.

TOP ATTRACTIONS

Kīhei. Thirty years ago, Kīhei was a dusty, dry non-destination. Now about one-third of the Maui population lives here in one of the fastest-growing towns in America. Development is still under way: a greenway for bikers and pedestrians is under construction, as is a multitude of new homes and properties. Traffic lights and mini-malls may not fit your notion of paradise, but Kīhei offers dependably warm sun, excellent beaches, and a front-row seat to marine life of all sorts. The county beach parks such as Kamaʻole I, II, and III have lawns, showers, and picnic tables. ■TIP→Remember: beach park or no beach park, the public has a right to the entire coastal strand but not to cross private property to get to it. Besides all the sun and sand, the town's relatively inexpensive condos and excellent restaurants make this a home base for many Maui visitors.

Mākena Beach State Park. Although it's commonly known as "Big Beach," its correct name is Oneloa ("long sand"), and that's exactly what it is—a huge stretch of heavenly golden sand without a house or hotel in sight. More than a decade ago, Maui citizens campaigned successfully to preserve this beloved beach from development. It's still wild, lacking in modern amenities (such as plumbing) but frequented by dolphins, turtles, and glorious sunsets. At the end of the beach farthest from Wailea, skim-boarders catch air. On the opposite end rises the beautiful hill called Pu'u Ōla'i, a perfect cinder cone. A climb over the steep rocks at this end leads to "Little Beach," which, although technically illegal, is clothing-optional. On Sundays, it's a mecca for drummers and island gypsies. On any day of the week watch out for the mean shore break—those crisp, aquamarine waves are responsible for more than one broken arm.

Maui Ocean Center. You'll feel as though you're walking from the seashore down to the bottom of the reef, and then through an acrylic tunnel in the middle of the sea at this aquarium, which focuses on Hawai'i and the Pacific. Special tanks get you close up with turtles, rays, sharks, and the unusual creatures of the tide pools. The center is part of a growing complex of retail shops and restaurants overlooking the harbor. ⊠ *Enter from Honoapi'ilani Hwy., Rte. 30, as it curves past Mā'alaea Harbor, Mā'alaea* ☎ *808/270–7000* ⊕ *www.mauioceancenter. com* ⊠ *$25 adults, $18 children 3–12* ☉ *Daily 9–5.*

Fodor'sChoice
★

Wailea. Wailea, the South Shore's resort community, is slightly quieter and drier than its West Side sister, Kā'anapali. The first two resorts were built here in the late 1970s. Soon a cluster of upscale properties sprung up, including the Four Seasons and the Fairmont Kea Lani. Check out the Grand Wailea Resort's chapel, which tells a Hawaiian love story in stained glass. The luxury of the resorts (edging on the excessive) and the simple grandeur of the coastal views make the otherwise stark landscape an outstanding destination. A handful of perfect little beaches, all with public access, front the resorts.

WORTH NOTING

'Āhihi-Kīna'u (La Pérouse Bay). Beyond Mākena Beach, the road fades away into a vast territory of black-lava flows, the result of Haleakalā's last eruption. Also known as La Pérouse Bay, this is where Maui received its first official visit by a European explorer—the French admiral Jean-François de Galaup, Comte de La Pérouse, in 1786. Before it ends, the

3

road passes through the 'Ahihi-Kīna'u Marine Preserve, an excellent place for morning snorkel adventures (*see Water Sports and Tours later in this chapter*). However, visitors should note that until August 2010 at the earliest, most of the area will be closed to the public, including unofficial trails to Kalua o Lapa, Kalaeloa (popularly known as "the Aquarium"), and Mokuha (also known as "the Fishbowl"). Access to northern portions of the reserve most used by the public will remain open during visiting hours. Some of these open areas are Waiala Cove and the coastal area along 'Ahihi Bay including the "Dumps" surf break. This is also the start of the Hoapili Trail, or "the King's Trail," where you can hike through the remains of one of Maui's ancient villages. For more information, you can visit the State Department of Land and Resources Web site at ⊕*hawaii.gov/dlnr*. ∎ TIP➔**Bring water and a hat, as there is little shade and no public facilities, and tread carefully over this culturally important landscape.**

★ **Coastal Nature Trail.** A paved beach walk allows you to stroll among Wailea's prettiest properties, restaurants, and rocky coves. The trail teems with joggers in the morning hours. The *makai*, or ocean, side is landscaped with exceptionally rare native plants. Look for the silvery *hinahina*, named after the Hawaiian moon goddess because of its color. In winter this is a great place to watch whales. ⊠*Accessible from Polo or Wailea Beach parks.*

ⵢ **Hawaiian Island Humpback Whale Sanctuary.** The sanctuary itself includes virtually all the waters surrounding the archipelago; the Education Center is located beside a restored ancient Hawaiian fishpond, in prime humpback-viewing territory. Whether the whales are here or not, the center is a great stop for youngsters curious to know how things work underwater. Interactive displays and informative naturalists will explain it all. Throughout the year, the center hosts intriguing activities, ranging from moonlight tidal-pool explorations to "Two Ton Talks." ⊠726 S. Kīhei Rd., Kīhei ☎808/879–2818 or 800/831–4888 ⊕*www.hawaii humpbackwhale.noaa.gov* ☞*Free* ⊗*Daily 10–3.*

ⵢ **Kealia Pond National Wildlife Reserve.** Long-legged stilts casually dip their beaks in the shallow waters of this Wildlife Reserve as traffic shuttles by. If you take time to read the interpretive signs on the new boardwalk, you'll learn that endangered hawksbill turtles return to the sandy dunes here year after year. Sharp-eyed birders may catch sight of occasional migratory visitors, such as a falcon or osprey. ⊠N. Kīhei Rd., Kīhei ☞*Free.*

Mā'alaea Small Boat Harbor. With only 89 slips and so many good reasons to take people out on the water, this active little harbor needs to be expanded. The Army Corps of Engineers has a plan to do so, but harbor users are fighting it—particularly the surfers, who say the plan would destroy their surf breaks. In fact, the surf here is world-renowned. The elusive spot to the left of the harbor called "freight train" rarely breaks, but when it does, it's said to be the fastest anywhere. ⊠Off Honoapi'ilani Hwy., Rte. 30.

Shops at Wailea. Louis Vuitton, Tiffany & Co., and the sumptuous Cos Bar lure shoppers to this elegant mall. Honolulu Coffee brews perfect shots of espresso to fuel those "shop-'til-you-drop" types. The kids can buy logo shirts in Pacific Sun while mom and dad ponder vacation ownership upstairs. Tommy Bahama's, Ruth's Chris, and Longhi's are all good dining options. ✉*3750 Wailea Alanui Dr.* ☎*808/891–6770* ⊕*www.shopsatwailea.com.*

CENTRAL MAUI

Kahului, where you most likely landed when you arrived on Maui, is the industrial and commercial center of the island. The area was developed in the early 1950s to meet the housing needs of the large sugarcane interests here, specifically those of Alexander & Baldwin. The company was tired of playing landlord to its many plantation workers and sold land to a developer who promised to create affordable housing. The scheme worked, and "Dream City," the first planned city in Hawai'i, was born.

West of Kahului, Wailuku, the county seat since 1950, is the most charming town in Central Maui—though it wasn't always so. Its name means "Water of Destruction," after the fateful battle in 'Īao Valley that pitted King Kamehameha the Great against Maui warriors. Wailuku was a politically important town until the sugar industry began to decline in the 1960s and tourism took hold. Businesses left the cradle of the West Maui Mountains and followed the new market to the shore, where tourists arrived by the boatload. Wailuku still houses the county government, but has the feel of a town that's been asleep for several decades. The interesting shops and offices now inhabiting Main Street's plantation-style buildings serve as reminders of a bygone era.

You can explore Central Maui comfortably in little more than a half day. These are good sights to squeeze in on the way to the airport, or if you want to combine sightseeing with shopping. Hikers may want to expand their outing to a full day to explore 'Īao Valley State Park.

TOP ATTRACTIONS

❸ **Bailey House.** This repository of the largest and best collection of
★ Hawaiian artifacts on Maui—including objects from the sacred island of Kaho'olawe—was first the Wailuku Seminary for Girls and then the home of missionary teachers Edward and Caroline Bailey. Built in 1833 on the site of the compound of Kahekili (the last ruling chief of Maui), the building was occupied by the Bailey family until 1888. Edward Bailey was something of a renaissance man: beyond being a missionary, he was also a surveyor, a naturalist, and an excellent artist. In addition to the fantastic Hawaiian collection, the museum displays a number of Bailey's landscape paintings, which provide a snapshot of the island during his time. There is missionary-period furniture, and the grounds include gardens with native Hawaiian plants and a fine example of a traditional canoe. The gift shop is one of the best sources on Maui for items that are actually made in Hawai'i. ✉*2375A Main St., Wailuku* ☎*808/244–3326* ⊕*www.mauimuseum.org* 💲*$5* ⊘*Mon.–Sat. 10–4.*

❷ **'Īao Valley State Park.** When Mark Twain saw this park, he dubbed it the
Fodor'sChoice Yosemite of the Pacific. Yosemite it's not, but it is a lovely deep valley
★

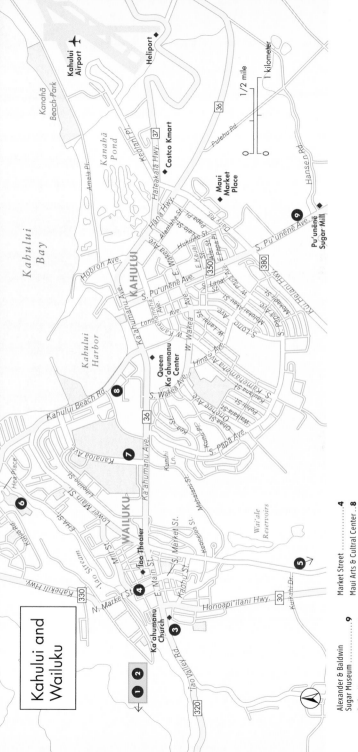

Kahului and Wailuku

Kahului Bay

Kanahā Beach Park

Kanahā Pond

Kahului Airport ✈

Heliport ◆

Kahului Harbor

Hobron Ave.

Amala Pl.

Keolani Pl.

Costco ◆ **Kmart** 37

Haleakalā Hwy. 36

Maui ◆ **Market Place**

Puʻunene **◆** 9 **Sugar Mill**

S. Puʻunene Ave.

Hansen Rd.

Pulehu Rd.

0 ──── 1/2 mile
0 ──── 1 kilometer

Hana Hwy.

E. Wakea Ave.

Kaʻahumanu Ave.

Alamaha St.

Kele St.

Hukilike St.

Papa Rd.

Dairy Rd.

E. Kauai St.

E. Lono Ave.

E. Papa Ave.

KAHULUI

S. Puʻunene Ave.

Lono Ave.

Lonohema Ave.

W. Kamehameha Ave.

S. Kamehameha Ave.

350 Alae St.

S. Lanai St.

W. Lanai St.

S. Lani St.

W. Lani St.

Moanalani St.

Npoanalaau St.

S. Papa Ave.

S. Lono Ave.

Moniwai St.

Kuihelani Hwy. 380

Queen ◆ **Kaʻahumanu Center**

S. Wakea Ave.

Kahului Beach Rd.

8

Kanaloa Ave.

7

Hina Ave.

S. Onehee Ave.

Papa Ave.

S. Kane St.

Kahili Ln.

Kulana Pl.

Onaehe Ave.

Ōnae St.

Kaiau Pl.

Hoomaha St.

Kapela St.

Wailana St.

Penu St.

Mahaolu St.

Kamehameha Ave.

Kea St.

Waiale Reservoirs

WAILUKU 36

Tao Theater ◆

E. Main St.

S. Market St.

S. High St.

Kaohu St.

Kaʻahumanu Ave.

Lower Main St.

Mill St.

Iao Stream

N. Market St.

330 Kahekili Hwy.

Hea Place

6

Eha St.

Kahili Rd.

Kaʻahumanu ◆ **Church**

3

320 Tao Valley Rd.

Honoapiʻilani Hwy.

Kuihati Dr.

30

5

with the curious 'Īao Needle, a spire that rises more than 2,000 feet from the valley floor. You can take an easy walk from the parking lot across 'Īao Stream and explore the thick, junglelike topography. This park has short, paved paths, where you can stop and meditate by the edge of a stream or marvel at the native plants and flowers (*see Golf, Hiking, and Outdoor Activities later in this chapter*). Locals come to jump from the rocks or bridge into the stream—this isn't recommended. Mist often rises if there has been a rain, which makes being here even more magical. ⊠ *Western end of Rte. 32* ⌂ *Free* ☉ *Daily 7–7.*

❶ Kepaniwai Park & Heritage Gardens. This county park is a memorial to Maui's cultural roots, with picnic facilities and ethnic displays dotting the landscape. Among the displays are an early-Hawaiian shack, a New England–style saltbox, a Portuguese-style villa with gardens, and dwellings from such other cultures as China and the Philippines. Next door, the Hawai'i Nature Center has an interactive exhibit and hikes good for children.

The peacefulness here belies the history of the area. During his quest for domination, King Kamehameha the Great brought his troops from the Big Island of Hawai'i to the Valley Isle in 1790 and waged a successful and particularly bloody battle against the son of Maui's chief, Kahekili, near Kepaniwai Park. An earlier battle at the site had pitted Kahekili himself against an older Big Island chief, Kalani'ōpu'u. Kahekili prevailed, but the carnage was so great that the nearby stream became known as Wailuku (water of destruction) and the place where fallen warriors choked the stream's flow was called Kepaniwai (the water dam). ⊠ *'Īao Valley Rd., Wailuku* ⌂ *Free* ☉ *Daily 7–7.*

❹ Market Street. An idiosyncratic assortment of shops makes Wailuku's Market Street (affectionately known as "Antiques Row") a delightful place for a stroll. Brown-Kobayashi and the Bird of Paradise Unique Antiques are the best for carry interesting collectibles and furnishings. Cafe Marc Aurel started out as a great espresso spot and has expanded to become a popular gathering place serving food and offering an excellent wine list. ⊠ *Wailuku 96793.*

WORTH NOTING

❾ Alexander & Baldwin Sugar Museum. "A&B," Maui's largest landowner, was one of the "Big Five" companies that spearheaded the planting, harvesting, and processing of sugarcane. Although Hawaiian cane sugar is now being supplanted by cheaper foreign versions—as well as by sugar derived from inexpensive sugar beets—the crop was for many years the mainstay of the Hawaiian economy. You can find the museum in a small, restored plantation manager's house next to the post office and the still-operating sugar refinery (black smoke billows up when cane is burning). Historic photos, artifacts, and documents explain the introduction of sugarcane to Hawai'i and how plantation managers brought in laborers from other countries, thereby changing the Islands' ethnic mix. Exhibits also describe the sugar-making process. ⊠ *3957 Hansen Rd., Pu'unēnē* ☎ *808/871–8058* ⌂ *$5* ☉ *Mon.–Sat. 9:30–4:30; last admission at 4.*

❻ Haleki'i-Pihana Heiau State Monument. Stand here at either of the two *heiau* and imagine the king of Maui surveying his domain. That's what

MAUI SIGHTSEEING TOURS

Maui is really too big to see all in one day, so tour companies offer specialized tours, visiting either Haleakalā or Hāna and its environs. A tour of Haleakalā and Upcountry is usually a half-day excursion and is offered in several versions by different companies for about $60 and up. The trip often includes stops at a protea farm and at Tedeschi Vineyards, Maui's only winery.

A Haleakalā sunrise tour starts before dawn so that you can get to the top of the dormant volcano before the sun peeks over the horizon. Because they offer island-wide hotel pickup, many sunrise trips leave around 2:30 AM.

A tour of Hāna is almost always done in a van, since the winding Road to Hāna just isn't built for bigger buses. Of late, Hāna has so many of these one-day tours that it seems as if there are more vans than cars on the road. Still, to many it's a more relaxing way to do the drive than behind the wheel of a car. Guides decide where you stop for photos. Tours run from $80 to $120.

The key is to ask how many stops you get and how many other passengers will be on board—otherwise you could end up on a packed bus, sightseeing through a window.

Most of the tour guides have been in the business for years and some have taken special classes to learn more about the culture and lore. They expect a tip ($1 per person at least), but they're just as cordial without one.

Maui Pineapple Plantation Tour. Explore one of Maui's pineapple plantations by going right into the fields in a company van. The 2¼-hour, $39.95 trip gives you firsthand experience of the operation and its history, some incredible views of the island, and the chance to pick a fresh pineapple for yourself. Two tours depart each weekday morning from the Kapalua Logo Shop. Reservations are required. ✉ *Maui Gold, Kapalua* ☎ *808/665–5491.*

Polynesian Adventure Tours. This company uses large buses with floor-to-ceiling windows. The drivers are fun and really know the island. ☎ *808/877–4242 or 800/622–3011* ⊕ *www.polyad.com.*

Roberts Hawai'i Tours. This is one of the state's largest tour companies, and its staff can arrange tours with bilingual guides if asked ahead of time. Eleven-hour trips venture out to Kaupo, the wild area past Hāna. ☎ *808/871–6226 or 866/898–2519 www.robertshawaii. com.*

Temptation Tours. Temptation Tours has targeted members of the affluent older crowd (though almost anyone would enjoy these tours) who don't want to be herded onto a crowded bus. Tours in plush six-passenger limovans explore Haleakalā and Hāna, and range from $110 to $249 per person. The "Hāna Sky-Trek" includes a return trip via helicopter. ☎ *808/877–8888 or 800/817–1234* ⊕ *www.temptation-tours.com.*

Tour da Food Maui. Maui resident Bonnie Friedman (a Fodor's contributor) guides small, customized food tours that include a couple of holes-in-the-wall some locals don't even know about. Tours leave Tuesday, Wednesday, and Thursday mornings and cost from $105 to $130 per person. ✉ *Wailuku96793* ☎ *808/242–8383* ⊕ *www.tourdafoodmaui.com.*

Kahekili, Maui's last fierce king, did, and so did Kamehameha the Great after he defeated Kahekili's soldiers. Today the view is most instructive. Below, the once-powerful 'Īao Stream has been sucked dry and boxed in by concrete. Before you is the urban heart of the island. The suburban community behind you is all Hawaiian Homelands—property owned solely by native Hawaiians. ⊠*End of Hea Pl., off Kuhio Pl. from Waiehu Beach Rd., Rte. 340, Kahului* ☏*Free* ⊙*Daily 7–7.*

❽ Maui Arts & Cultural Center. An epic fund drive by the citizens of Maui led to the creation of this $32 million facility. The top-of-the-line Castle Theater seats 1,200 people on orchestra, mezzanine, and balcony levels; rock stars play the A&B Amphitheater. The MACC (as it's called) also includes a small black box theater, an art gallery with interesting exhibits, and classrooms. The building itself is worth a visit: it incorporates work by Maui artists, and its signature lava-rock wall pays tribute to the skills of the Hawaiians. But the real draw is the Schaeffer International Gallery, which houses superb rotating exhibits. ⊠*One Cameron Way, Kahului* ☏*808/242–2787, 808/242–7469 box office* ⊕*www.mauiarts. org* ⊙*Weekdays 9–5.*

❼ Maui Nui Botanical Gardens. The fascinating plants grown on these seven ⟲ acres are representative of pre-contact Hawai'i. Both native and Polynesian-introduced species are cultivated—including ice-cream bananas, varieties of sweet potatoes and sugarcane, native poppies, hibiscus, and *anapanapa,* a plant that makes a natural shampoo when rubbed between your hands. Ethnobotany tours and presentations are offered on occasion. ⊠*150 Kanaloa Ave., 96793* ☏*808/249–2798* ⊕*www. mnbg.org* ⊙*Mon.–Sat. 8–4.*

❺ Maui Tropical Plantation & Country Store. When Maui's once-paramount ⟲ crop declined in importance, a group of visionaries decided to open an agricultural theme park on the site of this former sugarcane field. The 60-acre preserve, on Route 30 just outside Wailuku, offers a 30-minute tram ride through its fields with an informative narration covering growing processes and plant types. Children will probably enjoy the historical-characters exhibit as well as fruit tasting, coconut husking, and lei-making demonstrations, not to mention some entertaining spider monkeys. There's a restaurant on the property and a country store specializing in made in Maui products. ⊠*Honoapi'ilani Hwy., Rte. 30, Waikapu* ☏*808/244–7643* ☏*Free; tram ride with narrated tour $9.50* ⊙*Daily 9–5.*

UPCOUNTRY MAUI AND THE NORTH SHORE

North Shore action centers on the colorful town of Pā'ia and the windsurfing mecca, Ho'okipa Beach. Blasted by winter swells and wind, Maui's north shore draws water-sports thrill-seekers from around the world. But there's much more to this area of Maui than coastline. Inland, a lush, waterfall-fed Garden of Eden beckons.

As you venture up the mountain, you find yourself "Upcountry"—the name locals have given to the west-facing slope of Haleakalā. As you drive along you'll notice cactus thickets mingled with purple jacaranda, wild hibiscus, and towering eucalyptus trees. Upcountry is also fertile

Continued on page 196

ROAD TO HĀNA

As you round the impossibly tight turn, a one-lane bridge comes into view. Beneath its worn surface, a lush forested gulch plummets toward the coast. The sound of rushing water fills the air, compelling you to search the overgrown hillside for waterfalls. This is the Road to Hāna, a 55-mi journey into the unspoiled heart of Maui. Tracing a centuries-old path, the road begins as a well-paved highway in Kahului and ends in the tiny town of Hāna on the island's rain-gouged windward side.

★ Fodor's Choice Despite the twists and turns, the road to Hāna is not as frightening as it may sound. You're bound to be a little nervous approaching it the first time; but afterwards you'll wonder if somebody out there is making it sound tough just to keep out the hordes. The challenging part of the road takes only an hour and a half, but you'll want to stop often and let the driver enjoy the view, too. Don't expect a booming city when you get to Hāna. Its lure is its quiet timelessness. As the adage says, the journey *is* the destination.

During high season, the road to Hāna tends to clog—well, not clog exactly, but develop little choo-choo trains of cars, with everyone in a line of six or a dozen driving as slowly as the first car. The solution: leave early (dawn) and return late (dusk). And if you find yourself playing the role of locomotive, pull over and let the other drivers pass. You can also let someone else take the turns for you—several companies offer van tours, which make stops all along the way (*see Maui Sightseeing Tours box in this chapter*).

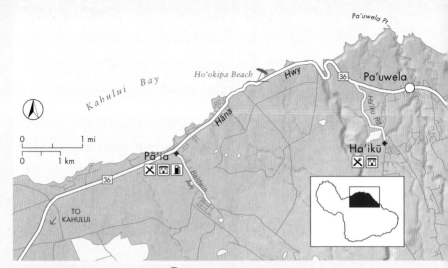

DRIVING THE ROAD TO HĀNA

Begin your journey in Pāʻia, the little town on Maui's North Shore. Be sure to fill up your gas tank here. There are no gas stations along Hāna Highway, and the station in Hāna closes by 6 PM. You should also pick up a picnic lunch. Lunch and snack choices along the way are limited to rustic fruit stands.

About 10 mi past Pāʻia, at the bottom of Kaupakalua Road, the roadside mileposts begin measuring the 36 mi to Hāna town. The road's trademark noodling starts about 3 mi after that. Once the road gets twisty, remember that many residents make this trip frequently. You'll recognize them because they're the ones zipping around every curve. They've seen this so many times before they don't care to linger. Pull over to let them pass.

All along this stretch of road, waterfalls are abundant. Roll down your windows. Breathe in the scent of guava and ginger. You can almost hear the bamboo growing. There are plenty of places to pull completely off the road and park safely. Do this often, since the road's curves make driving without a break difficult. ■ TIP→If you're prone to carsickness, be sure to take medication before you start this drive. You may also want to stop periodicially.

❶ **Twin Falls**. Keep an eye out for the fruit stand just after mile marker 2. Stop here and treat yourself to some fresh sugarcane juice. If you're feeling adventurous, follow the path beyond the stand to the paradisiacal waterfalls known as Twin Falls. Once a rough trail plastered with "no trespassing" signs, this treasured spot is now easily accessible. In fact, there's usually a mass of cars surrounding the fruit stand at the trail head. Several deep, emerald pools sparkle beneath waterfalls and offer excellent swimming and photo opportunities.

While this is still private property, the "no trespassing" signs have been replaced by colorfully painted arrows pointing away from residences and toward the falls. ■ TIP→Bring water shoes for crossing streams along the way. Swim at your own risk and beware: flash floods here and in all East Maui stream areas can be sudden and deadly. Check the weather before you go.

❷ **Huelo & Kailua.** Dry off and drive on past the sleepy country villages of Huelo (near mile marker 5) and Kailua (near mile marker 6). The little farm town of Huelo has two quaint churches. If you linger awhile, you could meet local residents and learn about a rural lifestyle you might not expect to find on the Islands. The same can be said for nearby Kailua,

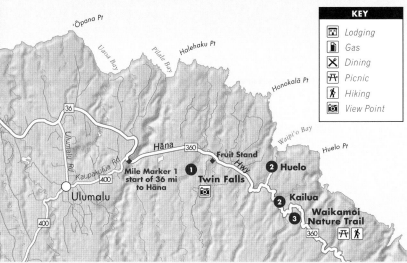

home to Alexander & Baldwin's irrigation employees.

❸ Waikamoi Nature Trail. Between mile markers 9 and 10, the Waikamoi Nature Trail sign beckons you to stretch your car-weary limbs. A short (if muddy) trail leads through tall eucalyptus trees to a coastal vantage point with a picnic table and barbecue. Signage reminds visitors QUIET, TREES AT WORK and BAMBOO PICKING PERMIT REQUIRED. Awapuhi, or Hawaiian shampoo ginger, sends up fragrant shoots along the trail.

❹ Puohokamoa Stream. About a mile farther, near mile marker 11, you can stop at the bridge over Puohokamoa Stream. This is one of many bridges you cross en route from Pā'ia to Hāna. It spans pools and waterfalls. Picnic tables are available, but there are no restrooms.

❺ Kaumahina State Wayside Park. If you'd rather stretch your legs and use a flush toilet, continue another mile to Kaumahina State Wayside Park (at mile marker 12). The park has a picnic area, restrooms, and a lovely overlook to the Ke'anae Peninsula. The park is open from 8 AM to 4 PM and admission is free. ☎ *808/984–8109.*

🕐 | **TIMING TIPS**

With short stops, the drive from Pā'ia to Hāna should take you between two and three hours one-way. Lunching in Hāna, hiking, and swimming can easily turn the round-trip into a full-day outing, especially if you continue past Hāna to the seven pools and Kīpahulu. If you go that far, you might consider continuing around the "back side" for the return trip. The scenery is completely different and you'll end up in beautiful Upcountry Maui. Since there's so much scenery to take in, we recommend staying overnight in Hāna. It's worth taking time to enjoy the waterfalls and beaches without being in a hurry. Try to plan your trip for a day that promises fair, sunny weather—though the drive can be even more beautiful when it's raining.

Ke'anae Peninsula

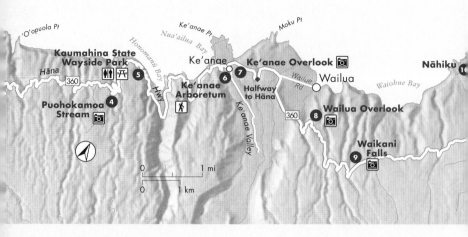

Near mile marker 14, before Keʻanae, you find yourself driving along a cliff side down into deep, lush Honomanū Bay, an enormous valley, with a rocky black-sand beach.

The Honomanū Valley was carved by erosion during Haleakalā's first dormant period. At the canyon's head there are 3,000-foot cliffs and a 1,000-foot waterfall, but don't try to reach them. There's not much of a trail, and what does exist is practically impassable.

6 Keʻanae Arboretum. Another 4 mi brings you to mile marker 17 and the Keʻanae Arboretum where you can add to your botanical education or enjoy a challenging hike into a forest. Signs help you learn the names of the many plants and trees now considered native to Hawaiʻi. The meandering Piʻinaʻau Stream adds a graceful touch to the arboretum and provides a swimming pond.

You can take a fairly rigorous hike from the arboretum if you can find the trail at one side of the large taro patch. Be careful not to lose the trail once you're on it. A lovely forest waits at the end of the 25-minute hike. Access to the arboretum is free.

7 Keʻanae Overlook. A half mile farther down Hāna Highway you can stop at the Keʻanae Overlook. From this observation point, you can take in the quilt-like effect the taro patches create below.

The people of Keʻanae are working hard to revive this Hawaiian agricultural art and the traditional cultural values that the crop represents. The ocean provides a dramatic backdrop for the patches. In the other direction there are awesome views of Haleakalā through the foliage. This is a great spot for photos.

■TIP→ Coming up is the halfway mark to Hāna. If you've had enough scenery, this is as good a time as any to turn around and head back to civilization.

8 Wailua Overlook. Between mile markers 20 and 21 you find Wailua Overlook. From the parking lot you can see Wailua Canyon, but you have to walk up steps to get a view of Wailua Village. The landmark in Wailua Village is a church made of coral, built in 1860.

Taro patch viewed from Hāna Highway

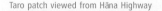

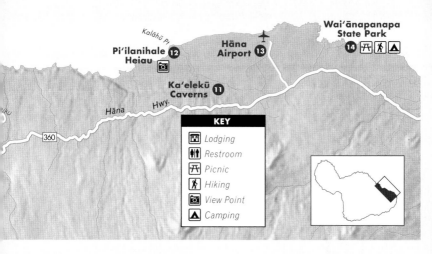

Once called St. Gabriel's Catholic Church, the current Our Lady of Fatima Shrine has an interesting legend surrounding it. As the story goes, a storm washed enough coral up onto shore to build the church and then took any extra coral back to sea.

⑨ Waikani Falls. After another ½ mi, past mile marker 21, you hit the best falls on the entire drive to Hāna, Waikani Falls. Though not necessarily bigger or taller than the other falls, these are the most dramatic falls you'll find in East Maui. That's partly because the water is not diverted for sugar irrigation; the taro farmers in Wailua need all the runoff. This is a particularly good spot for photos.

⑩ Nāhiku. At about mile marker 25 you see a road that heads down toward the ocean and the village of Nāhiku. In ancient times this was a busy settlement with hundreds of residents. Now only about 80 people live in Nāhiku, mostly native Hawaiians and some back-to-the-land types. A rubber grower planted trees here in the early 1900s, but the experiment didn't work out, and Nāhiku was essentially abandoned. The road ends at the sea in a pretty landing. This is the rainiest, densest part of the East Maui rain forest.

Coffee Break. Back on the Hāna Highway, about 10 minutes before Hāna town, you can stop for—of all things—espresso. The tiny, colorful **Nāhiku Ti Gallery and Coffee Shop** (between mile markers 27 and 28) sells local coffee, dried fruits and candies, and delicious (if pricey) banana bread. Sometimes the barbecue is fired up and you can try fish skewers or baked breadfruit (an island favorite nearly impossible to find elsewhere). The Ti Gallery sells Hawaiian crafts.

⑪ Kaʻelekū Caverns. If you're interested in exploring underground, turn left onto ʻUlaʻino Road, just after mile marker 31, and follow the signs to Kaʻelekū Caverns. **Maui Cave Adventures** points amateur spelunkers into a system of gigantic lava tubes, accentuated by colorful underworld formations.

You can take a self-guided, 30- to 45-min tour daily, from 10:30 to 4 PM for $11.95 per person. Flashlights are provided. Children under five are free with a paid adult. ☎808/248–7308 ⊕www.mauicave.com

Hāna

★ **⑫ Piʻilanihale Heiau.** Continue on ʻUlaʻino Road, which doubles back for a mile, loses its pavement, and even crosses a stream before reaching Kahanu Garden and Piʻilanihale Heiau, the largest prehistoric monument in Hawaiʻi. This temple platform was built for a great 16th-century Maui king named Piʻilani and his heirs. This king also supervised the construction of a 10-foot-wide road that completely encircled the island. (That's why his name is part of most of Maui's highway titles.)

Hawaiian families continue to maintain and protect this sacred site as they have for centuries, and they have not been eager to turn it into a tourist attraction. However, they now offer a brochure so you can tour the property yourself for $10 per person. Tours include the 122-acre **Kahanu Garden,** a federally funded research center focusing on the ethno-botany of the Pacific. The heiau and garden are open weekdays from 10 AM to 2 PM. ☎ 808/248–8912

⑬ Hāna Airport. Back on the Hāna Highway, and less than ½ mi farther, is the turnoff for the Hāna Airport. Think of Amelia Earhart. Think of Waldo Pepper. If these picket-fence runways don't turn your thoughts to the derring-do of barnstorming pilots, you haven't seen enough

old movies. Only the smallest planes can land and depart here, and when none of them happens to be around, the lonely wind sock is the only evidence that this is a working airfield. ☎ 808/248–8208

★ **⑭ Waiʻānapanapa State Park.** Just beyond mile marker 32 you reach Waiʻānapanapa State Park, home to one of Maui's only volcanic-sand beaches and some freshwater caves for adventurous swimmers to explore. The park is right on the ocean, and it's a lovely spot in which to picnic, camp, hike, or swim. To the left you'll find the black-sand beach, picnic tables, and cave pools. To the right you'll find cabins and an ancient trail which snakes along the ocean past blowholes, sea arches, and archaeological sites.

The tide pools here turn red several times a year. Scientists say it's explained by the arrival of small shrimp, but legend claims the color represents the blood of Popoʻalaea, a princess said to have been murdered in one of the caves by her husband, Chief Kaʻakea. Whichever you choose to believe, the drama of the landscape itself—black sand, green beach vines, azure water—is bound to leave a lasting impression.

With a permit you can stay in state-run cabins here for less than $45 a night—the price varies depending on the number of people—but reserve early. They often book up a year in advance. ☎ *808/984–8109*

⑮ Hāna. By now the relaxed pace of life that Hāna residents enjoy should have you in its grasp, so you won't be discouraged to learn that "town" is little more than a gas station, a post office, and a ramshackle grocery.

Hāna, in many ways, is the heart of Maui. It's one of the few places where the slow pulse of island life is still strong. The town centers on its lovely circular bay, dominated on the right-hand shore by a pu'u called Ka'uiki. A short trail here leads to a cave, the birthplace of Queen Ka'ahumanu. This area is rich in Hawaiian history and legend. Two miles beyond town another pu'u presides over a loop road that passes two of Hāna's best beaches—Kōkī and Hāmoa. The hill is called Ka Iwi O Pele (Pele's Bone). Offshore here, at tiny 'Ālau Island, the de-migod Maui supposedly fished up the Hawaiian islands.

Sugar was once the mainstay of Hāna's economy; the last plantation shut down in the '40s. In 1946 rancher Paul Fagan built the **Hotel Hāna-Maui** and stocked the surrounding pastureland with cattle. The cross you see on the hill above the hotel was put there in memory of Fagan. Now it's the ranch and

hotel that put food on most tables, though many families still farm, fish, and hunt as in the old days. Houses around town are decorated with glass balls and nets, which indicate a fisherman's lodging.

⑯ Hāna Cultural Center Museum. If you're determined to spend some time and money in Hāna after the long drive, a single turn off the highway onto Uakea Street, in the center of town, will take you to the Hāna Cultural Center Museum. Besides operating a well-stocked gift shop, it displays artifacts, quilts, a replica of an authentic *kauhale* (an ancient Hawaiian living complex, with thatch huts and food gardens), and other Hawaiiana. The knowledgeable staff can explain it all to you. The center is open 10 to 4 daily. ☎ *808/248–8622* ⊕ *www.hookele.com/hccm*

⑰ Hotel Hāna-Maui. With its surrounding ranch, the upscale hotel is the mainstay of Hāna's economy. It's pleasant to stroll around this beautifully rustic property. The library houses interesting, authentic Hawaiian artifacts. In the evening, while local musicians play in the casual lobby bar, their friends jump up to dance hula. The Sea Ranch cottages across the road, built to look like authentic plantation housing from the outside, are also part of the hotel. *See Where to Stay for more information.*

Hala Trees, Wai'ānapanapa State Park

Hāna

Don't be suprised if the mile markers suddenly start descending as you head past Hāna. Technically, Hāna Highway (Route 360) ends at the Hāna Bay. The road that continues south is Pi'ilani Highway (Route 31)—though everyone still refers to it as the Hāna Highway.

18 **Hāmoa Beach.** Just outside Hāna, take a left on Haneo'o Loop to explore lovely Hāmoa. Indulge in swimming or bodysurfing at this beautiful salt-and-pepper beach. Picnic tables, restrooms, and showers beneath the idyllic shade of coconut trees offer a more than comfortable rest stop.

The road leading to Hāmoa also takes you to **Koki Beach**, where you can watch the Hāna surfers mastering the swells and strong currents, and the seabirds darting over 'Ālau, the palm-fringed islet off the coast. The swimming is safer at Hāmoa.

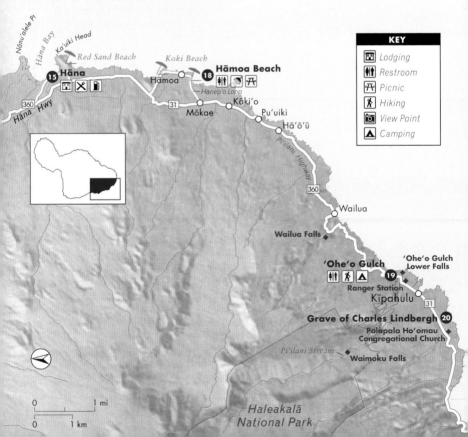

★ ⑲ **'Ohe'o Gulch.** Ten miles past town, at mile marker 42, you'll find the pools at 'Ohe'o Gulch. One branch of Haleakalā National Park runs down the mountain from the crater and reaches the sea here, where a basalt-lined stream cascades from one pool to the next. Some tour guides still call this area Seven Sacred Pools, but in truth there are more than seven, and they've never been considered sacred. You can park here—for a $10 fee—and walk to the lowest pools for a cool swim. The place gets crowded, since most people who drive the Hāna Highway make this their last stop.

If you enjoy hiking, go up the stream on the 2-mi hike to **Waimoku Falls.** The trail crosses a spectacular gorge, then turns into a boardwalk that takes you through an amazing bamboo forest. You can pitch a tent in the grassy campground down by the sea. *See Hiking in Golf, Hiking & Outdoor Activities.*

⑳ **Grave of Charles Lindbergh.** Many people travel the mile past 'Ohe'o Gulch to see the Grave of Charles Lindbergh. You see a ruined sugar mill with a big chimney on the right side of the road and then, on the left, a rutted track leading to Palapala Ho'omau Congregational Church. The simple one-room church sits on a bluff over the sea, with the small graveyard on the ocean side. The world-renowned aviator chose to be buried here because he and his wife, writer Anne Morrow Lindbergh, spent a lot of time living in the area. He was buried here in 1974. Since this is a churchyard, be considerate and leave everything exactly as you found it. Next to the churchyard on the ocean side is a small county park, good for a picnic.

Kaupō Road. The road to Hāna continues all the way around Haleakalā's "back side" through 'Ulupalakua Ranch and into Kula. The desert-like topography, with its grand vistas, is unlike anything else on the island, but the road itself is bad, sometimes impassable in winter, and parts of it are unpaved. Car-rental agencies call it off-limits to their passenger cars and there

TROPICAL DELIGHTS

The drive to Hāna wouldn't be as enchanting without a stop or two at one of the countless fruit and flower stands alongside the highway. Every $1/2$ mi or so a thatched hut tempts passersby with apple bananas (a smaller firmer variety), liliko'i (passion fruit), avocados, or starfruit just plucked from the tree. Leave a few dollars in the can for the folks who live off the land. Huge bouquets of tropical flowers are available for a handful of change, and some farms will ship.

is no emergency assistance available. The danger and dust from increasing numbers of speeding jeep drivers are making life tough for the residents, especially in Kaupō, with its 4 mi of unpaved road. The small communities around East Maui cling tenuously to the old ways. Please keep that in mind if you do pass this way. If you can't resist the adventure, try to make the drive just before sunset. The light slanting across the mountain is incredible. At night, giant potholes, owls, and loose cattle can make for some difficult driving. The bridge that was damaged in a 2006 earthquake has been repaired, allowing visitors to once again drive all the way around East Maui. Please note, however, that the condition of the road remains rough.

ranch land; cowboys still work the fields of the historic 20,000-acre 'Ulupalakua Ranch and the 32,000-acre Haleakalā Ranch. Keep an eye out for *pueo*, Hawai'i's native owl, which hunts these fields during daylight hours.

Most travelers cruise through the North Shore on their way to Hāna. You can explore Pā'ia in an hour. If you poke around the area's beaches and restaurants, you have a day's outing, especially if you head up Upcountry. From Kīhei or Kā'anapali it takes between 45 minutes and an hour to get to Pā'ia or Makawao. Tedeschi Winery and other Upcountry destinations are farther, at least another half hour along Kula Highway. It's good to combine a Haleakalā crater expedition with a tour of Upcountry and a North Shore meal.

TOP ATTRACTIONS

Fodor'sChoice
★ **Haleakalā National Park.** *See the Golf, Hiking, and Outdoor Activities section later in this chapter for information about this park, one of Maui's top attractions.*

Fodor'sChoice
★ **Ho'okipa Beach.** There's no better place on this or any other island to watch the world's finest windsurfers in action. The surfers know five different surf breaks here by name. Unless it's a rare day without wind or waves, you're sure to get a show. ■TIP➡It's not safe to park on the shoulder. Use the ample parking lot at the county park entrance. ⊠2 mi past Pā'ia on Rte. 36.

Makawao. This once-tiny town has managed to hang on to its country charm (and eccentricity) as it has grown in popularity. The district was originally settled by Portuguese and Japanese immigrants who came to Maui to work the sugar plantations and then moved Upcountry to establish small farms, ranches, and stores. Descendants now work the neighboring Haleakalā and 'Ulupalakua ranches. Every July 4 the

> ### CREAM PUFFS, YUM!
>
> One of Makawao's most famous landmarks is **Komoda Store & Bakery** (3674 Baldwin Ave.; 808/572–7261)—a classic mom-and-pop store that has changed little in three-quarters of a century—where you can get a delicious cream puff if you arrive early enough. They make hundreds but sell out each day.

paniolo set comes out in force for the Makawao Rodeo. The crossroads of town—lined with chic shops and down-home eateries—reflects a growing population of people who came here just because they liked it. For those seeking lush greenery rather than beachside accommodations, there are great, secluded little bed-and-breakfasts in and around the town. ⊠Intersection of Baldwin and Makawao Aves.

★ **Pā'ia.** This little town was once a sugarcane enclave, with a mill and plantation camps. The town boomed during World War II when the marines set up camp in nearby Ha'ikū. The old HC&S sugar mill finally closed and no sign of the military remains, but the town continues to thrive. In the '70s Pā'ia became a hippie town as dropouts headed for Maui to open boutiques, galleries, and unusual eateries. In the '80s windsurfers discovered nearby Ho'okipa Beach and brought an international flavor to Pā'ia. Eclectic boutiques supply everything from high fashion to hemp oil candles. The restaurants provide excellent people-watching and an array of dining options. Pāʻia is the last place to snack before the pilgrimage to Hāna. ⊠*Intersection of Hāna Hwy. (Hwy. 36) and Baldwin Ave.*

WORTH NOTING

★ **Aliʻi Kula Lavender.** Reserve a spot for tea or lunch at this lavender farm with a falcon's view. It's *the* relaxing remedy for those suffering from too much sun, shopping, or golf. Owners Aliʻi and Lani lead tours through winding paths of therapeutic lavender varieties, proteas, succulents, and rare Maui wormwood. Their logo, a larger-than-life dragonfly, darts above chefs who are cooking up lavender-infused shrimp appetizers out on the lānai. The gift shop abounds with the farm's own innovative lavender products. ⊠*1100 Waipoli Rd., Kula* ☎*808/878–3004* ⊕*www.mauikulalavender.com* ⊡*$12 for walking tours; combine with a lunch basket for $37 per person* ⚚*Reservations essential for group tours* ☉*Daily 9–4, walking tours leave 5 times a day.*

Haʻikū. At one time this area vibrated around a couple of enormous pineapple canneries. Both have been transformed into rustic warehouse malls. At Haʻikū cannery you can snack on pizza at Colleen's or get massaged by the students at Spa Luna. Up Kokomo Road is a large puʻu capped with a grove of columnar pines, and the **4th Marine Division Memorial Park.** During World War II American GIs trained here for battles on Iwo Jima and Saipan. Locals nicknamed the cinder cone Giggle Hill because it was a popular hangout for Maui women and their favorite servicemen. ⊠*Intersection of Haʻikū and Kokomo Rds.*

Hui Noʻeau Visual Arts Center. The main house of this nonprofit cultural center on the old Baldwin estate, just outside the town of Makawao, is an elegant two-story Mediterranean-style villa designed in the 1920s by the defining Hawaiʻi architect C. W. Dickey. "The Hui" is the grande dame of Maui's well-known arts scene. The exhibits are always satisfying, and the grounds might as well be a botanical garden. The Hui also offers classes and maintains working artists' studios. ⊠*2841 Baldwin Ave., Makawao* ☎*808/572–6560* ⊡*Free* ☉*Daily 10–4.*

Kēōkea. More of a friendly gesture than a town, this tiny outpost is the last bit of civilization before Kula Highway becomes the winding backside road, heading east around to Hāna. A coffee tree pushes through the sunny deck at Grandma's Coffee Shop, the morning watering hole for Maui's cowboys who work at ʻUlupalakua or Kaupō ranch. Kēōkea Gallery next door sells some of the most original artwork on the island. ■TIP➔The only restroom for miles is across the street at the public park, and the view makes stretching your legs worth it.

Surfing Goat Dairy. It takes goats to make goat cheese and they've got plenty of both at this 42-acre farm. Tours range from "casual" to "grand" and particularly delight children. If you have the time, both the two-hour grand tour (twice a month) and the "Evening Chores & Milking Tour" are educational and fun. The owners make more than two dozen kinds of goat cheese, from the plain, creamy "Udderly Delicious" to more exotic cheeses that include other, sometimes tropical, ingredients. All varieties are available for purchase in the dairy store, along with gift baskets and even goat milk soaps. ✉️*3651 Ōmaopio Rd., Kula* 📞*808/878–2870* 🌐*www.surfinggoatdairy.com* 💵*$7–$25* 🕐*Mon. –Sat. 10–5, Sun. 10–2; check ahead for tour schedule.*

Tedeschi Vineyards and Winery. You can tour the winery and its historic grounds, the former Rose Ranch, and sample the island's only wines: a pleasant Maui Blush, Maui Champagne, and Tedeschi's annual Maui Nouveau. The top-seller, naturally, is the pineapple wine. The tasting room is a cottage built in the late 1800s for the frequent visits of King Kalākaua. The cottage also contains the **'Ulupalakua Ranch History Room,** which tells colorful stories of the ranch's owners, the *paniolo* tradition that developed here, and Maui's polo teams. The old General Store may look like a museum, but in fact it's an excellent pit stop. ✉️*Kula Hwy., 'Ulupalakua Ranch* 📞*808/878–6058* 🌐*www.mauiwine. com* 💵*Free* 🕐*Daily 9–5, tours at 10:30 and 1:30, and 3.*

BEACHES

Updated by Bonnie Friedman

Of all the beaches in the Hawaiian islands, Maui's are some of the most diverse. You'll find the pristine, palm-lined shores you expect with waters as clear and inviting as sea-green glass, but you'll also discover rich red- and black-sand beaches, craggy cliffs with surging whitecaps, and year-round sunsets that quiet the soul. As on the other isles, all of Maui's beaches are public—but that doesn't mean it's not possible to find a secluded cove where you can truly get away from the world.

The island's leeward shores (the South Shore and West Maui) have the calmest, sunniest beaches. Hit the beach early, when the aquamarine waters are as accommodating as bathwater. In summer, afternoon winds can be a sandblasting force, which can chase even the most dedicated sun worshippers away. From November through May, the South and West beaches are also great spots to watch the parade of whales that spend the winter and early spring in Maui's waters.

Windward shores (the North Shore and East Maui) offer more adventurous beach-going. Beaches face the open ocean (rather than other islands) and tend to be rockier and more prone to powerful swells. This is particularly true in winter, when the North Shore becomes a playground for experienced big-wave riders and windsurfers. Don't let this keep you away completely, however. Some of the island's best beaches are those remote slivers of volcanic sand found on the wild windward shore.

The sandy crescent of Nāpili Beach on West Maui is a lovely place to wait for sunset.

WEST MAUI

West Maui beaches are legendary for their glittering aquamarine waters banked by long stretches of golden sand. Reef fronts much of the western shore, making the underwater panorama something to behold. The beaches listed here start in the north at Kapalua and head south past Kā'anapali and Lahaina. Note that there are a dozen roadside beaches to choose from on Route 30; those listed here are the ones we like best.

"Slaughterhouse" (Mokulē'ia) Beach. The island's northernmost beach is part of the Honolua-Mokuleia Marine Life Conservation District. "Slaughterhouse" is the surfers' nickname for what is officially Mokuleia. When the weather permits, this is a great place for body-surfing and sunbathing. Concrete steps and a green railing help you get down the sheer cliff to the sand. The next bay over, Honolua, has no beach but offers one of the best surf breaks in Hawai'i. Often you can see competitions happening there; look for cars pulled off the road and parked in the pineapple field. ⊠ *Mile marker 32 on Rte. 30 past Kapalua* ☞ *No facilities.*

Kapalua Bay Beach. Kapalua has been recognized by many travel magazines as one of the world's best beaches. Walk through the tunnel at the end of Kapalua Place and you'll see why—the beach fronts a pristine bay good for snorkeling, swimming, and general lazing. Located just north of Nāpili Bay, this lovely, sheltered shore often remains calm late into the afternoon, although there may be strong currents offshore. Snorkeling is easy here and there are lots of colorful reef fish to see. This area is quite popular and is bordered by the Kapalua Resort, so don't expect to have the beach to yourself. ⊠ *From Rte. 30, turn onto*

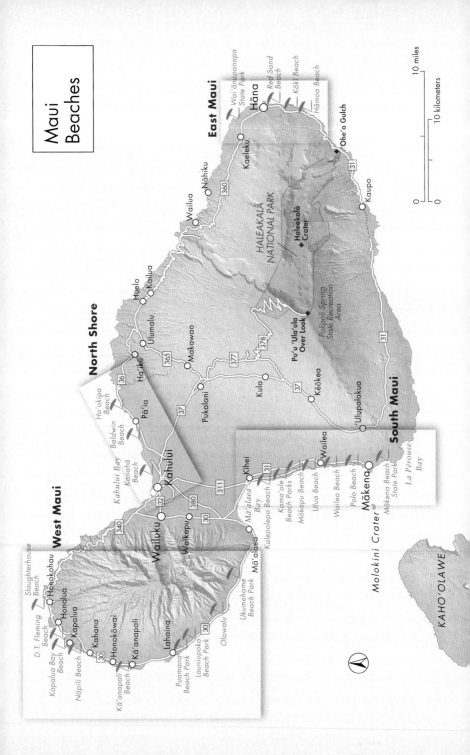

Maui
Beaches

West Maui

North Shore

East Maui

Slaughterhouse
Beach

D.T. Fleming
Beach

Honokohau

Honolua

Kapalua

Kahana

Honokowai

Kā'anapali

Lahaina

Kapalua Bay
Beach

Nāpili Beach

Kā'anapali
Beach

Puamana
Beach Park

Launiupoko
Beach Park

Olowalu

Ukumehame
Beach Park

Mā'alaea

Waikapu

Waihe'e

Wailuku

Kahului

Pā'ia

Ho'okipa
Beach

Baldwin
Beach

Kanahā
Beach

Kahului Bay

Ha'ikū

Huelo

Ulumalu

Makawao

Pukalani

Kula

Kēōkea

'Ulupalakua

Kailua

Wailua

Nāhiku

Kaeleku

Wai'ānapanapa
State Park

Hāna

Red Sand
Beach

Kōki Beach

Hāmoa Beach

Ohe'o Gulch

Kaupo

HALEAKALĀ
NATIONAL PARK

Haleakalā
Crater

Pu'u 'Ula'ula
Over Look

Polipoli Spring
State Recreation
Area

South Maui

Mā'alaea
Bay

Kihei

Kalepolepo Beach

Kama'ole
Beach Parks

Mōkapu Beach

Ulua Beach

Wailea Beach

Wailea

Polo Beach

Mākena

Mōkena Beach
State Park

La Pérouse
Bay

Molokini Crater

KAHO'OLAWE

36
340
32
380
30
311
37
365
31
378
377
360
31
30

10 miles

10 kilometers

Kapalua Pl., walk through tunnel
✆*Toilets, showers, parking lot.*

☾ **Nāpili Beach.** Surrounded by sleepy
Fodor'sChoice condos, this round bay is a turtle-
★ filled pool lined with a sparkling
white crescent of sand. Sunbathers
love this beach, which is also a terrific sunset spot. The shore break is
steep but gentle and it's easy to keep
an eye on kids here as the entire
bay is visible from any point in the
water. The beach is right outside
the Nāpili Kai Beach Club, a popular little resort for honeymooners,
only a few miles south of Kapalua.

✉*5900 Lower Honoapi'ilani Hwy., look for Nāpili Pl. or Hui Dr.*
✆*Showers, parking lot.*

☾ **Kā'anapali Beach.** Stretching from the Sheraton Maui at its northernmost
★ end to the Hyatt Regency Maui at its southern tip, Kā'anapali Beach
is lined with resorts, condominiums, restaurants, and shops. If you're
looking for quiet and seclusion, this is not the beach for you. But if
you want lots of action, lay out your towel here. The center section in
front of Whalers Village is also called "Dig Me Beach," and it is one
of Maui's best people-watching spots: catamarans, windsurfers, and
parasailers head out from here while the beautiful people take in the
scenery. A cement pathway weaves along the length of this 3-mi-long
beach, leading from one astounding resort to the next.

The drop-off from Kā'anapali's soft, sugary sand is steep, but waves
hit the shore with barely a rippling slap. The area at the northernmost
end (in front of the Sheraton Maui), known as Keka'a, was, in ancient
Hawai'i, a *lele*, or jumping-off place for spirits. It's easy to get into the
water from the beach to enjoy the prime snorkeling among the lava rock
outcroppings. ✉*Follow any of 3 Kā'anapali exits from Honoapi'ilani
Hwy. and park at any hotel* ✆*Toilets, showers, parking lot.*

Launiupoko State Wayside Park. Launiupoko is the beach park of all beach
parks. Both a surf break and a beach, it offers a little something for
everyone with its inviting stretch of lawn, soft white sand, and gentle
waves. The shoreline reef creates a protected wading pool, perfect for
small children. Outside the reef, beginner surfers will find good longboard rides. From the long sliver of beach (good for walking), you'll
enjoy superb views of neighbor islands, and landside, of deep valleys jet-
ting through the West Maui Mountains. Because of its endless sunshine
and serenity—not to mention its many amenities—Launiupoko draws
a crowd on the weekends, but there's space for everyone (and overflow
parking across the street). ✉*On Rte. 30, just south of Lahaina at mile
marker 18* ✆*Toilets, showers, picnic tables, grills/firepits.*

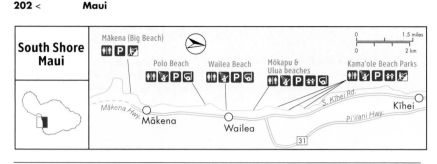

THE SOUTH SHORE

Sandy beach fronts nearly the entire southern coastline of Maui, from Kīhei at the northern end to Mākena at the southern tip. The farther south you go, the better the beaches get. Kīhei has excellent beach parks right in town, with white sand, showers, restrooms, picnic tables, and barbecues. Good snorkeling can be found along the beaches' rocky borders. As good as Kīhei is, Wailea is even better. Wailea's beaches are cleaner, facilities tidier, and views even more impressive. ■ TIP→Note that break-ins have been reported at many of these beach parking lots. As you head out to Mākena, the terrain gets wilder. Bring lunch, water, and sunscreen with you. The following South Shore beaches are listed from north Kīhei southeast to Mākena.

Kama'ole I, II, and III. Three steps from South Kīhei Road, you can find three golden stretches of sand separated by outcroppings of dark, jagged lava rocks. You can walk the length of all three beaches if you're willing to get your feet wet. The northernmost of the trio, Kama'ole I (across from the ABC Store, in case you forgot your sunscreen), offers perfect swimming with a sandy bottom a long way out and an active volleyball court. If you're one of those people who likes your beach sans sand, there's also a great lawn for you to spread out on at the south end of the beach. Kama'ole II is nearly identical minus the lawn. The last beach, the one with all the people on it, is Kama'ole III, perfect for throwing disk or throwing down a blanket. This is a great family beach, complete with a playground, volleyball net, barbecues, kite flying, and frequently, rented inflatable castles—a birthday-party must for every cool kid living on the island.

Locally—and quite disrespectfully, according to native Hawaiians—known as "Kam" I, II, and III, all three beaches have great swimming and lifeguards. In the morning the water can be as still as a lap pool. Kama'ole III offers terrific breaks for beginning bodysurfers. ■ TIP→The public restrooms have seen better days; decent facilities are found at convenience stores and eateries across the street. ⊠ *S. Kīhei Rd., between Ke Ali'i Alanui Rd. and Keonekai Rd.* ↻ *Lifeguard, toilets, showers, picnic tables, grills/firepits, playground, parking lot.*

Keawakapu Beach. Who wouldn't love Keawakapu with its long stretch of golden sand, near-perfect swimming, and stunning views of the crater and Kaho'olawe? It's great fun to walk or jog this beach south into Wailea as the path is lined with over-the-top residences. It's best here

BEST BEACHES

Maui has miles and miles of great beaches, so how do you choose where to park your towel? Here are some that are sure to satisfy.

BEST FOR FAMILIES

Baldwin Beach, the North Shore. The long, shallow, calm end closest to Kahului is safe even for toddlers—with adult supervision, of course.

Kama'ole III, the South Shore. There's sand, gentle surf, a playground, volleyball net, and barbecues—what more could a family want?

BEST OFFSHORE SNORKELING

Olowalu, West Maui. The beach remains shallow far offshore and there's plenty to see.

Ulua, the South Shore. It's beautiful and the kids can enjoy the tide pools while the adults experience the excellent snorkeling.

BEST SURFING

Ho'okipa, the North Shore. This is a great surfing spot, and one of the best windsurfing beaches in the world, though it's not for beginners.

Honolua Bay, West Maui. One bay over from Mokulē'ia Beach (north of Kapalua) you'll find one of the best surf breaks in Hawai'i.

BEST SUNSETS

Kapalua Bay, West Maui. The ambience here is as stunning as the sunset.

Keawakapu, the South Shore. Since most active beachgoers enjoy this gorgeous spot before mid-afternoon when the wind picks up, it's never crowded at sunset. ■TIP➔Bring a picnic.

BEST FOR SEEING AND BEING SEEN

Kā'anapali Beach, West Maui. The portion of this popular beach that fronts Whalers Village is called "Dig Me"—need we say more?

Wailea Beach, the South Shore. At this beach fronting the ultraluxurious Four Seasons and Grand Wailea resorts, you never know who might be "hiding" in that private cabana!

in the morning as the winds pick up in the afternoon (beware of irritating sand storms). Keawakapu has two entrances: one at the Mana Kai Maui Resort (look for the blue SHORELINE ACCESS sign and the parking at Kilohana Street), and the second at the dead end of Kīhei Road. Toilets are portable. ⊠ *S. Kīhei Rd., at Kilohana St.* ☞ *Toilets, showers, parking lot.*

Mōkapu & Ulua. Look for a little road and public parking lot next to the Wailea Marriott. This gets you to Mōkapu and Ulua beaches. Though there are no lifeguards, families love this place. Reef formations create tons of tide pools for kids to explore and the beaches are protected from major swells. Snorkeling is excellent at Ulua, the beach to the left of the entrance. Mōkapu, to the right, tends to be less crowded. ⊠ *North of Wailea Marriott resort* ☞ *Toilets, showers, parking lot.*

Polo Beach. From Wailea Beach you can walk to this small, uncrowded crescent fronting the Fairmont Kea Lani resort. Swimming and snorkeling are great here and it's a good place to whale-watch. As at Wailea Beach, private cabanas occupy prime sandy real estate, but there's plenty of room for you and your towel, and even a nice grass picnic area. The pathway connecting the two beaches is a great spot to jog or leisurely take in awesome views of nearby Molokini and Kahoʻolawe. Rare native plants grow along the *makai* side of the path; the honey-sweet smelling one is *naio*, or false sandalwood. ⊠ *Wailea Alanui Dr., south of Fairmont Kea Lani resort entrance* ☞ *Toilets, showers, picnic tables, grills/firepits, parking lot.*

Fodor'sChoice **Mākena (Big Beach).** Locals successfully fought to give Mākena—one
★ of Hawaiʻi's most breathtaking beaches—state-park protection. Also known as "Big Beach," this stretch of deep-golden sand abutting sparkling aqua water is 3,000 feet long and 100 feet wide. It's never crowded, no matter how many cars cram into the lots. The water is fine for swimming, but use caution. ■TIP➔ The shore drop-off is steep and swells can get deceptively big. Despite the infamous "Mākena cloud," a blanket that rolls in during the early afternoon and obscures the sun, it rarely rains here. For a dramatic view of Big Beach, climb Puʻu Ōlaʻi, the steep cinder cone near the first entrance. Continue over the cinder cone's side to discover "Little Beach"—clothing-optional by popular practice. (Officially, nude sunbathing is illegal in Hawaiʻi.) On Sunday, free spirits of all kinds crowd Little Beach's tiny shoreline for a drumming circle and bonfire. Little Beach has the island's best bodysurfing (no pun intended). Skim-boarders catch air at Big Beach's third entrance. Each of the three paved entrances has portable toilets. ⊠ *Off Wailea Alanui Dr.* ☞ *Toilets, parking lot.*

THE NORTH SHORE

Many of the folks you see jaywalking in Pāʻia sold everything they owned to come to Maui and live a beach bum's life. Beach culture abounds on the North Shore. But these folks aren't sunbathers; they're big-wave riders, windsurfers, or kiteboarders. The North Shore is their challenging sports arena. Beaches here face the open ocean and tend to be rougher and windier than beaches elsewhere on Maui—but don't let that scare you off. On calm days, the reef-speckled waters are truly beautiful and offer a quieter and less commercial beach-going experience than the leeward shore. Beaches below are listed from Kahului (near the airport) eastward to Hoʻokipa.

Kanahā Beach. Windsurfers, kiteboarders, joggers, and picnicking families like this long, golden strip of sand bordered by a wide grassy area with lots of shade. The winds pick up in the early afternoon, making for the best kiteboarding and windsurfing conditions—if you know what

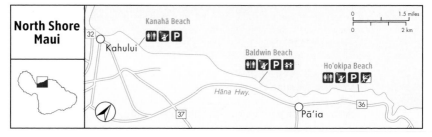

you're doing, that is. The best spot for watching kiteboarders is at the far left end of the beach. ✉ *Drive through airport and make right onto car-rental road (Koeheke); turn right onto Amala Pl. and take any left (there are 3 entrances) into Kanahā* ☞ *Toilets, showers, picnic tables, grills/firepits, parking lot.*

☾ **Baldwin Beach.** A local favorite, just west of Pā'ia town, Baldwin Beach
★ is a big stretch of comfortable white sand. This is a good place to lie out, jog, or swim, though the waves can sometimes be choppy and the undertow strong. Don't be afraid of those big brown blobs floating beneath the surface, they're just pieces of seaweed awash in the surf. You can find shade along the beach beneath the ironwood trees, or in the large pavilion, a spot regularly overtaken by local parties and community events.

The long, shallow pool at the Kahului end of the beach is known as "Baby Beach." Separated from the surf by a flat reef wall, this is where ocean-loving families bring their kids (and sometimes puppies) to practice a few laps. The view of the West Maui Mountains is hauntingly beautiful from here. ✉ *Hāna Hwy., 1 mi west of Baldwin Ave.* ☞ *Lifeguard, toilets, showers, picnic tables, grills/firepits, parking lot.*

★ **Ho'okipa Beach.** If you want to see some of the world's finest windsurfers in action, hit this beach along Hāna Highway. The sport was largely developed right at Ho'okipa and has become an art and a career to some. This beach is also one of Maui's hottest surfing spots, with waves as high as 20 feet. This is not a good swimming beach, nor the place to learn windsurfing, but it's great for hanging out and watching the pros. Bust out your telephoto lens at the cliff-side lookout to capture the aerial acrobatics of board-sailors and kiteboarders. ✉ *2 mi past Pā'ia on Rte. 36* ☞ *Toilets, showers, picnic tables, grills/firepits, parking lot.*

EAST MAUI AND HĀNA

Hāna's beaches will literally stop you in your tracks—they're that beautiful. Black and red sands stand out against pewter skies and lush tropical foliage creating picture-perfect scenes, which seem too breathtaking to be real. Rough conditions often preclude swimming, but that doesn't mean you can't explore the shoreline. Beaches below are listed in order from the west end of Hāna town eastward.

Fodor'sChoice **Wai'ānapanapa State Park.** Small but rarely crowded, this beach will
★ remain in your memory long after visiting. Fingers of white foam rush onto a black volcanic pebble beach fringed with green beach vines and palms. Swimming here is both relaxing and invigorating: strong currents bump smooth stones up against your ankles while seabirds flit above a black, jagged sea arch draped with vines. At the edge of the parking lot, a sign tells you the sad story of a doomed Hawaiian princess. Stairs lead through a tunnel of interlocking Polynesian *hau* branches to an icy cave pool—the secret hiding place of the ancient princess. ■ TIP➔**You can swim in this pool, but be wary of mosquitoes!** In the other direction, a 3-mi, dramatic coastal path continues beyond the campground, past sea arches, blowholes, and cultural sites all the way to Hāna town. Grassy tent sites and rustic cabins that accommodate up to six people

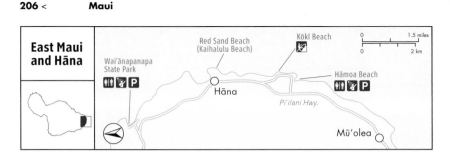

are available by reservation only; call ahead for information. ⊠*Hāna Hwy. near mile marker 32* ☞*Toilets, showers, picnic tables, grills/ firepits, parking lot.*

★ **Red Sand Beach (Kaihalulu Beach).** Kaihalulu Beach, better known as Red Sand Beach, is unmatched in its raw and remote beauty. It's not simple to find but when you round the last corner of the trail and are confronted with the sight of it, your jaw is bound to drop. Earthy red cliffs tower above the deep maroon sand beach and swimmers bob about in a turquoise blue lagoon formed by volcanic boulders just offshore (it's like floating around in a giant natural bathtub). It's worth spending a night in Hāna just to make sure you can get here early and have some time to enjoy it before anyone else shows up. ■TIP➔Getting here is not easy and you have to pass through private property along the way—do so at your own risk. You need to tread carefully up and around Ka'uiki (the red cinder hill); the cliff-side cinder path is slippery and constantly eroding. Hiking is not recommended in shoes without traction, or in bad weather. By popular practice, clothing on the beach is optional. ⊠*At end of U'akea Rd. past baseball field. Park near community center, walk through grass lot to trail below cemetery* ☞*No facilities.*

Kōkī Beach. You can tell from the trucks parked every which way alongside the road that this is a favorite local surf spot. ■TIP➔Watch conditions before swimming or bodysurfing, because the riptides here can be mean. Look for awesome views of the rugged coastline and a sea arch on the left end. *Iwa,* or white-throated frigate birds, dart like pterodactyls over 'Alau islet offshore. ⊠*Haneo'o Loop Rd., 2 mi east of Hāna town* ☞*No facilities.*

Hāmoa Beach. Why did James Michener describe this stretch of salt-and-pepper sand as the most "South Pacific" beach he'd come across, even though it's located in the North Pacific? Maybe it was the perfect half-moon shape, speckled with the shade of palm trees. Perhaps he was intrigued by the jutting black coastline, often outlined by rain showers out at sea, or the pervasive lack of hurry he felt here. Whatever it was, many still feel the lure. The beach can be crowded but nonetheless relaxing. Expect to see a few chaise longues and a guest-only picnic area set up by the Hotel Hāna-Maui. At times, the churning surf might intimidate beginning swimmers, but bodysurfing can be great here. ⊠*½ mi past Kōkī Beach on Haneo'o Loop Rd., 2 mi east of Hāna town* ☞*Toilets, showers, picnic tables, parking lot.*

WATER SPORTS AND TOURS

Updated by
Eliza Escaño-
Vasquez

Getting into (or onto) the water will be the highlight of your Maui trip. At Lahaina and Māʻalaea harbors, you can board boats for snorkeling, scuba diving, deep-sea fishing, whale-watching, parasailing, and sunset cocktail adventures. You can learn to surf, catch a ferry to Lānaʻi, or grab a seat on a fast inflatable raft. Along the leeward coastline, from Kāʻanapali on the West Shore all the way down to Waiala Cove on the South Shore, you can discover great snorkeling and swimming. If you're a thrill-seeker, head out to the North Shore and Hoʻokipa, where surfers, kiteboarders, and windsurfers catch big waves and big air.

BOOGIE BOARDING AND BODYSURFING

Bodysurfing and "sponging" (as boogie boarding is called by the regulars) are great ways to catch some waves without having to master surfing—and there's no balance or coordination required. A boogie board (or "sponge") is softer than a hard, fiberglass surfboard, which means you can ride safely in the rough-and-tumble surf zone. If you get tossed around (which is half the fun), you don't have a heavy surfboard nearby to bang your head on, but you do have something to hang onto. Serious spongers invest in a single short-clipped fin to help propel them into the wave.

The technique for catching waves is the same with or without a board. Swim out to where the swell is just beginning to break, and position yourself toward shore. When the next wave comes, lie on your board (if you have one), kick like crazy, and catch it! You'll feel the push of the wave as you glide in front of the gurgling, foamy surf. When bodysurfing, put your arms over your head, bring your index fingers together (so you look like the letter "A"), and stiffen your body like a board to achieve the same effect. If you don't like to swim too far out, stick with boogie boarding and bodysurfing close to shore. Shorebreak (if it isn't too steep) can be exhilarating to ride. You'll know it's too steep if you hear the sound of slapping when the waves hit the sand. You're looking for waves that curl over and break farther out, then roll, not slap onto the sand. Always watch first to make sure the conditions aren't too strong.

BEST SPOTS

D.T. Fleming Beach (✉ *Honoapiʻilani Hwy., below the Ritz-Carlton, Kapalua* offers great surf almost daily along with some nice amenities: ample parking, restrooms, a shower, grills, picnic tables, and a daily lifeguard. However, caution is advised, especially during winter months when the current and undertow can get rough.

Kamaʻole III (✉ *S. Kîhei Rd.*) is another good spot for bodysurfing and boogie boarding. It has a sandy floor, with 1- to 3-foot waves breaking not too far out. It's often crowded late into the day, especially on weekends when local kids are out of school. Don't let that chase you away—the waves are wide enough for everyone.

On the North Shore, **Pāʻia Bay** (✉ *Just before Pāʻia town, beyond large community building and grass field*) has waves suitable for spongers

DID YOU KNOW?

Wai'ānapanapa State Park in East Maui has a black volcanic-sand beach and a lovely 3-mi path along the coast. It's a great place to hike, picnic, or camp.

and bodysurfers. ■TIP→Park in the public lot across the street and leave your valuables at home, as this beach is known for break-ins.

EQUIPMENT

Most condos and hotels have boogie boards available to guests—some in better condition than others (but beat-up boogies work just as well for beginners). You can also pick up a boogie board from any discount shop, such as Kmart or Long's Drugs, for upward of $30.

Auntie Snorkel. You can rent decent boogie boards here for $5 a day, or $15 a week. ⊠2439 S. Kīhei Rd., Kīhei ☎808/879–6263.

Honolua Surf. "Waverider" boogie boards with smooth undersides (better than the bumpy kind) can be rented from this surf shop for $8

a day, or $35 a week (with a $100 deposit). ⊠2411 S. Kīhei Rd., Kīhei ☎808/874–0999 ⊠845 Front St., Lahaina ☎808/661–8848.

DEEP-SEA FISHING

If fishing is your sport, Maui is your island. In these waters you'll find 'ahi, *aku* (skipjack tuna), barracuda, bonefish, *kawakawa* (bonito), mahimahi, Pacific blue marlin, ono, and *ulua* (jack crevalle). You can fish year-round and you don't need a license. ■TIP→Because boats fill up fast during busy seasons (Christmas, spring break, tournament weeks), consider making reservations before coming to Maui.

Plenty of fishing boats run out of Lahaina and Mā'alaea harbors. If you charter a private boat, expect to spend in the neighborhood of $700 to $1,000 for a thrilling half-day in the swivel seat. You can share a boat for much less if you don't mind close quarters with a stranger who may get seasick, drunk, or worse . . . lucky! Before you sign up, you should know that some boats keep the catch. They will, however, fillet a nice piece for you to take home. And if you catch a real beauty, you might even be able to have it professionally mounted.

■TIP→Don't go out with a boater who charges for the fish you catch—that's harbor robbery. You're expected to bring your own lunch and nonglass beverages. (Shop the night before; it's hard to find snacks at 6 AM.) Boats supply coolers, ice, and bait. 10% to 20% tips are suggested.

BOATS AND CHARTERS

★ **Finest Kind Inc.** A record 1,118-pound blue marlin was reeled in by the crew aboard *Finest Kind,* a lovely 37-foot Merritt kept so clean you'd never guess the action it's seen. Ask Captain Dave about his pet frigate bird—he's been around these waters long enough to befriend other expert fishers. This family-run company operates four boats and specializes in live bait. ⊠ *Lahaina Harbor, Slip 7* ☏ *808/661–0338* ⊕ *www. finestkindsportfishing.com.*

Kai Palena Sportfishing. Captain Fuzzy Alboro runs a serious and highly recommended operation on the 32-foot Die Hard. Check-in is at 2:45 AM, and he takes a maximum of six people per trip. The cost is from $200 for a shared boat to $1,100 for a private charter; add 7% tax. ⊠ *511 Pikanele St., Lahaina Harbor, Slip 10* ☏ *808/878–2362.*

Strike Zone. This is one of the few charters to offer morning bottom-fishing trips (for smaller fish such as snapper), as well as deep-sea trips (for the big ones—ono, 'ahi, mahimahi, and marlin). Strike Zone is a 43-foot Delta that offers plenty of room (16-person max). Lunch and soft drinks are included. The catch is shared with the entire boat. The cost is $168 per adult and $148 per child for a pole; spectators can ride for $78, plus 7% tax. The four- and six-hour bottom-fishing trips run Monday, Wednesday, Friday, and Saturday; the six-hour deep-sea trips run Tuesday, Thursday, and Sunday, all weather-permitting. All trips leave at 6:30 AM. ⊠ *Māʻalaea Harbor, Slip 64, Māʻalaea* ☏ *808/879–4485.*

KAYAKING

Kayaking is a fantastic way to experience Maui's coast up close. Floating aboard a "plastic popsicle stick" is easier than you might think, and allows you to cruise out to vibrant, living coral reefs and waters where dolphins and even whales roam. Kayaking can be a leisurely paddle or a challenge of heroic proportion, depending on your ability, the location, and the weather. ■ TIP→ **Though you can rent kayaks independently, we recommend taking a guide.** An apparently calm surface can hide extremely strong ocean currents—and you don't *really* want to take an unplanned trip to Tahiti! Most guides are naturalists who will steer you away from surging surf, lead you to pristine reefs, and point out camouflaged fish, like the stalking hawkfish. Not having to schlep your gear on top of your rental car is a bonus. A half-day tour runs around $75. Custom tours can be arranged.

If you decide to strike out on your own, tour companies will rent kayaks for the day with paddles, life vests, and roof racks, and many will meet you near your chosen location. Ask for a map of good entries and plan to avoid paddling back to shore against the wind (schedule extra time for the return trip regardless). For beginners, get there early before the trade wind kicks in, and try sticking close to the shore. When you're ready to snorkel, secure your belongings in a dry pack onboard and drag your boat by its bowline behind you. (This isn't as bad as it sounds). ■ TIP→ The 'Āhihi-Kīnaʻu Natural Area Reserve, at the southernmost point of South Maui, is closed to all activities until July 31, 2010. You may not kayak, dive, or snorkel in the reserve before this date. Closure is to allow the coral reef system in the area to recover from overuse.

BEST SPOTS

In West Maui, past the steep cliffs on the Honoapiʻilani Highway and before you hit Lahaina, there's a long stretch of inviting coastline, including **Ukumehame** and **Olowalu** (⊠ *Between mile markers 12 and 14* *on Rte. 30*) beaches. This is a good spot for beginners; entry is easy and there's much to see in every direction. If you want to snorkel, the best visibility is farther out at Olowalu, at about 25 feet depth. ■ TIP→Watch for sharp kiawe thorns buried in the sand on the way into the water.

Mākena Landing (⊠ *Off Mākena Rd.*) is an excellent taking-off point for a South Maui adventure. Enter from the paved parking lot or the small sandy beach a little south. The bay itself is virtually empty, but the right edge is flanked with brilliant coral heads and juvenile turtles. If you round the point on the right, you come across **Five Caves,** a system of enticing underwater arches. In the morning you may see dolphins, and the arches are havens for lobsters, eels, and spectacularly hued butterfly fish. Check out the million-dollar mansions lining the shoreline and guess which celebrity lives where. ■ TIP→ Regulators, activity operators, and the public are immersed in a hot debate about shore access to this area due to concerns over conservation, safety, and economic issues. At press time, commercial kayaking was prohibited at Mākena Landing; if you want to kayak here, you'll need to rent equipment and come on your own.

EQUIPMENT AND TOURS

Kelii's Kayak Tours. One of the highest-rated kayak outfitters on the island, Kelii's offers combo trips where one can paddle, surf, snorkel, or hike to a waterfall. They can take up to eight people per guide. Trips are available on the island's North, South, and West shores, and range from $54 to $149, plus 4.4% tax. ⊠ *Kīhei* ☎ *888/874–8652 or 808/874–7652* ⊕ *www.keliiskayak.com.*

Fodor'sChoice **South Pacific Kayaks.** These guys pioneered recreational kayaking on
★ Maui—they know their stuff. Guides are friendly, informative, and eager to help you get the most out of your experience; we're talking true, fun-loving, kayak geeks. Some activity companies show a strange lack of care for the marine environment; South Pacific stands out as adventurous *and* responsible. They offer a variety of trips leaving from both West Maui and South Shore locations, including an advanced four-hour "Molokini Challenge." ☎ *800/776–2326 or 808/875–4848* ⊕ *www.southpacifickayaks.com.*

KITEBOARDING

Catapulting up to 40 feet in the air above the breaking surf, kiteboarders hardly seem of this world. Silken kites hold the athletes aloft for precious seconds—long enough for the execution of mind-boggling tricks—then deposit them back in the sea. This new sport is not for the weak-kneed. No matter what people might tell you, it's harder to learn than windsurfing. The unskilled (or unlucky) can be caught in an upwind and carried far out in the ocean, or worse—dropped smack on the shore. Because of insurance (or the lack thereof), companies are not allowed to rent equipment. Beginners must take lessons, and then purchase their own gear. Devotees swear after your first few lessons, committing to buying your kite is easy.

LESSONS

Aqua Sports Maui. "To air is human," or so they say at Aqua Sports, which calls itself the local favorite of kiteboarding schools. They've got a great location right near Kite Beach, at the west (left) end of Kanahā Beach, and offer basic through advanced kiteboarding lessons. Rates start at $210 for a three-hour basics course taught by certified instructors. ✉ *90 Amala Pl., near Kite Beach, Kahului* ☎ *808/242–8015* ⊕ *www. mauikiteboardinglessons.com.*

Hawaiian Sailboarding Techniques. Pro kiteboarder and legendary windsurfer Alan Cadiz will have you safely ripping in no time at lower Kanahā Beach Park. A "Learn to Kitesurf" package starts at $225 for a three-hour private lesson, which includes all equipment. As opposed to observing from the shore, instructors paddle after students on a chaseboard to give immediate feedback. HST is in the Hi Tech Surf & Sports store, located in the Triangle Square shopping center. ✉ *425 Koloa St., Kahului* ☎ *808/871–5423 or 800/968–5423* ⊕ *www.hstwindsurfing.com.*

PARASAILING

Parasailing is an easy, exhilarating way to earn your wings: just strap on a harness attached to a parachute, and a powerboat pulls you up and over the ocean from a launching dock or a boat's platform. ■ TIP➜Keep in mind, parasailing is limited to West Maui, and "thrill craft"—including parasails—are prohibited in Maui waters during humpback whale–calving season, December 15 to May 15.

West Maui Parasail. Launch 400 feet above the ocean for a bird's-eye view of Lahaina, or be daring at 800 feet for smoother rides and better views. The captain will be glad to let you experience a "toe dip" or "freefall" if you request it. For safety reasons, passengers weighing less than 100 pounds must be strapped together in tandem. Hour-long trips departing from Lahaina Harbor, Slip #15, and Kāʻanapali Beach include eight- to 10-minute flights and run from $65 for the 400-foot ride to $75 for the 800-foot ride. Observers must pay $30 each. ☎ *808/661–4060* ⊕ *www. westmauiparasail.com.*

RAFTING

The high-speed, inflatable rafts you find on Maui are nothing like the raft that Huck Finn used to drift down the Mississippi. While passengers grip straps, these rafts fly, skimming and bouncing across the sea. Because they're so maneuverable, they go where the big boats can't—secret coves, sea caves, and remote beaches. Two-hour trips run around $50, half-day trips upward of $100. ■ TIP➜Although safe, these trips are not for the faint of heart. If you have back or neck problems or are pregnant, you should reconsider this activity.

TOURS

Blue Water Rafting. One of the only ways to get to the stunning Kanaio Coast (the roadless southern coastline beyond ʻĀhihi-Kīnaʻu), this rafting tour begins trips conveniently at the Kīhei boat ramp. Dolphins, turtles, and other marine life are the highlight of this adventure, along with sea caves, lava arches, and views of Haleakalā. Two-hour trips start at $49 plus tax; longer trips cost $90 to $115 and include a deli lunch. ✉2777 *South Kīhei Rd., Kīhei* ☎808/879–7238 ⊕*www.blue waterrafting.com.*

Ocean Riders. This West Maui tour crosses the ʻAuʻAu channel to Lānaʻi's Shipwreck Beach, then circles the island for 70 minutes of remote coast. For snorkeling, the "back side" of Lānaʻi is one of Hawaiʻi's unsung marvels. Tours—$129 plus tax per person—depart from Mala Wharf, at the northern end of Front Street and include snorkel gear, a fruit breakfast, and a deli lunch. ✉*Lahaina* ☎808/661–3586 ⊕*www.maui-oceanriders.com.*

SAILING

With the islands of Molokaʻi, Lānaʻi, Kahoʻolawe, and Molokini a stone's throw away, Maui waters offer visually arresting backdrops for sailing adventures. Sailing conditions can be fickle, so some operations throw in snorkeling or whale-watching, and others offer sunset cruises. Winds are consistent in summer, but variable in winter, and afternoons are generally windier all throughout the year. Prices range from around $40 for two-hour trips to $80 for half-day excursions. ■TIP➔You won't be sheltered from the elements on the trim racing boats, so be sure to bring a hat (one that won't blow away), a light jacket or cover-up, sunglasses, and extra sunscreen.

BOATS AND CHARTERS

America II. This one-time America's Cup contender offers an exciting, intimate alternative to crowded catamarans. For fast action, try a morning trade-wind sail. Sunset sails are generally calmer—a good choice if you don't want to spend two hours fully exposed to the sun. Plan to bring a change of clothes, because you will get wet. Snack and beverages are provided. No one under five years old is permitted. ✉*Harbor Slip #6, Lahaina* ☎808/667–2195 ⊕*www.sailingonmaui.com.*

Paragon. If you want to snorkel and sail, this is your boat. Many snorkel cruises claim to sail but actually motor most of the way; Paragon is an exception. Both Paragon vessels (one catamaran in Lahaina, the other in Māʻalaea) are ship-shape, and crews are competent and friendly. Their mooring in Molokini Crater is particularly good, and they often stay after the masses have left. The Lānaʻi trip includes a picnic lunch on the beach, snorkeling, and an afternoon blue water swim. Extras on their trips to Lānaʻi include mai tais and sodas, hot and cold pūpū (Hawaiian tapas), and champagne. A similar spread comes with the sunset sail, which departs from Lahaina Harbor every Monday, Wednesday, and Friday. ✉*Lahaina and Māʻalaea Harbors* ☎808/244–2087 *or* 800/441–2087 ⊕*www.sailmaui.com.*

Trilogy Excursions. With more than 35 years of sailing tradition, not to mention a commitment to Hawaiiana and the ecosystem, Trilogy remains a favorite of locals and visitors alike. It is one of only two companies that sail to Molokini. A two-hour sail starts at $59. Alcohol is not provided. Book online for a 10% discount. ✉*Māʻalaea*

Harbor, Slip 99, Lahaina Harbor, or by the Kāʻanapali Beach Hotel
☎808/661–4743 or 888/225–6284 ⊕www.sailtrilogy.com.

SCUBA DIVING

Maui is just as scenic underwater as it is on dry land. It's common to see huge sea turtles, eagle rays, and small reef sharks, not to mention many varieties of angelfish, parrotfish, eels, and octopi. Unlike other popular dive destinations, most of the species are unique to this area. For example, of Maui's 450 species of reef fish, 25% are endemic to the island. Dives are best in the morning, when visibility can hold a steady 100 feet. If you're a certified diver, you can rent gear at any Maui dive shop simply by showing your PADI or NAUI card. If you're not certified, hook up with a dive shop for an introductory underwater tour ($100–$160). Tours include tanks and weights. ■TIP➜Before signing on with any of these outfitters, it's a good idea to ask a few pointed questions about your guide's experience, the weather outlook, and the condition of the equipment.

BEST SPOTS

Honolua Bay (⊠Between mile markers 32 and 33 on Rte. 30, look for narrow dirt road to left) has beach entry. This West Maui marine preserve is alive with many varieties of coral and tame tropical fish, including large ulua, kāhala, barracuda, and manta rays. With depths of 20 to 50 feet, this is a popular summer dive spot, good for all levels. ■TIP➜High surf often prohibits winter dives.

Only 3 mi offshore, **Molokini Crater** is world renowned for its deep, crystal clear, fish-filled waters. A crescent-shaped islet formed by the eroding top of a volcano, the crater is a marine preserve ranging 10 to 80 feet in depth. The numerous tame fish and brilliant coral dwelling within the crater make it a popular introductory dive site. On calm days, exploring the back side of Molokini (called Back Wall) can be a dramatic sight for advanced divers—giving them visibility of up to 150 feet. The enormous dropoff into the ʻAlalākeiki Channel (to 350 feet) offers awesome seascapes, black coral, and chance sightings of larger pelagic fish and sharks.

On the South Shore, a popular dive spot is **Mākena Landing,** also called **Five Graves** or **Five Caves.** About ⅓ mi down Mākena Road, you'll feast on underwater delights—caves, ledges, coral heads, and an outer reef home to a large green sea-turtle colony (called "Turtle Town"). ■TIP➜Entry is rocky lava, so be careful where you step. This area is for the more experienced diver. Rookies can enter farther down Mākena Road at Mākena Landing, and dive to the right.

EQUIPMENT AND TOURS

★ **Ed Robinson's Diving Adventures.** Ed wrote the book, literally, on Molokini. Because he knows so much, he includes a "Biology 101" talk with every dive. An expert marine photographer, he offers diving instruction and boat charters to South Maui, the backside of Molokini, and Lānaʻi. Weekly night dives are available, and there's a 10% discount if you book three or more days. Check out the Web site for good info and

DIVING 101

If you've always wanted gills, Hawai'i is a good place to get them. Although the bulky, heavy equipment seems freakish on shore, underwater it allows you to move about freely, almost weightlessly. As you descend into another world, you slowly grow used to the sound of your own breathing and the strangeness of being able to do so 30-plus feet down.

Most resorts offer introductory dive lessons in their pools, which allow you to acclimate to the awkward breathing apparatus before venturing out into the great blue. If you aren't starting from a resort pool, no worries. Most intro dives take off from calm, sandy beaches, such as Ulua or Kā'anapali. If you're bitten by the deep-sea bug and want to continue diving, you should get certified. Only certified divers can rent equipment or go on more adventurous dives, such as night dives, open-ocean dives, and cave dives.

There are several certification companies, including PADI, NAUI, and SSI. PADI, the largest, is the most comprehensive. Once you begin your certification process, stick with the same company. The dives you log will not apply to another company's certification. (Dives with a PADI instructor, for instance, will not count toward SSI certification). Remember that you will not be able to fly or go to the airy summit of Haleakalā within 24 hours of diving. Open-water certification will take three to four days and cost around $350. From that point on, the sky . . . or rather, the sea's the limit!

links on scuba sites, weather, and sea conditions. ✉ *50 Koki St., Kīhei* ☎ *808/879–3584 or 800/635–1273* ⊕ *www.mauiscuba.com.*

Maui Dive Shop. With six locations island-wide, Maui Dive Shop offers scuba charters, diving instruction, and equipment rental. Excursions, offering awe-inspiring beach and boat dives, go to Molokini Back Wall (most advanced dive), Shipwreck Beach on Lāna'i, and more. Night dives and customized trips are available, as are full SSI and PADI certificate programs. ✉ *1455 S. Kīhei Rd., Kīhei* ☎ *808/879–3388 or 800/542–3483* ⊕ *www.mauidiveshop.com.*

Shaka Divers. Shaka provides personalized dives including a great four-hour intro dive ($79), a refresher course ($89), scuba certification ($375), and shore dives ($59) to Mākena, Ulua, Five Graves (at Mākena Landing), Turtle Town, Bubble Cave, Black Sand Beach, and more. Typical dives last about an hour, with 30 to 45 feet visibility. Dives can be booked on short notice, with afternoon tours available (hard to find on Maui). Shaka also offers night dives and torpedo scooter dives. The twilight two-tank dive is nice for day divers who want to ease into night-diving. A fun bit of trivia: owner Shaka Doug holds the world record for thickest diving logbook and most bubble rings, 34, blown in one breath. ✉ *24 Hakoi Pl., Kīhei* ☎ *808/250–1234* ⊕ *www.shakadivers.com.*

Snorkelers can see adorable green sea turtles around Maui.

SNORKELING

No one should leave Maui without ducking underwater to meet a sea turtle, moray eel, or *humuhumunukunukuāpua'a*—the state fish. Visibility is best in the morning, before the wind picks up.

There are two ways to approach snorkeling—by land or by sea. Daily around 7 AM, a parade of boats heads out to Lāna'i or Molokini Crater, that ancient cone of volcanic cinder off the coast of Wailea. Boat trips offer some advantages—deeper water, seasonal whale-watching, crew assistance, lunch, and gear. But you don't need a boat; much of Maui's best snorkeling is found just steps from the road. Nearly the entire leeward coastline from Kapalua south to 'Āhihi-Kīna'u offers prime opportunities to ogle fish and turtles. If you're patient and sharp-eyed, you may glimpse eels, octopi, lobsters, eagle rays, and even a rare shark or monk seal.

BEST SPOTS

Snorkel sites here are listed from north to south, starting at the northwest corner of the island.

On the west side of the island, just north of Kapalua, **Honolua Bay** (⊠ *Between mile markers 32 and 33 on Rte. 30, dirt road to left*), Marine Life Conservation District has a superb reef for snorkeling. When conditions are calm, it's one of the island's best spots with tons of fish and colorful corals to observe. ■ TIP→ Make sure to bring a fish key with you, you're sure to see many species of triggerfish, filefish, and wrasses. The coral formations on the right side of the bay are particularly dramatic and feature pink, aqua, and orange varieties. Take care entering the water, there's no beach and the rocks and concrete ramp can be slippery.

The northeast corner of this windward-facing bay periodically gets hammered by big waves in winter and high-profile surf contests are held here. Avoid the bay then, and after a heavy rain (you'll know because Honolua stream will be running across the access path).

Just minutes south of Honolua, dependable **Kapalua Bay** (⊠ *From Rte. 30, turn onto Kapalua Pl., and walk through tunnel*) beckons. As beautiful above the water as it is below, Kapalua is exceptionally calm, even when other spots get testy. Needle and butterfly fish dart just past the sandy beach, which is why it's sometimes crowded. ■ TIP➔ Sand can be particularly hot here, watch your toes!

Fodor'sChoice We think **Black Rock** (⊠ *In front of Kāʻanapali Sheraton Maui, Kāʻanapali
★ Pkwy.*), at the northernmost tip of Kāʻanapali Beach, is tops for snorkelers of any skill level. The entry couldn't be easier—dump your towel on the sand in front of the Sheraton Maui resort and in you go. Beginners can stick close to shore and still see lots of action. Advanced snorkelers can swim beyond the sand to the tip of Black Rock, or Kekaʻa Point, to see larger fish and eagle rays. One of the underwater residents, a turtle named "Volkswagen" for its hefty size, can be found here. He sits very still; you must look closely. Equipment can be rented on-site. Parking, in a small lot adjoining the hotel, is the only hassle.

Along Honoapiʻilani Highway (Route 30) there are several favorite snorkel sites including the area just out from the cemetery at **Hanakaoʻo Beach Park** (⊠ *Near mile marker 23 on Rte. 30*). At depths of 5 and 10 feet, you can see a variety of corals, especially as you head south toward **Waihikuli Wayside Park. Olowalu** (⊠ *South of Olowalu General Store on Rte. 30, at mile marker 14*) is good for a quick underwater tour, though the best spot is a ways out, at depths of 25 feet or more. Closer to shore, the visibility can be hit or miss, but if you're willing to venture out about 50 yards, you'll have easy access to an expansive coral reef with abundant fish life—no boat required. Swim offshore toward the pole sticking out of the reef. Except for during a south swell, this area is calm and good for families with small children; turtles are plentiful. Boats sometimes stop nearby (they refer to this site as "Coral Gardens") on their return trip from Molokini.

Excellent snorkeling is found down the coastline between Kīhei and Mākena. The best spots are along the rocky fringes of Wailea's beaches, **Mōkapu, Ulua, Wailea,** and **Polo,** off Wailea Alanui Drive. Find one of the public parking lots sandwiched between Wailea's luxury resorts, and enjoy these beaches' sandy entries, calm waters with relatively good visibility, and variety of fish species. Of the four beaches, Ulua has the best reef. You can glimpse a box-shaped puffer fish here, and listen to snapping shrimp and parrot fish nibbling on coral.

Between Maui and neighboring Kahoʻolawe, 3 mi offshore from Wailea, is the world-famous **Molokini Crater**. Its crescent-shaped rim provides a sanctuary for birds and marine life and draws masses of snorkel and dive tours year-round. Most snorkeling tour operators offer a Molokini trip. The journey to this sunken crater takes more than 90 minutes from Lahaina, an hour from Māʻalaea, and half an hour from the South Shore.

At the very southernmost tip of paved road in South Maui lies 'Āhihi-Kīna'u (⊠*Just before end of Mākena Alanui Rd., follow marked trails through trees*) Natural Area Reserve, also referred to as La Pérouse Bay. Despite its barren, lava-scorched landscape, the area recently gained such popularity with adventurers and activity purveyors that it had to be closed to commercial traffic and is temporarily closed to all foot traffic (until July 31, 2010). If you're visiting Maui after this date, be sure to visit. A ranger is stationed at the parking lot to assist visitors. It's difficult terrain and sometimes crowded, but if you make use of the rangers' suggestions (stay on marked paths, wear sturdy shoes to hike in and out), you can experience some of the reserve's outstanding treasures, such as the sheltered cove known as the "Fish Bowl." ■TIP➔Be sure to bring water, this is a hot and unforgiving wilderness.

EQUIPMENT

Most hotels and vacation rentals offer free use of snorkel gear. Beachside stands fronting the major resort areas rent equipment by the hour or day. ■TIP➔Don't shy away from asking for instructions, a snug fit makes all the difference in the world. A mask fits if it sticks to your face when you inhale deeply through your nose. Fins should cover your entire foot (unlike diving fins, which strap around your heel). If you're squeamish about using someone else's gear (or need a prescription lens), pick up your own at any discount shop. Costco and Long's Drugs have better prices than ABC stores; dive shops have superior equipment.

Maui Dive Shop. You can rent pro gear (including optical masks, boogie boards, and wet suits) from six locations island-wide. Pump these guys for weather info before heading out, they'll know better than last night's news forecaster, and they'll give you the real deal on conditions. ⊠*1455 S. Kīhei Rd., Kīhei* ☎*808/873–3388* ⊕*www.mauidiveshop.com.*

Snorkel Bob's. If you need gear, Snorkel Bob's will rent you a mask, fins, and a snorkel, and throw in a carrying bag, map, and snorkel tips for as little as $9 per week. Avoid the circle masks and go for the split-level ($22 per week), it's worth the extra cash. ⊠*Nāpili Village Hotel, 5425 Lower Honoapi'ilani Hwy., Nāpili* ☎*808/669–9603* ⊠*Dickenson Square, Dickenson St., Lahaina* ☎*808/662–0104* ⊠*1279 S. Kīhei Rd., #310, Kīhei* ☎*808/875–6188* ⊠*Kamaole Beach Center, 2411 S. Kīhei Rd., Kīhei* ☎*808/879–7449* ⊕*www.snorkelbob.com.*

TOURS

Molokini Crater, a crescent about 3 mi off the shore of Wailea, is the most popular snorkel cruise destination. You can spend half a day floating above the fish-filled crater for about $80. Some say it's not as good as it's made out to be, and that it's too crowded, but others consider it to be one of the best spots in Hawai'i. Visibility is generally outstanding and fish are incredibly tame. Your second stop will be somewhere along the leeward coast, either "Turtle Town" near Mākena or "Coral Gardens" toward Lahaina. ■TIP➔Be aware that on blustery mornings, there's a good chance the waters will be too rough to moor in Molokini and you'll end up snorkeling some place off the shore, which you could have driven to for free. For the safety of everyone on the boat, it's the captain's prerogative to choose the best spot for the day.

Snorkel cruises vary slightly—some serve mai tais and steaks whereas others offer beer and cold cuts. You might prefer a large ferryboat to a smaller sailboat, or vice versa. Whatever trip you choose, be sure you know where to go to board your vessel; getting lost in the harbor at 6 AM is a lousy start to a good day. ■TIP➔Bring sunscreen, an underwater camera (they're double the price onboard), a towel, and a cover-up for the windy return trip. Even tropical waters get chilly after hours of swimming, so consider wearing a rash guard. Wet suits can usually be rented for a fee. Hats without straps will blow away, and valuables should be left at home.

★ **Ann Fielding's Snorkel Maui.** For a personal introduction to Maui's undersea universe, this guided tour is the undisputable authority. A marine biologist, Fielding—formerly with the University of Hawai'i, Waikīkī Aquarium, and the Bishop Museum, and the author of several guides to island sea life—is the Carl Sagan of Hawai'i's reef cosmos. She'll not only show you fish, but she'll also introduce you to *individual* fish. This is a good first experience for dry-behind-the-ears types. Snorkel trips cost $95 per adult, and include a snack and equipment. Groups travel to shoreline snorkel sites by car; these are not boat tours. ☎808/572–8437 ⊕www.maui.net/~annf.

Maui Classic Charters. This company offers two top-rate snorkel trips at a good value. Hop aboard the *Four Winds II,* a 55-foot, glass-bottom catamaran, for one of the most dependable snorkel trips around. You'll spend more time than the other charter boats do at Molokini and enjoy turtle-watching on the way home. The trip includes optional snuba ($49 extra), Continental breakfast, and a deluxe barbecue lunch, beer, wine, and soda. For a faster ride, try the *Maui Magic,* Mā'alaea's fastest power cat. This boat takes fewer people (45 max) than some of the larger vessels, and as an added bonus, they offer snuba and play Hawaiian music on the ride. This one's good for kids. Trips range from $98 to $109; book online at least seven days in advance for a $10 discount. ⊠*Mā'alaea Harbor Slips #55 and #80* ☎808/879–8188 or 800/736–5740 ⊕www.mauicharters.com.

Paragon. With this company, you get to snorkel and sail—they have some of the fastest vessels in the state. As long as conditions are good, you'll hit prime snorkel spots in Molokini, Lāna'i, and occasionally, Coral Gardens. The Lāna'i trip includes a Continental breakfast, a picnic lunch on the beach, snacks, open bar, a snorkel lesson, and plenty of time in the water. The friendly crew takes good care of you, making sure you get the most value and enjoyment from your trip. ⊠*Mā'alaea Harbor Slip 72, or Lahaina Harbor* ☎808/244–2087 ⊕www.sailmaui.com.

☾ **Trilogy Excursions.** The longest-running operation on Maui is the Coon family's Trilogy Excursions. In terms of comprehensive offerings, this company's got it: they have six beautiful multi-hulled sailing vessels at three departure sites. All excursions are manned by energetic crews who will keep you entertained with stories of the islands and plenty of corny jokes. A full-day catamaran cruise to Lāna'i includes Continental breakfast and a deli lunch onboard; a guided van tour of the island; a "Snorkeling 101" class; and time to snorkel in the waters of

Lāna'i's Hulopo'e Marine Preserve (Trilogy has exclusive commercial access). There is a barbecue dinner on Lāna'i and an optional dolphin safari. The company also offers a Molokini and Honolua Bay snorkel cruise. Many people consider a Trilogy excursion the highlight of their trip. ⊠*Mā'alaea Harbor Slip #99, or Lahaina Harbor* ☎*808/661–4743 or 888/225–6284* ⊕*www.sailtrilogy.com.*

SURFING

Maui's diverse coastline has surf for every level of waterman or -woman. Waves on leeward-facing shores (West and South Maui) tend to break in gentle sets all summer long. Surf instructors in Kīhei and Lahaina can rent you boards, give you onshore instruction, and then lead you out through the channel, where it's safe to enter the surf. They'll shout encouragement while you paddle like mad for the thrill of standing on water—some will even give you a helpful shove. These areas are great for beginners, the only danger is whacking a stranger with your board or stubbing your toe against the reef.

The North Shore is another story. Winter waves pound the windward coast, attracting water champions from every corner of the world. Adrenaline addicts are towed in by Jet Ski to a legendary, deep-sea break called *Jaws.* Waves here periodically tower upward of 40 feet, dwarfing the helicopters seeking to capture unbelievable photos. The only spot for viewing this phenomenon (which happens just a few times a year) is on private property. So, if you hear the surfers next to you crowing about Jaws "going off," cozy up and get them to take you with them.

Stand-up paddle surfing, where you stand on a longboard and paddle out with a canoe oar, is the new "comeback kid" of surf sports. Paddleboarding requires even more balance and coordination than regular surfing. But these days you can almost always see at least one lone paddler amid the pack—watch for them.

Whatever your skill, there's a board, a break, and even a surf guru to accommodate you. A two-hour lesson is a good intro to surf culture. Surf camps are becoming increasingly popular, especially with women. One- or two-week camps offer a terrific way to build muscle and self-esteem simultaneously. **Maui Surfer Girls** (⊕*www.mauisurfergirls.com*) immerses adventurous young ladies in wave-riding wisdom during overnight, one-, and two-week camps. Coed camps are sponsored by **Action Sports Maui** (⊕*www.actionsportsmaui.com*).

BEST SPOTS

Beginners can hang 10 at Kīhei's **Cove Park** (⊠*S. Kīhei Rd., Kīhei*), a sometimes crowded but reliable 1- to 2-foot break. Boards can easily be rented across the street, or in neighboring Kalama Park parking lot. The only bummer is having to balance the 9-plus-foot board on your head while crossing busy South Kīhei Road. But hey, that wouldn't stop world-famous longboarder Eddie Aikau, now would it?

Long- or short-boarders can paddle out anywhere along Lahaina's coastline. One option is at **Launiupoko State Wayside** (⊠ *Honoapiʻilani Hwy. near mile marker 18*). The east end of the park has an easy break, good for beginners. Even better is **Ukumehame** (⊠ *Honoapiʻilani Hwy. near mile marker 12*), also called "Thousand Peaks." You'll soon see how the spot got its name; the waves here break again and again in wide and consistent rows, giving lots of room for beginning and intermediate surfers.

Other **good surf spots** in West Maui include "Grandma's" at **Papalaua Park,** just after the *pali* (cliff)—where waves are so easy a grandma could ride 'em; **Puamana Beach Park** for a mellow longboard day; and **Lahaina Harbor,** which offers an excellent inside wave for beginners (called "Breakwall"), as well as the more-advanced outside (a great lift if there's a big south swell). Near-perfect waves can also be seen at **Honolua Bay,** on the northern tip of West Maui, 2 mi north of D.T. Fleming Park.

For advanced wave riders, **Ho'okipa Beach Park** (⊠ *2 mi past Pāʻia on Hāna Hwy.*) boasts several well-loved breaks, including "Pavilions," "Lanes," "the Point," and "Middles." Surfers have priority until 11 AM, when windsurfers move in on the action. ■ TIP→**Competition is stiff here, and the attitudes can be "agro." If you don't know what you're doing, consider watching from the shore.**

You can get the wave report each day by checking page 2 of the *Maui News,* logging onto the Glenn James weather site at ⊕ *www.hawaii weathertoday.com,* or calling ☎ *808/871–5054* (for the weather forecast) or ☎ *808/877–3611* (for the surf report).

EQUIPMENT AND LESSONS

Big Kahuna Adventures. Rent surfboards (soft-top long boards) here for $20 for two hours, or $30 for the day. The shop also offers surf lessons, and rents kayaks and snorkel gear. Located across from Cove Park. ⊠ *Island Surf Bldg., 1993 S. Kīhei Rd. #2, Kīhei* ☎ *808/875–6395* ⊕ *www.bigkahunaadventures.com.*

★ **Goofy Foot.** Surfing "goofy foot" means putting your right foot forward. They might be goofy, but we like the right-footed gurus here. Their safari shop is just plain cool and only steps away from "Breakwall," a great beginner's spot in Lahaina. Two-hour classes with five or fewer students are $65, and six-hour classes with lunch and an ocean-safety course are $250. ⊠ *505 Front St., Ste. 123, Lahaina* ☎ *808/244–9283* ⊕ *www.goofyfootsurfschool.com.*

Hi-Tech Surf Sports. Locals hold Hi-Tech in the highest regard. They have some of the best boards, advice, and attitudes around. Rent surfboards for $20 per day; $112 for the week. They rent even their best models— choose from long boards, short boards, and hybrids. All rentals come with board bags, roof rags, and oh yeah, wax. ⊠ *425 Koloa St., Kahului* ☎ *808/877–2111* ⊕ *www.htmaui.com.*

★ **Nancy Emerson School of Surfing.** Nancy's motto is "If my dog can surf, so can you." Instructors here will get even the most shaky novice riding with their "Learn to Surf in One Lesson" program. A two-hour group lesson (six students max) is $78. Nancy currently lives in Australia, but private lessons with her equally qualified instructors are $165–$200 for two hours. Semiprivate lessons with two people are $130 per person. Multiple-day sessions start at $350. They provide the boards and rash guards. ⊠*505 Front St., Ste. 224B, Lahaina* ☎*808/244–7873* ⊕*www. mauisurfclinics.com.*

WHALE-WATCHING

From November through May, whale-watching becomes one of the most popular activities on Maui. During the season, all outfitters offer whale-watching in addition to their regular activities, and most do an excellent job. Boats leave the wharves at Lahaina and Māʻalaea in search of humpbacks, allowing you to enjoy the awe-inspiring size of these creatures in closer proximity.

As it's almost impossible *not* to see whales in winter on Maui, you'll want to prioritize: is adventure or comfort your aim? If close encounters with the giants of the deep are your desire, pick a smaller boat that promises sightings. Those who think "green" usually prefer the smaller, quieter vessels that produce the least amount of negative impact to the whales' natural environment. If an impromptu marine-biology lesson sounds fun, go with the Pacific Whale Foundation. Two-hour forays into the whales' world are around $30. For those wanting to sip mai tais as whales cruise calmly by, stick with a sunset cruise on a boat with an open bar and pūpū ($40 and up). ■TIP→Afternoon trips are generally rougher because the wind picks up, but some say this is when the most surface action occurs.

Every captain aims to please during whale season, getting as close as legally possible (100 yards). Crew members know when a whale is about to dive (after several waves of its heart-shaped tail) but rarely can predict breaches (when the whale hurls itself up and almost entirely out of the water). Prime-viewing space (on the upper and lower decks, around the railings) is limited, so boats can feel crowded even when half full. If you don't want to squeeze in beside strangers, opt for a smaller boat with fewer bookings. Don't forget to bring sunscreen, sunglasses, light long sleeves, and a hat you can secure. Winter weather is less predictable and at times can be extreme, especially as the wind picks up. Arrive early to find parking.

BEST SPOTS

From December 15 to May 1 the Pacific Whale Foundation has naturalists stationed in two places—on the rooftop of their headquarters and at the scenic viewpoint at **Papawai Point Lookout** (⊠*Rte. 30, 3 mi west of Mâ'alaea Harbor*). Just like the commuting traffic, whales cruise along the *pali*, or cliff-side, of West Maui's Honoapiʻilani highway all day long. ■TIP→Make sure to park safely before craning your neck out to see them.

Humpback whale calves are plentiful in winter; this one is breaching off West Maui.

The northern end of **Keawakapu Beach** (⊠ *S. Kīhei Rd. near Kilohana Dr.*) seems to be a whale magnet. Situate yourself on the sand or at the nearby restaurant, and you're bound to see a mama whale patiently teaching her calf the exact technique of flipper-waving.

BOATS AND CHARTERS

Pacific Whale Foundation. This nonprofit organization pioneered whale-watching back in 1979 and now runs four boats, with 15 trips daily. As the most recognizable name in whale-watching, the crew (with a certified marine biologist on-board) offers insights into whale behavior (do they *really* know what those tail flicks mean?) and suggests ways for you to help save marine life worldwide. The best part about these trips is the underwater hydrophone that allows you to actually listen to the whales sing. Trips meet at the Foundation's store, where you can buy whale paraphernalia, snacks, and coffee—a real bonus for 8 AM trips. Passengers are then herded much like migrating whales down to the harbor. These trips are more affordable than others, but you'll be sharing the boat with about 100 people in stadium seating. Once you catch sight of the wildlife up close, however, you can't help but be thrilled. ⊠ *Māʻalaea and Lahaina harbors* ☎ *800/942–5311 or 808/249–8811* ⊕ *www.pacificwhale.org.*

Trilogy Excursions. Trilogy whale-watching trips consist of smaller crowds of about 20 to 30 passengers, and include beverages and snacks, an on-board marine naturalist, and hydrophones (microphones that detect underwater sound waves). Trips are $39 plus tax. Book online for a discount. ⊠ *Loading at the Kāʻanapali Beach Hotel* ☎ *808/661–4743 or 888/225–6284* ⊕ *www.sailtrilogy.com.*

The Humpback's Winter Home

The humpback whales' attraction to Maui is legendary. More than half the Pacific's humpback population winters in Hawai'i, especially in the waters around the Valley Isle, where mothers can be seen just a few hundred feet offshore training their young calves in the fine points of whale etiquette. Watching from shore it's easy to catch sight of whales spouting, or even breaching—when they leap almost entirely out of the sea, slapping back onto the water with a huge splash.

At one time there were thousands of the huge mammals, but a history of overhunting and marine pollution dwindled the world population to about 1,500. In 1966 humpbacks were put on the endangered species list. Hunting or harassing whales is illegal in the waters of most nations, and in the United States, boats and airplanes are restricted from getting too close. The word is still out, however, on the effects military sonar testing has on marine mammals.

Marine biologists believe the humpbacks (much like the humans) keep returning to Hawai'i because of its warmth. Having fattened themselves in subarctic waters all summer, the whales migrate south in the winter to breed, and a rebounding population of thousands cruise Maui waters. Winter is calving time, and the young whales, born with little blubber, probably couldn't survive in the frigid Alaskan waters. No one has ever seen a whale give birth here, but experts know that calving is their main winter activity, since the 1- and 2-ton youngsters suddenly appear while the whales are in residence.

The first sighting of a humpback whale spout each season is exciting and reassuring for locals on Maui. A collective sigh of relief can be heard, "Ah, they've returned." In the not-so-far distance, flukes and flippers can be seen rising above the ocean's surface. It's hard not to anthropomorphize the tail-waving, it looks like such an amiable, human gesture. Each fluke is uniquely patterned, like a human's fingerprint, and used to identify the giants as they travel halfway around the globe and back.

WINDSURFING

Something about Maui's wind and water stirs the spirit of innovation. Windsurfing, invented in the 1950s, found its true home at Ho'okipa in 1980. Seemingly overnight, windsurfing pros from around the world flooded Maui's North Shore. Equipment evolved, amazing film footage was captured, and a new sport was born.

If you're new to the action, you can get lessons from the experts islandwide. For a beginner, the best thing about windsurfing is (unlike surfing) you don't have to paddle. Instead, you have to hold on like heck to a flapping sail, as it whisks you into the wind. Needless to say, you're going to need a little coordination and balance to pull this off. Instructors start you on a beach at Kanahā, where the big boys go. Lessons range from two-hour introductory classes to five-day advanced "flight school." If you're an old salt, pick up tips and equipment from the companies below.

BEST SPOTS

After **Ho'okipa Bay** (⊠*2 mi past Pā'ia on Hāna Hwy.*) was discovered by windsurfers three decades ago, this windy beach 10 mi east of Kahului gained an international reputation. The spot is blessed with optimal wave-sailing wind and sea conditions, and can offer the ultimate aerial experience.

In summer the windsurfing crowd heads south to **Kalepolepo Beach** (⊠*S. Kīhei Rd. near Ohukai St.*). Trade winds build in strength and by afternoon a swarm of dragonflysails can be seen skimming the whitecaps, with the West Maui mountains as a backdrop.

A great site for speed, **Kanahā Beach Park** (⊠*Behind Kahului Airport*) is

ON THE SIDELINES

Few places lay claim to as many windsurfing tournaments as Maui. In March the **PWA Hawaiian Pro-Am Windsurfing** competition gets under way at Ho'okipa Beach. In June the **Da Kine Windsurfing Classic** lures top windsurfers to Kanahā Beach, and in November the **Aloha Classic World Wave Sailing Championships** takes place at Ho'okipa. For competitions featuring amateurs as well as professionals, check out the **Maui Race Series** (☎*808/877–2111*), six events held at Kanahā Beach in Kahului in summer.

dedicated to beginners in the morning hours, before the waves and wind really get roaring. After 11 AM, the professionals choose from their quiver of sails the size and shape best suited for the day's demands. This beach tends to have smaller waves and forceful winds—sometimes sending sailors flying at 40 knots. ■TIP➜If you aren't ready to go pro, this is a great place for a picnic while you watch from the beach.

EQUIPMENT AND LESSONS

Action Sports Maui. The quirky, friendly professionals here will meet you at Kanahā, outfit you with your sail and board, and guide you through your first "jibe" or turn. They promise your learning time will be cut in half. Don't be afraid to ask lots of questions. Lessons are held at 9 AM every morning except Sunday at Kanahā, and start at $69 for a two-hour class. Three- and five-day courses cost $225 and $375. ⊠*6 E. Waipuilani Rd., Kīhei* ☎*808/871–5857* ⊕*www.actionsportsmaui.com.*

Hi-Tech Surf & Sports. Known locally as Maui's finest windsurfing school, Hawaiian Sailboarding Techniques (HST, located in Hi-Tech) brings you quality instruction by skilled sailors. Founded by Alan Cadiz, an accomplished World Cup Pro, the school sets high standards for a safe, quality windsurfing experience. Intro classes start at $79 for 2½ hours, gear included. Hi-Tech itself offers excellent equipment rentals; $50 gets you a board, two sails, a mast, and roof racks for 24 hours. ⊠*425 Koloa St., Kahului* ☎*808/877–2111* ⊕*www.htmaui.com.*

Second Wind. Located in Kahului, this company rents boards with two sails for $46 per day. Boards with three sails go for $49 per day. Intro classes start at $79. ⊠*11 Hāna Hwy., Kahului* ☎*808/877–7467.*

GOLF, HIKING, AND OUTDOOR ACTIVITIES

Updated by
Heidi Pool

You may come to Maui to sprawl out on the sand, but it won't take long before you realize there's much more to Maui than the beach. For a relatively small island, Maui's interior landscapes vary wildly, from the moonlike surface of Haleakalā Crater to the glistening green rain forest of 'Īao Valley State Park. Whether you're exploring waterfalls on a day hike, riding horseback through ranchlands, soaring on a zipline, taking an exhilarating bicycle ride down Haleakalā, or teeing off on a world-class golf course, there's plenty to keep you busy.

AERIAL TOURS

Helicopter flight-seeing excursions can take you over the West Maui Mountains, Hāna, Haleakalā Crater, even the Big Island lava flow, or the islands of Lāna'i and Moloka'i. This is a beautiful, exciting way to see the island, and the only way to see some of its most dramatic areas and waterfalls. Tour prices usually include a DVD of your trip so you can relive the experience at home. Prices run from about $200 for a half-hour rain-forest tour to over $500 for a 90-minute mega-experience that includes a champagne toast on landing. Generally the 45- to 50-minute flights are the best value, and if you're willing to chance it, considerable discounts may be available if you call last minute or book online.

Blue Hawaiian Helicopters. Blue Hawaiian has provided aerial adventures in Hawai'i since 1985, and has been integral in some of the filming Hollywood has done on Maui. Its new EcoStar helicopters are air-conditioned and have noise-blocking headsets for all passengers. Flights are 30 to 90 minutes and cost $220 to $560. Charter flights are also available. ⊠*Kahului Heliport, Hangar 105, Kahului* ☎*808/871–8844 or 800/745–2583* ⊕*www.bluehawaiian.com.*

Sunshine Helicopters. Sunshine offers tours of Maui, Lāna'i, and Moloka'i, as well as the Big Island, in its Black Beauty AStar or WhisperStar aircraft. A pilot-narrated DVD of your actual flight is available for purchase. Prices start at $200 for 30 to 105 minutes. First-class seating is available for an additional fee. ⊠*Kahului Heliport, Hangar 107, Kahului* ☎*808/270–3999 or 866/501–7738* ⊕*www.sunshinehelicopters.com.*

BIKING

Maui County biking is safer and more convenient than in the past, but long distances and mountainous terrain keep it from being a practical mode of travel. Still, painted bike lanes enable cyclists to travel all the way from Mākena to Kapalua, and you'll see hardy souls battling the trade winds under the hot Maui sun.

Several companies offer guided downhill bike tours down Haleakalā. This activity is a great way to see the summit of the world's largest dormant volcano and enjoy an easy, gravity-induced bike ride, but isn't for those not confident in their ability to handle a bike. The ride is inherently dangerous due to the slope, sharp turns, and the fact that you're riding down an actual road with cars on it. That said, the guided bike companies do take every safety precaution. A few companies are now offering unguided (or as they like to say "self-guided") tours where they provide you with the bike and transportation to the top and then you're free to descend at your own pace. Sunrise is downright brisk at the summit, so dress in layers.

■TIP→ Haleakalā National Park no longer allows commercial downhill bicycle rides within the park's boundaries. As a result, tour amenities and routes vary by company. Be sure to ask about sunrise viewing from the Haleakalā summit, if this is an important feature for you.

BEST SPOTS

Though it's changing, at present there are few truly good spots to ride on Maui. Street bikers will want to head out to scenic **Thompson Road** (⊠ *Off Rte. 37, Kula Hwy., Keokea*). It's quiet, gently curvy, and flanked by gorgeous views on both sides. Plus, because it's at a higher elevation, the air temperature is cooler and the wind lighter. The coast back down toward Kahului is worth the ride up.

EQUIPMENT AND TOURS

Cruiser Phil's Volcano Riders. Owner Phil Feliciano ("Cruiser Phil") has been in the downhill bicycle industry for 25 years. He offers sunrise and morning tours, which cost $150, and include hotel pick-up and drop-off, Continental breakfast at the company's base in Kahului, a van tour of the summit, and a guided 28-mi ride down the mountain. Riders will make a no-host meal stop in either Kula or Pāʻia. Participants should be at least 15 and under 65 years old; be at least 5 feet tall and weigh no more than 275 pounds; and have ridden a bicycle in the past 12 months. ⊠ *58-A Amala Pl., Kahului* ☎ *808/893–2332 or 877/764–2453* ⊕ *www.cruiserphil.com.*

Haleakalā Bike Company. If you're thinking about an unguided Haleakalā bike trip, consider one of the trips offered by this company. Meet at the Old Haʻikû Cannery and take their van shuttle to the summit. Along the way you'll learn about the history of the island, the volcano, and other Hawaiiana. Unlike the guided trips, food is not included although there are several spots along the way down to stop, rest, and eat. The simple, mostly downhill route takes you right back to the cannery where you started. HBC offers bike sales, rentals, and services. Prices range from $69 to $115. ⊠ *810 Haʻikū Rd., Suite 120, Haʻikū* ☎ *808/575–9575 or 888/922–2453* ⊕ *www.bikemaui.com.*

Island Biker. This is the premier bike shop on Maui when it comes to rental, sales, and service. They offer 2005 Specialized standard front-shock bikes, road bikes, and full-suspension mountain bikes. Daily or weekly rates range $50 to $150, and include a helmet, pump, water bottle, flat-repair kit and spare tube. They can suggest various routes appropriate for mountain or road biking, or you can join them in a biweekly group ride. ⊠ *415 Dairy Rd., Kahului* ☎ *808/877–7744* ⊕ *www.islandbikermaui.com.*

West Maui Cycles. Servicing the west side of the island, WMC offers an assortment of cycles including cruisers for $15 per day ($60 per week); hybrids for $30 per day ($120 per week); and Cannondale road bikes and front-suspension Giantbikes for $50 per day ($200 per week). Sales and service are available. ✉ *1087 Limahana Pl., No. 6, Lahaina* ☎ *808/661–9005* ⊕ *www.westmauicycles.com.*

GOLF

Maui's natural beauty and surroundings offer some of the most jaw-dropping vistas imaginable on a golf course. Holes run across small bays, past craggy lava outcrops, and up into cool, forested mountains. Most courses feature mesmerizing ocean views, some close enough to feel the salt in the air. And although many of the courses are affiliated with resorts (and therefore a little pricier), the general public courses are no less impressive. Green fees listed here are the highest course rates per round on weekdays and weekends for U.S. residents. (Some courses charge non–U.S. residents higher prices.) Discounts are often available for resort guests and for those who book tee times on the Web. Rental clubs may or may not be included with green fees. ■TIP➜Cheaper twilight fees are usually offered; call individual courses for information.

Fodor's Choice ★ **Dunes at Maui Lani.** This is Robin Nelson (1999) at his minimalist best, a bit of British links in the middle of the Pacific. Holes run through ancient, lightly wooded sand dunes, 5 mi inland from Kahului Harbor. Thanks to the natural humps and slopes of the dunes, Nelson had to move very little dirt and created a natural beauty. During the design phase he visited Ireland, and not so coincidentally the par-3 third looks a lot like the Dell at Lahinch: a white dune on the right sloping down into a deep bunker and partially obscuring the right side of the green—just one of several blind to semi-blind shots here. Popular with residents, this course has won several awards including "Best 35 New Courses in America" by *Golf Magazine* and "Five Best Kept Secret Golf Courses in America" by *Golf Digest.* ✉ *380 Kuihelani Hwy., Kahului* ☎ *808/873–0422* ⊕ *www.dunesatmauilani.com* ⛳ *18 holes. 6841 yds. Par 72. Slope 136. Green fee: $99* ⚲ *Facilities: Driving range, putting green, golf carts, rental clubs, pro shop, golf academy/lessons, restaurant, bar.*

★ **Kā'anapali Golf Resort.** The Royal Kā'anapali (North) Course (1962) is one of three in Hawai'i designed by Robert Trent Jones Sr., the godfather of modern golf architecture. The greens average a whopping 10,000 square feet, necessary because of the often-severe undulation. The par-4 18th hole (into the prevailing trade breezes, with out-of-bounds on the left, and a lake on the right) is notoriously tough. The Kā'anapali Kai (South) Course (Arthur Jack Snyder, 1976) shares similar seaside-into-the-hills terrain, but is rated a couple of strokes easier, mostly because putts are less treacherous. ✉ *2290 Kā'anapali Pkwy., Lahaina* ☎ *808/661–3691* ⊕ *www.kaanapali-golf.com* ⛳ *North Course: 18 holes. 6,500 yds. Par 71. Slope 126. Green Fee: $235. South Course: 18 holes. 6400 yds. Par 70. Slope 124. Green Fee: $195* ⚲ *Facilities: Driving range, putting green, rental clubs, golf carts, lessons, restaurant, bar.*

Fodor's Choice ★ **Kapalua Resort.** Perhaps Hawai'i's best-known golf resort and the crown jewel of golf on Maui, Kapalua hosts the PGA Tour's first event each January: the Mercedes Championships at the Plantation Course at Kapalua. Ben Crenshaw and Bill Coore (1991) tried to incorporate traditional shot values in a very nontraditional site, taking into account slope, gravity, and the prevailing trade winds. The par-5 18th, for instance, plays 663 yards from the back tees (600 yards from the resort tees). The hole drops 170 feet in elevation, narrowing as it goes to a partially guarded green, and plays downwind and down-grain. Despite the longer-than-usual distance, the slope is great enough and the wind at your back usually brisk enough to reach the green with two well-struck shots—a truly unbelievable finish to a course that will challenge, frustrate, and reward the patient golfer.

The Bay Course (Arnold Palmer and Francis Duane, 1975) is the more traditional of Kapalua's courses, with gentle rolling fairways and generous greens. The most memorable hole is the par-3 fifth, with a tee shot that must carry a turquoise finger of Onelua Bay. The Kapalua Golf Academy (⊠ *1000 Office Rd.* ☎ *808/665–5455 or 877/527–2582*) offers 23 acres of practice turf and 11 teeing areas, a special golf fitness gym, and an instructional bay with video analysis. Each of the courses has a separate clubhouse. The Bay Course: ⊠ *300 Kapalua Dr., Kapalua* ☎ *808/669–8044 or 877/527–2582* ⊕ *www.kapaluamaui. com/golf* ⚑ *18 holes. 6600 yds. Par 72. Slope 133. Green Fee: $215* ⚐ *Facilities: Driving range, putting green, rental clubs, pro shop, lessons, restaurant, bar*. The Plantation Course: ⊠ *2000 Plantation Club Dr., Kapalua* ☎ *808/669–8044 or 877/527–2582* ⊕ *www.kapaluamaui. com/golf* ⚑ *18 holes. 7411 yds. Par 73. Slope 135. Green Fee: $295* ⚐ *Facilities: Driving range, putting green, golf carts, pull carts, rental clubs, pro shop, golf academy/lessons, restaurant, bar.*

Fodor$Choice
★
Mākena Resort. Robert Trent Jones Jr. and Don Knotts (not the Barney Fife actor) built the first course at Mākena in 1981. A decade later Jones was asked to create 18 totally new holes and blend them with the existing course to form the North and South courses, which opened in 1994. Both courses—sculpted from the lava flows on the western flank of Haleakalā—offer quick greens with lots of breaks, and plenty of scenic distractions. On the North Course, the fourth is one of the most picturesque inland par-3s in Hawai'i, with the green guarded on the right by a pond. The sixth is an excellent example of option golf: the fairway is sliced up the middle by a gaping ravine, which must sooner or later be crossed to reach the green. Although trees frame most holes on the North Course, the South Course is more open. This means it plays somewhat easier off the tee, but the greens are trickier. The view from the elevated tee of the par-5 10th is lovely with the lake in the foreground mirroring the ocean in the distance. The par-4 16th is another sight to see, with the Pacific running along the left side. **Note:** At this writing, the South Course was scheduled to be closed for part of 2009. Call to confirm. ⊠ *5415 Mākena Alanui, Mākena* ☎ *808/891–4000* ⊕ *www.princeresortshawaii.com/maui-golf.php* ⚑ *North Course: 18 holes. 6567 yds. Par 72. Slope 135. Green fee: $200. South Course: 18 holes. 6630 yds. Par 72. Slope 133. Green fee: $200* ⚐ *Facilities: Driving range, putting green, golf carts, rental clubs, pro shop, golf academy/lessons, restaurant, bar.*

BEFORE YOU HIT THE FIRST TEE . . .

Golf is golf, and Hawai'i is part of the United States, but island golf nevertheless has its own quirks. Here are a few tips to make your golf experience in the Islands more pleasant.

■ All resort courses and many daily fee courses provide rental clubs. In many cases, they're the latest lines from top manufacturers. This is true for both men and women, as well as left-handers, which means you don't have to schlep clubs across the Pacific.

■ Come spikeless—very few Hawai'i courses still permit metal spikes. And most of the resort courses require a collared shirt.

■ Maui is notorious for its trade winds. Consider playing early if you want to avoid the wind, and remember that while it'll frustrate you at times and make club selection difficult, you may very well see some of your longest drives ever.

■ In theory you can play golf in Hawai'i 365 days a year, but there's a reason the Hawaiian Islands are so green. An umbrella and light jacket can come in handy.

■ Unless you play a muni or certain daily fee courses, plan on taking a cart. Riding carts are mandatory at most courses and are included in the green fees.

Pukalani Golf Course. At 1,110 feet above sea level, Pukalani (Bob E. and Robert L. Baldock, 1970) provides one of the finest vistas in all Hawai'i. Holes run up, down, and across the slopes of Haleakalā. The trade wind tends to come up in the late morning and afternoon. This—combined with frequent elevation change—makes club selection a test. The fairways tend to be wide, but greens are undulating and quick. ⊠ *360 Pukalani St., Pukalani* ☎ *808/572–1314* ⊕ *www.pukalanigolf. com* ⏱. *18 holes. 6962 yds. Par 72. Slope 127. Green fee: $78* ⌐ *Facilities: Driving range, putting green, rental clubs, golf carts, pro shop, restaurant, bar.*

Fodor'sChoice ★ **Wailea.** Wailea is the only Hawai'i resort to offer three different courses: Gold, Emerald, and Old Blue. Designed by Robert Trent Jones Jr., these courses share similar terrain, carved into the leeward slopes of Haleakalā. Although the ocean does not come into play, its beauty is visible on almost every hole. ■ TIP→ **Remember, putts break dramatically toward the ocean.**

Jones refers to the Gold Course at Wailea (1993) as the "masculine" course. Host to the Championship Senior Skins Game in January, it's all trees and lava and regarded as the hardest of the three courses. The trick here is to note even subtle changes in elevation. The par-3 eighth, for example, plays from an elevated tee across a lava ravine to a large, well-bunkered green framed by palm trees, the blue sea, and tiny Molokini. The course has been labeled a "thinking player's" course because it demands strategy and careful club selection. The Emerald Course at Wailea (1994) is the "feminine" layout with lots of flowers and bunkering away from greens. Although this may seem to render the bunker benign, the opposite is true. A bunker well in front of a green disguises the distance to the hole. Likewise, the Emerald's extensive flower beds are designed to be dangerous distractions because of their beauty. The Gold and Emerald share a clubhouse, practice facility, and 19th hole (watering hole and restaurant). Judging elevation change is also key at Wailea's first course, the Old Blue Course (Arthur Jack Snyder, 1971). Fairways and greens

WORD OF MOUTH

"Hike in the ʻĪao Valley. It's quiet, green, lush, and a totally different experience than the west side of Maui."

—Erin74

3

tend to be wider and more forgiving than on the Gold or Emerald, and run through colorful flora that includes hibiscus, wiliwili, bougainvillea, and plumeria. Old Blue Course: ✉ *120 Kaukahi St., Wailea* ☎ *808/875–7450 or 888/328–6284* ⊕ *www.waileagolf.com* ⚐ *18 holes. 6765 yds. Par 72. Slope 129. Green fee: $225* ⚲ *Facilities: Driving range, putting green, golf carts, rental clubs, pro shop, golf academy/ lessons, restaurant, bar.* Gold and Emerald Courses: ✉ *100 Wailea Golf Club Dr., Wailea* ☎ *808/875–7450 or 888/328–6284* ⊕ *www. waileagolf.com* ⚐ *Gold Course: 18 holes. 6653 yds. Par 72. Slope 132. Green fee: $225. Emerald Course: 18 holes. 6407 yds. Par 72. Slope 130. Green fee: $225* ⚲ *Facilities: Driving range, putting green, golf carts, rental clubs, pro shop, golf academy/lessons, restaurant, bar.*

HANG GLIDING AND PARAGLIDING

Hang Gliding Maui. Armin Engert will take you on an instructional powered hang-gliding trip out of Hāna Airport in East Maui. With more than 7,500 hours in flight and a perfect safety record, Armin flies you 1,000 feet over Maui's most beautiful coast. A 30-minute flight lesson costs $130, and a 60-minute lesson is $220. This is easily one of the coolest things you can do in Hāna. Snapshots of your flight from a wing-mounted camera cost an additional $30, and a 34-minute DVD of the flight is available for $70. Reservations are required. ✉ *Hāna Airport, Hāna* ☎ *808/572–6557* ⊕ *www.hangglidingmaui.com.*

Proflyght Paragliding. Proflyght is the only paragliding outfit on Maui to offer solo, tandem, and instruction at Polipoli Spring State Recreation Area. The leeward slope of Haleakalā lends itself perfectly to paragliding with breathtaking scenery and upcountry air currents that increase and rise throughout the day. Polipoli creates tremendous thermals that allow one to peacefully descend 3,000 feet to the landing zone. Owner–pilot Dexter Clearwater boasts a perfect safety record with tandems and student pilots since taking over the company in 2002. Ask and Dexter will bring along his flying duck Chuckie or his paragliding puppy Daisy. Prices start at $75, with full certification available. ✉ *Polipoli State Park, Kula* ☎ *808/874–5433* ⊕ *www.paraglidehawaii.com.*

HIKING

Hikes on Maui range from coastal seashore to verdant rain forest to alpine desert. Orchids, hibiscus, ginger, heliconia, and anthuriums grow wild on many trails, and exotic fruits like mountain apple, lilikoi (passion fruit), thimbleberry, and strawberry guava provide refreshing snacks for hikers. Ironically, much of what you see in lower altitude forests is alien, brought to Hawai'i at one time or another by someone hoping to improve upon nature. Plants like strawberry guava and ginger may be tasty, but they grow over native forest plants and have become serious, problematic weeds.

The best hikes get you out of the imported landscaping and into the truly exotic wilderness. Hawai'i possesses some of the world's rarest plants, insects, and birds. Pocket field guides are available at most grocery or drug stores and can really illuminate your walk. Before you know it you'll be nudging your companion and pointing out trees that look like something out of a Dr. Suess book. If you watch the right branches quietly you can spot the same Honeycreepers or Happy-face Spiders scientists have spent their lives studying.

BEST SPOTS

Fodor's Choice
★ Going into **Haleakalā Crater**—the best hiking on the island—is like going to a different planet. In the early 1960s NASA actually brought moon-suited astronauts here to practice "walking on the moon." You'll traverse black sand and wild lava formations, follow the trail of blooming silverswords, watch for *nēnē*, and witness tremendous views of big sky and burnt-red cliffs. There are 30 mi of moderate to strenuous trails, two camping areas, and three cabins. If you're in shape, you can do a day hike descending from the summit (along Sliding Sands Trail) to the crater floor. Be sure to ask a ranger about water availability before starting your hike. Bring plenty of warm, layered clothing. It may be scorching hot during the day, but it can get very chilly after dark. If you have time, consider camping here amid the cinder cones, lava flows, and all that loud silence.

⇨ *For more information, see Haleakalā National Park feature in this section.*

'Ohe'o Gulch (⊠ *Rte. 31, 10 mi past Hāna town*) is a branch of Haleakalā National Park. Famous for the Pool of Ohe'o (the area is sometimes called the "Seven Sacred Pools"), the cascading gulch is the starting point of one of Maui's best hikes—the Pipiwai Trail, a 2-mi trek upstream to the 400-foot **Waimoku Falls.** Follow signs from the parking lot up the road, past the bridge overlook, and uphill into the forest. Along the way you can take side trips and swim in the stream's basalt-lined pools. The trail bridges a sensational gorge and passes onto a boardwalk through a mystifying forest of giant bamboo. This stomp through muddy and rocky terrain takes around three hours to fully enjoy. It's best done early in the morning, before the touring crowds arrive (though it can never truly be called crowded). A $10 national park fee applies, which is valid for one week and can be used at Haleakalā's summit as well. Down at the grassy sea cliffs, you can camp, no permit required, although you can stay only three nights. Toilets, grills, and tables are available here, but there's no water and open fires aren't allowed. Part of the road to Kaupo, beyond One'o Gulch, that was damaged in a 2006 earthquake has been repaired and is once again open. ■**TIP➔Check with officials at Haleakalā National Park (☎808/572–4400; dial 0 during the recorded message to speak to a representative during office hours) before traveling beyond 'Ohe'o Gulch.**

A much-neglected hike is the coastal **Hoapili Trail** (⊠ *Follow Mākena Alanui to end of paved road at La Pérouse Bay, walk through parking lot along dirt road, follow signs*) beyond the 'Āhihi-Kīna'u Natural Area Reserve. Named after a bygone Hawaiian king, it follows the shoreline, threading through the remains of ancient Hawaiian villages. The once-thriving community was displaced by one of Maui's last lava flows. Later, King Hoapili was responsible for overseeing the creation of an island-wide highway. This remaining section, a wide path of stacked lava rocks, is a marvel to look at and walk on, though it's not the easiest surface for the ankles. (It's rumored to have once been covered in grass.) You can wander over to the Hanamanioa lighthouse, or quietly ponder the rough life of the ancients. Wear sturdy shoes and bring extra water. This is brutal territory with little shade and no facilities. Beautiful, yes. Accommodating, no.

> **KEEP IN MIND**
>
> Wear sturdy shoes while hiking; you'll want to spare your ankles from a crash course in loose lava rock. When hiking near streams or waterfalls, be extremely cautious—flash floods can occur at any time. Do not drink stream water or swim in streams if you have open cuts; bacteria and parasites are not the souvenir you want to take home with you. Wear sunscreen, a hat, and layered clothing, and be sure to drink plenty of water (even if you don't feel thirsty). At upper elevations, the weather is guaranteed to be extreme—alternately chilly or blazing.

★ One of Maui's great wonders, **'Īao Valley** is the site of a famous battle to unite the Hawaiian islands. Out of the clouds, the **'Īao Needle,** a tall chunk of volcanic rock, stands as a monument to the long-ago lookout for Maui warriors. Today, there's nothing warlike about it: the valley is a peaceful land of lush, tropical plants, clear pools and a running stream, and easy, enjoyable walks.

Anyone (including your grandparents) can take the easy hike from the parking lot at 'Īao Valley State Park. On your choice of two paved walkways, you can cross the 'Īao Stream and explore the junglelike area. Ascend the stairs for spectacular views of Central Maui, or pause in the garden of Hawaiian heritage plants and marvel at the local youngsters hurling themselves from the bridge into the chilly pools below. ⊠ *To get to 'Īao Valley State Park, go through Wailuku and continue to the west end of Route 32. The road dead-ends into the parking lot.* ☎ *808/984–8109* ⊙ *Open daily 7 AM–7 PM* ☞ *Facilities available.*

GOING WITH A GUIDE

Fodor'sChoice **Friends of Haleakalā National Park.** This nonprofit offers day and overnight service trips into the crater, and in the Kipahulu region. The purpose of your trip, the service work itself, isn't too much—mostly removing invasive plants and light cabin maintenance. Chances are you'll make good friends and have more fun than on a hike you'd do on your own. Trip leader Farley, or one of his equally knowledgeable cohorts, will take you to places you'd never otherwise see, and teach you about the native flora and birds along the way. Bring your own water; share food in group dinners. Admission is free. ☎ *808/248–7660* ⊕ *www.fhnp.org.*

Fodor's Choice

★ **Hike Maui.** Hike Maui is the oldest hiking company on the Islands. Its waterfall and rain forest, mountain ridge, crater, coastline, and combination hikes are led by enthusiastic trained naturalists who weave botany, geology, ethnobotany, culture, and history into the outdoor experience. Prices range from $75 to $154 for excursions of 3 to 10 hours (discounts are available for advance, online bookings). Hike Maui supplies waterproof day packs, rain ponchos, first-aid gear, water bottles, lunch and/or snacks for the longer hikes, and transportation to the site. ☎808/879–5270 ⊕*www.hikemaui.com.*

Maui Eco Adventures. For excursions into remote areas, Maui Eco Adventures is your choice. The ecologically minded company leads hikes into private or otherwise inaccessible areas. Hikes, which can be combined with kayaking, mountain biking, or sailing trips, explore botanically rich valleys in Kahakuloa and East Maui, as well as Hāna, Haleakalā, and more. They also offer a hike/kayak combination at Kapalua Bay, and a Haleakalā Heli-Hike with Sunshine Helicopters. Guides are botanists, mountaineers, boat captains, and backcountry chefs. Excursions are priced from $80 for a "waterfall experience" to $400 for the Heli-Hike. ⊠*180 Dickenson St., Suite 101, Lahaina* ☎*808/661–7720 or 877/661–7720* ⊕*www.ecomaui.com.*

★ **Sierra Club.** A great avenue into the island's untrammeled wilderness is Maui's chapter of the Sierra Club. Rather than venturing out on your own, join one of the club's hikes into pristine forests and valley isle watersheds, or along ancient coastal paths. Several hikes a month are led by informative naturalists who carry first aid kits and arrange waivers to access private land. Some outings include volunteer service, but most are just for fun. Bring your own food and water, sturdy shoes, and a suggested donation of $5—a true bargain. ⌂*Box 791180, Pā'ia 96779* ☎*808/573–4147* ⊕*www.hi.sierraclub.org/maui.*

HORSEBACK RIDING

Several companies on Maui offer horseback riding that's far more appealing than the typical hour-long trudge over a dull trail with 50 other horses.

GOING WITH A GUIDE

Fodor's Choice

★ **Maui Stables.** Hawaiian-owned and run, this company provides a trip back in time, to an era when life moved more slowly and reverently—though galloping is allowed, if you're able to handle your horse! Educational tours begin at the stable in remote Kipahulu (near Hāna), and pass through several historic Hawaiian sites. Before heading up into the forest, your guides intone the words to a traditional *oli*, or chant, asking for permission to enter. By the time you reach the mountain pasture overlooking Waimoku Falls, you'll feel lucky to have been a part of the tradition. Both morning and afternoon rides are available at $150 per rider. ⊠*Between mile markers 40 and 41 on Hwy. 37, Hāna* ☎*808/248–7799* ⊕*www.mauistables.com.*

Fodor's Choice

★ **Mendes Ranch.** Family-owned and run, Mendes operates out of the beautiful ranchland of Kahakuloa on the windward slopes of the West Maui Mountains. Two-hour morning and afternoon trail rides ($110) are

Continued on page 241

HALEAKALĀ NATIONAL PARK

HALEAKALA CRATER

From the Tropics to the Moon! Two hours, 38 mi, 10,023 feet—those are the unlikely numbers involved in reaching Maui's highest point, the summit of the volcano Haleakalā. Nowhere else on earth can you drive from sea level (Kahului) to 10,023 feet (the summit) in only 38 mi. And what's more shocking—in that short vertical ascent, you'll journey from lush, tropical-island landscape to the stark, moonlike basin of the volcano's enormous, otherworldly crater.

Established in 1916, Haleakalā National Park covers an astonishing 27,284 acres. Haleakalā "Crater" is the centerpiece of the park though it's not actually a crater. Technically, it's an erosional valley, flushed out by water pouring from the summit through two enormous gaps. The mountain has terrific camping and hiking, including a trail that loops through the crater, but the chance to witness this unearthly landscape is reason enough for a visit.

THE CLIMB TO THE SUMMIT

To reach Haleakalā National Park and the mountain's breathtaking summit, take Route 36 east of Kahului to the Haleakalā Highway (Route 37). Head east, up the mountain to the unlikely intersection of Haleakalā Highway and Haleakalā Highway. If you continue straight the road's name changes to Kula Highway (still Route 37). Instead, turn left onto Haleakalā Highway—this is now Route 377. After about 6 mi, make a left onto

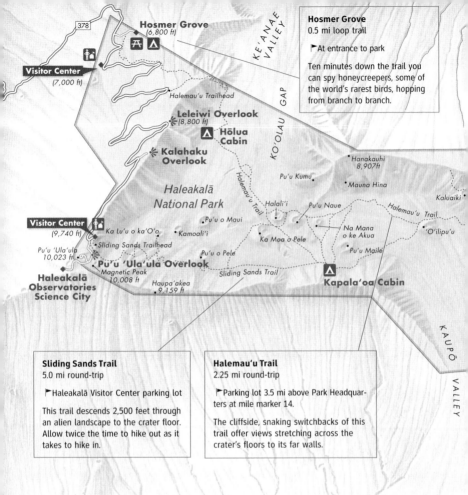

Hosmer Grove
(6,800 ft)

378

Visitor Center
(7,000 ft)

Halemau'u Trailhead

KE'ANAE VALLEY

Hosmer Grove
0.5 mi loop trail

▶At entrance to park

Ten minutes down the trail you can spy honeycreepers, some of the world's rarest birds, hopping from branch to branch.

Leleiwi Overlook
(8,800 ft)

Hōlua Cabin

Kalahaku Overlook

KO'OLAU GAP

Hanakauhi 8,907ft

Pu'u Kumu

Mauna Hina

Kaluaiki

Haleakalā National Park

Halali'i

Halemau'u Trail

Pu'u Naue

Halemau'u Trail

'O'ilipu'u

Visitor Center
(9,740 ft)

Ka Lu'u o ka'O'o

Pu'u o Maui

Kamoali'i

Sliding Sands Trailhead

Na Mana o ke Akua

Ka Moa o Pele

Pu'u Maile

Pu'u 'Ula'ula
10,023 ft

Pu'u 'Ula'ula Overlook

Magnetic Peak 10,008 ft

Pu'u o Pele

Sliding Sands Trail

Haleakalā Observatories Science City

Haupa'akea 9,159 ft

Kapala'oa Cabin

KAUPŌ VALLEY

Sliding Sands Trail
5.0 mi round-trip

▶Haleakalā Visitor Center parking lot

This trail descends 2,500 feet through an alien landscape to the crater floor. Allow twice the time to hike out as it takes to hike in.

Halemau'u Trail
2.25 mi round-trip

▶Parking lot 3.5 mi above Park Headquarters at mile marker 14.

The cliffside, snaking switchbacks of this trail offer views stretching across the crater's floors to its far walls.

Crater Road (Route 378). After several long switchbacks (look out for downhill bikers!) you'll come to the park entrance.

■TIP→Before you head up Haleakalā, call for the latest park weather conditions (☎866/944–5025). Extreme gusty winds, heavy rain, and even snow in winter are not uncommon. Because of the high altitude, the mountaintop temperature is often as much as 30 degrees cooler than that at sea level. Be sure to bring a jacket. Also make sure you have a full tank of gas. No service stations exist beyond Kula.

There's a $10 per car fee to enter the park; but it's good for three days and can

be used at 'Ohe'o Gulch (Seven Sacred Pools), so save your receipt.

6,800 feet, Hosmer Grove. Just as you enter the park, Hosmer Grove has campsites and interpretive trails (*see* Hiking & Camping *on the following pages*). Park rangers maintain a changing schedule of talks and hikes both here and at the top of the mountain. Call the park for current schedules.

7,000 feet, Park Headquarters/Visitor Center. Not far from Hosmer Grove, the Park Headquarters/Visitor Center (open daily from 8 to 4) has trail maps and displays about the volcano's origins

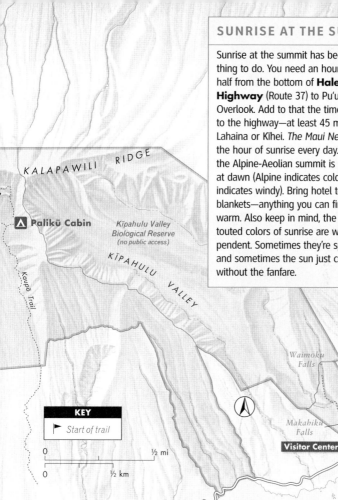

KALAPAWILI RIDGE

△ **Palikū Cabin**

Kīpahulu Valley
Biological Reserve
(no public access)

KĪPAHULU VALLEY

Kaupō Trail

Waimoku
Falls

31

KEY

▶ Start of trail

Makahiku
Falls

Kuloa Point

Visitor Center

'Ohe'o
Gulch

0   ½ mi

0   ½ km

PACIFIC OCEAN

SUNRISE AT THE SUMMIT

Sunrise at the summit has become the thing to do. You need an hour and a half from the bottom of **Haleakalā Highway** (Route 37) to Pu'u 'Ula'ula Overlook. Add to that the time of travel to the highway—at least 45 minutes from Lahaina or Kīhei. *The Maui News* posts the hour of sunrise every day. Remember the Alpine-Aeolian summit is *freezing* at dawn (Alpine indicates cold, Aeolian indicates windy). Bring hotel towels, blankets—anything you can find to stay warm. Also keep in mind, the highly touted colors of sunrise are weather-dependent. Sometimes they're spectacular and sometimes the sun just comes up without the fanfare.

and eruption history. Hikers and campers should check-in here before heading up the mountain. Maps, posters, and other memorabilia are available at the gift shop.

8,800 feet, Leleiwi Overlook. Continuing up the mountain, you come to Leleiwi Overlook. A short walk to the end of the parking lot reveals your first awe-inspiring view of the crater. The small hills in the basin are volcanic cinder cones (called *pu'u* in Hawaiian), each with a small crater at its top, and each the site of a former eruption.

WHERE TO EAT

KULA LODGE (✉ Haleakalā Hwy., Kula ☎ 808/878–2517) serves hearty breakfasts from 7 to 11 AM, a favorite with hikers coming down from a sunrise visit to Haleakalā's summit, as well as those on their way up for a late-morning tramp in the crater. Spectacular ocean views fill the windows of this mountainside lodge.

If you're here in the late afternoon, it's possible you'll experience a phenomenon called the Brocken Specter. Named after a similar occurrence in East Germany's

Silversword

10,023 feet, Pu'u 'Ula'ula Overlook.
The highest point on Maui is the Pu'u 'Ula'ula Overlook, at the 10,023-foot summit. Here you find a glass-enclosed lookout with a 360-degree view. The building is open 24 hours a day, and this is where visitors gather for the best sunrise view. Dawn begins between 5:45 and 7, depending on the time of year. On a clear day you can see the islands of Moloka'i, Lāna'i, Kaho'olawe, and Hawai'i (the Big Island). On a *really* clear day you can even spot O'ahu glimmering in the distance.

■TIP→The air is very thin at 10,000 feet. Don't be surprised if you feel a little breathless while walking around the summit. Take it easy and drink lots of water. Anyone who has been scuba diving within the last 24 hours should not make the trip up Haleakalā.

On a small hill nearby, you can see **Science City**, an off-limits research and communications center straight out of an espionage thriller. The University of Hawai'i maintains an observatory here, and the Department of Defense tracks satellites.

For more information about Haleakalā National Park, contact the **National Park Service** (☎808/572–4400, ⊕www.nps.gov/hale).

HIKING & CAMPING

Exploring Haleakalā Crater is one of the best hiking experiences on Maui. The volcanic terrain offers an impressive diversity of colors, textures, and shapes—almost as if the lava has been artfully sculpted. The barren landscape is home to many plants, insects, and birds that exist nowhere else on earth and have developed intriguing survival mechanisms, such as the sun-reflecting, hairy leaves of the silversword, which allow it to survive the intense climate.

Stop at park headquarters to register and pick up trail maps on your way into the park.

Harz Mountains, the "specter" allows you to see yourself reflected on the clouds and encircled by a rainbow. Don't wait all day for this because it's not a daily occurrence.

9,000 feet, Kalahaku Overlook. The next stopping point is Kalahaku Overlook. The view here offers a different perspective of the crater, and at this elevation the famous silversword plant grows amid the cinders. This odd, endangered beauty grows only here and at the same elevation on the Big Island's two peaks. It begins life as a silver, spiny-leaf rosette and is the sole home of a variety of native insects (it's the only shelter around). The silversword reaches maturity between 7 and 17 years, when it sends forth a 3- to 8-foot-tall stalk with several hundred tiny sunflowers. It blooms once, then dies.

9,740 feet, Haleakalā Visitor Center. Another mile up is the Haleakalā Visitor Center (open daily from sunrise to 3 PM). There are exhibits inside, and a trail from here leads to White Hill—a short easy walk that will give you an even better view of the valley.

1-Hour Hike. Just as you enter Haleakalā National Park, **Hosmer Grove** offers a short 10-minute hike, and an hour-long, $^1/_2$-mi loop trail into the Waikamoi Cloud Forest that will give you insight into Hawai'i's fragile ecology. Anyone can go on the short hike, whereas the longer trail through the cloud forest is accessible only with park ranger–guided hikes. Call park headquarters for the schedule. Facilities here include six campsites (no permit needed, available on a first-come, first-served basis), pit toilets, drinking water, and cooking shelters.

4-Hour Hikes. Two half-day hikes involve descending into the crater and returning the way you came. The first, **Halemau'u Trail** (trailhead is between mile markers 14 and 15), is 2.25 mi round-trip. The cliffside, snaking switchbacks of this trail offer views stretching across the crater's pu'u-speckled floor to its far walls. On clear days you can peer through the Ko'olau Gap to Hāna. Native flowers and shrubs grow along the trail, which is typically misty and cool (though still exposed to the sun). When you reach the gate at the bottom, head back up.

The other hike, which is 5 mi round-trip, descends down **Sliding Sands Trail** (trailhead is at the Haleakalā Visitor Center) into an alien landscape of reddish black cinders, lava bombs, and silverswords. It's easy to imagine life before humans in the solitude and silence of this place. Turn back when you hit the crater floor.

■TIP→ Bring water, sunscreen, and a reliable jacket. These can be demanding hikes if you're unused to the altitude. Take it slowly to acclimate, and give yourself additional time for the uphill return trip.

8-Hour Hike. The recommended way to explore the crater in a single, but full day is to go in two cars and ferry yourselves back and forth between the head of **Halemau'u Trail** and the summit. This way, you can hike from the summit down **Sliding Sands Trail**, cross the crater's floor, investigate the **Bottomless Pit** and **Pele's Paint Pot**, then climb out on the **switchback trail** (**Halemau'u**). When you emerge, the shelter of your waiting car will be very welcome (this is an 11.2-mi hike). If you don't have two cars, hitching a ride from Halemau'u back to the summit should be relatively safe and easy.

■ TIP→ Take a backpack with lunch, water, sunscreen, and a reliable jacket for the beginning and end of the 8-hour hike. This is a demanding trip, but you will never regret or forget it.

Overnight Hike. Staying overnight in one of Haleakalā's three cabins or two wilderness campgrounds is an experience like no other. You'll feel like the only person on earth when you wake up inside this enchanted, strange landscape. Nēnē and 'u'au (endangered storm petrels) make charming neighbors. The cabins, each tucked in a different corner of the crater's floor, are equipped with 12 bunk beds, wood-burning stoves, fake logs, and kitchen gear.

Hōlua cabin is the shortest hike, less than 4 hours (3.7 mi) from Halemau'u Trail. **Kapala'oa** is about 5 hours (5.5 mi) down Sliding Sands Trail. The most cherished cabin is **Palikū,** a solid eight-hour (9.3-mi) hike starting from either trail. It's nestled against the rain-forested cliffs above the Kaupō Gap. To reserve a cabin you have to apply to the National Park Service at least 60 days in advance and hope the lottery system is kind to you. Tent campsites at Hōlua and Palikū are free and easy to reserve on a first-come, first-served basis.

■ TIP→ Toilets and nonpotable water are available—bring iodine tablets to purify the water. Open fires are not allowed and packing out your trash is mandatory.

For more information on hiking or camping, or to reserve a cabin, contact the National Park Service (⊠ Box 369, Makawao 96768 ☎ 808/572–4459 ⊕ www.nps.gov/hale).

OPTIONS FOR EXPLORING

If you're short on time you can drive to the summit, take a peek inside, and drive back down. But the "House of the Sun" is really worth a day, whether you explore by foot, horseback, or helicopter.

BIKING

At this writing, all guided bike tours inside park boundaries were suspended indefinitely while park officials study the safety of this activity. However, the tours continue but now start outside the boundary of the park. The park is still open to individual bikes for a $5 fee. There are no bike paths, however—just the same road that is used by vehicular traffic.

HELICOPTER TOURS

Viewing Haleakalā from above can be a mind-altering experience, if you don't mind dropping $200+ per person for a few blissful moments above the crater. Most tours buzz Haleakalā, where airspace is regulated, then head over to Hanā in search of waterfalls.

HORSEBACK RIDING

Several companies offer half-day, full-day, and even overnight rides into the crater. On one half-day ride you descend into the crater on Sliding Sands Trail and have lunch before you head back.

For complete information on any of these activities, ⇨ *see Golf, Hiking and Outdoor Activities.*

available with an optional barbecue lunch ($20). Cowboys will take you cantering up rolling pastures into the lush rain forest to view some of Maui's biggest waterfalls. Mendes caters to weddings and parties and offers private trail rides on request. Should you need accommodations they have a home and bunk for rent right on the property. ✉ *Hwy. 340, Wailuku* ☎ *808/244–7320 or 808/871–8222* ⊕ *www. mendesranch.com.*

Pi'iholo Ranch. The local wranglers here will lead you on a rousing ride through family ranchlands—up hillside pastures, beneath a eucalyptus canopy, and past many native trees. Morning and afternoon "country" rides last two hours and cost $120. Their well-kept horses navigate the challenging terrain easily, but hold on when axis deer pass by! Private rides and lessons are available. ✉ *End of Waiahiwi Rd., Makawao* ☎ *808/357–5544* ⊕ *www.piiholo.com.*

TENNIS

Most courts charge by the hour but will let players continue after their initial hour for free, provided no one is waiting. In addition to the facilities listed below, many hotels and condos have courts open to nonguests for a fee. The best free courts are the five at the **Lahaina Civic Center** (✉ *1840 Honoapi'ilani Hwy., Lahaina* ☎ *808/661–4685*), near Wahikuli State Park. They're available on a first-come, first-served basis.

Kapalua Tennis Garden. This complex, home to the Kapalua Tennis Club, serves the Kapalua Resort with 10 courts, four lighted for night play, and a pro shop. You'll pay $14 an hour if you're a guest, $16 if you're not. ✉ *100 Kapalua Dr., Kapalua* ☎ *808/669–5677.*

Wailea Tennis Club. The club has 11 Plexipave courts (its famed grass courts are, sadly, a thing of the past), lessons, rentals, and ball machines. On weekday mornings clinics are given to help you improve ground strokes, serve, volley, or doubles strategy. Rates are $15 per hour, per person, with three lighted courts available for night play. ✉ *131 Wailea Ike Pl., Kihei* ☎ *808/879–1958 or 800/332–1614.*

ZIPLINE TOURS

Since Skyline Eco Adventures opened their first zipline tour on the slope of Haleakalā in 2002, two other companies have opened tours, and Skyline has opened a second venue at Kā'anapali. With ziplining, you can satisfy your inner Tarzan by soaring high above deep gulches and canyons. A harness keeps you supported on each ride. There are weight restrictions, and you should wear closed-toe athletic-type shoes and expect to get dirty. ■ TIP➔ Although zipline tours are completely safe, you may want to reconsider this activity if you are uncomfortable with heights or have serious back or joint problems.

Kapalua Adventures Mountain Outpost. Opened in 2008, the zipline at Kapalua Adventures Mountain Outpost has almost 2 mi of parallel lines, enabling two riders to zip side by side. You can do just one zip or a combination, which could include the Giant Swing. Prices range from $60 to $299. You must be at least 10 years old and weigh between 60 and 250 pounds. The Mountain Outpost also has a high-ropes challenge course, and a 35-foot pole from which you can leap to catch a trapeze several feet away. ✉ *2000 Village Rd., Kapalua* 📞*808/665–4386 or 877/665–4386* 🌐*www.kapalua.com/adventures.*

Piʻiholo Ranch Zipline. The Piʻiholo Ranch complex, opened in 2008, has six ziplines—five parallel lines and one quadruple—plus a 12-person climbing tower. Ziplines range from 500 to 3,200 feet, with the latter being one of the 10 longest lines in the world. Prices are $140 for four lines and $190 for five lines. You must be at least 10 years old and weigh between 60 and 275 pounds. Nonparticipants can watch the action from the shady "tree-house" observation deck. ✉ *Piʻiholo Rd., Makawao* 📞*808/572–1717* 🌐*www.piiholo.com.*

Skyline Eco Adventures. Skyline Eco Adventures operates in two locations on Maui: the original course on the slope of Haleakalā, and the newer venue at 1,000 feet above Kāʻanapali. Good-natured guides give expert instruction and have you "zipping" confidently in no time. You must be at least 10 years old, weigh between 80 and 260 pounds, and be able to hike a moderate distance over uneven terrain in order to participate. For the Haleakalā tour ($89), dress in layers, as it can get chilly at the 4,000-plus foot elevation, especially in the morning. The Kāʻanapali tour ($150) includes breakfast or lunch. Advance reservations are suggested, especially in summer, and discounts are available for online bookings. 📞*808/878–8400* 🌐*www.zipline.com.*

SHOPPING

Updated by Eliza Escaño-Vasquez

Whether you're searching for a dashboard hula dancer or an original Curtis Wilson Cost painting, you can find it on Front Street in Lahaina or at the Shops at Wailea. Art sales are huge in the resort areas, where artists regularly show up to promote their work. Alongside the flashy galleries are standards like Quicksilver and ABC store, where you can stock up on swim trunks, sunscreen, and flip-flops.

Don't miss the great boutiques lining the streets of small towns like Pāʻia and Makawao. You can purchase boutique fashions and art while strolling through these charming,

> **BEST MADE-ON-MAUI GIFTS**
>
> ■ *Koa* jewelry boxes from **Maui Hands.**
>
> ■ Fish-shape sushi platters and bamboo chopsticks from the **Maui Crafts Guild.**
>
> ■ Black pearl pendant from **Maui Divers.**
>
> ■ Handmade Hawaiian quilt from **Hāna Coast Gallery.**
>
> ■ Fresh plumeria lei, made by you!

quieter communities. Notably, several local designers—Tamara Catz, Letarte, and Maui Girl—all produce top-quality island fashions. In the neighboring galleries, local artisans turn out gorgeous work in a range of prices. Special souvenirs include rare hardwood bowls and boxes, prints of sea life, Hawaiian quilts, and blown glass.

Specialty food products—pineapples, coconuts, or Maui onions—and "Made in Maui" jams and jellies make great, less-expensive souvenirs. Cook Kwee's Maui Cookies have gained a following, as have Maui Potato Chips. Coffee sellers now offer Maui-grown-and-roasted beans alongside the better-known Kona varieties. Remember that fresh fruit must be inspected by the U.S. Department of Agriculture before it can leave the state, so it's safest to buy a box that has already passed inspection.

Business hours for individual shops on the island are usually 9 to 5, seven days a week. Shops on Front Street and in shopping centers tend to stay open later (until 9 or 10 on weekends).

WEST MAUI

SHOPPING CENTERS

Lahaina Cannery Mall. In a building reminiscent of an old pineapple cannery are 50 shops and an active stage. The mall hosts free events year-round (like the Keiki Hula Festival and annual ice-sculpting competition). Recommended stops include Na Hoku, purveyor of striking Hawaiian heirloom jewelry and pearls; Totally Hawaiian Gift Gallery; and Kite Fantasy, one of the best kite shops on Maui. An events schedule is on the Web site. ⊠ *1221 Honoapi'ilani Hwy., Lahaina* ☏ *808/661–5304* ⊕ *www.lahainacannerymall.com.*

Lahaina Center. Island department store Hilo Hattie Fashion Center anchors the complex and puts on a free hula show at 2:30 PM every Wednesday. In addition to Hard Rock Cafe, Warren & Annabelle's Magic Show, and a four-screen cinema, you can find a replica of an ancient Hawaiian village complete with three full-size thatch huts built with 10,000 feet of Big Island *'ōhi'a* wood, 20 tons of *pili* grass, and more than 4 mi of handwoven coconut *senit* (twine). There's all that *and* validated parking. ⊠ *900 Front St., Lahaina* ☏ *808/667–9216.*

Whalers Village. Chic Whalers Village has a whaling museum and more than 50 restaurants and shops. Upscale haunts include Louis Vuitton and Tiffany & Co. The complex also offers some interesting diversions: Hawaiian artisans display their crafts daily; hula dancers perform on an outdoor stage weeknights from 6:30 to 7:30; sunset jazz is featured every first Sunday of the month; and Taiko drums and island rhythms beat on Saturday. ⊠ *2435 Kā'anapali Pkwy., Kā'anapali* ☏ *808/661–4567.*

BOOKSTORES

Fodor'sChoice **Old Lahaina Book Emporium.** Down a narrow alley you will find this book-
★ store stacked from floor to ceiling with new and antique finds. Spend a few moments (or hours) browsing the maze of shelves filled with mystery, sci-fi, nature guides, art, military history, and more. Collectors can scoop up rare Hawaiian memorabilia: playing cards, coasters, rare editions, and out-print-books chronicling Hawai'i's colorful past. ⊠ *In the alley next door, 834 Front St., Lahaina* ☏ *808/661–1399* ⊕ *www. oldlahainabookemporium.com.*

CLOTHING

Hilo Hattie Fashion Center. Hawai'i's largest manufacturer of aloha shirts and *mu'umu'u* also carries brightly colored blouses, skirts, and children's clothing. ✉*Lahaina Center, 900 Front St., Lahaina* ☎*808/667–7911.*

Honolua Surf Company. If you're not in the mood for a matching aloha shirt and *mu'umu'u* ensemble, check out this surf shop—popular with young men and women for surf trunks, casual clothing, and accessories. ✉*845 Front St., Lahaina* ☎*808/661–8848.*

Maggie Coulombe. Maggie Coulombe's cutting-edge fashions have the style of SoHo and the heat of the Islands. The svelte, body-clinging designs are definitely worth a look. ✉*505 Front St., Lahaina* ☎*808/ 662–0696.*

FOOD

Lahaina Square Shopping Center Foodland. This Foodland serves West Maui and is open daily from 6 AM to midnight. ✉*840 Waine'e St., Lahaina* ☎*808/661–0975.*

Safeway. Safeway has three stores on the island open 24 hours daily. ✉*Lahaina Cannery Mall, 1221 Honoapi'ilani Hwy., Lahaina* ☎*808/ 667–4392.*

GALLERIES

Lahaina Galleries. Works of both national and international artists are displayed at the gallery's two locations in West Maui. ✉*828 Front St., Lahaina* ☎*808/667–2152* ✉*In the Shops at Wailea, 3750 Wailea Alanui Dr., Wailea* ☎*808/874–8583* ⊕*www.lahainagalleries.com.*

Lahaina Printsellers Ltd. Hawai'i's largest selection of original antique maps and prints pertaining to Hawai'i and the Pacific is available here. You can also buy museum-quality reproductions and original oil paintings from the Pacific Artists Guild. A second, smaller shop is at 505 Front Street. ✉*Whalers Village, 2435 Kā'anapali Pkwy., Kā'anapali* ☎*808/667–7617* ⊕*www.printsellers.com.*

Martin Lawrence Galleries. Martin Lawrence displays the works of noted mainland artists, including Andy Warhol and Keith Haring, in a bright, friendly gallery. ✉*Lahaina Market Pl., Front St. and Lahainaluna Rd., Lahaina* ☎*808/661–1788* ⊕*www.martinlawrence.com.*

Village Gallery. This gallery, with two locations on the island, showcases the works of such popular local artists as Betty Hay Freeland, Wailehua Gray, Margaret Bedell, George Allen, Joyce Clark, Pamela Andelin, Stephen Burr, and Macario Pascual. ✉*120 Dickenson St., Lahaina* ☎*808/661–4402* ✉*Ritz-Carlton, 1 Ritz-Carlton Dr., Kapalua* ☎*808/669–1800* ⊕*www.villagegalleriesmaui.com.*

JEWELRY

Jessica's Gems. Jessica's has a good selection of Hawaiian heirloom jewelry, and its Lahaina store specializes in black pearls. ⊠ *Whalers Village, 2435 Kā'anapali Pkwy., Kā'anapali* ☎ *808/661–4223* ⊠ *858 Front St., Lahaina* ☎ *808/661–9200* ⊕ *www.jessicasgems.com.*

Lahaina Scrimshaw. Here you can buy brooches, rings, pendants, cuff links, tie tacks, and collector's items adorned with intricately carved sailors' art. ⊠ *845A Front St., Lahaina* ☎ *808/661–8820* ⊠ *Whalers Village, 2435 Kā'anapali Pkwy., Kā'anapali* ☎ *808/661–4034.*

Maui Divers. This company has been crafting gold and coral into jewelry for more than 40 years. ⊠ *640 Front St., Lahaina* ☎ *808/661–0988* ⊕ *www.lahainascrimshaw.net.*

CENTRAL MAUI

SHOPPING CENTERS

Maui Marketplace. On the busy stretch of Dairy Road, just outside the Kahului Airport, this behemoth marketplace couldn't be more conveniently located. The 20-acre complex houses several outlet stores and big retailers, such as Pier One Imports, Sports Authority, and Borders Books & Music. Sample local food at the Kau Kau Corner food court. ⊠ *270 Dairy Rd., Kahului* ☎ *808/873–0400.*

Queen Ka'ahumanu Center. This is Maui's largest mall with 75 stores, a movie theater, an active stage, and a food court. The mall's interesting rooftop, composed of a series of manta ray–like umbrella shades, is easily spotted. Stop at Camellia Seeds for what the locals call "crack seed," a snack made from dried fruits, nuts, and lots of sugar. Other stops here include mall standards such as Macy's, Pacific Sunwear, and American Eagle Outfitters. ⊠ *275 Ka'ahumanu Ave., Kahului 96732* ☎ *808/877–3369* ⊕ *www.queenkaahumanucenter.com.*

CLOTHING

Bohemia. Find vintage Hawaiiana, top-quality designer resale, *and* new pieces by upscale designers like Letarte, Chanel, Roberto Cavalli and Juicy Couture, all at affordable prices. ⊠ *105 N. Market St., Wailuku* ☎ *808/244–9995.*

Hi-Tech. Stop here immediately after deplaning to stock up on surf trunks, windsurfing gear, bikinis, and sundresses. ⊠ *425 Koloa Rd., Kahului* ☎ *808/877–2111.*

FOOD

Maui Coffee Roasters. This café and roasting house near Kahului Airport is the best stop for Kona and Island coffees. The salespeople give good advice and will ship items. You even get a free cup of joe in a signature to-go cup when you buy a pound of coffee. ⊠ *444 Hāna Hwy., Unit B, Kahului* ☎ *808/877–2877* ⊕ *www.mauicoffeeroasters.com.*

Safeway. Safeway has three stores on the island open 24 hours daily. ⊠ *170 E. Kamehameha Ave., Kahului* ☎ *808/877–3377.*

THE SOUTH SHORE

SHOPPING CENTERS

Azeka Place Shopping Center. Azeka II, on the *mauka* (toward the mountains) side of South Kīhei Road, has the Coffee Store (the place for iced mochas), Who Cut the Cheese (the place for aged gouda), and the Nail Shop (the place for shaping, waxing, and tweezing). Azeka I, the older half on the *makai* side of the street, has a decent Vietnamese restaurant and Kīhei's post office. ⊠*1280 S. Kīhei Rd., Kīhei* ☎*808/879–5000.*

Kīhei Kalama Village Marketplace. This is a fun place to investigate. Shaded outdoor stalls sell everything from printed and hand-painted T-shirts and sundresses to jewelry, pottery, wood carvings, fruit, and gaudily painted coconut husks—some, but not all, made by local craftspeople. ⊠*1941 S. Kīhei Rd., Kīhei* ☎*808/879–6610.*

Rainbow Mall. This mall is one-stop shopping for condo guests—it offers video rentals, Hawaiian gifts, plate lunches, and a liquor store. ⊠*2439 S. Kīhei Rd., Kīhei* ☎*808/879–1145* ⊕*www.rainbowmallmaui.com.*

Shops at Wailea. Stylish, upscale, and close to most of the resorts, this mall brings high fashion to Wailea. Luxury boutiques such as Gucci, Fendi, Cos Bar, and Tiffany & Co. have shops, as do less-expensive chains like Gap, Guess, and Tommy Bahama. Several good restaurants face the ocean, and regular Wednesday-night events include live entertainment, art exhibits, and fashion shows. ⊠*3750 Wailea Alanui Dr., Wailea* ☎*808/891–6770* ⊕*www.shopsatwailea.com.*

CLOTHING

Cruise. This upscale resort boutique has sundresses, swimwear, sandals, bright beach towels, and a few nice pieces of resort wear. ⊠*In the Grand Wailea, 3850 Wailea Alanui Dr., Wailea* ☎*808/875–1234.*

Hilo Hattie Fashion Center. Hawai'i's largest manufacturer of aloha shirts and *mu'umu'u* also carries brightly colored blouses, skirts, and children's clothing. ⊠*297 Pi'ikea Ave., Kīhei* ☎*808/875–4545.*

Sisters & Company. Opened by four sisters, this little shop has a lot to offer—current brand-name clothing such as True Religion and Da-nang, locally made jewelry, beach sandals, and gifts. Sister No. 3, Rhonda, runs a tiny, ultrahip hair salon in back while Caroline, Sister No. 2, offers mani-pedis. ⊠*1913 S. Kīhei Rd., Kīhei* ☎*808/875–9888.*

Tommy Bahama's. It's hard to find a man on Maui who *isn't* wearing a TB-logo aloha shirt. For better or worse, here's where you can get yours. Make sure to grab a Barbados Brownie on the way out at the restaurant attached to the shop. ⊠*Shops at Wailea, 3750 Wailea Alanui Dr., Wailea* ☎*808/879–7828.*

FOOD

Foodland. In Kīhei town center, this is the most convenient supermarket for those staying in Wailea. It's open round-the-clock. ⊠*1881 S. Kīhei Rd., Kīhei* ☎*808/879–9350.*

Safeway. Safeway has three stores on the island open 24 hours daily. ⊠*277 Piikea Ave., Kīhei* ☎*808/891–9120.*

Continued on page 250

ALL ABOUT LEIS

Leis brighten every occasion in Hawai'i, from birthdays to bar mitzvahs to baptisms. Creative artisans weave nature's bounty—flowers, ferns, vines, and seeds—into gorgeous creations that convey an array of heartfelt messages: "Welcome," "Congratulations," "Good luck," "Farewell," "Thank you," "I love you." When it's difficult to find the right words, a lei expresses exactly the right sentiments.

WHERE TO BUY THE BEST LEIS

These florists carry a nice variety of leis: **A Special Touch** (Emerald Plaza, 142 Kupuohi St., Ste. F-1, Lahaina, 808/661—3455); **Kahului Florist** (Maui Mall, 70 E. Ka'ahumanu Ave., Kahului, 808/877–3951 or 800/711—8881); **Nāpili Florist** (5059 Nāpilihau St., Lahaina, 808/669–4861); and **Kīhei-Wailea Flowers by Cora** (1280 S. Kīhei Rd., Ste. 126, Kīhei, 808/879-7249 or 800/339—0419). **Costco, Kmart, Wal-Mart**, and **Safeway** sell basic leis, such as orchid and plumeria.

LEI ETIQUETTE

■ To wear a closed lei, drape it over your shoulders, half in front and half in back. Open leis are worn around the neck, with the ends draped over the front in equal lengths.

■ Pīkake, ginger, and other sweet, delicate blossoms are "feminine" leis. Men opt for cigar, crown flower, and ti leaf, which are sturdier and don't emit as much fragrance.

■ Leis are always presented with a kiss, a custom that supposedly dates back to World War II when a hula dancer fancied an officer at a U.S.O. show. Taking a dare from members of her troupe, she took off her lei, placed it around his neck, and kissed him on the cheek.

■ You shouldn't wear a lei before you give it to someone else. Hawaiians believe the lei absorbs your *mana* (spirit); if you give your lei away, you'll be giving away part of your essence.

ORCHID

Growing wild on every continent except Antarctica, orchids—which range in color from yellow to green to purple—comprise the largest family of plants in the world. There are more than 20,000 species of orchids, but only three are native to Hawai'i—and they are very rare. The pretty lavender vanda you see hanging by the dozens at local lei stands has probably been imported from Thailand.

MAILE

Maile, an endemic twining vine with a heady aroma, is sacred to Laka, goddess of the hula. In ancient times, dancers wore maile and decorated hula altars with it to honor Laka. Today, "open" maile leis usually are given to men. Instead of ribbon, interwoven lengths of maile are used at dedications of new businesses. The maile is untied, never snipped, for doing so would symbolically "cut" the company's success.

'ILIMA

Designated by Hawai'i's Territorial Legislature in 1923 as the official flower of the island of O'ahu, the golden 'ilima is so delicate it lasts for just a day. Five to seven hundred blossoms are needed to make one garland. Queen Emma, wife of King Kamehameha IV, preferred 'ilima over all other leis, which may have led to the incorrect belief that they were reserved only for royalty.

PLUMERIA

This ubiquitous flower is named after Charles Plumier, the noted French botanist who discovered it in Central America in the late 1600s. Plumeria ranks among the most popular leis in Hawai'i because it's fragrant, hardy, plentiful, inexpensive, and requires very little care. Although yellow is the most common color, you'll also find plumeria leis in shades of pink, red, orange, and "rainbow" blends.

PĪKAKE

Favored for its fragile beauty and sweet scent, pīkake was introduced from India. In lieu of pearls, many brides in Hawai'i adorn themselves with long, multiple strands of white pīkake. Princess Kaiulani enjoyed showing guests her beloved pīkake and peacocks at Āinahau, her Waikīkī home. Interestingly, pīkake is the Hawaiian word for both the bird and the blossom.

KUKUI

The kukui (candlenut) is Hawai'i's state tree. Early Hawaiians strung kukui nuts (which are quite oily) together and burned them for light; mixed burned nuts with oil to make an indelible dye; and mashed roasted nuts to consume as a laxative. Kukui nut leis may not have been made until after Western contact, when the Hawaiians saw black beads from Europe and wanted to imitate them.

UPCOUNTRY, THE NORTH SHORE, AND HĀNA

CLOTHING

Biasa Rose. This boutique offers hip island styles for the whole family. Charming gifts—pillows, napkins, photo albums—are on display along with comfy cotton Splendid and James Perse tees, airy tunics, and vintage aloha shirts. There's a consignment area in the back where you can score designer pieces on a dime. ⊠ *104 Hāna Hwy., Pā'ia* ☎ *808/579–8602.*

Fodor'sChoice ★ **Maui Girl.** This is *the* place for swimwear, cover-ups, beach hats, and sandals. Maui Girl designs its own suits and imports teenier versions from Brazil as well. Tops and bottoms can be purchased separately, greatly increasing your chances of finding a suit that actually fits. ⊠ *13 Baldwin Ave., Pā'ia* ☎ *808/579–9266.*

Moonbow Tropics. If you're looking for an aloha shirt that won't look out of place on the mainland, make a stop at this little store, which sells the best-quality shirts on the island. ⊠ *36 Baldwin Rd., Pā'ia* ☎ *808/579–8592.*

Pink By Nature. Stay ahead of the style curve with coveted lines like Ella Moss, Tart, and Paige Denim. Owner Desiree Martinez's penchant for refined nautical details and easy wearability keeps this rustic store stocked with select pieces from Free People and T-Bag, or showstoppers from local designers Fighting Eel and Tamara Catz. Trendsetting moms can gush about adorable vintage onesies and baby tanks by Annie K. for the wee fashionista-in-training. ⊠ *3663 Baldwin Ave., Makawao* ☎ *808/572–9576.*

Fodor'sChoice ★ **Tamara Catz.** This Maui designer already has a worldwide following, and her sarongs and super-stylish beachwear have been featured in many fashion magazines. If you're looking for a sequined bikini or a delicately embroidered sundress, this is the place to check out. And for the blushing beach bride, Catz has recently launched a bridal line that is superhaute. ⊠ *83 Hāna Hwy., Pā'ia* ☎ *808/579–9184.*

FOOD

Mana Foods. Stock up on local fish and grass-fed beef for your barbecue here. You can find the best selection of organic produce on the island, as well as a great bakery and deli at this typically crowded health-food store. ⊠ *49 Baldwin Ave., Pā'ia* ☎ *808/579–8078.*

GALLERIES

★ **Hāna Coast Gallery.** One of the best places to shop on the island, this 3,000-square-foot gallery has fine art and jewelry on consignment from local artists. ⊠ *Hotel Hāna-Maui, Hāna Hwy., Hāna* ☎ *808/248–8636 or 800/637–0188.*

Fodor'sChoice ★ **Maui Crafts Guild.** This is one of the more interesting galleries on Maui. Set in a two-story wooden building alongside the highway, the Guild is crammed with treasures. Resident artists craft everything in the store—from Norfolk-pine bowls to *raku* (Japanese lead-glazed) pottery to original sculpture. The prices are surprisingly low. ⊠ *43 Hāna Hwy., Pā'ia* ☎ *808/579–9697.*

JEWELRY

Maui Master Jewelers. The exterior of this shop is as rustic as all the old buildings of Makawao, so there's no way to prepare yourself for the elegance of the handcrafted jewelry displayed within. ✉ *3655 Baldwin Ave., Makawao* ☎ *808/572–6000.*

SPAS

Updated by Eliza Escaño-Vasquez

Traditional Swedish massage and European facials anchor most spa menus, though you'll also find shiatsu, ayurveda, aromatherapy, and other body treatments drawn from cultures across the globe. *Lomi lomi,* traditional Hawaiian massage involving powerful strokes down the length of the body, is a regional specialty passed down through generations. Many treatments incorporate local plants and flowers. *Awapuhi,* or Hawaiian ginger, and *noni,* a pungent-smelling fruit, are regularly used for their therapeutic benefits. *Limu,* or seaweed, and even coffee is employed in rousing salt scrubs and soaks. And this is just the beginning.

★ **Heavenly Spa by Westin at the Westin Maui.** An exquisite 80-minute Lavender Body Butter treatment is the star of this spa's menu, thanks to a partnership with a local lavender farm. Other options include cabana massage (for couples, too) and water lily sunburn relief with green tea. The facility is flawless, and it's worth getting a treatment just to sip lavender lemonade in the posh ocean-view waiting room. The open-air yoga studio and the gym offer energizing workouts. Bridal parties can request a private area within the salon. ✉ *Westin Kāʻanapali, 2365 Kāʻanapali Pkwy., Kāʻanapali* ☎ *808/661–2588* ⊕ *www.westinmaui. com* ☞ *$130 50-minute massage, $285 day spa packages; Hair salon, hot tub, sauna, steam room. Gym with: cardiovascular machines, free weights, weight-training equipment. Services: aromatherapy, body wraps, facials, hydrotherapy, massage, Vichy shower. Classes and programs: aquaerobics, yoga.*

Fodor'sChoice **Honua Spa at Hotel Hāna-Maui.** A bamboo gate opens into an outdoor
★ sanctuary with a lava-rock pool and hot tub; at first glimpse this spa seems to have been organically grown, not built. The decor here can hardly be called decor—it's an abundant, living garden. Taro varieties, orchids, and ferns still wet from Hāna's frequent downpours nourish the spirit as you rest with a cup of jasmine tea, or take an invigorating dip in the plunge pool. Signature aromatherapy treatments utilize Honua, the spa's own sumptuous blend of sandalwood, coconut, ginger, and vanilla orchid essences. The Hâna Wellness package is a blissful eight hours of treatments, which can be shared between the family, or enjoyed alone. ✉ *Hotel Hāna-Maui, Hāna Hwy., Hāna* ☎ *808/270–5290* ⊕ *www. hotelhanamaui.com* ☞ *$140 60-minute massage, $265 spa packages; Hair salon, hot tubs (indoor and outdoor), sauna, steam room. Gym with: cardiovascular machines, free weights, weight-training equipment. Services: aromatherapy, body wraps, facials, hydrotherapy, massage. Classes and programs: meditation, Pilates, yoga.*

Fodor's Choice
★

Spa at Four Seasons Resort. The Four Seasons' hawklike attention to detail is reflected here. Thoughtful gestures like fresh flowers beneath the massage table (to give you something to stare at), organic herbal tea in the "relaxation room," and your choice of music begin to ease your mind and muscles before your treatment even begins. The spa is genuinely stylish and serene, and the therapists are among the best. Thanks to an exclusive partnership, the spa offers treatments created by celebrity skin-care specialist Kate Somerville. The "Ultimate Kate" is 80 minutes of super hydrating, collagen-increasing magic, incorporating light therapy and powerful, tingling products that literally wipe wrinkles away. ⊠ *3900 Wailea Alanui Dr., Wailea* ☎ *808/874–8000 or 800/334–6284* ⊕ *www. fourseasons.com* ✆ *$150 50-minute massage, $450 3-treatment packages; Hair salon, steam room. Gym with: cardiovascular machines, free weights, weight-training equipment. Services: aromatherapy, body wraps, facials, hydrotherapy, massage. Classes and programs: aquaerobics, meditation, personal training, Pilates, Spinning, tai chi, yoga.*

> ### BUDGET-FRIENDLY SPAS
>
> If hotel spa prices are a little intimidating, try **Spa Luna** (⊠ *810 Ha'ikū Rd., Ha'ikū* ☎ *808/575–2440*), a day spa, which is also an aesthetician's school. In the former Ha'ikū Cannery, it offers services ranging from massage to microdermabrasion. You can opt for professional services, but the student clinics are the real story here. The students are subject to rigorous training, and their services are offered at a fraction of the regular cost ($30 for a 50-minute massage).

Fodor's Choice
★

Spa Grande, Grand Wailea Resort. Built to satisfy an indulgent Japanese billionaire, this 50,000-square-foot spa makes others seem like well-appointed closets. Slathered in honey and wrapped up in the steam room (if you go for the Ali'i honey steam wrap), you'll feel like royalty. All treatments include a loofah scrub and a trip to the *termé*, a hydrotherapy circuit including a Roman Jacuzzi, furo bath, plunge pool, powerful waterfall and Swiss jet showers, and five therapeutic baths. (Soak for 10 minutes in the moor mud to relieve sunburn or jellyfish stings.) To fully enjoy the baths, plan to arrive an hour before your treatment. Free with treatments, the termé is also available separately for $55 for two hours. At times—especially during the holidays—this wonderland can be crowded. ⊠ *3850 Wailea Alanui Dr., Wailea* ☎ *808/875–1234 or 800/888–6100* ⊕ *www.grandwailea.com* ✆ *$150 50-minute massage, $255 half-day spa packages; Hair salon, hot tub, sauna, steam room. Gym with: cardiovascular machines, free weights, racquetball, weight-training equipment. Services: aromatherapy, body wraps, facials, hydrotherapy, massage, Vichy shower. Classes and programs: aquaerobics, cycling, Pilates, qigong, yoga.*

Spa Kea Lani, Fairmont Kea Lani Hotel Suites & Villas. This small spa is a little cramped, but nicely appointed: fluffy robes and Italian mints greet you upon arrival. We recommend the excellent *lomi lomi* massage—a series of long, soothing strokes combined with gentle stretching, or the *ili ili* hot stone therapy. Both treatments employ indigenous healing oils: rich *kukui* nut, kava, and noni, and tropical fragrances. Poolside massages by the divinely serene adult pool can be reserved on the spot. Not in a lounging mood? Check out the state-of-the-art 1,750-square-foot fitness center. ⊠ *4100 Wailea Alanui Dr., Wailea* ☎ *808/875–4100 or 800/441–1414* ⊕ *www.kealani.com* ☞ *$145 50-minute massage, $340 spa packages; Hair salon, steam room. Gym with: cardiovascular machines, free weights, weight-training equipment. Services: aromatherapy, body wraps, facials, hydrotherapy, massage, Vichy shower. Classes and programs: aquaerobics, yoga.*

★ **Waihua Spa, Ritz-Carlton, Kapalua.** This gorgeous 17,500-square-foot spa reopened as part of the hotel's recent renovation. Enter this blissful maze where floor-*to*-ceiling riverbed stones lead to serene treatment rooms, couples' *hales* (cabanas), and a wet grotto with a Jacuzzi, dry sauna, and steam rooms. With cucumber water in hand, hang out in the co-ed waiting area, where sliding glass doors open to a whirlpool overlooking a taro patch garden. Get any rough skin exfoliated with a pineapple papaya scrub; then wash it off in a private outdoor shower garden before indulging in a traditional *lomilomi* massage (traditional Hawaiian massage involving powerful strokes down the length of the body). The spa's caviar of beauty treatments uses advanced oxygen technology to tighten mature skin. ⊠ *1 Ritz-Carlton Dr., Kapalua* ☎ *808/669–6200 or 800/262–8440* ⊕ *www.ritzcarlton.com* ☞ *$150 50-min massage, $375 half-day spa packages. Hair salon, hot tubs (outdoor and indoor), sauna, steam room. Gym with: cardiovascular machines, free weights, weight-training equipment. Services: aromatherapy, body wraps, facials, massage. Classes and programs: aquaerobics, cycling, nutrition, Pilates, yoga.*

ENTERTAINMENT AND NIGHTLIFE

Updated by
Eliza Escaño-
Vasquez

Looking for wild island nightlife? We can't promise you'll always find it here. This quiet island has little of Waikīkī's after-hours decadence, and the club scene (if you want to call it that) can be quirky, depending on the season and the day of the week. But sometimes Maui will surprise you with a big-name concert, outdoor festival, or world-class DJ. Lahaina and Kīhei are your best bets for action. Outside of those towns, you might be able to hit an "on" night in Pāʻia (North Shore) or Makawao (Upcountry), mostly on weekend nights. Your best bet? Pick up the free *MauiTime Weekly,* or Thursday's edition of the *Maui News,* where you'll find a listing of all your after-dark options, island-wide.

ENTERTAINMENT

ARTS CENTER

★ **Maui Arts & Cultural Center.** The hub of all highbrow arts and quality performances has an events calendar that features everything from rock to reggae to Hawaiian slack-key guitar, international dance and circus troupes, political and literary lectures, art films, cult classics—you name it. Each Wednesday (and occasionally Friday) evening, the MACC hosts movie selections from the Maui Film Festival. The complex includes the 1,200-seat Castle Theater, a 4,000-seat amphitheater for large outdoor concerts, the 350-seat McCoy Theater for plays and recitals, and a courtyard café offering preshow dining and drinks. For information on current events, check the Events Box Office (☎808/242–7469 ⊕www. mauiarts.org) or *Maui News*. (⊠*1 Cameron Way, above harbor on Kahului Beach Rd., Kahului* ☎808/242–2787).

DINNER CRUISES AND SHOWS

There's no better place to see the sun set on the Pacific than from one of Maui's many boat tours. You can find a tour to fit your mood, anything from a quiet, sit-down dinner to a festive, beer-swigging booze cruise. Note, however, that many cocktail have recently put a cap on the number of free drinks offered with open bars, instead including a limited number of drinks per ticket.

Dinner cruises typically feature music and are generally packed—which is great if you're feeling social, but you might have to fight for a good seat. You can usually get a much better meal at one of the local restaurants. Most nondinner cruises offer *pūpū* and an open bar. Winds are consistent in summer, but variable in winter—sometimes making for a rocky ride. If you're worried about sea sickness, you might consider a catamaran, which is much more stable than a mono-hull. Take Dramamine before the trip, and if you feel sick, sit in the shade (but not inside the cabin), place a cold rag or ice on the back of your neck, and *breathe* as you look at the horizon. Tours leave from Māʻalaea or Lahaina harbors. Be sure to arrive at least 15 minutes early.

Kaulana **Cocktail Cruise.** This two-hour sunset cruise prides itself on its live music and festive atmosphere. Accommodating up to 100 people, the cruise generally attracts a rowdier, more boisterous crowd. *Pūpū*, such as meatballs, crab and shrimp platters, and teriyaki pineapple chicken are served, and there is a full bar (two drinks included). Freshly baked chocolate chip cookies are passed around toward the end of the trip. ⊠*Lahaina Harbor, Slip 3* ☎800/621–3601 ⊕*www. tombarefoot.com/maui/kaulana_sunset.html* ⊠$49 ⊙*Mon., Wed. and Fri. 4:30–7:30* PM.

Paragon **Champagne Sunset Sail.** This 47-foot catamaran brings you a performance sail within a personal setting. Limited to groups of 24 (with private charters available), you can spread out on deck and enjoy the gentle trade winds. An easygoing, attentive crew will serve you hot and cold *pūpū*, such as grilled chicken skewers, spring rolls, and a fruit platter, along with beer, wine, mai tais, and champagne at sunset. ⊠*Loading Dock, Lahaina Harbor* ☎808/244–2087 ⊕*www.sailmaui. com* ⊠$47.60 adult, $33.15 child 4–12, free for children 3 and under ⊙*Mon., Wed., Fri. evenings only; call for check-in times*.

Pride **Charters.** A 65-foot catamaran built specifically for Maui's waters, the *Pride of Maui* has a spacious cabin, dance floor, and large upper deck for unobstructed viewing. Evening cruises include cocktails and an impressive spread of baby back ribs, grilled chicken, roasted veggies, artichoke dip, and penne pasta salad. Desserts include tropical cake and assorted tarts. ⊠*Māʻalaea Harbor, Māʻalaea* ☎877/867–7433 ⊕*www. prideofmaui.com* ⊠$69.95 ⊙*Tues., Thurs., and Sat. 5–7:30* PM.

Spirit of Lahaina **Dinner Cruise.** This double-deck, 65-foot catamaran offers a family-style dinner cruise, featuring appetizers, warm taro rolls, freshly grilled steak, *huli-huli* chicken (barbecued with flavors like brown sugar cane, ginger, and soy), shrimp skewered on sugarcane, and fabulous desserts. The trip also features contemporary Hawaiian music, hula, and a comedy magic show that will definitely cure you of any motion sickness. ⊠ *Slip 4, Lahaina Harbor* ☎ *808/662–4477* ⊕ *www. spiritoflahaina.com* ⌗ *$99 adult, $59 child* ⊙ *Daily 5–7:15* PM.

LŪ'AU

★ **Feast at Lele.** "Lele" is an older, more traditional name for Lahaina. This feast redefines the lū'au by crossing it with island-style fine dining in an intimate beach setting. Each course of this succulent sit-down meal expresses the spirit of specific island culture—Hawaiian, Samoan, Tongan, Tahitian—and don't forget dessert. Dramatic Polynesian entertainment accompanies the dinner, along with excellent wine and liquor selections. This is the most expensive lū'au on the island for a reason: Lele is top-notch. ⊠ *505 Front St., Lahaina* ☎ *808/667–5353* ⌕ *Reservations essential* ⊕ *www.feastatlele.com* ⌗ *$110 adult, $80 child 2–12* ⊙ *Nightly at 5:30* PM *in winter, 6* PM *in summer.*

Fodor's Choice **Old Lahaina Lū'au.** Many consider this the best lū'au on Maui; it's cer-
★ tainly the most traditional. Located right on the water, at the northern end of town, the Old Lahaina Lū'au is small, personal, and as authentic as it gets. Sitting either at a table or on a *lauhala* mat, you'll dine on all-you-can-eat Hawaiian cuisine: pork *laulau* (wrapped with taro sprouts in tī leaves), a'hi *poke* (pickled raw tuna, tossed with herbs and seasonings), *lomilomi* salmon (rubbed with onions and herbs), Maui-style mahimahi, *haupia* (coconut pudding), and more. At sunset the show begins a historical journey that relays key periods in Hawai'i's history, from the arrival of the Polynesians to the influence of the missionaries and, later, tourism. The tanned, talented performers will charm you with their music, chanting, and variety of hula styles (modern and *kahiko*, the ancient way of communicating with the gods). But if it's fire dancers you want to see, you won't find them here, as they aren't considered traditional. Although it's performed nightly, this lū'au sells out regularly. Make your reservations when planning your trip to Maui. You can cancel up until 10 AM the day of the scheduled show. ⊠ *1251 Front St., makai of Lahaina Cannery Mall, Lahaina* ☎ *808/667–1998* ⌕ *Reservations essential* ⊕ *www.oldlahainaluau.com* ⌗ *$92 adult, $62 child 2–12* ⊙ *Nightly at 5:15* PM *in winter, 5:45* PM *in summer.*

Wailea Beach Marriott Honua'ula Lū'au. The Marriott lū'au presents a high-quality show, an open bar, a tasty buffet, and a sunset backdrop that can't be beat. The stage is placed right next to the water, and the show features an *imu* (underground oven) ceremony to start, and Polynesian dancers performing a blend of modern acrobatics (including an impressive fire-knife dance) and traditional hula. ⊠ *3700 Wailea Alanui Dr.* ☎ *808/879–1922* ⊕ *www.marriotthawaii.com* ⌕ *Reservations essential* ⌗ *$94 adult ($104 for premium seating), $49 child 6–12 ($78 for premium seating)* ⊙ *Mon. and Thurs.–Sat. 5* PM.

FILM

In the heat of the afternoon, a theater may feel like paradise. There are megaplexes showing first-run movies in Kukui Mall (Kīhei), Lahaina Center, and Maui Mall and Ka'ahumanu Shopping Center (Kahului).

★ **Maui Film Festival.** In this ongoing celebration, the Maui Arts & Cultural Center features art-house films every Wednesday (and sometimes Friday) evening at 5 and 7:30 PM, accompanied by live music, dining, and poetry in the Candlelight Café. In summer an international week-long festival attracts big-name celebrities to Maui for cinema under the stars. ☎808/579–9244 recorded program information ⊕www.mauifilmfestival.com.

THEATER

For live theater, check local papers for events and showtimes.

☾ **"'Ulalena" at Maui Theatre.** One of Maui's hottest tickets, "'Ulalena" is a
★ 75-minute musical extravaganza that is well received by audiences and Hawaiian-culture experts alike. Cirque de Soleil–inspired, the ensemble cast (20 singer-dancers and a five-musician orchestra) mixes native rhythms and stories with acrobatic performance. High-tech stage wizardry gives an inspiring introduction to island culture. It has auditorium seating, and beer and wine are for sale at the concession stand. There are dinner-theater packages in conjunction with top Lahaina restaurants. ✉878 Front St., Lahaina ☎808/661–9913 or 877/688–4800 ⊕www.mauitheatre.com ⚓Reservations essential ✉$59.50–$129.50 for a dinner package ☺Tues.–Sat. at 6:30 PM.

Warren & Annabelle's. This is one show not to miss—it's serious comedy with an amazing sleight of hand. Magician Warren Gibson entices guests into his swank nightclub with red carpets and a gleaming mahogany bar, and plies them with à la carte appetizers (coconut shrimp, crab cakes), desserts (rum cake, crème brûlée), and "smoking cocktails." Then, he performs tableside magic while his ghostly assistant, Annabelle, tickles the ivories. This is a nightclub, so no one under 21 is allowed. ✉Lahaina Center, 900 Front St., Lahaina ☎808/667–6244 ⊕www.hawaiimagic.com ⚓Reservations essential ✉$56 or $94.50, including food and drinks ☺Mon.–Sat. at 5 and 7:30 PM.

NIGHTLIFE

Your best bet when it comes to bars on Maui? If you walk by and it sounds like it's happening, go in. If you want to scope out your options in advance, be sure to check the free *Maui Time Weekly*, found at most stores and restaurants, to find out who's playing where. The *Maui News* also publishes an entertainment schedule in its Thursday edition of the "Maui Scene." With an open mind (and a little luck), you can usually find a good scene for fun.

WEST MAUI

The Cellar 744. This late-night subterranean spot, formerly known as Paradice Bluz, re-opened in late 2008 without any major renovation but with cushy new lounge seating having replaced its pool tables. Tuesday features hip-hop and reggae but if you're jonesing for some bass-heavy funky house, Friday will give you the necessary fix. ✉*744 Front St., Lahaina* ☎*808/661–3744* ⊕*www.thecellar744maui.com.*

Cool Cat Café. One could easily miss this casual 1950's-style diner while strolling through Lahaina. Tucked in the second floor of the Wharf Cinema Center, its semi-outdoor area plays host to rockin' local music nightly. The entertainment lineup covers jazz, contemporary Hawaiian, and traditional island rhythms. It doesn't hurt that the kitchen dishes out specialty burgers, fish that's fresh from the harbor, and delicious homemade sauces from the owner's family recipes. ✉*658 Front St., Lahaina* ☎*808/667–0908* ⊕*www.coolcatcafe.com.*

Hard Rock Cafe. You've seen one Hard Rock Cafe, you've seen them all. However, Maui's Hard Rock brings you Reggae Monday, featuring our beloved local reggae star Marty Dread. $5 cover, 10 PM. ✉*Lahaina Center, 900 Front St., Lahaina* ☎*808/667–7400.*

Mai Tai Lounge. You have to pass through a lot of "bling" to get to this swanky joint. Perched atop a jewelry store, the oceanfront lounge has a DJ who spins hip-hop, Hawaiian, and reggae music on Friday and Saturday evenings. You might want to ask the bartender to ease up on the ice. ✉*839 Front St., Lahaina* ☎*808/661–5288* ☽*11–11.*

THE SOUTH SHORE

Ambrosia Blues and Jazz Club. For or a chill night out, Ambrosia is a South Maui favorite. It's a cozy hangout for blues, jazz, and folk music, as well as the occasional absinthe drink. The crowd is more sophisticated—less rowdy, but a lot of fun. ✉*1913 S. Kīhei Rd., Kīhei* ☎*808/891–1011* ⊕*www.ambrosiamaui.com* ☽*5 PM–2 AM.*

Lulu's. Lulu's could be your favorite bar in any beach town. It's a second-story, open-air tiki and sports bar, with a pool table, small stage, and dance floor to boot. The most popular night is Salsa Thursday, with dancing and lessons until 11. Wednesday is karaoke night, Friday is classic rock night, and Saturday features guest hip-hop DJs. ✉*1945 S. Kīhei Rd., Kīhei* ☎*808/879–9944.*

★ **Mulligan's on the Blue.** Frothy pints of Guinness and late-night fish-and-chips—who could ask for more? Sunday nights feature foot-stomping Irish jams that will have you dancing a jig, and singing something about "a whiskey for me-Johnny." Other nights bring in various local bands. ✉*Blue Golf Course, 100 Kaukahi St., Wailea* ☎*808/874–1131.*

South Shore Tiki Lounge. Good eats are paired with the island's most progressive DJs in this breezy, tropical tavern. Local DJs are featured every day of the week; if you're craving some old-school hip-hop, Thursday is your night. ✉*1913-J S. Kihei Rd., Kihei* ☎*808/874–6444* ⊕*www.southshoretikilounge.com.*

WHAT'S A LAVA FLOW?

Can't decide between a piña colada or strawberry daiquiri? Go with a Lava Flow—a mix of light rum, coconut and pineapple juice, and a banana, with a swirl of strawberry puree. Add a wedge of fresh pineapple and a paper umbrella, and mmm . . . good. Try one at Lulu's in Kīhei.

UPCOUNTRY AND THE NORTH SHORE

Casanova Italian Restaurant and Deli. Casanova can bring in some big acts, which in the past have included Kool and the Gang, Los Lobos, and Taj Majal. Most Friday and Saturday nights, though, it attracts a hip, local scene with live bands and eclectic DJs spinning house, funk, and world music. Don't miss the costume theme nights. Wednesday is for Wild Wahines (code for ladies drink half price), which can be more on the smarmy side. Cover $5 to $25. ⊠*1188 Makawao Ave., Makawao* ☎*808/572–0220.*

Charley's. The closest thing to country Maui has to offer, Charley's is a down-home, divey bar in the heart of Pāʻia. It also hosts disco, house, industry, and lounge nights. ⊠*142 Hāna Hwy., Pāʻia* ☎*808/579–9453.*

Jacques. Who can resist a venue once voted by locals as the "best place to see suspiciously beautiful people from around the world"? On Friday nights, the crowd spills onto the cozy streets of Pāʻia, as funky DJs spin Latino, world lounge, salsa, and live jazz. ⊠*120 Hāna Hwy., Pāʻia* ☎*808/579-8844.*

WHERE TO EAT

By Carla Tracy

In the mid-1990s, Maui and the rest of Hawaiʻi emerged as a gastronomic force, as menus were infused with bold flavors, colors, and the freshest island ingredients. Hawaiʻi Regional Cuisine (Modern Hawaiian fare) was born, and whether you're dining at an upscale restaurant or a beach café, you're likely to be the beneficiary.

Forget old clichés of island chefs dishing up bland Dover sole and iceberg lettuce. Instead, picture nori fettuccine with fresh *ʻopihi* (limpets) and Hoʻokipa Bay *limu* (seaweed) poke salad made with chunks of yellowfin tuna and blood-orange dressing. Imagine desserts that bend all culinary conventions, such as macadamia-nut tacos packed with tropical fruits and *likoʻi* (passion fruit) custard.

This sustainable style of cooking is no flash in the pan. Maui now has everything from award-winning goat cheese to a host of lavender food products. Many of Hawaiʻi Regional Cuisine's original 12 chefs still live on Maui and remain successful restaurateurs: Beverly Gannon of Hāliʻimaile General Store, Peter Merriman of Hula Grill, and Mark Ellman of Mala Ocean Tavern and Penne Pasta, to name a few. Countless chefs in small mom-and-pop shops also buy locally and support the vast agricultural resources found on island.

If you want to get off the beaten path and hunt down ethnic and local-style restaurants, you can eat well at thrifty prices. Check out historic Wailuku, Upcountry Makawao, or little Pāʻia on the North Shore. You will find quality bistros, cafés, and sushi bars.

WHAT IT COSTS				
¢	$	$$	$$$	$$$$
RESTAURANTS under $10	$10–$17	$18–$26	$27–$35	over $35

Restaurant prices are for a main course at dinner.

WEST MAUI

LAHAINA

¢ ✕**Aloha Mixed Plate.** Set right on the ocean in Lahaina, this walk-up
HAWAIIAN open-air bar and restaurant under the shade trees is a great casual place
for 'ono grinds—"good food" in Hawaiian slang. Chinese roast duck,
Hawaiian laulau (leaf-wrapped bundles of meats and fish) plate, and
Korean kalbi ribs (marinated and cooked on a grill) are indicative of
the mixed-plate culture that's part of Hawai'i. The plates go well with
drinks such as the Lava Flow, Peachy Passion, and Hawaiian Punch.
This place is well regarded by locals and is a good pit stop for lunch.
⊠*1286 Front St., Lahaina* ☏*808/661–3322* ═*AE, D, DC, MC, V.*

$$$ ✕**Chez Paul.** Open since 1975, this intimate restaurant in tiny Olowalu
FRENCH (between Mâ'alaea and Lahaina) remains the is the oldest French res-
taurant in the state of Hawai'i. Owner-chef Patrick Callarec hails from
Provence, and he honed his skills at many Ritz-Carltons. Let the Edith
Piaf music and sensual artwork transport you to France as you dine on
whole duck à l'orange; seared papio Provençale in the niçoise style with
shrimp; or rack of lamb *paniolo*-style with fruit marinade. For dessert,
try the pineapple tart tatin with tapioca pudding and caramel sauce.
Chef Patrick is a lively firebrand, so do chat him up. The restaurant's
offbeat exterior belies the elegant interior, which is complete with linen-
draped tables and a wine cellar. ⊠*Honoapi'ilani Hwy., 4 mi south of
Lahaina, Olowalu* ☏*808/661–3843* ⌃*Reservations essential* ═*AE,
D, MC, V* ⊘*No lunch.*

$ ✕**Cilantro.** The flavors of Old Mexico are given new life here, where
MEXICAN the tortillas are hand-pressed and no fewer than nine chilies are used
to create the salsas. Owner Paris Nabavi, a former high-end food and
beverage pro, spent three years visiting authentic eateries in 40 Mexi-
can cities. Let him take you south of the border with spinach, mush-
room, and poblano enchiladas (a first-place winner in Taste of Lahaina);
or scallops and prawns chile relleno with ancho tomato sauce, crema
fresca, and roasted corn. The rotisserie chicken tacos with jicama slaw
are also mouthwatering—and healthful. Look for Nabavi's collection
of tortilla presses worn from duty, now hand-painted and displayed
up on the wall. ⊠*Old Lahaina Center, 170 Papalaua Ave., Lahaina*
☏*808/667–5444* ═*AE, MC, V.*

$$$$ ✕**Gerard's.** French-born owner and top Lahaina chef Gerard Reversade
FRENCH honors the French tradition yet adds an island twist in such exquisite
Fodor's Choice dishes as appetizers as shrimp sautéed in hazelnut oil, and 'ahi and
★ smoked salmon carpaccio with lemon Chantilly. The rack of lamb Per-
sillade offers a mint and lemon jus crust and is served with potatoes au
gratin and stuffed tomatoes. You will be in heaven with the pineapple
tart tatin à la mode. Located in the Plantation Inn, Gerard's resembles
a country estate with balustrades and gingerbread lattice work. Birds
chirp on the palms, mangos hang on the trees in the courtyard, and fans
spin overhead. Antique furnishings and wallpaper along with a wide
veranda for dining make this perfect for special occasions. A first-class
wine list and celebrity-spotting round out the experience. ⊠*Plantation
Inn, 174 Lahainaluna Rd., Lahaina* ☏*808/661–8939* ═*AE, D, DC,
MC, V* ⊘*No lunch.*

¢
HAWAIIAN

✕**Honokowai Okazuya.** Don't expect to sit down at this miniature restaurant sandwiched between a dive shop and a salon—this is strictly a take-out joint. It has quite a good reputation with the locals, so it's always packed. Sink your teeth into mahimahi with lemon capers, ono with a sun-dried tomato sauce, or spicy kung pao chicken. Or try chicken *katsu* (Japanese-style breaded and fried chicken), pork, and peas piled with the requisite two scoops of rice and macaroni-potato salad. You'll also find lighter fare such as vegetarian plates, sandwiches, and Chinese food. The spicy eggplant is delicious, and the fresh chow fun noodles (flat, wide Chinese rice noodles) are purchased quickly. ⊠*3600-D Lower Honoapi'ilani Hwy., Lahaina* ☎808/665–0512 ⊟*No credit cards* ⊘*Closed Sun.*

$$$$
AMERICAN

✕**Lahaina Grill.** Open since 1990, Lahaina Grill lost the "David Paul's" part of its name late in 2007, but under the latest owner Jurg Munch, executive chef at the Mandarin Oriental in Hong Kong for years, the celebrated updated American food and the service remain consistent. Beautifully designed with stamped-tin ceilings, splashy artwork, and overhead fans, it is part of an elegant older building and has an extensive wine cellar and an in-house bakery. Try the seared 'ahi with foie gras or the crispy-fried blue corn–crusted chile relleno filled with Hawaiian Big Island prawns, scallops, and Monterey Jack cheese. Save room for the scrumptious triple-berry pie. Smaller portions are available at the bar. ⊠*127 Lahainaluna Rd., Lahaina 96761* ☎808/667–5117 ⊟*AE, DC, MC, V* ⊘*No lunch.*

$$$$
ITALIAN

✕**Longhi's.** A Lahaina landmark, Longhi's has been drawing in throngs of visitors since 1976, serving great Italian pasta as well as sandwiches and seafood, beef, and chicken dishes from the menu created by Bob Longhi, "the man who loves to eat." The pasta is homemade and the in-house bakery turns out breakfast pastries, desserts, and pizza bread, the latter complimentary with your meal. Definitely for two, the signature lobster Longhi includes two lobsters over linguine and pomodoro sauce with mussels, clams, and prawns. Another must try is the fillet Longhi, served with red and yellow bell peppers. There are two spacious, open-air levels from which to choose; and there's a second Maui restaurant on the South Shore, at the Shops at Wailea. ⊠*888 Front St., Lahaina* ☎808/667–2288 ⊟*AE, D, DC, MC, V*⊠ Maui Prince, 5400 Mākena Alanui Rd., Mākena ☎ 808/874—1111⊟ *AE, MC, V.*

$$
MODERN
HAWAIIAN

✕**Mala Ocean Tavern.** On the water's edge, above the tide-tossed rocks, stands this cheery yellow-walled, open-air restaurant owned by noted Hawai'i Regional Cuisine chef Mark Ellman and his wife, Judy. The menu, composed of mostly organic and locally sourced ingredients, includes flavorful flatbreads and a Kobe burger with Maytag blue cheese. Don't miss the calamari, battered and fried with lemon slices and served with a spicy mojo verde (jalapeño cilantro pesto). This is a good place to try moi, the famed fish of Hawaiian royalty, wok-fried with ginger and spicy black-bean sauce. Fans of the Caramel Miranda dessert at Avalon (Ellman's former restaurant) can find it here. In the evening, the bar is a coveted hangout, and weekend brunch is lively. In addition, the much bigger Mala Ocean Tavern opened in Wailea in mid-2008 as a co-venture between Ellman and a number of celeb partners, including Clint Eastwood and Alice Cooper. ✉*1307 Front St., Lahaina* ☏*808/667–9394* 🖃*AE, MC, V.*

$$$
SEAFOOD

✕**Pacific'O.** You can sit outdoors at umbrella-shaded tables near the water's edge, or find a spot in the breezy, marble-floor interior of this seafood haven. All the produce comes from the owner's Upcountry organic farm, just as it does at its sister restaurant I'o. The exciting menu features the appropriately named bling bling, which is grilled petit filet mignon topped with Gorgonzola cheese and ginger butter; and poached lobster with potato du jour and tempura asparagus. Another fun dish is fresh 'ahi-and-ono tempura, in which the two kinds of fish are wrapped around *tobiko* (flying-fish roe), then wrapped in nori, and wok-fried. For dessert, try the banana pineapple *lumpia* served hot with homemade banana ice cream. ✉*505 Front St., Lahaina* ☏*808/667–4341* 🖃*AE, D, DC, MC, V.*

$
ITALIAN

✕**Penne Pasta.** A couple of blocks off the beaten path in Lahaina, little Penne Pasta packs a powerhouse of a menu, as might be expected from a place owned by chef Mark Ellman of the Mala Ocean Tavern. Heaping plates of reasonably priced, flavorful pasta and low-key, unobtrusive service make this restaurant the perfect alternative to an expensive night in the resort areas. House favorites are cheesy baked penne in tomato cream sauce and linguine in clam sauce with lemon butter. The osso buco (Wednesday's special) is a lamb shank with fettuccine, lamb ragout, and salad. The salade niçoise overflows with olives, peppers, garlic 'ahi, and potatoes. Couples should split a salad and entrée, as portions are large. ✉*180 Dickenson St., Lahaina* ☏*808/661–6633* 🖃*AE, D, DC, MC, V* ☉*No lunch weekends.*

KĀ'ANAPALI

$$$
MODERN
HAWAIIAN

✕**Hula Grill.** Genial chef-restaurateur Peter Merriman, the pied piper and founder of Hawai'i Regional Cuisine has teamed with TS Restaurant Group in this bustling, family-oriented restaurant. They have recreated a 1930s Hawaiian beach house, and every table has an ocean view. You can also dine on the beach, toes in the sand, at the Barefoot Bar, where Hawaiian entertainment is presented every evening. Lunch items include such tasty dishes as shrimp, spinach, and Asian pear salad and Bahn Mi, a Vietnamese steak sandwich using local Maui Cattle Co. beef. Two types of fresh fish are offered nightly, often with lobster risotto or mango-jasmine rice and fresh local vegetables. Children of all ages scream for the ice-cream sandwich made with baked brownies and drizzled with raspberry sauce. ✉*Whalers Village, 2435 Kā'anapali Pkwy., Kā'anapali* ☏*808/667–6636* 🖃*AE, DC, MC, V.*

$$$$
CONTINENTAL

✕**Son'z at Swan Court.** Robin Leach once named this the most romantic restaurant in the world in *Lifestyles of the Rich and Famous*, and it's perfect for couples celebrating special occasions. Descend the grand staircase into an amber-lit dining room soaring ceilings and a massive artifical lagoon with swans, waterfalls, and tropical gardens. Choose your evening's libation from one of 3,000 bottles of wine, the largest cellar in the state. Must-haves on include tiger shrimp penne à la vodka; goatcheese ravioli of fresh Kula corn, edamame, and Hamakua mushrooms; and *opakapaka* (blue snapper) served with artichokes, sweet-potato hash browns, and tomato puree. ✉*Hyatt Regency Maui, Kā'anapali*

Beach Resort, 200 Nohea Kai Dr., Kāʻanapali ☎808/661–1234 ☐*AE,*
D, DC, MC, V ☉*No lunch.*

KAPALUA AND VICINITY

$$$$ ✕**The Banyan Tree.** The signature restaurant of the Ritz-Carlton, Kapalua
MODERN is better than ever after the resort's late 2007 makeover. Drink in views
HAWAIIAN of the Pailolo Channel and Molokaʻi from the new outdoor bar and
lounge with covered terrace. Indoors are light fixtures and artwork
inspired by sea urchins and vibrant corals. The *dukka* (Middle Eastern
spices) delivered with your bread is a tip that this elegant dining hall
offers plenty of worldly influences. Chef Ryan Urig excels with pine-
nut-crusted ʻahi with cucumber noodles and Thai-basil pesto; crispy ehu
with creamy Surfing Goat Dairy cheese polenta with beets and watercress; and Kona lobster with ginger-carrot risotto, tarragon, and coral
butter. The open-beam restaurant's subdued atmosphere is sometimes
charged with the sounds of live world music by Ranga Pae. ⊠*Ritz-Car-*
lton, Kapalua, 1 Ritz-Carlton Dr., Kapalua ☎808/669–6200 ☐*AE,*
D, DC, MC, V.

¢ ✕**The Gazebo Restaurant.** Even locals will stand in line up to half an
DINER hour to have diner fare at a table overlooking the beach at this slightly
hard-to-find restaurant, an open-air gazebo (albeit an old and funky
one) overlooking magnificent Nāpili Bay. Sunsets are phenomenal, and
turtle and spinner dolphin sightings are common. The food is standard
diner fare, but it's thoughtfully prepared. Breakfast choices include pancakes with macadamia-nuts, pineapple, and bananas; and the Kahuna
omelet with Portuguese sausage, mushrooms, onions, bacon, avocado,
and pepper-jack cheese. At lunch, there are satisfying bacon and avocado burgers and Southwestern salads. The friendly resort staff puts out
coffee for those waiting in line. ⊠*Nāpili Shores Resort, 5315 Lower*
Honoapiʻilani Hwy., Nāpili ☎808/669–5621 ☐*No credit cards* ☉*No*
dinner.

$$$ ✕**Kai.** The popular sushi bar in the Ritz-Carlton, Kapalua takes design
JAPANESE inspiration from the arrival of the ancient Hawaiians over the sea.
Hand-carved ceiling beams resemble outrigger canoes, and the back
wall of the bar glows like lava. This is a great place to meet your
friends and lift your chopsticks to rainbow roll and fresh ʻahi sashimi
before you head to the neighboring Alaloa Lounge. The menu also
includes hot Japanese entrées such as baked crab dynamite, but your
best bet is to let Tokyo native, chef Tadashi Yoshino, design the meal.
His top sellers include tuna tataki salad in ponzu sauce and the Yamato
Roll with fresh hamachi (yellowtail) and spicy tuna. The kitchen is
open until 9 PM. ⊠*Ritz-Carlton, Kapalua, 1 Ritz-Carlton Dr., Kapalua*
☎808/669–6200 ☐*AE, D, DC, MC, V.*

$$$ ✕**Pineapple Grill.** With a menu built almost entirely around local ingre-
MODERN dients, Pineapple Grill attracts those foodies who appreciate exceptional
HAWAIIAN Pacific Island cuisine such as stuffed Kamuela vine-ripened tomatoes,
ʻahi and salmon tartare, Molokaʻi sweet potatoes, and Maui Gold
pineapple upside-down cake for dessert. A Maui Seafood Watch par-
ticipant, the restaurant only serves seafood that has been harvested sus-
tainably. So go on—order the Kona lobster. The restaurant also features
Wine Spectator's annual top 100 wines by the glass. At night, you can

witness spectacular sunsets overlooking the golf greens and the Pacific; the outdoor tables facing the West Maui Mountains can be even nicer than those with an ocean view. There's live entertainment and 50% off the bar menu every Wednesday night. ✉ *200 Kapalua Dr., Kapalua* ☎ *808/669–9600* ▤ *AE, D, DC, MC, V.*

$$$
MEDITERRANEAN

✕ **Plantation House Restaurant.** It's hard to decide which is better here, the food or the view. Perched high above Kapalua's coastline, this estate-like restaurant at the Plantation Course has the misty Maui Mountains behind, and views of Moloka'i and the Pailolo Channel in front. The menu is on par with the surroundings and features Mediterranean flavors blended with local ingredients. Longtime Chef Alex Stanislaw began doing the sustainability thing even before it became widespread. He uses neighboring Kapalua Farms' vegetables and prepares two or three fresh Hawaiian fish seven different ways nightly. A favorite is the Venice: panko-crusted and sautéed fish on risotto with Kula sugar peas, O'ahu asparagus, and Pacific shrimp. Breakfast here is luxurious; try the Bloody Mary with pickled asparagus and one of the famous Benedicts. ✉ *Plantation Course Clubhouse, 2000 Plantation Club Dr., past Kapalua* ☎ *808/669–6299* ▤ *AE, MC, V.*

$$$
MODERN
HAWAIIAN

✕ **Roy's Kahana Bar & Grill.** Founder Roy Yamaguchi is a James Beard Award–winning chef who now has almost 40 restaurants to his name from Japan to Florida. This is one of his first, and regulars keep returning for his Hawaiian-fusion specialties and private-label wines and beers. Favorites include Kona kampachi tataki with sizzling yuzu soy and sesame snap peas; crisp Sonoma duck breast with Makawao mushroom risotto cake; and pepper-seared scallops and seared white shrimp with saffron rice. Locals know to order the incomparable chocolate soufflé immediately after being seated. Both branches, in Kahana and Kīhei, are in supermarket parking lots—it's not the view that excites; it's the fantastic food and the welcoming and professional service. ✉ *Kahana Gateway Shopping Center, 4405 Honoapi'ilani Hwy., Kahana* ☎ *808/669–6999* ▤ *AE, D, DC, MC, V* ✉ *Safeway Shopping Center, 303 Pi'ikea Ave., Kīhei* ☎ *808/891–1120* ▤ *AE, D, DC, MC, V..*

$$
PACIFIC RIM

✕ **Sansei Seafood Restaurant & Sushi Bar.** One of the best-loved restaurants on the island, Sansei is Japanese with a Hawaiian twist. Inspired dishes include *panko* (Japanese bread crumb) -crusted 'ahi sashimi roll, rock shrimp in creamy garlic aioli, spicy fried calamari, and the signature mango-and-crab-salad roll. Those who love French cuisine will appreciate the decadent foie gras nigiri sushi. Desserts such as deep-fried tempura ice cream are worth the calories. The Kapalua location uses colors such as pumpkin, butterscotch, and sage that all add a tasty touch. Both this and the Kīhei location are popular karaoke hangouts, serving late-night sushi at half price. ✉ *600 Office Rd., Kapalua* ☎ *808/669–6286* ▤ *AE, D, MC, V* ⊗ *No lunch* ✉ *Kīhei Town Center, 1881 S. Kīhei Rd., Kīhei* ☎ *808/879–0004* ▤ *AE, D, MC, V* ⊗ *No lunch.*

THE SOUTH SHORE

KĪHEI AND MĀ'ALAEA

$$
AMERICAN
Fodor'sChoice
★

Cafe O'Lei. This is where locals go on their day off. Chef-owners Michael and Dana Pastula are known to dish up fabulously fresh tastes at affordable prices. Huge portions at lunch and dinner include Manoa lettuce wraps filled with chicken, mushrooms, and water chestnuts; crab cakes; and quinoa salads packed with local eggplant and creamy goat cheese. Order sushi from the bar in back or baked clams and giant tiger prawns from the brick oven. Other popular items are fresh fish, macadamia-nut chicken breast, and Asian short ribs. Gauze curtains separate tables nicely set with white linens and bright tableware, and the spacious octagonal bar is great for sharing pūpū and sipping cocktails. The Pastulas also have Café O'Lei restaurants in Kahului and Wailuku. ⊠ *2439 S. Kīhei Rd., Kīhei* ☎ *808/891–1368* ⊟ *AE, MC, V.*

$
VEGETARIAN

✕ **Joy's Place.** You may see Joy in the back of this small spot, whipping up one of the fantastic, vitamin-packed soups that reflect her healthful culinary wizardry. Try a sandwich or collard-green wrap filled with veggies and a creamy spread, or a nut burger and nondairy cheese. Joy's is also known for free-range turkey sandwiches, and they poach tuna for fresh tuna salad. Organic cookies and vegan brownies top it off. If you have a hint of a cold, a spicy potion called Cold Buster can ward it off. ⊠ *In Island Surf Bldg., 1993 S. Kīhei Rd., Suite 17, Kīhei* ☎ *808/879–9258* ⊟ *MC, V.*

¢
AMERICAN

✕ **Kihei Caffe.** People-watching is fun over a cup of coffee at this casual breakfast and lunch joint right on the main drag in Kîhei. Hearty, affordable portions will prepare you for a day of surfing across the street at Kalama Park. The bowl-shaped egg scramble is tasty and almost enough for two, or try signature dishes such as loco moco (a hamburger patty and over-easy egg on top of scoops of rice in a bowl, slathered in brown gravy), pork fried rice, and chorizo and eggs. Opakapaka (blue snapper) with *liliko'i* (passion fruit) beurre blanc is popular lunch fare, and fish preparations change daily. The resident rooster, one of many that live under the building, may come a-beggin' for some of your muffin. This place closes at 3. ⊠ *1945 S. Kīhei Rd., Kīhei* ☎ *808/879–2230* ⊟ *MC, V* ⊗ *No dinner.*

$$
AMERICAN

✕ **Mā'alaea Grill.** Large French doors are kept open so that you can view Mâ'alaea Harbor and feel the ocean breezes in this casual seaside restaurant. The teak and bamboo furniture, open kitchen, and walk-in wine cellar lend sophistication to this otherwise happily relaxed establishment. Enjoy the light but satisfying blackened mahimahi with tropical fruit salsa, kiawe-wood-grilled New York steak with house-made onion rings, or shrimp prepared a variety of ways: coconut fried, sautéed Provençale, or garlic grilled with pesto. Live jazz music is performed Wednesday through Sunday. This may be one of the only restaurants on Maui in which you can enjoy ocean views until 9 PM, as the harbor and Kîhei beyond are backlighted. ⊠ *In the Harbor Shops, 300 Mā'alaea Rd., Mā'alaea* ☎ *808/243–2206* ⊟ *AE, MC, V.*

$$$$
ITALIAN

✕ **Sarento's on the Beach.** The setting right on spectacular Keawakapu Beach, with views of the islands of Molokini and Kaho'olawe, at this upscale Italian restaurant is irresistible. Chef Geno Sarmiento heads the kitchen which turns out such gems as wild tiger shrimp served over house-made ravioli of ricotta cheese, Yukon Gold potato puree, and white truffle oil; seafood *fra diavolo (*in a tomato sauce spiced with chilies*); and* swordfish saltimbocca, a strangely successful entrée with a prosciutto, Bel Paese cheese, radicchio, and porcini sauce. Meat lovers should try the fall-off-the-bone tender osso buco. The wine list includes some great finds. ✉*2980 S. Kīhei Rd., Kīhei* ☎*808/875–7555* ▭*AE, D, DC, MC, V* ⊘*No lunch.*

$$
AMERICAN

✕**Stella Blues.** Parked in humble Azeka Mauka marketplace, this affordable spot wins die-hard fans for unpretentious service and cuisine in an open-beam, warmly lit dining room that's unexpectedly classy. The menu is a major hit, especially with families, and the bar is great for surfer-dude watching. Comfort food of every sort is served at breakfast, lunch, and dinner, including grilled New York steak (dry-aged and all-natural from Maui Cattle Co.); Sunshine Daydream seafood stew in a white saffron tomato broth; and yellow coconut curry for vegetarians. The ample Bananas Foster Our Way features vanilla ice cream topped with caramelized bananas, macadamia nuts, and whipped cream. ✉*1279 S. Kīhei Rd., Kīhei* ☎*808/874–3779* ▭*AE, D, DC, MC, V.*

$
THAI

✕**Thailand Cuisine.** Fragrant tea and coconut-ginger chicken soup begin a satisfying meal at this excellent Thai restaurant, set unassumingly in the back of a casual shopping mall. The care that goes into the decor here—reflected in the glittering Buddhist shrines, fancy napkin folds, and matching blue china—also applies to the cuisine. Take an exotic journey with pad thai noodles; beef salad with scallions, tomatoes, cucumber, and mint; or yellow curry with potatoes, carrots and your choice of protein. ✉*In Kukui Mall, 1819 S. Kīhei Rd., Kīhei* ☎*808/875–0839* ▭*AE, D, DC, MC, V.*

$$$$
SEAFOOD
Fodor's Choice
★

✕**Waterfront Restaurant.** The Smith family lures you in hook, line, and fresh catch at this well-regarded harborside establishment with an outstanding wine list. Sit in cushy leather booths or on the lānai and choose from six types of fresh fish prepared in nine different ways, including baked in buttered parchment paper; captured in ribbons of angel-hair potato; and topped with tomato salsa, smoked chili pepper, and avocado. The varied menu also lists an outstanding rack of lamb and veal scaloppine. Visitors like to come early to dine at sunset on the outdoor patio. Enter Māʻalaea at the Maui Ocean Center and then follow the blue WATERFRONT RESTAURANT signs to the third condominium Come early if you want to dine at sunset on the lānai. ✉*50 Hauʻoli St., Māʻalaea* ☎*808/244–9028* ▭*AE, D, DC, MC, V* ⊘*No lunch.*

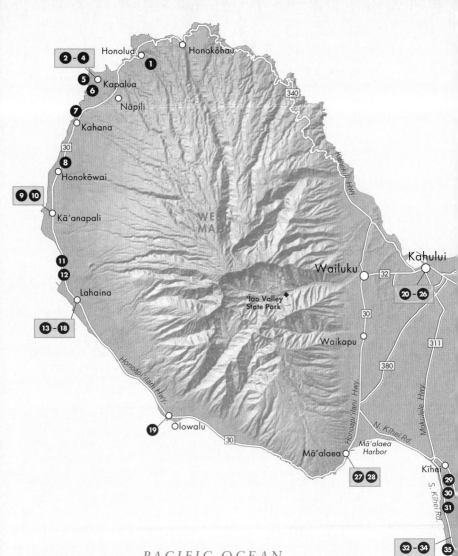

Where to Eat on Maui

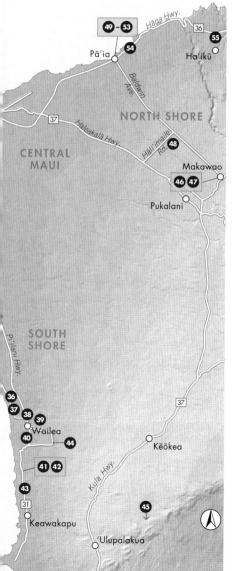

$ ✕**WokStar International Noodle Café.**
VEGETARIAN   This fun, easy-on-the-budget eatery, across the street from the humpback whale sculpture in Kīhei, has a walk-up counter and picnic tables. The name may imply that it's part of some global conglomerate, but this is the first and only one of its kind. You'll find everything from Thai red curry with seasonal vegetables to Japanese miso ramen soup and Balinese stir-fries. The young owners try to stay open until midnight seven nights a week for those hungry after "pub crawling" through the many nearby bars and lounges. ⊠ *Kīhei Kalama Village, 1913D S. Kihei Rd., Kihei* ☎ *808/495–0066* ⊟ *AE, MC, V.*

> ### SUSHI FOR ALL
>
> On Maui, there's a sushi restaurant for everyone—even those who don't like sushi! Sansei has the most diverse menu: everything from lobster ravioli to sea urchin. People love designer rolls such as the "69"—unagi eel slathered in sweet sauce paired with crab, or the "caterpillar"—avocado and tuna wrapped around rice, complete with radish-sprout antennae!

WAILEA AND MĀKENA

$$$$ ✕**Capische.** Hidden up at the quiet Diamond Hawaii Resort & Spa, this
ITALIAN   Italian restaurant is one local patrons would like kept secret. A circular
Fodor'sChoice   stone atrium with soaring ceilings gives way to a small piano lounge,
★   where you can find some of the best sunset views on the island. It's as romantic as it gets, and you'll want to be dressed up for your date. Capische favorites include cioppino, braised lamb shank with lemon risotto, and truffle grilled 'ahi with sautéed butternut squash, Kula corn sauce, and wilted frisée. Intimate and well conceived, this restaurant, with its seductive flavors and ambience, ensures a lovely night out. Il Teatre downstairs is owner-chef Brian Etheredge's fine-dining concept, where he designs and cooks your menu in front of you. ⊠ *Diamond Hawaii Resort & Spa, 555 Kaukahi St., Wailea* ☎ *808/879–2224* ⊟ *AE, D, DC, MC, V* ⊘ *No lunch.*

$$$$ ✕**Ferraro's Bar & Restorante.** Overlooking Wailea Beach, this outdoor
ITALIAN   Italian restaurant at the Four Seasons Resort Maui is beautiful both day and night, with unparalleled service. For lunch, indulge in a lobster sandwich, salade niçoise, or a *bento* (Japanese divided box filled with savory items). At dinner you might begin your feast with the arugula and endive salad and move on to the lobster risotto and veal Milanese while enjoying live classical music. Try the wine list's excellent Italian choices, and if chef Michael Cantin is offering one of his periodic tasting menus—such as white Alba truffles in fall—go for it. ⊠ *Four Seasons Resort Maui at Wailea, 3900 Wailea Alanui Dr., Wailea* ☎ *808/874–8000* ⊟ *AE, D, DC, MC, V.*

$$$ ✕**Hakone.** The Japanese food served at this popular restaurant in the
JAPANESE   Maui Prince Hotel has a great reputation with locals. Saturday, the all-you-can-eat Japanese Buffet ($48) draws them in like moths to a flame. Indulge in seaweed salads, kabocha pumpkin and cranberries, miso butterfish, shrimp tempura, and kalbi beef. The regular menu offers numerous dishes of raw, cooked, hot, cold, sweet, and savory items. Impeccably fresh sushi, traditional cooked dishes, and an impressive sake list round out the menu. You may even get a degree in sake to take

home with you if you try one of the samplers. The ambience takes you into the heart of Tokyo with its shoji screens, austere look, and servers dressed in kimonos. ✉ *Maui Prince, 5400 Mākena Alanui Rd., Mākena* ☎ *808/874–1111* 🖃 *AE, MC, V* ⊘ *No lunch.*

$$$$ ✕ **Joe's.** Owners Joe and Beverly Gannon, who run the immensely popu-
AMERICAN lar Hāliʻimaile General Store in Upcountry Maui, have brought their flair for food to this comfortable treetop-level restaurant at the Wailea Tennis Club. Views include the sparkling Pacific on one side and vistas of Haleakalā on the other. This place is named after Joe, who's been in show biz for decades, instead of his celebrity chef wife. So his gold records and other memorabilia hang on the walls. Friendly service and the best burger on the island draw residents as well as visitors. Top menu items include Joe's favorite meat loaf, grilled thick-cut pork chop, seafood potpie, and Joe's pastry chef daughter Cheech's chocolate bread pudding. ✉ *131 Wailea Ike Pl., Wailea* ☎ *808/875–7767* 🖃 *AE, MC, V* ⊘ *No lunch.*

$$ ✕ **Matteo's.** Chef Matteo Mitsura—a bona-fide Italian—may be heard
ITALIAN singing as he pounds dough in the kitchen of this miraculous pizzeria.
☺ (Trust us, discovering handsomely-sized Margherita and Portofino piz-
zas for $17 in Wailea is truly a miracle.) Handmade pastas are loaded with luxurious braised lamb, wild mushrooms, and fresh-shaved Par-
mesan. Located on the Wailea Blue golf course, this casual, open-air restaurant benefits from gentle trade winds in the afternoon and a sky full of stars at night. A voluptuous wine list, and desserts such as tira-
misu top it off. ✉ *100 Wailea Ike Dr., Wailea 96753* ☎ *808/874–1234* 🖃 *AE, D, MC, V.*

$$$$ ✕ **Nick's Fishmarket Maui.** This romantic spot serves fresh seafood using
SEAFOOD the simplest preparations. Savor the grilled ʻahi mignon served medium rare with polenta fries and sauce au poivre; or the seared diver scal-
lops with herb gnocchi, local mushrooms, asparagus tips, and Parme-
san nage. Everyone seems to love the Greek Maui Wowie salad made with local onions, tomatoes, avocado, feta cheese, and bay shrimp. The service is formal—even theatrical—but it befits the beautiful food presentations and extensive wine list. If you are a repeat diner, the staff will probably remember what drink is your favorite. ✉ *Fairmont Kea Lani, 4100 Wailea Alanui Dr., Wailea* ☎ *808/879–7224* 🖃 *AE, D, DC, MC, V* ⊘ *No lunch.*

$$$$ ✕ **Spago.** Celebrity chef and owner Wolfgang Puck wisely brought his
PACIFIC RIM fame to this gorgeous, popular-with-celebs restaurant set lobby level and oceanfront at the Four Seasons Resort Maui. Giant sea-anemone prints, modern-art-inspired lamps, and views of the shoreline give you something to look at while waiting. The cutting-edge menu delivers with appetizers such as spicy ʻahi *poke* in sesame miso cones and entrées such as Thai seafood in red coconut curry; pan-roasted organic free-
range chicken breast; and lamb chops with spicy Hunan eggplant, sweet peas, and chili mint vinaigrette. Chef Cameron Lewark's tasting menu, paired with wines, is a treat. ✉ *Four Seasons Resort Maui at Wailea, 3900 Wailea Alanui Dr., Wailea* ☎ *808/879–2999* 🖃 *AE, D, DC, MC, V* ⊘ *No lunch.*

CENTRAL MAUI

KAHULUI

¢   ✕ **Ba Le.** Tucked into a mall's food court is the best, cheapest Vietnam-
VIETNAMESE   ese fast food on the island. The famous soups, or *pho,* come laden
with seafood or rare beef, fresh basil, bean sprouts, and lime. Tasty
sandwiches are served on crisp French rolls—lemongrass chicken is a
favorite. The word is out, so the place gets busy at lunchtime, though
the wait is never long. Make sure to try one of the flavored tapiocas for
dessert and take home some freshly baked croissants. Also check out
Ba Le's latest incarnation in Wailuku. ⊠*Kau Kau Corner food court,
Maui Marketplace, 270 Dairy Rd., Kahului* ☎*808/877–2400* ⊟*AE,
D, DC, MC, V.*

$$ ✕ **Dragon Dragon.** Whether you're a party of 10 or 2, this is the place
CHINESE   to share Cantonese West Lake beef soup, honey walnut prawns, and
lamb-back ribs with garlic sauce. Tasteful, simple decor that focuses
on feng shui and sharp angles complements the solid Chinese menu.
Dim sum is served at lunch only. Can't decide what to order? Try the
set meals for two, four, or six people. The restaurant shares parking
with the Maui Megaplex and makes a great pre- or postmovie stop.
⊠*In Maui Mall, 70 E. Ka'ahumanu Ave., Kahului* ☎*808/893–1628*
⊟*AE, D, MC, V.*

$$ ✕ **Marco's Grill & Deli.** Outside Kahului Airport, this convenient eatery
ITALIAN   (look for the green awning) serves Italian food in Central Maui. Owner
Marco Defanis was a butcher in his former life, and his meatballs and
sausages are housemade. Homemade pastas appear on the extensive
menu, along with an unforgettably good Reuben sandwich and tiramisu. Even the coffee, served in Mad Hatter–size cups, is made by
nearby Maui Coffee Roasters; you can buy packages to take home.
The local business crowd fills the place for breakfast, lunch, and dinner.
⊠*444 Hāna Hwy., Kahului* ☎*808/877–4446* ⊟*AE, D, DC, MC, V.*

WAILUKU

$ ✕ **A.K.'s Café.** Nearly hidden between auto-body shops and karaoke
HAWAIIAN   bars is this wonderful, bright café serving good Hawaiian fare. Affordable, tasty entrées such as grilled tenderloin with wild mushrooms or
garlic-crusted ono with ginger relish come with a choice of two sides.
The flavorful dishes are healthy, too—Chef Elaine Rothermal previously
instructed island nutritionists on how to prepare health-conscious versions of local favorites. (She's trying to get away from that somewhat,
as most people like the bad stuff.) Try the Hawaiian french-fried sweet
potatoes or the poi, the Hawaiian classic made from taro root. Single
musicians entertain you on the weekends. ⊠*1237 Lower Main, Wailuku* ☎*808/244–8774* ⊟*D, MC, V* ☻*Closed Sun.*

¢   ✕ **Maui Bake Shop.** Wonderful breads baked in old brick ovens (dating to
AMERICAN   1935), hearty lunch fare, and irresistible desserts make this a popular
lunch spot in Central Maui. Baker José Krall was trained in his home-
land of France, and his wife, Claire, is a Maui native whose friendly face
you often see when you walk in. Standouts include the focaccia, Caesar
salads, and homemade soups. José also creates impressive wedding and

other specialty cakes. ⊠*2092 Vineyard St., Wailuku* ☎*808/242–0064* ▭*AE, D, MC, V* ⊘*Closed Sun. No dinner.*

$$
THAI
✕**Saeng's Thai Cuisine.** Choosing a dish from the six-page menu here requires determination, but the food is worth the effort, and most dishes can be tailored to your taste buds: hot, medium, or mild. Begin with angel wings (chicken wings stuffed with carrots and bean-thread noodles); move on to such entrées as Poh Teak (spicy seafood soup), Evil Prince Chicken (cooked in coconut sauce with Thai herbs), or red-curry shrimp; and finish up with tea and tapioca pudding. Asian artifacts, flowers, and a waterfall decorate the dark dining room, and tables on a veranda satisfy lovers of the outdoors. ⊠*2119 Vineyard St., Wailuku* ☎*808/244–1567* ▭*AE, MC, V.*

$$
VIETNAMESE
Fodor's Choice
★
✕**A Saigon Café.** The only storefront sign announcing this delightful Vietnamese hideaway is one reading open. Once you find it, treat yourself to *banh hoi chao tom*, more commonly known as "shrimp pops burritos" (ground marinated shrimp, steamed and grilled on a stick of sugarcane). Wok-fried or steamed whole opakapaka is always available, and vegetarian fare is well represented—try the green-papaya salad. The simple white interior serves as a backdrop for Vietnamese carvings, and booths make for some privacy. Owner Jennifer Nguyen really makes the place, so ask to talk story with her if she's in. ⊠*1792 Main St., Wailuku* ☎*808/243–9560* ▭*D, MC, V.*

UPCOUNTRY

$$$
ITALIAN
✕**Casanova Italian Restaurant & Deli.** An authentic Italian dinner house and nightclub, this place is smack in the middle of *paniolo* (cowboy) country, yet it remains an Upcountry institution. The pizzas, baked in a brick wood-burning oven imported from Italy, are the best on the island, especially the *tartufo*, or truffle oil pizza. All entrées come with either creamy risotto, steamy polenta, or garlicky mashed potatoes. The daytime deli serves outstanding sandwiches and espresso. After dining hours, local and visiting entertainers heat up the dance floor. ⊠*1188 Makawao Ave., Makawao* ☎*808/572–0220* ▭*D, DC, MC, V.*

$$$
MODERN
HAWAIIAN
✕**Hāli'imaile General Store.** What do you do with a lofty wooden building surrounded by sugarcane and pineapple fields that was a tiny town's camp store in the 1920s? If you're Beverly and Joe Gannon, you invent a now legendary restaurant known for Hawai'i Regional Cuisine. This landmark celebrated 20 successful years in 2008, and it continues to wow with bamboo steamer fish with dumplings; Kurobuta pork shank; and Asian bouillabaisse with green tea noodles. For lunch, dig into the Kobe beef burger with fontina cheese; or the Brie-and-grape quesadilla with sweet-pea guacamole. The back room houses a rotating art exhibit, courtesy of some of the island's top artists. The restaurant even has its own cookbook, but Beverly will never reveal the recipe for her famous "crab" dip. ⊠*900 Hāli'imaile Rd., take left exit halfway up Haleakalā Hwy., Hāli'imaile* ☎*808/572–2666* ▭*MC, V.*

$$
MEXICAN
✕**Polli's.** The sign at the front reads, "Come in and Eat or We'll Both Starve" and the interior is plastered with colorful sombreros and other cantina knickknacks. Menu items include such Mexican standards as enchiladas, chimichangas, and fajitas; and you can request any item on

the menu with seasoned tofu or vegetarian taco mix—and the meat-less dishes are just as good as the real thing. A special treat are the *buñuelos*—light pastries topped with cinnamon, maple syrup, and ice cream. Call ahead and ask for the nightly promotion. The bar is always packed with the same regulars, just as it has been for decades. ⊠ *1202 Makawao Ave., Makawao* ☎ *808/572–7808* ⊟ *AE, D, DC, MC, V.*

THE NORTH SHORE

$ ✕ **Cafe Des Amis.** Papier-mâché wrestlers pop out from the walls at this
FRENCH small creperie. French crepes with Gruyère, and Indian wraps with lentil curry are among the choices, all served with wild greens and sour cream or chutney on the side. The giant curry bowls are mild but tasty, served with delicious chutney. For dessert there are crepes, of course, filled with chocolate, Nutella, cane sugar, or banana. The people-watching in eccentric Pā'ia makes it worth the wait—so do the smoothies. ⊠ *42 Baldwin Ave., Pā'ia* ☎ *808/579–6323* ⊟ *AE, D, MC, V.*

$ ✕ **Colleen's.** On the main road in jungly Ha'ikū, this is the neighborhood
AMERICAN hangout for windsurfers, yoga teachers, and just plain beautiful people. Many regulars prefer takeout on their way home from commutes in the touristy areas. At breakfast, pastries tend to be jam-packed with berries and nuts, rather than being flaky and full of butter. Sandwiches are especially good, served on giant slices of homemade bread. For dinner you can't go wrong with the 'ahi niçoise salad, pepper-crusted mahimahi, or red-ale-and-mango-glazed ribs with sour cream and herb mashed potatoes. ⊠ *In Ha'ikū Cannery, 810 Kokomo Rd., Ha'ikū* ☎ *808/575–9211* ⊟ *AE, DC, MC, V.*

$$ ✕ **Flatbread Company.** Sit inside this popular pizzeria and watch the chef
PIZZA stir the giant cauldron of organic fresh tomatoes over kiawe wood
☺ and sweeten it with maple syrup. Next to him, another chef caramelizes organic onions. Every item on the menu screams that it's fresh, sustainable, and oh-so-good for you. Wood-fired pizzas are baked in a primitive clay oven, and meats include nitrate-free pepperoni and free-range pork. Partake in the "Mopsy's Pork Pie" with *kālua* (baked underground) pork, barbecue sauce, and pineapple goat cheese; or the "Pele's Pesto" with Roma tomatoes, goat cheese, and olives. Portions are large and service is prompt and friendly, despite the near-constant crowds. It can get hot inside with all of those clay ovens, so dress accordingly or opt to sit in the breezy courtyard. ⊠ *375 Hāna Hwy., Pā'ia* ☎ *808/579–8989. MC, V.*

$ ✕ **Jacques North Shore.** An amiable French chef, Jacques Pauvert, won the
ECLECTIC hearts of the windsurfing crowd when he opened this hip, ramshackle bar and restaurant. It's a youthful hangout with fairly sophisticated fare for the price, and makes a great dating spot for twentysomethings on a budget. French-Caribbean dishes like Jacques' Crispy Little Poulet (chicken) reveal the owner's expertise. The outdoor seating can be a little chilly at times; coveted spots at the sushi bar inside are snatched up quickly. On Friday nights, a DJ moves in and the dining room becomes a packed dance floor. ⊠ *120 Hāna Hwy., Pā'ia* ☎ *808/579–8844* ⊟ *AE, D, MC, V.*

$$$$
SEAFOOD
Fodor'sChoice
★

✕**Mama's Fish House.** For 35 years Mama's has been *the* Maui destination for special occasions. A stone- and shell-engraved path leads you up to what would be, in an ideal world, a good friend's house. The Hawaiian nautical theme is hospitable and fun—the menu even names which boat reeled in your fish. Despite its high prices—even for Maui—the restaurant is always full; dinner reservations start at 4:30 PM. The daily catch baked in a creamy caper sauce or steamed in traditional lū'au leaves is outstanding—and worth the cash. Follow up with the Polynesian Pearl—a gorgeous affair of chocolate mousse and passion-fruit cream. A tiny fishing boat is perched above the entrance to Mama's, about 1½ mi east of Pā'ia on Hāna Highway. ⊠*799 Poho Pl., Kū'au* ☎*808/579–8488* ⚑*Reservations essential* ⊟*AE, D, DC, MC, V.*

$$
LATIN AMERICAN

✕**Milagro's.** Delicious fish tacos are found at this corner restaurant, along with a selection of fine tequilas and Latin-fusion recipes that ignite the taste buds. For instance, try the lava-rock grilled 'ahi burrito with house-made beans and rice; and the seafood enchiladas with 'ahi, ono, and mild green Anaheim chile sauce. The location at the junction of Baldwin Avenue and Hāna Highway makes watching the scene from under the awning shade a lot of fun, but but the constant stream of traffic makes it a bit noisy. Mostly tourists dine here as it's such a convenient location. Lunch and happy hour (3 to 5) are the best values; prices jump at dinnertime. ⊠*3 Baldwin Ave., Pā'ia* ☎*808/579–8755* ⊟*AE, D, DC, MC, V.*

$
SEAFOOD

✕**Pā'ia Fishmarket Restaurant.** The line leading up to the counter of this tiny corner fish market should attest to the popularity of the tasty fish sandwiches—though the great location on the corner of Hāna Highway and Baldwin Avenue, right in the middle of Pā'ia, doesn't hurt. Bench seating is somewhat grimy (you aren't the only one to have enjoyed fries here), but you will find a good fish sandwich. Don't bother with the other items—go for your choice of fillet on a soft bun with a dollop of slaw and some grated cheese. As we say in Hawai'i, *'ono* (delicious)! ⊠*2A Baldwin Ave., Pā'ia* ☎*808/579–8030* ⊟*AE, DC, MC, V.*

WHERE TO STAY

Updated
by Bonnie
Friedman

Maui's accommodations run the gamut from a rural B&B listed on the State and National Historic Registers to one particularly over-the-top, super-opulent mega-resort. But hey, each to his or her own taste, right? In between the extremes, there's something for every vacation style and budget. If the latest and greatest is your style, be prepared to spend a small fortune. Newly renovated properties like the Ritz-Carlton, Kapalua, and the Four Seasons Resort Maui at Wailea and the newest condo complexes may well set you back at least $600 a night, though the weakened economy has brought more deals. Ask for these wherever you stay, and consider the alternatives.

Although there aren't many of them, small bed-and-breakfasts are charming. They tend to be in residential or rural neighborhoods around the island, sometimes beyond the resort areas of West Maui and the South Shore. The B&Bs offer both a personalized experience and a window onto local life. The prices tend to be the lowest available on Maui, often less than $200 per night. Because Maui County is in the midst of a controversy over the licensing of B&Bs and transient vacation rentals, our best advice is to ask whether a property is licensed by the county. You might even ask for the permit number, which should be posted on the property's Web site.

Apartment and condo rentals are perfect for modest budgets, for two or more couples traveling together, and for families. Not only are the nightly rates lower than hotel rooms, but "eating in" (all have kitchens) is substantially less expensive than dining out, especially over a week or two.

There are literally hundreds of these units, ranging in size from studios to luxurious four-bedrooms with multiple baths, all over the island. The vast majority are along the sunny coasts—from Mākena to Kīhei on the South Shore and Lahaina up to Kapalua on West Maui. Prices are dependent on the size of the unit and its proximity to the beach, as well as on the amenities and services offered. For about $250 a night, you can get a perfectly lovely one-bedroom apartment without many frills or flourishes, close to but probably not on the beach. Many rentals have minimum stays (usually three to five nights), and don't forget to ask if a discount is offered on stays of a week or more.

Most of Maui's resorts—several are mega-resorts—have opulent gardens, fantasy swimming pools, championship golf courses, and the latest "must," full-service fitness centers and spas offering everything from hot-rock treatments to beachside massage. Expect to spend at least $350 a night at any one of the resort hotels; they are all located in the Wailea and Mākena resort area on the South Shore and Kāʻanapali and Kapalua on West Maui.

At all hotels, ask about discounts and deals (free nights with longer stays, for example), which have proliferated.

Along with the condos listed in this chapter, which operate like hotels and offer hotel-like amenities, Maui has condos you can rent through central booking agents; *see the box on Vacation Rental Companies in this section.* Most agents represent more than one condo complex (some handle single-family homes as well), so be specific about what kind of price, space, facilities, and amenities you want.

WHAT IT COSTS				
¢	$	$$	$$$	$$$$
HOTELS under $100	$100–$180	$181–$260	$261–$340	over $340

Hotel prices are for two people in a double room in high season. Condo price categories reflect studio and one-bedroom rates. Prices do not include 11.41% tax.

WEST MAUI

3

Along the coast, West Maui is a long string of small communities, beginning with Lahaina at the south end and meandering north into Kāʻanapali, Honokowai, Kahana, Nāpili, and Kapalua. Here's the breakdown on what's where: Lahaina is the business district with all the shops, shows, restaurants, historic buildings, churches, and rowdy side streets. Kāʻanapali is all glitz: fancy resorts set on Kāʻanapali Beach. Honokowai, Kahana, and Nāpili are quiet little nooks characterized by comfortable condos built in the late 1960s. All face the same direction and get the same consistently hot, humid weather. Kapalua, at the northern tip, faces windward, and has a cooler climate and slightly more rain. It has become synonymous with the utmost in luxury in accommodations from hotels to condos to residences.

LAHAINA

$–$$
B&B/INN

Lahaina Inn. An antique jewel in the heart of town, this two-story wooden building is classic Lahaina and will transport romantics back to the turn of the 20th century. The small rooms and shine with authentic period furnishings, including antique lamps and bed headboards. You can while away the hours in a wooden rocking chair on your balcony, sipping coffee and watching Old Lahaina town come to life. Beverages are served in the Community Room, which has a microwave and toaster for guests. The renowned restaurant Lahaina Grill is downstairs. **Pros:** just a half block off Front Street, the location is within easy walking distance of shops, restaurants, and historical attractions; lovely antiques. **Cons:** rooms are really small, bathrooms particularly so; some street noise. ⊠*127 Lahainaluna Rd., Lahaina* ☎*808/661–0577 or 800/669–3444* ⊕*www.lahainainn.com* ⤴*10 rooms, 2 suites* ⏣*In-room: no TV. In-hotel: no elevator, public Internet, no-smoking rooms* ⊟*AE, MC, V.*

$$–$$$
B&B/INN

Plantation Inn. Charm and some added amenities set this inn, tucked into a corner of a busy street in the heart of Lahaina, apart. Filled with Victorian and Asian furnishings, it's reminiscent of a southern plantation home. Secluded lānai draped with hanging plants face a central courtyard, pool, and a garden pavilion perfect for morning coffee. Each guest room or suite is decorated differently, with hardwood floors, French doors, slightly dowdy antiques, and four-poster beds. (We think number 10 is nicest.) Suites have kitchenettes and whirlpool baths. A generous breakfast is included in the room rate, and one of Hawaiʻi's best French restaurants, Gerard's, is on-site. Breakfast, coupled with free parking in downtown Lahaina, makes this a truly great value, even if it's 10 minutes from the beach. **Pros:** guests have full privileges at the sister Kāʻanapali Beach Hotel, 3 mi north; walk to shops, sights, and restaurants. **Cons:** Lahaina Town can be noisy, Wi-Fi connection is hit-or-miss (try the lānai). ⊠*174 Lahainaluna Rd., Lahaina* ☎*808/667–9225 or 800/433–6815* ⊕*www.theplantationinn. com* ⤴*15 rooms, 4 suites* ⏣*In-room: safe, kitchen (some), refrigerator, Wi-Fi. In-hotel: restaurant, pool, no elevator* ⊟*AE, D, DC, MC, V.*

WHERE TO STAY IN WEST MAUI

	Property Name	Worth Noting	Cost $	Pools	Beach	Golf Course	Tennis Courts	Gym	Spa	Children's Programs	Rooms	Restaurants	Other	Location
	Hotels & Resorts													
❸	Hyatt Regency Maui	130-ft water slide	365–580	1	yes	priv.	6	yes	yes	3–12	806	5		Kā'anapali
❻	Kā'anapali Beach Hotel	Hula & lei-making classes	235–485	1	yes	priv.	3				432	3		Kā'anapali
⑮	Mauian Hotel	On Nāpili Bay	120–280	1	yes						44		no TVs	Nāpili
⑰ ★	Ritz-Carlton, Kapalua	Environmental education center	505–875	1	yes	priv.	10	yes	yes	5–12	463	6	shops	Kapalua
❾	Royal Lahaina Resort	New tower wing	235–650	3	yes	priv.	11				333	2		Kā'anapali
❼	Sheraton Maui	Nightly torch-lighting ritual	360–680	1	yes		3	yes	yes	5–12	540	2		Kā'anapali
❺	The Westin Maui Resort	The Heavenly Spa	525–810	5	yes	priv.	2	yes	yes	5–12	758	2		Kā'anapali
	Rentals													
❿	Aston Mahana at Kā'anapali	Spacious rooms	391–715	1	yes		2				215		kitchens	Honokowai
⑪	Aston at Papakea Resort	Cultural classes	315–650	2			4			5–12	364		kitchens	Honokowai
❹	Kā'anapali Ali'i	Kā'anapali Ali'i	405–675	2	yes	yes	6				264			kitchens
⑬	Mahina Surf Oceanfront Resort	Free parking and phone	170–320	1							50		kitchens	Mahinahina
⑫	Makani Sands	Small private beach	180–435	1	yes						21		kitchens	Honokowai
❽	Maui Eldorado	On golf course	259–419	3	yes	yes					204		kitchens	Kā'anapali
⑯	Nāpili Kai Beach Club	Outstanding beach	275–965	4	yes					6–10	163		some kitchens	Nāpili
⑭	Sands of Kahana	Kids' putting green	265–500	2	yes		3				162		kitchens	Kahana
	B&Bs & Inns													
❷	Lahaina Inn	Historic property	165–225								12	1	no TVs	Lahaina
❶	Plantation Inn	Gerard's restaurant	189–310	1							19	1		Lahaina

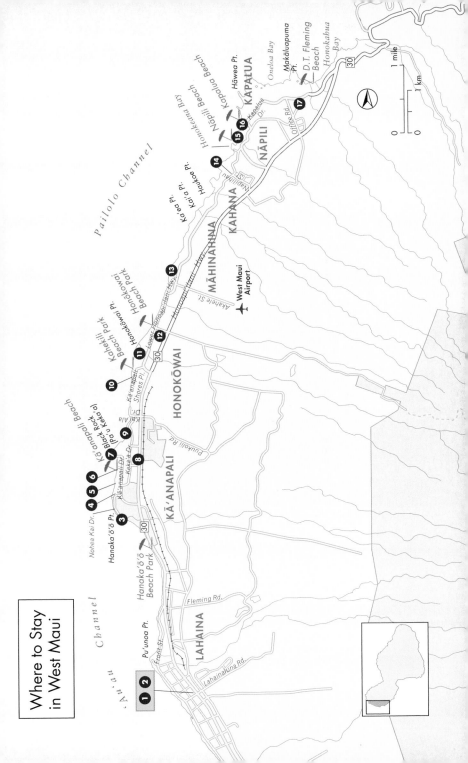

Where to Stay in West Maui

Pailolo Channel

'Au'au Channel

KAPALUA
Honokahua Bay
D.T. Fleming Beach
Makāluapuma Pt.
Oneloa Bay
Honokahua Bay
Kapalua Dr.
Kapalua Beach
Nāpili Beach
Hāwea Pt.
Honokeana Bay

NĀPILI
Olihoa Rd.

KAHANA
Napilihau St.
Haukoe Pt.
Kai'a Pt.

MĀHINAHINA
Ka'eo Pt.
West Maui Airport
Akahele St.

HONOKŌWAI
Lower Honoapi'ilani Hwy.
Honokōwai Beach Park
Honokōwai Pt.
Kahekili Beach Park
Kā'anapali Shores Pl.
Ka'Ala Dr.
Puukolii Rd.

KĀ'ANAPALI
Kā'anapali Beach
Black Rock (Pu'u Keka'a)
Keka'a Dr.
Kā'anapali Dr.
Nohea Kai Dr.
Hanaka'ō'ō Pt.
Hanaka'ō'ō Beach Park

LAHAINA
Pu'unoa Pt.
Front St.
Fleming Rd.
Lahainaluna Rd.

30

1 mile
1 km

KĀ'ANAPALI AND VICINITY

$$$–$$$$
RENTALS

☷ **Aston at Papakea Resort.** Although this oceanfront condominium with studios to two-bedrooms units has no beach, there are several close by. And with classes on swimming, snorkeling, pineapple cutting, and more, you'll have plenty to keep you busy. Papakea has built-in privacy because its units are spread

out among 11 low-rise buildings on some 13 acres of land; bamboo-lined walkways between buildings and fish-stocked ponds add to the serenity. Fully equipped kitchens and laundry facilities make longer stays easy here. There are air-conditioning units in the living rooms of each condo. **Pros:** units have large rooms, lovely garden landscaping. **Cons:** no beach in front of property, pool can get crowded, no on-site shops or restaurants. ✉ *3543 Lower Honoapi'ilani Hwy., Honokōwai* ☎ *808/669–4848 or 800/922–78665* ⊕ *www.resortquesthawaii.com* ⤥ *364 units* ♿ *In-room: kitchen, Wi-Fi, laundry facilities. In-hotel: tennis courts, pools, children's programs (ages 5–12)* ☰ *AE, MC, V.*

$$$–$$$$
RENTALS

☷ **Aston Mahana at Kā'anapali.** Though the address claims Kā'anapali, this 12-story condominium complex is really in quiet, neighboring Honokōwai. All of the studio and one- and two-bedroom units in this building are oceanfront, with views of the ocean and nearby islands, and the spacious rooms and living areas can accommodate families easily. Built in 1974, the property has been regularly updated since, but the decor in individually owned units may vary. An elegant pool faces a sandy beach, which isn't, unfortunately, recommended for swimming because of the shallow reef. **Pros:** the private lānai and floor-to-ceiling windows are great for watching Maui's spectacular sunsets, daily maid service. **Cons:** high-rise with an elevator; not on a swimming beach. ✉ *110 Kā'anapali Shores Pl., Honokōwai* ☎ *808/661–8751* ⊕ *www.themahana.com* ⤥ *215 units* ♿ *In-room: safe, kitchen, Ethernet, Wi-Fi (some), laundry facilities. In-hotel: tennis courts, pool, beachfront, concierge, public Wi-Fi* ☰ *AE, MC, V.*

$$$$
RESORT

☷ **Hyatt Regency Maui Resort & Spa.** Fantasy landscaping with splashing waterfalls, swim-through grottoes, a lagoonlike swimming pool, and a 130-foot waterslide wow guests of all ages at this active Kā'anapali resort. Stroll through the lobby past museum-quality art, brilliant parrots, and South African penguins (as we said, this is not reality). The Hyatt is not necessarily Hawaiian, but it is photogenic. The grounds are the big deal, but rooms are elegantly decorated with plantation-style wood furniture; each has a private sitting area and lānai. At the southern end of Kā'anapali Beach, this resort is in the midst of the action. Also on the premises is Spa Moana, an oceanfront, full-service facility. **Pros:** nightly lū'au show on-site, recent upgrades of linens, refurbished restaurant. **Cons:** it can be difficult to find a space in self-parking, the hotel staff's service can be uneven. ✉ *200 Nohea Kai Dr., Kā'anapali* ☎ *808/661–1234 or 800/233–1234* ⊕ *www.maui.hyatt.com* ⤥ *815 rooms* ♿ *In-room: safe, refrigerator, Ethernet. In-hotel: 5 restaurants,* bars, golf courses, tennis courts, pool, gym, spa, beachfront, children's programs (ages 3–12) ✉AE, D, DC, MC, V.

$$$$
RENTALS
⬚ **Kāʻanapali Aliʻi.** Four 11-story buildings are laid out so well that the feeling of seclusion you enjoy may make you forget you're in a condo complex. Instead of tiny units, you'll be installed in an ample (1,500–1,900 square feet) one- or two-bedroom apartment. All units have great amenities: a chaise in an alcove, a sunken living room, a whirlpool, and a separate dining room, though some of the furnishings are dated. It's the best of both worlds: home-like condo living with hotel amenities—daily maid service, an activities desk, small store with video rentals, and 24-hour front-desk service. **Pros:** large, comfortable units on the beach, good location in heart of the action in Kāʻanapali Resort. **Cons:** elevators are notoriously slow, crowded parking, no on-site restaurant. ✉50 Nohea Kai Dr., Kāʻanapali ☎808/667–1400 or 800/642–6284 ⊕www.kaanapalialii.com ⛵264 units ♨In-room: safe, kitchen, DVD. In-hotel: golf course, tennis courts, pools, beachfront, laundry facilities ✉AE, D, DC, MC, V.

$$$–$$$$
HOTEL
⬚ **Kāʻanapali Beach Hotel.** Older but still attractive, this small hotel is full of aloha. Locals say that it's one of the few resorts on the island where visitors can get a true Hawaiian experience. The entire staff takes part in the hotel's ongoing Poʻokela program to learn about the history, traditions, and values of Hawaiian culture, and shares its knowledge and stories with guests. Also, you can take complimentary classes in authentic hula dancing, lei-making, lauhala weaving, and ʻukulele playing. The spacious rooms are decorated with Hawaiian motifs, wicker, and rattan; each has a lānai and faces the beach beyond the courtyard. The departure ceremony makes you want to come back. **Pros:** exceptional Hawaiian culture program, friendly staff. **Cons:** a bit run-down, no fine-dining option on site, fewer amenities than other places along this beach. ✉2525 Kāʻanapali Pkwy., Kāʻanapali ☎808/661–0011 or 800/262–8450 ⊕www.kbhmaui.com ⛵432 rooms ♨In-room: safe, refrigerator, Ethernet. In-hotel: 3 restaurants, bar, pool, beachfront ✉AE, D, DC, MC, V.

$–$$
RENTALS
⬚ **Makani Sands.** Centrally located in Honokawi on the lower road between two roads that access West Maui's main highway, this slightly older complex offers an economical way to see West Maui. Rooms have wide lānai, which hang over a small sandy beach below. The corner rooms (ending in 01) are best, with wraparound views. A small freshwater pool is available for cooling off. The back bedrooms may be noisy at night, as they're close to the road. **Pros:** beachfront, reasonable rates. **Cons:** older buildings, few amenities, road noise. ✉3765 Lower Honoapiʻilani Hwy., Honokōwai ☎808/669–8223 or 800/227–8223 ⊕www.makanisands.com ⛵21 units ♨In-room: kitchen, DVD, dial-up, Wi-Fi (some). In-hotel: pool, beachfront, laundry facilities ✉AE, MC, V.

$$$–$$$$
RENTALS
⬚ **Maui Eldorado.** The Kāʻanapali golf course's fairways wrap around this fine condo complex that offers several perks, most notably air-conditioning in the units and access to a fully outfitted beach cabana on a semiprivate beach. The complex itself isn't exactly on the beach—it's a quick golf-cart trip away. While guests at other resorts get scolded for

dragging lounge chairs onto neighboring resort beaches, here you can relax in luxury. Not only will you have beach chairs at your disposal, but a full kitchen and lounge area at the cabana, too. The privately owned units are tastefully decorated with modern appliances and have spacious bathrooms. These condos are a good value for pricey Kā'anapali. **Pros:** privileges at five resort golf courses, daily maid service. **Cons:** not right on beach, some distance from attractions of the Kā'anapali Resort, some units are privately owned so condition of units may vary. ✉2661 Keka'a Dr., Kā'anapali ☎808/661–0021 ⊕www.mauieldorado.com ⇱204 units ⚴ In-room: kitchen, Internet. In-hotel: golf course, pools, laundry facilities, concierge ☐AE, D, DC, MC, V.

$$$–$$$$
RESORT

Royal Lahaina Resort. Major upgrades have taken place here since 2006, including renovation of the rooms in the 12-story Lahaina Kai Tower. The 333-room tower has Hawaiian canoe–theme rooms with dark teak furnishings set against light-colored walls, plush beds with 300-count Egyptian cotton linens, sound systems with an iPod and docking station, and 32-inch, high-definition flat-screen TVs. The resort's quaint low-rise cottages were scheduled to be replaced with individually owned luxury villas but those plans are on hold. So, you can still stay in one of the 27 plantation-style cottages that have been updated with new bedding, furnishings, and amenities. Another option at the Royal Lahaina Resort is the Kā'anapali Ocean Inn where you can stay for less money and a little less comfort (it's a three-story building with no elevator), but enjoy the services and amenities of the resort. To experience the spirit of the hotel's early days, head to the poolside Don the Beachcomber bar, billed as "the Home of the Original Mai Tai," where the retro-Tiki style of Hawai'i's early days as a vacation paradise lives on. **Pros:** on-site lū'au nightly, variety of accommodation types, tennis ranch with 11 courts and pro shop. **Cons:** older property still in need of updating. ✉2780 Keka'a Dr., Kā'anapali ☎808/661–3611 or 800/447–6925 ⊕www.hawaiianhotels.com ⇱333 rooms ⚴ In-room: safe, refrigerator, Internet, Wi-Fi. In-hotel: 2 restaurants, tennis courts, pools, beachfront ☐AE, D, DC, MC, V.

$$$$
RESORT

Sheraton Maui Resort & Spa. Set among dense gardens on Kā'anapali's best stretch of beach, the Sheraton offers a quieter, more low-key atmosphere than its neighboring resorts. The open-air lobby has a crisp, cool look with understated furnishings and decor, and sweeping views of the pool area and beach. The majority of the spacious rooms come with ocean views; only one of the six buildings has rooms with mountain or garden views. All rooms have plenty of amenities, including a 32-inch flat-screen TV with video games and on-command movies; all

3

suites also have Bose stereo systems. The huge swimming pool looks like a natural lagoon, with rock waterways and wooden bridges; and the Spa at Black Rock has been renovated and expanded. Best of all, the hotel sits next to and on top of the 80-foot-high Puʻu Kekaʻa (Black Rock), from which divers leap in a nightly torch-lighting and cliff-diving ritual. **Pros:** luxury resort with terrific beach location, great snorkeling right off the beach. **Cons:** extensive property can mean a long walk from your room to the lobby, restaurants, and beach; staff not overly helpful. ⊠ *2605 Kāʻanapali Pkwy., Kāʻanapali* ☎ *808/661–0031 or 888/488–35358* ⊕ *www.sheraton-maui.com* ⇨ *508 rooms, 32 suites* △ *In-room: safe, refrigerator, Ethernet. In-hotel: 2 restaurants, bar, tennis courts, pool, gym, spa, beachfront, children's programs (ages 5–12), laundry facilities, public Wi-Fi* ⊟ *AE, D, DC, MC, V.*

$$$$ 🖼 **The Westin Maui Resort & Spa.** The cascading waterfall in the lobby
RESORT   of this hotel gives way to an "aquatic playground" with five heated swimming pools, abundant waterfalls (15 at last count), lagoons complete with pink flamingos, and a premier beach. The water features combined with a spa and fitness center and privileges at two 18-hole golf courses make this an active resort—great for families. Relaxation is by no means forgotten, though. The 15,000-square-foot Heavenly Spa has 16 treatment rooms and a yoga studio. Elegant dark-wood furnishings in the rooms accentuate the crisp linens of the chain's "Heavenly Beds." Rooms in the Beach Tower are newer and slightly larger than those in the Ocean Tower. Farther up the beach, the newly built Westin Kāʻanapali Ocean Resort Villas offers studio and one-bedroom units with full kitchens. The Villas have their own restaurants, tennis courts, and three pools, including one for kids with a pirate ship. **Pros:**complimentary shuttle between both Westin properties and to Lahaina, where parking can be difficult; activity programs for all ages; one pool just for adults. **Cons:** you could end up with fantasy overload, luxury chain hotel can seem a bit stuffy at times. ⊠ *2365 Kāʻanapali Pkwy., Kāʻanapali* ☎ *808/667–2525 or 888/488–3535* ⊕ *www.star wood.com/hawaii* ⇨ *758 rooms, 500 studios, 521 1-bedroom units* △ *In-room: Ethernet. In-hotel: 6 restaurants, bar, pools, gym, spa, beachfront, children's programs (all ages), public Wi-Fi* ⊟ *AE, D, DC, MC, V.*

KAPALUA AND VICINITY

$–$$ 🖼 **Mahina Surf Oceanfront Resort.** Mahina Surf stands out from the many
RENTALS   condo complexes lining the oceanside stretch of Honoapiʻilani Highway by being both well-managed and affordable. You won't be charged fees for parking, check-out, or local phone use, and discount car rentals are available. The individually owned units are typically overdecorated (lots of rattan furniture, silk flowers, and decorative items), but each one has a well-equipped kitchen and an ocean view. The quiet complex is a short amble away from Honokowai's grocery shopping, beaches, and restaurants. **Pros:** oceanfront barbecues, no "hidden" fees. **Cons:** set among relatively nondescript condominium complexes, oceanfront but with rocky shoreline rather than a beach. ⊠ *4057 Lower Honoapiʻilani Hwy., Mahinahina* ☎ *808/669–6068 or 800/367–60864* ⊕ *www.mahina*

surf.com ➥ 50 units 🛏 In-room: safe, kitchen, Ethernet. In-hotel: pool, laundry facilities, concierge ☐ MC, V.

$–$$
HOTEL

🛏 **Mauian Hotel.** If you're looking for a quiet place to stay, this nostalgic hotel way out in Nāpili may be for you. The rooms have neither TVs nor phones—such noisy devices are relegated to the 'Ohana Room, where a Continental breakfast is served daily. The simple two-story buildings date from 1959 but have been renovated with bright islander furnishings. Rooms include well-equipped kitchens. Best of all, the 2-acre property opens out onto lovely Nāpili Bay. **Pros:** reasonable rates, friendly staff. **Cons:** older building, few amenities ✉ 5441 Lower Honoapi'ilani Hwy., Nāpili ☎ 808/669–6205 or 800/367–5034 9 ⊕ www.mauian.com ➥ 44 rooms 🛏 In-room: no a/c, no phone, kitchen, no TV. In-hotel: pool, beachfront, laundry facilities, public Wi-Fi ☐ AE, D, MC, V.

$$$–$$$$
☺
RENTALS

🛏 **Nāpili Kai Beach Resort.** On 10 beautiful beachfront acres—the beach here is one of the best on West Maui for swimming and snorkeling—the Nāpili Kai draws a loyal following. Hawaiian-style rooms have plantation-themed furnishings with shoji doors opening onto a private lānai. The rooms closest to the beach have no air-conditioning, but ceiling fans usually suffice. "Hotel" rooms have only mini-refrigerators and coffeemakers, whereas studios and suites have fully equipped kitchenettes. This is a family-friendly place, with children's programs and free classes in hula and lei-making. A 5th Night Free package is offered seasonally. **Pros:** free kids' hula performance every week, fantastic swimming and sunning beach, old Hawaiian feel. **Cons:** older property, some might call it "un-hip." ✉ 5900 Lower Honoapi'ilani Hwy., Nāpili ☎ 808/669–6271 or 800/367–5030 ⊕ www.napilikai. com ➥ 163 units 🛏 In-room: no a/c (some), kitchen (some), Ethernet. In-hotel: pools, beachfront, children's programs (ages 6–10), laundry service, concierge ☐ AE, D, MC, V.

$$$$
RESORT
Fodor's Choice
★

🛏 **Ritz-Carlton, Kapalua.** After a multimillion-dollar going-over, this elegant hillside property reopened in early 2008 with upgraded accommodations, spa, restaurants, and pool, along with a new education center and an enhanced Hawaiian sense of place, making it one of Maui's most notable resorts. Refurbished guest rooms and 107 newly-created one- and two-bedroom condominium residential suites (some of which are available for rent) are decorated in themes incorporating the rich colors of the ocean, mountains, and rain forests that surround the resort. The expanded spa facility includes a fitness center, yoga studio, 15 treatment rooms, private outdoor shower gardens, and Hawaiian design elements. Set amid the lush grounds of the resort, the renovated multilevel pool and hot tubs are open 24 hours. There is a new Environmental Education Center, as well as a full-time cultural advisor who instructs employees and guests in Hawaiian traditions. Although not set directly on the sand, the Ritz does front D.T. Fleming beach, recognized as one of America's best. **Pros:** luxury and service you'd expect from a Ritz, newly renovated, many cultural and recreational programs. **Cons:** can be windy on the grounds and at the pool, the hotel is not on the beach and is far from major attractions such as Lahaina and Haleakalā. ✉ 1 Ritz-Carlton Dr., Kapalua ☎ 808/669–6200 or 800/262–8440 ⊕ www.ritzcarlton.com/resorts/kapalua ➥ 463 rooms 🛏 In-room: safe, Wi-Fi. In-hotel: 6 restaurants, bar, tennis courts, pool,

Ritz-Carlton, Kapalua

gym, spa, beachfront, children's programs (ages 5–12), laundry service ⊟*AE, D, DC, MC, V.*

$$–$$$

RENTALS

⊡ **Sands of Kahana.** Meandering gardens, spacious rooms, and an on-site restaurant distinguish this large condominium complex. Primarily a time-share property, a few units are available as vacation rentals; those are managed by Sullivan Properties. The upper floors benefit from their height—matchless ocean views stretch away from private lānai. The oceanfront penthouse, which accommodates up to eight, is a bargain at $495 during peak season. One-, two- and three-bedroom units are also available in the rental pool. Kids can enjoy their own swimming pool area near a putting green and ponds filled with giant koi. **Pros:** spacious units at reasonable prices, restaurant on the premises. **Cons:** you may be approached about buying a unit, street-facing units may get a bit noisy. ⊠*4299 Lower Honoapi'ilani Hwy., Kahana* ☎*808/669–0400* 🖷*808/669–8409* ⊕*www.sands-of-kahana.com* ⟳*162 units* ⌂*In-room: no a/c (some), kitchen, Ethernet. In-hotel: restaurant, tennis courts, pools, beachfront, concierge* ⊟*AE, D, MC, V.*

THE SOUTH SHORE

The South Shore is composed of two main communities: resort-filled Wailea and down-to-earth Kīhei. In general, the farther south you go, the fancier the accommodations get. ■TIP→**North Kīhei tends to have great prices, but it has windy beaches scattered with seaweed. (This isn't a problem if you don't mind driving five to 10 minutes to save a few bucks.)** As you travel down South Kīhei Road, you can find condos both fronting and across the street from inviting beach parks, and close to shops and restaurants. Once you hit Wailea, the opulence quotient takes a giant leap—this is the land of perfectly groomed resorts. Wailea and West Maui's Kāʻanapali continuously compete over which is more exclusive and which has better weather—in our opinion it's a draw.

KĪHEI

$$–$$$

RENTALS

⊡ **Hale Hui Kai.** Bargain hunters who stumble across this small three-story condo complex of two-bedroom units will think they've died and gone to heaven. The beachfront units are older, but many of them have been renovated. Some have marble countertops in the kitchens and all have outstanding views. But never mind the interior; you'll want to spend all of your time outdoors—in the shady lava-rock lobby that overlooks a small pool perfect for kids, or on gorgeous Keawakapu Beach just steps away. Light sleepers should avoid the rooms just above the neighboring restaurant, Sarento's, but do stop in there for dinner. **Pros:** far enough from the noise and tumult of "central" Kīhei, close enough to all the conveniences. **Cons:** "older" can sometimes mean a bit shabby, nondescript '70s architecture. ⊠*2994 S. Kīhei Rd., Kīhei* ☎*808/879–1219 or 800/809–6284* ⊕*www.halehuikaimaui.com* ⟳*40 units* ⌂*In-room: no a/c (some), safe, kitchen, DVD. In-hotel: pool, beachfront, laundry facilities* ⊟*D, DC, MC, V.*

$$–$$$

RENTALS

Ⓒ

⊡ **Kamaʻole Sands.** At this south Kīhei property, a good choice for the active traveler, there are tennis and volleyball courts to keep you in shape, and the ideal family beach (Kamaʻole III) is just across the street.

CONDO COMFORTS

When you stay in a condo, you'll want to find the best places for food shopping, takeout, and other comforts. Here's a rundown of the best sports around Maui.

WEST MAUI

Foodland. This large grocery store should have everything you need, including video rentals and a Starbucks. ⊠ *Old Lahaina Center, 845 Waine'e St., Lahaina* ☎ *808/661-0975.*

Gaby's Pizzeria and Deli. The friendly folks here will toss a pie for takeout. ⊠ *505 Front St., Lahaina* ☎ *808/661-8112.*

The Maui Fish Market. It's worth stopping by this little fish market for an oyster or a cup of fresh-fish chowder. You can also get live lobsters and fillets marinated for your barbecue. ⊠ *4405 Lower Honoapi'ilani Hwy., Honokowai* ☎ *808/665-9895.*

SOUTH SHORE

Eskimo Candy. Stop here for fresh fish or fish-and-chips. ⊠ *2665 Wai Wai Pl., Kīhei* ☎ *808/879-5686.*

Safeway. Find every variety of grocery at this giant superstore. ⊠ *277 Pi'ikea Ave., Kīhei* ☎ *808/891-9120.*

Who Cut the Cheese. This shop has great party foods. ⊠ *Azeka Marketplace, 1279 S. Kīhei Rd., Suite 309, Kīhei* ☎ *808/874-3930.*

CENTRAL MAUI

Safeway. Newly renovated to look more like a gourmet grocery than a supermarket, this store has a deli, prepared foods section, and bakery that are all fantastic. There's a great wine selection, tons of produce, and a flower shop where you can treat yourself to a fresh lei. ⊠ *170 E. Ka'ahumanu Ave., Kahului* ☎ *808/877-3377.*

UPCOUNTRY

Pukalani Terrace Center. Stop by for pizza, a bank, post office, hardware store, and Starbucks. There's also a **Foodland** (☎ *808/572-0674*), which has fresh sushi and a good seafood section in addition to the usual grocery store fare. ⊠ *55 Pukalani St., Pukalani.*

NORTH SHORE

Ha'ikū Cannery. This marketplace is home to **Ha'ikū Grocery** (☎ *808/575-9291*), a somewhat limited grocery store where you can find the basics: veggies, meats, wine, snacks, and ice cream. Also part of the cannery are a few restaurants, along with a laundromat, pharmacy, and yoga studio. The post office is across the street. ⊠ *810 Ha'ikū Rd., Ha'ikū.*

Ten four-story buildings wrap around 15 acres of grassy slopes with swimming pools, a small waterfall, and barbecues. Condos with one to three bedrooms are equipped with modern conveniences, but there's a relaxed, almost retro feel to the place. All units have two bathrooms, kitchens, laundry facilities, and private lānai. The property has a 24-hour front desk and an activities desk. **Pros:** in the seemingly endless strip of Kīhei condos, this stands out for its pleasant grounds and well-cared-for units. **Cons:** for some, the complex of buildings is bit too "city"; all buildings look alike, so remember a landmark so you can find your unit. ⊠ *2695 S. Kīhei Rd., Kīhei* ☎ *808/270–1200* ⊕ *www.castleresorts.com* ⤴ *309 units* ☌ *In-room: kitchen, DVD, Ethernet (some), Wi-Fi (some). In-hotel: tennis courts, pool* ═ *AE, D, DC, MC, V.*

WHERE TO STAY ON THE SOUTH SHORE

	Property Name	Worth Noting	Cost $	Pools	Beach	Golf Course	Tennis Courts	Gym	Spa	Children's Programs	Rooms	Restaurants	Other	Location
	Hotels & Resorts													
3	Fairmont Kea Lani	Villas available	485–4,000	3	yes	priv.		yes	yes	5–13	450	4	shops	Wailea
★ 4	Four Seasons Resort	Luxurious	495–12,800	3	yes	priv.	2	yes	yes	5–12	380	3	poolside cabanas	Wailea
5	Grand Wailea Resort	Spa Grande	700–15,000	3	yes	priv.		yes	yes	5–12	780	5	shops	Wailea
11	Mana Kai Maui	Fabulous beach	190–438	1	yes						158	1		Kihei
13	Maui Coast Hotel	Beach across the street	265–345	1			2				265	1		Kihei
6	Wailea Beach Marriott Resort & Spa	Package deals avail.	350–600	3	yes	priv.		yes	yes		546	2	large rooms	Wailea
	Rentals													
10	Hale Hui Kai	Oceanfront lounge	225–385	1	yes						40		kitchens	Kihei
12	Kama'ole Sands	Beach across the street	305–555	1			4				204		kitchens	Kihei
1	Mākena Surf	Secluded gated community	625–1,800	2	yes	priv.	4				107		kitchens	Wailea
14	Maui Sunseeker Resort	Beach across the street	109–295	1							17		kitchens	Kihei
2	Polo Beach Club	Location, location, location	445–800	1	yes	priv.					71		kitchens	Wailea
8	Wailea 'Ekahi	Studios available	275–1,400	4	yes	priv.					300		kitchens	Wailea
7	Wailea 'Elua	Gated community	275–1,400	2	yes	priv.					150		kitchens	Wailea
9	Wailea 'Ekolu	Hillside view	275–1,400	2	no	priv.					160		kitchens	Wailea

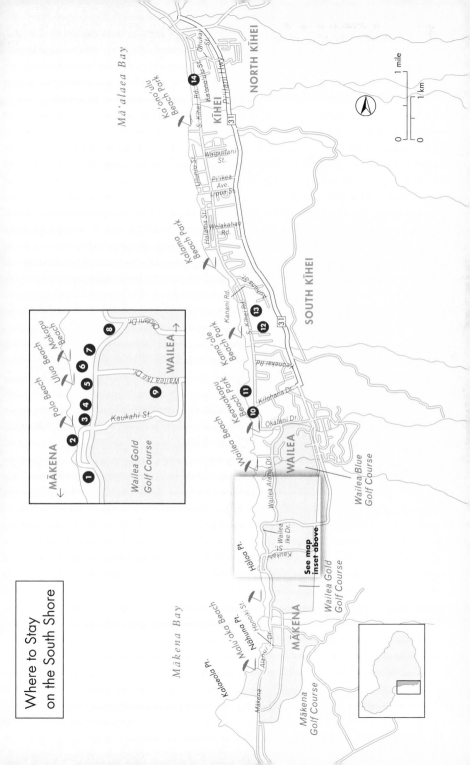

Where to Stay
on the South Shore

$$–$$$
HOTEL
☾ **Mana Kai Maui.** An unsung hero of South Shore hotels, this place may be older than its competitors, but you cannot get any closer to gorgeous Keawakapu Beach than this. Hotel rooms with air-conditioning are remarkably affordable for the location. One- and two-bedroom condos—very well-priced—with private lānai benefit from the hotel amenities, such as daily maid service and discounts at the oceanfront restaurant downstairs. Also, prices are discounted for stays of seven nights and longer. The ocean views are marvelous; you may see the visiting humpback whales. **Pros:** arguably the best beach on the South Shore, great value, Maui Yoga Path is on property and offers classes (additional cost). **Cons:** older property, the decor of some of the individually decorated condos is a little rough around the edges. ⊠ *2960 S. Kīhei Rd., Kīhei* ☎ *808/879–2778 or 800/367–5242* ⊕ *www.crhmaui. com* ⬈ *50 hotel rooms, 57 1-bedroom condos, 57 2-bedroom condos* ⬧ *In-room: safe, refrigerator, dial-up (some), Wi-Fi (some). In-hotel: restaurant, pool, beachfront, laundry facilities* ▭ *MC, V.*

$$$–$$$$
HOTEL
Maui Coast Hotel. You might never notice this lovely hotel because it's set back off the street, but it's worth a look. The standard rooms are fine—very clean and modern—but the best deal is to pay a little more for one of the suites. In these you'll get an enjoyable amount of space and jet nozzles in the bathtub. All rooms and suites have lānai. You can sample nightly entertainment by the large, heated pool or work out in the fitness center until 10 PM. The 6-mi-long stretch of Kama'ole Beach I, II, and III is across the street. **Pros:** closest thing to a boutique hotel on the South Shore; Spices Restaurant on property is open for breakfast, lunch, and dinner. **Cons:** right in the center of Kīhei, so traffic and some street noise are issues. ⊠ *2259 S. Kīhei Rd., Kīhei* ☎ *808/874–6284 or 800/895–6284* 🖷 *808/875–4731* ⊕ *www.mauicoasthotel.com* ⬈ *151 rooms, 114 suites* ⬧ *In-room: safe, refrigerator. In-hotel: 2 restaurants, tennis courts, pool, laundry service* ▭ *AE, D, DC, MC, V.*

$–$$
RENTALS
Maui Sunseeker Resort. The care put into this small North Kīhei property, which is particularly popular with a gay and lesbian clientele, is already noticeable from the sign on the road. A great value for the area, it's private and relaxed. You can opt for the simple but attractively furnished studio and one-bedroom units, or the incredible, more expensive penthouse decked out in French Provincial antiques (really); all have kitchenettes and full baths. There's a lovely gazebo with two gas grills in the courtyard. The 4-mi stretch of beach across the street isn't the best for swimming, but it's great for strolling and watching windsurfers, whales (in winter), and sunsets. **Pros:** impeccably maintained; there's a hair salon and a wedding officiate on property. **Cons:** no pool; no frills. ⊠ *551 S. Kīhei Rd., Kīhei* ☎ *808/879–1261 or 800/532–6284* ⊕ *www. mauisunseeker.com* ⬈ *17 units* ⬧ *In-room: kitchen, DVD. In-hotel: no elevator, laundry facilities, public Wi-Fi* ▭ *AE, D, MC, V.*

WAILEA

$$$$
RESORT
☾ **Fairmont Kea Lani Hotel Suites & Villas.** Gleaming white spires and tiled archways are the hallmark of a stunning resort that's particularly good for families. Spacious suites have microwaves, stereos, and marble bathrooms. The villas are the real lure, though. Each is two-story and has a private plunge pool, two (or three) large bedrooms, a laundry room, and

a fully equipped kitchen—barbecue and margarita blender included. Best of all, maid service does the dishes. A fantastic haven for families, the villas are side by side, creating a sort of miniature neighborhood. Request one on the end, with an upstairs sundeck. The resort also boasts a new restaurant, Kō, and offers a small, almost private beach. **Pros:** for families, this is the best of the South Shore luxury resorts; on-site Caffe Ciao serves up good, casual Italian fare; adjacent deli good for picnic fare. **Cons:** some feel the architecture and design scream anything but Hawai'i, great villas but prices put them out of range for many. ✉ *4100 Wailea Alanui Dr., Wailea* ☎ *808/875–4100 or 800/659–4100* ⊕ *www. kealani.com* ⌁ *413 suites, 37 villas* ⌂ *In-room: kitchen (some), refrigerator, DVD, Ethernet. In-hotel: 3 restaurants, bar, pools, gym, spa, beachfront, children's programs (ages 5–13)* ▤ *AE, D, DC, MC, V.*

$$$$
RESORT
Fodor's Choice
★

Four Seasons Resort Maui at Wailea. Impeccably stylish, subdued, and relaxing describe most Four Seasons properties; this one fronting award-winning Wailea beach is no exception. Thoughtful luxuries—like Evian spritzers poolside and room-service attendants who toast your bread in-room—earned this Maui favorite its reputation. The property has an understated elegance, with beautiful floral arrangements, courtyards, and private cabanas. Most rooms have an ocean view (avoid those over the parking lot in the North Tower), and terry robes and whole-bean coffee grinders are among the amenities. Choose among three restaurants, including Wolfgang Puck's Spago and Duo. The spa is small but expertly staffed and impeccably appointed, or you can opt for poolside spa mini-treatments. Honeymooners: request Suite 301, with its round tub and private lawn. **Pros:** the most low-key elegance on Maui, known for exceptional service. **Cons:** extremely expensive; for some, a bit too pretentious. ✉ *3900 Wailea Alanui Dr., Wailea* ☎ *808/874–8000 or 800/ 332–3442* ⊕ *www.fourseasons.com/maui* ⌁ *305 rooms, 75 suites* ⌂ *In-room: safe, refrigerator, Ethernet. In-hotel: 3 restaurants, bars, tennis courts, pool, gym, spa, beachfront, bicycles, children's programs (ages 5–12)* ▤ *AE, D, DC, MC, V.*

$$$$
RESORT

Grand Wailea Resort Hotel & Spa. Following a renovation of all rooms in 2007, "Grand" is no exaggeration for this opulent, sunny 40-acre resort with elaborate water features such as a "canyon riverpool" with slides, caves, a Tarzan swing, and a water elevator. Tropical garden paths meander past artwork by Léger, Warhol, Picasso, Botero, and noted Hawaiian artists—sculptures even hide in waterfalls. Spacious ocean-view rooms are outfitted with stuffed chaises, comfortable desks, and oversize marble bathrooms. Spa Grande, also upgraded in 2007, is the island's most comprehensive spa facility, offering everything from mineral baths to massage. For kids, Camp Grande has a full-size soda fountain, game room, and movie theater. Definitely not the place to go for a quiet retreat or for attentive service, the resort is astounding or way over the top, depending on your point of view. **Pros:** you can meet every vacation need without ever leaving the property, many shops. **Cons:** at these prices, service should be extraordinary, and it isn't; sometimes too much is too much. ✉ *3850 Wailea Alanui Dr., Wailea* ☎ *808/875–1234 or 800/888–6100* ⊕ *www.grandwailea.com* ⌁ *728 rooms, 52 suites* ⌂ *In-room: safe, Ethernet. In-hotel: 5 restaurants,*

Four Seasons Resort Maui at Wailea

bars, pools, gym, spa, beachfront, children's programs (ages 5–12) ▭*AE, D, MC, V.*

$$$$
RENTALS

🏨 **Mākena Surf.** For travelers who've done all there is to do on Maui and just want simple but luxurious relaxation, this is the spot. The security-gate entrance gives way to manicured landscaping dotted with palm trees. The secluded complex is designed so that it's hard to tell from the road that they're actually three-story buildings. "B" building is ocean-front; "A," "C," and "G" are the best value, just a bit farther from the shore. Water aerobics and tennis clinics are regularly offered. Privacy envelops the grounds—which makes the place a favorite with visiting celebrities. **Pros:** get away from it all, still close enough to "civiliza-tion." **Cons:** too secluded and "locked-up" for some, Hawaiian legend has it that spirits may have been disturbed here. ✉*3750 Wailea Alanui Dr., Wailea* ☎*808/879–1595 or 800/367–5246* ⊕*www.drhmaui.com* ⤴*107 units* ⚐*In-room: safe, kitchen, DVD, Wi-Fi, laundry facilities. In-hotel: tennis courts, pools, beachfront* ▭*AE, MC, V.*

$$$$
RENTALS

🏨 **Polo Beach Club.** Lording over a hidden section of Polo Beach, this wonderful old eight-story property somehow manages to stay under the radar. From your giant corner window, you can look down at the Fairmont Kea Lani villas and know you've scored the same great locale at a fraction of the price (and also including daily housekeeping service). Individually owned one- and two-bedroom apartments are well cared for and feature top-of-the-line amenities, such as stainless-steel kitchens, marble floors, and valuable artwork. An underground parking garage keeps vehicles out of the blazing Kīhei sun. **Pros:** you can pick fresh herbs for dinner out of the garden, beach fronting the building is a beautiful, very private crescent of sand. **Cons:** some may feel isolated. ✉*3750 Wailea Alanui Dr., Wailea* ☎*808/879–1595 or 800/367–5246* 🖷*808/874–3554* ⊕*www.drhmaui.com* ⤴*71 units* ⚐*In-room: kitchen, DVD, Wi-Fi. In-hotel: pool, beachfront, laundry facilities* ▭*AE, MC, V.*

$$$$
RESORT

🏨 **Wailea Beach Marriott Resort & Spa.** The Marriott was built before cur-rent construction laws, so rooms sit much closer to the crashing surf than at most resorts. If you like to be lulled to sleep by the sound of the ocean, this is the place. Wailea Beach is a few steps away, as are the Shops at Wailea. In 2007, the hotel completed a $60 million renovation with redesigned guest rooms, the new 10,000-square-foot Mandara Spa, a gorgeous, adults-only "Serenity" pool, and Maui celebrity chef Mark Ellman's Mala Ocean Tavern. All rooms have private lānai and have been restyled with a contemporary residential feel; the new mat-tresses, quilts, and bed linens make for a great night's sleeep. You have golf privileges at three nearby courses, as well as tennis privileges at the Wailea Tennis Club. **Pros:** spa is one of the best in Hawai'i, Mala restaurant is outstanding, near good shopping. **Cons:** it's not techni-cally "beachfront" but has a rocky shore, so you must walk left or right to sit on the sand; building exteriors are showing their age. ✉*3700 Wailea Alanui Dr., Wailea* ☎*808/879–1922 or 800/922–7866* ⊕*www. waileamarriott.com* ⤴*499 rooms; 47 suites* ⚐*In-room: safe, Ethernet. In-hotel: 2 restaurants, pools, gym, spa, beachfront, children's programs (ages 5–12), laundry service* ▭*AE, D, DC, MC, V.*

$$$–$$$$
RENTALS
⊡ **Wailea 'Ekahi, 'Elua, and 'Ekolu.** The Wailea Resort started out with three upscale condominium complexes named, appropriately, 'Ekahi, 'Elua, and 'Ekolu (One, Two, and Three). The individually owned units, managed by Destination Resorts Hawai'i, represent some of the best values in this high-class neighborhood; there's a wide range of prices. All benefit from daily housekeeping, air-conditioning, high-speed Internet, free long distance, lush landscaping, and preferential play at the neighboring world-class golf courses and tennis courts. You're likely to find custom appliances and sleek furnishings befitting the million-dollar locale. ■TIP→The concierges here will stock your fridge with groceries—even hard-to-find dietary items—for a nominal fee. 'Ekolu, farthest from the water, is the most affordable, and benefits from a hillside view; 'Ekahi is a large V-shaped property focusing on Keawakapu Beach; 'Elua has 24-hour security and overlooks Ulua Beach. **Pros:** probably the best value in this high-rent district; close to good shopping and dining. **Cons:** the oldest complexes in the neighborhood, it can be tricky to find your way around the buildings. ⊠*3750 Wailea Alanui Dr., Wailea* ☎*808/879–1595 or 800/367–5246* ⊕*www.drhmaui.com* ⟡*594 units* ⚴*In-room: kitchen, DVD, Wi-Fi, laundry facilities. In-hotel: pools, beachfront* ☐*AE, MC, V.*

CENTRAL MAUI

Kahului and Wailuku, the commercial, residential, and government centers that make up Central Maui, are not known for their lavish accommodations, but there are options that meet some travelers' needs perfectly.

$
B&B/INN
Fodor'sChoice
★
⊡ **The Old Wailuku Inn at Ulupono.** Built in 1924 and listed on the State and National Register of Historic Places, this home may be the ultimate Hawaiian B&B. Each room is decorated with the theme of a Hawaiian flower, and the flower motif appears in the heirloom Hawaiian quilt on each bed. Other features include 10-foot ceilings and floors of native hardwoods; some rooms have delightful whirlpool tubs. The first-floor rooms have private gardens. A newer addition has three gorgeous rooms, each with a standing spa shower and bed coverings designed by Hawai'i's premier fabric designer, Sig Zane. A hearty and delicious breakfast is included. **Pros:** the charm of old Hawai'i, knowledgeable innkeepers, walking distance to Maui's best ethnic restaurants. **Cons:** closest beach is a 20-minute drive away, you may hear some traffic at certain times. ⊠*2199 Kaho'okele St., Wailuku* ☎*808/244–5897 or 800/305–4899* ⊕*www.mauiinn.com* ⟡*10 rooms* ⚴*In-room: VCR, Ethernet. In-hotel: no elevator* ☐*AE, D, DC, MC, V.*

UPCOUNTRY

Upcountry accommodations (those in Kula, Makawao, and Hāli'imaile) are generally on country properties—with the exception of Kula Lodge—and are privately owned vacation rentals. At high elevation, these lodgings offer splendid views of the island, temperate weather, and a "getting away from it all" feeling—which is actually the case, as most shops and restaurants are a fair drive away, and beaches even farther. You'll definitely need a car here.

VACATION RENTALS

There are many real-estate companies that specialize in short-term vacation rentals. They may represent an entire resort property, most of the units at one property, or even individually owned units. The companies listed here have a long history of excellent service to Maui visitors.

AA Oceanfront Condominium Rentals. As the name suggests, the specialty is "oceanfront." With rental units in more than 25 condominium complexes from the northernmost reaches of *Kīhei* all the way to Wailea, there's something for everyone at prices that range from $130 to $435 a night. ⊠ *1279 S. Kīhei Rd., Kīhei* ☎ *808/879–7288 or 800/488–6004* ⊕ *www.aaoceanfront.com*

Aston Hotels & Resorts. Formerly ResortQuest, the company manages hotels and condos throughout the islands, including nine properties on Maui. Most are on or near the beach, concentrated in the resort areas of Kā'anapali and Kīhei and Wailea. Studios to three-bedroom units range in price from $120 to $695 per night. The company offers some interesting value-added programs like "Kids Stay, Play and Eat Free." ⊠ *2511 S. Kīhei Rd, Kīhei* ☎ *808/879–5445 or 800/822–4409* ⊕ *www.resortquesthawaii.com*

Bello Maui Vacations. The Bellos are Maui real estate experts and have a full range of vacation rentals in 20 South Shore condominium complexes. They also have gorgeous houses for rent. Condos start at right around $100 per night (most are $200 or less); a seven-bedroom oceanfront estate rents for $1,500 per night. ⊠ *115 E. Lipoa #101, Kīhei* ☎ *808/879–3328 or 800/541–3060* ⊕ *www.bellomauivacations.com*

Chase 'n Rainbows. Family owned and operated, this is the largest property management company on West Maui, with the largest selection of rentals from studios to three-bedrooms. Rentals are everywhere from Lahaina town up to Kahana. Prices range from about $100 to $525 per night. The company has been in business since 1980, and it's good. ⊠ *118 Kupuohi St., Lahaina* ☎ *808/667–7088 or 800/367–6092* ⊕ *www.chasenrainbows.com*

Destination Resorts. If it's the South Shore luxury of Wailea and Mākena luxury you seek, look no further. This company has a full complement of many dozens of condominiums and villas ranging in size from studios to four bedrooms, and in price from a $240 a night for a studio at Wailea 'Ekahi, an older property, to more than $3,500 for the new Wailea Villas. The company offers excellent personalized service and is known for particularly fine housekeeping services. ⊠ *3750 Wailea Alanui Dr., Wailea* ☎ *808/879–1595 or 866/384–1365* ⊕ *www.drhmaui.com*

Mā'alaea Bay Realty & Rentals. Mā'alaea, a little strip of condominiums within the isthmus that links Central and West Maui, is often overlooked, but it shouldn't be. This company has 140 one-, two-, and three-bedroom units from $100 to $235 per night. The wind is usually strong here, but there's a nice beach, a harbor, and some good shopping and decent restaurants. ⊠ *280 Hau'oli St., Mā'alaea* ☎ *808/244–5627 or 800/367–6084* ⊕ *www.maalaeabay.com*

$–$$
B&B/INN

The Banyan Tree House. If a taste of rural Hawai'i life in plantation days is what you crave, you'll find it here. The setting is pastoral—the 2-acre property is lush with tropical foliage, has an expansive lawn, and is fringed with huge monkeypod and banyan trees. The cottages (bedrooms, really, with updated baths and kitchenettes) are simple and functional. The gem, though, is the 1927 plantation house with

its sprawling living and dining rooms, a kitchen any cook will adore, and a lānai that will take you back in time. The configuration of the property allows for lots of combinations; you can rent one, two, or all three bedrooms in the house or even add the adjoining one-bedroom cottage. And you can rent the entire property for a family reunion or a retreat and have access to a large activities room complete with audio and video capabilities. **Pros:** one cottage and the pool are outfitted for travelers with disabilities, you can walk to Makawao town for dining and shopping. **Cons:** the furniture in the cottages is pretty basic, few amenities. ⊠*3265 Baldwin Ave., Makawao* ☎*808/572–9021* ⊕*www.banyantreehouse.com* ⟿*7 rooms* ⟲*In-room: kitchen, Wi-Fi. In-hotel: pool, laundry facilities* ▤*AE, D, V, MC.*

$–$$
B&B/INN
Fodor's Choice
★

Hale Ho'okipa Inn. A handsome 1924 Craftsman-style house in the heart of Makawao town, this inn on both the Hawai'i and the National Historic Registers provides a great base for excursions to the Haleakalā or to Hāna. Owner Cherie Attix has furnished it with antiques and fine art, and she allows guests to peruse her voluminous library of Hawai'i-related books. She's also a fount of local knowledge. The house is divided into three single rooms, each prettier than the next, and the South Wing, which sleeps four and includes the kitchen. Two rooms have wonderful claw-foot tubs. The grounds are lush and serene complete with koi pond and the biggest Norfolk Pine tree you've ever seen. **Pros:** genteel rural setting, price includes full island-style breakfast including organic fruit from the garden. **Cons:** a 20-minute drive to the nearest beach; this is not the sun, sand, and surf surroundings of travel posters. ⊠*32 Pakani Pl., Makawao* ☎*808/572–6698* 📠*808/572–2580* ⊕*www.maui-bed-and-breakfast.com* ⟿*3 rooms, 1 suite* ⟲*In-room: TV, Wi-Fi* ▤ *MC, V.*

$–$$
HOTEL

Kula Lodge. Don't expect a local look despite being out in the country: the lodge inexplicably resembles a chalet in the Swiss Alps, and two units even have gas fireplaces. Charming and cozy in spite of the nontropical ambience, it's a good spot for a short romantic stay. Units are in two wooden cabins; four have lofts in addition to the ample bed space downstairs. On 3 acres, the lodge has striking, expansive views of Haleakalā and two coasts, enhanced by the surrounding tropical gardens. The property has an art gallery and a protea store that will pack flowers for you to take home; next door you'll find a gourmet and gift shop. **Pros:** a quiet and peaceful place in the country, excellent

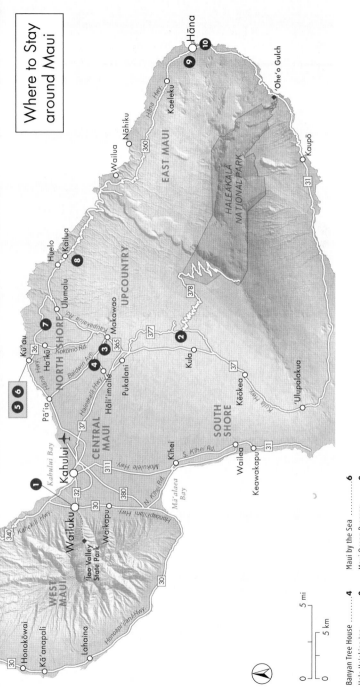

Where to Stay around Maui

Banyan Tree House **4**
Hale Ho'okipa Inn **3**
Hāna Kai-Maui Resort
Condominiums **9**
Hotel Hāna-Maui **10**
Inn at Mama's
Fish House **5**
Kula Lodge **2**

Maui by the Sea **6**
Maui Ocean Breezes **8**
Old Wailuku Inn **1**
Pu'ukoa Maui Rentals **7**

The Old Wailuku Inn at Ulupono

Hale Ho'okipa Inn

shopping right next door. **Cons:** it's a long, long way to the beach; in the winter, it can get downright cold. ⊠*15200 Haleakalā Hwy., Rte. 377, Kula* ☎*808/878–1535 or 800/233–1535* ⊕*www.kulalodge.com* ⤳*5 units* ⚭*In-room: no a/c, no phone, no TV. In-hotel: restaurant, no elevator* ⊟*AE, MC, V.*

THE NORTH SHORE

You won't find any large resorts or condominium complexes along the North Shore, yet there are a variety of accommodations along the coastline from the surf town of Pā'ia, through tiny Kū'au, and along the rainforested Hāna Highway through Ha'ikū. Some are oceanfront but not necessarily beachfront (with sand); instead, look for tropical gardens overflowing with ginger, bananas, papayas, and nightly bug symphonies. Some have heart-stopping views or the type of solitude that seeps in, easing your tension before you know it. You may encounter brief, powerful downpours, but that's what make this part of Maui green and lush. You'll need a car to enjoy staying on the North Shore.

$–$$
B&B/INN

⌂**The Inn at Mama's Fish House.** Nestled in gardens adjacent to one of Maui's most popular dining spots, Mama's Fish House ($$$$), these well-maintained one- and two-bedroom cottages have a retro-Hawaiian style with rattan furnishings and local artwork. Each has a kitchen and a private garden patio. There is a small beach in front of the property known as Kū'au Cove. It's best to make reservations for the restaurant when you book your accommodations or you may not get a table. **Pros:** daily maid service, free parking, next to Ho'okipa Beach. **Cons:** Mama's Fish House is very popular, so there can be a lot of people around in the evenings (it's more mellow during the day). ⊠*799 Pono Pl., Kū'au* ☎*808/579–9764 or 800/860–4852* ⊕*www.mamasfishhouse.com* ⤳*9 units* ⚭*In-room: safe, kitchen, DVD, Wi-Fi. In-hotel: restaurant, laundry facilities* ⊟*AE, D ,DC, M. VC.*

$$
RENTALS

⌂**Maui by the Sea.** Just past Pā'ia, on the other side of a stucco wall from Hāna Highway, this cute, small but clean one-bedroom apartment decorated with tropical prints and Hawaiian quilts is bright and airy. You can park your car in the garage below and climb the stairs to this second-floor unit, which has a broad lānai with a gas grill and a dining table. The lānai captures gentle cooling breezes, and it has a fantastic ocean view. You're just steps away from the ocean here, although there is no sand beach, just a rocky access; Tavares Bay is a mere 200 yards away for launching windsurfing or swimming. **Pros:** free interisland, mainland, and Canada phone calls; host is lifelong Maui resident and will share island stories with you. **Cons:** road noise from Hāna Highway, room for only one or two people, another house is right next door, no resort amenities. ⊠*523 Hāna Hwy., Pā'ia* ☎*808/579–9865* ⊕*www.mauibythesea.com* ⤳*1 unit* ⚭*In-room: kitchen, DVD, Ethernet. In-hotel: laundry facilities* ⊟*AE, MC, V*

$
RENTALS

⌂**Maui Ocean Breezes.** The warm ocean breeze rolls through these pretty rentals and shoos the mosquitoes away, making this a perfect spot if you want quiet, gorgeous scenery. The decor is both whimsical and calming—expect colorfully painted walls and sheer curtains. The saltwater pool is fed by a waterfall. Fully equipped kitchens and Wi-Fi make these studios an ideal home away from home. Allergy-prone travelers can relax here—no chemicals or pesticides are used on the property. Although it seems far from civilization, you are only five minutes from Haʻikū and 10 from Pāʻia. **Pros:** good for people sensitive to harsh chemicals. **Cons:** 15 minutes from closest beach, rather remote location; the owner prefers stays of seven nights or longer, though will negotiate depending on availability. ✉ *240 N. Holokai Rd., Haʻikū* ☎ *808/572–2775* ⊕ *www.mauivacationhideaway.com* 🛏 *3 units* ⚐ *In-room: no a/c, kitchen, Wi-Fi. In-hotel: pool, no elevator, laundry facilities* ⊟ *MC, V.*

¢
RENTALS
🏠 **Puʻukoa Maui Rentals.** Off a peaceful cul-de-sac in a residential area, these two well-maintained and immaculately clean homes offer studio and one-bedroom accommodations. Studios have an efficiency-style kitchen with a small refrigerator, hot plate, microwave, toaster oven, and coffeemaker. One-bedroom apartments have fully-equipped kitchens, a separate bedroom, and a large living area. All units have private bathrooms and a lānai or patio, some with ocean views. The large yard with tropical flowers and fruit trees is great for a sunset barbecue or just relaxing. **Pros:** very clean, reasonable rates, good spot for a group attending a wedding or family reunion. **Cons:** it's about a 10-minute drive to the beach, no hot tub, set in quiet residential area. ✉ *Puʻukoa Pl., Haʻikū* ☎ *808/573–2884* ⊕ *www.puukoa.com* 🛏 *7 rooms* ⚐ *In-room: no a/c, kitchen, DVD, Wi-Fi. In-hotel: no elevator* ⊟ AE, MC, V.

B&Bs

Additional B&Bs on Maui can be found by contacting **Bed & Breakfast Hawaiʻi** (☎ *808/822–7771 or 800/733–1632* ⊕ *www.bandb-hawaii.com*). **Bed and Breakfast Honolulu** (☎ *808/595–7533 or 800/288–4666* ⊕ *www.hawaiibnb.com*) is another good source. It's always a good idea to ask specifically if a property is licensed by the County of Maui.

HĀNA

Why stay in Hāna when it's so far from everything? In a world where everything moves at high speed, Hāna still travels on horseback, ambling along slowly enough to smell the flowers. But old-fashioned and remote do not mean tame—this is a wild coast, known for heart-stopping scenery and downpours. Leave city expectations behind: the single grocery may run out of milk, and the only videos to rent may be several years old. The dining options are slim. ■ TIP→ **If you're staying for several days, or at a vacation rental, stock up on groceries before you head out to Hāna.** Even with these inconveniences, Hāna is a place you won't want to miss.

$$–$$$
RENTALS
🏠 **Hāna Kai-Maui Resort Condominiums.** Perfectly situated close to Hāna Bay, this resort complex has a long history (it opened in 1970) and excellent reputation for visitor hospitality. And all you have to do is take your morning coffee out onto the lānai of any of these lovely units to know why Hāna is often referred to as "heavenly." All units are tastefully and comfortably furnished with tropical-pattern fabrics and light-colored

Hotel Hāna-Maui

wood, with well-equipped kitchens with all the appliances, table settings, and tools you need to prepare meals. They even have 100% Egyptian cotton sheets on the beds. **Pros:** It's a stone's throw to Hāna Bay, where you can take a swim or have a Roselani Mac Nut ice cream cone at Tutu's. **Cons:** Early to bed and early to rise—no nightlife or excitement here. ⊠ *1533 Uakea Rd., Hāna* ☏ *808/248–8426 or 800/346–2772* ⊕ *www.hanakaimaui.com* ⟿ *6 studios, 11 1-bedroom* ⚿ *In-room: kitchen, no TV, Wi-Fi* ⊟ *MC, V.*

$$$$
HOTEL
Fodor's Choice
★

🖫 **Hotel Hāna-Maui.** Small, secluded, and quietly luxurious, with unobstructed views of the Pacific, this tranquil property is a departure from the usual resort destinations on Maui. Here, horses nibble wild grass on the sea cliff nearby. Spacious rooms (680 to 830 square feet) have bleached-wood floors, authentic kapa-print fabric furnishings, and sumptuously stocked minibars at no extra cost. Spa suites and a heated *watsu* (massage performed in warm water) pool complement a state-of-the-art spa-and-fitness center. The Sea Ranch Cottages with individual hot tubs are the best value. A shuttle takes you to beautiful Hāmoa Beach. **Pros:** if you want to get away from it all, there's no better or more beautiful place; spa is incredibly relaxing. **Cons:** everything moves slowly; if you can't live without your Blackberry, this is not the place for you; it's oceanfront but does not have a sandy beach (red- and black-sand beaches are nearby). ⊠ *5031 Hāna Hwy.* ⌂ *Box 9, Hāna 96713* ☏ *808/248–8211 or 800/321–4262* ⊕ *www.hotelhanamaui.com* ⟿ *69 rooms, 47 cottages, 1 house* ⚿ *In-room: refrigerator, no TV, dial-up. In-hotel: 2 restaurants, bar, tennis courts, pools, gym, spa, no elevator, public Internet* ⊟ *AE, D, DC, MC, V.*

MAUI ESSENTIALS

TRANSPORTATION

AIR TRAVEL

Updated by
Cathy Sharpe

You can fly to Maui from the mainland United States or from Honolulu. Flight time from the West Coast to Maui is about five hours; from the Midwest, expect about an eight-hour flight; and coming from the East Coast will take about 10 hours, not including layovers. Maui is the most visited of the Neighbor Islands and therefore the easiest to connect to on an interisland flight. Honolulu–Kahului is one of the most heavily traveled air routes in the nation.

AIRPORTS AND
CARRIERS

The Kahului Airport is Maui's only airport with direct service from the mainland. It's smallish and easy to navigate; the main disadvantage is its distance from the major resort destinations. A wide range of airlines now fly nonstop from various West Coast cities to Kahului. If you're staying in West Maui, you might choose to fly into the Kapalua–West Maui Airport. Aloha Airlines, go! Airlines, Hawaiian Airlines, Island Air and Pacific Wings are interisland carriers with several flights daily between Oʻahu and the Kahului and/or Kapalua–West Maui airports. They are all competitively priced, and if you're relatively flexible with dates and times, you should have no problem securing a one-way fare of less than $30. *See Travel Smart Hawaiʻi for airline contact information.*

Tiny Hāna in East Maui has a single airstrip, served by commuter planes from Honolulu and charter flights from Kahului and Kapalua. Flying here is a great option if you want to avoid the long and windy drive to Hāna from one of the other airports.

TO AND FROM THE AIRPORTS The best way to get from the airport to your destination—and to see the island itself—is in your own rental car. Most major car-rental companies have desks or courtesy phones at each airport and can provide a map and directions to your hotel. It will take you about an hour, with traffic in your favor, to get from Kahului Airport to a hotel in Kapalua or Kāʻanapali and 30 to 40 minutes to go to Kīhei or Wailea.

Maui Airport Taxi serves the Kahului Airport. A number of taxi companies make frequent passes through the Kapalua–West Maui Airport. If you don't see a cab upon your arrival into Kapalua, you can call La Bella Taxi for island-wide service. Call Kīhei Taxi if you're staying in the Kīhei, Wailea, or Mākena area. Charges from Kahului Airport to Kāʻanapali run about $87; to Lahaina, about $75; and to Wailea, about $57.

SpeediShuttle offers transportation between the Kahului Airport and hotels, resorts, and condominium complexes throughout the island. There is an online reservation and fare-quote system for information and bookings.

If you're flying into Hāna Airport and staying at the Hotel Hāna-Maui, your flight will be met by a hotel van. If you have reserved a rental car, the agent will usually know your arrival time and meet you. Otherwise you can call Dollar Rent A Car to pick you up.

Contacts Dollar Rent A Car (☎ 800/800–4000). **Kīhei Taxi** (☎ 808/879–3000). **La Bella Taxi** (☎ 808/242–8011). **Maui Airport Taxi** (☎ 808/877–0907). **Speedi-Shuttle Hawaiʻi** (☎ 877/242–5777 ⊕ *www.speedishuttle.com*).

BUS AND SHUTTLE TRAVEL

Maui Bus, operated by Roberts Hawaiʻi, offers eleven routes in and between various central, south, and west Maui communities, seven days a week, including all holidays. Passengers can travel in and around Wailuku, Kahului, Lahaina, Kāʻanapali, Kapalua, Kīhei, Wailea, Māʻalaea, and Upcountry (including Pukalani, Hāliʻimaile, Haʻikū and Pāʻia). The Upcountry Islander route includes a stop at Kahului Airport. The Kahului and Wailuku loops are free and all other fares are $1.

If you're staying in the right hotel or condo, a few shuttles can get you around the area. Akina Tours has a shuttle that runs between Wailea's resorts, golf courses, tennis courts and Shops at Wailea, free of charge, hourly from about 6:30 AM to 6 PM. The free Kā'anapali Trolley Shuttle runs within the resort area between 9 AM and 11 PM and stops automatically at all hotels and at condos when requested. All Kā'anapali hotels have copies of schedules.

Contacts Akina Tours (☎ *808/879–2828* ⊕ *www.akinatours.com*). **Roberts Hawai'i** (☎ *808/871–4838* ⊕ *www.co.maui.hi.us/bus*).

CAR TRAVEL

To really see the island, you'll need a car. Maui has bad roads in beautiful places. Roads generally have two lanes, and sometimes only one—ancient highways that bridge staggering valleys in testimony to their bygone engineers. Maui's landscape is extraordinarily diverse for such a small island. Your sense of place (and the weather) seem to change every few miles. If you drive to the summit of Haleakalā, you can rise from palm-lined beaches to the rare world inhabited by silverswords in less than two hours. On the Road to Hāna, you'll drive into and out of the rain, with rainbows that seem to land on the hood of your car. Maui's two difficult roads are Hāna Highway (Rte. 360) and an 8-mi scenic stretch between Kapalua and Wailuku. If you're going to attempt the partially paved, patched, and bumpy road between Hāna and 'Ulupalakua, take a four-wheel-drive vehicle. Be forewarned: rental-car companies prohibit travel on roads they've determined might damage the car. If you break down, you're on your own for repairs.

CAR RENTAL   During peak seasons—summer, and Christmas through Easter—be sure to reserve your car well ahead of time. Expect to pay about $35 to $40 a day—before taxes, insurance, and extras—for a compact car from one of the major companies. You can get a less-expensive deal from one of the locally owned budget companies. There's a $3 daily road tax on all rental cars in Hawai'i.

Budget, Dollar, and National have courtesy phones at the Kapalua–West Maui Airport; Hertz and Alamo are nearby. All of the above, plus Avis, Enterprise, and Thrifty, have desks at or near Maui's major airport in Kahului. Quite a few locally owned companies rent cars on Maui, including Aloha Rent-A-Car, which will pick you up at Kahului Airport or leave a vehicle for you if your flight comes in after-hours.

Contacts Aloha Rent-A-Car (☎ *808/877–4477 or 877/452–5642* ⊕ *www.aloha rentacar.com*).

MOPED   To rent a moped, you need to be 18 years of age (24 years of age to rent
RENTAL   a motorcycle) and have a driver's license and credit card. Be especially careful navigating roads that have no designated bicycle lanes. Note that helmets are optional on Maui, but eye protection is not.

Hula Hogs in Kīhei can outfit you with a moped for $50 a day. Motorcycle rentals start at about $105 per day. On the West Side, Aloha Toys Exotic Cars is a little pricier, and specializes in exotic auto rentals, Jeeps, Harleys, and mopeds.

Contacts Aloha Toys Exotic Cars (✉ *640 Front St., Lahaina* ☎ *808/891–0888 or 888/883–1212* ⊕ *www.alohatoystore.com*). **Hula Hogs** (✉ *Azeka Place, 1279 S. Kīhei Rd., Kīhei* ☎ *808/875–7433* ⊕ *www.hulahogs.com*).

FERRY TRAVEL

There is daily ferry service between Lahaina, Maui, and Mānele Bay, Lāna'i, with Expeditions Lāna'i Ferry. The 9-mi crossing costs $50 cash (or $52 if you pay with a credit card) round-trip, per person and takes about 45 minutes or so, depending on ocean conditions (which can make this trip a rough one). Moloka'i Ferry offers twice daily ferry service between Lahaina, Maui and Kaunakakai, Moloka'i. Travel time is about 90 minutes each way and the one-way fare is $42.40 per person (including taxes and fees); a book of six one-way tickets costs $196.10 (including taxes and fees). Reservations are recommended for both ferries.

At this writing, Hawai'i Superferry, a high-speed interisland ferry with routes between Honolulu and Kahului, Maui, has suspended service. Consult the Supperferry Web site for updates, or go to www.gohawaii.com.

Contacts Expeditions Lāna'i Ferry (☎ 800/695–2624 ⊕ www.go-lanai.com). **Hawaii Superferry** (☎ 877/443–3779 ⊕ www.hawaiisuperferry.com). **Molokai Ferry** (☎ 866/307–6524 ⊕ www.molokaiferry.com).

BY TAXI

You'd be smart to use taxis just for the areas in which they're located, as most destinations are spread out over long distances. The county rate is $3.50 for the first tenth of a mile and $.30 for each tenth of a mile after that. For short hops between hotels and restaurants, taxis can be a convenient way to go, but you'll have to call ahead. Even busy West Maui doesn't have curbside taxi service.

Ali'i Cab covers West Maui. Arthur's Limousine Service offers a chauffeured super-stretch Lincoln complete with bar and two TVs for $122 per hour. Arthur's fleet also includes less grandiose Lincoln Town Cars for $91 per hour. Both require a two-hour minimum. Classy Taxi offers limos, convertibles, and a 1929 Model A Ford Phaeton for a regular cab's fare. Kīhei Taxi serves Central Maui. Wailea Limousine Service provides vans, Cadillacs, and limousines on the South Shore. Despite the name, they also service the Lahaina area.

Contacts Ali'i Cab (☎ 808/661–3688). **Arthur's Limousine Service** (☎ 808/871–5555 or 877/408–9559 ⊕ www.arthurslimo.com). **Classy Taxi** (☎ 808/665–0003). **Kīhei Taxi** (☎ 808/879–3000). **Wailea Limousine Service** (☎ 808/875–4114, 808/661–4114 in Lahaina).

CONTACTS AND RESOURCES

EMERGENCIES

In an emergency, dial **911** to reach an ambulance, the police, or the fire department.

For emergency road service, there's a Honolulu-based AAA. A dispatcher will send a tow truck, but you will need to tell the driver where to take your car. Don't forget to carry your membership card with you.

For medical assistance in West Maui, call Doctors on Call. Or try West Maui Health Care Center, a walk-in clinic at Whalers Village. It's open daily from 7:30 AM to 8 PM. Kīhei Clinic Medical Services in South Maui is geared to working with visitors in Kīhei and Wailea.

Doctors Doctors on Call (✉ *Hyatt Regency Maui, Nāpili Tower, Suite 100, 200 Nohea Kai Dr., Lahaina* ☎ *808/667–7676*). **Kīhei Clinic Medical Services** (✉ *2349 S. Kīhei Rd., Suite D, Kīhei* ☎ *808/879–1440*). **West Maui Health Care Center** (✉ *2435 Kā'anapali Pkwy., Suite H-7, Kā'anapali* ☎ *808/667–9721*).

Emergency Services AAA (☎ *800/222–4357*). **Coast Guard Rescue Center** (☎ *800/552–6458*).

Hospitals Hāna Medical Center (✉ *4590 Hāna Hwy., Hāna* ☎ *808/248–8294*). **Kula Hospital** (✉ *100 Keokea Pl., Kula* ☎ *808/878–1221*). **Maui Memorial Hospital** (✉ *221 Mahalani St., Wailuku* ☎ *808/244–9056*).

Pharmacies Kīhei Professional Pharmacy (✉ *41 E. Lipoa, Kīhei* ☎ *808/879–8499*). **Kmart Stores** (✉ *424 Dairy Rd., Kahului* ☎ *808/871–5677*). **Valley Isle Pharmacy** (✉ *130 Prison St., Lahaina* ☎ *808/661–4747*).

VISITOR INFORMATION

Before you go, contact the Hawai'i Visitors & Convention Bureau (HVCB) for general information and to order "The Islands of Aloha" free visitor guide featuring maps, photos, and information on accommodations, transportation, activities, visitor attractions, entertainment, and dining. Take a virtual visit to the islands on the Web, which can be helpful in planning many aspects of your vacation. The HVCB site has a calendar section that allows you to see what local events are in place during the time of your stay. You can also check out the Maui Visitors Bureau site.

Contacts Hawai'i Visitors & Convention Bureau (✉ *2270 Kalakaua Ave., Suite 801, Honolulu* ☎ *808/923–1811, 800/464–2924 to order free visitor guide* ⊕ *www. gohawaii.com*). In the U.K. contact the **Hawai'i Visitors & Convention Bureau** (⌖ *36 Southwark Bridge Rd., London SE1 9EU* ☎ *020/7202–6384* ⊕ *www.gohawaii. com*). **Maui Visitors Bureau** (⊕ *www.visitmaui.com*).

The Big Island

WORD OF MOUTH

"The BI is a study in contrasts . . . From the white (or black, or even green) sand beaches, you can drive an hour and be in a chilly misty rain forest full of tree ferns. Drive another 15 minutes and you are in the blazing sun in the middle of a totally alien landscape consisting entirely of black volcanic glass."

—azuresky

WELCOME TO THE BIG ISLAND

TOP REASONS TO GO

★ **Hawai'i Volcanoes National Park:** Catch the lava fireworks at night and explore newly made land, lava tubes, steam vents, and giant craters.

★ **Waipi'o Valley:** Experience a real-life secret garden, the remote spot known as the Valley of the Kings.

★ **Kealakekua Bay Double Feature:** Kayak past spinner dolphins to the Captain Cook Monument, then go snorkeling along the fabulous coral reef.

★ **The Heavens:** Stargaze through gigantic telescopes on snow-topped Mauna Kea.

★ **Hidden Beaches:** Discover one of the Kohala Coast's lesser-known gems.

1 Kohala District and Waimea. The sparkling turquoise of the Kohala Coast is home to all those long, white-sand beaches and the expensive resorts that go with them. Ranches sprawl across the cool, upland meadows surrounding Waimea (Kamuela)—this is *paniolo* (cowboy) country.

2 Kailua-Kona. A seaside town bustling with tourists.

3 South Kona and Kealakekua Bay. Younger residents and transplants have turned defunct coffee farms into lively art communities overlooking Kealakekua Bay.

4 Ka'ū and Ka Lae (South Point). Green-sand beaches and moonlike lava fields make up the stunning southern part of the island. This is the home of Hawai'i Volcanoes National Park, which continues to grow, as active Kīlauea Volcano sends lava spilling into the ocean, creating new land.

5 Volcano Village. Volcano is a cozy town with an artsy vibe, and makes a great base for exploring nearby Hawai'i Volcanoes National Park.

6 Puna. This part of the island, most recently covered by lava, has brand-new, jet-black beaches punctuated with volcanically heated hot springs.

7 Hilo. The rainy side of the island takes its name from the large fishing town of Hilo, nicknamed the City of Rainbows.

8 Hāmākua Coast. Waterfalls, dramatic cliffs, hidden valleys, the greenest green you'll ever see, rain forests, and exotic flowers await on the Hāmākua Coast.

GETTING ORIENTED

You could fit all of the other Hawaiian islands into the Big Island and still have some room left over—hence the name. Locals refer to the island by side: Kona to the west and Hilo to the east. Most of the resorts, condos, and restaurants are crammed into 30 mi of the sunny Kona side, while rainy, tropical Hilo is much more residential.

HĀMĀKUA COAST

240 Honoka'a
Waimea 19 (Māmalahoa Hwy.)
Kamuela

8 Hawai'i Belt Rd.

Kamuela
Airport

HĀMĀKUA

Saddle Rd.

Mauna Kea
13,769 ft

NORTH HILO

19

200

Hilo Bay

HILO 7 Hilo

200 Saddle Rd.

11 Hilo International Airport (General Lyman Field)

SOUTH HILO

Stainback Hwy.

130

Kūlani Honor Camp
Ola'a Rain Forest

Pāhoa 132

PUNA

Mauna Loa
13,679

Hawai'i Belt Rd.

Volcano Village 6

130

Kilauea
4,069 ft 5

Kilauea Crater

11

Hawai'i Volcanoes National Park

KA'Ū

4

Hawai'i Belt Rd.

Punalu'u

0   15 mi
0   15 km

Honu'apo Bay

Waikapuna Bay

Pu'u Nāhāhā Point

Ka Lae (South Point)

BIG ISLAND PLANNER

When You Arrive

The Big Island's two airports are directly across the island from each other. Kona International Airport on the west side is about a 10-minute drive from Kailua-Kona and 30 to 45 minutes from the Kohala Coast. On the east side, Hilo International Airport, 2 mi from downtown Hilo, is about 40 minutes from Volcanoes National Park. A 2½-hour drive connects Hilo and Kailua-Kona.

Timing Is Everything

You can see humpback whales clearly off the western coast of the island from about January until May. The Ironman Triathlon takes place every October in Kailua-Kona. Shortly after the Ironman, the first 10 days of November are devoted to the Kona Coffee Cultural Festival—each day brings numerous caffeinated events including a cooking competition, a picking competition, a barista competition, and of course the cupping competition, which is all about the taste and quality of each coffee. Coffee connoisseurs from all over the world flock to Kona for the festival, and the whole west side of the island goes crazy for coffee.

Renting a Car

You will need a car on the Big Island. Get a four-wheel-drive vehicle if you're at all interested in exploring. Some of the island's best sights (and most beautiful beaches) are at the end of rough or unpaved roads. ■TIP➔ Talk to the agency in advance if you want to pick up a car at one airport and drop it off at the other. Though they allow this, most charge an additional fee of up to $50. If you arrange it ahead of time, they can often be talked into waiving the fee.

Most agencies make you sign an agreement that you won't drive on the Saddle Road, the path to Mauna Kea and its observatories. Though smoothly paved, the Saddle Road is remote, winding, unlighted, and bereft of gas stations. Harper's, a local rental company, is the sole exception.

Dining and Lodging on the Big Island

Hawai'i is a melting pot of cultures, and nowhere is this more apparent than in its cuisine. From lū'au and "plate lunches" to sushi and steak, there's no shortage of interesting flavors and presentations. The same "buy local" trend that is spreading through the rest of the country is really taking hold on the Big Island. This is a giant shift from years past, in which everything but the pineapple was imported, and it's a happy trend for visitors, who get to taste juicy, flavorful Waimea tomatoes and creamy handmade Hāmākua goat cheese.

Whether you're looking for a quick snack or a multicourse meal, we cover the best eating experiences the island has to offer.

Choosing vacation lodging is a tough decision, but fret not—our expert writers and editors have done most of the legwork.

Looking for a tropical forest retreat, a big resort, or a private vacation rental? We give you all details you need to book a place that suits your style. Quick tips: Reserve your room far in advance. Be sure to ask about discounts and special packages (hotel Web sites often have Internet-only deals).

Island Hopping

There is enough on the Big Island to keep visitors active and entertained for weeks. However, if you're spending more than 10 days here, you might be interested in checking out one of the other islands and comparing notes. Maui is the Big Island's closest neighbor—on a sunny day you can see it clearly from the Kohala Coast—and the flight there is barely half an hour. For nightlife-deprived visitors, a weekend trip to check out the lively bars and restaurants on Maui might be the perfect solution. If you're visiting in October, consider hopping to Maui for its famous Halloween party. Go, Hawaiian, and Island Air all offer island-hopping flights, usually at low prices.

Remember to book your island-hopping flights as soon as you decide to hop—the flights are small and can fill up fast, particularly during Halloween when many Big Islanders make their way to Maui, and during Christmas and Thanksgiving when locals hop to the neighbor islands to visit family.

If you're planning a longer trip and considering including a few islands, ⇨see the Travel Smart chapter for more information.

Island Driving Times

Due to the Big Island's size, it can take quite a bit of time to get from one region of the island to another. Added to that, the island's increasing traffic problems are making driving times even longer, particularly between Kona and the Kohala Coast, and Kona to Kealakekua Bay and Kau.

The state is working on widening Highway 19, which circles the island, and the hope is that the wider highway will cut down on traffic. In the meantime, the following are average driving times between some of the Big Island's most popular sights.

Kailua-Kona to Kealakekua Bay	15 minutes
Kailua-Kona to Kohala Coast	30 minutes
Kailua-Kona to Waimea	45 minutes
Kailua-Kona to Hāmākua Coast	1 hour
Kailua-Kona to Volcano	2 hours
Kailua-Kona to Hilo	2.5 hours
Kohala Coast to Waimea	25 minutes
Kohala Coast to Hāmākua Coast	40 minutes
Hilo to Volcano	30 minutes

Will I See Flowing Lava?

The best time to see lava is at night. However, you may or may not see flowing lava. Anyone who tries to tell you they can guarantee it or predict it is lying or trying to sell you something. Your best bet is to call the visitor center at the national park before you head out; even at that you could be pleasantly surprised or utterly disappointed. Keep in mind that the volcano is a pretty amazing sight even if it's not spewing fire.

The hike out to the closest viewing station to the flowing lava depends on the current location of the lava eruption site, and can range from 20 minutes to four hours each way.

The best way to handle it is to head out in the late afternoon, arrive at the viewing station by nightfall, and then start the trek back when you've had your fill of Pele's fireworks. ■TIP➜ Bring a flashlight and be prepared for some rough going over the lava fields at night.

There may be viewing stations along the way as well, so you don't necessarily have to make the entire journey. In fact, depending on how the lava is flowing, a viewing station farther from the lava could actually afford better views. ⇨See the Volcanoes National Park feature for more information.

4

1 DAY ITINERARIES

The following one-day itineraries will take you to our favorite spots on the island.

Hike Volcanoes. Devote a full day (at least) to Volcanoes National Park. Head out to Kīlauea Iki trail—a 4-mi loop at the summit—by late morning. Grab a sandwich at the Volcano House when you're finished and take in their fantastic views of the craters. After lunch, head down Chain of Craters Road to the coast and potential active lava flows. Bring water, snacks, and a flashlight if you intend to hike where the lava flows into the ocean. Start your hike during the day (by 4 PM or earlier) to ensure that you're as close as you can safely be when night falls and to prepare yourself for a spectacular lava show.

Black & Green Sand. Check out some of the unusual beaches you'll only find on the Big Island. Start with a hike into Green Sand beach and plan to spend some time here, dipping into the bay's turquoise waters and marveling at the surreal beauty of this spot. Then hop into the car and head a half hour south to Punalu'u, the island's best-known black-sand beach and favorite resting place of the Hawaiian sea turtle. There are usually a few turtles happily on the beach.

Majestic Waterfalls & Kings' Valleys. Take a day to enjoy the splendors of the Hāmākua Coast, a jagged stretch of coastline that embodies all things tropical. Any gorge you see on the road indicates a waterfall waiting to be explored. For a sure bet, head to the beautiful Waipi'o Valley. Book a horseback, hiking, or 4WD tour or walk on in yourself (just keep in mind that it's an arduous hike back up). Once in the valley, take your first right to get to the black-sand beach. Take a moment to sit here—the ancient Hawaiians believed this was where souls crossed over to the afterlife. Whether you believe it or not, there's something unmistakably special about this place. Waterfalls abound in the valley, depending on recent rainfall. Your best bet is to follow the river from the beach to the back of the valley, where a waterfall and its lovely pool await.

Volcano Hot Springs & Boiling Pots. Most tourists skip Puna. Venture into this remote area for a morning, and you'll be rewarded with lava tube hikes (Kīlauea Caverns of Fire), volcanically heated pools (Ahalanui Beach Park), and tide pools brimming with colorful coral, fish, and the occasional turtle (Kapoho). Head to Hilo in the afternoon to catch a glimpse of the Boiling Pots waterfalls, Banyan Drive, and Queen Lili'uokalani Gardens, before dining at one of Hilo's great restaurants.

Underwater Day. Explore the colorful reefs off the Big Island's coast for one day and we defy you to stop thinking about the world beneath the waves when you're back on land. Our favorite spots include Two Step (near the Place of Refuge), Kealakekua Bay, and the Kapoho Tide Pools. Early morning is the best time to see the Hawaiian spinner dolphins that frolic off this coast, but you're likely to see turtles any time of day, along with yellow and white angelfish, spotted moray eels, trumpet fish, and myriad other tropical varieties.

Sun & Stars. Spend the day lounging on a Kohala Coast beach (Hāpuna, Kauna'oa—also known as Mauna Kea—or Kua Bay), but throw jackets and boots in the car because you'll be catching the sunset from Mauna Kea's summit. Bundle up and stick around after darkness falls for some of the world's best stargazing. Book a tour or head straight for the visitor center, join their free tour of the summit at sunset, and return to the center to use their telescopes.

Written by
Peter Serafin
& Amy
Westervelt
Updated by
Meredith
Wertz

Nicknamed "The Big Island," Hawai'i the island is a micro-cosm of Hawai'i the state. From long white-sand beaches and crystal clear bays to rain forests, waterfalls, lū'au, exotic flowers, and birds, all things quintessentially Hawaiian are well represented here. But an assortment of happy surprises also distinguish the Big Island from the rest of Hawai'i—an active volcano (Kīlauea) oozing red lava and creating new earth every day, the clearest place in the world to view stars in the night sky (Mauna Kea), and some seriously good cof-fee (Kona, of course).

4

GEOLOGY

Home to 10 of the world's 13 climate zones, this is the land of fire (thanks to active Kīlauea Volcano) and ice (compliments of not-so-active Mauna Kea, topped with snow and expensive telescopes).

At just under a million years old, Hawai'i is the youngest of the Hawai-ian Islands. The east rift zone on Kīlauea has been spewing lava inter-mittently since January 3, 1983. Mauna Loa's explosions caused some changes back in 1984, and she's due to blow again any minute. These two are the only of the island's five volcanoes considered active; Mauna Kea and Hualālai are dormant, while Kohala is extinct.

FLORA AND FAUNA

Sugar was the main agricultural and economic staple of all the Islands, but especially the Big Island. The drive along the Hāmākua Coast from Hilo illustrates recent agricultural developments on the island. Sugarcane stalks have been replaced by orchards of macadamia-nut trees, eucalyptus, and specialty crops (from lettuce to strawberries). Macadamia nuts on the Big Island supply 90% of the state's yield, and coffee continues to be big business, dominating the mountains above Kealakekua Bay. Orchids keep farmers from Honok'a to Pāhoa afloat, and small organic farms produce meat, fruits, vegetables, and even goat cheese for high-end resort restaurants.

HISTORY

Though no longer home to the capital, the state's history is nonethe-less rooted in that of its namesake island, Hawai'i. Kamehameha, the greatest king in Hawaiian history and the man credited with uniting the Islands, was born here, raised in Waipi'o Valley, and died peace-fully in Kailua-Kona. The other man who most affected the history of Hawai'i, Captain James Cook, spent the bulk of his time here, docked in Kealakekua Bay (he landed first in Kaua'i, but had little contact with the natives there). Thus it was here that Western influence was first felt, and from here that it spread to the rest of the Islands.

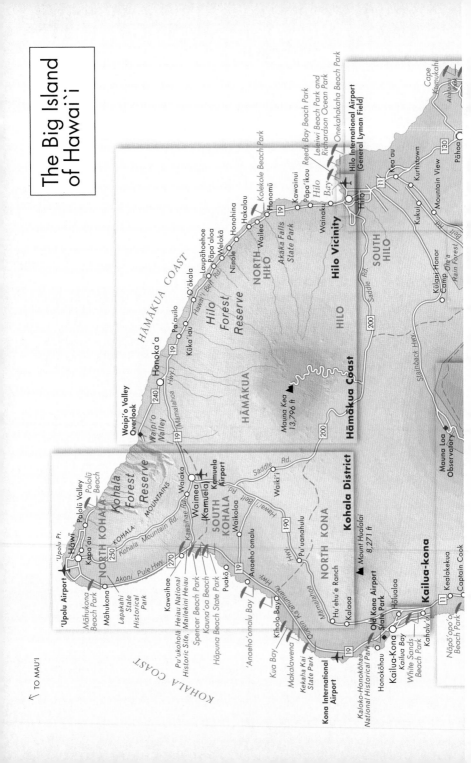

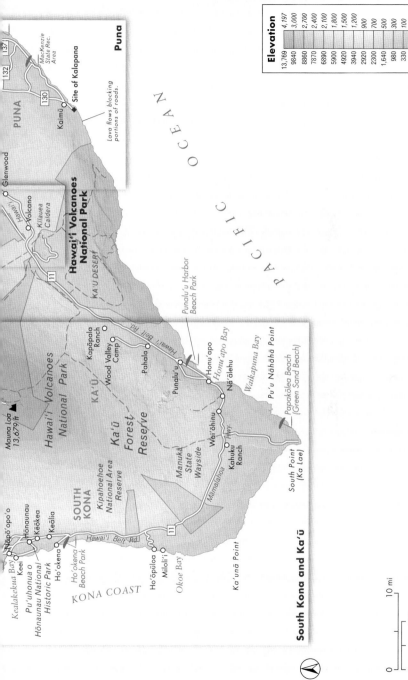

Elevation

feet	meters
13,769	4,197
9840	3,000
8860	2,700
7870	2,400
6890	2,100
5900	1,800
4920	1,500
3940	1,200
2920	900
2300	700
1,640	500
980	300
330	100

South Kona and Ka'ū

0   10 mi

0   10 km

PACIFIC OCEAN

Puna

MacKenzie State Rec. Area

Site of Kalapana

Lava flows blocking portions of roads.

Kaimū

PUNA

Glenwood

Volcano

Kīlauea Caldera

Hawai'i

Hawai'i Volcanoes National Park

KA'Ū DESERT

Punalu'u Harbor Beach Park

Honu'apo

Honu'apo Bay

Nā'ālehu

Waikapuna Bay

Pu'u Nāhāhā Point

Papakōlea Beach (Green Sand Beach)

South Point (Ka Lae)

Mauna Loa 13,679 ft

Hawai'i Volcanoes National Park

KA'Ū

Kapāpala Ranch

Wood Valley Camp

Pahala

Punalu'u

Ka'ū Forest Reserve

Kīpahoehoe National Area Reserve

SOUTH KONA

Manukā State Wayside

Wai'ōhinu

Kahuku Ranch

Māmalanoa

Kona COAST

Hawai'i Belt Rd.

Hawai'i Belt Rd.

Nāpō'opo'o

Kealakekua Bay

Keei

Pu'uhonua o Hōnaunau National Historic Park

Hōnaunau

Keōkea

Keālia

Ho'okena

Ho'okena Beach Park

Ho'ōpūloa

Miloli'i

Okoe Bay

Ka'unā Point

ON THE BIG ISLAND TODAY

The Big Island is in a period of great change. In the last few years, Wal-Mart, Kmart, and Costco opened; development went wild; and real estate prices skyrocketed. These sorts of things make locals unhappy. Work is underway to counteract some of the poorly planned development of the island. New developments are required by law to consult with a Hawaiian cultural expert, and most of the island's hotels have a Hawaiian historian on staff to teach visitors about the ancient customs and keep developers from breaking with Hawaiian traditions any more than is absolutely necessary.

EXPLORING THE BIG ISLAND

The first secret to enjoying the Big Island: rent a car, ideally one with four-wheel drive. The second: stay more than three days, or return again and again to really explore this fascinating place. With 266 mi of coastline made up of white coral, black lava, and a dusting of green-olivine beaches, interspersed with lava cliffs, emerald gorges, and splashing waterfalls, the Big Island can be overwhelming. Depending on the number of days you have available, it would be best to divide your time between the Hilo and Kona sides of the island in order to take in the attractions of each.

THE KOHALA DISTRICT AND WAIMEA

If you had only a weekend to spend on the Big Island, this is probably where you'd want to go, for a mix of the island's best beaches and swankiest hotels just minutes from ancient valleys and temples, waterfalls, and funky artist enclaves.

North of Kona International Airport, along Highway 19, brightly colored bougainvillea stands out in relief against miles of black lava fields stretching as far as the eye can

> **WORD OF MOUTH**
>
> "North Kohala is the birthplace of King Kamehameha, and it is lush, rural, charming, and historical. Be sure to check out the local papers for festivals and events. Pretty much everything is wonderful on the Big Island (except for Kona traffic)."
> —Kailani

see. Most of the lava flows, spreading from the mountain to the sea, are from the last eruptions of Mt. Hualālai, in 1800 and 1801. They are interrupted only by the green oases of irrigated golf courses surrounding the glamorous luxury resorts along the Kona-Kohala Coast. Just up the hill from Kohala, past Saddle Road (the route to Mauna Kea), Waimea offers a completely different experience from the rest of the island. Rolling green hills, large open pastures, cool evening breezes and morning mists, cattle everywhere, and regular rodeos are just a few of the surprises you'll stumble upon here in *paniolo* (Hawaiian for "cowboy") country. This is also where some of the island's top resort chefs are sent out to pasture, which makes Waimea an ideal place to find yourself stranded at dinnertime. Rounding the northern tip of the island, the arid coast suddenly gives way to the lush green valley of

Pololū in North Kohala, home of the sugar-plantations-turned-artsy enclaves of Hāwī and Kapaʻau. On the weekends, the pristine Kohala beaches are a meeting ground for both worlds, with tourists and locals alike enjoying the warm sun, white sand, and clear blue waters.

TOP ATTRACTIONS

Hāwī & Kapaʻau. These neighboring villages thrived during plantation days. There were hotels, saloons, and theaters—even a railroad. Today, both towns are blossoming once again, thanks to strong local communities and an influx of artists keen on honoring the towns' past. Old historic buildings have been restored and now hold shops, galleries, and eateries. In Kapaʻau, browse through the extensive

> ### GRAFFITI
>
> The black-lava fields lining Highway 19 are littered with white-coral graffiti. The first thing everyone asks is "where do the white rocks come from?" The answer is this: they're bits of coral from the ocean. Now that we know that coral isn't totally expendable, no one starts from scratch anymore. If you want to write a message in the lava, use the coral that's already out there. No one's message lasts for long, but that's part of the fun. Some local couples even have a tradition of writing their names in the same spot on the lava fields every year on their anniversary.

Hawaiian collection of the **Kohala Book Shop** (✉ 54-3885 Akoni Pule Hwy. 96755 ☎ 808/889–6400 ⊕ www.kohalabooks.com), the largest used bookstore in the state. ✉ Hwy. 270, North Kohala.

NEED A BREAK? If you're looking for something sweet, the **Kohala Coffee Mill** serves Tropical Dreams (✉ 55-3214 Akoni Pule Hwy., Hāwī 96719 ☎ 808/889–5577) ice cream that is da kine (translation: awesome, amazing—pick any superlative).

Kohala Mountain Road Lookout. The lookout here provides a splendid view of the Kohala Coast and Kawaihae Harbor far below. On clear days, you can see well beyond the resorts. It's one of the most scenic spots on the island and great for a picnic. Often, thick fog drifts in, casting an eerie mist over it all. ✉ Kohala Mountain Rd., Hwy. 250.

★ **Moʻokini Heiau.** This National Historic Landmark, an isolated heiau (an ancient place of worship), is so impressive in size it may give you goose bumps. Its foundations date to about AD 480, but the high priest Paʻao from Tahiti expanded it several centuries later to offer sacrifices to please his gods. You can still see the lava slab where hundreds of people were sacrificed, which gives this place a truly haunted feel. A nearby sign marks the place where Kamehameha I was born in 1758. The area is now part of the Kohala Historical Sites State Monument. ✉ Turn off Hwy. 270 at sign for ʻUpolu Airport, near Hāwī, and hike or drive in a four-wheel-drive vehicle 1½ mi southwest ☎ 808/974–6200.

Parker Ranch Historic Homes. The homes chronicle the life of John Palmer Parker (and his descendants), who founded Parker Ranch in 1847. Parker married the granddaughter of King Kamehameha and bought 2 acres of land from the king for the sum of $10. The original family residence, Mānā, "the house of spirit," is built entirely from native woods such as koa. Puʻōpelu, added to the estate in 1879, was the residence of Richard

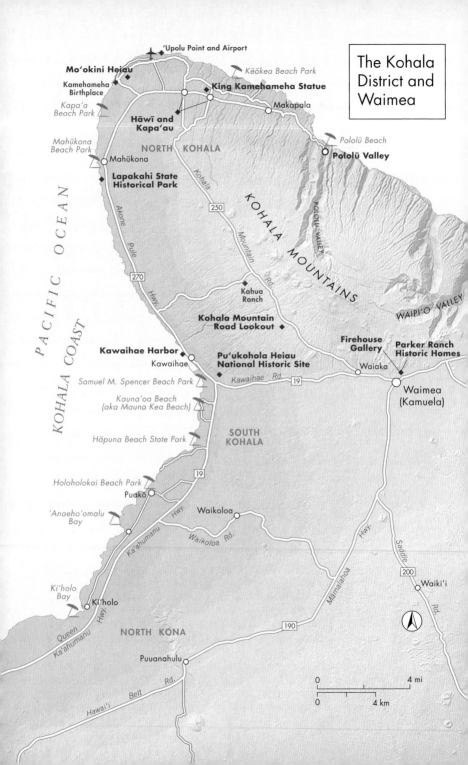

The Kohala
District and
Waimea

'Upolu Point and Airport

Mo'okini Heiau

Kamehameha
Birthplace

Kēōkea Beach Park

King Kamehameha Statue

*Kapa'a
Beach Park*

Makapala

Hāwī and
Kapa'au

*Mahūkona
Beach Park*

NORTH KOHALA

Mahūkona

Pololū Beach

Pololū Valley

Lapakahi State
Historical Park

Kohala

250

PACIFIC OCEAN

Akone Pule

270

KOHALA MOUNTAINS

POLOLŪ VALLEY

Mountain Rd.

Kahua
Ranch

WAIPI'O VALLEY

KOHALA COAST

Kohala Mountain
Road Lookout

Kawaihae Harbor

Kawaihae

Pu'ukohola Heiau
National Historic Site

Firehouse
Gallery

Parker Ranch
Historic Homes

Waiaka

Samuel M. Spencer Beach Park

Kawaihae Rd.

19

Waimea
(Kamuela)

*Kauna'oa Beach
(aka Mauna Kea Beach)*

SOUTH
KOHALA

Hāpuna Beach State Park

Holoholokai Beach Park

19

Puakō

Waikoloa

'Anaeho'omalu
Bay

Ka'ahumanu Hwy.

Waikoloa Rd.

Mamalahoa Hwy.

Saddle Rd.

200

Waiki'i

*Ki'holo
Bay*

Ki'holo

NORTH KONA

190

Queen Ka'ahumanu Hwy.

Puuanahulu

Hawai'i Belt Rd.

0   4 mi

0   4 km

Smart, a sixth-generation Parker who expanded the house to make room for his European art collection. The Mānā Road Tour and the Cattle Country Tour explore Parker Ranch, Hawaii's oldest working cattle ranch, and offer insight into the intriguing Parker family history. Also available are horseback rides, ATV rides, hunting expeditions, and walking tours. Stop by the Gear Up & Go desk at the Parker Ranch Shopping Center for information before visiting the homes. ⊠*Parker Ranch Shopping Center, 67-1185 Māmalahoa Hwy., Waimea* ☎*808/885–7655 or 808/885–5433, 877/885–7999* ⊕*www.parker ranch.com* ⊠*Homes $10* ⊙ *Homes Tues.–Sat. 10–5.*

> **WAIMEA OR KAMUELA?**
>
> Both, actually. The name of the Waimea post office is Kamuela, while the name of the town itself is Waimea. Some say the post office is named for the son of the founder of Parker Ranch.

Pololū Valley. A steep trail leads through this lush green valley and down to black-sand Pololū Beach, which edges a rugged coastline ribboned by silver waterfalls. ⊠*End of Hwy. 270.*

★ **Puʻukoholā Heiau National Historic Site.** In 1790 a prophet told King Kamehameha I to build a *heiau* (temple) on top of Puʻukoholā (Hill of the Whale) and dedicate it to the war god Kūkāʻilimoku by sacrificing his principal rival, Keōua Kūahuʻula. By doing so the king would achieve his goal of conquering the Hawaiian Islands. The prophecy came true in 1810. A short walk over arid landscape leads from the visitor center to **Puʻukoholā Heiau** and to **Mailekini Heiau,** a navigational aid constructed about 1550. An even older temple, dedicated to the shark gods, lies submerged just offshore. For safety reasons, visitors are no longer able to actually enter the heiaus. ⊠*Just off Hwy. 270, 62-3601 Kawaihae Rd., Kawaihae* ☎*808/882–7218* ⊕*www.nps.gov* ⊠*Free* ⊙*Daily 7:45–4:55.*

WORTH NOTING

Firehouse Gallery. Walk across the Parker Ranch Shopping Center parking lot to a historic 77-year-old fire station, now a gallery, to glimpse what the artists in Hāmākua and Kohala are up to. The Waimea Arts Council sponsors free *kaha kiʻis* (one-person shows). ⊠*Near main stoplight in Waimea, toward Kailua-Kona on Hwy. 190, Waimea* ☎*808/887–1052.*

Kawaihae Harbor. This commercial harbor, where the first cattle in Hawaiʻi came ashore in 1793, is a hub of activity. It's especially busy on weekends, when paddlers and local fishing boats float on the waves. Second in size only to Hilo Harbor on the east coast, the harbor is often home to the *Makaliʻi,* one of three Hawaiian sailing canoes. King Kamehameha I and his men launched their canoes from here when they set out to conquer the Islands. ⊠*Kawaihae Harbor Rd. off Hwy. 270.*

King Kamehameha Statue. This is the original of the statue in front of the Judiciary Building on King Street in Honolulu. It was cast in Florence in 1880 but lost at sea when the German ship transporting it sank near the Falkland Islands. A replica was shipped to Honolulu. Two years later an American sea captain found the original in a Port Stanley (Falkland

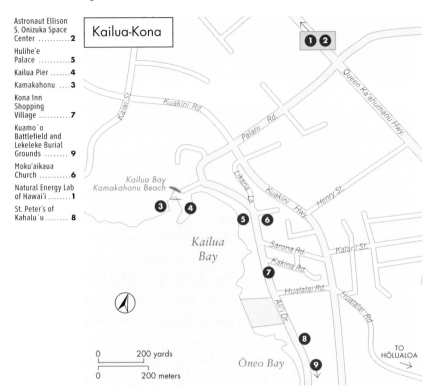

Islands) junk yard and brought it to the Big Island. The legislature voted
to erect it near Kamehameha's birthplace. Every year, on King Kamehameha Day (June 11), a magnificent abundance of floral lei adorns the
image of Hawai'i's great king. It's in front of the old Kohala Courthouse
next to the highway. ⊠ *Hwy. 270, Kapa'au.*

★ **Lapakahi State Historical Park.** A self-guided, 1-mi walking tour leads
through the ruins of the once-prosperous fishing village Koai'e, which
dates as far back as the 15th century. Displays illustrate early Hawaiian fishing and farming techniques, salt gathering, games, and legends.
A park guide is often on-site to answer questions. Since the shoreline
near the state park is an officially designated Marine Life Conservation District, and part of the site itself is considered sacred, swimming
is discouraged. For some reason a distinction is made between swimming and snorkeling, which is fortunate because the snorkeling here is
superb. ⊠ *Hwy. 270, between Kawaihae and Māhukona, North Kohala*
🕾 *808/974–6200 or 808/882–6207* 🖃 *Free* ☉ *Daily 8–4.*

**NEED A
BREAK?**

If you're in the mood for a steaming latte and a warm pastry, stop by
Waimea Coffee Company (⊠ *Parker Sq., 65-1279 Kawaihae Rd., Waimea*
🕾 *808/885–8915*), sit out on their veranda, and try to believe you're in
Hawai'i and not West Virginia.

KAILUA-KONA

A surprising number of historic sites are tucked among the open-air restaurants and trinket shops that line Aliʻi Drive, the main drag of Kailua-Kona. Not just your average touristy seaside village, Kailua-Kona is where King Kamehameha I died in 1819 and where his successor, King Liholiho, broke the ancient *kapu* (roughly translated as "forbidden," it was the strict code of conduct Islanders were compelled to follow) by publicly sitting and eating with women. The following year, on April 4, 1820, the first Christian missionaries came ashore here, changing the Islands forever. If you want to know more about the village's fascinating past, arrange for a 75-minute guided walking tour with the **Kona Historical Society** (✉ *81-6551 Māmalahoa Hwy.* ☎ *808/323–3222* ⊕ *www.konahistorical.org*).

Kailua-Kona enjoys year-round sunshine—except for the rare deluge. Mornings offer cooler weather, smaller crowds, and more birds singing in the banyan trees, but afternoon outings are great for cool drinks while gazing out over the ocean.

■ TIP➔The easiest place to park in town is at King Kamehameha's Kona Beach Hotel ($3 per hour). Some free parking is also available: when you enter Kailua via Palani Road (Highway 190), turn left onto Kuakini Highway; drive for a half block, and turn right into the small marked parking lot. Walk *makai* (toward the ocean) on Likana Lane a half block to Aliʻi Drive and you'll be in the heart of Kailua-Kona.

TOP ATTRACTIONS

OFF THE
BEATEN
PATH

Hōlualoa. Hugging the hillside above Kealakekua Bay, the tiny village of Hōlualoa is just up Hualālai Road from Kailua-Kona. A charming surprise, it's the kind of place where locals sit on their porches or in front of the stores and shoot the breeze all day long. It's comprised almost entirely of galleries in which all types of artists, from woodworkers to jewelry-makers and more traditional painters, work in their studios in back and sell the finished product up front. Formerly coffee country, there are still quite a few coffee farms offering free tours and cups of joe. Duck into the only café in town, the cleverly named **Hōluakoa Cafe** (✉ *76-5900 Mamalahoa Hwy.96725* ☎ *808/322–2233*), and grab a cup to sip while you stroll through town.

❺ ★ **Huliheʻe Palace.** Fronted by a wrought-iron gate decorated with an elaborate crest, Huliheʻe Palace is one of only three royal palaces in the United States. The two-story residence was built by Governor John Adams Kuakini in 1838, a year after he completed Mokuʻaikaua Church. It's constructed of local materials, including lava, coral, koa wood, and ʻōhiʻa timber. The oversize doors and furniture bear witness to the size of some of the Hawaiian people. On weekday afternoons hula schools rehearse on the grounds. Huliheʻe Palace is operated by the Daughters of Hawaiʻi, a nonprofit focused on maintaining the heritage of the Islands. Free concerts are given regularly. ■ TIP➔Huliheʻe Palace suffered fairly severe damage in the October 2006 earthquakes. Due to ongoing repairs, limited tours are conducted. Call ahead for the day's schedule. ✉ *75-5718 Aliʻi Dr.* ☎ *808/329–1877* ⊕ *www.huliheepalace.org* 🖾 *$5* ⊙ *Weekdays 9–4, weekends 10–4.*

7 Kona Inn Shopping Village. Originally a hotel, the Kona Inn was built in 1928 to woo a new wave of wealthy travelers. As newer condos and resorts opened along the Kona and Kohala coasts, it lost much of its appeal and was transformed into a mall with dozens of clothing boutiques, art galleries, gift shops, and island-style eateries. Broad lawns with coconut trees on the ocean side are lovely for afternoon picnics. Prior to the construction of the inn, the personal *heiau* of King Liholiho stood on this shore. ⊠ *75-5744 Ali'i Dr96740.*

NEED A BREAK?   If it's late afternoon, it's time to unwind with one of those umbrella drinks. For cocktails head to the **Kona Inn Restaurant** (⊠ *75-5744 Ali'i Dr.* ☎ *808/329–4455*), a local favorite.

1 Natural Energy Lab of Hawai'i. Driving south from the Kona International Airport toward Kailua-Kona you'll spot a large mysterious group of buildings with a photovoltaic (solar) panel installation just inside its gate. Although it looks like a top-secret military station, this is the site of the Natural Energy Lab of Hawaii, NELHA for short, where scientists, researchers, and entrepreneurs are developing and marketing everything from new uses for solar power to energy-efficient air-conditioning systems and environmentally friendly aquaculture techniques. Visitors are welcome at the lab, and there are 1½-hour tours for those interested in learning more about the experiments being conducted. ⊠ *73-4460 Queen Ka'ahumanu Hwy. 101* ☎ *808/329–7341, 808/329–8073 for tour information* ⊕ *www.nelha.org* ⧉ *Free, $8 tour* ☉ *Weekdays 8–4; tours Tues., Wed., Thurs. at 10.*

WORTH NOTING

2 Astronaut Ellison S. Onizuka Space Center. This informative museum 7 mi north of Kailua-Kona, at the airport, was opened as a tribute to Hawai'i's first astronaut, who was killed in the 1986 *Challenger* disaster. The space center has computer-interactive exhibits. You can launch a miniature rocket and rendezvous with an object in space, feel the effects of gyroscopic stabilization, participate in hands-on science activities, and view educational films. ⊠ *Keāhole–Kona International Airport, Kailua-Kona* ☎ *808/329–3441* ⧉ *$3 adult, $1 child (12 and under)* ☉ *Daily 8:30–4:30.*

4 Kailua Pier. Though most fishing boats use Honokōhau Harbor, this pier dating from 1918 is still a hub of ocean activity. Outrigger canoe teams practice, and tour boats depart throughout the day. Each October nearly 1,800 international athletes swim 2.4 mi from the pier to begin the grueling Ironman Triathlon. ⊠ *Next to King Kamehameha's Kona Beach Hotel; seawall is between Kailua Pier and Hulihe'e Palace on Ali'i Dr.*

3 Kamakahonu. King Kamehameha I spent his last years, from 1812 to ★ 1819, near what is now King Kamehameha's Kona Beach Hotel. Part of what was once a 4-acre homestead complete with several houses and religious sites has been swallowed by Kailua Pier, but a replica of the temple, **Ahu'ena Heiau,** keeps history alive. Free tours start from King Kamehameha's Kona Beach Hotel. ⊠ *75-5660 Palani Rd.* ☎ *808/327–0123* ⧉ *Free, Donations accepted* ☉ *Tours available on request (reservations only).*

⑨ Kuamo'o Battlefield and Lekeleke Burial Grounds. In 1819 an estimated 300 Hawaiians were killed on this vast, black-lava field. After the death of his father, Kamehameha I, Liholiho was crowned king; shortly thereafter he ate at the table of women, thereby breaking an ancient *kapu*. Chief Kekuaokalani, who held radically different views about religious traditions, unsuccessfully challenged King Liholiho in battle. The site of the battle is now filled with terraced graves. ⊠*South end of Ali'i Dr.*

⑥ Moku'aikaua Church. A thatch hut, erected on this site by missionaries
★ in 1820, served as the first Christian church on the Islands. A more permanent structure was built in 1836 with black stone from an abandoned *heiau*. The stone was mortared with white coral and topped by an impressive steeple. Inside, behind a panel of gleaming koa wood, is a model of the brig *Thaddeus*. ⊠*75-5713 Ali'i Dr.* ☎*808/329–0655.*

NEED A BREAK? The laid-back Island Lava Java (⊠ **75-5799 Ali'i Dr. 96740** ☎**808/327–2161**), in the Ali' Sunset Plaza, has great coffee and the best and biggest cinnamon rolls on the island. In the afternoon stop by for fresh fish or *kālua* pig tacos, sandwiches, fruit smoothies, and ice cream. The large outdoor seating area has a bird's-eye view of the ocean. Locals hang out here to read the paper, play board games, or just watch the surf.

⑧ St. Peter's of Kahalu'u. The definition of "quaint" with its crisp white-and-blue trim, this tiny old-fashioned steeple church sits on the rocks overlooking the ocean near Kahalu'u Beach. It has appeared on many a Kailua-Kona postcard, and its charm and views bring hundreds of visitors every year. ⊠*Ali'i Dr., north of mile marker 5, 96740.*

SOUTH KONA AND KEALAKEKUA BAY

South of Kailua-Kona, Highway 11 hugs splendid coastlines, leaving busy streets behind. A detour along the winding narrow roads in the mountains above takes you straight to the heart of coffee country, where lush plantations and jaw-dropping views offer a taste of what Hawai'i was like before the resorts took over. Take a tour at one of the coffee farms to find out what the big deal is about Kona coffee. A half-hour back on the highway will lead

WORD OF MOUTH

"My husband was never a coffee drinker until he had Kona coffee. We brought several bags of Kona beans home and keep them in the freezer—he drinks half a pot every morning now. We're on the last bag . . . I told him that's fine, we'll just have to go back to the Big Island and get some more!"   —luvtravl

you to magical Kealakekua Bay, where Captain James Cook arrived in 1778, changing the Islands forever. Hawaiian spinner dolphins frolic in the bay, now a marine preserve nestled alongside impossibly high green cliffs more reminiscent of Ireland than posters of Hawai'i. Snorkeling and kayaking are superb here, so you may want to rent a kayak along Highway 11 and bring your snorkel gear to spend a few hours exploring the coral reefs. The winding road above Kealakekua Bay is home to a quaint little painted church, as well as several reasonably priced B&Bs

COFFEE-FARM TOURS

Several coffee farms around the South Kona and Upcountry Kona coffee-belt area from Hōlualoa to Hōnaunau welcome visitors. You'll learn about the whole process, from cherry-picking (coffee beans are commonly referred to as "cherries" because of their red husks) to roasting and packaging. Often, macadamia nuts are also for sale, and the brew, of course, is always ready. Some tours are self-guided, and most are free, with the exception of Kona Coffee Living History Farm.

Bay View Coffee Farm. ⬠ P.O. Box 680, Honaunau., 96726 ☎ 808/328-9658 or 800/662-5880.

Greenwell Farms. ⬠ 81-6581 Māmalahoa Hwy., Kealakekua ☎ 808/323-2862.

Hōlualoa Kona Coffee Company. ⬠ 77-6261 Old Māmalahoa Hwy., Hwy. 180, Hōlualoa ☎ 808/322-9937 or 800/334-0348.

Kona Coffee Living History Farm. ⬠ 81-6551 Māmalahoa Hwy., Kealakekua ☎ 808/323-3222.

Royal Kona Coffee Museum & Coffee Mill. ⬠ 83-5427 Māmalahoa Hwy., next to tree house in Hōnaunau ☎ 808/328-2511.

with stunning views. The communities surrounding the bay (Kainaliu and Captain Cook) are brimming with local and transplanted artists, making them great places to stop for a meal, some unique gifts, or an afternoon stroll.

TOP ATTRACTIONS

Captain Cook Monument. No one knows for sure what happened on February 14, 1779, when English explorer Captain James Cook was killed on this spot. He had chosen Kealakekua Bay as a landing place in November 1778. Cook, arriving during the celebration of Makahiki the harvest season, was welcomed at first. Some Hawaiians saw him as an incarnation of the god Lono. Cook's party sailed away in February 1779, but a freak storm forced his damaged ship back to Kealakekua Bay. The Hawaiians were not so welcoming this time. Cook's godly status was revoked when he was bested by a simple storm, and various confrontations arose. The theft of a longboat brought Cook and an armed party ashore to reclaim it. One thing led to another: shots were fired, daggers and spears were thrown, and Captain Cook fell, mortally wounded. Strangely enough, this didn't deter other Westerners from visiting the Islands; Captain James Cook and his party had effectively introduced the Hawaiian Islands to the world. A 27-foot-high obelisk marks the spot where Captain Cook died on the shore of Kealakekua Bay. Locals like to point out that the land the monument sits on is British territory (to clarify: the British government owns the land that the monument occupies, but it's still U.S. territory). The three-hour 2½-mi hike to get to the monument begins at the trailhead 100 yards off Highway 11 on Nāpōʻopoʻo Road. Look for the downslope trail opposite three large royal palm trees. You can also kayak across the bay to the monument.

FodorśChoice ★ **Kealakekua Bay.** Though it suffered some damage in the October 2006 earthquakes (a large chunk of the cliffs overhead broke off), this bay remains one of the most beautiful spots on the island. Dramatic cliffs

Kealakekua Bay is one of the most beautiful spots on the Big Island.

surround crystal-clear, turquoise water chock-full of stunning coral and tropical fish. Before the arrival of Captain Cook in the late 18th century, this now tranquil state marine park and sanctuary lay at the center of Hawaiian life. Historians consider Kealakekua Bay to be the birthplace of the post-contact era.

NEED A BREAK?

Before or after winding down Nāpōʻopoʻo Road, treat yourself to awesome views of Kealakekua Bay at the **Coffee Shack** (✉ *83-5799 Māmalahoa Hwy.* ☎ *808/328–9555* ⊕ *www.coffeeshack.com*), a deli and pizza place with just nine tables on an open, breezy lānai. The bread and pastries are home-baked, the eggs Benedict is a local breakfast favorite, the sandwiches are generous, and the staff is friendly.

★ **Puʻuhonua O Hōnaunau (Place of Refuge).** This 180-acre National Historic Park was once a safe haven for women in times of war as well as for *kapu* breakers, criminals, and prisoners of war—anyone who could get inside the 1,000-foot-long wall, which was 10 feet high and 17 feet thick, could avoid punishment. **Hale-o-Keawe Heiau,** built in 1650 as the burial place of King Kamehameha I's ancestor Keawe, has been restored. South of the park, tide pools offer another delight—most notably the crowd of sea turtles feeding there regularly. Demonstrations of poi pounding, canoe making, and local games are occasionally scheduled. ✉ *Rte. 160, about 20 mi south of Kailua-Kona* ☎ *808/328–2288* ⊕ *www. nps.gov/puho* 🎫 *$3 per person, $5 per vehicle* ☉ *Park daily 6 AM– 8 PM; visitor center daily 8 AM–4 PM.*

WORTH NOTING

Greenwell Store. Established in 1850, the homestead of Henry N. Greenwell served as cattle ranch, sheep station, store, post office, and family home all in one. Now, all that remains is the 1875 stone structure, which is listed on the National Register of Historic Places. It houses a fascinating museum that has exhibits on ranching and coffee farming. It's also headquarters for the **Kona Historical Society**, which organizes walking tours of Kailua-Kona. ⊠ *81-6551 Māmalahoa Hwy.* ☎ *808/323–3222* ⊕ *www.konahistorical.org* ✉ *$7 adult, $4 child (12 and under)* ☉ *Weekdays 10–2.*

Kainaliu. Like many of the Big Island's old plantation towns, Kainaliu is experiencing a bit of a renaissance. In addition to a ribbon of funky old stores, many of them traditional Japanese family-operated shops, a handful of new galleries and shops have sprung up in the last several years. ⊠ *Hwy. 11, mile markers 112–114.*

St. Benedict's Painted Church. The walls, columns, and ceiling of this Roman Catholic church depict colorful biblical scenes through the paintbrush of Belgian-born priest Father Velghe. Mass is still held every weekend. The view of Kealakekua Bay from the entrance is amazing. ⊠ *Painted Church Rd. off Hwy. 160, Hōnaunau* ☎ *808/328–2227.*

KA'Ū AND KA LAE (SOUTH POINT)

The most desolate region of the island, Ka'ū is nonetheless home to some spectacular sights. Mark Twain wrote some of his finest prose here, where macadamia-nut farms, green-sand beaches, and tiny villages offer largely undiscovered beauty. The 50-mi drive from Kailua-Kona to windswept South Point, where the first Polynesians came ashore as early as AD 750, winds away from the ocean through a surreal moonscape of lava-covered forests. Past South Point, glimpses of the ocean return and hidden Green Sand Beach tempts hikers to stop awhile before the highway narrows and returns to the coast, passing verdant cattle pastures and sheer cliffs on the way to the black-sand beach of Punalu'u, the nesting place of the Hawaiian sea turtle.

TOP ATTRACTIONS

Fodor's Choice
★ **Hawai'i Volcanoes National Park.**
See highlighted feature in this chapter.

★ **Ka Lae (South Point).** Windswept Ka Lae is the southernmost point of land in the United States. A few abandoned structures were used in the 19th and early 20th centuries to lower cattle and produce to ships anchored below the cliffs. It's thought that the first Polynesians came ashore here. Check out the old canoe-mooring holes that are carved through the rocks, possibly by settlers from Tahiti as early as AD 750. Some artifacts, thought to have been left by early voyagers who never settled here, date to AD 300. Driving down to the point, you pass Kama'oa Wind Farm; although the rows of windmill turbines are still fueled by the nearly constant winds sweeping across this coastal plain, the equipment and facilities are falling into disrepair due to neglect. Continue down the road (parts at the end are unpaved, but driveable), bear left when the

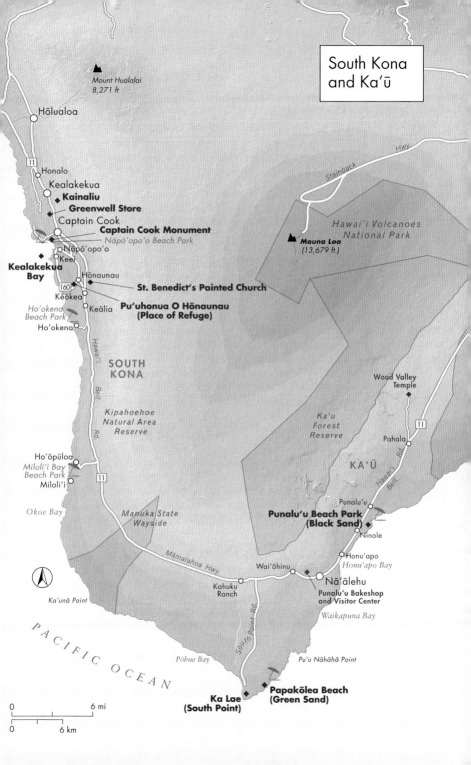

South Kona and Ka'ū

Mount Hualalai
8,271 ft

Hōlualoa

11
Honalo

Kealakekua

Kainaliu

Greenwell Store

Captain Cook

Captain Cook Monument

Nāpō'opo'o Beach Park

Nāpō'opo'o

Keei

Kealakekua Bay

Hōnaunau

160
Keōkea

St. Benedict's Painted Church

Keālia

Pu'uhonua O Hōnaunau (Place of Refuge)

Ho'okena Beach Park

Ho'okena

Hawai'i Belt Rd.

SOUTH KONA

Kipahoehoe Natural Area Reserve

Ho'ōpūloa

Miloli'i Bay Beach Park

Miloli'i

Okoe Bay

Manuka State Wayside

11

Stainback Hwy.

Hawai'i Volcanoes National Park

Mauna Loa
(13,679 ft.)

Wood Valley Temple

Ka'ū Forest Reserve

Pahala

11

KA'Ū

Hawai'i Belt Rd.

Punalu'u

Punalu'u Beach Park (Black Sand)

Ninole

Honu'apo

Honu'apo Bay

Māmalahoa Hwy.

Wai'ōhinu

Nā'ālehu

Punalu'u Bakeshop and Visitor Center

Waikapuna Bay

Kahuku Ranch

South Point Rd.

Pōhue Bay

PACIFIC OCEAN

Ka'unā Point

Pu'u Nāhāhā Point

Ka Lae (South Point)

Papakōlea Beach (Green Sand)

0   6 mi

0   6 km

road forks and park in the lot at the end; walk past the boat hoists toward the little lighthouse. South Point is just past the lighthouse at the southernmost cliff. ⊠ *Turn right past mile marker 70 on Māmalahoa Hwy., then drive 12 mi down South Point Rd.*

NEED A BREAK?
Punaluʻu Bakeshop & Visitor Center (⊠ *Hwy. 11, Nāʻālehu* 🕾 *808/929–7343* ⊙ *Daily 9–5*) is a bit of a tourist trap, but it's also a good spot to grab a snack before heading back out on the road. Try some Portuguese sweet bread or a homemade ice-cream sandwich paired with some local Kaʻū coffee (that's right, not Kona, but equally tasty).

Papakōlea Beach (Green Sand Beach). It takes awhile to get down and even longer to get back, but where else are you going to see green sand? Add to that the fact that the rock formations surrounding the beach are surreally beautiful, and this is a detour worth taking. ⊠ *2½ mi northeast of South Point.*

Punaluʻu Beach Park (Black Sand Beach). This easily accessed beach is well worth at least a short stop for two reasons: it's a beautiful black-sand beach, and it's where the Hawaiian sea turtles like to nest so the water's swarming with them. The turtles are used to people by now, and they'll swim right alongside you. ⊠ *Turn right down driveway into beach off Hwy. 11 south. Beach is well marked off hwy.*

OFF THE BEATEN PATH
Pahala. About 16 mi east of Nāʻālehu, beyond Punaluʻu Beach Park, Highway 11 flashes past this little town. You'll miss it if you blink. Pahala is a perfect example of a former sugar-plantation town. Behind it, along a wide cane road, you enter Wood Valley, once a prosperous community, now just a road heavily scented by eucalyptus trees, coffee blossoms, and night-blooming jasmine. Here you can find **Wood Valley Temple** (🕾 *808/928–8539*), a quiet Tibetan Buddhist retreat that welcomes guests who seek serenity and solitude.

VOLCANO VILLAGE

Few visitors realize that in addition to "the Volcano" there's also Volcano, the town. Conveniently located next to—you guessed it—Hawaiʻi Volcanoes National Park, Volcano Village is a charming little hamlet in the woods that offers a dozen or so inns and B&Bs, a decent Thai restaurant, some killer (although strangely expensive) pizza, and a handful of things to see and do that don't include the village's namesake. For years, writers, artists, and meditative types have been coming to the Volcano to seek inspiration, and many of them have settled in and around Volcano Village. Artist studios (open to the public by appointment) are scattered throughout the hills, and writers' retreats are hidden in the tranquil rain forests surrounding the area. If you plan to explore the Volcano, spending a night or two in Volcano Village is the ideal way to go about it.

TOP ATTRACTIONS

Kīlauea Caverns of Fire. Strap on a miner's hat and gloves and get ready to explore the underbelly of the world's largest active volcano. Tours through these fascinating caves and lava tubes underneath the volcano must be arranged in advance but are well worth a little extra planning. The largest lava tube in the world is here—40 mi long, it has 80-foot ceilings and is 80 feet wide. Tours can range from safe and easy (suitable for children five years old and up) to long and adventurous. ⊠ *Off Hwy. 11, between Kurtistown and Mountain View* ☎ *808/217–2363* ⊕ *www.kilaueacavernsoffire.com* 🖃 *$29 for walking tour* 🕘 *By appointment only.*

Volcano Garden Arts. On the former Hopper Estate, the Volcano Garden Arts complex includes a gallery, several acres of landscaped sculpture gardens, and dozens of art studios all housed in redwood buildings built in 1908. The grounds are immaculately maintained, and there are several trails leading up to and through the surrounding rain forest. There's a new and delicious vegetarian café, and a recently renovated one-bedroom "artist's cottage" is available for rent on the estate grounds as well. ⊠ *19-3834 Old Volcano Rd.* ☎ *808/985–8979* ⊕ *www.volcanogardenarts.com* 🖃 *Free* 🕘 *Mon.–Sat. 10–4, Sun. 11–4.*

Volcano Golf Course and Country Club. Don't let the "country club" bit fool you. This is nothing like the snooty courses on the Kohala coast. First off, the green fees are way lower; second, the course is well maintained but not overly manicured; and third, there are rarely crowds, so play is continuous and moves quickly. The course itself is reasonably challenging—an 18-hole, par 72 course—but the real draws are the views and the location. It might be the only course in the world built on an active volcano (Kīlauea). ⊠ *Pi'i Mauna Dr., down road from entrance to Volcanoes National Park, toward 30 mile marker* ☎ *808/967–7331* ⊕ *www.volcanogolfshop.com* 🖃 *$71* 🕘 *Daily 7–5.*

Volcano Winery. The wines here are good, but not amazing. The primary reason to visit is the novelty of the winery itself—wine produced from an active volcano is undeniably interesting and appealing. And it makes for a great, unique (and fairly reasonable) gift to bring home. The winery is in a pleasant setting, looking out over the vineyard and nearby golf course; staff are friendly and helpful; and the gift store has a well-chosen selection of local crafts and other goods. ⊠ *35 Pi'i Mauna Dr.* ☎ *808/967–7772* ⊕ *www.volcanowinery.com* 🖃 *Free tasting* 🕘 *Daily 10–5:30.*

PUNA

The Puna District is a wild place in every sense of the word. The jagged black coastline is changing all the time; the trees are growing out of control to form canopies over the few paved roads; the land is dirt-cheap and there are no building codes; and the people, well, there's something about living in an area that could be destroyed by lava at any moment (as Kalapana was in 1990) that makes the laws of modern society seem silly. So it is that Puna has its well-deserved reputation as the "outlaw" region of the Big Island. That said, it's a unique place that's well worth a detour, especially if you're in this part of the island anyway. There are volcanically heated springs, tide pools bursting with interesting sea life, and some mighty fine people-watching opportunities in Pāhoa, a funky little town that the outlaws call home. This is also farm country (yes,

Continued on page 334

HAWAI'I VOLCANOES NATIONAL PARK

Exploring the surface of the world's most active volcano—from the moonscape craters at the summit to the red-hot lava flows on the coast to the kīpuka, pockets of vegetation miraculously left untouched—is the ultimate ecotour and one of Hawai'i's must-dos.

The park sprawls over 520 square miles and encompasses Kīlauea and Mauna Loa, two of the five volcanoes that formed the Big Island nearly half a million years ago. Kīlauea, youngest and most rambunctious of the Hawaiian volcanoes, erupted at its summit from the 19th century through 1982. Since then, the top of the volcano had been more or less quiet, frequently shrouded in mist; an eruption in the Halema'uma'u Crater in 2008 ended this period of relative inactivity.

Kilauea's eastern side sprang to life on January 3, 1983, shooting molten lava four stories high. This eruption has been ongoing, and lava flows are generally steady and slow, appearing and disappearing from view. Over 500 acres have been added to Hawai'i's eastern coast since the activity began, and scientists say this eruptive phase is not likely to end anytime soon.

If you're lucky, you'll be able to catch creation at its most elemental—when molten lava meets the ocean, cools, and solidifies into brand-new stretches of coastline. Even if lava-viewing conditions aren't ideal, you can hike 150 miles of trails; camp amid wide expanses of 'a'ā (rough) and *pahoehoe* (smooth) lava; or sip cocktails at Volcano House, a hotel perched on the rim of Kīlauea Caldera. There's nothing quite like it.

🏠 P.O. Box 52, Hawai'i Volcanoes National Park, HI 96718

☎ 808/985–6000

🌐 www.nps.gov/havo

💳 $10 per vehicle; $5 for pedestrians and bicyclists. Ask about passes. Admission is good for seven consecutive days.

🕐 The park is open daily, 24 hours. Kīlauea Visitor Center: 7:45 am–5 pm. Thomas A. Jaggar Museum: 8:30–5. Volcano Art Center Gallery: 9–5.

(top) Kīlauea Iki Trail
(left) Fuming rim of Pu'u' Ō'ō, source of the current eruption

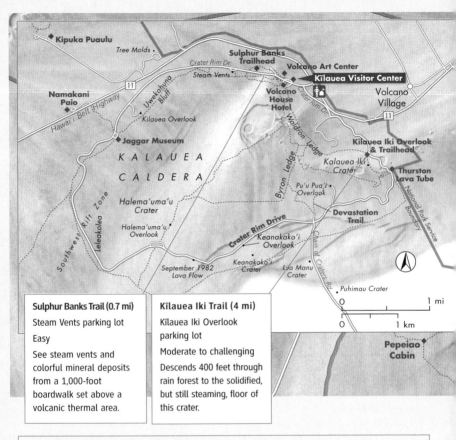

Sulphur Banks Trail (0.7 mi)

Steam Vents parking lot

Easy

See steam vents and colorful mineral deposits from a 1,000-foot boardwalk set above a volcanic thermal area.

Kīlauea Iki Trail (4 mi)

Kīlauea Iki Overlook parking lot

Moderate to challenging

Descends 400 feet through rain forest to the solidified, but still steaming, floor of this crater.

SEEING THE SUMMIT

The best way to explore the summit of Kīlauea is to cruise 11-mile Crater Rim Drive, which encircles the volcano's massive caldera. Volcano House's dining room offers front-row views of this eerie, awe-inspiring spot, which bears an uncanny resemblance to those old Apollo moon photos.

Depending on the number of stops you make, it'll take one to three hours to complete the circuit. Highlights include sulfur and steam vents, a walk-through lava tube, and the southwest rift zone—deep fissures, fractures, and gullies along Kīlauea's flanks.

There's also Halemaʻumaʻu Crater, an awesome depression in Kīlauea Caldera measuring 3,000 feet across and nearly 300 feet deep. When skies are clear, this is a good place to see Mauna Loa and Mauna Kea.

The Thomas A. Jaggar Museum offers breathtaking looks at Halemaʻumaʻu and Kīlauea Caldera, geologic displays, video presentations of volcanic eruptions, and exhibits of seismographs once used by volcanologists at the adjacent Hawaiian Volcano Observatory (not open to the public).

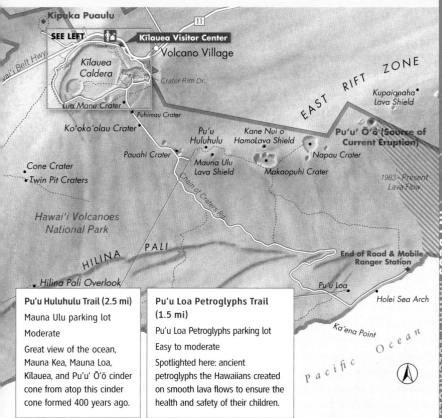

Pu'u Huluhulu Trail (2.5 mi)

Mauna Ulu parking lot

Moderate

Great view of the ocean, Mauna Kea, Mauna Loa, Kīlauea, and Pu'u' Ō'ō cinder cone from atop this cinder cone formed 400 years ago.

Pu'u Loa Petroglyphs Trail (1.5 mi)

Pu'u Loa Petroglyphs parking lot

Easy to moderate

Spotlighted here: ancient petroglyphs the Hawaiians created on smooth lava flows to ensure the health and safety of their children.

SEEING LAVA

Before you head out to find flowing lava, pinpoint the safe viewing spots at the Visitor Center. One of the best places usually is at the end of 19-mile Chain of Craters Road. Magnificent plumes of steam rise where the rivers of liquid fire meet the sea.

There are three guarantees about lava flows in HVNP. First: They constantly change. Second: Because of that, you can't predict when and where you'll be able to see them. Third: New land formed when lava meets the sea is highly unstable and can collapse at any time. Never go into areas that have been closed.

■TIP→The view of brilliant red-orange lava flowing from Kīlauea's east rift zone is most dramatic at night.

People watching lava flow at HVNP

PLANNING YOUR TRIP TO HVNP

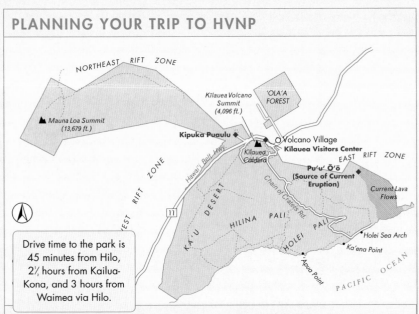

NORTHEAST RIFT ZONE

Kīlauea Volcano
Summit
(4,096 ft.)

'OLA'A
FOREST

▲ Mauna Loa Summit
(13,679 ft.)

Kipuka Puaulu ◆

O Volcano Village
Kīlauea Visitors Center

Kīlauea
Caldera

EAST RIFT ZONE

**Pu'u' Ō'ō
(Source of Current
Eruption)**

Current Lava
Flows

WEST RIFT ZONE

Hawai'i Belt Hwy.

Chain of Craters Rd.

KA'U DESERT

HILINA PALI

HOLEI PALI

11

Holei Sea Arch

Ka'ena Point

Apua Point

PACIFIC OCEAN

Drive time to the park is
45 minutes from Hilo,
2¼ hours from Kailua-
Kona, and 3 hours from
Waimea via Hilo.

Lava entering the ocean

WHERE TO START

Begin your visit at the Visitor Center, where you'll find maps, books, and DVDs; information on trails, ranger-led walks, and special events; and current weather, road, and lava-viewing conditions. Free volcano-related film showings, lectures, and other presentations are regularly scheduled.

WEATHER

Weather conditions fluctuate daily, sometimes hourly. It can be rainy and chilly even during the summer; the temperature usually is 14° cooler at the 4,000-foot-high summit of Kīlauea than at sea level.

Expect hot, dry, and windy coastal conditions at the end of Chain of Craters Road. Bring rain gear, and wear layered clothing, sturdy shoes, sunglasses, a hat, and sunscreen.

Photographer on lava table filming lava flow into ocean

FOOD

Volcano House has the only food concessions at HVNP; it's a good idea to bring your own favorite snacks and beverages. Stock up on provisions in Volcano Village, 1½ miles away.

PARK PROGRAMS

Rangers lead daily walks into different areas; check with the Visitor Center for details as times and destinations depend on weather conditions.

Over 60 companies hold permits to lead hikes at HVNP. Good choices are Hawai'i Forest & Trail (www.hawaii-forest.com), Hawaiian Walkways (www.hawaiianwalkways.com), and Native Guide Hawai'i (www.nativeguidehawaii.com).

CAUTION

"Vog" (volcanic smog) can cause headaches; breathing difficulties; lethargy; irritations of the skin, eyes, nose, and throat; and other health problems. Pregnant women, young children, and people with asthma and heart conditions are most susceptible, and should avoid areas such as Halema'uma'u Crater where fumes are thick.

Wear long pants and boots or closed-toe shoes with good tread for hikes on lava. Stay on marked trails and step carefully. Lava is composed of 50% silica (glass) and can cause serious injury if you fall.

Carry at least 2 quarts of water on hikes. Temperatures near lava flows can rise above 100°F, and dehydration, heat exhaustion, and sunstroke are common consequences of extended exposure to intense sunlight and high temperatures.

Remember that these are active volcanoes, and eruptions can cause parts of the park to close at any time. Check the park's Web site or call ahead for last-minute updates before your visit.

Volcanologists inspecting a vent in the East Rift Zone

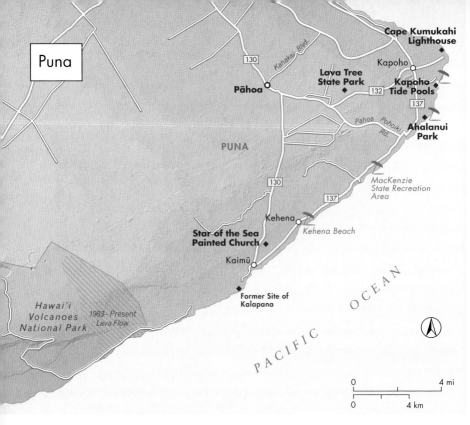

that kind of farm, but also the legal sort). Local farmers grow everything from orchids and anthuriums to papayas, bananas, and macadamia nuts. Several of the island's larger, rural residential subdivisions are between Kea'au and Pāhoa, including Hawaiian Paradise Park, Orchidland Estates, Hawaiian Acres, Hawaiian Beaches, and others.

The roads connecting Pāhoa to Kapoho and the Kalapana coast form a loop that's about 25 mi long; driving times are from two to three hours, depending on the number of stops you make and the length of time at each stop. There are long stretches of the road that may be completely isolated at any given point; this can be a little scary at night, but beautiful and tranquil during the day.

TOP ATTRACTIONS

Ahalanui Park. This park was established with a federal grant in the mid-1990s to replace those lost to the lava flows at Kalapana. It's 2½ mi south of the intersection of highways 132 and 137 on the Kapoho Coast, southeast of Pāhoa town. There's a half-acre pond fed by thermal freshwater springs mixed with seawater, which makes for a relaxing soak. Facilities include portable restrooms, outdoor showers, and picnic tables; no drinking water is available. ⊠ *Hwy. 137, 2½ mi south of junction of Hwy. 132, Puna.*

Cape Kumukahi Lighthouse. The lighthouse, 1½ mi east of the intersection of highways 132 and 137, was miraculously unharmed during the 1960 volcano eruption here that destroyed the town of Kapoho. The lava flowed directly up to the lighthouse's base but instead of pushing it over, actually flowed around it. According to Hawaiian legend, Pele, the volcano goddess, protected the Hawaiian fisherfolk by sparing the lighthouse. The lighthouse itself is a simple metal-frame structure with a light on top, similar to a tall electric-line transmission tower. Seeing the hardened lava flows skirting directly around the lighthouse is worth the visit. ⊠*Past intersection of Hwys. 132 and 137, Kapoho.*

Kapoho Tide Pools. This network of tide pools at the end of Kapoho-Kai Road is great for a swim or a snorkel, or even just a beautiful view of new coastline. Take the road to the end, turn left, and park. Some of the pools are on private property, but those closest to the ocean, Waiʻōpae (ponds), are open to all. ⊠*End of Kapoho-Kai Rd., off Hwy. 137.*

Pāhoa. Sort of like an outlaw town from the Wild West, but with renegade Hawaiians instead of cowboys, this little town is all wooden boardwalks and rickety buildings. The secondhand stores, tie-dye clothing boutiques, and art galleries in quaint old buildings are fun to wander through, but Pāhoa is not the best spot to go wandering around at night. Pāhoa's main street boasts a handful of island eateries, the best of which is **Luquin's Mexican Restaurant.** ⊠*Turn southeast onto Hwy. 130 at Keaʻau, drive 11 mi to right turn marked Pāhoa.*

WORTH NOTING

Lava Tree State Park. Tree molds that rise like blackened smokestacks formed here in 1790 when a lava flow swept through theʻōhiʻa forest. Some reach as high as 12 feet. The meandering trail provides close-up looks at some of Hawaiʻi's tropical plants and trees. There are restrooms and a couple of picnic pavilions and tables. ■TIP➜Mosquitoes live here in abundance, so be sure to bring repellent. ⊠*Hwy. 132, Puna District* 🕾808/974–6200 🎟*Free* ⊙*Daily 30 min before dawn–30 min after dusk.*

Star of the Sea Painted Church. This historic church, now a community center, was moved to its present location in 1990 just ahead of the advancing lava flow that destroyed the Kalapana area. The church, which dates from the 1930s, was built by a Belgian Catholic missionary priest, Father Evarest Gielen, who also did the detailed paintings on the church's interior. Though similar in style, the Star of the Sea and St. Benedict's were actually painted by two different Belgian Catholic missionary priests. Star of the Sea also has several lovely stained-glass windows. ⊠*Hwy. 130, 1 mi north of Kalapana.*

HILO

When compared to Kailua-Kona, Hilo is often described as "the real Hawaiʻi." With fewer tourists than residents, more historic buildings, and more Hawaiian cultural events, life does seem more Hawaiian on this side of the island. This quaint, traditional fishing village stretches from the banks of the Wailuku River to Hilo Bay, where a few hotels line stately Banyan Drive. The wonderful old buildings that make up

Hilo's downtown have recently been spruced up as part of a revitalization effort. Nearby, the 30-acre Queen Lili'uokalani Gardens, a formal Japanese garden with arched bridges and waterways, was created in the early 1900s to honor the area's Japanese sugar-plantation laborers. It also became a safety zone after a devastating tidal wave swept away businesses and homes on May 22, 1960, killing 60 people.

One of the main reasons visitors have tended to steer clear of the east side of the island is its weather. With an average rainfall of 130 inches per year, it's easy to see why Hilo's yards are so green, its buildings so weather-worn. Hilo's beauty lies in its rain forests and waterfalls, very unlike the hot and dry white-sand beaches of the Kohala Coast. But when the sun does shine, the snow glistens on Mauna Kea, 25 mi in the distance, and the town sparkles. Most days the rain blows away by noon, leaving behind the colorful arches that earn Hilo its nickname: the City of Rainbows.

TOP ATTRACTIONS

⑩ Banyan Drive. The more than 50 leafy banyan trees with aerial roots ★ dangling from their limbs were planted some 60 to 70 years ago by visiting celebrities. You'll find such names as Amelia Earhart and Franklin Delano Roosevelt on plaques affixed to the trees. ⊠*Begin at Hawai'i Naniloa Resort, 93 Banyan Dr.*

⑨ Hilo Farmers' Market. An abundant and colorful market draws farmers ★ and shoppers from all over the island. Bright orchids, anthuriums, and birds-of-paradise create a feast for the eyes, while exotic vegetables, tropical fruits, and baked goods create a feast for the stomach. Don't dawdle, as it closes in the early afternoon. ⊠*Mamo and Kamehameha Sts.* ⊙ *Wed. and Sat. 6:30* AM*–2:30* PM.

⑯ 'Imiloa Astronomy Center. Hilo's new astronomy center is part Hawaiian cultural center, dedicated to sharing the spiritual significance of Mauna Kea, and part observatory, filled with the magic of the stars. ⊠*600 'Imiloa Pl., at UH Hilo Science & Technology Park, off Nowelo and Komohana* ☎*808/969–9700* ⊕*www.imiloahawaii.org* ⊠*$17.50* ⊙*Tues.–Sun. 9–4 plus holiday Mon.*

⑪ Queen Lili'uokalani Gardens. Fish-filled ponds, stone lanterns, half-★ moon bridges, elegant pagodas, and a ceremonial teahouse make this 30-acre park a favorite Sunday destination. It was designed to honor Hawai'i's first Japanese immigrants. ⊠*Banyan Dr. at Lihiwai St.* ☎*808/961–8311.*

⑮ Pe'epe'e Falls. Four separate streams fall into a series of circular pools, forming the Pe'epe'e Falls. The resulting turbulent action—best seen after a good rain—has earned this stretch of the Wailuku River the name Boiling Pots. ■ TIP→ **There's no swimming allowed in the pools at the falls, or anywhere in the Wailuku River, due to dangerous currents and undertows.** ⊠*3 mi northwest of Hilo on Waiānuenue Ave.; keep right when road splits and look for green sign for Boiling Pots.*

⑭ Rainbow Falls. After a hard rain, these falls thunder into the Wailuku Riv-★ er gorge. If the sun peeks out in the morning hours, rainbows form above the mist. ⊠*Take Waiānuenue Ave. west of town 1 mi; when road forks, stay on right of Waiānuenue Ave.; look for Hawaiian warrior sign.*

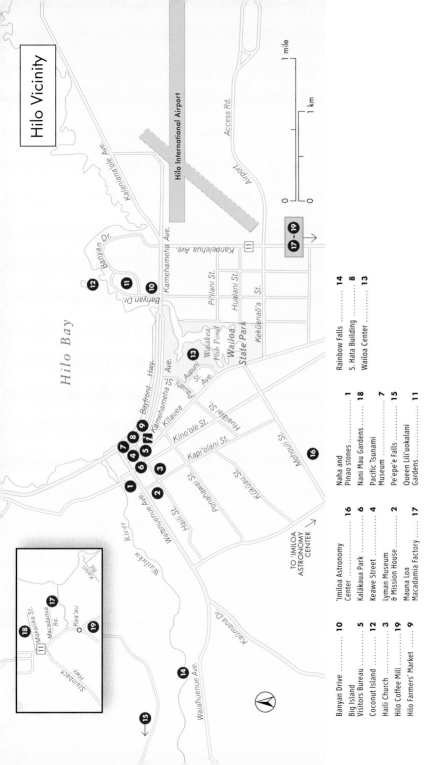

Hilo Vicinity

Hilo Bay

Hilo International Airport

Banyan Dr.

Kalaniana'ole Ave.

Kamehameha Ave.

Kanoelehua Ave.

Pi'ilani St.

Hualani St.

Kekūanāo'a St.

Waiākea Fish Pond

Wailoa State Park

Auaui St.

Paukū St.

Kīlauea Ave.

Bayfront Hwy.

Kamehameha Ave.

Kino'ole St.

Kapi'olani St.

Hualālai St.

Ponahawai St.

Haili St.

Kūkila St.

Kīlauea St.

Mohouli St.

Waiānuenue Ave.

River

Waiākea

TO 'IMILOA ASTRONOMY CENTER

1 mile

1 km

Airport Access Rd.

Kalākaua Dr.

Waiānuenue Ave.

Wailuku

Kaiolu Rd.

Makalika St.

Macadamia Rd.

Kea'au

Stainback Hwy.

Banyan Drive **10**
Big Island Visitors Bureau **5**
Coconut Island **12**
Haili Church **3**
Hilo Coffee Mill **19**
Hilo Farmers' Market **9**

'Imiloa Astronomy Center **16**
Kalākaua Park **6**
Keawe Street **4**
Lyman Museum & Mission House **2**
Mauna Loa Macadamia Factory **17**

Naha and Pinao stones......... **1**
Nani Mau Gardens **18**
Pacific Tsunami Museum **7**
Pe'epe'e Falls **15**
Queen Lili'uokalani Gardens **11**

Rainbow Falls **14**
S. Hata Building **8**
Wailoa Center **13**

WORTH NOTING

⑤ Big Island Visitors Bureau. Marked by a red-and-white Hawaiian warrior sign, the bureau is worth a visit for brochures, maps, and up-to-date, friendly insider advice. ⊠*250 Keawe St., at Haili St.* ☎*808/961–5797* ⊕*www.bigisland.org* ☉ *Weekdays 8–4:30.*

⑫ Coconut Island. This small island, just offshore from Liliʻuokalani Gardens, is accessible via a footbridge. It was considered a place of healing in ancient times. Today children play in the tide pools while fisherfolk try their luck. ⊠*Liliʻuokalani Gardens, Banyan Dr.*
★

③ Haili Church. This church was originally constructed in 1859 by New England missionaries, but the church steeple was rebuilt in 1979 following a fire. Haili Church is known for its choir, which sings hymns in Hawaiian during services. ⊠*211 Haili St.* ☎*808/935–4847.*

⑲ Hilo Coffee Mill. With all the buzz about Kona coffee, it's easy to forget that coffee is produced throughout the rest of the island as well. The Hilo Coffee Mill is a pleasant reminder of that fact. In addition to farming its own coffee on-site, the mill partners with several local small coffee farmers in East Hawaiʻi in an effort to put the region on the world's coffee map. Even if you don't have time for the tour, the mill's café is a great pit stop on the way to the volcano. ⊠*17-995 Volcano Rd., between mile markers 12 and 13, Mountain View* ☎*808/968–1333* ⊕*www.hilocoffeemill.com* ⊠*Free* ☉ *Weekdays 7–4.*

⑥ Kalākaua Park. King Kalākaua, who revived the hula, was the inspiration for Hilo's Merrie Monarch Festival. A bronze statue, erected in 1988, depicts the king with a taro leaf in his left hand to signify the Hawaiian peoples' bond with the land. The park also features a huge spreading banyan tree and small fishponds, but no picnic or recreation facilities. In a local tradition, families that have had recent funerals often leave leftover floral displays and funeral wreaths along the fishpond walkway as a way of honoring and celebrating their loved ones. ⊠*Kalākaua and Kinoʻole Sts .*

NEED A BREAK?

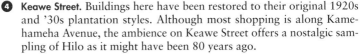

For breads and sandwiches, soups, mouthwatering apple pies, croissants, and biscotti, O'Keefe & Sons Bread Bakers (⊠ *374 Kinoʻole St.* ☎ *808/934-9334*) is the place to go. The tiny retail shop is filled with specialties such as five-grain sourdough, banana bread, and cinnamon toast.

④ Keawe Street. Buildings here have been restored to their original 1920s and '30s plantation styles. Although most shopping is along Kamehameha Avenue, the ambience on Keawe Street offers a nostalgic sampling of Hilo as it might have been 80 years ago.

② Lyman Museum & Mission House. Built in 1839 for David and Sarah Lyman, Congregationalist missionaries, the Lyman House is the oldest frame building on the island. In the adjacent museum, dedicated in 1973, there's a realistic magma chamber, exhibits on the islands' formation, and an interesting section on Hawaiian flora and fauna. ⊠*276 Haili St.* ☎*808/935–5021* ⊕*www.lymanmuseum.org* ⊠*$10 adult, $3 child (6–17)* ☉*Mon.–Sat. 10–4:30.*

17 Mauna Loa Macadamia Factory. Acres of macadamia trees lead to a processing plant with viewing windows. A videotape depicts the harvesting and preparation of the nuts, and there are free samples in the visitor center. Children can run off their energy on the nature trail. ✉*16-701 Macadamia Rd. off Hwy. 11, 5 mi south of Hilo* ☎*808/966–8618* ⊕*www.maunaloa.com* ⊗*Daily 8:30–5:30.*

1 Naha and Pinao Stones. These two huge, oblong stones are legendary. The Pinao stone is purportedly an entrance pillar of an ancient temple built near the Wailuku River. Kamehameha I is said to have moved the 5,000-pound Naha stone when he was still in his teens. Legend decreed that he who did so would become king of all the Islands. They're in front of the Hilo Public Library. ✉*300 Waiānuenue Ave.*

18 Nani Mau Gardens. The name means "forever beautiful" in Hawaiian, and that's a good description of this 20-acre botanical garden ★ filled with several varieties of fruit trees and hundreds of varieties of ginger, orchids, anthuriums, and other exotic plants. A botanical museum details the history of Hawaiian flora. ✉*421 Makalika St., off Hwy. 11* ☎*808/959–3500* ⊕*www.nanimau.com* 🎟*$10, tram tour $7* ⊗*Daily 10–3.*

7 Pacific Tsunami Museum. A memorial to all those who lost their lives in ↻ the tragedies that have struck this side of the island, this small museum offers a poignant history of tsunamis. ✉*130 Kamehameha Ave.* ☎*808/935–0926* ⊕*www.tsunami.org* 🎟*$7 adult, $3 child (17 and under)* ⊗*Mon.–Sat. 9–4.*

8 S. Hata Building. Erected as a general store in 1912 by Sadanosuke Hata and his family, this historic structure now houses shops, restaurants, offices, and a museum called Mokupapapa: Discovery Center for Hawaii's Remote Coral Reefs. During World War II the Hatas were interned and the building confiscated by the U.S. government. When the war was over, a daughter repurchased it for $100,000. A beautiful example of Renaissance-revival architecture, it won an award from the state for the authenticity of its restoration. ✉*308 Kamehameha Ave., at Mamo St.*

13 Wailoa Center. This circular exhibition center, adjacent to Wailoa State Park, has shows by local artists that change monthly. There's also a photographic exhibit of the 1946 and 1960 tidal waves. Just in front of the center is a 12-foot-high bronze statue of King Kamehameha I, made in Italy in the late 1980s. Check out his gold Roman sandals. ✉*Pi'opi'o St. off Kamehameha Ave.* ☎*808/933–0416* ⊗*Mon., Tues., Thurs., and Fri. 8:30–4:30, Wed. noon–4:30.*

HĀMĀKUA COAST

The spectacular waterfalls, mysterious jungles, emerald fields, and stunning ocean vistas along Highway 19 northwest of Hilo are collectively referred to as the Hilo–Hāmākua Heritage Coast. Brown signs featuring a sugarcane tassel reflect the area's history: thousands of acres of sugarcane are now idle, with no industry to support since "King Sugar" left the island in the early 1990s. The 45-mi drive winds through little

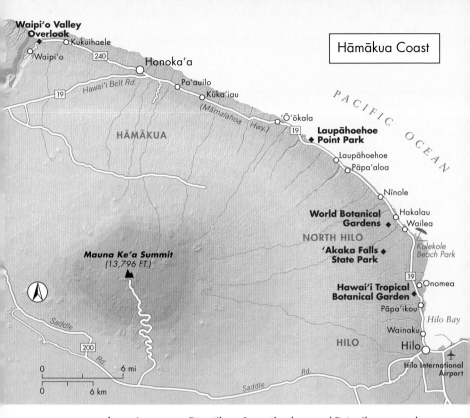

Waipiʻo Valley Overlook

Kukuihaele

Waipiʻo

240

Honokaʻa

Hawaiʻi Belt Rd.

Paʻauilo

Kūkaʻiau

(Māmalahoa Hwy.)

ʻŌʻōkala

19

HĀMĀKUA

PACIFIC OCEAN

19

Laupāhoehoe Point Park

Laupāhoehoe

Pāpaʻaloa

Nīnole

Hakalau

World Botanical Gardens

Wailea

NORTH HILO

Kolekole Beach Park

Mauna Keʻa Summit (13,796 FT.)

ʻAkaka Falls State Park

Hawaiʻi Tropical Botanical Garden

Onomea

Saddle

Pāpaʻikou

Hilo Bay

Wainaku

200

HILO

Hilo

Saddle Rd.

0   6 mi

0   6 km

Hilo International Airport

plantation towns, Pāpaʻikou, Laupāhoehoe, and Paʻauilo among them. It's a great place to wander off the main road and see "real" Hawaiʻi—untouched valleys, overgrown banyan trees, tiny coastal villages. In particular, ■ TIP→ the "Heritage Drive," a 4-mi loop just off the main highway, is well worth the detour. Once back on Highway 19, you'll pass the road to Honokaʻa, which leads to the end of the road bordering Waipiʻo Valley, ancient home to Hawaiian royalty. The isolated valley floor has maintained the ways of old Hawaiʻi, with taro patches, wild horses, and a handful of houses.

Night will undoubtedly be falling by the time you've had your fill of Hāmākua, but don't worry: the return to Hilo via Highway 19 only takes about an hour, or you can go south on the same road to stop for dinner in Waimea (30 minutes) before heading back to the Kohala Coast resorts (another 25 to 45 minutes).

TOP ATTRACTIONS

★ **ʻAkaka Falls State Park.** A meandering 10-minute loop trail takes you to the best spots to see the two cascades, **ʻAkaka** and **Kahuna**. The 400-foot Kahuna Falls is on the lower end of the trail. The majestic upper ʻAkaka Falls drops more than 442 feet, tumbling far below into a pool drained by Kolekole Stream amid a profusion of fragrant white, yellow, and red torch ginger. ✉ *4 mi inland off Hwy. 19, near Honomū* ☎ *808/974–6200* ✉ *Free* ☉ *Daily 7–7.*

Mauna Keʻa. Mauna Keʻa is the antithesis of the typical island experience. Freezing temperatures and arctic conditions are common at the summit, and snowstorms can occur year-round. It's also home to Lake Waiau, one of the highest lakes in the world. The summit—at 13,796 feet—is reputedly the clearest place in the world for viewing the night sky; it's also an outstanding place to see the sun rise and set. To get there, you'll need a four-wheel-drive vehicle. Make sure to stop at the **Onizuka Center for International Astronomy Visitor Information Station** (☎ *808/961–2180* ⊕ *www.ifa.hawaii.edu/info/vis* ☉ *Daily 9 AM–10 PM*), at a 9,300-foot elevation, both to get information about the mountain and to acclimate to the altitude. On weekends the Onizuka Center offers escorted summit tours, heading up the mountain in a caravan. Reservations are not required for the free tours, which depart at 1 PM. The center is the best amateur observation site on the planet, with three telescopes and a knowledgeable staff. It hosts nightly stargazing sessions from 6 to 10. To get here from Hilo, which is about 34 mi away, take Highway 200 (Saddle Road), and turn right at mile marker 28 onto the John A. Burns Way, which is the access road to the summit.

If you haven't rented a four-wheel-drive vehicle, don't want to deal with driving to the summit, or don't want to fight for space at the telescopes to see the stars, consider booking a tour. Most listed here provide parkas, telescopes, and meals. Excursion fees range from about $110 to $197. **Arnott's Lodge & Hiking Adventures** (☎ *808/969–7097* ⊕ *www.arnottslodge.com*) leaves from Hilo and is a bit cheaper than the others because it does not provide dinner. **Hawaiʻi Forest & Trail** (☎ *808/331–8505 or 800/464–1993* ⊕ *www.hawaii-forest.com*) stops for dinner along the way at a historic ranch. **Mauna Kea Summit Adventures** (☎ *808/322–2366* ⊕ *www.maunakea.com*) specializes in tours to the mountain. It was the first company to do so, so it has a bit more cred than the rest of the pack.

Waipiʻo Valley. Though completely off the grid today, Waipiʻo was once the center of Hawaiian life; somewhere between 4,000 and 20,000 people made it their home between the 13th and 17th centuries. In 1780 Kamehameha I was singled out here as a future ruler by reigning chiefs. In 1791 he fought Kahekili in his first naval battle at the mouth of the valley. In 1823 the first white visitors found 1,500 people living in this Eden-like environment amid fruit trees, banana groves, taro fields, and fishponds. The 1946 tidal wave drove most residents to higher ground. Now, as then, waterfalls frame the landscape, but the valley has become one of the most isolated places in the state. To preserve this pristine part of the island, commercial transportation permits are limited—only four outfits offer organized valley trips—and Sunday the valley rests. The walk down into the valley is less than a mile—start at the four-wheel-drive road leading down from the lookout point—but keep in mind, the climb back up is strenuous, especially in the hot sun.

If climbing back out of the valley is not an appealing prospect, or if your time is limited, consider taking a guided tour. Costs range from about $50 to $165, depending on the company. **Waipi'o Ridge Stables** (☎808/775–1007 ⊕*www.waipioridgestables.com*) and **Na'alapa Stables** (☎*808/775–0419* ⊕*www.naalapastables.com*) offer horseback riding trips around the valley's edge and down into the Waipi'o Valley. Other outfitters include **Waipi'o Valley Shuttle** (☎*808/775–7121*), which drives those afraid of wrecking their rental cars into the valley and around to the waterfalls. **Waipi'o Valley Wagon Tours** (☎*808/775–9518* ⊕*www.waipiovalleywagontours.com*) takes you on a 1½-hour tour through the valley in mule-drawn wagons.

★ **Waipi'o Valley Overlook.** Bounded by 2,000-foot cliffs, the Valley of the Kings was once a favorite retreat of Hawaiian royalty. Waterfalls drop 1,200 feet from the Kohala Mountains to the valley floor. Horses roam narrow trails and rocky streams. Sheer cliffs make access difficult. Only four-wheel-drive vehicles should attempt the steep road from the overlook. ⊠*Follow Hwy. 240 8 mi northwest of Honoka'a.*

WORTH NOTING

★ **Hawai'i Tropical Botanical Garden.** Eight miles north of Hilo, stunning coastline views appear around each curve of the 4-mi scenic jungle drive that accesses the privately owned nature preserve beside Onomea Bay. Paved pathways in this 17-acre botanical garden lead past ponds, waterfalls, and more than 2,000 species of plants and flowers, including palms, bromeliads, ginger, heleconia, orchids, and ornamentals. ⊠*27-717 Old Māmalahoa Hwy., Pāpa'ikou* ☎*808/964–5233* ⊕*www. hawaiigarden.com* ≊*$15 adult, $5 child (6–16)* ☉*Daily 9–4.*

Honoka'a. In 1881 Australian William Purvis planted the first macadamia-nut trees in Hawai'i near what is now this funky little town. But Honoka'a's true heyday came when sugar was king in the early part of the 20th century. During World War II, this was the place for soldiers stationed around Waimea to cut loose. Today, little eateries and stores crammed with knickknacks, secondhand goods, and antiques occupy its historic buildings. ⊠*Mamane St., Hwy. 240.*

NEED A BREAK?	A quick stop at Tex Drive-In (⊠ *45-690 Pakalana St. and Hwy. 19* ☎ *808/775–0598*) will give you a chance to taste the snack that made it famous: *malasada,* a puffy, doughy doughnut without a hole. These deep-fried beauties are best eaten hot. They also come in cream-filled versions, including vanilla, chocolate, and coconut.

Laupāhoehoe Point Park. Come here to watch the surf pound the jagged black rocks at the base of the stunning point. This is not a safe place for swimming, however. Still vivid in the minds of longtime area residents is the 1946 tragedy in which 21 schoolchildren and three teachers were swept to sea by a tidal wave. ⊠*On northeast coastline, Hwy. 19, makai side, north of Laupāhoehoe* ☎*808/961–8311* ≊*Free* ☉*Daily 6–11.*

⟳ **World Botanical Gardens.** About 300 acres of former sugarcane land are slowly giving way to a botanical center, which includes native Hawaiian plants such as orchids, palms, gingers, hibiscus, and heliconias. In the 10-acre arboretum children love to wind their way through a maze made of shrubs. From within the gardens you have access to splendid views of one of the prettiest waterfalls on the isle, triple-tiered

DID YOU KNOW?

The dramatic ʻAkaka Falls is only one of the hundreds of waterfalls on the Hāmākua Coast. Many falls tumble into pristine swimming holes, so bring your swimsuit when you explore this area.

BIG ISLAND SIGHTSEEING TOURS

Guided tours on the island are great for specific things: seeing Mauna Kea, exploring Waipi'o Valley, maybe even touring Volcanoes National Park (especially if your time is short). Sticking to a guided tour the whole time, though, would not be a great idea. Half the fun of the island is in exploring it on your own. Plus, if you stick to a guided tour, you'll only see the major tourist attractions, none of the Big Island's many hidden treasures.

Local tour-bus operators conduct volcano tours and circle-island tours, with pickup at the major resorts. Costs range from $38 to $160, depending on pickup location and length of tour. The circle-island tour is a full 12-hour

day, but Jack's and Polynesian Adventure Tours also offer half-day tours to the volcano, Mauna Kea observatory, and around Kailua-Kona.

Hawai'i Forest & Trail. ☎ *808/331–8505 in Kona, 800/464–1993* ⊕ *www.hawaii-forest.com.*

Jack's Tours. ☎ *808/329-2555 in Kona, 808/961–6666 in Hilo, 800/442–5557* ⊕ *www.jackstours.com.*

Polynesian Adventure Tours. ☎ *808/329–8008 in Kona, 800/622-3011* ⊕ *www.polyad.com.*

Roberts Hawai'i. ☎ *808/329–1688 in Kona, 808/966–5483 in Hilo, 800/831–5541* ⊕ *www.robertshawaii.com.*

Umauma Falls. For those preferring to avoid the fee, pull over near the entrance, and walk about a quarter of a mile for a decent, unobstructed view of the falls. ⊠ *Hwy. 19, from Hilo just past mile marker 16* ☎ *808/963–5427* ⊕ *www.wbgi.com* ▤ *$13* ☉ *Daily 9–5:30.*

BEACHES

Don't believe anyone who tells you that the Big Island lacks beaches.

It's not so much that the Big Island has fewer than the other islands, just that there's more island so getting to the beaches can be slightly less convenient. That said, there are plenty of those perfect white beaches you think of when you hear "Hawai'i," and the added bonus of black- and green-sand beaches, thanks to the age of the island and its active volcanoes. New beaches appear—and disappear—regularly. In 1989 a black-sand beach, Kamoamoa, formed when molten lava shattered as it hit cold ocean waters; it was closed by new lava flows in 1992.

The bulk of the island's beaches are on the northwest part of the island, along the Kohala Coast. Black-sand beaches and green-sand beaches are in the southern region, along the coast nearest the volcano. Remember that the black and green sand is not a souvenir. There's only so much, and everyone wants to enjoy these spots for years to come. On the eastern side of the island, beaches tend to be of the rocky-coast–surging-surf variety, but there are still a few worth visiting, and this is where the Hawaiian shoreline is at its most picturesque.

Note that many beaches have dangerous undertows. Rip currents and pounding shore breaks may cause serious risk anywhere at any time.

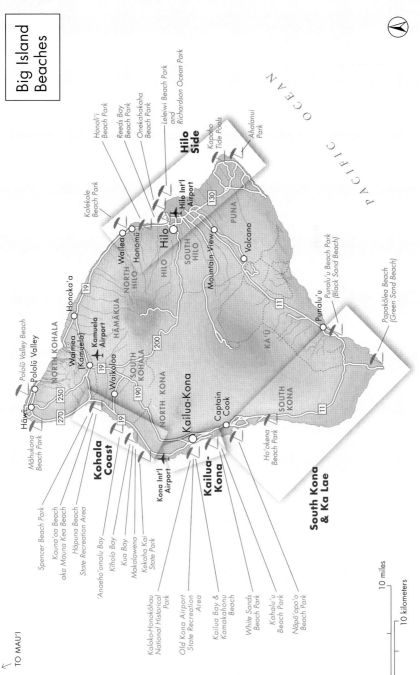

Big Island
Beaches

TO MAU'I

PACIFIC OCEAN

Hilo
Side

Honoli'i
Beach Park

Reeds Bay
Beach Park

Onekahakaha
Beach Park

Leleiwi Beach Park
and
Richardson Ocean Park

Kapoho
Tide Pools

Ahalanui
Park

Kolekole
Beach Park

Hilo Int'l
Airport

130

Wailea
Honomū
Hilo
Hilo

PUNA

NORTH
HILO

Volcano

Honoka'a

19

Kamuela
Airport

HĀMĀKUA

SOUTH
HILO

Mountain View

Waimea
(Kamuela)

Waikoloa

19

NORTH KOHALA

SOUTH
KOHALA

200

Hāwī

270
250

Pololū Valley

Pololū Valley Beach

KA'U

11

Punalu'u

Punalu'u Beach Park
(Black Sand Beach)

Papakōlea Beach
(Green Sand Beach)

Māhukona
Beach Park

Spencer Beach Park

Kauna'oa Beach
aka Mauna Kea Beach

Hāpuna Beach
State Recreation Area

Kohala
Coast

'Anaeho'omalu Bay

Kīholo Bay

Kua Bay

Makalawena

Kekaha Kai
State Park

Kaloko-Honokōhau
National Historical
Park

Old Kona Airport
State Recreation
Area

Kailua Bay &
Kamakahonu
Beach

White Sands
Beach Park

Kahalu'u
Beach Park

Nāpō'opo'o
Beach Park

Kona Int'l
Airport

Kailua-
Kona

Kailua-Kona

NORTH KONA

190

19

Captain
Cook

SOUTH KONA

Ho'okena
Beach Park

South Kona
& Ka Lae

11

PACIFIC OCEAN

0   10 miles

0   10 kilometers

Few public beaches have lifeguards. To swim safely, try to stick to those with lifeguards, keep an eye out for warning signs, and get into the water only when you see other swimmers. (The presence of surfers is not an indication that the area is safe for swimmers.)

KOHALA COAST

Most of the white sandy beaches are found on the Kohala Coast, which is, understandably, home to the majority of the island's first-class resorts. Hawai'i's beaches are public property. The resorts are required to provide public access to the beach, so don't be frightened off by a guard shack and a fancy sign. There is some limited public parking as well. The resort beaches aside, there are some real hidden gems on the Kohala Coast accessible only by boat, four-wheel drive, or a 15- to 20-minute hike. It's well worth the effort to get to at least one of these. ■TIP➜ The west side of the tends to be calmer, but the surf still gets rough in winter. The beaches here are listed in order from north (farthest from Kona) to south.

Pololū Valley Beach. One of the most beautiful spots on the island, Pololū is a wide, fine black-sand beach bordered by sheer green cliffs. Follow Highway 270 to its end at Pololū Valley, the northernmost point of the island. The trail down to the beach is rocky and can be slippery after a rain. It's steep, too, so expect about a 10-minute jaunt down and a more difficult half-hour hike back up. Take a rest here and there and check out the views. ■TIP➜The surf is almost always rough and the currents are strong, so it's not an ideal spot for swimming or snorkeling, but dipping in close to shore is relatively safe. ⊠ *End of Hwy. 270* ☞ *No facilities.*

Māhukona Beach Park. This used to be a fairly busy harbor when sugar was the economic staple of Kohala. Now it's a great swimming hole and an underwater museum of sorts. Remnants of shipping machinery and what looks like an old boat are easily visible in the clear water. No sandy beach here, but there's a ladder off the old dock that makes getting in the water easy. Snorkeling is decent as well, but it's only worth a visit on tranquil days. ⊠ *Off Hwy. 270, between mile markers 14 and 15, Māhukona* ☎ *808/961–8311* ☞ *Toilets, showers, picnic tables, grills, parking lot.*

☺ **Spencer Beach Park.** This spot is popular with local families because of its reef-protected waters. It's safe for swimming year-round, which makes it an excellent spot for a lazy day at the beach. The water is clear, but there aren't loads of fish here, so it's not a great snorkeling spot. It's a smaller beach, gently sloping with white sand and a few pebbles. You can walk from here to Pu'ukoholā Heiau National Historic Site. ⊠ *Off Hwy. 270, uphill from Kawaihae Harbor* ☎ *808/961–8311* ☞ *Lifeguard, toilets, showers, picnic tables, grills, parking lot.*

Fodor'sChoice **Kauna'oa Beach** *(Mauna Kea Beach).* Hands-down one of the most beau-
★ tiful beaches on the island, Kauna'oa is a long white crescent of sand. The beach, which fronts the Mauna Kea Beach Hotel, slopes very gradually. It's a great place for snorkeling. When conditions permit, there are good body- and board surfing also. Currents can be strong, and powerful winter waves can be dangerous, so be careful. At this writing, the

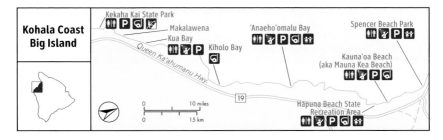

Mauna Kea Beach Hotel was closed for repairs to damages sustained in the 2006 earthquake, but the hotel's outdoor Hau Tree gazebo bar and restrooms are still open to beachgoers. ■ TIP➔ Public parking is limited to only 30 spots, so it's best to arrive before 10 am. ⊠ Off Hwy. 19; entry through gate to Mauna Kea Beach Resort ⌦ Lifeguard, toilets, showers, parking lot.

Fodor'sChoice **Hāpuna Beach State Recreation Area.**
★ Guidebooks usually say it's a toss-up between Hāpuna and Kauna'oa for "best beach" on the island, but, although Kauna'oa is beautiful most locals give the prize to Hāpuna. There is ample parking so you don't have to get here early, although it can fill up by midday.

WORD OF MOUTH

"The Hāpuna beach is great, free of anything but soft sand. If you want a beach, the Hāpuna beach and the Mauna Kea beach are the best swimming beaches in the [Kohala] area."   —sandinmytoes

And while the north end of the beach fronts the Hāpuna Beach Prince Hotel, it's still a public beach and not just for hotel guests. The beach itself is a long (½-mi), white, perfect crescent, wide enough to hold half the island on a holiday weekend and not feel crowded. The turquoise water is very calm in summer, with just enough rolling waves to make bodysurfing or boogie-boarding fun. ■ TIP➔ In winter, surf can be very rough. Hāpuna tends to get a little windy in the late afternoon; even that can have a benefit, as everyone else leaves just in time to give you a private, perfect sunset. ⊠ Hwy. 19, near mile marker 69, at Hāpuna Beach Prince Hotel ☎ 808/974–6200 ⌦ Lifeguard, toilets, showers, food concession, picnic tables, grills/firepits, parking lot.

★ **'Anaeho'omalu Beach (A-Bay).** This expansive beach, at the Waikoloa Beach Marriott, is perfect for swimming, windsurfing, snorkeling, and diving. It's a well-protected bay, so even when surf is rough on the rest of the island, it's fairly calm here. Snorkel gear, kayaks, and boogie boards are available for rent at the north end. Be sure to wander around the ancient fishponds. A walking trail follows the coastline to the Hilton Waikoloa Village next door, passing by tide pools and ponds. Footwear is recommended for the trail. ⊠ Follow Waikoloa Beach Dr. to Kings' Shops, then turn left; parking lot and beach right-of-way south of Waikoloa Beach Marriott ⌦ Toilets, showers, food concession, picnic tables, parking lot.

Kīholo Bay. A new gravel road to the shoreline makes Kīholo Bay an absolute must-see (previously you'd have to hike over lava for 20 minutes).

Thanks to Mauna Loa, what was once the site of King Kamehameha's gigantic fishpond is now several freshwater ponds encircling a beautiful little bay. The water's a bit cold and hazy because of the mix of fresh and salty water, but there are tons of green sea turtles here, and the snorkeling is great. If you follow the shoreline southwest toward Kona, just past the big yellow house is another public beach where you'll find some naturally occurring freshwater pools inside a lava tube. This area, called Queen's Bath, is as cool as it sounds. ✉ *Hwy. 19, gravel road between mile markers 82 and 83* ☞ *Toilets, showers, parking lot.*

Kua Bay. Locals are pretty unhappy about the newly paved road leading to Kua Bay, the northernmost beach in the stretch of coast that comprises Kekaha Kai (Kona Coast) State Park. At one time you had to hike over a few miles of unmarked, rocky trail to get here, which kept many people out. It's easy to understand why the locals would be so protective. This is one of the most beautiful bays you will ever see— the water is crystal clear, deep aquamarine, and peaceful in summer. Rocky shores on either side keep the beach from getting too windy in the afternoon. ■TIP➡The surf here can get very rough in winter. ✉ *Hwy. 19, north of mile marker 88* ☞ *No facilities.*

Makalawena. Makalawena is a long white crescent, dotted with little coves and surrounded by dunes and trees. The sand is powdery fine, the water is perfect, and the place is deserted. If it weren't so hard to get to, this would be the unanimous choice for best beach on the island. Like Kua Bay, Mahai'ula and Ka'elehuluhulu, it is within Kekaha Kai State Park, but it is the most remote. You have to rent a boat and anchor there, walk 20 minutes on a rough coastal trail over lava rock terrain, or take a brutal four-wheel-drive jaunt over the lava. (You still have to walk the last five to 10 minutes.) But it's worth it. Makalawena is more than just a great beach—it's a truly magical place. An afternoon here is a recipe for delirious happiness. Locals body board here occasionally, but a jetty on the north end of the beach creates a calm area for swimming even when the surf's up a bit. Did we mention that there are wild goats hanging around on the trail leading to the beach? There's a freshwater pond that beats hosing off at one of those water-spigot showers at the marked public beaches. ✉ *Hwy. 19, between mile markers 88 and 89; if you're walking, park in lot at Kekaha Kai (Kona Coast) State Park and follow footpath along shore* ☞ *No facilities.*

Kekaha Kai (Kona Coast) State Park. Beyond the park's entrance, at the end of two 1½-mi-long unpaved roads, you can find two sandy beaches: Mahai'ula to the south, and Ka'elehuluhulu to the north. In calm weather, they're great for swimming. You can hike along a historic 4½-mi trail from one to the other, but be prepared for the heat and bring lots of drinking water. ✉ *Hwy. 19, sign about 2 mi north of Keāhole– Kona International Airport marks rough road* ☎808/327–4958 or 808/974–6200 ☞ *Parking lot at entrance; Mahai'ula: Toilets, picnic area; Ka'elehuluhulu: No facilities.*

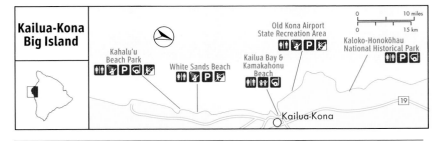

KAILUA-KONA

Most of the coastline around Kona is rocky, so there aren't the white sandy beaches found in Kohala. What you will discover, though, is excellent snorkeling and scuba diving, some calm swimming spots, and decent surf conditions. Beaches are listed from north to south.

Kaloko–Honokōhau National Historical Park. This 1,160-acre park near Honokōhau Harbor has three beaches, all good for swimming. 'Ai'opio (☞ *Toilets*), a few yards north of the harbor, is a small beach with calm, protected swimming areas (good for kids) and great snorkeling in the water near the archaeological site of Hale o Mono. **Honokōhau Beach** (☞ *No facilities*), a ¾-mi stretch with ruins of ancient fishponds, is also north of the harbor. At the north end of the beach, a historic trail leads *mauka* (toward the mountain) across the lava to a pleasant freshwater pool called Queen's Bath. A Hawaiian settlement until the 19th century, the area is being developed as a cultural and historical site. 'Alula (☞ *No facilities*) is a slip of white sand at the south end of the harbor, a short walk over lava to the left of the harbor entrance. For information about the park, visit its headquarters, a 5- to 10-minute drive away. ✉ *74-425 Kealakehe Pkwy., off Hwy. 19* ☎ *808/329–6881* ⊕ *www.nps.gov* ⊗ *Park road gate 8* AM–3:30 PM ☞ *Toilets, food concession, parking lot.*

Old Kona Airport State Recreation Area. The unused runway—great for jogging—is still visible above this palm-tree-lined beach at Kailua Park. The beach has a sheltered, sandy inlet with tide pools for children, and there are usually very few people there during the week. An offshore surfing break known as Old Airport is popular with local surfers. ✉ *North end of Kuakini Hwy., Kailua-Kona* ☎ *808/327–4958 or 808/974–6200* ☞ *Toilets, showers, picnic tables, parking lot.*

Kailua Bay & Kamakahonu Beach. Next to King Kamehameha's Kona Beach Hotel, this little square of white sand is the only beach in downtown Kailua-Kona. Protected by the harbor, the calm water makes this a perfect spot for kids; for adults it's a great place for a swim and a lazy beach day. The water is surprisingly clear for being surrounded by an active pier. Snorkeling can be good, especially if you move south from the beach. There's a kiosk with snorkeling, paddle boarding, and kayaking equipment rentals. ■ TIP➔ A little family of sea turtles likes to hang out next to the seawall, so keep an eye out. ✉ *Ali'i Dr.* ☞ *Toilets.*

The calm Kailua Bay is an excellent spot for rowing, snorkeling, and swimming.

White Sands, Magic Sands, or Disappearing Sands Beach. Now you see it, now you don't. Overnight, winter waves wash away this small white-sand beach on Ali'i Drive just south of Kailua-Kona. In summer you'll know you've found it when you see the body- and board surfers. Though not really a great beach, this is a really popular summer hangout for young locals and a great place to get your boogie (board) on. ✉ *Ali'i Dr., 4½ mi south of Kailua-Kona* ☎ *808/961–8311* ☞ *Lifeguard, toilets, showers, food concession, parking lot.*

Kahalu'u Beach Park. This spot was a favorite of King Kalākaua, whose summer cottage is on the grounds of the neighboring Outrigger Keauhou Beach Resort. Kahalu'u is popular with commoners, too, and on weekends it gets crowded. This is, however, one of the best snorkeling spots on the island—it's a good place to see fish up close, as they are used to snorkelers. This is also the best place on the island to try surfing, as the waves are relatively small and lessons and board rentals are available. ■ TIP➔ Beware—a strong riptide during high surf pulls swimmers away from shore. ✉ *Ali'i Dr., 5½ mi south of Kailua-Kona* ☎ *808/961–8311* ☞ *Lifeguard, toilets, showers, food concession, picnic tables, parking lot.*

SOUTH KONA AND KA'Ū

You wouldn't expect to find sparkling white-sand beaches in the moonscape of South Kona and Ka'ū, and you won't. What you will find is something a bit more rare and well worth the visit: black- and green-sand beaches. And there's the chance to see the endangered Hawaiian green sea turtles close up. Beaches are listed from north to south.

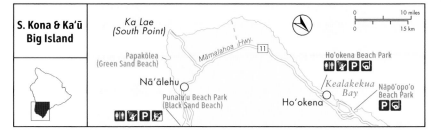

Nāpō'opo'o Beach Park. There's no real beach here, but don't let that deter you—this is a great spot. Kealakekua Bay is protected by impossibly high green cliffs, so the water's always very calm and clear. Swimming is great here, but bring a mask along, as the snorkeling in this marine reserve is amazing; your chances of seeing Hawaiian spinner dolphins are very good, especially if you come in the early morning. If you enter the water from the short pier at the left side of the parking lot, you'll see coral and fish almost immediately. This is also a great kayaking spot, and several stands along the highway rent kayaks, in addition to snorkel gear. Another great way to enjoy this marine preserve is to take a snorkel, scuba, or glass-bottom boat tour from Keauhou Bay. Fair Wind Cruises *(see Snorkeling in this chapter)* is the only operation allowed to dock in Kealakekua Bay. ⊠ *End of Nāpō'opo'o Rd., off Hwy. 11, Kealakekua Bay* ☎ *808/961–8311* ☞ *Parking lot.*

Ho'okena Beach Park. Driving south from Kealakekua Bay, you can see the sign for Ho'okena Beach Park. The road down to the beach is narrow and steep, but the views are great. (Plus you'll feel like you're venturing off the beaten path.) The salt-and-pepper beach is on the small side and is mostly frequented by the people from the nearby village; it's rarely crowded, except on weekends. By Hawaiian standards, this is an average beach (the water's nice for swimming, and there's a bit of snorkeling to the left, but nothing amazing), but that still makes it great for the rest of us. Plus it's the only white-sand beach on this part of the island. ⊠ *2-mi drive down road bordered by ruins of stone wall off Hwy. 11, 23 mi south of Kailua-Kona* ☎ *808/961–8311* ☞ *Toilets, showers, picnic tables, parking lot.*

★ **Papakōlea Beach (Green Sand Beach).** Tired of the same old gold-, white-, or black-sand beach? Then how about a green-sand beach? You'll need good hiking shoes to get to this greenish black crescent, one of the most unusual beaches on the island. It lies at the base of Pu'u o Mahana, at Mahana Bay, where a cinder cone formed during an early eruption of Mauna Loa. The greenish tint is caused by an accumulation of olivine crystals that form in volcanic eruptions. The dry barren landscape is totally surreal. The surf is often rough, and swimming is hazardous due to strong currents, so caution is advised. Take the road toward the left at the end of the paved road to Ka Lae (South Point) about 12 mi off Highway 11. Park at the end of the road. (Anyone trying to charge you for parking is running a scam.) Hikers can follow the 2-mi coastal trail, which will end in a steep and dangerous descent down the cliff side on an unimproved trail. Note: while hikers can cross the private Hawaiian Home Lands without a permit to get to the beach, those wanting to take a 4WD vehicle along the rugged coast trail supposed to first contact the Department of Hawaiian Home Lands in Hilo (☎808/974–4250). However, there is very rarely anyone around actually checking for permits. ■TIP→There is no guarantee of open access to 4WD vehicles, so check first. ⊠2½ mi northeast of South Point, off Hwy. 11 ☞No facilities.

★ **Punalu'u Beach Park (Black Sand Beach).** The endangered Hawaiian green sea turtle nests in the black sand of this beautiful and easily accessible beach. You can see them feeding on the seaweed along the surf break or napping on the sand. You can even swim with the turtles; they're used to people and will swim along right next to you. (Resist the urge to touch them, though.) However, strong shoreward currents make being in the water here a hazard. Don't venture far out, and avoid going out past the boat ramp as very strong rip currents are active. ■TIP→ It's quite rocky in the water, even close to shore—you might want to bring a pair of reef shoes if you plan to swim. The beach is a long black-sand crescent backed by low dunes with some rocky outcroppings at the shoreline. ⊠Hwy. 11, 27 mi south of Hawai'i Volcanoes National Park ☎808/961–8311 ☞Showers, toilets across road, grills, firepits, parking lot.

HILO SIDE

There are no real beaches along the jagged cliffs of the Hāmākua Coast, but there are a few surf spots and swimming holes worth an afternoon stop. These spots are rarely crowded, and they're surrounded by lush rain forest. Hilo isn't exactly known for its beautiful white beaches, but there are a few gems and plenty of opportunities to dip into streams and waterfalls if the ocean is being uncooperative. Puna's few beaches have some unique attributes—swaths of black sand, volcano-heated springs, and a coastline that is beyond dramatic (sheer walls of lava rock dropping into the bluest ocean you've ever seen). Beaches are listed from north to south.

Kolekole Beach Park. The Kolekole River meets the ocean at this small beach between 'Akaka and Umauma Falls. Although there's a rocky shoreline, the river is calm and great for swimming. There's even a rope swing tied to a banyan tree on the opposite side. Local surfers like this spot in the winter. ⊠Off Hwy. 19 ☎808/961–8311 ☐Free ☉Daily 6–11 ☞Toilets, showers, picnic tables, grills, parking lot.

Honoli'i Beach Park. There aren't many places along the east Hawai'i coastline to catch the waves when the surf's up, but this is one of the best. It's popular among the local surf crowd, and it's fun to watch the surfers paddle out when the surfing is good. The sandy beach is minimal here, a mix of sand and coral rubble debris along the mostly rocky coast. There's limited parking beside the narrow roadside. ⊠1½ mi north of Hilo on Hwy. 19 ☎808/961–8311 ☞Toilets.

Reeds Bay Beach Park. Safe swimming, proximity to downtown Hilo, and a freshwater-fed swimming hole called "the Ice Pond" are the

enticements of this cove. ⊠*Banyan Dr. and Kalaniana'ole Ave., Hilo* ☎*808/961–8311* ⚲*Toilets, showers, parking lot.*

Onekahakaha Beach Park. A white-sand beach with a shallow, enclosed tide pool makes this a favorite for Hilo families with small children. ⊠*Kalaniana'ole Ave., 3 mi east of Hilo* ☎*808/961–8311* ⚲*Life-guard, toilets, showers, picnic tables, parking lot.*

Leleiwi Beach Park and Richardson Ocean Park. There's hardly any sand here, but these two beaches make up one beautiful spot—laced with bays, inlets, lagoons, and pretty parks. The grassy area is ideal for picnics. Snorkeling can be great, as turtles and dolphins frequent this area. ⊠*2349 Kalaniana'ole Ave., 4 mi east of Hilo* ☎*808/961–8311* ⚲*Lifeguard (on weekends), picnic tables, parking lot.*

Kapoho Tide Pools. Snorkelers will find tons of colorful coral and the fish who feed off it in this network of tide pools at the end of Kapoho-Kai Road. Take the road to the end. Then turn left and park. Some of the pools have been turned into private swimming pools; those closest to the ocean are open to all. The pools are usually very calm, and some are volcanically heated. It's best to come during the week, as the pools can get crowded on the weekend. ⊠*End of Kapoho-Kai Rd., off Hwy. 137* ⚲*No facilities.*

Ahalanui Park. This 3-acre beach park, also known as Pū'āla'a, has a ½-acre pond heated by volcanic steam and surrounded by big, beautiful coconut palms. There's nothing like swimming in this warm pool, but the nearby ocean is rough. ⊠*Hwy. 137, 2½ mi south of junction of Hwy. 132* ☎*808/961–8311* ⚲*Lifeguard, toilets, showers, picnic tables, grills.*

WATER SPORTS AND TOURS

The ancient Hawaiians, who took much of their daily sustenance from the ocean, also enjoyed playing in the water. In fact, surfing was the sport of kings. Though it's easy to be lulled into whiling away the day baking in the sun, getting into and onto the water will be a highlight of your trip to the Big Island.

All of the Hawaiian Islands are surrounded by the Pacific Ocean, making them some of the world's greatest natural playgrounds. But certain experiences are even better on the Big Island: nighttime scuba dives with manta rays; deep-sea fishing in Kona's fabled waters, where dozens of

Pacific blue marlin of 1,000 pounds or more have been caught; kayaking among the dolphins in Kealakekua Bay; and sighting humpback whales on a whale-watching cruise.

As a general rule, the waves are gentler here than on other Islands, but there are a few things to be aware of before heading to the shore: don't turn your back on the ocean; conditions can change quickly, so keep your eyes open; obey lifeguards and park rangers and heed the advice of outfitters from whom you rent equipment.

BOOGIE BOARDING AND BODYSURFING

According to the movies, in the Old West there was always friction between cattle ranchers and sheep ranchers. Some will say the same situation exists between surfers and boogie boarders. Sure, there's some good-natured trash-talking between the groups, but nothing more. The truth is, boogie boarding is a blast. The only surfers who don't do it are hardcore surfing purists, and almost none of that type lives on this island.

■TIP➔ Novice boogie boarders should use smooth-bottom boards, wear protective clothing (or at least T-shirts), and catch shore waves only. You'll need a pair of short fins to get out to the bigger waves offshore (not recommended for newbies). As for bodysurfing, just catch a wave and make like Superman going faster than a speeding bullet.

BEST SPOTS

When conditions are right, **Hāpuna Beach State Recreation Area** (⊠ *Hwy. 19, near mile marker 69*) is fabulous. The water is very calm in summer, with just enough rolling waves for bodysurfing or boogie boarding. But this beach isn't known as the "broken-neck capital" for nothing. Ask the lifeguards about conditions before heading into the water in winter. Much of the sand at **White Sands, Magic Sands, or Disappearing Sands Beach Park** (⊠ *Ali'i Dr., 4½ mi south of Kailua-Kona*) washes out to sea and forms a sandbar just offshore. This causes the waves to break in a way that's great for intermediate or advanced boogie boarding. ■TIP➔There can be nasty rip currents at high tide. If you're not using fins, wear reef shoes because of the rocks.

North of Hilo, **Honoli'i Cove** (⊠ *Access road off Hwy. 19, just past mile marker 4*) is the best boogie boarding–surfing spot on the east side of the island.

EQUIPMENT

Equipment rental shacks are all over the place. Boogie board rental rates are $5 to $12 per day and $50 to $60 per week.

Orchid Land Surf Shop. ⊠ *262 Kamehameha Ave., Hilo* ☎ *808/935–1533* ⊕ *www.orchidlandsurf.com.*

Pacific Vibrations. ⊠ *75-5702 Likana La., at Ali'i Dr., Kailua-Kona* ☎ *808/ 329–4140.*

DEEP-SEA FISHING

Along the Kona Coast you can find some of the world's most exciting "blue-water" fishing. Although July, August, and September are peak months, with the best fishing and a number of tournaments, charter fishing goes on year-round. You don't have to compete to experience the thrill of landing a Pacific blue marlin or other big-game fish. More than 60 charter boats, averaging 26 to 58 feet, are available for hire, most of them out of **Honokōhau Harbor,** north of Kailua-Kona.

For an exclusive charter, prices generally range from $350 to $700 for a half-day trip (about four hours) and $600 to $950 for a full day at sea (about eight hours). For share charters, rates range from $100 to $140 per person for a half-day and $200 for a full day. If fuel prices continue increasing, expect charter costs to rise. Most boats are licensed to take up to six passengers, in addition to the crew. Tackle, bait, and ice are furnished, but you'll usually have to bring your own lunch. You won't be able to keep your catch, although if you ask, many captains will send you home with a few fillets.

Big fish are weighed in daily at **Honokōhau Harbor's Fuel Dock.** Show up at 11 AM to watch the weigh-in of the day's catch from the morning charters, or 3:30 PM for the afternoon charters. If you're lucky, you'll get to see a "grander" weighing in at 1,000-plus pounds. A surprising number of these are caught just outside Kona Harbor.

Kona hosts a variety of fishing tournaments, but the Big Kahuna is the **Hawaiian International Billfish Tournament** (☎808/329–6155 ⊕*www. kona-billfish.com*), held in August since 1959. Billfish, of course, are majestic marlin. If you're in town, you can find a number of tournament-related activities. Pay attention to the list of winners, as it helps you choose which boat to charter.

BOATS AND CHARTERS

Charter Locker. This fleet of four boats ranging from 38 to 53 feet is a good bet for both novices and experts. Operating since 1964, Charter Locker is one of the respected old-timers at Honokohau Harbor. They can also book you on the luxurious *Blue Hawai'i,* which has air-conditioned staterooms for overnight trips. ☎808/326–2553 ⊕*www. charterlocker.com.*

Honokōhau Harbor Charter Desk. With 50 boats on the books, this place can take care of almost anyone. You can make arrangements through your hotel activity desk, but we suggest you go down to the desk at the harbor and look things over for yourself. ⊠*74-381 Kealakehe Pkwy., Kailua-Kona* ☎*808/329–5735 or 888/566–2487* ⊕*www.charterdesk.com.*

Illusions Sportfishing. Captain Tim Hicks is one of Kona's top fishing tourney producers with several years experience. The 39-foot *Illusions* is fully equipped with galley, restrooms, an air-conditioned cabin for guest comfort, plus the latest in fishing equipment. Half-day exclusive charters begin at $550, full day exclusives at $850. ☎*808/960–7371* ⊕*www.illusionssportfishing.com.*

Pamela Big Game Fishing. This family-operated company has been in the business since 1967. The 38-foot *Pamela* is captained by Peter Hoogs.

They've also got an informative Web site with information on sportfishing. Half-day exclusive charters begin at $600, full-day exclusives at $950. ☎808/329–3600 or 800/762–7546 ⊕www.konabiggame fishing.com.

KAYAKING

Kayaks are great for observing Hawai'i's diverse marine life and serene shores. When you venture out, however, be sure to respect Hawai'i's waters. Almost a third of marine mammals here are unique to the Big Island. Coral reefs are endangered, so many bays are protected marine reserves. A reputable kayak shop can brief you on proper conduct and recommend places with manageable currents.

BEST SPOTS

The likelihood of seeing dolphins makes **Kealakekua Bay** (⊠*Bottom of Nāpō'opo'o Rd., south of Kailua-Kona*) one of the most popular kayak spots on the Big Island. The bay is usually calm, and the kayaking is not difficult except during high surf. If you're there in the morning, you're likely to see spinner dolphins. Depending on your strength and enthusiasm, you'll cross the bay in 30–60 minutes and put in at the ancient canoe landing about 50 yards to the left of the **Captain Cook Monument.** The monument marks the landfall of Captain James Cook in 1778, the first European to visit Hawai'i. The coral around the monument itself is too fragile to land a kayak, but it makes for fabulous snorkeling. There are several rental outfitters on Highway 11 between mile markers 110 and 113.

Ōneo Bay (⊠*Ali'i Dr., south of Kailua-Kona*) is usually quite a placid place to kayak. It's easy to get to and great for all skill levels. If you can't find a parking spot along Ali'i Drive, there's a parking lot across the street near the farmers' market.

Hilo Bay (⊠*2349 Kalaniana'ole Ave., about 4 mi east of Hilo*) is a favorite kayak spot. The best place to put in is at **Richardson's Ocean Beach Park.** Most afternoons you can share the bay with local paddling clubs. Stay inside the breakwater unless the ocean is calm (or you're feeling unusually adventurous). Conditions range from extremely calm to quite choppy.

EQUIPMENT, LESSONS, AND TOURS

Aloha Kayak Co. This Honalo outfitter offers guided Wet-N-Wild Kayak Snorkel/Cave Tours out of Keauhou Bay—a four-hour morning tour ($89 per person) and a 2½-hour afternoon version ($65 per person). The morning tour includes sandwich lunch, snacks, and cold drinks; the afternoon tour includes snacks and drinks. New popular guided tours include the Turtle Kayak Adventure at the Place of Refuge ($129 per person) and the six-hour Kayak Tour from Kealakekua Bay to the Captain Cook Monument ($159 per person.) Daily kayak rental rates: single $35, double $60. ⊠79-7248 Mamalahoa Hwy., Honalo ☎808/322–2868 or 877/322–1444 ⊕www.alohakayak.com.

Kona Boys. This full-service outfitter handles kayaks, boogieboards, surf boards, and related equipment, including the new craze, stand-up paddle boards for $25 per hour and $67 per day. The units are located on the highway above Kealakekua Bay and at Kamakahonu Beach next to the King Kamehameha Kona Beach Hotel. Single-seat kayaks are $47, doubles $67. Dive kayaks with a well for an air tank are also available. They also lead guided trips to Kealakekua (half day for $159 per person) and give stand-up paddle board lessons (2½ hours for $159 per person.). ☒79-7539 *Mamalahoa Hwy., Kealakekua* ☒*75–5660 Palani Rd. Kailua-Kona* ☎*808/328–1234* ⊕*www. konaboys.com.*

Ocean Safari's Kayak Adventures. On the 3½-hour tours that begin in Keauhou Bay, you can visit sea caves along the coast, then swim

> ### DOLPHINS AT REST
>
> Kealakekua Bay is a designated marine refuge where the dolphins return to rest after feeding. Kayakers occasionally pursue the dolphins in an aggressive way. Because of the actions of a few, some environmental activists are working to close the bay to all kayakers. Those who charge after dolphins may be videotaped and have complaints filed against them (as well as suffer the ephemeral but very real consequences of behaving without the aloha spirit). If you behave in a calm, nonthreatening manner, the dolphins are very likely to come to you.

ashore for a snack, snorkeling, and perhaps some cliff jumping. The kayaks are on the beach so you don't have to hassle with transporting them. The cost is $64 per person. A two-hour dolphin–whale tour leaves at 7 AM on Tuesday. It's $35 per person. ☒*End of Kamehameha III Rd., Kailua-Kona* ☎*808/326–4699* ⊕*www.oceansafariskayaks.com.*

SAILING

Maile Charters. Ralph Blancato and Kalia Potter offer unique around-the-Islands sailing adventures that range from half-day excursions to five-day journeys to Maui, Moloka'i, or Lāna'i. Private cabins and hot showers keep you comfortable, and island-style meals keep you satisfied. Fees start at $979 for a sunset sail charter to $5,950 for five days. ☒*Kawaihae Harbor, Kawaihae* ☎*808/960–9744 or 800/726–7245* ⊕*www.adventuresailing.com.*

SCUBA DIVING

With its steep undersea drop-offs, the Big Island has some of the most dramatic diving in the Hawaiian Islands. Although there's diving on the Hilo side, the Kona coast is much better. Two-tank dives average $100–$150 depending on whether you're already certified and whether you're diving from a boat or from shore. Instruction with PADI, SDI, or TDI certification in three to five days costs $400–$650. Most instructors rent out dive equipment and snorkel gear, and many rent underwater cameras. A few organize otherworldly manta-ray dives at night, or whale-watching cruises in season.

The Kona Coast's relatively calm waters and colorful coral reefs are excellent for scuba diving.

BEST SPOTS

Hāpuna Beach State Recreation Area (⊠ *Hwy. 19, near mile marker 69*), in Kohala, can be a good shore dive. Just south of the state park is **Puako** (⊠ *Puako Rd., off Hwy. 19*). Public access to the beach from Puako Road provides easy entry to some fine reef diving. Deep chasms, sea caves, rock arches, and more abound plus varied marinelife.

The water is usually very clear at **Pawai Bay Marine Reserve** (⊠ *Just north of Old Kona Airport Beach Park, at beginning of Kuakini Hwy.*). This bay near Kailua-Kona has numerous underwater sea caves, arches, and rock formations, plus lots of marine life. It can be busy with snorkel boats but is an easy dive spot. **Plane Wreck Point,** off Keāhole Point, is for expert divers only. Damselfish, fantail, and filefish hover around in the shadows.

One of Kona's best night dive spots is **Manta Village** (⊠ *Off Sheraton Keauhou Bay Resort at Keauhou*). A booking with a scuba/snorkel night dive operator is required for the short boat ride to the area. If you're a diving or snorkeling fanatic, it's well worth it for the experience of seeing the manta rays.

Dive boats come to **Puʻuhonua O Hōnaunau** *(Place of Refuge)* (⊠ *Rte. 160, about 20 mi south of Kailua-Kona* ⊕ *www.nps.gov/puho*) for the steep drop-offs and dramatic views. You can also get in the water from the shore on the north end.

EQUIPMENT, LESSONS, AND TOURS

There are quite a few good dive shops on the Kona coast. Most are happy to take on all customers, but a few focus on specific types of trips.

★ **Aloha Dive Company.** Native-born Hawaiian and PADI master dive instructor Mike Nakachi, together with wife Buffy (a registered nurse and PADI dive instructor) and Earl Kam (a videographer and PADI dive master) have been instructing since 1990. Although they'll take anybody, they're biased in favor of experienced divers who want unique locations and know how to take care of themselves in deep water. Their boat is fast enough to take you places other companies can't reach. They're fun people with great attitudes and operate the only true *kamā'aina* (Hawai'i born-and-raised) outfitter around. ⊠*Kailua-Kona96745* ☎*808/325–5560* ⊕*www.alohadive.com.*

Jack's Diving Locker. The best place for novice and intermediate divers (certified to 60 feet), Jack's Diving Locker has trained and certified tens of thousands of divers since opening in 1981. The company has three boats that can each take 10 to 18 divers. It does a good job looking out for customers and protecting the coral reef. Before each charter the dive master briefs divers on various options and then everyone votes on where to go. Jack's also runs the biggest dive shop on the island, and has classrooms and a dive pool for beginning instruction. ⊠*75-5813 Ali'i Dr., Kailua-Kona* ☎*808/329–7585* ⊕*www.jacksdivinglocker.com.*

★ **Pacific Rim Divers.** This fantastic husband-and-wife operation (with homemade snacks!) is all about enjoying and respecting the Big Island's reefs. They love what they do, they know their stuff, and they have a real knack for finding everything from tiny shrimp to daunting hammerheads. ⊠*Honokōhau Harbor, 74-425 Kealakehe Pkwy., Kailua-Kona* ☎*808/334–1750* ⊕*www.pacificrimdivers.com.*

SNORKELING

Although the snorkeling on the Hilo side is passable (except for the Kapoho tide pools, which are stunning), the real action is on the Kona side where colorful tropical fish frequent the lava outcroppings and coral reefs. It's easy to arrange a do-it-yourself snorkeling tour by renting masks and snorkels from any of the many diving outfits in Kailua-Kona or at the resorts.

Many snorkel cruises are also available. Shop for prices at kayak, scuba, and sailing outfitters; ask about the size of the boat, and be sure you know what equipment and food is included. Also find out what the extras (mask defogger, dry bags, or underwater cameras) will cost.

BEST SPOTS

★ **Kealakekua Bay** (⊠*Bottom of Nāpō'opo'o Rd., south of Kailua-Kona*) is, hands-down, the best snorkel spot on the island, with fabulous coral reefs around the Captain Cook monument and generally calm waters. Besides, you'll probably get to swim with dolphins. Overland access is difficult, so you'll want to opt for one of several guided snorkel cruises or kayak across the bay to get to the monument. ■TIP➔ Be on the lookout for kayakers who might not notice you swimming beneath them, and stay on the ocean side of the buoys near the cliffs.

The snorkeling just north of the boat launch at **Pu'uhonua O Hōnaunau (Place of Refuge)** (⊠*Rte. 160, about 20 mi south of Kailua-Kona* ⊕*www.*

nps.gov/puho) is almost as good as Kealakekua Bay, and it's much easier to reach. It's also a popular scuba diving spot.

Since ancient times, the waters around **Kahalu'u Beach Park** (⊠ *Ali'i Dr., 5½ mi south of Kailua-Kona*) have been a traditional net fishing area. The swimming is good, and the snorkeling is even better. You'll see angelfish, parrotfish, needlefish, pufferfish, and a lot more. ■TIP➔**Don't stray too far, as dangerous and unpredictable currents swirl outside the bay, and resist temptation to feed the fish.**

Kapoho Tide Pools (⊠ *End of Kapoho-Kai Road, off Hwy. 137*) has the best snorkeling on the Hilo side. Fingers of lava from the 1960 flow that destroyed the town of Kapoho jut into the sea to form a network of tide pools. Conditions near the shore are excellent for beginners, and challenging enough farther out for experienced snorkelers.

EQUIPMENT, LESSONS, AND TOURS

Captain Zodiac Raft Expedition. The exciting four-hour trip on an inflatable raft takes you along the Kona Coast to explore gaping lava-tube caves, search for dolphins and turtles, and snorkel around Kealakekua Bay. The cost is $93 for adults, $78 for kids ages 4–12. ⊠ *Honokōhau Harbor, Kailua-Kona* ☎*808/329–3199* ⊕*www.captainzodiac.com.*

★ **Fair Wind Cruises.** This outfit offers both a 4½-hour morning snorkeling and 3½-hour afternoon excursions to Kealakekua Bay, and a 5-hour luxury cruise on the Hula Kai that sails into three different secret snorkeling spots a day. Snorkel gear is included (ask about prescription masks), but bring your own towel. On morning cruises you'll get a Continental breakfast and a barbecue lunch. These trips are great for families with small kids, as there is lots of pint-size flotation equipment and underwater viewing devices for those who don't want to use a mask–snorkel setup. Morning cruises cost $119 for adults, $75 for kids ages 4–12 and $29 for kids 3 and under. Afternoon cruises cost $75 for adults, $45 for kids ages 4–12, and are free for kids 3 and under. Hula Kai cruises are $155 per person, which includes an alcoholic beverage and two gourmet meals. ⊠*78-7130 Kaleiopapa St., Keauhou Bay, Kailua-Kona* ☎*808/322–2788 or 800/677–9461* ⊕*www.fair-wind.com.*

Snorkel Bob's. You're likely to see his wacky ads in your airline inflight magazine. The company actually delivers what it promises, and you can make reservations online before beginning your trip. ⊠*75-5831 Kahakai St., Kailua-Kona* ☎*808/329–0770 or 800/262–7725* ⊕*www. snorkelbob.com.*

SUBMARINE TOURS

ⓒ **Atlantis VII Submarine.** Want to stay dry while exploring the undersea Fodor'sChoice world? Climb aboard the 48-foot *Atlantis VII* submarine anchored ★ off Kailua Pier, across from King Kamehameha's Kona Beach Hotel in Kailua-Kona. A large glass dome in the bow and 13 viewing ports on the sides allow clear views of the aquatic world more than 100 feet down. This is a great trip for kids and nonswimmers. Each one-hour voyage costs $90 for adults and $45 for children under 12. The company

Continued on page 364

SNORKELING IN HAWAI'I

The waters surrounding the Hawaiian Islands are filled with life—from giant manta rays cruising off the Big Island's Kona Coast to humpback whales giving birth in Maui's Mā'alaea Bay. Dip your head beneath the surface to experience a spectacularly colorful world: pairs of milletseed butterflyfish dart back and forth, red-lipped parrotfish snack on coral algae, and spotted eagle rays flap past like silent spaceships. Sea turtles bask at the surface while tiny wrasses give them the equivalent of a shave and a haircut. The water quality is typically outstanding; many sites afford 30-foot-plus visibility. On snorkel cruises, you can often stare from the boat rail right down to the bottom.

Certainly few destinations are as accommodating to every level of snorkeler as Hawai'i. Beginners can tromp in from sandy beaches while more advanced divers descend to shipwrecks, reefs, craters, and sea arches just offshore. Because of Hawai'i's extreme isolation, the island chain has fewer fish species than Fiji or the Caribbean—but many of the fish that are here exist nowhere else. The Hawaiian waters are home to the highest percentage of endemic fish in the world.

The key to enjoying the underwater world is slowing down. Look carefully. Listen. You might hear the strange crackling sound of shrimp tunneling through coral, or you may hear whales singing to one another during winter. A shy octopus may drift along the ocean's floor beneath you. If you're hooked, pick up a waterproof fishkey from Long's Drugs. You can brag later that you've looked the Hawaiian turkeyfish in the eye.

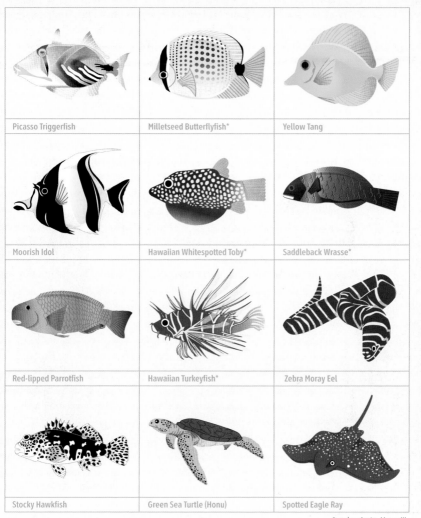

Picasso Triggerfish | Milletseed Butterflyfish* | Yellow Tang

Moorish Idol | Hawaiian Whitespotted Toby* | Saddleback Wrasse*

Red-lipped Parrotfish | Hawaiian Turkeyfish* | Zebra Moray Eel

Stocky Hawkfish | Green Sea Turtle (Honu) | Spotted Eagle Ray

*endemic to Hawai'i

POLYNESIA'S FIRST CELESTIAL NAVIGATORS: HONU

Honu is the Hawaiian name for two native sea turtles, the hawksbill and the green sea turtle. Little is known about these dinosaur-age marine reptiles, though snorkelers regularly see them foraging for *limu* (seaweed) and the occasional jellyfish in Hawaiian waters. Most female honu nest in the uninhabited Northwestern Hawaiian Islands, but a few sociable ladies nest on Maui and Big Island beaches. Scientists suspect that they navigate the seas via magnetism—sensing the earth's poles. Amazingly, they will journey up to 800 miles to nest—it's believed that they return to their own birth sites. After about 60 days of incubation, nestlings emerge from the sand at night and find their way back to the sea by the light of the stars.

also operates on Oʻahu and Maui. ☎808/329–6626 or 800/548–6262 ⊕ www.atlantisadventures.com.

SURFING

You won't find the world-class waves of Oʻahu or Maui on the Big Island, but there are decent waves and a thriving surf culture. Expect high surf in winter and much calmer activity during summer. The surf scene is much more active on the Kona side.

Among the best places to catch the waves are **Pine Trees** (⊠ *Off Hwy. 11 and south of Kona Airport and Natural Energy Lab of Hawaiʻi on an unimproved beach road*) and **Kahaluʻu Beach Park** (⊠ *Aliʻi Dr., 5½ mi south of Kailua-Kona next to Sheraton Keauhou Beach Hotel*). **Banyans** (⊠ *Aliʻi Dr. near Kona Bali Kai condos*) is popular with local surfers. **Old Kona Airport State Recreation Area** (⊠ *Kuakini Rd. at old Kona Airport*) is also a good place for catching wave action, and safe for beginners. On the east side near Hilo, try **Honoliʻi Cove** (⊠ *Access road off Hwy. 19, just past mile marker 4*).

EQUIPMENT AND LESSONS

Orchid Land Surf Shop. ⊠ *262 Kamehameha Ave., Hilo* ☎808/935–1533 ⊕ www.orchidlandsurf.com.

Pacific Vibrations. ⊠ *75-5702 Likana La., at Aliʻi Dr., a block south of Kailua Pier, Kailua-Kona* ☎808/329–4140.

WHALE-WATCHING

Each winter humpback whales migrate from the waters off Alaska to the warm Hawaiian ocean to give birth and care for their newborns. Recent reports indicate that the whale population is on the upswing—a few years ago one even ventured into the mouth of Hilo Harbor, which marine biologists say is quite rare. Humpbacks are spotted here from early December through the end of April, but other species can be seen year-round. Most ocean tour companies offer whale outings during the season, but the operators who do it fulltime are much more familiar with whale behavior and you're more likely to have a quality whale-watching experience. ■ TIP➜ **If you take the morning cruise, you're likely to see dolphins as well.**

Captain Dan McSweeney's Year-Round Whale Watching Adventures. This is probably the most experienced small operation on the island. Captain Dan McSweeney offers three-hour trips on his 40-foot boat. In addition to humpbacks in the winter, he'll show you some of the six other whale species that live off the Kona Coast year-round. Three-hour tours cost $70 per adult and $60 for kids 90 lbs and under (snacks and juices included). McSweeney guarantees you'll see a whale or he'll take you out again free. ⊠ *Honokōhau Harbor, Kailua-Kona* ☎808/322–0028 or 888/942–5376 ⊕ www.ilovewhales.com.

WINDSURFING

Windsurfers will find good waters and winds in the coves and bays along the Kohala Coast. The surf is usually choppy when the wind comes up but not so much that windsurfers can't get out. Unlike surfing, windsurfing requires no paddling. Instead, you have to hang on to a sail flapping in the wind and pick up speed. Coordination and balance are crucial. One of the best windsurfing locations on the Big Island is at **'Anaeho'omalu Beach** (✉ *Follow Waikoloa Beach Dr. to Kings' Shops, then turn left*) on the Kohala Coast. The beach is near the Waikoloa Beach Marriott.

EQUIPMENT & LESSONS

Ocean Sports. This concession fronting the Waikoloa Beach Resort rents boards and teaches windsurfing on the beach. ✉ *69-275 Waikoloa Beach Dr., Waikoloa* ☎ *808/886–6666 or 888/724–5924* ⊕ *www. hawaiioceansports.com.*

GOLF, HIKING, AND OUTDOOR ACTIVITIES

AERIAL TOURS

There's nothing quite like the aerial view of a waterfall that drops a couple thousand feet into multiple pools, or seeing lava flow to the ocean, where clouds of steam billow into the air. Although there have been a few cases of pilots violating flight paths and altitudes over resident communities in recent years, most operators are reputable and fly with strict adherence to FAA safety rules. How to get the best experience for your money? ■ TIP➔ **Before you hire a company, be a savvy traveler and ask the right questions. What kind of aircraft do they fly? Do they have two-way headsets so you can talk with the pilot? What is their safety record?**

Blue Hawaiian Helicopters. Conveniently located near the Kohala Coast resorts, Blue Hawaiian is the best way to explore the beauty of the whole island in just a few hours. The Big Island Spectacular soars through nine of the Island's 13 climate zones, swooping by waterfalls that cascade down 3,000-foot valley walls and hovering above the active volcano's lava. ✉ *Waikoloa Heliport, Waikoloa* ☎ *808/961–5600 or 800/786–BLUE* ⊕ *www.bluehawaiian.com* .

Mokulele Airlines. In addition to regular interisland scheduled flights, this commuter line offers a 1½-hour Circle Island Tour in a nine-passenger single-engine aircraft. The air tour departs Kona Airport and goes over Hawai'i Volcanoes National Park, the Hilo-Hāmākua Coast, and the Kohala Coast. Rates are $349 per person; ask about senior discounts. ☎ *808/326–7070 or 866/260–7070* ⊕ *www.mokulele.com.*

Paradise Helicopters. Paradise operates from Kona, but your best bet is flying out of Hilo on its four-passenger MD-500 aircraft. Everyone has a window seat in these highly maneuverable helicopters, and you can even select the "doors off" option for better viewing. Communicate with the friendly and knowledgeable pilots over two-way headsets. Another exciting option is the new Volcano & Waipio Hike which includes a

3½-mi hike in Waipio Valley, complete with a picnic lunch and the chance to swim in a waterfall. The 50-minute Volcano & Waterfall Adventure (from Hilo) is $230 per person or $259 per person with the "doors off"; the top-of-the-line four-hour Volcanoes & Valley Adventure (from Kona) is $610 per person, including lunch; the Volcanoe Waipio Hike tour is $672 per person. ⊠ *Hilo Airport, Kona Airport* ☏ *808/969–7392* ⊕ *www.paradisecopters.com.*

Sunshine Helicopters. Ride the "Black Beauties" on these exciting air tours that take in the ocean cliffs and valleys of the Kohala-Hāmākua Coast, or, from Hilo, the formations of the Kīlauea Volcano. Narrated tours range from 45 minutes to two hours; the longer tour covers both regions. Afterward, you can buy a DVD of your flight experience. ⊠ *Helipad at Hāpuna Beach Prince Hotel and Hilo Airport* ☏ *Hāpuna Beach Prince Hotel: 808/882–1223, Hilo: 808/969–7501 or 800/469–3000* ⊕ *www. sunshinehelicopters.com.*

ATV TOURS

A different way to experience the Big Island's rugged coastline and wild ranch lands is through an off-road adventure. At higher elevations, weather can be nippy and rainy, but views can be awesome. Protective gear is provided. Prices range from $85 to $249 per person, depending on tour length and specifics.

ATV Outfitters Hawai'i. ⊠ *53-324 Lighthouse Rd., Between 24 and 25 mile markers on Hwy. 270, Kapa'au* ☏ *808/889–6000 or 888/288–7288* ⊕ *www.atvoutfittershawaii.com.*

Kahuā Ranch ATV Rides. ⊠ *Hwy. 250, 10 mi north of Waimea* ☏ *808/ 882–7954 or 808/882–4646* ⊕ *www.kahuaranch.com.*

Waipi'o Ride the Rim. ⊠ *Waipi'o Valley Artworks Bldg., 48-5416 Kukuihaele Rd., Kukuihaele* ☏ *808/775–1007 or 877/757–1414* ⊕ *www. ridetherim.com.*

BIKING

Fodor's Choice ★ *Mountain Bike* magazine voted **Kulani Trails** the best ride in the state. To reach the trailhead from the intersection of Highway 11 and Highway 19, take Highway 19 south about 4 mi, then turn right onto Stainback Highway and continue on 2½ mi, then turn right at the Waiakea Arboretum. Park near the gate. This technically demanding ride, which passes majestic eucalyptus trees, is for advanced cyclists.

The **Old Puna Trail** (⊠ *Trailhead: From Hwy. 130, take Kaloli Rd. to Beach Rd.*) is a 10½-mi ride through the subtropical jungle in Puna, one of the island's most isolated areas. You'll start out on a cinder road, which becomes a four-wheel-drive trail. If it's rained recently, you'll have to deal with some puddles—the first few of which you'll gingerly avoid until you give in and go barreling through the rest of them for the sheer fun of it. This is a great ride for all abilities that takes about 90 minutes.

EQUIPMENT

If you want to strike out on your own, there are several rental shops in Kailua-Kona and a couple in Waimea and Hilo. Resorts rent bicycles that can be used around the properties. Most outfitters listed can provide a bicycle rack for your car.

Bike Works. This branch operation of Hawaiian Pedals caters to more advanced bicyclists and Ironman wannabes with its rentals of deluxe road bikes and full-suspension mountain bikes, starting at $40 a day. ✉ *Hale Hana Centre, 74-5583 Luhia St., Kailua-Kona* ☎ *808/326–2453* ⊕ *www.hpbikeworks.com.*

Cycle Station. This shop, which has a variety of bikes to rent, from road sport to racing bikes, hybrids to tandems, will also deliver to and pick up at hotels. It also has trailers for toddlers. Daily rentals range from $20 for a hybrid to $75 for a road or mountain racing bikes. ✉ *Kamanu St., Kailua-Kona* ☎ *808/327–0087* ⊕ *www.cyclestationhawaii.com.*

Hawaiian Pedals. For those who prefer comfort over speed, Hawaiian Pedals rents seven-speed cruisers and hybrids starting at $20 for 24 hours. ✉ *Kona Inn Shopping Village, 75-5744 Ali'i Dr., Kailua-Kona* ☎ *808/329–2294* ⊕ *www.hpbikeworks.com.*

GOING WITH A GUIDE

Orchid Isle Bicycling. Geared to cyclists of varying abilities, options range from challenging 3,500-foot climbs up Kohala Mountain to downhill-only rides. Half-day tours cover 8 to 55 mi and start at $125 per person. ✉ *73-5619 Kauhole St., Kailua-Kona* ☎ *808/327–0087 or 800/219–2324* ⊕ *www.cyclekona.com.*

Volcano Bike Tours. Discover craters, steaming vents, and lava tubes on the four- to five-hour Kilauea Volcano Summit to Sea & Wine Tasting Tour or bike through rain forests and lava landscapes to an active lava flow on the six- to seven-hour "Bike to Pele" Bike Adventure. The tours are $130 per person and include lunch or dinner and beverages. The trips cover mostly downhill and level terrain. ✉ *2352 Kalanianaole St., Hilo* ☎ *808/934–9199 or 888/934–9199* ⊕ *www.bikevolcano.com.*

GOLF

For golfers, the Big Island is a big deal, starting with the Mauna Kea Golf Course, which opened in 1964 and remains one of the state's top courses after a refurbishment in 2008.

Black lava and deep blue sea are the predominant themes on the island. Most of the best courses are concentrated along the Kona Coast, statistically the sunniest spot in the Hawaiian archipelago.

Green Fees: Green fees listed here are the highest course rates per round on weekdays for U.S. residents. Courses with varying weekend rates are noted in the individual listings. (Some courses charge non-U.S. residents higher prices.) ■ TIP→Discounts are often available for resort guests and for those who book tee times on the Web. Twilight fees are usually offered; call individual courses for information.

★ **Big Island Country Club.** Set 2,000 feet above sea level on the slopes of Mauna Kea, the Big Island Country Club is rather out of the way but well worth the drive. Pete and Perry Dye (1997) created a gem that plays through upland woodlands—more than 2,500 trees line the fairways. On the par-5 15th, a giant tree in the middle of the fairway must be avoided with the second shot. Five lakes and a meandering natural mountain stream mean water comes into play on nine holes. The

most dramatic is on the par-3 17th, where Dye creates a knockoff of his infamous 17th at the TPC at Sawgrass. ⊠ *71-1420 Māmalahoa Hwy., Kailua-Kona* ☎ *808/325–5044* ⊕ *www.intrawest.com* ⚑ *18 holes. 7075 yds. Par 72. Green fee: $109* ⚐ *Facilities: Driving range, putting green, rental clubs, golf carts, pro shop, lessons.*

Fodor'sChoice
★
Hāpuna Golf Course at Mauna Kea Beach Resort. Mauna Kea's second course, Hāpuna, was created by Arnold Palmer and Ed Seay in 1992. Hāpuna is a links-style course that rises to 600 feet elevation, providing views of the ocean and elevation-change challenges. Trees are a factor on most holes at Mauna Kea, but they seldom are at Hāpuna. Palmer and Seay put a premium on accuracy off the tee, and are more forgiving with approaches. ⊠ *62-100 Kauna'oa Dr., Kohala Coast* ☎ *808/880–3000* ⊕ *www.hapunabeachprincehotel.com* ⚑ *18 holes. 6534 yds. Par 72. Green fee: $165* ⚐ *Facilities: Driving range, putting green, golf carts, rental clubs, pro shop, lessons, restaurant, bar.*

★ **Hualālai Resort.** Named for the volcanic peak that is the target off the first tee, the Nicklaus Course at Hualālai is semiprivate, open only to guests of the adjacent Four Seasons Resort Hualālai. From the forward and resort tees, this is perhaps Jack Nicklaus's most friendly course in Hawai'i, but the back tees play a full mile longer. The par-3 17th plays across convoluted lava to a seaside green, and the view from the tee is so lovely, you may be tempted to just relax on the koa bench and enjoy the scenery. ⊠ *100 Ka'ūpūlehu Dr., Kohala Coast* ☎ *808/325–8480* ⊕ *www.fourseasons.com/hualalai* ⚑ *18 holes. 7117 yds. Par 72. Green fee: $250* ⚐ *Facilities: Driving range, putting green, pull carts, golf carts, rental clubs, lessons, pro shop, restaurant, bar.*

★ **Kona Country Club.** This venerable country club offers two very different tests with the aptly named Ocean and Ali'i Mountain courses. The Ocean Course (William F. Bell, 1967) is a bit like playing through a coconut plantation, with a few remarkable lava features—such as the "blowhole" in front of the par-4 13th, where sea water propelled through a lava tube erupts like a geyser. The Ali'i Mountain Course (front nine, William F. Bell, 1983: back nine, Robin Nelson and Rodney Wright, 1992) plays a couple of strokes tougher than the Ocean and is the most delightful split personality you may ever encounter. Both nines share breathtaking views of Keauhou Bay, and elevation change is a factor in most shots. The most dramatic view on the front nine is from the tee of the par-3 5th hole, one of the best golf vistas in Hawai'i. The back nine is links-style, with less elevation change— except for the par-3 14th, which drops 100 feet from tee to green, over

Most of the Big Island's top golf courses are located on the sunny Kona Coast.

a lake. The routing, the sight lines and framing of greens, and the risk-reward factors on each hole make this one of the single best nines in Hawai'i. ⊠78-7000 Ali'i Dr., Kailua-Kona ☎808/322–2595 ⊕www.konagolf.com ⎯⎱ Ocean Course: 18 holes. 6806 yds. Par 72. Green fee: $165. Mountain Course: 18 holes. 6673 yds. Par 72. Green fee: $150 ⌒Facilities: Driving range, putting green, golf carts, rental clubs, lessons, restaurant, bar.

Mākālei Country Club. Set on the slopes of Hualālai, at an elevation of 2,900 feet, Mākālei is one of the rare Hawai'i courses with bent-grass putting greens, which means they're quick and without the grain associated with Bermuda greens. Former PGA Tour official Dick Nugent (1994) designed holes that play through thick forest and open to provide wide ocean views. Elevation change is a factor on many holes, especially the par-3 15th, with the tee 80 feet above the green. ⊠72-3890 Hawai'i Belt Rd., Kailua-Kona ☎808/325–6625 ⎯⎱ 18 holes. 7041 yds. Par 72. Green fee: $89 before 11 AM; $65 after 11 AM ⌒Facilities: Driving range, putting green, golf carts, rental clubs, pro shop, lessons, restaurant.

Mauna Kea Golf Course. This prestigious and challenging golf course was designed by Robert Trent Jones Sr. in 1964, and it has stayed in the family. Jones' son, Rees Jones, and his company restored and modernized the course tee-to-green in 2008, adding new grasses to the tees, greens, fairways and roughs, and a new irrigation system. The clubhouse restaurant, Number 3, was also rebuilt. Note that at this writing the course was considering becoming private—call or check the Web site before visiting. ⊠62-100 Mauna Kea Beach Dr., Kohala

Coast ☎808/882–5400 ⊕*www.maunakearesort.com* ⚐*18 holes. 6737 yds. Par 72. Green fee: $210* ⚐*Facilities: Driving range, putting green, golf carts, rental clubs, pro shop, lessons, restaurant, bar.*

WORD OF MOUTH

". . . On the Big Island you also have an entire coastline of great golf courses. I'm told that rainfall on the Kohala coast averages 9 inches a year, so while the courses are lush, the weather is generally warm and dry. There are great courses at Mauna Lani (two courses and a good restaurant at the clubhouse). . . . There is also a renowned golf school at Mauna Lani if you want to take a few lessons." —Leburta

Fodor's Choice ★ **Mauna Lani Resort.** Black lava flows, lush green turf, white sand, and the Pacific's multihues of blue define the 36 holes at Mauna Lani. The South Course includes the par-3 15th across a turquoise bay, one of the most photographed holes in Hawai'i. But it shares "signature hole" honors with the seventh. A long par-3, it plays downhill over convoluted patches of black lava, with the Pacific immediately to the left and a dune to the right. The North Course plays a couple of shots tougher. Its most distinctive hole is the 17th, a par-3 with the green set in a lava pit 50 feet deep. The shot from an elevated tee must carry a pillar of lava that rises from the pit and partially blocks your view of the green. ✉*68-1310 Mauna Lani Dr., Kohala Coast* ☎*808/885–6655* ⊕*www.maunalani.com* ⚐*North Course: 18 holes. 6601 yds. Par 72. Green fee: $260 before 1 PM, $180 after 1 PM. South Course: 18 holes. 6436 yds. Par 72. Green fee: $260 before 1 PM, $180 after 1 PM* ⚐*Facilities: Driving range, putting green, golf carts, rental clubs, pro shop, lessons, restaurant, bar.*

Volcano Golf & Country Club. Just outside Volcanoes National Park— and barely a stout drive from Halema'uma'u Crater—Volcano is by far Hawai'i's highest course. At 4,200 feet elevation, shots tend to fly a bit farther than at sea level, even in the often cool, misty air. Because of the elevation and climate, Volcano is one of the few Hawai'i courses with bent-grass putting greens. The course is mostly flat and holes play through stands of Norfolk pines, flowering *lehua* trees, and multitrunk *hau* trees. The uphill par-4 15th doglegs through a tangle of *hau*. ✉*Pi'i Mauna Dr., off Hwy. 11, Volcanoes National Park* ☎*808/967–7331* ⊕*www.volcanogolfshop.com* ⚐*18 holes. 6106 yds. Par 72. Green fee: $70 mornings, $57 afternoon* ⚐*Facilities: Driving range, putting green, golf carts, rental clubs, restaurant, bar.*

Fodor's Choice ★ **Waikoloa Beach Resort.** Robert Trent Jones Jr. built the Beach Course at Waikoloa (1981) on an old flow of crinkly 'a'ā lava, which he used to create holes that are as artful as they are challenging. The third tee, for instance, is set at the base of a towering mound of lava. The par-5 12th plays through a chute of black lava to an ocean-side green, the blue sea on the right coming into play on the second and third shots. At the King's Course at Waikoloa (1990), Tom Weiskopf and Jay Morrish built a very links-esque track. It turns out lava's natural humps and declivities remarkably replicate the contours of seaside Scotland. But there are a few island twists—such as seven lakes. This is "option golf" as Weiskopf and Morrish provide different risk-reward tactics on

Continued on page 374

BIRTH OF THE ISLANDS

How did the volcanoes of the Hawaiian Islands evolve here, in the middle of the Pacific Ocean? The ancient Hawaiians believed that the volcano goddess Pele's hot temper was the key to the mystery; modern scientists contend that it's all about plate tectonics and one very hot spot.

Plate Tectonics & the Hawaiian Question: The theory of plate tectonics says that the Earth's surface is comprised of plates that float around slowly over the planet's molten interior. The vast majority of earthquakes and volcanic eruptions occur near plate boundaries—the San Francisco earthquakes in 1906 and 1989, for example, were the result of activity along the nearby San Andreas Fault, where the Pacific and North American plates meet. Hawai'i, more than 1,988 miles from the nearest plate boundary, is a giant exception. For years scientists struggled to explain the island chain's existence—if not a fault line, what caused the earthquakes and volcanic eruptions that formed these islands?

What's a hotspot? In 1963, J. Tuzo Wilson, a Canadian geophysicist, argued that the Hawaiian volcanoes must have been created by small concentrated areas of extreme heat beneath the plates. Wilson hypothesized that there is a hotspot beneath the present-day position of the Big Island. Its heat produced a persistent source of magma by partly melting the Pacific Plate above it. The magma, lighter than the surrounding solid rock, rose through the mantle and crust to erupt onto the sea floor, forming an active seamount. Each flow caused the seamount to grow until it finally emerged above sea level as an island volcano. Plausible so far, but why then, is there not one giant Hawaiian island?

HAWAIIAN CREATION MYTH

Holo Mai Pele, often played out in hula, is the Hawaiian creation myth. Pele sends her sister Hi'iaka on an epic quest to fetch her lover Lohi'au. Overcoming many obstacles, Hi'iaka reaches full goddess status and falls in love with Lohi'au herself. When Pele finds out, she destroys everything dear to her sister, killing Lohi'au and burning Hi'iaka's 'ohi'a groves. Each time lava flows from a volcano, 'ohi'a trees sprout shortly after, in a constant cycle of destruction and renewal.

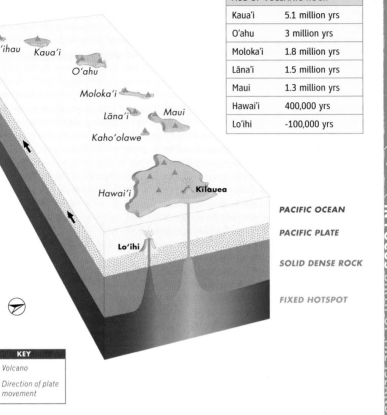

AGE OF VOLCANIC ROCK	
Kaua'i	5.1 million yrs
O'ahu	3 million yrs
Moloka'i	1.8 million yrs
Lāna'i	1.5 million yrs
Maui	1.3 million yrs
Hawai'i	400,000 yrs
Lo'ihi	-100,000 yrs

PACIFIC OCEAN

PACIFIC PLATE

SOLID DENSE ROCK

FIXED HOTSPOT

KEY

▲ Volcano

◄ Direction of plate movement

Volcanoes on the Move: Wilson further suggested that the movement of the Pacific Plate itself eventually carries the island volcano beyond the hotspot. Cut off from its magma source, the island volcano becomes dormant. As the plate slowly moved, one island volcano would become extinct just as another would develop over the hotspot. After several million years, there is a long volcanic trail of islands and seamounts across the ocean floor. The oldest islands are those farthest from the hotspot. The exposed rocks of Kaua'i, for example, are about 5.1 million years old, but those on the Big Island are less than .5 million years old, with new volcanic rock still being formed.

An Island on the Way: Off the coast of the Big Island, the volcano known as Lo'ihi is still submerged but erupting. Scientists long believed it to be a retired seamount volcano, but in the 1970s they discovered both old and new lava on its flanks, and in 1996 it erupted with a vengeance. It is believed that several thousand years from now, Lo'ihi will be the newest addition to the Hawaiian Islands.

Ironman and Friends

Run annually since 1978, the Ironman Triathlon World Championship (☎ *808/329–0063* ⊕ *www.ironmanlive. com*) is the granddaddy of them all. For about a week prior to Race Day (the third Saturday of October), Kailua-Kona takes on the air of an Olympic Village as top athletes from across the globe arrive to compete for glory and $580,000 in prize money at the world's premiere swim/bike/run endurance event. To watch the nearly 1,800 competitors push themselves to the ultimate in this grueling event is an inspiring testament to the human spirit. The competition starts at Kailua Pier with a 2.4-mi open-water swim, immediately followed by a 112-mi bicycle ride, then a 26.2-mi marathon. The Ironman wouldn't happen without the 7,000 volunteers who donate their time and services. To volunteer, register online at the Ironman Web site.

The **Honu Half-Ironman Triathlon** (☎ *808/329–0063* ⊕ *www.honuhalf ironman.com*) in late May or early June is an Ironman "farm team event." Participants swim at Hāpuna beach, bike the Ironman course, and run on the Mauna Lani resort grounds.

Supermen and women do the Ironman. A few notches down on the difficulty scale, but still extremely challenging, is the **Lavaman Triathlon** (⊕ *www.lava mantriathlon.com*) held at the end of March or beginning of April. The race occurs along the Kohala Coast, with a 1.5-km swim in Anaeho'omalu Bay, a 40-km bike along Queen K. and a 10-km run through, yes, you guessed it, a lava field.

For the most current race information, check out the **Big Island Race Schedule** (⊕ *www.bigislandraceschedule.com/ race_links.html*).

each hole. Beach and King's have separate clubhouses. **Beach Course:** ⊠ *1020 Keana Pl., Waikoloa* ☎ *808/886–6060* ⊕ *www.waikoloagolf. com* 🏌 *18 holes. 6566 yds. Par 70. Green fee: $195* ☞ *Facilities: Driving range, putting green, golf carts, rental clubs, lessons, restaurant, bar.* **Kings' Course:** ⊠ *600 Waikoloa Beach Dr., Waikoloa* ☎ *808/886–7888* ⊕ *www.waikoloagolf.com* 🏌 *18 holes. 6594 yds. Par 72. Green fee: $195* ☞ *Facilities: Driving range, putting green, golf carts, rental clubs, lessons, restaurant, bar.*

Waikoloa Village Golf Course. A 20-minute drive from Waikoloa Beach Resort, Robert Trent Jones Jr.'s Waikoloa Village (1972) is not affiliated with the resort. It is, however, the site of the annual Waikoloa Open, one of the most prestigious tournaments in Hawai'i. Holes run across rolling hills with sweeping mountain and ocean views. ⊠ *68-1792 Melia St., Waikoloa* ☎ *808/883–9621* ⊕ *www.waikoloa.org* 🏌 *18 holes. 6230 yds. Par 72. Green fee: $80* ☞ *Facilities: Driving range, putting green, golf carts, rental clubs, lessons, restaurant, bar.*

HIKING

Meteorologists classify the world's weather into 13 climates. Ten are here on the Big Island, and you can experience as many of them as you like. The ancient Hawaiians blazed trails across their archipelago, and many of these paths can still be used today. Part of the King's Trail at ʻAnaehoʻomalu winds through a field of lava rocks covered with prehistoric carvings called petroglyphs, meant to communicate stories of births, deaths, marriages, and other family events. Plus, the serenity of remote beaches, such as Papakōlea Beach (Green Sand Beach), is accessible only to hikers.

For information on all Big Island's state parks, contact the **Department of Land and Natural Resources, State Parks Division** (⊠ *75 Aupuni St., Hilo* ☎ *808/974–6200* ⊕ *www. state.hi.us/dlnr/dsp/hawaii.html*).

4

BEST SPOTS

See Hawaiʻi Volcanoes National Park feature in this chapter.

At **Kekaha Kai (Kona Coast) State Park** (⊠ *Hwy. 19, sign about 2 mi north of Keāhole–Kona International Airport marks rough road*), two 1½-mi-long unpaved roads lead to the Mahaiʻula Beach and Kua Bay sections of the park. Mahaiʻula has a sandy beach with a picnic area. A 4½-mi hike north along the Ala Kahakai historic coastal trail leads to Kua Bay. Midway, a hike to the summit of Puʻu Kuʻili, a 342-foot-high cinder cone, offers an excellent view of the coastline. It's dry and hot with no drinking water, so be sure to pack sunscreen and bottled water.

The **Mauna Kea Trail** (⊠ *Trailhead at Onizuka Visitors Center*) ascends from the visitor center (9,200 feet) to the 13,000-foot summit. The difficult, four-hour trek rewards the hardy with glimpses of endangered species, a stunning view of the primeval Lake Waiau, and a fabulous vantage point from the top of the world (you look down on the sunset). Because of the difficulty of the trail and the low-oxygen environment, it's a very tough hike even for the most fit. This trek is not recommended for children under 16, pregnant women, or those with respiratory problems.

GUIDED HIKES

To get to some of the best trails and places, it's worth going with a skilled guide. Costs range from $115 to $225, and hikes include picnic meals and gear such as binoculars, ponchos, and walking sticks. The outfitters mentioned here also offer customized adventure tours.

Hawaiʻi Forest & Trail. Expert naturalist guides take you to hidden waterfalls in North Kohala, through the 4,000-year-old craters at Mount Hualālai (the volcano that created all those lava fields along the coast), and on bird-watching expeditions throughout the island. In addition to its other expeditions, the company offers tours in Pinzgauers (Austrian all-terrain vehicles) that are perfect for groups, especially those that include off-road junkies. It also offers tours into lava tubes and through normally inaccessible areas of Hawaiʻi Volcanoes National Park. ☎ *808/331–8505 or 800/464–1993* ⊕ *www.hawaii-forest.com.*

Hawaiian Walkways. Hawaiian Walkways conducts several tours—waterfall hikes, coastal adventures, flora and fauna explorations, and jaunts through Hawai'i Volcanoes National Park—as well as custom-designed trips. ☎808/775–0372 or 800/457–7759 ⊕*www.hawaiianwalkways.com.*

HORSEBACK RIDING

With its *paniolo* heritage, the Big Island is a great place for equestrians. Riders can gallop through green Upcountry pastures, ride to Kealakekua Bay to see the Captain Cook Monument, or saunter into Waipi'o Valley for a taste of old Hawai'i.

King's Trail Rides O'Kona. Riders take an excursion (two hours of riding) to a secluded bay north of Kealakekua Bay for snorkeling. (All your gear is provided, except for fins and reef walkers.) The cost is $135 on weekdays and $150 on weekends and holidays and includes lunch. ⊠*Hwy. 11, mile marker 111, Kealakekua* ☎808/323–2388 or 808/345–0616 ⊕*www.konacowboy.com.*

Na'alapa Stables. This company is a good bet, especially for novice riders. The horses are well trained, and the stable is well run. Rides through the Waipi'o Valley cross freshwater streams and pass a black-sand beach. Rides depart twice daily from Waipi'o Valley Artworks and begin at $89. ⊠*Off Hwy. 240, Kukuihaele* ☎808/775–0419 ⊕*www.naalapastables.com.*

Waipi'o Ridge Stables. Two different rides around the rim of Waipi'o Valley are offered—a 2½-hour trek for $85 and a five-hour hidden-waterfall adventure (with swimming) for $165. Riders meet at Waipi'o Valley Artworks. ⊠*Off Hwy. 240, Kukuihaele* ☎808/775–1007 or 877/757–1414 ⊕*www.waipioridgestables.com.*

SKIING

Where else but Hawai'i can you surf, snorkel, and snow ski on the same day? In winter, the 13,796-foot Mauna Kea (Hawaiian for "white mountain") has snow at higher elevations—and along with that, skiing. No lifts, no manicured slopes, no faux-Alpine lodges, no apres-ski nightlife—but the chance to ski some of the most remote (and let's face it, unlikely) runs on earth. Some people even have been known to use boogie boards as sleds, but we don't recommend it. As long as you're up there, fill your cooler with the white stuff for a snowball fight on the beach with local kids.

Ski Guides Hawai'i. ✐*Box 1954, Kamuela 96743* ☎808/885–4188, 808/884–5131 off-season ⊕*www.skihawaii.com.*

TENNIS

Many of the island's resorts allow non-guests to play for a fee. They also rent rackets, balls, and shoes. On the Kohala Coast, **DiDonato Facility Management** (☎808/886–2222 ⊕*www.kohalatennis.com*) handles the tennis facilities at the Mauna Lani Resort, Fairmont Orchid Hawai'i and Hilton Waikoloa Village. In Kailua-Kona there's the Outrigger Keauhou Beach Resort, King Kamehameha's Kona Beach Hotel, and the Royal Kona Resort.

Contact the **County of Hawai'i Department of Parks and Recreation** (✉ *25 Aupuni St., Hilo* ☎ *808/961–8311* ⊕ *www.hawaii-county.com/directory/ dir_parks.htm*) for information on all public courts.

In Kailua-Kona, you can play for free at the **Kailua Playground** (✉ *75-5794 Kuakini Hwy., Kailua-Kona* ☎ *808/961–8311*). Tennis courts are available at **Old Kona Airport State Recreation Area** (✉ *North end of Kuakini Hwy., Kailua-Kona* ☎ *808/327–4958 or 808/974–6200*).

On the Hilo side, there's a small fee to play on the eight courts (three lighted for night play) at **Hilo Tennis Stadium** (✉ *Ho'olulu County Park, Pi'ilani and Kalanikoa Sts., Hilo* ☎ *808/961–8720*).

ZIPLINE TOURS

Big Island Eco-Adventures Zip Line Canopy Tour. Soar above the treetops of North Kohala with the Big Island's first zip line. This four-hour round-trip excursion with a *very* bumpy off-road ride lets you zip along eight separate lines past waterfalls, native Albizia and Ironwood forests, and deep gulches. Waiting for your turn is a bit tedious, and the price is a little steep considering only a small snack is included. However, this is a unique and fun way to discover the Big Island. ✉ *Off Akoni Pule Hwy just past 24 mile marker Kapa'au* ☎ *808/889–5111* ⊕ *www.bigisland ecoadventures.com* ⌂ *$159* ⊘ *Sun. private parties only.*

SHOPPING

Residents like to complain that there isn't much to shop for on the Big Island, but unless you're searching for winter coats or high-tech toys, you can find plenty to deplete your pocketbook. Kailua-Kona has a range of souvenirs from far-flung corners of the globe. Resorts along the Kohala Coast have high-quality clothing and accessories. Galleries and boutiques, many showcasing the work of local artists, fill historic buildings in Waimea and North Kohala.

In general, stores and shopping centers on the Big Island open at 9 or 10 AM and close by 6 PM. Hilo's Prince Kūhiō Shopping Plaza stays open until 9 weekdays. In Kona, most shops in shopping plazas that are geared to tourists remain open until 9. Big outlets such as Wal-Mart are open until midnight.

KOHALA COAST

SHOPPING CENTERS

Kawaihae Harbor Center. This harborside shopping plaza houses a dive shop, a bathing-suit store, restaurants, and art galleries, including the Harbor Gallery. ✉ *Hwy. 270, Kawaihae.*

Kings' Shops at Waikoloa Beach Resort. Here you can find fine stores such as Under the Koa Tree, with its upscale gift items crafted by artisans, along with high-end outlets such as DFS Galleria, Tiffany & Co., and Louis Vuitton and several other specialty resort shops and boutiques. At the other end of the spectrum, there is a convenience store, but the prices are stiff. For dining options, head to Roy's Waikoloa Bar & Grill and Merriman's Market Café. Entertainment and activities also take place at the Kings' Shops, from Hawaiian music and arts and crafts to petroglyph tours. ⊠ *250 Waikoloa Beach Dr., Waikoloa Beach Resort Waikoloa* ☎ *808/886–8811* ⊕ *www.waikoloabeachresort.com*

Queens' MarketPlace at Waikoloa Beach Resort. The Kohala Coast's newest shopping and dining experience is the Queens' MarketPlace. Find "aloha wear" at Reyn's and Blue Ginger Family, great bathing suits at multiple surf shops, and top-notch shades at Sunglass Hut. There are also trendy boutiques, jewelry stores, and island-style gift shops. Island Gourmet Markets is well-stocked, albeit expensive, while the food court is perfect for quick, affordable meals. Additional dining options include Romano's Macaroni Grill and Sansei Seafood Restaurant & Sushi Bar. Like the Kings' Shops, there are cultural classes and performances here, and the island's largest entertainment venue, the Waikoloa Bowl at the Queens' Gardens, is right next door. ⊠ *201 Waikoloa Beach Dr., Waikoloa Beach Resort Waikoloa* ☎ *808/886–8822* ⊕ *www.waikoloabeachresort.com.*

Shops at Mauna Lani. In an effort to keep up with the Joneses, or in this case the Hiltons, Mauna Lani has opened its own collection of shops and restaurants, including Big Island Sports Coalition, a high-performance fitness outfitter; Tori Richard by Quiet Storm, featuring upscale resort attire; and steak houses by Tommy Bahama and Ruth's Chris. There is also a Foodland Farms—one of the best places on the Kohala Coast to stock up on groceries and fresh seafood. On some evenings there are 30-minute, complimentary shows with hula and music by the prominent Lim Family. ⊠ *68-1400 Mauna Lani Dr., Mauna Lani Resort Kohala Coast* ☎ *808/885–9501* ⊕ *www.shopsatmaunalani.com.*

BOOKS AND MAPS

Kohala Book Shop. In the historic Old Nanbu Hotel, the state's largest used-book store contains one of the most complete Hawaiian and Pacific collections. There are also some rare first editions. ⊠ *54-3885 Akoni Pule Hwy., Kapaʻau* ☎ *808/889–6400.*

CLOTHING

As Hāwī Turns. This North Kohala shop, in the historic 1932 Toyama Building, adds a sophisticated touch to resort wear with items made of hand-painted silk. There are vintage and secondhand treasures as well. ⊠ *Akoni Pule Hwy., Hāwī* ☎ *808/889–5023.*

HAWAIIAN ARTS AND CRAFTS

Remote North Kohala has a remarkable number of galleries in its old restored plantation buildings.

Ackerman Fine Art Gallery. Painter Gary Ackerman, his wife, Yesan, and their daughter, Camille, have a fine and varied collection of gifts for sale in their side-by-side gallery and gift shop near the King Kamehameha statue. ⊠ *54-3878 Akoni Pule Hwy., Kapaʻau* ☎ *808/889–5971.*

Elements Jewelry & Fine Crafts. Be sure to stop at the Old Nanbu Hotel, built in 1898. In the front window of his store, John Flynn creates exquisite jewelry such as delicate silver leis and gold waterfalls. The shop also showcases carefully chosen gifts, including unusual ceramics and glass. ⊠ *54-3885 Akoni Pule Hwy., Kapaʻau* ☎*808/889–0760.*

The Gallery-Hilton Waikoloa Village. Find high-quality original works of art from raku pottery, wood turnings, and hand-blown and fused glass to paintings and clay, wood, and bronze sculptures. Everything is made by artists that reside in Hawaii, particularly on the Big Island. ⊠*69-425 Waikoloa Beach Dr., Hilton Waikoloa Village Waikoloa* ☎*808/886–2199* ⊕*www.thegalleryhwv.com.*

Rankin Gallery. Watercolorist and oil painter Patrick Louis Rankin runs this shop in the old Wo On Store, next to the Chinese community and social hall, the Tong Wo Society. ⊠ *53-4380 Akoni Pule Hwy., Kapaʻau* ☎*808/889–6849.*

Swerdlow Art Gallery. This is a great little gallery with Swerdlow's studio in the back and unique, beautiful paintings and prints in the front. Swerdlow also showcases the work of other local artists, offering everything from paintings to prints and etched glass, plus a range of gift items and interesting home objets d'art. ⊠ *54-3862 Akoni Pule Hwy., Kapaʻau* ☎*808/889–0002.*

WAIMEA

SHOPPING CENTERS

Parker Ranch Center. With a snazzy ranch-style motif, this shopping hub includes a supermarket, coffee shop, natural foods store, and some clothing boutiques. The Gear Up & Go desk for the Parker Ranch Historic Homes is also here. ⊠*67-1185 Māmalahoa Hwy., Waimea.*

Parker Square. Browse around boutiques here and in the adjacent **High Country Traders,** where you may find hand-stitched Hawaiian quilts. ⊠*65-1279 Kawaihae Rd., Waimea.*

HAWAIIAN ARTS AND CRAFTS

Dan DeLuz's Woods. Master bowl-turner Dan DeLuz creates works of art from 50 types of exotic wood grown on the Big Island. The shop features a variety of items—from picture frames to jewelry boxes—made from koa, monkeypod, mango, kiawe, and other fine local hardwoods. ⊠*64-1013 Māmalahoa Hwy., Waimea* ☎*808/885–5856* ⊠*Hwy. 19, Mountain View* ☎*808/968–6607.*

Gallery of Great Things. At this Parker Square shop, you might fall in love with the Niʻihau shell lei ranging from $150 to $7,000. More affordable are koa mirrors and other high-quality artifacts from around the Pacific basin. ⊠*65-1279 Kawaihae Rd., Waimea* ☎*808/885–7706.*

Harbor Gallery. For fine art, furniture, and decorative pieces made with koa and other native woods, be sure to stop here. The gallery is next to Harbor Grill. ⊠*Kawaihae Harbor Center, Hwy. 270, Kawaihae* ☎*808/882–1510.*

KAILUA-KONA

SHOPPING CENTERS

Coconut Grove Marketplace. Just south of Kona Inn Shopping Village, this meandering labyrinth of airy buildings hides coffee shops, boutiques, ethnic restaurants, and an exquisite gallery. ⊠ *75-5795–75-5825 Ali'i Dr.*

Kaloko Industrial Park. Developed for local consumers, this shopping plaza has outlets such as Costco Warehouse and Home Depot. It's useful for off-the-beaten-path finds. ⊠ *Off Hwy. 19 and Hina Lani St., near Keāhole-Kona International Airport.*

Kona Marketplace. On the *makai* side of Ali'i Drive, in the heart of Kailua-Kona and extending for an entire block along Kailua Bay, the village is crammed with boutiques selling bright beach wraps and knickknacks. ⊠ *75-5744 Ali'i Dr.*

Makalapua Center. Just north of Kona, off Highway 19, Islanders find bargains at Kmart and island-influenced clothing, jewelry, and housewares at the large Macy's, along with one of the island's largest movie theaters. ⊠ *Kamakaeha Ave. at Hwy. 19, Kailua-Kona.*

CANDIES AND CHOCOLATES

Kailua Candy Company. The chocolate here is made with locally grown cacao beans from the Original Hawaiian Chocolate Factory. Of course, tasting is part of the fun. Through a glass wall you can watch the chocolate artists at work. ⊠ *In Koloko Industrial Area, Kamanu and Kauholo Sts., Kailua-Kona* ☎ *808/329–2522.*

CLOTHING

'A'ama Surf & Sport. This boutique has some cool button-ups for men, along with unbelievably cute suits for women in a variety of unusual styles and fabrics. There's a branch on Henry, across the street from the Crossroads Shopping Center. ⊠ *75-5741 Kuakini Hwy.* ☎ *808/326–7890* ⊠ *75-1002 Henry St.* ☎ *808/326–7890.*

★ **Hilo Hattie.** The well-known clothier matches his-and-her aloha wear and carries a huge selection of casual clothes, slippers, jewelry, and souvenirs. Call for free transportation from nearby hotels. ⊠ *75-5597 Palani Rd., Kopiko Plaza, Kailua-Kona* ☎ *808/329–7200.*

Honolua Surf Company. Surfer chic, compliments of Roxy, Volcom, and the like: this is a great place to look for a bikini or board shorts or to pick up a cool, casual T-shirt. ⊠ *75-5744 Ali'i Dr., Kona Inn Shopping Village, Kailua-Kona* ☎ *808/329–1001.*

Miss M. Kealakekua is home to the first high-end designer boutique on the Big Island. They carry squeal-worthy contemporary clothing from designers like Carlos Miele, Barbara Bui, and Catherine Malandrino. If these names are familiar, we don't need to tell you to expect high prices. ⊠ *79-7491 Māmalahoa Hwy., Kealakekua* ☎ *808/322–2260.*

Paradise Found. In the upcountry town of Kainaliu, as well as in two of Kailua-Kona's shopping centers, this reputable spot carries contemporary silk and rayon clothing. ⊠ *Māmalahoa Hwy. 11, Kainaliu* ☎ *808/322–2111* ⊠ *Keauhou Shopping Center, 78-6831 Ali'i Dr., Kailua-Kona* ☎ *808/324–1177.*

Yamaya. The only shop in downtown that favors trendier threads for women, Yamaya sells mainland standards like Miss Me and Level 99 Jeans, dresses by Akualani, and Gaya shoes and purses. ⊠ *75-5744 Ali'i Dr., Kona Inn Shopping Village Kailua-Kona* ☎ *808/329–8606.*

HAWAIIAN ARTS AND CRAFTS

Hōlualoa Gallery. In the little coffee town of Hōlualoa, this is one of several excellent galleries that crowd the narrow street. It carries stunning raku (Japanese lead-glazed pottery). ⊠ *76-5921 Māmalahoa Hwy., Hōlualoa* ☎ *808/322–8484.*

★ **Kimura's Lauhala Shop.** Men can pick up an authentic *lauhala* hat here for some stylish sun protection. ⊠ *Māmalahoa Hwy. and Hualalai Rd., Hōlualoa* ☎ *808/324–0053.*

Kona Arts Center. There's an entire community of artists at work in this complex; feel free to drop in if the doors are open. ⊠ *Māmalahoa Hwy., Hōlualoa.*

Showcase Gallery. With artwork from more than 100 of Hawai'i's most talented artists, it will be hard to choose which piece to buy. Browse jewelry, sculpture, ceramics, photography, hand-blown glass, and more. ⊠ *78-6831 Ali'i Dr., Keauhou Shopping Center Kailua-Kona* ☎ *808/322–9711* ⊕ *www.keauhoushoppingcenter.com* ☾ *Mon.–Sat. 10–6, Sun. noon–5.*

MARKETS

★ **Ali'i Gardens Marketplace.** More a flea market than a farmers' market, this cluster of vendor stalls has everything from beautiful tropical flowers to locally grown coffee. It's open daily 9 to 5. ⊠ *75-6129 Ali'i Dr., 1½ mi south of Kona Inn Shopping Village, Kailua-Kona* ☎ *808/334–1381.*

Kona Farmers' Market. This low-key farmers' market is filled with produce, coffee, and macadamia nuts from around the region. It's held in the parking lot of the Kona Inn Shopping Village Wednesday through Sunday from 7 until 4. ⊠ *75-7544 Ali'i Dr., park at Kona Inn Shopping Village parking lot, Kailua-Kona.*

Kona International Market. The new kid on the block, housed in an open-air facility, has attracted vendors away from a lot of other island markets to sell flowers, local produce, Hawaiian crafts, clothes, and random collectibles. It's open Tuesday through Sunday 9 to 5. ⊠ *On Luhia St., in Kailua-Kona's Old Industrial Area.*

HILO

SHOPPING CENTERS

Hilo Shopping Center. This rather dated shopping plaza has several air-conditioned shops and restaurants. Great cookies, cakes, and baked goodies are at Lanky's Pastries. There's plenty of free parking. ⊠ *345 Kekuanaoa St. at Kīlauea Ave., Hilo.*

Prince Kūhiō Shopping Plaza. Hilo's most comprehensive mall, Prince Kūhiō Shopping Plaza is where you can find Macy's for fashion, Safeway for food, and Longs Drugs for just about everything else, along with several other shops and boutiques. ⊠ *111 E. Puainako St., at Hwy. 11, Hilo* ☎ *808/959–3555.*

Waiakea Center. Here you can find a Borders Books & Music, Island Naturals, and a Wal-Mart. If all the shopping makes you hungry, there's also a food court. ⊠*315-325 Maka'ala St. at Kanoelehua Ave., across from Prince Kūhiō Shopping Plaza, at Hwy. 11, Hilo* ☎*808/792-7225.*

BOOKS AND MAGAZINES

Basically Books. This shop stocks one of Hawai'i's largest selections of maps and charts, including topographical and relief maps. It also has Hawaiiana books, with great choices for children. ⊠*160 Kamehameha Ave., Hilo* ☎*808/961-0144 or 800/903-6277.*

CANDIES AND CHOCOLATE

★ **Big Island Candies.** This chocolate factory lets you tour and taste before you buy. ⊠*585 Hinano St., Hilo* ☎*808/935-8890.*

CLOTHING

★ **Hilo Hattie.** The well-known clothier matches his-and-her aloha wear and carries a huge selection of casual clothes, slippers, jewelry, and souvenirs. Call for free transportation from selected hotels. ⊠*Prince Kūhiō Shopping Plaza, 111 E. Puainako St., Hilo* ☎*808/961-3077.*

★ **Sig Zane Designs.** This acclaimed boutique sells distinctive island wearables with bold colors and motifs. ⊠*122 Kamehameha Ave., Hilo* ☎*808/935-7077.*

GIFTS

Dragon Mama. Step into this spot to find authentic Japanese fabrics, futons, and antiques. ⊠*266 Kamehameha Ave., Hilo* ☎*808/934-9081.*

Fuku-Bonsai Cultural Center. In addition to selling and shipping miniature *brassaia lava* plantings and other bonsai plants, this place on the way to Volcano has interesting exhibits of different ethnic styles of pruning. ⊠*17-856A Ola'a Rd., Kurtistown* ☎*808/982-9880.*

Hoaloha. If you're driving north from Hilo, take time to browse through this shop and pick up a colorful *pareu* (beach wrap). ⊠*Last Chance Store, off Hwy. 240, Kukuihaele*

Most Irresistible Shop. This place lives up to its name by stocking unique gifts from around the Pacific, be it coconut-flavored butter or whimsical wind chimes. ⊠*256 Kamehameha Ave., 96720* ☎*808/935-9644.*

Waipi'o Valley Artworks. In this remote gallery you can find finely crafted wooden bowls, koa furniture, paintings, and jewelry—all made by local artists. ⊠*48-5416 Kukuihaele Rd., off Hwy. 240, Kukuihaele* ☎*808/775-0958.*

MARKETS

★ **Hilo Farmers' Market.** The farmers here sell a profusion of tropical flowers, high-quality produce, and macadamia nuts, while local craftspeople sell clothing, jewelry, art, and collectibles. This colorful, open-air market—the most popular in the state—opens for business Wednesday and Saturday from 6:30 AM to 2:30 PM. ⊠*Kamehameha Ave. and Mamo St., Hilo.*

SPAS

Ho'ōla Spa at the Sheraton Keauhou Bay. The Sheraton Keauhou Bay occupies one of the prettier corners of the island, with an unbeatable view from most parts of the hotel. That said, it's too bad that the Ho'ōla Spa fails to truly take advantage of its location. Although there are plenty of windows with pretty views of the bay, the spa lacks the outdoor treatment areas other island spas are known for. Still, the spa menu includes a variety of locally influenced treatments, and the warm lava-rock massage is a little slice of heaven. The packages are an excellent deal, combining several services for far less than you would pay à la carte. For couples, the spa offers an ocean-side massage that takes place on a balcony overlooking the water, followed by a dip in a whirlpool bath. ⊠*78-128 Ehukai St., Kailua-Kona* ☎*808/930–4900* ⊕*www.hawaiianrainforest.com* ☞*$120 50-min lomi lomi massage; $225–$410 packages. Hair salon, hot tub, sauna, steam room. Services: aromatherapy, body scrubs and wraps, facials, massages, waxing.*

★ **Kohala Sports Club & Spa at the Hilton Waikoloa Village.** The orchids that run riot in the rain forests of the Big Island suffuse the signature treatments at the Kohala Sports Club & Spa. By the end of the Orchid Isle Wrap, you're completely immersed in the scent and in bone-deep relaxation. The island's volcanic character is also expressed in several treatments, as well as in the design of the lava-rock soaking tubs. Locker rooms are outfitted with a wealth of beauty and bath products. The extensive hair and nail salon could satisfy even Bridezilla with its updo consultations and luxe pedicure stations. The fitness center is well-equipped, but group classes that roam across the beautifully manicured resort grounds—like tai chi on the lawn or walking meditation at Buddha Point—are much more appealing. ⊠*Hilton Waikoloa Village, 69-425 Waikoloa Beach Dr., Waikoloa* ☎*808/886–2828 or 800/445–8667* ⊕*www.kohalaspa.com* ☞*$160 50-min massage. Hair salon, hot tubs (indoor and outdoor), sauna, steam room. Gym with: cardiovascular machines, free weights, weight-training equipment. Services: aromatherapy, body scrubs and wraps, facials, massage. Classes and programs: chi kung, personal training, Pilates, spinning, tai chi, total body training, yoga.*

★ **Mamalahoa Hot Tubs and Massage.** Tucked into a residential neighborhood above Kealekekua, this little gem is a welcome alternative to the large resort spas. Soaking tubs are made of the finest quality wood, tropical plants and flowers abound, and each tub is enclosed in its own little gazebo, with portholes in the roof for your star-gazing pleasure. Tastefully laid out and run, there's no seedy "hot tub party" vibe here, just a pleasant soak followed by, if you like, an hour-long massage. Mamalahoa offers *lomi lomi*, Swedish, deep tissue, and a Hawaiian hot stone massage performed with lava rocks collected from around the island. In addition to its secret hideaway ambience, Mamalahoa's prices are lower than any other spa on the island. ⊠ *81-1016 St. John's Rd.,*

Kealekekua, south of Kailua-Kona ☎*808/323–2288* ⊕*www.mamala hoa-hottubs.com* ☞*$30 60-min soak; $95 30-min soak plus 60-min massage* ⊙*By appointment only. Open Wed.–Sat. noon–9.*

★ **Mandara Spa at the Waikoloa Beach Marriott Resort.** Overlooking the hotel's main pool with a distant view of the ocean, Mandara offers a very complete if not unique spa menu, with more available facial options than you'll find at the island's other spas. Mandara operates spas throughout the world and on a number of cruise lines, and they are managing this one for Marriott, using Elemis and La Therapie products in spa and salon treatments. The spa menu contains the usual suspects—*lomi lomi*, a variety of facials, scrubs, and wraps—but they do incorporate local ingredients where appropriate (lemon and ginger in the scrubs, warm coconut milk in the wraps), and the new facilities, designed in a style that combines 20th-century modern American with traditional Asian motifs, are beautiful. ⊠*69-275 Waikoloa Beach Dr., Waikoloa* ☎*808/886–8191* ⊕*www.mandaraspa.com* ☞*$144 50-min lomi lomi massage; $269–$527 half-day packages. Hair salon, steam room. Services: aromatherapy, body scrubs and wraps, facials, massage.*

Fodor's Choice   **Mauna Lani Spa.** If you're looking for a one-of-a-kind experience, this is
★   your destination. Most treatments take place in outdoor *hales* (houses) surrounded by lava rock. Incredible therapists offer a mix of the old standbys (*lomi lomi* massage, moisturizing facials) and innovative treatments, many of which are heavily influenced by ancient traditions and incorporate local products. *Watsu* therapy takes place in an amazing pool filled by the adjacent lava tube. Meant to re-create the feeling of being in a womb, the 50-minute or 80-minute therapy is essentially an underwater massage. The aesthetic treatments on the menu incorporate high-end products from Epicuren and Emminence, so a facial will have a real and lasting therapeutic effect on your skin. ⊠*Mauna Lani Resort, 68-1365 Pauoa Rd., Kohala Coast* ☎*808/881–7922 or 808/885–6622* ⊕*www.maunalani.com* ☞*$159 50-min massage; $335–$465 packages. Hair salon, hot tubs (outdoor), sauna, steam room. Gym with: cardiovascular machines, free weights, weight-training equipment. Services: aquatic therapy, baths, body wraps, facials, massage, scrubs. Classes and programs: aerobics, kickboxing, personal training, Pilates, Spinning, weight training, yoga.*

Spa Without Walls at the Fairmont Orchid Hawai'i. This is possibly the best massage on the island, partially due to having the best setting. Massages face the ocean or a waterfall. Though most people will probably opt for the ocean, both settings are absolutely peaceful. There are other great treatments as well, including facials, a linu (detoxifying) wrap, and coffee and vanilla scrubs, but the massages are the best thing going. ⊠*Fairmont Orchid Hawai'i, 1 N. Kanikū Dr., Kohala Coast* ☎*808/887–7540 or 808/885–2000* ⊕*www.fairmont.com* ☞*$159 50-min lomi lomi massage; $319–$349 packages. Sauna, steam room. Gym with: cardiovascular machines, free weights, weight-training equipment. Services: baths, body wraps, facials, massage, scrubs. Classes and programs: aquaerobics, guided walks, meditation, personal training, yoga.*

ENTERTAINMENT AND NIGHTLIFE

ENTERTAINMENT

If you're the sort of person who doesn't come alive until after dark, you're going to be lonely on the Big Island. Blame it on the plantation heritage. People did their cane-raising in the morning. Still, there are a few lively bars on the island, a handful of great local playhouses, half a dozen or so movie houses, and plenty of musical entertainment to keep you occupied. And let's not forget the lū'au. These fantastic dance and musical performances are combined with some of the best meals on the island and are plenty of fun for the whole family.

4

HULA

★ For hula lovers, the biggest show of the year and the largest event of its kind in the world is the annual **Merrie Monarch Hula Festival** (⊠ *101 Aupuni St., Suite 1014-A1, Hilo* ☎ *808/935–9168* ⊕ *www.merrie monarchfestival.org*). Honoring the legacy of King David Kalākaua, Hawai'i's last king, the festival is staged in Hilo at the spacious Edith Kanaka'ole Stadium during the first week following Easter Sunday. Hula *hālau* (schools) compete in various classes of ancient and modern dance styles. You need to reserve accommodations and tickets up to a year in advance.

The new kid on the block is the **Moku O Keawe International Festival** (⊠ *Waikoloa Beach Resort, Kohala Coast96720* ☎ *808/886–8822* ⊕ *www.mokuokeawe.org*). In the beginning of November, top hula troupes from Hawai'i and Japan take the stage for an exciting competition under the stars at the Waikoloa Beach Resort's Waikoloa Bowl. During the day, cultural workshops and a made-in-Hawai'i Marketplace round out the celebration of rich Hawaiian culture.

LŪ'AU AND POLYNESIAN REVUES

KOHALA
COAST AND
WAIKOLOA

Fairmont Orchid. The Fairmont's "Gathering of the Kings Polynesian Feast" offers the most entertainment bang for your resort buck. However, keep in mind that this is not your traditional lū'au. The show is slickly produced and well choreographed, incorporating both traditional and modern dance and choreography as well as beautiful costumes. The meal offers more variety than most, with options representing all of the early Hawaiian settlers, including those from New Zealand, Hawaii, Tahiti, and Samoa. ⊠ *1 N. Kaniku Dr., Kohala Coast* ☎ *808/885–2000* ⊕ *www.fairmont.com/orchid* ⊠ *$104* ⊙ *Sat. at 6.*

Hilton Waikoloa Village. The Hilton seats 400 people outdoors at the Kamehameha Court, where the acclaimed Polynesian group Tihati Productions performs a lively show, "The Legends of the Pacific." A buffet dinner provides samplings of Hawaiian food as well as fish, beef, and chicken to appeal to all tastes. ⊠ *69-425 Waikoloa Beach Dr., Waikoloa* ☎ *808/886–1234* ⊕ *www.hiltonwaikoloavillage.com* ⊠ *$95* ⊙ *Tues. and Fri. at 6.*

★ **Kona Village Resort.** The lū'au here is one of the most traditional on the Islands. As in other lū'au, activities include the steaming of a whole pig in the *imu* (ground oven). The Wednesday night show focuses solely

CLOSE UP

Hawai'i's Hippy Hippy Shake

Legends immortalize Laka as the goddess of hula, a gentle deity who journeyed from island to island, sharing the dance with all who were willing to learn. Laka's graceful movements, spiritual and layered with meaning, brought to life the history, traditions, and genealogy of the islanders. Ultimately taught by parents to children and by *kumu* (teachers) to students, the hula preserved the culture of these ancient peoples without a written language.

Some legends trace the origins of hula to Moloka'i, where a family named La'ila'i was said to have established the dance at Ka'ana. Eventually the youngest sister of the fifth generation of La'ila'i was given the name Laka, and she carried the dance to all the Islands in the Hawaiian chain.

Another legend credits Hi'iaka, the volcano goddess Pele's youngest sister, as having danced the first hula in the *hala* groves of Puna on the Big Island. Hi'iaka and possibly even Pele were thought to have learned the dance from Hōpoe, a mortal and a poet also credited as the originator of the dance.

In any case, hula thrived until the arrival of puritanical New England missionaries, who with the support of Queen Ka'ahumanu, an early Christian convert, attempted to ban the dance as an immoral activity throughout the 19th century.

Though hula may not have been publicly performed, it remained a spiritual and poetic art form, as well as a lively celebration of life presented during special celebrations in many Hawaiian homes. David Kalākaua, the popular "Merrie Monarch" who was king from 1874 to 1891, revived the hula. Dancers were called to perform at official functions.

Gradually, ancient hula, called *kahiko,* was replaced with a lively, updated form of dance called *'auana* (modern). Modern costumes of fresh ti-leaf or raffia skirts replaced the voluminous *pa'u* skirts made of *kapa* (cloth made of beaten bark), and the music became more melodic. Such tunes as "Lovely Hula Hands," "Little Grass Shack," and the "Hawaiian Wedding Song" are considered hula *'auana.* Dancers might wear graceful *holomu'u* with short trains or ti-leaf skirts with coconut bra tops.

In 1963 the Merrie Monarch Festival was established in Hilo and has since become the most prestigious hula competition in the state. It's staged annually the weekend after Easter, and contestants of various *halau* (hula schools) compete in the categories of Miss Aloha Hula, hula *kahiko* (ancient), and hula *'auana* (modern). For more information, contact the **Merrie Monarch Hula Festival** (☎*808/935-9168* ⊕ *www.merrie monarchfestival.org*).

on Hawaiian traditions and music, while Friday night incorporates Polynesian dancing, music, and traditions as well. The dancing, done on a stage over a lagoon, is magical. ⊠ *Queen Ka'ahumanu Hwy., 6 mi north of Kona International Airport, Kailua-Kona* ☎*808/325-5555 or 808/325-4273* ⊕*www.konavillage.com* 🗨*$98, includes one mai tai and a flower lei for the ladies* ☉ *Wed. and Fri. doors open at 5, imu ceremony at 6, dinner at 6:45, show at 7:45.*

Mauna Kea Beach Hotel. Every Tuesday, on the gracious North Pointe Lū'au Grounds of the Mauna Kea Beach Hotel, you can sample the best of Hawaiian cuisine while listening to the enchanting songs of Nani Lim Yap and Traditions Hawai'i at one of the first lū'au on the Big Island. Chefs come together here to create a traditional Hawaiian *pa'ina* (dinner feast), which includes the classic *kālua* (roasted in an underground oven) pig. ✉ *62-100 Mauna Kea Beach Dr., Kohala Coast* ☎ *808/882–7222* ⊕ *www.maunakeabeachhotel.com* ☒ *$86* ☽ *Tues. at 6.*

Waikoloa Beach Marriott. At this celebration, entertainment includes a Samoan fire dance as well as songs and dances of various Pacific cultures. Traditional Hawaiian dishes are served alongside more familiar fare. ✉ *69-275 Waikoloa Beach Dr., Waikoloa* ☎ *808/886–6789* ⊕ *www.marriott.com* ☒ *$80, including open bar* ☽ *Wed. and Sun. 5–8:30.*

KAILUA-KONA **King Kamehameha's Kona Beach Hotel.** Witness the royal court arrive by canoe at the Island Breeze Lū'au, a beachfront event, which includes a 22-item buffet, an open bar, and a show. ✉ *75-5660 Palani Rd., Kailua-Kona* ☎ *808/326–4969 or 808/329–8111* ⊕ *www.islandbreezeluau.com* ☒ *$73* ☽ *Tues.–Fri. and Sun. 5:30–8:30.*

Sheraton Keauhou Bay. The newest addition to the Big Island's lū'au scene, Firenesia, with Island Breeze Productions, tells the story of a young man traveling through Polynesia with traditional hula and storytelling. This lū'au is entertaining, and the open bar doesn't hurt either. ✉ *75-5852 Ali'i Dr., Kailua-Kona* ☎ *808/930–4900* ⊕ *www.sheratonkeauhou.com or www.firenesia.com* ☒ *$79.95* ☽ *Mon. at 4:30.*

SUNSET CRUISES

★ **Champagne Sunset Sail with Ocean Sports.** Sail the Kohala Coast in luxury with Ocean Sports, and experience a new perspective of the Big Island from the sea. If you're lucky, there may be a dolphin or whale sighting. The cruise includes a buffet dinner, champage, and an open bar. ✉ *Kawaihae Harbor, Kawaihae* ☎ *808/886–6666 or 888/724–5924* ⊕ *www.hawaiioceansports.com* ☒ *$100 per adult, $50 per child* ☽ *Check-in 4–4:15 PM, depending on sunset.*

★ **Evening on the Reef: Sunset & Glass Bottom Dinner Cruise.** Hop aboard the Spirit of Kona, a 70-foot double deck catamaran, and discover dolphins, manta rays, turtles, and scores of tropical fish through two large glass bottom walls—even after dark thanks to special lighting. Then catch a famous Kona sunset, and jam to live local entertainment on Blue Sea Cruises' newest trip. The 2-hour cruise is $88 per person, including a dinner buffet and mai tai. ✉ *Kailua-Kona Pier, Kailua-Kona* ☎ *808/331–8875* ⊕ *www.blueseacruisesinc.com* ☽ *Daily, check in varies with sunset.*

MUSIC

Waikoloa Bowl Concert Series at the Waikoloa Beach Resort. The newest and largest entertainment complex on the Kohala Coast is the Waikoloa Bowl at the Queens' Gardens, Waikoloa Beach Resort. First-rate concerts (think Earth, Wind & Fire) are held under the stars on this sprawling lawn and festivals, such as the Moku O Keawe International Festival and the Big Island Film Festival, take place here as well. ✉*201 Waikoloa Beach Dr., Waikoloa Beach Resort, Waikoloa* ☎*808/886–8822* ⊕*www.waikoloanights.com.*

THEATER

Aloha Angel Performing Arts Center. Local talent stages musicals and Broadway plays at this charming old plantation center near Kailua-Kona. ✉*Aloha Angel Theatre Café, 79-7384 Māmalahoa Hwy., Kainaliu* ☎*808/322–2323.*

Kahilu Theater. For legitimate theater, the little town of Waimea is your best bet. The Kahilu Theater hosts regular internationally acclaimed performances. ✉*Parker Ranch Center, 67-1185 Māmalahoa Hwy., Waimea* ☎*808/885–6868.*

BARS AND CLUBS

KOHALA DISTRICT

Blue Dragon. Previously Blue Dolphin, this restaurant and bar is newly renovated and perfect for a good time. During the week, Blue Dragon is more of a restaurant than a bar, but on Friday and Saturday nights, everyone's here for drinks rather than food, and the music bumps it up a notch to rock-n-roll for moves on the dance floor. ✉*61-3616 Kawaihae Rd., Kawaihae* ☎*808/882–7771*

Honu Bar. This elegant spot at the Mauna Lani Bay Hotel & Bungalows has a nice dance floor for weekend revelry. Delicious appetizers, imported cigars, and fine cognacs make this a popular spot on the Kohala Coast. ✉*68-1400 Mauna Lani Dr., Kohala Coast* ☎*808/885–6622.*

Malolo Lounge. A favorite after-work spot for employees from the surrounding hotels, this lounge in the Hilton Waikoloa Village offers decent music, friendly bartenders, and a pool table. ✉*425 Waikoloa Beach Dr., Waikoloa* ☎*808/886–1234.*

Sansei Seafood Restaurant & Sushi Bar. Sansei is the new hot spot for the locals on Friday and Saturday evenings. With late-night karaoke, half-priced sushi and appetizers, and drink specials from 10 PM to 1 AM, this is where you'll find the crowd. ✉*201 Waikoloa Beach Dr., 801, Queens' MarketPlace, Waikoloa* ☎*808/886–6286*

KAILUA-KONA

Huggo's on the Rocks. Jazz, country, and even rock bands perform at this popular restaurant, so call ahead to find out what's on. Outside, people often dance in the sand to Hawaiian songs. ✉*75-5828 Kahakai Rd., at Ali'i Dr., Kailua-Kona* ☎*808/329–1493.*

Lulu's. On weekends, the young crowd gyrates until late in the evening to hot dance music—hip-hop, R&B, and rock—spun by a professional DJ. ✉*75-5819 Ali'i Dr., Kailua-Kona* ☎*808/331–2633.*

BEST SUNSET MAI TAIS

Crystal Blue at the Sheraton Keauhou (Kailua-Kona). Fantastic sunset views from plush lounge chairs, followed by spotlighted glimpses of nearby manta rays.

Huggo's on the Rocks (Kailua-Kona). Literally on the rocks, this sand-floored bar has strong drinks and live music Friday and Saturday.

Kawaihae Harbor Grill (Kohala). Views off the deck of the upstairs Seafood Bar, great food in the restaurant next door, and well-poured drinks.

Kona Inn (Kailua-Kona). Wide, unobstructed view, in the middle of downtown, best mai tais on the island.

Wai'oli Lounge in the Hilo Hawaiian Hotel (Hilo). A nice view of Coconut Island, live music most nights and karaoke others.

Oceans Sports Bar & Grill. This is the current hot spot in Kona—a sports bar in the back of the Coconut Grove Marketplace. There's a pool table and an outdoor patio, and this place really gets hopping on most weekend evenings. ⊠ *Coconut Grove Marketplace, 75-5811 Ali'i Dr., Kailua-Kona* ☎ *808/327–9494.*

WHERE TO EAT

Between star chefs and a crop (pun intended) of quality new local farms, the Big Island restaurant scene has been heating up in the past couple of years. In the past it used to be a pleasant surprise for visitors to discover a gourmet meal on the island, now food writers from national magazines are praising the chefs of the Big Island for their ability to turn the local bounty into inventive blends of the island's cultural heritage. Drawn by reviews and the reputations of some world-renowned chefs, the Big Island has become a destination for foodies on vacation.

Hotels along the Kohala Coast invest in cutting-edge chefs who use the freshest local ingredients, creating intriguing blends of flavors that reflect the island's varied cultural backgrounds. As the bulk of Big Island tourism is on the Kona coast, the majority of restaurants are here as well, and they tend to be a bit pricey. There are also some great choices in Upcountry Waimea, North Kohala (in Kawaihae and Hāwī, both a short drive from the resort area) and on the east side of the island in Hilo. Less populated areas like Ka'ū, the Hāmākua Coast, and Puna offer limited choices for dinner, but usually at least one or two spots that do a decent plate lunch. A handful of excellent little eateries have recently cropped up in Kainaliu, near Kealakekua Bay.

WHAT IT COSTS					
	¢	$	$$	$$$	$$$$
Restaurants	under $10	$10–$17	$18–$26	$27–$35	over $35

Prices are for one main course at dinner.

KOHALA

$$
PACIFIC RIM
Fodor'sChoice
★

✕ **Bamboo Restaurant.** It's out of the way, but the food at this spot in the heart of Hāwī is good and the service and ambience have a Hawaiian–country flair. Creative entrées feature fresh island fish prepared several ways. The Thai-style fish combines lemongrass, Kaffir lime leaves, and coconut milk; it's best washed down with a passion-fruit margarita or passion-fruit iced tea. Bamboo accents, bold local artwork, and an old unfinished wooden floor make the restaurant cozy. Local musicians entertain on Friday or Saturday evenings. ⊠ *Hwy. 270, Hāwī* ☎ *808/889–5555* ▤ *MC, V* ⊗ *Closed Mon. No dinner Sun.*

$$
SEAFOOD

✕ **Blue Dragon.** From farm to table, Blue Dragon is known for Big Island ingredients with crispy, fresh vegetables and produce from their own farm, Touching the Earth, down the road in Hāwī. Their fish travels a short distance as well, straight off the boat at the Kawaihae Harbor. Seafood dishes have a Mediterranean influence, and the pūpū menu is packed. Try the yummy crab cakes, ceviche, and beet salad. Formerly the Blue Dolphin, the Blue Dragon has a great new look, while keeping its old open-air atmosphere. Nightly entertainment adds a nice beat with mellow tunes during the week, but with rock and roll on Friday and Saturday nights, either eat early, ask for terrace seating, or just skip it. ⊠ *61-3616 Kawaihae Rd., Kawaihae* ☎ *808/882–7771* ▤ *D, DC, MC, V* ⊗ *No lunch.*

$$$$
MODERN
HAWAIIAN
Fodor'sChoice
★

✕ **Brown's Beach House at the Fairmont Orchid Hawai'i.** This waterfront wonder is well worth the splurge—the menu is inventive (but not too inventive), and the wine list is excellent. Though you can order steak here, the seafood is really where it's happening. Their crab-crusted ono is a little piece of heaven, sitting on

clouds of wasabi mashed potatoes. Leave room for dessert; the sweets change regularly, but they're always worth the indulgence. Local musicians play on the grassy knoll outside. ⊠ *Fairmont Orchid Hawai'i, 1 N. Kanikū Dr., Kohala Coast* ☎ *808/885–2000* ▤ *AE, D, DC, MC, V* ⊗ *No lunch.*

$$
ITALIAN

✕ **Café Pesto.** This branch of Café Pesto, in the quaint harbor town of Kawaihae, is just as popular as its sibling in Hilo. Exotic pizzas (with chili-grilled shrimp, shiitake mushrooms, and cilantro crème fraîche, for example), Asian-inspired pastas and risottos, and fresh seafood reflect the ethnic diversity of the island. Local microbrews and a full-service bar make this a good place to end the evening, and the lounge-y bar area with sofas and comfy chairs is a great place to grab a drink while you're waiting for a table. ⊠ *61-3665 Akoni Pule Hwy., Kawaihae Harbor Center, Hwy. 270, Kawaihae* ☎ *808/882–1071* ▤ *AE, D, DC, MC, V.*

$$$$
PACIFIC RIM

✕ **CanoeHouse at the Mauna Lani Bay Hotel & Bungalows.** The open-air, beachfront setting is stunning, and as the CanoeHouse was among the first on the island to offer Pacific Rim fusion, it does it very well. With influences drawn from time spent in Hong Kong, the chef has recreated the menu to add unique dishes, many with Asian flair. The blackened 'ahi and scallops dish is a standout, and the wide variety of fresh fish is always cooked to perfection. But the ahualoa goat cheese and potato "ravioli" is a must, especially with corn, mushrooms, and tomatoes straight from Big Island farms. The wine list is also great, and the location and attentive service complete the experience. ⊠*Mauna Lani Bay Hotel & Bungalows, 68-1400 Mauna Lani Dr., Kohala Coast* ☎*808/885–6622* ⊟*AE, D, DC, MC, V* ⊘*No lunch.*

$$$$
MODERN
HAWAIIAN
★

✕**Coast Grille at Hāpuna Beach Prince Hotel.** This is a beautiful spot, with high ceilings and a lānai overlooking the ocean. The Coast Grille offers a well-rounded seafood menu, including loads of fresh oysters, clams and mussels from the oyster bar, and a wide variety of cuisine, from pan seared diver scallops and Kona crab fettuccine to batik East Indian curry. The servers exude the Aloha Spirit; however, the food is only average, and for the price you'd do a lot better at one of the neighboring resorts' restaurants. ⊠*Hāpuna Beach Prince Hotel, 62-100 Kauna'oa Dr., Kohala Coast* ☎*808/880–3192 or 808/880–3023* ⊟*AE, D, DC, MC, V* ⊘*No lunch.*

$$$
ITALIAN

✕**Donatoni's at Hilton Waikoloa Village.** This romantic restaurant overlooking the boat canal resembles an Italian villa and serves scrumptious dishes with the subtle sauces of northern Italy. From spaghetti with shrimp, scallops, island fish, clams, and calamari to fresh Kona Kampachi, the kitchen sets out to please, although some may find the pasta prices tough to justify. Be sure to look over the Italian wine and champagne list. ⊠*69-425 Waikoloa Beach Dr., Waikoloa* ☎*808/886–1234* ⊟*AE, D, DC, MC, V* ⊘*No lunch.*

$$$$
MODERN
HAWAIIAN

✕**Hale Samoa at Kona Village Resort.** Formal and romantic, this Kona Village restaurant has a magical atmosphere, especially at sunset. In a Samoan setting with screens and candles, you can feast on five-course prix-fixe dinners that change daily. Specialties may include sautéed abalone raised at the aqua-farm up the street, papaya-and-coconut bisque, duck stuffed with andouille sausage, or wok-charred prime strip loin. ⊠*Kona Village Resort, Hwy. 19, 12 mi north of Kailua-Kona, North Kona Coast* ☎*808/325–5555* ⚠*Reservations essential* ⊟*AE, D, MC, V* ⊘*Closed Tues. and Fri.*

$$$$
MODERN
HAWAIIAN

✕**Kamuela Provision Company at Hilton Waikoloa Village.** Tables set along a breezy lānai and a sweeping view of the Kohala coast are the perfect accompaniments to the elegant yet down-to-earth Hawai'i regional cuisine. The lānai offers the best seats in the house—get there by 5:30 if you want to score a seat for the sunset. Popular are the bouillabaisse with fresh island seafood and the fillet of beef with tempura lobster. This is a great place to sip cocktails—the adjacent Wine Bar makes for a romantic evening in itself, with more than 40 labels available by the glass. ⊠*Hilton Waikoloa Village, 69-425 Waikoloa Beach Dr., Waikoloa* ☎*808/886–1234* ⊟*AE, D, DC, MC, V* ⊘*No lunch.*

$$
SEAFOOD

✕**Kawaihae Harbor Grill & Seafood Bar.** This little restaurant is always packed—there's something about the crisp green-and-white 1850s building, along with the scent of fresh local seafood being sautéed with garlic, that draws people in. The food downstairs at the Harbor Grill is a bit more than some want to pay for basics like grilled mahimahi and fish-and-chips, but the Seafood Bar, upstairs in a separate structure that also dates from the 1850s, serves a dynamite and well-priced bar menu with sandwiches and *pūpū* (appetizers), and a good lunch as well. The upstairs area is also a bit more fun and casual than downstairs; it's been a hot spot since it opened in 2003. ⊠ *61-3642 Kawaihae Harbor, Hwy. 270, Kawaihae* ☎ *808/882–1368* ⊟ *MC, V.*

$$$

JAPANESE

★

✕ **Kenichi Pacific.** At this contemporary restaurant the shrimp tempura stashed in a sushi roll is still warm at first bite, and creative innovations include edamame (soybean) paper instead of rice paper on specialty rolls and freshly grated wasabi from Japan. The 'ahi pepper steak and island *ono* are first-rate, while the dynamite shrimp is made from a 20-year-old original recipe. Kenichi's fifth restaurant location, this one in the shops at the Mauna Lani, has hip, Hawaiian character complete with accents from the prestigious designer Sig Zane. However, locals still rave about the Big Island's pioneer Kenichi Pacific in Kailua-Kona. ⊠ *Shops at Mauna Lani, 68-1330 Mauna Lani Dr., 111 Kohala Coast* ☎ *808/881–1515* ⊟ *AE, D, DC, MC, V* ⊘ *No lunch.*

$$

MEDITERRANEAN

✕ **Merriman's Market Café.** From Peter Merriman, one of Hawai'i's star chefs, comes a more affordable alternative to his upscale Waimea and Maui restaurants. The Mediterranean-influenced menu includes a variety of pasta dishes, tasty appetizers, and some of the island's best salads. It's delicious, but the options are limited. Its huge patio has quickly become a favorite for locals and visitors alike, which means you could have a bit of a wait for a table. ⊠ *Kings' Shops at Waikoloa Beach Resort, 250 Waikoloa Beach Dr., Waikoloa* ☎ *808/886–1700* ⊟ *AE, D, MC, V.*

$$$$

JAPANESE

✕ **Norio's Sushi Bar & Restaurant.** Norio's is great, but it's pricey for sushi and there are sushi restaurants of equal or higher caliber with lower prices down the road (Kenichi Pacific), or north of Kohala in Hawi (Sushi Rock). Still, if you're staying at one of the resorts nearby, Norio's is a solid choice. Sashimi and sushi are lovingly prepared with the freshest possible fish. The flounder, 'ahi, and abalone are not to be missed. Equally delicious hot dishes include baked sea scallops and miso butterfish. The assortment of tropical drinks is tasty, as is the sinfully good chocolate fondue, served with an assortment of tropical fruits. ⊠ *Fairmont Orchid Hawai'i, 1 N. Kaniku Dr., Kohala Coast* ☎ *808/885–2000* ⊟ *AE, D, DC, MC, V* ⊘ *Closed Tues. and Wed. No lunch.*

$$$–$$$$

MODERN

HAWAIIAN

Fodor'sChoice

★

✕ **Pahui'a at the Four Seasons Resort Hualālai.** *Pahui'a* means "aquarium," so it's fitting that a 9- by 4-foot aquarium in the entrance casts a dreamy light through this exquisite restaurant. Presentation is paramount, and the food tastes as good as it looks. Asian-influenced dishes stand out for their layers of flavor. Don't miss the prosciutto-wrapped Kona Blue Kampachi, or the Pacific seafood ragout served with a red pepper-coconut sauce. In keeping with the island-wide trend, the restaurant is featuring special prix-fixe dinner menus that change seasonally and focus on local produce, meats, and fish. Breakfasts are superb; the lemon ricotta pancakes are so good they should be illegal. Reserve a table on the patio and you may be able to spot whales while dining.

Four Seasons Resort Hualālai, 100 Ka'ūpūlehu Dr., North Kona Coast ☎*808/325–8000* ═*AE, D, DC, MC, V* ⊘*No lunch.*

$–$$

ITALIAN

✕**Romano's Macaroni Grill.** Ample portions and decent prices (compared to the Kohala Coast choices) make the Macaroni Grill a preferred dining destination. Yes, this is a chain restaurant with little Hawaiian influence, but the family style platters are ideal for take-out, the servers are attentive, and the food is well prepared. The brick oven pizzas are a hit, along with the option to create your own dish from six pastas, seven sauces, and 13 seasonal ingredients, and a meal can easily be made from the antipasti. Sit outside for a cool breeze and good people watching—the restaurant is located in the Queens' MarketPlace. ⊠ *69-201 Waikoloa Beach Dr., Suite 1010, Waikoloa Beach Resort-Waikoloa* ☎*808/443–5515* ═ *AE, D, DC, MC, V.*

$$$$

MODERN
HAWAIIAN

✕**Roy's Waikoloa Bar & Grill.** Combine friendly service with fresh, local ingredients fused with Asian and European sauces and spices, and you have Roy's Waikoloa. The menu changes daily, but if you're lucky you'll catch Roy's misoyaki butterfish, Szechuan style baby back ribs, or the blackened 'ahi. And if you're looking for a light meal, you can easily fill up on the enormous selection of great appetizers, and the extensive by-the-glass wine list offers good pairing options. The standard island dessert is a variation of a molton lava cake, but according to the coconut wireless, Roy's dark chocolate soufflé is by far the best; it's complemented with raspberry sauce and vanilla ice cream. Be forewarned that the place tends to get noisy. ⊠*Kings' Shops at Waikoloa Village, 250 Waikoloa Beach Dr., Kohala Coast* ☎*808/886–4321* ⊕*www.roys restaurant.com* ═*AE, D, DC, MC, V.* ⊘*No lunch.*

$$$$

STEAK

✕**Ruth's Chris Steakhouse.** Located in the shops at Mauna Lani, the new Hawaii location of the popular Lousiana steak-house chain serves the same sizzling steaks and heaping sides the restaurant is known for throughout the country. Steaks come topped with melted butter or with entrée complements such as blue cheese crust or four jumbo shrimp. Tasty, heavy, classic sides, which are à la carte, include creamed spinach, fresh asparagus with hollandaise sauce, and potatoes au gratin. Several prime time specials, island vegetables, and a wide wine selection make this spot a favorite for visitors and residents alike. ⊠*68-1330 Mauna Lani Dr., Kohala Coast 96743* ☎*808/887–0800* ═*AE, D, MC, V* ⊘*No lunch.*

$$

JAPANESE

✕**Sansei Seafood Restaurant & Sushi Bar.** Chef D.K. Kodama does it again with his fourth Hawai'i location, this time on the Big Island. Sansei has won awards from major magazines so expectations are high . . . and met. For the optimal experience, order a variety of the appetizers and rolls to taste several dishes. Favorites include the panko crusted 'ahi sashimi sushi roll, Japanese calamari salad, and tender butterfish marinated and seared in sake and sweet miso. Still hungry? D.K.'s crab ramen with Asian truffle broth is considered the stomach topper. On Friday and Saturday nights, the full bar comes alive with late night karaoke, half-price sushi and appetizers, and drink specials from 10 PM to 1 AM. Or, if you want to get an early start, there are also specials from 5:30 PM to 6 PM. ⊠ *201 Waikoloa Beach Dr., 801 Queens' MarketPlace, Waikoloa* ☎*808/886–6286* ═*AE, D, DC, MC, V* ⊘*No lunch.*

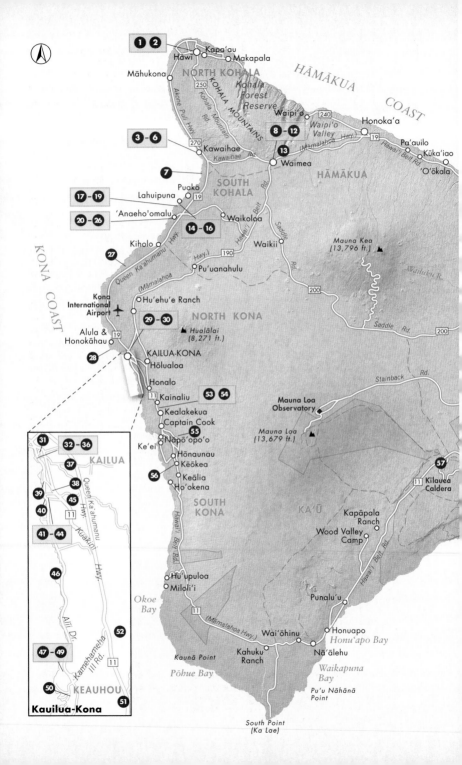

Where to Eat on the Big Island

$ ✕**Sushi Rock.** In Hāwī's funky With-
JAPANESE   out Boundaries shop, Sushi Rock isn't big on ambience—its narrow dining room is brightly painted and casually decorated with various Hawaiian and Japanese knick-knacks—but hungry locals and visiting couples flock here for some of the island's freshest raw fish. In addition to lots of new-wave California-style rolls and Hawaiʻi Regional sushi, the menu includes a variety of cooked seafood, noodle dishes, and salads. Everything is plated beautifully and served either at the sushi bar, at one of the handful of indoor tables, or on the covered back patio. There's also a full bar. ⊠ *55-3435 Akoni Pule Hwy., Hāwī* ☎ *808/889–5900* ▤ *MC, V* ⊙ *Closed Wed.*

$$$$ ✕**Tommy Bahama's Tropical Café.** It's funny that a chain known for its
MODERN   "Hawaiian-ness" would start in California and then one day end up in
HAWAIIAN   Hawaii, but that is Tommy Bahama's story. In an open-air space above the Tommy Bahama store in the shops at Mauna Lani, the restaurant does a good job of making guests forget they're in a shopping complex. And the food is decent, although derivative of other menus on the island. The macadamia-crusted *opakapaka* (Pacific red snapper) is a standout. Some of the best items, and best values, on the menu are actually in the appetizer section—the *poke* is outstanding—and on the salad list, which includes a fresh take on a roasted beet and spinach salad with hearts of palm and a *lilikoi* (passion fruit) infused dressing. Desserts are decadent and meant for sharing. ⊠ *68-1330 Mauna Lani Dr., #102* ☎ *808/881–8686* ▤ *AE, D, DC, MC, V.*

$–$$ ✕**Tres Hombres Beach Grill.** The food is decent, if a bit pricey, but what
MEXICAN   you come here for are the marvelous margaritas. They're in all sorts of tropical flavors, including *lilikoʻi* (passion fruit). Lunch is the usual Mexican combination platters (tacos, enchiladas, chiles rellenos) as well as burgers and sandwiches. Dinner entrées include fresh fish, killer fajitas, bean-and-rice combinations, and steaks. ⊠ *Kawaihae Harbor Center, Hwy. 270, Kawaihae* ☎ *808/882–1031* ▤ *MC, V.*

WAIMEA

$$$ ✕**Daniel Thiebaut Restaurant.** This fine-dining restaurant features the cre-
MODERN   ations of respected local chef Thiebaut in a quaint little yellow building
HAWAIIAN   that once housed the historic Chock In Store, which catered to the ranching community beginning in 1900. The store's redwood countertop now serves as one long community dining table. Collectibles abound, such as antique porcelain pieces. The French-Asian menu includes an amazing appetizer of sweet-corn crab cake with a lemongrass, coconut, and lobster sauce. Other signature dishes include Hunan-style rack of lamb

---

BEST BREAKFAST

Café 100 (Hilo). Local destination for *loco moco* on the Hilo side.

Coffee Shack (Kealekekua). Homemade everything plus the best view on the island—try the delicious lūʻau bread, smoothies, or eggs Benedict with homemade English muffins.

Ken's House of Pancakes (Hilo). Like IHOP, but with Spam.

Pahu iʻa at the Four Seasons Hualālai (Kohala). Hands-down the best fancy breakfast on the island.

served with eggplant compote and the fresh catch of the day—straight from Kawaihae Harbor. It's also notorious for the all-you-can-eat Sunday brunch. ✉65-1259 *Kawaihae Rd., Waimea* ☎808/887–2200 ▤*AE, D, DC, MC, V* ⊗*No lunch Sat.*

¢ ✗**Hawaiian Style Café.** Whatever you do, do not miss the most popular
HAWAIIAN place among locals for heaping plates of Hawaiian style specialties at incredibly cheap prices. The famed Loco Moco (rice with a hamburger patty, fried egg, and brown gravy) is the best, along with spam, rice, and eggs, and teriyaki chicken. Normally open for breakfast and lunch, be warned that the café closes if it runs out of food or has another engagement. ✉ *65-1290 Kawaihae Rd, Waimea* ☎808/885–4295 ▤*No credit cards* ⊗*Closed Sat. No dinner.*

$ ✗**Huli Sue's BBQ and Grill.** Huli Sue's serves large portions of updat-
MODERN ed Hawaiian classics in a casual little restaurant along the highway
HAWAIIAN between Waimea and Honoka'a. The barbecue menu, which includes your choice of meat (classics like ribs, pork roast, brisket) with one of four sauces, is melt-in-your-mouth delicious. The menu includes many other options, including a baked potato stuffed with your choice of meat, cilantro sour cream, and Fontina cheese, a variety of curry dishes, and a handful of fantastic appetizers, such as the crab, smoked pepper, onion, and Fontina quesadilla. Salads, with produce from a nearby farm, are great too. ✉*64-957 Mamalahoa Hwy. (Hwy. 11)* ☎*808/885–6268* ▤*AE, D, DC, MC, V.*

$$$ ✗**Merriman's.** This is the signature restaurant of Peter Merriman, one
MODERN of the pioneers of Hawai'i regional cuisine. Merriman's is the home
HAWAIIAN of the original wok-charred 'ahi, usually served with buttery Wain-
Fodor's Choice aku corn. If you prefer meat, try the Kahuā Ranch lamb, raised to the
★ restaurant's specifications, or the prime Kansas City Cut steak, grilled to order. The wine list includes 22 selections poured by the glass, and the staff is refreshingly knowledgeable. For true foodies, Merriman's now offers a farmers' market tour—four hours spent browsing around local ranches and food stands, culminating in a fantastic five-course meal using produce and meat bought throughout the day. ✉*'Opelo Plaza, 65-1227 'Opelo Rd., Waimea* ☎*808/885–6822* ⌂*Reservations essential* ▤*AE, MC, V.*

$ ✗**Pau Pizza.** Sauces and dressings made from scratch accompany home-
ITALIAN made super-thin and crispy pizza, sandwiches, soups, and salads at this quick-service, organic café. The menu changes every few days, depending on what the farmers bring to the chefs, but you can always score a large slice of the daily pizza and side salad for only $8. The butternut squash soup is great with the grilled heirloom tomato, mozzarella, and arugula on fresh-baked ciabatta bread. Stop here on your way to the volcano, or the beach, and grab their "Food on the Run" special for a picnic or late night pizza. ✉ *65-1227 Opelo Rd., Waimea* ☎*808/885–6325* ▤*AE, DC, MC, V* ⊗*Closed Sun.*

$ ✗**Tako Taco.** Housed in a small, brightly painted hut, Tako Taco feels
MEXICAN more like a mainland burrito joint than an island Mexican food restaurant, and its authentic food makes it hugely popular with both locals, who line up for to-go orders, and visitors who snag one of the plastic booths and eat in. With a focus on fresh ingredients, Tako Taco whips

up awesome tacos, burritos, Mexican salads, enchiladas, rellenos, and seriously *ono* (Hawaiian slang for "tasty") quesadillas fresh to order. The tomatillo pineapple salsa is the bee's knees, and they're also now serving top-shelf margaritas, along with local beers and wine. Stop in on Friday evenings for live music. ✉*64-1066A Mamalahoa Hwy.* ☎*808/887–1717* ⊟*MC, V.*

KAILUA-KONA

$ ✕**Ba-Le.** Comparable to Kona Mix Plate in terms of prices, food qual-
HAWAIIAN ity, and local cred, Ba-Le serves a great plate lunch. It also has tasty Vietnamese-influenced food, such as their popular croissant sandwiches stuffed with mint, lemongrass, sprouts, and your choice from a variety of Vietnamese-style meats. ✉*Kona Coast Shopping Center, 74-5588 Palani Rd., Kailua-Kona* ☎*808/327–1212* ⊟*MC, V.*

$ ✕**Bangkok House Thai Restaurant.** It may not look like much, with its
THAI small, dark interior and tired carpets, but Bangkok House is the local go-to for good Thai food. One of few Thai restaurants on the island to add enough spice to their sauces, Bangkok serves up tasty curries, satays, and soups, along with a random assortment of Chinese entrées. The Rainbow salad, panang curry, and spring rolls are all standouts. Save room for homemade lychee ice cream. ✉*75-5626 Kuakini Hwy., in King Kamehameha Mall* ☎*808/329–7764* ⊟*D, DC, MC, V* ◷*Closed Sat. No lunch Sun.*

$ ✕**Big Island Grill.** This typical, local
HAWAIIAN Hawaiian restaurant looks like an old coffee shop or a Denny's—it's dark and nondescript inside, with booths along the walls and basic tables with bingo hall chairs in the middle of the room. Local families love it for the huge portions of pork chops, chicken *katsu*, and an assortment of fish specialties at very reasonable prices. "Biggie's" also serves a great breakfast—the prices and portions make this a good place to take large groups or families. ✉*75-5702 Kuakini Hwy.* ☎*808/326–1153* ⊟*AE, MC, V* ◷*Closed Sun.*

> ### WORD OF MOUTH
>
> "While in Kailua-Kona, we had dinners at the Big Island Grill. It was the best dinner out during our week here—the mud pie will forever be a part of family lore." —bon_voyage

$ ✕**Boston Basil's.** This tiny traditional trattoria serves solid, family-style
ITALIAN Italian food and great pizzas at very good prices. The atmosphere is the same you'll find at hundreds of Italian restaurants in the U.S.—the table-cloths are checkered, the candles are in Chianti bottles, there's spaghetti on the menu, and it always feels a little hot and greasy inside. But you can't beat the location in downtown Kailua-Kona, right across the street from the ocean. ✉*75-5707 Ali'i Dr., Kailua-Kona* ☎*808/326–7836* ⊟*MC, V.*

$$ ✕**Bubba Gump Shrimp Company.** Okay, it's a chain, and a chain that cen-
AMERICAN ters on a Tom Hanks movie, no less. However, it has one of the largest oceanfront patios on the island, and the food's not bad, once you get past the silly names. The dynamite shrimp is good, and the "Pear & Berry" salad (a combination of raspberries, strawberries, pears, and pecans) is the perfect size for lunch. Too bad they're no longer doing

breakfast—they used to be one of the best in town for it. ✉ *75-5776 Ali'i Dr., Kailua-Kona* ☎ *808/331–8442* ▭ *AE, D, DC, MC, V.*

$$$
PACIFIC RIM
✕**Fish Hopper.** The Hawaii location of the popular Monterey, California, restaurant has an expansive menu, with inventive fresh fish specials alongside the fish-and-chips and clam chowder the original restaurant is known for. The owners spent serious time and money renovating the old and funky Ocean View Inn, and the restaurant itself is lovely— lots of koa wood, Hawaiian art, and an open-air floor plan that takes advantage of the ocean view. The food is decent, but may not feel worth the price. However, the wine list is outstanding, and there are frequent bottle specials, so this is a great spot for wine and appetizers with a view. It's also currently the only ocean-view restaurant in town to serve breakfast. ✉ *75-5683 Ali'i Dr.* ☎ *808/326–2002* ▭ *AE, D, MC, V.*

¢
AMERICAN
✕**Harbor House.** It's nothing fancy—an old wooden bar, and dozens of plastic tables and chairs scattered about the covered patio next to the docks at Honokohau Harbor—but Harbor House is a local favorite for fresh fish a few hours off the boat and extra-large icy schooners of Kona Brewing Company ale. ✉ *74-425 Kealakehe Pkwy., Suite 4, Honokohau Harbor* ☎ *808/326–4166* ▭ *AE, MC, V.*

$$$$
PACIFIC RIM
★
✕**Huggo's.** This is the only restaurant in town with prices and atmosphere comparable to the splurge restaurants at the Kohala-coast resorts. Open windows extend out over the rocks at the ocean's edge, and at night you can almost touch the manta rays drawn to the spotlights. Relax with a cocktail for two and feast on fresh local seafood; the catch changes daily, and the nightly chef's special is always a good bet. **Huggo's on the Rocks,** next door, is a great outdoor bar with a floor of sand; it has become a popular Friday night hangout with live music and drinks. Huggo's on the Rocks is also the perfect place to stick your toes in the sand and enjoy a delicious, reasonably priced lunch. ✉ *75-5828 Kahakai Rd., off Ali'i Dr., Kailua-Kona* ☎ *808/329–1493* ▭ *AE, D, DC, MC, V.*

$$
MODERN
HAWAIIAN
✕**Jackie Rey's Ohana Grill.** Uphill from downtown Kailua-Kona, this bright green open-air restaurant is a popular lunch destination, and increasingly crowded for dinner as well, thanks to the chef's fantastic poke, perfectly prepared local seafood dishes, and a few juicy meat standouts, including Korean-style short ribs and a delicious blackened prime rib on select evenings. At lunchtime, the fresh fish sandwiches with wasabi mayo are excellent, and the fries are crisped to perfection. On the lighter side, inventive salads keep it healthy but flavorful. ✉ *Pottery Terrace, 75-5995 Kuakini Hwy., Kailua-Kona* ☎ *808/327–0209* ▭ *AE, D, MC, V* ⊗ *No lunch weekends.*

$$$
PACIFIC RIM
✕**Kai at the Sheraton Keauhou Bay.** Facing Keauhou Bay, Kai has a primo view. The enormous windows are left open most of the time, making it almost feel like an outdoor restaurant. The Pacific Rim fusion menu is limited, but each entrée is good, from the fresh local fish to the brined and roasted hormone-free chicken. The seared 'ahi appetizer is not to be missed. Breakfast is a good bet as well; very reasonable, great buffet, and the view during the daytime is just about perfect. ✉ *78-128 Ehukai St., Kailua-Kona* ☎ *808/930–4900* ▭ *AE, D, DC, MC, V.*

4

$ ╳**Kanaka Kava.** A popular local hangout, and not just because da kava
HAWAIIAN makes you mellow. Their *pūpū* (Hawaiian hors d'oeuvre) rock! Fresh poke, smoky, tender bowls of pulled kālua pork, and healthy sautéed veggies are available in fairly large portions for less than you'll pay anywhere else on the island. Seating is at a premium at their outdoor bar, but don't be afraid to share a table and make friends. ⊠*75-5803 Ali'i Dr., Space B6, in Coconut Grove Marketplace* ☎*808/883–6260* ⊟*No credit cards.*

$$$ ╳**Kenichi Pacific.** With its black-lacquer tables and lipstick-red ban-
JAPANESE quettes, Kenichi's original Big Island outlet seems a little out of place
★ in this small strip mall. The location keeps many tourists from finding it, even though it's been open for several years now. This is where everyone in Kailua-Kona goes when they feel like splurging on top-notch sushi. It's a little on the spendy side, but it's worth it. The sashimi is so fresh it melts in your mouth, and the signature rolls are inventive and tasty. ⊠*Keauhou Shopping Center, 78-6831 Ali'i Dr., D-125, Kailua-Kona* ☎*808/322–6400* ⊟*AE, D, DC, MC, V* ◷*No lunch.*

$$ ╳**Kona Brewing Company & Brewpub.** This large and cheery spot with
AMERICAN a huge outdoor patio features an excellent and varied menu includ-ing pulled-pork quesadillas, gourmet pizzas, and a killer spinach salad with Gorgonzola cheese, macadamia nuts, and strawberries. Go for the beer tasting menu to sample an assortment of their microbrews. ⊠*75-5629 Kuakini Hwy., off Kaiwi St. at end of Pawai Pl., Kailua-Kona* ☎*808/329–2739* ⊟*AE, D, MC, V.*

$ ╳**Kona Mix Plate.** Don't be surprised if you find yourself rubbing elbows
HAWAIIAN with lots of hungry locals at this inconspicuous Kona lunch spot. The antithesis of a tourist trap, this casual island favorite with fluores-cent lighting and wooden tables is all about the food. Try the teriyaki chicken, shrimp tempura, or *katsu*—a chicken breast fried with bread crumbs and served with a sweet sauce. ⊠*341 Palani St., Kailua-Kona* ☎*808/329–8104* ⊟*No credit cards* ◷*Closed Sun.*

$$$$ ╳**La Bourgogne.** A genial husband-and-wife team owns this relax-
FRENCH ing, country-style bistro with dark-wood walls and private, romantic booths. The traditional French menu has classics such as escargots, beef with a cabernet sauvignon sauce, rack of lamb with roasted garlic and rosemary, and a less-traditional venison with a pomegranate glaze. Call well in advance for reservations. ⊠*77-6400 Nālani St., Kailua-Kona* ☎*808/329–6711* ⌕*Reservations essential* ⊟*AE, DC, MC, V* ◷*Closed Sun. and Mon. No lunch.*

¢ ╳**Los Habaneros.** A surprising find in the corner of this shopping mall,
MEXICAN next to the movie theater, Habaneros serves up tasty, fresh, and fast Mexican food for low low prices. Our favorites are usually the day's specials, which can be anything from enchilada plates to homemade sopes and chiles rellenos. Their giant burritos are also a solid pick, stuffed with meat, beans, cheese, and all the fixings. ⊠*78-631 Ali'i Dr., Keauhou Shopping Center, Keauhou* ☎*808/324–4688* ⊟*No credit cards* ◷*Closed Sun.*

$ ╳**Mixx Bistro.** Kona never knew it needed a wine bar until it got Mixx,
CAFÉ but now the town would seem strange without it. In addition to their

fantastic wine and cheese delivery service, Mixx serves up a tasty menu of bistro-inspired *pūpū* (appetizers) ranging from super healthy plates of sautéed veggies and tofu to what they claim are "the Island's best fries." And then of course there's the cheese plate. And the wine. *Sigh.* Live music keeps the patio lively most nights and Sunday afternoons. ✉*75-5626 Kuakini Hwy., in King Kamehameha Mall* ☎*808/329–7334* ⊕*www. konawinemarket.com* ⊟*AE, D, DC, MC, V* ⊘*No lunch weekends.*

$$
MEXICAN

×**Pancho & Lefty's.** Across the street from the Kona Marketplace, this typical Tex-Mex place is great for nachos and margaritas (watch out, they pour 'em strong) on a lazy afternoon. It's also a great place from which to watch the Ironman triathletes running below during the race in October. ✉*75-5719 Ali'i Dr., Kailua-Kona* ☎*808/326–2171* ⊟*AE, MC, V.*

$
FRENCH

×**Peaberry & Galette.** This little creperie is a welcome addition to the neighborhood. It serves Illy espresso, excellent sweet and savory crepes, and rich desserts like lemon cheesecake and chocolate mousse that are made fresh daily. It's got a cool, urban-café vibe, and is a nice place to hang for a bit if you're waiting for a film at the theater next door, or just feel like taking a break from paradise to sip a decent espresso and flip through the latest *W*. ✉*Keauhou Shopping Center, 78-6831 Ali'i Dr., Kailua-Kona* ☎*808/322–6020* ⊟*MC, V.*

$
AMERICAN

×**Quinn's Almost by the Sea.** OK, Quinn's is a bit of a dive. That said, it does have a few things going for it—some of the best ono sandwiches on the island, for example. It's also open until 11 PM, later than almost every other restaurant in Kailua-Kona (except Denny's). If time gets away from you on a drive to South Point, Quinn's is awaiting your return with a cheap beer and a basket of excellent calamari. ✉*75-5655A Palani Rd., Kailua-Kona* ☎*808/329–3822* ⊟*MC, V.*

¢
MEXICAN

×**Tacos El Unico.** An array of authentic soft-taco choices (beef and chicken, among others), burritos, quesadillas, and great homemade tamales. Order at the counter, take a seat outside at one of a dozen yellow tables with blue umbrellas, and enjoy all the good flavors served up in those red plastic baskets. ✉*Kona Marketplace, 75-5729 Ali'i Dr., Kailua-Kona* ☎*808/326–4033* ⊟*No credit cards.*

$
THAI

×**Thai Rin Restaurant.** The Thai owner at this old-timer in Ali'i Sunset Plaza is likely to take your order, cook it, and bring it to your table himself. The menu includes five curries, a green-papaya salad, and a popular platter that combines spring rolls, satay, beef salad, and *tom yum* (lemongrass soup). ✉*75-5799 Ali'i Dr., Kailua-Kona* ☎*808/329–2929* ⊟*AE, D, DC, MC, V.*

¢
HAWAIIAN

×**U-Top-It.** Tucked behind the shops and cafés of the Coconut Grove Marketplace, U-Top-It is a local favorite breakfast joint. Opened by a former Kona Village resort chef, all dishes at U-Top-It are built upon the restaurant's terrific taro pan crepes, which guests can choose to top with any combination of over 100 different toppings ranging from straightforward fruit or egg combinations to more unusual toppings. At lunchtime, try pairing one of the crepes with beef or chicken teriyaki. ✉*75-5799 Ali'i Dr., Coconut Grove Marketplace* ☎*808/329–0092* ⊟*AE, D, DC, MC, V* ⊘*Closed Mon.*

4

CLOSE UP

The Plate Lunch Tradition

To experience island history first-hand, take a seat at one of Hawai'i's ubiquitous "plate lunch" eateries, and order a segmented Styrofoam plate piled with rice, macaroni salad, and maybe some fiery pickled vegetable condiment. On the sugar plantations, native Hawaiians and immigrant workers from many different countries ate together in the fields, sharing food from their kaukau kits, the utilitarian version of the Japanese bento lunchbox. From this melting pot came the vibrant language of pidgin and its equivalent in food: the plate lunch.

At beaches and events, you can probably see a few tiny kitchens-on-wheels, another excellent venue for sampling plate lunch. These portable restaurants

are descendants of lunch wagons that began selling food to plantation workers in the 1930s. Try the deep-fried chicken *katsu* (rolled in Japanese panko flour and spices). The marinated beef teriyaki is another good choice, as is miso butterfish. The noodle soup, *saimin*, with its Japanese fish stock and Chinese red-tinted barbecue pork, is a distinctly local medley. Koreans have contributed spicy barbecue *kal-bi* ribs, often served with chili-laden *kimchi* (pickled cabbage). Portuguese bean soup and tangy Filipino *adobo* stew are also favorites. The most popular Hawaiian contribution to the plate lunch is the *laulau*, a mix of meat and fish and young taro leaves, wrapped in more taro leaves and steamed.

$ ✕**Wasabi's.** A tiny little place tucked into the back of the Coconut
JAPANESE   Plaza on Ali'i, Wasabi's five little tables tend to be occupied by the west side's Japanese population, here for some of the best sashimi on the island. Prices may seem steep, but the fish is of the highest quality. Fans of Americanized sushi rolls will find the familiar California and spicy tuna rolls here, along with a few unique inventions. And for those who will never be hip to the raw fish thing, teriyaki, *udon*, and sukiyaki options abound. ✉ *75-5803 Ali'i Dr., Coconut Grove Marketplace* ☎ *808/326–2352* ⊟ *AE, MC, V.*

SOUTH KONA

$ ✕**Aloha Theatre Café.** With an emphasis on healthy, organic fare, this
AMERICAN   friendly café adjacent to the Aloha Theatre serves tasty, mostly good-for-you options on a lānai overlooking Kealakekua Bay and the orchards above it. Choose from an assortment of egg dishes and pastries from the all-day breakfast menu; burgers, fish sandwiches, and salads for lunch; and pasta, grilled fish, or steak for dinner, all at very reasonable prices. The only problem here is that service is glacially slow—even the locals complain, so you know it's bad; plan on chilling out on their veranda, taking in the views for awhile. ✉ *79-7384 Mamalahoa Hwy., Kainaliu* ☎ *808/322–3383* ⊟ *D, DC, MC, V.*

$ ✕**Coffee Shack.** There's really no flaw to this place. The view is stun-
AMERICAN   ning, the service is excellent even when it's busy (which is most of the
★   time), and the eggs Benedict and hot Reuben sandwich are the best on the island. Breads and pastries are all homemade, and the coffee is

strong and tasty. On your way to nowhere in particular, stop by for a Hawaiian smoothie, an iced honey mocha latte, or homemade lū'au bread—all worth a detour. In the evening, enjoy gourmet pizza and an amazing sunset view. ✉83-5799 *Mamalahoa Hwy.* ☎808/328–9555 ⊟D, DC, MC, V ⊗*No dinner.*

$$ ✕**Ke'ei Café.** This beautiful restaurant is in a plantation-style building
ECLECTIC 15 minutes south of Kona. Delicious dinners with Brazilian, Asian, and
Fodor'sChoice European flavors utilize fresh ingredients provided by local farmers.
★ Try the Thai red curry or wok-seared 'ahi accompanied by a selection from the extensive wine list. The owners are Brazilian, so the *caipirinhas* are outstanding if you're tired of mai tais. ✉79-7511 *Māmalahoa Hwy.*, *1/2 mi south of Kainaliu, Hōnaunau* ☎808/322–9992 ⚞*Reservations essential* ⊟*No credit cards* ⊗*Closed Sun. and Mon for dinner. Closed weekends for lunch.*

$ ✕**Manago Hotel.** About 20 minutes south of Kailua-Kona, Manago is
AMERICAN a time-warp experience. A vintage neon sign identifies the hotel, and
★ Formica tables, ceiling fans, and Venetian blinds add to the flavor of this film-noir spot. The pork chops are its claim to fame, and the fresh fish is excellent as well, especially ono and butterfish. Unless you request otherwise, the fish is all sautéed with a special butter-garlic concoction (always good, don't worry). Meals come with rice for the table and an assortment of side dishes that changes from time to time, but usually includes macaroni-potato-tuna salad, some sort of braised tofu and a sautéed veggie dish. ✉82-6155 *Māmalahoa Hwy.*, *Captain Cook* ☎808/323–2642 ⊟D, DC, MC, V ⊗*Closed Mon.*

$$ ✕**Teshima's.** Locals show up at this small, neighborhood restaurant
JAPANESE 15 minutes south of Kailua-Kona whenever they're in the mood for fresh sashimi, puffy shrimp tempura, or *hekka* (beef and vegetables cooked in an iron pot) at a reasonable price. Teshima's doesn't look like much, inside or out, but it's been crowded since 1929 for a reason. You might also want to try a *teishoku* (tray) of assorted Japanese delicacies, or the popular bento box lunch. The service is laid-back and friendly. ✉79-7251 *Māmalahoa Hwy.*, *Honalo* ☎808/322–9140 ⊟*No credit cards.*

VOLCANO

$$ ✕**Kiawe Kitchen.** Everyone around here says the same thing: "Kiawe has
ITALIAN awesome pizza, but it's a little expensive." And it's true—the wood-fired pizza at this warm and pretty Italian eatery, with red walls and wood floors, has a perfect thin crust and an authentic Italian taste, but you have to be prepared to spend around $15 on a typical pie, plus $2 per topping. Food options are limited in this area, though. Go for it. ✉19-4005 *Old Volcano Rd.*, *Volcano* ☎808/967–7711 ⊟MC, V.

$$$ ✕**Kīlauea Lodge.** Chef Albert Jeyte combines contemporary trends with
CONTINENTAL traditional cooking styles from the mainland, France, and his native Hamburg, Germany. The menu changes daily, and features such entrées as venison, duck à l'orange with an apricot-mustard glaze, and authentic *hasenpfeffer* (braised rabbit) served with Jeyte's signature sauerbraten. The coconut-crusted Brie appetizer is huge, melty, and absolutely delicious. Built in 1937 as a YMCA camp, the restaurant still has the

original "Friendship Fireplace" made from stones from around the world. The roaring fire, koa-wood tables, and warm lighting make the dining room feel like a cozy lodge. ✉ *19-3948 Old Volcano Hwy., Volcano Village* ☎ *808/967-7366* ▭ *AE, MC, V* ⊗ *No lunch. Open for breakfast.*

$ ✕ **Lava Rock Café.** This is a decent place to grab a sandwich or a coffee
AMERICAN   and check your e-mail before heading to the Volcano, but stay away from dinner here. Though it's not perfect, Lava Rock is a good place to stop if you want to take a picnic into the park: once inside, the park's concessionaires sell bland, overpriced food. ✉ *19-3972 Old Volcano Hwy., behind Kīlauea General Store, Volcano* ☎ *808/967-8526* ⊗ *No dinner Sun. and Mon.* ▭ *MC, V.*

$$ ✕ **Thai Thai Restaurant.** The food is authentic, and the prices are reason-
THAI   able at this little Volcano Village find. A steaming hot plate of curry is the perfect antidote to a chilly day on the volcano. The chicken satay is excellent—the peanut dipping sauce the perfect match of sweet and spicy. Be careful when you order, as "medium" is more than spicy enough even for hard-core chili addicts. The service is warm and friend-ly and the dining room is pleasant, with white tablecloths, Thai art, and a couple of silk wall hangings ✉ *19-4084 Old Volcano Rd., Volcano* ☎ *808/967-7969* ⊗ *No lunch Wed.* ▭ *AE, D, DC, MC, V.*

$ ✕ **Volcano Golf & Country Club.** This restaurant doesn't feel much like a
AMERICAN   country club—it's simple and not at all fancy with oak tables filled with local old-timers talking story and chowing down on greasy local favor-ites. Locals love this spot for its large portions and classic breakfasts: ordering the breakfast burger (with fried egg, cheese, and your choice of meat) and a cup of local coffee is the way to go. If it's lunchtime, you can't beat the burgers. ✉ *Pi'i Mauna Dr., off Hwy. 11, Volcano* ☎ *808/967-8228* ⊗ *No dinner* ▭ *AE, D, DC, MC, V.*

HILO

$$$ ✕ **Big Island Pizza.** If spending $20 on a large pizza is something you
ITALIAN   just can't come to grips with, steer clear of Big Island Pizza. If, on the other hand, you can rationalize paying more for a pie that's topped with things like Black Tiger shrimp, scallops, and chunks of crabmeat (the "Ali'i Feast"), then order up and get ready for a little slice of heaven. There are only a handful of tables for eating in, but they do a brisk take-out business and also deliver to the eastern side of the island. ✉ *760 Kilauea Ave.* ☎ *808/934-8000* ▭ *AE, D, MC, V.*

¢   ✕ **Blane's Drive-In.** With a vast menu second only to Ken's House of
HAWAIIAN   Pancakes, Blane's serves up everything from standard hamburgers to chicken *katsu*. There's a mean plate lunch with tons of fresh fish for only $8. At one point it was a real drive-in, with car service. Now, cus-tomers park, order at the window, and then eat at one of the few picnic tables provided or take their food to go. ✉ *217 Wainuenue Ave., Hilo* ☎ *808/969-9494* ▭ *D, DC, MC, V.*

¢   ✕ **Café 100.** This popular local restaurant is famous for its tasty *loco*
HAWAIIAN   *moco*, prepared in more than a dozen ways, and its dirt-cheap breakfast and lunch specials. (You can stuff yourself for $3 if you order right.) The word restaurant, or even café, is used liberally here—you order at

a window and eat on one of the outdoor benches provided—but you come here for the food and prices, not the ambience. ✉ *969 Kīlauea Ave., Hilo* ☎ *808/935–8683* ▭ *AE, DC, MC, V* ⏲ *Closed Sun.*

$$ ITALIAN ✕ **Café Pesto.** This is one of the few places on the island where you can find a hearty, healthy salad and brick oven pizza with a twist of local seafood and produce. Try the Wild Mushroom & Artichokes pizza with fresh oyster, shiitake mushrooms, and rosemary Gorgonzola sauce. Overlooking the Hilo Bay, the causal restaurant also serves unique Italian dishes, such as sesame soy marinated Island fish rolled with pesto, red onions, and cheese and served with coconut crusted calamari and Oregon wasabi snow crab Caesar salad. ✉ *308 Kamehameha Ave., Hilo* ☎ *808/969–6640* ▭ *AE, D, DC, MC, V.*

4

$$ AMERICAN ✕ **Hilo Bay Café.** What this eatery lacks in setting—it's in a strip mall that contains OfficeMax and Wal-Mart—it makes up for with modern decor and fantastic food. When in season, the out-of-this-world heirloom tomato salad puts any mainland variation to shame. The menu changes every few months, but the vegan offerings, from the garlic fries to the potpie, are always good enough to seduce meat-eaters. Other excellent options include macadamia nut praline seared scallops, Guinness onion rings with sun dried tomato ketchup, and any of the salads (the beet salad is a standout). Prices are exceedingly reasonable given the quality of the food. ✉ *315 Maka'ala St., Hilo* ☎ *808/935–4939* ▭ *AE, DC, MC, V* ⏲ *No lunch Sun.*

$ AMERICAN ✕ **Ken's House of Pancakes.** For years this 24-hour coffee shop between the airport and the hotels along Banyan Drive has been a gathering place for Hilo residents. As its name implies, Ken's serves good pancakes, but there are about 180 other tasty local specialties and American diner–inspired items from which to choose. Wednesday is prime rib night. ✉ *1730 Kamehameha Ave., Hilo* ☎ *808/935–8711* ▭ *AE, D, DC, MC, V.*

$ HAWAIIAN ✕ **Kūhiō Grille.** There's no ambience to speak of, and water is served in unbreakable plastic, but if you're searching for local fare—that eclectic and undefinable fusion of ethnic cuisines—Kūhiō Grille is a must. Sam Araki serves a 1-pound *laulau* (a steamed bundle of taro leaves and pork) that is worth the trip. This diner at the edge of Hilo's largest mall opens at 6 AM. ✉ *Prince Kūhiō Shopping Plaza, 111 E. Puainako St., at Hwy. 11* ☎ *808/959–2336* ▭ *AE, MC, V.*

$ MEXICAN ✕ **Luquin's Mexican Restaurant.** Long an island favorite for tasty, albeit greasy, Mexican grub, Luquin's is still going strong in the funky town of Pahoa. Tacos are great here (go for crispy), especially when stuffed with grilled, seasoned local fish. Chips are warm and salty, the salsa's got some kick, and the beans are thick with lard and topped with melted cheese. Not something you'd eat before a long swim, but perfect after a long day of exploring. ✉ *15-2942 Pahoa Village Rd., Pahoa* ☎ *808/965–9990* ▭ *AE, D, DC, MC, V.*

$ THAI ✕ **Naung Mai.** There's not much to this downtown eatery: five tables, three booths, and chef-owner Sukanya Heideman hard at work in the kitchen. It's a bit hard to find, but fresh, reasonably priced meals make it worth seeking out. It may be the best Thai food on the island. For those who like to pair spicy curry with cold beer, feel free to pick up a six-pack at the grocery store up the street. ⊠*86 Kīlauea Ave., Hilo* 🕾*808/934–7540* ➡*D, DC, MC, V.*

$ ✕**Reuben's Mexican Restaurant.** It's not the best Mexican food you've

MEXICAN ever had, but if you're in Hilo and you're jonesing for some chile verde, Reuben's has got you pretty well covered. You could make a meal out of their warm chips and salsa alone, and they're known for pouring a stiff margarita. Fancy? No. Authentic? *Mas o menos* (more or less). Sometimes you just want a greasy plate of nachos and a margarita. ⊠*336 Kamehameha Ave., Hilo* 🕾*808/961–2552* ➡*No credit cards.*

$$ ✕**The Seaside.** The Nakagawa family has been running this eatery since

SEAFOOD the early 1920s. The latest son to manage the place has spruced it up a bit with tablecloths and candles, but the decor is still bare bones. No matter, since it serves some of the freshest fish on the island. (Not a surprise, as the fish come from the restaurant's own aqua farm.) Islanders travel great distances for the furikake salmon. Not a fish eater? Try the grilled lamb chops, chicken, or prime rib. Arrive before sunset and request a table on the patio for a view of the egrets roosting around the fishponds. ⊠*1790 Kalaniana'ole Ave., Hilo* 🕾*808/935–8825* ➡*AE, DC, MC, V* ⊘*Closed Mon. No lunch.*

$ ✕**Sombat's Fresh Thai Cuisine.** The name says it all. Sombat Parente uses

THAI only the freshest local ingredients to prepare authentic and tasty Thai treats like pumpkin curry, spring rolls with lime sauce, and green papaya salad. In fact, many of the items on the menu come directly from Sombat's own garden. The weekday lunch plate special is a steal ($7 for an entrée plus rice and salad, $8 for two entrée choices, and $9 for three). And if you can't leave the island without it, Sombat's infamous pad thai sauce is available to take home in jars. ⊠*88 Kanoelehue Ave., Waiakea Kai Plaza, Hilo* 🕾*808/969–9336* ➡*AE, D, DC, MC, V* ⊘*Closed Sun.*

WHERE TO STAY

You'll almost always be able to find a room on the Big Island, but you might not get your first choice if you wait until the last minute. Make reservations six months to a year in advance if you're visiting during the winter season (December 15 through April 15). The week after Easter Sunday, when the Merrie Monarch Festival is in full swing, all of Hilo's rooms are booked. Kailua-Kona is packed in mid-October during the Ironman World Triathlon Championship. (Even tougher than trying to find a room at these times is trying to find a rental car.)

There are literally hundreds of vacation condo rentals in Kailua-Kona, and along the Kohala Coast, which is a good way to get more space and save some money by eating in (although it's easy to amass a huge bill at the grocery store, so you still have to be careful).

The bulk of the island's resorts are on the beaches of the Kohala Coast, and many offer package deals throughout the year. If you choose a B&B, inn, or an out-of-the-way hotel, explain your expectations fully and ask plenty of questions before booking. Be clear about your travel and location needs. Some places require stays of two or three days. No matter where you stay, you'll want to rent a car—preferably one with four-wheel drive.

Members of the Big Island–based Hawai'i Island Bed & Breakfast Association are listed with phone numbers and rates in a comprehensive online brochure. In order to join this network, B&Bs must be evaluated every year and meet fairly stringent minimum requirements.

Hawai'i Island Bed & Breakfast Association (⊕*www.stayhawaii.com*). **Hawai'i's Best Bed & Breakfasts** (☎*808/985–7488 or 800/262–9912* ⊕*www.bestbnb.com*). For information on camping at county parks, including Spencer Beach Park, contact the **Department of Parks and Recreation** (⊠*25 Aupuni St., Hilo* ☎*808/961–8311* ⊕*www. hawaii-county.com*).

WHAT IT COSTS					
	¢	$	$$	$$$	$$$$
HOTELS	under $100	$100–$180	$181–$260	$261–$340	over $340

Prices are for two people in a standard double room in high season. Condo price categories reflect studio and one-bedroom rates. Prices do not include 11.41% tax.

KOHALA COAST

$$$–$$$$
B&B/INN
Fodor's Choice
★

▦**Ahu Pohaku Ho'omaluhia Hawai'i Island Eco Retreat.** Ahu Pohaku is set above the cliffs of North Kohala near Pololu valley. As the name implies, it has plenty of "green" credentials: the retreat generates its own solar power, uses a water catchment tank, and grows almost all of its own food. Beautiful hardwood floors are built from sustainably harvested woods, and rooms take advantage of natural light and ventilation to keep energy usage low. Surrounded by 60 acres, 20 of which are a dedicated conservation area, the retreat feels both luxurious and completely hidden from the world. Rooms are large and bright, with ocean views. Most have private balconies, and all are equipped with large bathrooms that include both soaking tubs and showers. Three meals a day are prepared from the retreat's garden supply, augmented by additions from local farms. **Pros:** stunning location, new and beautiful construction with no expense spared, eco-friendly. **Cons:** not within walking distance of restaurants, no pool, off the beaten path. ⊠*54-250 Maluhia Rd.,* ☎*808/889–6336* ⊕*www.hawaii-island-retreat.com* ⬟*9 rooms* ⌂*In-room: no a/c, no phone, no TV, Wi-Fi. In-hotel: restaurant, laundry facilities, Internet terminal, Wi-Fi, parking (free), no-smoking rooms* ☰*AE, MC, V.*

$$$
RENTAL

▦**Aston Shores at Waikoloa.** Villas with red-tile roofs are set amid landscaped lagoons and waterfalls at the edge of the championship Waikoloa Village Golf Course. The spacious condo units—the ground floor and upper floor are available separately—are privately owned, so furnishings vary from unit to unit. Sliding glass doors open onto large lānai. All units have complete kitchens with washer-dryers, and come with maid service. Check the Web site for deals. **Pros:** good prices, great location, self-sufficient condos with maid service. **Cons:** no access to resort amenities, fee for Internet access. ⊠*69-1035 Keana Pl., Waikoloa* ☎*808/886–5001 or 877/997–6667* ⊕*www.astonhotels.*

WHERE TO STAY ON THE KOHALA COAST & WAIMEA

	Property Name	Worth Noting	Cost $	Pools	Beach	Golf Course	Tennis Courts	Gym	Spa	Children's Programs	Rooms	Restaurants	Other	Location
Hotels & Resorts														
8	Fairmont Orchid Hawai'i	Massages on the beach	449–899	1	yes	yes	10	yes	yes	5–12	540	4	shops	South Kohala
★ 1	Four Seasons Resort Hualālai	King's Pond snorkeling	725–1,215	6	yes	yes	8	yes	yes	5–12	274	3		North Kona
11	Hāpuna Beach Prince Hotel	Fantastic beach	350–560	1	yes	yes	5	yes	yes	5–12	350	5		South Kohala
3	Hilton Waikoloa Village	Dolphin Quest program	249–499	3	yes	yes	8	yes	yes	5–12	1297	9	shops	Waikoloa
★ 2	Kona Village Resort	2 lū'au options	660–1,475	2	yes	Yes	3	yes	yes	5–17	125	2	no a/c phone or TV	North Kona
12	Mauna Kea Beach Hotel	Re-opened in 2009	450	1	yes	Yes	11	yes	yes	5–12	258	4	shops	South Kohala
9	Mauna Lani Bay Hotel	Renowned golf & spa	445–935	1	yes	yes	6	yes	yes	5–12	350	5		South Kohala
4	Waikoloa Beach Marriott	Newly renovated	425–565	2	yes	yes	0	yes	yes	5–12	565	1		Waikoloa
16	Waimea Country Lodge	Large rooms	120–140								21		kitchens (some)	Waimea
Condos & Vacation Rentals														
17	Aloha Vacation Cottages	Private, close to beach	145–165								2		kitchens	Waimea
5	Aston Shores, Waikoloa	Great package deals	224–400	1	yes		1	yes			80		kitchens	Waikoloa
7	Kolea at Waikoloa Beach Resort	Great location	250–800	1				yes			13		kitchens	Waikoloa
10	Mauna Lani Point, Islands	Waterfall pool	395–820	1							83		kitchens	South Kohala
6	Vista Waikoloa	Large lānai	180–300	1			0	yes			122		kitchens	Waikoloa
18	Waimea Gardens Cottage	Mountainside stream	150–180								3		kitchens	Waimea
B&Bs & Inns														
19	Aaah, The Views!	Streamside, those views	135–195								3		kitchens	Waimea
★ 14	Ahu Pohaku Ho'omaluhia	Eco-resort	300–450								9		no a/c phone or TV	North Kohala
13	Hale Ho'onanea	Great deal	110–140								3		no a/c	Kawaihae
15	Jacaranda Inn	Good breakfast, big rooms	159–225, cottage 450								9		no phone, no TV	Waimea

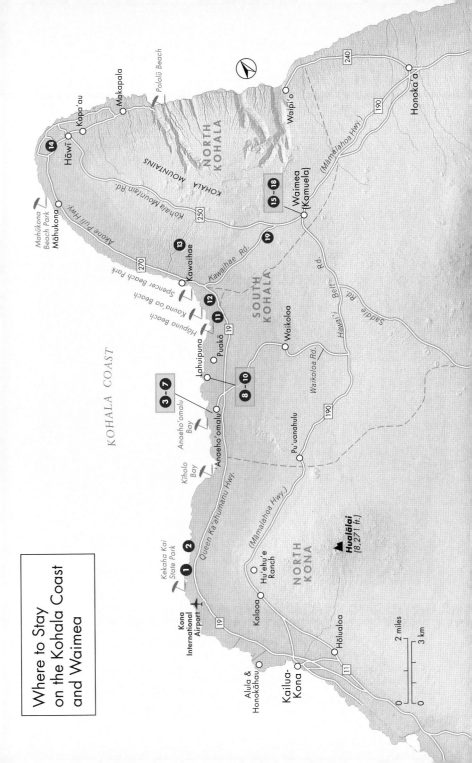

Where to Stay
on the Kohala Coast
and Waimea

Ahu Pohaku Ho'omaluhia Hawaii Island Eco Retreat

com ⟿80 units ⚷In-room: safe, kitchen, Internet. In-hotel: tennis courts, pool, gym, laundry facilities, parking (free), no-smoking rooms ⊟AE, D, DC, MC, V.

$$$$ ⛾**Fairmont Orchid Hawai'i.** The Fair-

RESORT mont is a megaresort in every sense of the word—huge, crowded, expensive, with grand staircases, domed ceilings, chandeliers, and marble everywhere. If you're looking for a unique, intimate experience, this is

not your hotel, but with its antiques and 32 acres of beachfront gardens the Orchid provides the perfect old-school hotel experience for some. Its restaurants are also among the best on the island, with a large variety of options ranging from sushi to modern Hawaiian cuisine to an upscale steak house. The fabulous "Gold Floor" of the hotel includes free breakfast and a daily wine and hors d'oeuvres hour. **Pros:** oceanfront location, great restaurants, executive floor. **Cons:** mammoth resort lacks personal feel, outdated room decor. ⊠1 N. Kanikū Dr., Kohala Coast ☎808/885–2000 or 800/845–9905 ⊕www.fairmont/orchid.com ⟿486 rooms, 54 suites ⚷In-room: safe, refrigerator, Wi-Fi. In-hotel: 4 restaurants, room service, bars, golf courses, tennis courts, pool, gym, spa, beachfront, diving, water sports, bicycles, children's programs (ages 5–12), laundry service, Internet terminal, Wi-Fi, parking (paid), some pets allowed, no-smoking rooms ⊟AE, D, DC, MC, V.

$$$$ ⛾**Four Seasons Resort Hualālai.** Beautiful views everywhere, polished

RESORT wood floors, brand-new furnishings and linens in warm earth and cool

♺ white tones, and Hawaiian artwork make Hualālai a peaceful retreat.

Fodor'sChoice Ground-level rooms have outdoor garden showers. Bungalows are large

★ and cozy, with down comforters and spacious slate-floor bathrooms. One of the five pools, called King's Pond, is a brackish pond with loads of fish and two manta rays that guests have the opportunity to feed daily. The main infinity pool looks like something out of an ad for an expensive liquor—it's long and peaceful, surrounded by cabanas and palm trees with a clear view to the ocean beyond. The on-site Hawaiian Cultural Center honors the grounds' spiritual heritage, and the sports club and spa offer top-rate health and fitness options. Hualālai's golf course hosts the Senior PGA Tournament of Champions. Despite its quiet luxury, the resort is also super kid-friendly, with a great activities program, and a few pool options for families. The downside is this: despite valiant efforts to the contrary, the Four Seasons doesn't feel much like Hawai'i; add to that the number of guests who will be squawking on their cell phones next to you at the pool (despite the sign reading NO CELL PHONES), and you can see why some folks avoid this place. Still, it is beautiful, the restaurants are fantastic, the rooms are more than comfortable, and the service is definitely of Four Seasons quality. **Pros:** beautiful location, island's best restaurants. **Cons:** can be noisy poolside, doesn't feel Hawaiian. ⊠72-100 Ka'ūpūlehu Dr. ⛫Box 1269, North Kona, 96745 ☎808/325–8000, 800/819–5053, or 888/340–5662 ⊕*www.fourseasons.com* ↻*243 rooms, 31 suites* ⌂*In-room: safe, DVD, Wi-Fi. In-hotel: 3 restaurants, room service, bars, golf course, tennis courts, pools, gym, spa, beachfront, water sports, children's programs (ages 5–12), laundry facilities, laundry service, Internet terminal, Wi-Fi, parking (free), some pets allowed, no-smoking rooms* ▭*AE, D, DC, MC, V.*

$ ⌧**Hale Ho'onanea.** A comfortable
B&B/INN home with three detached guest suites, this 3-acre property in the Kohala Estates lives up to the English translation of its name, "House of Relaxation." From its bluff above the ocean you can watch the sun rise over Mauna Kea and set over the Pacific, and view the sparkling beauty

KOHALA CONDO COMFORTS

There are fewer stores and takeout options on the Kohala Coast, but, as the condos are all associated with resorts, most of your needs will be met. If you require anything not provided by the management, the Queens' MarketPlace at Waikoloa Beach Resort (⊠150 Waikoloa Beach Dr., Waikoloa ☎808/886–8822) is the place to go. There's a new gourmet grocery store that is not exactly cheap, but you're paying for the convenience of not having to drive into town. There is also a food court with a couple of decent, affordable dining choices.

ty of Hawai'i's night sky. The rooms are comfortable and spacious, if not terribly beautiful; the views and grounds make up for what the rooms lack, as does the price in this neck of the woods (less than half the nightly rate of the Kohala Coast resorts). **Pros:** detached suites, panoramic ocean views from private lānai, good price for the neighborhood. **Cons:** not within walking distance to restaurants, no pool. ⊠*Kohala Estates, 59-513 Ala Kahua Dr., Kawaihae* ☎*808/882–1653 or 877/882–1653* ⊕*www.houseofrelaxation.com* ↻*3 suites* ⌂*In-room: no a/c, kitchen, DVD, Wi-Fi. In-hotel: parking (free)* ▭*MC, V.*

$$$$ ⌧**Hāpuna Beach Prince Hotel.** Often more reasonably priced than its
HOTEL neighbors, the Hāpuna Beach Prince is no less luxurious and happens to
♻ be sitting on a corner of the best beach on the island. Initially designed with business travelers in mind, rooms at the Hāpuna Prince are spacious, with large marble bathrooms and plenty of in-room amenities. However, the spacious rooms and beachfront location have turned the hotel into more of a family vacation destination than a business hotel, which means that couples seeking a romantic getaway might be disappointed by the number of kids playing Marco Polo at the pool. Still, the place is large enough to escape from other guests if you so desire, and the staff is exceedingly helpful. The golf course, designed by Arnold Palmer and Ed Seay, has topped many a "best courses" list. **Pros:** extra-large rooms, full or partial ocean views from most rooms, direct access to one of island's best beaches. **Cons:** tons of kids around the pool can make it noisy, big resort atmosphere lacks intimacy. ⊠*62-100 Kauna'oa Dr., Kohala Coast* ☎*808/880–1111 or 800/882–6060* ⊕*www.hapunabeachprincehotel.com* ↻*314 rooms, 36 suites* ⌂*In-room: safe, refrigerator, DVD, Internet. In-hotel: 5 restaurants, bars, golf course, pool, gym, spa, beachfront, diving, watersports, children's programs*

Four Seasons Resort Hualālai

Kona Village Resort

KOHALA VACATION RENTAL COMPANIES

Along the Kohala Coast, there are two main resort pockets, **Waikoloa Beach Resort** (⊕ *www.waikoloabeachresort. com*) and **Mauna Lani**, with several condominium and town house communities as well as private homes. Both areas border championship golf courses and pristine beaches and feature several new shops and restaurants. A few miles north is **Mauna Kea Resort** (☎ *808/880–3490* ⊕ *www. maunakearesortrentals.com*), which also has a selection of luxury vacation rentals.

Since most vacation properties are owned by individual families, there are several property management companies to choose from. Browse their Web sites to find your best value, as prices tend to vary, and there are often specials during the off-season. Or, you can follow the new trend and rent directly from the owner to avoid additional fees. Although these units tend to have a more personal touch with less wear and tear, there are no guarantees on the amenities or service, as it depends soley on the owner.

To start, check out **Vacation Rentals by Owner** (⊕ *www.vrbo.com*) for a wide selection of individually listed condos. **South Kohala Management** (☎ *800/882–4252* or *808/883–8500* ⊕ *www.southkohala.com*) and **Coldwell Banker** (☎ *808/329–3545* ⊕ *www.escapetoextraordinary.com*) have numerous options in both Waikoloa and Mauna Lani, as do **Aldridge Associates** (☎ *800/662–5642* or *808/883–8300* ⊕ *www.alohahawaiivacations.com*) and **Waikoloa Realty** (☎ *808/883–9951* ⊕ *www.waikoloa-realty.com*). For the Waikoloa Colony Villas and the Shores at Waikoloa try **Aston Hotels & Resorts** (☎ *877/997–6667* ⊕ *www.astonhotels. com*). **Outrigger** (☎ *800/688–7444* ⊕ *www.outrigger.com*) features the Palm Villas and Fairways at Mauna Lani and the Waikoloa Beach and Fairway Villas at Waikoloa. **Kolea Vacations** (☎ *888/565–3244* ⊕ *www.koleavacations.com*) has high-end vacation rentals at Kolea and Hali'i Kai, plus private estates, while **Classic Resorts** (☎ *800/642–6284* or *808/885–5022* ⊕ *www.classicresorts.com*) handles the two Mauna Lani properties that we list.

(ages 5–12), laundry services, Internet terminal, Wi-Fi, parking (free), no-smoking rooms ▭*AE, D, DC, MC, V.*

$$$–$$$$
RESORT
Ⓒ

🏨 **Hilton Waikoloa Village.** Dolphins chirp in the lagoon; a pint-size daredevil zooms down the 175-foot waterslide; a bride poses on the grand staircase; a fire-bearing runner lights the torches along the seaside path at sunset—these are some of the scenes that may greet you at this 62-acre megaresort. Shaded pathways lined with a multimillion-dollar Pacific Island art collection connect the three tall buildings; Swiss-made trams and Disney-engineered boats shuttle those weary of the long hallways and meandering paths. The stars of **Dolphin Quest** (☎ *800/248–3316* ⊕*www.dolphinquest.org*) are the resort's pride and joy; reserve in advance for an interactive learning session. Though there's no ocean beach, there is a seaside trail to 'Anaeho'omalu Bay, aka A-Bay, one of the island's most pleasant beaches. An artificial sand beach borders the 4-acre resort lagoon. Modern rooms in neutral tones have private lānai and are large enough to accommodate the families that flock here. **Pros:** a kid's idea of paradise, lots of restaurant and activity options. **Cons:** gigantic, crowded, and often noisy, restaurants are pricey. ✉ *69-425 Waikoloa Beach Dr., Waikoloa* ☎ *808/886–1234 or 800/445–8667* ⊕ *www.hiltonwaikoloavillage.com* ⌁ *1,240 rooms, 57 suites* ♿ *In-room: safe, refrigerator, Internet. In-hotel: 9 restaurants, room service, bars, golf courses, tennis courts, pools, gym, spa, beachfront, diving, water sports, bicycles, children's programs (ages 5–12), laundry facilities, laundry service, Internet terminal, Wi-Fi, parking (paid), some pets allowed, no-smoking rooms* ▭ *AE, D, DC, MC, V.*

$$$–$$$$
RENTAL

🛈 **Kolea at Waikoloa Beach Resort.** Set just steps from the beach along the Kohala Coast, with access to a private chef, nanny, in-house masseuse, or personal concierge make this the ultimate in luxury. The two- or three-bedroom units have a large, open living area connected by retractable doors to a lānai with a gas grill, bar, and sink—perfect for a barbecue. (Grab gourmet groceries down the road at the Queens' MarketPlace.) Relax at the infinity pool while your keiki (children) splash in the waterfall at the sandy-bottom kid's pool. Kolea Vacations caters to families, and cribs, high chairs, and toys are available for a fee. For execs, all units come equipped with fax machines, printers, and copiers, so business can be done in paradise, if needed. **Pros:** prime location, online service to book activities prior to arrival, free, unlimited phone calls to mainland. **Cons:** costly, minimum 3-nights stay (7-nights during holidays), security deposit required. ✉ *68-100 Kolea Kai Circle, off Waikoloa Beach Dr., Waikoloa Beach Resort, Waikoloa* ☎ *888/565–3244* ⊕ *www.koleavacations.com* ⌁ *12 units, 1 villa* ♿ *In-room: kitchen, DVD, Wi-Fi. In-hotel: pool, gym, beachfront, laundry facilities, Wi-Fi, parking (free), no-smoking rooms* ▭ *AE, MC, V.*

$$$$
RESORT
Fodor'sChoice
★

🛈 **Kona Village Resort.** The most Hawaiian of the Kohala Coast resorts, Kona Village was one of the first, and it makes a real effort to keep modern life at bay. Without phones, televisions, or radios, the Kona Village is in a time warp—the perfect place for couples or families to get away from it all in their own thatch-roof *hale* (house) near the resort's sandy beach. Built on the grounds of an ancient Hawaiian village, the bungalows reflect styles of South Seas cultures—Tahitian, Samoan, Māori, Fijian, or Hawaiian. The Royal oceanfront rooms have private hot tubs. Some of the bungalows are oceanfront, some nestled in a rain-forest-like setting of ponds and gardens, and no matter where you hair from and how crowded the resort is, you'll feel like this is your own little hideaway. The beach here is long and idyllic, with sea turtles nesting in the sand around a calm, turquoise bay. **Pros:** detached bungalows afford ultimate privacy, sea turtles nest on the resort's private beach, all meals and many activities included. **Cons:** somewhat isolated location, no phones in rooms. ✉ *Queen Ka'ahumanu Hwy., Box 1299, North Kona* ☎ *808/325–5555 or 800/367–5290* ⊕ *www.konavillage. com* ⌁ *125 bungalows* ♿ *In-room: no a/c, no phone, safe, refrigerator,* *no TV. In-hotel: 2 restaurants, bars, tennis courts, pools, gym, spa, beachfront, diving, water sports, bicycles, children's programs (ages 5–17), laundry facilites, laundry service, Internet terminal, Wi-Fi, parking (free), no-smoking rooms ☐AE, DC, MC, V.*

$$$$
HOTEL
★
Mauna Kea Beach Hotel. The grande dame of Kohala Coast, the Mauna Kea Beach Hotel opened in 1965, and has long been regarded as one of the world's premier vacation resort hotels. It is now even better than ever after a multi-million dollar restoration, though it still radiates the original trademark character of understated elegance. Guest rooms feature new furnishings, a media hub, and a private bath lānai. Refreshed restaurants and the addition of the Mandara Spa, fitness center, and shops complete the package. Additionally, the hotel borders one of the islands' finest white-sand beaches, Kauna'oa. The rejuvenated rooms and deluxe amenities, coupled with the traditional Hawaiian vibe and the amazing beach, make Mauna Kea hard to beat. Shuttles operate between the Mauna Kea and the adjacent Hāpuna Beach Prince Hotel, allowing guests to use the facilities at both hotels. **Pros:** brand new rooms and amenities, personalized check-in, outstanding service. **Cons:** fee for Internet access. ✉*62-100 Mauna Kea Beach Dr., Kohala Coast* ☎*808/882–7222 or 886/977–4589* ⊕*www.maunakeabeachhotel.com* ⬎*258 rooms, 8 suites* ⬧*In-room: safe, refrigerator, DVD, Internet. In-hotel: 4 restaurants, golf courses, tennis courts, pool, gym, spa, beachfront, children's programs (age 5–12), parking (free), no-smoking rooms* ☐*AE, D, DC, MC, V.*

$$$$
HOTEL
Mauna Lani Bay Hotel & Bungalows. A Kohala Coast classic, popular with honeymooners and anniversary couples for decades, the elegant Mauna Lani is still one of the most beautiful resorts on the island. The open-air lobby has ceilings near the stratosphere, ocean views, and a constant, pleasant breeze. The vast majority of the large, recently renovated rooms have ocean views, and all have a large lānai. The resort is known for its two spectacular golf courses and award-winning spa, and recently opened a collection of shops and restaurants. **Pros:** beautiful design, award-winning spa, each room has a large private lānai. **Cons:** so-so restaurants, lacks kid-friendly features. ✉*68-1400 Mauna Lani Dr., Kohala Coast* ☎*808/885–6622 or 800/367–2323* ⊕*www.maunalani.com* ⬎*335 rooms, 10 suites, 5 bungalows* ⬧*In-room: safe, refrigerator, Wi-Fi. In-hotel: 5 restaurants, room service, bars, golf courses, tennis courts, pools, gym, spa, beachfront, diving, water sports, children's programs (ages 5–12), laundry service, Internet terminal, Wi-Fi, parking (free), no-smoking rooms* ☐*AE, D, DC, MC, V.*

$$$$
RENTAL
Mauna Lani Point Villas and the Islands of Mauna Lani Condominiums. Surrounded by the emerald greens of a world-class ocean-side golf course, spacious two-story suites at Islands of Mauna Lani offer a private, independent home away from home. The privately owned units, individually decorated according to the owners' tastes, have European cabinets and oversize soaking tubs in the main bedrooms. The Mauna Lani Point villas are closer to the beach, which means they're priced a little higher, but that extra dough pays for an ocean view from the lānai of most units. At both properties you're steps away from the Mauna Lani resort, where you have access to golf, tennis, spa facilities, and restaurants.

Pros: privacy, but with access to resort amenities, soaking tubs, extra-large units. **Cons:** can get very pricey, a bit farther from restaurants. ✉ *68-1050 Mauna Lani Point Dr., Kohala Coast* ☎ *808/885–5022 or 800/642–6284* ⊕ *www.classicresorts.com* ⌕ *83 units* ⌂ *In-room: kitchen, DVD, Internet (some). In-hotel: pool, laundry facilities, parking (free), no-smoking rooms* ⊟ *AE, DC, MC, V.*

$$

RENTAL

⌨ **Vista Waikoloa.** Older than most of the condo complexes along the Kohala Coast, the two-bedroom, two-bath Vista condos offer ocean views and a great value for this part of the island. All are large and well appointed, with two lānai per unit. The complex is walking distance to A-Bay, the King's Shops at Waikoloa, the new Queens' Market-Place, and the restaurants and amenities of Hilton Waikoloa Village. **Pros:** centrally located, reasonably priced, very large units. **Cons:** hit or miss on decor, some owners charge (refundable) security deposits, most units are outdated. ✉ *Waikoloa Beach Resort, 69-1010 Keana Pl.* ☎ *808/886–3594* ⊕ *www.vistawaikoloa.com* ⌕ *122 units* ⌂ *In-room: kitchen. In-hotel: pool, gym, hot tub, laundry facilities, parking (free), no-smoking rooms* ⊟ *AE, D, DC, MC, V.*

$$$$

RESORT

⌨ **Waikoloa Beach Marriott.** The most affordable resort on the Kohala Coast, the Waikoloa Beach Marriott covers 15 acres bordering the white-sand beach of 'Anaeho'omalu Bay and encompasses ancient fishponds, historic trails, and petroglyph fields. All of the Marriott's rooms, some of them very recently completed, have low-slung, sleek modern beds framed with dark wood that contrasts nicely with bright white linens and Hawaiian art in a rainbow of tropical colors. The oversize cabana rooms overlook the lagoon. Dining is not the hotel's strong suit, but the Waikoloa Beach Grill, plus the tons of restaurants at the King's Shops, Queen's MarketPlace, and the next-door Hilton, offer plenty of choices within walking distance. The hotel's Mandara Spa offers a full range of treatments in a spacious new wellness center. **Pros:** great location at a great price, brand new hotel, well-designed interiors. **Cons:** no standout restaurants, there is no real Hawaiian ambience. ✉ *69-275 Waikoloa Beach Dr., Waikoloa* ☎ *808/886–6789 or 800/228–9290* ⊕ *www.marriott.com* ⌕ *555 rooms, 10 suites* ⌂ *In-room: safe, refrigerator, Internet. In-hotel: restaurant, bars, golf courses, pools, gym, spa, beachfront, water sports, children's programs (ages 5–12), laundry facilities, laundry service, Internet terminal, Wi-Fi, parking (paid), no-smoking rooms* ⊟ *AE, D, DC, MC, V.*

WAIMEA

$

B&B/INN

⌨ **Aaah, The Views!** This tranquil and pretty stream-side mountain home in upcountry Waimea is lovingly tended by owners Erika and Derek Stuart. Rooms are clean and bright, with lots of windows to enjoy the views. The house has a sauna and an in-house massage therapist as well. **Pros:** away from it all, beautiful countryside views, on-site yoga and massage. **Cons:** not kid-friendly, no pool, must drive to area restaurants and attractions. ✉ *66-1773 Alaneo St., off Akulani, just past mile marker 60 on Hwy. 19, Waimea* ☎ *808/885–3455* ⊕ *www.aaahtheviews.com* ⌕ *3 rooms* ⌂ *In-room: kitchen (some), refrigerator, Wi-Fi. In-hotel: parking (free), no-smoking rooms* ⊟ *MC, V.*

$ ▥**Aloha Vacation Cottages.** Set on several acres of North Kohala proper-
RENTAL ty, these two rental cottages don't look like much from the outside, but
inside they are newly upgraded, clean, comfortable, and well stocked
with beach toys—from kayaks to snorkels—towels and mats, books,
cable TV, DVDs, you name it. They even come with a laptop computer
for your use. The price is right, and they are just a 10-minute drive from
the Kohala Coast. **Pros:** each cottage equipped with gas grill and large
lānai, free Wi-Fi, 10-minute drive from great beaches. **Cons:** somewhat
remote location, can't walk to restaurants or stores, no pool. ⬭*Box
1395, Waimea 96743* ☎*877/875–1722 or 808/885–6535* ⊕*www.aloha
cottages.net* ⬐*2 units* ⬕*In-room: no a/c, kitchen, DVD, Wi-Fi. In-
hotel: laundry facilites, parking (free), no-smoking rooms* ▭*AE, D,
DC, MC, V.*

$–$$ ▥**Jacaranda Inn.** Charming inside and out, the lavender Jacaranda Inn
B&B/INN can be spotted from miles away. Built in 1897, the sprawling estate was
★ once the home of the manager of Parker Ranch; it's been redecorated
in hues of raspberry and lavender, with lots of koa wood accents. Most
of the rooms have hot tubs. A separate nearby cottage that sleeps six
has been recently renovated with new hardwood floors, a stone fireplace, and large outdoor hot tub. **Pros:** country charm, hot tubs in
most rooms, walking distance to Waimea restaurants. **Cons:** no pool,
lots of purple, pricey for the area. ✉*65-1444 Kawaihae Rd., Waimea*
☎*808/885–8813* ⊕*www.jacarandainn.com* ⬐*8 suites, 1 cottage*
⬕*In-room: no a/c, no phone, refrigerator (some), no TV. In-hotel: Wi-
Fi, parking (free), no-smoking rooms* ▭*MC, V.*

$ ▥**Waimea Country Lodge.** In the heart of cowboy country, this mod-
HOTEL est ranch house–style lodge offers views of the green, rolling slopes of
Mauna Kea. It's so quiet you forget you're close to busy Waimea. The
rooms are large and clean, with Hawaiian quilts lending an authentic
touch. A handful of studios with kitchenettes are also available. **Pros:**
affordable, large rooms equipped with kitchenettes, charge meals to
your room at one of the island's best restaurants (Merriman's). **Cons:**
rooms could use some updating, no pool. ✉*65-1210 Lindsey Rd.,
Waimea* ☎*808/885–4100 or 800/367–5004* ⊕*www.castleresorts.com/
WCL* ⬐*21 rooms* ⬕*In-room: no a/c, kitchen (some), Internet. In-
hotel: laundry facilities, parking (free), no-smoking rooms* ▭*AE, D,
DC, MC, V* ⍓*CP.*

$ ▥**Waimea Gardens Cottage.** Charming country cottages surrounded by
RENTAL flowering private gardens contain surprisingly luxe suites that look like
★ they just leapt out of a glossy magazine. One (Kohala) includes a full
kitchen and the others (Waimea and the Garden Studio) a kitchenette,
and all are stocked with provisions (including fresh farm eggs) for a
hearty self-serve Continental breakfast. Both have their own private
gardens, beautiful hardwood floors, and bathrooms equipped with rain-
head showers and large soaking tubs. The grounds are full of birds and
plant life that will make you want to move in for good. **Pros:** no detail
left out, beautiful self-contained cottages, gardens, complete privacy.
Cons: pricey for the area, requires payment in full six weeks prior to
arrival. ⬭*Box 563, Kamuela 96743* ☎*808/885–8550* ⊕*www.waimea
gardens.com* ⬐*2 cottages, 1 studio* ⬕*In-room: no a/c, kitchen, DVD,*

Wi-Fi. *In-hotel: Internet terminal, parking (free), no-smoking rooms* ▭*No credit cards.*

KAILUA-KONA

$$$–$$$$
RENTAL
▦**Aston Kona by the Sea.** Complete modern kitchens, tile lānai, and washer-dryer units can be found in every suite of this comfortable ocean-front condo complex. The nearest sandy beach is 2 mi away, but the pool is next to the ocean and many of the rooms have ocean views. **Pros:** oceanfront, quiet and peaceful. **Cons:** no beach, not many kid-friendly features. ⊠*75-6106 Aliʻi Dr., Kailua-Kona* ☎*808/327–2300 or 877/997–6667* ⊕*www.astonhotels.com* ⤶*37 1-bedroom units, 41 2-bedroom units* ⚘*In-room: safe, kitchen, Internet. In-hotel: pool, beachfront, laundry facilities, Wi-Fi, parking (free), no-smoking rooms* ▭*AE, D, DC, MC, V.*

$
RENTAL
☾
▦**Casa de Emdeko.** A large and pretty complex on the *makai* (ocean-front) side of Aliʻi Drive, Casa de Emdeko offers a few more amenities than most condo complexes, including an on-site convenience store that makes great sandwiches, a sandy oceanfront area for sunbathing, and both fresh and saltwater pools. All units have lānai, with either garden or ocean views. **Pros:** oceanfront fresh- and saltwater pools, on-site convenience store. **Cons:** quality can be hit or miss depending on owner, some units are close to high-traffic road. ⊠*75-6082 Aliʻi Dr., Kailua-Kona* ☎*808/329–2160* ⊕*www.casadeemdeko.org* ⤶*106 units* ⚘*In-room: kitchen, DVD (some), Internet (some). In-hotel: pools, laundry facilities, parking (free), no-smoking rooms* ▭*AE, MC, V.*

$
B&B/INN
▦**Hale Hualalai.** Perfect for couples, Hale Hualalai has two suites with exposed beams, hardwood floors, hot tubs, and private lānai. Perhaps the most memorable aspect of Hale Hualalai is the food—owner Lonn Armour was a professional chef for 20 years, and cooks up a break-fast that puts other B&B offerings to shame. **Pros:** gourmet breakfast with Kona coffee, new and tastefully decorated house, whirlpool tubs. **Cons:** not kid-friendly, removed from local beaches and restaurants. ⊠*74-4968 Māmalahoa Hwy., Hōlualoa* ☎*808/326–2909* ⊕*www. hale-hualalai.com* ⤶*2 suites* ⚘*In-room: no a/c, no phone, refrigera-tor, Wi-Fi. In-hotel: Wi-Fi, parking (free)* ▭*MC, V.*

$$$–$$$$
B&B/INN
★
▦**Hōlualoa Inn.** Six spacious rooms are available in this beautiful cedar home on a 40-acre coffee country estate, 4 mi above Kailua Bay and steps away from the artists' town of Hōlualoa. A lavish breakfast includes estate-grown coffee as well as homemade breads and mac-adamia-nut butter. Rooftop gazebos inspire quiet, relaxing moments, and for stargazers there's a telescope. **Pros:** within walking distance to small village, well appointed with wood floors and lots of windows, panoramic views, infinity pool. **Cons:** a bit far away from beaches and restaurants, expensive for location. ⊠*76-5932 Māmalahoa Hwy., Box 222, Hōlualoa* ☎*808/324–1121 or 800/392–1812* ⊕*www.holualoa inn.com* ⤶*6 rooms* ⚘*In-room: no a/c, no TV, Wi-Fi. In-hotel: pool, laundry facilities, Wi-Fi, parking (free), no kids under 13, no-smoking rooms* ▭*AE, D, DC, MC, V.*

$
RENTAL
▦**Kona Magic Sands.** Cradled between two small beaches, this condo complex is great for swimmers and sunbathers in summer (the sand at

WHERE TO STAY ON THE KONA COAST AND UPCOUNTRY

	Property Name	Worth Noting	Cost $	Pools	Beach	Golf Course	Tennis Courts	Gym	Spa	Children's Programs	Rooms	Restaurants	Other	Location
	Hotels & Resorts													
13	Kona Tiki Hotel	Oceanfront lānai	72–96	1							15		no a/c	Kailua-Kona
3	Manago Hotel	Great local food	36–64								64	1	no a/c, no TV	Captain Cook
7	Outrigger Keauhou	Close to Kahulu'u Beach	165–359	1	yes		6	yes	yes		312	1		Kailua-Kona
14	Royal Kona Resort	Good rates for oceanfront	180–330	1	yes		4	yes	yes		436	1		Kailua-Kona
5	Sheraton Keauhou	Cool pool with slide	199–460	1	yes		2	yes	yes	5–12	521	1		Kailua-Kona
	Condos & Vacation Rentals													
9	Aston Kona by the Sea	Oceanfront pool	280–464	1							78		kitchens	Kailua-Kona
10	Casa de Emdeko	Oceanfront saltwater pool	100–150	2							106		kitchens	Kailua-Kona
8	Kona Magic Sands	Ocean view from all units	115–150	1							37	1	kitchens	Kailua-Kona
11	Kona Nalu	Huge lānai, ocean views	210–300	1	yes						4		kitchens	Kailua-Kona
12	Kona Pacific	Ocean view from pool, BBQ	75–180	1							80		kitchens	Kailua-Kona
6	Outrigger Kanaloa at Kona	Three pools	249–499	3			2				166		kitchens	Kailua-Kona
	B&Bs & Inns													
2	Aloha Guesthouse	Eco-conscious	126–280								5			South Kona
15	Hale Hualalai	Outstanding breakfast	160								2			Hōlualoa
4	Hōlualoa Inn	Beautiful interior	270–375	1							6		no TV	Hōlualoa
1	Kalaekilohana	Hot breakfast, cozy linens	189–249								4		no phone, no TV	Ka'u

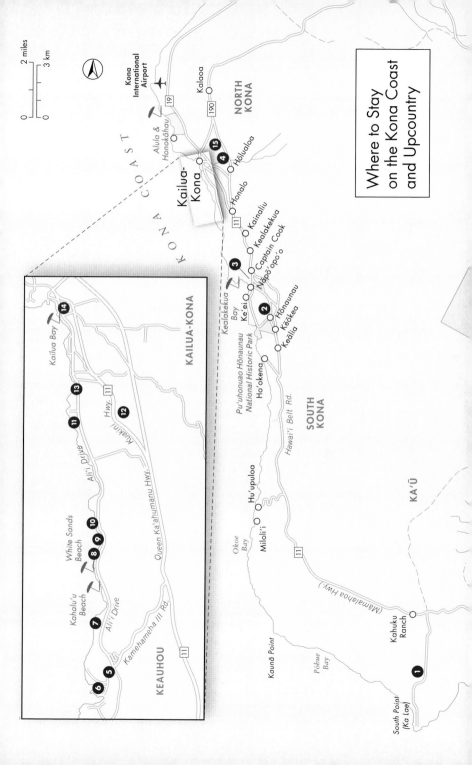

Where to Stay
on the Kona Coast
and Upcountry

Magic Sands Beach washes away in winter). Units vary because they're individually owned, but all the studios are oceanfront, spacious, and light. Some units have enclosed lānai, and all have an ocean view. **Pros:** next door to popular beach, ocean view from all units. **Cons:** studios only, some units are dated. ⊠ *77-6452 Ali'i Dr., Kailua-Kona* 🕾 *808/329–9393 or 800/622–5348* ⊕ *www.konahawaii.com* 🌫 *37 units* ⚠ *In-room: no a/c (some), kitchen. In-hotel: restaurant, bar, pool, beachfront, laundry facilities, parking (free), no-smoking rooms.* ⊟ *DC, MC, V.*

$$–$$$ ⊡ **Kona Nalu.** One of the nicest complexes on the ocean side of Ali'i,
RENTAL Kona Nalu units are large and beautifully furnished with super-size
★ lānai, and ocean views from all units. The pool is tiny, but they have a small sandy beach for lying in the sun, and the complex itself is small so you won't be fighting for poolroom. **Pros:** extra-large units, ocean views. **Cons:** not within walking distance to stores or restaurants, sandy beach doesn't provide safe ocean entry. ⊠ *76-6212 Ali'i Dr., 96740* 🕾 *808/329–6438* ⊕ *www.sunquest-hawaii.com* 🌫 *4 units* ⚠ *In-room: no a/c (some), kitchen, DVD (some), Internet (some). In-hotel: pool, beachfront, laundry facilities, parking (free), no-smoking rooms* ⊟ *DC, MC, V.*

¢–$ ⊡ **Kona Pacific.** Once a hotel, the Kona Pacific gives you plenty of space.
RENTAL The one-bedroom units, which comfortably sleep four, are the size of
★ two large hotel rooms, with a full kitchen and usually two bathrooms. There are ocean views from the lānai of most units and the pool. This large and well-maintained complex is just at the edge of Kailua-Kona, within walking distance of shops and restaurants. Note that the acceptance of credit cards varies with the unit owners. **Pros:** very large units, some with two lānai, ocean-view pool, well-maintained complex. **Cons:** some units in better shape than others, some units get noise from nearby highway. ⊠ *75-5865 Walua Rd., 96740* 🕾 *808/329–6140* ⊕ *www. vrbo.com* 🌫 *80 units* ⚠ *In-room: kitchen. In-hotel: pool.*

¢ ⊡ **Kona Tiki Hotel.** The best thing about this three-story walk-up budget
HOTEL hotel, about a mile south of Kailua-Kona, is that all the units have lānai right next to the ocean. The rooms are modest but pleasantly decorated. You can sunbathe by the seaside pool, where a complimentary Continental breakfast is served. Some would call this place old-fashioned; others would say it's local, has a certain kitschy charm, and is the best deal in town. **Pros:** very low price, ocean-front lānai and pool, convenient location. **Cons:** older hotel, no beach, doesn't accept credit cards. ⊠ *75-5968 Ali'i Dr., Kailua-Kona* 🕾 *808/329–1425* ⊕ *www.konatiki. com* 🌫 *15 rooms* ⚠ *In-room: no a/c, no phone, kitchen (some), refrigerator, no TV, Wi-Fi. In-hotel: pool, beachfront, Wi-Fi, parking (free), no-smoking rooms* ⊟ *No credit cards.*

$$$ ⊡ **Outrigger Kanaloa at Kona.** The 16-acre grounds provide a peaceful
RENTAL and verdant background for this low-rise condominium complex bordering the Keauhou-Kona Country Club. It's walking distance from the golf course and within a five-minute drive of the nearest beaches (Kahalu'u and White Sands). Large units have koa-wood cabinetwork and washer-dryers; some oceanfront villas have private hot tubs. **Pros:** oceanfront restaurant in complex, across the street from acclaimed golf course, three pools with hot tubs. **Cons:** not within walking distance to

KAILUA-KONA VACATION RENTALS

When booking a condo, remember that most are individually owned and that most owners outsource the rental process. Renters make arrangements through property management companies. **Kona Coast Vacations** (⊕ *www.konacoastvacations.com*) looks after several vacation rentals on the Kona side of the island, as does **Knutson and Associates** (⊕ *www.konahawaiirentals.com*). **Keauhou Property Management** (⊕ *www.konacondo.net*) has condos along the Kona coast, just south of Kailua-Kona around Keauhou Bay. **CJ Kimberly Realty** (⊕ *www.cjkimberly. com*) offers fantastic deals on some oceanfront homes and condos. **Kolea Vacations** (⊕ *www.koleavacations. com*) lists dozens of condos at the Kolea at Waikoloa complex as well as a stunning oceanfront home on Ali'i in Kailua-Kona. **Hawaiian Beach Rentals** (⊕ *www.hawaiianbeachrentals. com*) and **Tropical Villa Vacations** (⊕ *www.tropicalvillavacations.com*) are excellent for high-end, ocean-, or beachfront homes. **Vacation Rental By Owner** (⊕ *www.vrbo.com*) has homes and condos for rent all over the island. You can browse any of these Web sites for photos of available units to find the perfect one.

beach, some owners don't manage their rentals well. ⊠ *78-261 Manukai St., Kailua-Kona* ☎ *808/322–9625, 808/322–2272, or 800/688–7444* ⊕ *www.outrigger.com* ⟲ *166 units* ⟳ *In-room: no a/c (some), safe, kitchen, DVD (some). In-hotel: tennis courts, pools, laundry facilities, Wi-Fi, parking (free), no-smoking rooms* ⊟ *AE, D, DC, MC, V.*

$$–$$$
RESORT

⌂ **Outrigger Keauhou Beach Resort.** Although it has won awards for preserving its unique history (the grounds include a *heiau*, a sacred fishpond, and a replica of the summer home of King David Kalākaua), the Outrigger Keauhou Beach Resort is not doing such a hot job at preserving the guest accommodations. That said, if you can find a good rate, this is still a good place to stay, mainly for its proximity to Kahalu'u, one of the best snorkeling beaches on the island. **Pros:** large rooms, unique history, next to one of the island's best snorkeling beaches. **Cons:** restaurant has gone downhill, hotel needs a face-lift. ⊠ *78-6740 Ali'i Dr., Kailua-Kona* ☎ *808/322–3441 or 800/462–6262* ⊕ *www.outrigger. com* ⟲ *309 rooms, 3 suites* ⟳ *In-room: safe, refrigerator, Internet. In-hotel: restaurant, bar, tennis courts, pool, gym, spa, beachfront, laundry facilities, laundry service, Internet terminal, Wi-Fi, parking (paid), no-smoking rooms* ⊟ *AE, D, DC, MC, V.*

$$
RESORT

⌂ **Royal Kona Resort.** This is a great option if you're on a budget. The Royal Kona has seen better days, but the owners are finally doing a bit of renovation, and the hotel has greatly improved, as has the quality of food and service at its restaurant. The location is great, the lobby, pool, and restaurant are right on the water, and most of the hotel's large, lānai-front rooms have been recently updated. The hotel is within walking distance of Kailua-Kona. Make sure to book online, where the rates can be as much as 50% less than the rack rates, and select rooms in the Ali'i or Lagoon tower if you'd like a recently refurbished room. **Pros:** convenient location, waterfront pool, low prices. **Cons:** older hotel, oceanfront lagoon is often closed, staff are sometimes grumpy.

✉ *75-5852 Ali'i Dr., Kailua-Kona* ☎ *808/329–3111 or 800/222–5642* ⊕ *www.royalkona.com* ⇝ *428 rooms, 8 suites* ⚿ *In-room: safe, refrigerator, Wi-Fi. In-hotel: restaurant, bar, tennis courts, pool, gym, spa, beachfront, laundry facilities, laundry service, Wi-Fi, parking (paid), no-smoking rooms* ☐AE, D, DC, MC, V.

$$$–$$$$
RESORT
☺
★

🏨 **Sheraton Keauhou Bay Resort & Spa.** For the big-resort style of the Kohala Coast at a less astronomical price, the Sheraton is a good bet. Longtime Big Island visitors might remember it as the old Kona Surf. Left empty for several years, the hotel still shows some of its wear and tear, but the new owners have gone to great lengths to restore it to its former glory. The lobby, with floor to ceiling windows and carved marble architectural elements, is particularly stunning. The only remnants of the old hotel in the bright and modern Sheraton rooms are the small and unimpressive bathrooms. On the up side, many of the rooms have great views of the bay, and all have the Sheraton's signature Sweet Sleeper beds, which ensure a good night's sleep. The big selling point for those traveling with kids is the pool, one of the coolest on the island, with a slide, waterfalls, and an ocean view. **Pros:** fantastic pool, manta rays on view nightly, resort style at lower price. **Cons:** no beach, only one restaurant. ✉ *78-128 Ehukai St., Kailua-Kona* ☎ *808/930–4900* ⊕ *www.sheratonkeauhou.com* ⇝ *511 rooms, 10 suites* ⚿ *In-room: safe, refrigerator, Wi-Fi. In-hotel: restaurant, bar, tennis courts, pool, gym, spa, beachfront, children's program (ages 5–12), laundry facilties, laundy service, Internet terminal, Wi-Fi, parking (paid), no-smoking rooms* ☐AE, D, DC, MC, V.

SOUTH KONA & KA'Ū

$–$$
B&B/INN

🏨 **Aloha Guesthouse.** In the hills above Kealakekua Bay, Aloha Guesthouse offers quiet elegance, complete privacy, and ocean views from every room. With a focus on nature, the house is furnished in earth tones. The bath products are 100% organic, and the yummy full breakfasts are as close to organic as they can muster. Common areas include a kitchenette, a high-definition television, a DVD library, and a computer with high-speed Internet. **Pros:** eco-conscious, full breakfast, views of Kealakekua Bay. **Cons:** remote location, no grocery stores or restaurants within walking distance, not recommended for kids. ✉ *Old Tobacco Rd., off Hwy. 11 near mile marker 104, Honaunau* ☎ *808/328–8955* ⊕ *www.alohaguesthouse.com* ⇝ *5 rooms* ⚿ *In-room: no a/c, no phone,* refrigerator, DVD, Wi-Fi. In-hotel: laundry facilities, Wi-Fi, parking (free), some pets allowed, no-smoking rooms ⊟AE, MC, V.

$$
B&B/INN

⚏**Kalaekilohana.** You wouldn't really expect to find a top-notch B&B in Kaʻū, but just up the road from South Point, this charming yellow house offers large, comfortable private suites with beautifully restored hardwood floors, private lānai with ocean and mountain views, and big, comfy beds decked out with high-thread-count sheets and fluffy down comforters. For breakfast, enjoy their gourmet choices and full table service. Guests can also look forward to a nightly talk story filled with plenty of great advice from their hosts, as this is one of the only Hawaiian-owned bed B&Bs on the island. There is also a concentration on Hawaiian cultural arts, including lei-making classes. **Pros:** luxurious beds, beautifully restored house, delicious breakfast. **Cons:** strange location, no pool. ⊠94-2152 South Point Rd., Nāʻālehu ☎808/939–8052 ⊕www.kau-hawaii.com ⬐4 suites ⬧In-room: no a/c, no phone, no TV, Wi-Fi. In-hotel: laundry facilities, Wi-Fi, parking (free), no kids under 10, no-smoking rooms ⊟MC, V.

¢
HOTEL

⚏**Manago Hotel.** This historic hotel is a good option if you want to escape the touristy thing but still be close to everything on the island. Don't let the front TV room creep you out—you have not checked into an old folks' home. The place has an authentic Hawaiʻi vibe, and the restaurant is one of the best on the island. Dwight Manago—whose grandparents, Kinzo and Osame Manago, built the main building in 1917—has maintained one Japanese-style room with tatami mats and a furo, a traditional Japanese bath, and this is the room to book. The other rooms are nothing special, but they're clean, and those in the newer wing have great views high above the Kona Coast. **Pros:** local color, rock-bottom prices, terrific on-site restaurant. **Cons:** a bit run-down, not the best sound insulation between rooms. ⊠81-6155 Māmalahoa Hwy., Box 145, Captain Cook ☎808/323–2642 ⊕www.managohotel. com ⬐64 rooms, 42 with bath ⬧In-room: no a/c, no TV, Wi-Fi. In-hotel: restaurant, bar, Wi-Fi, parking (free) ⊟D, DC, MC, V.

VOLCANO

$–$$
HOTEL/RENTAL

⚏**Chalet Kīlauea Collection.** The Collection comprises three inns and lodges and five vacation houses in and around Volcano Village, with accommodations ranging from no-frills dorm-style bedrooms in a historic house to a plantation mansion with its own six-person hot tub. The **Lokahi Lodge** ($122–$147) provides cozy rooms in a country lodge with plenty of exposed beams and wood, and comfy beds with custom-made raised wooden bed frames. For those looking for a bit more privacy, the **Volcano Cottages** are dispersed vacation homes and cottage rentals around Volcano Village. The Collection's most reasonably priced offering is the **Volcano Hale** ($62–$72 double-occupancy room), which has a communal kitchen, bathroom, and fireplace. **Pros:** large variety of lodging types to choose from, hot tub, fireplace. **Cons:** staff and management changes frequently, which can sometimes make service suffer. ⊠19-4178 Wright Rd., Volcano Village ☎808/967–7786 or 800/937–7786 ⊕www.volcano-hawaii.com ⬐14 rooms, 3 suites, 5 houses ⬧In-room: no a/c, no phone (some), kitchen (some), refrigerator (some), DVD (some). In-hotel: Internet terminal, parking (free), no-smoking rooms ⊟D, DC, MC, V.

$
RENTAL
Hale Ohia Cottages. A stately and comfortable Queen Anne–style mansion, Hale Ohia was built in the 1930s as a summer place for a wealthy Scotsman. The namesake Ohia cottage, large enough for a family, has a full kitchen. The ʻIhilani cottage is the cushiest of the group; built into an old water tank, it's naturally lighted, beautifully designed, and completely private. Continental breakfast is left in your refrigerator while you're away in the afternoon so that you can enjoy it at your leisure in the morning. **Pros:** unique architecture, recently refurbished rooms, plenty of props for volcano excursions (they stock extra umbrellas, flashlights, etc.). **Cons:** property cat roams around, which could be problematic for guests with allergies. ⊠11-3968 Hale Ohia Rd., off Hwy. 11, Volcano ☎808/967–7986 ⊕www.haleohia.com ⇨4 rooms, 3 cottages, 1 suite ⌂In-room: no a/c, no phone, kitchen (some), refrigerator (some), Wi-Fi. In-hotel: Wi-Fi, parking (free), no-smoking rooms ⊟MC, V.

$-$$
HOTEL
★
Kīlauea Lodge. A mile from the entrance of Hawaiʻi Volcanoes National Park, this cheery yellow lodge was initially built as a YMCA camp in the 1930s. Now it's a pleasant inn, tastefully furnished with European antiques. Rooms have rich quilts and Hawaiian photographs, and the honeymoon deluxe room has a wood-burning fireplace. A charming two-bedroom cottage with a gas fireplace and a private balcony is perfect for romance. Cottages off the main property include Piʻi Mauna House, on the fairway of the Volcano Golf Course. Rates include a full hot breakfast at the Lodge's restaurant, which has an excellent dinner menu as well. **Pros:** great restaurant, close to volcano, fireplaces. **Cons:** overpriced for area, limited breakfast selection. ⊠19-3948 Old Volcano Hwy., 1 mi northeast of Volcano Store ⌂Box 116, Volcano Village 96785 ☎808/967–7366 ⊕www.kilauealodge.com ⇨11 rooms, 3 cottages ⌂In-room: no a/c, no phone (some), no TV (some), Wi-Fi. In-hotel: restaurant, bar, Wi-Fi, parking (free), no-smoking rooms ⊟AE, MC, V.

¢-$
B&B/INN
My Island Bed & Breakfast Inn. Gordon and Joann Morse, along with their daughter Kiʻi, opened their historic home and 7-acre botanical estate to visitors in 1985. The oldest in Volcano, it was built in 1886 by the Lyman missionary family. There are two rooms sharing one bath and one room with a private bath in the main house. Scattered around the area are three garden apartments and one fully equipped guesthouse. You won't start the day hungry after the expanded Continental

---

HAWAIʻI ON A BUDGET

Kona Tiki Hotel (Kailua-Kona). Oceanfront, all rooms have ocean views, walking distance to downtown.

Manago Hotel (South Kona). Historic, Japanese theme, clean, some oceanfront rooms, super reasonable, excellent restaurant.

Nāmakani Paio Cabins (Volcano Village). Close to the Volcano, cheap, clean, recently renovated.

Royal Kona Resort (Kailua-Kona). Old-school Hawaiʻi, oceanfront, great bar, good package deals, close to downtown Kailua-Kona.

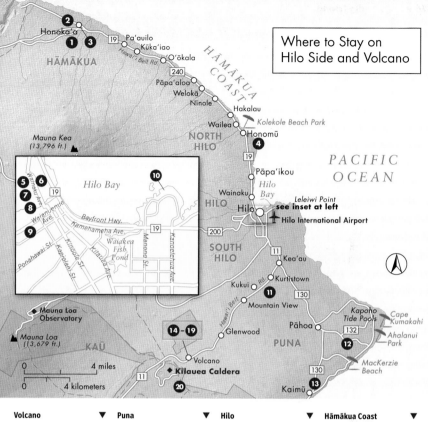

Where to Stay on Hilo Side and Volcano

breakfast. **Pros:** historic home, hosts are island experts. **Cons:** remote location, some shared bathrooms. ✉19-3896 Old Volcano Hwy., Volcano Village 🏠 Box 100, Volcano 96785 ☎808/967–7216 ⊕www. myislandinnhawaii.com ➡6 rooms, 4 with bath; 1 guesthouse 🛏️In-room: no a/c, no phone, refrigerator (some), no TV (some). In-hotel: Wi-Fi, parking (free), no-smoking rooms ▭DC, MC, V.

¢

CABINS

☺

🖥️**Nāmakani Paio Cabins.** These recently remodeled cabins, managed by Volcano House, are for those who are into roughing it. The simple cabins are at the end of a long, deserted road. Inexpensive and clean, each has a double bed, two bunk beds, and electric lights. Bring extra blankets, as it gets cold at night. Each cabin also has a grill outside, but you must bring your own firewood. **Pros:** beautiful location in the forest, linens are supplied, 3 mi from Hawai'i Volcanoes National Park. **Cons:** maximum of 4 people, additional charge for second and third guests. ✉1 Crater Rim Dr., Hawai'i Volcanoes National Park ☎808/967–7321 ➡10 cabins 🛏️In-room: no a/c, no phone, no TV. In-hotel: parking (free), no-smoking rooms ▭AE, D, DC, MC, V.

$–$$

RENTAL

🖥️**Volcano Places.** A collection of lovely vacation homes, the accommodations range from a simple cottage in the rain forest to a stunning Craftsman-style house with its own spa room. Many can accommodate up to eight people comfortably. All come equipped with full kitchens. **Pros:** unique architecture, rain-forest location, total privacy. **Cons:** can't always select the exact property you want, prices of more expensive units are high for the area. ✉19-3951 Laukapua, Volcano ☎808/967–7990 ⊕www.volcanoplaces.com ➡4 cottages 🛏️In-room: no a/c, kitchen, DVD, Wi-Fi. In-hotel: laundy facilities (some), Wi-Fi, parking (free), no-smoking rooms ▭MC, V.

$$

RENTAL

★

🖥️**Volcano Teapot Cottage.** A near-perfect spot for couples seeking a romantic getaway, this cute two-bedroom red-and-white cottage is completely private. The claw-foot bathtub, hot tub, and fireplace add to the general coziness. Continental breakfast is included, and the restaurants in Volcano Village are nearby. **Pros:** claw-foot tub, hot tub, fireplace, recently enlarged bathroom. **Cons:** isolated location, maximum of two people. ✉19-4041 Kilauea Rd., Volcano Village 🏠 Box 511, Volcano 96785 ☎808/967–7112 ⊕www.volcanoteapot.com ➡1 cottage 🛏️In-room: no a/c, kitchen, DVD, Wi-Fi. In-hotel: laundy facilities, Wi-Fi, parking (free), no kids, no-smoking rooms ▭AE, MC, V.

PUNA

¢–$

B&B/INN

🖥️**Bed & Breakfast Mountain View.** This modern home is surrounded by rolling forest and farmland. The secluded 4-acre estate has extensive floral gardens and a fishpond. Owners Linus and Jane Chao are longtime Big Island art educators and have an art studio on the lower level where they teach classes. Some special packages include art lessons. The house itself is a virtual art gallery with varied displays in oil, acrylic, water-color, and Oriental brush paintings. **Pros:** reasonable prices, local artist hosts, beautiful landscaping. **Cons:** rooms could use some updating, location is remote. ✉South Kulani Rd., Kurtistown ☎808/968–6868 or 888/698–9896 ⊕www.bbmtview.com ➡4 rooms, 2 with shared bath ☁ In-room: no a/c, no phone, refrigerator (some), DVD. In-hotel: parking (free), no kids under 5, no-smoking rooms ▭MC, V.

$ 🖫 **Plumeria Hill Bed & Breakfast.** A relatively new B&B near the popular
B&B/INN   steam vent caves in Opihikao in the Puna region, Plumeria Hill offers two beautiful suites, each with its own private entrance, two queen beds covered with Hawaiian quilts, and large floor-to-ceiling windows with ocean views. It doesn't get more Hawaiian than the Puna region, with its wild rain forest and reputation for outlaw locals, and Plumeria Hill's hosts do a great job of providing modern luxury amid this wilderness. **Pros:** wildly beautiful location, massage therapist on-site, proximity to volcano and steam vent caves. **Cons:** remote location, only two rooms, must drive to get to nearest restaurant. ✉ 13-1264 Kamaʻili Rd., off Hwy. 130 just past mile marker 15, Pāhoa ☎ 808/965–8810 ⊕ www. plumeriahill.com ⇨ 2 suites ☁ In-room: no a/c, no phone, kitchen, DVD, Wi-Fi. In-hotel: Wi-Fi, parking (free), no-smoking ▭ No credit cards †◯| CP.

¢–$ 🖫 **Yoga Oasis.** This center, on 26 tropical acres, has a bit of a commune
B&B/INN   feel. With its exposed redwood beams, Balinese doorways, and imported art, Yoga Oasis draws those who seek relaxation and rejuvenation, and perhaps a free yoga lesson or two. A 1,600-square-foot state-of-the-art yoga and gymnastics space, with 18-foot ceilings, crowns this friendly retreat. You're close to hot springs and black-sand beaches, and the volcano is a 45-minute drive away. Bathrooms are shared. **Pros:** daily yoga, one yoga class and hot breakfast included in price, low prices. **Cons:** remote location, shared bathrooms in the main building. ✉ Pohoiki Rd., Box 1935, Pāhoa ☎ 808/965–8460 or 800/274–4446 ⊕ www.yogaoasis.org ⇨ 5 rooms with shared bath, 4 bungalows, 1 cottage ☁ In-room: no a/c, no phone, no TV, Wi-Fi. In-hotel: Wi-Fi, laundry service, parking (free), no-smoking rooms ▭MC, V.

HILO

$ 🖫 **Dolphin Bay Hotel.** A glowing lava flow sign marks the office and
HOTEL   bespeaks owner John Alexander's passion for the volcano. Stunning
☪   lava pictures adorn the common area, and Alexander is a great source
★   of information for visiting the park and for exploring the back roads of Hilo. Units in the 1950s-style motor lodge are modest, but clean and inexpensive. Coffee and fresh fruit are offered daily. Four blocks from Hilo Bay, in a residential area called Puʻueʻo, the hotel borders a verdant 2-acre Hawaiian garden with jungle trails and shady places to rest. Guests of the hotel return repeatedly, and it's ideal for families who seek a home base. **Pros:** great value, extremely helpful and pleasant staff, rates go down every night you stay. **Cons:** located along a busy road; basic, motel-style rooms. ✉ 333 ʻIliahi St., Hilo ☎ 808/935–1466 ⊕ www. dolphinbayhotel.com ⇨ 13 rooms, 4 1-bedroom units, 1 2-bedroom unit ☁ In-room: no a/c, no phone, kitchen. In-hotel: laundry facilities, Wi-Fi, parking (free), no-smoking rooms ▭MC, V.

$$$–$$$$ 🖫 **The Falls at Reed's Island.** Legend has it this property was once the
RENTAL   playground of the Aliʻi (royalty), and it's easy to see why. Set upon volcanic rocks, tucked away in a rainforest and fronting a 25-foot waterfall along the Wailuku River, this is the place to get away from it

all. However, depsite the illusion of a secluded island, this house is less than 2 mi from historic Hilo town. All sides of the home face the river or gorge, and the kitchen window frames the waterfall. The kitchen and three bedrooms (each with a private bath) are connected by a screened lanai and feature large windows and simple furnishings. **Pros:** waterfall in your backyard, extremely private, serene and romantic, soaking tubs. **Cons:** two-night minimum, reservations must be made far in advance, cleaning fee. ⊠ *286 Kaiulani St., Hilo* ☎ *808/935–7920* ⊕ *www.reeds island.com* ⇨ *1 house* ⚲ *In-room: no a/c, Wi-Fi. In-hotel: laundry facilities, Wi-Fi, parking (free), no-smoking rooms* ▭ *D, MC, V.*

$
B&B/INN   🏠 **Hale Kai.** On a bluff above Hilo Bay, this 5,400-square-foot modern home is 2 mi from downtown Hilo. Three impeccable rooms with patios have been freshly painted and spruced up by new owners Maria Macias and Ricardo Zepeda, as has the private loft, which is ideal for families. All rooms have grand ocean views and are within earshot of lapping waves. Fresh flowers add a warm, European touch. Maria and Ricardo serve a full hot breakfast every morning on an outdoor deck or in the kitchen's bay-window dining area. **Pros:** delicious hot breakfast, panoramic views, privacy. **Cons:** removed from town, no kids allowed. ⊠ *111 Honoli'i Place, Hilo* ☎ *808/935–6330* ⊕ *www. halekaihawaii.com* ⇨ *3 rooms, 1 suite* ⚲ *In-room: no a/c, no phone, Wi-Fi. In-hotel: pool, Wi-Fi, parking (free), no kids under 13, no-smoking rooms* ▭ *MC, V.*

$–$$
HOTEL   🏨 **Hilo Hawaiian Hotel.** Though it shows its age, this older hotel, with large bay-front rooms offering spectacular views of Mauna Kea and Coconut Island, is one of the most pleasant lodgings on Hilo Bay. Street-side rooms overlook the golf course. Most accommodations have private lānai. **Pros:** Hilo Bay views, private lānai, large rooms. **Cons:** rooms sorely in need of renovation, prices high for quality of rooms. ⊠ *71 Banyan Dr., Hilo* ☎ *808/935–9361, 800/367–5004 from mainland, 800/272–5275 interisland* ⊕ *www.hilohawaiian.com* ⇨ *268 rooms, 18 suites* ⚲ *In-room: refrigerator, Internet. In-hotel: restaurant, bar, pool, beachfront, laundry facilities, laundry service, Internet terminal, parking (paid), no-smoking rooms* ▭ *AE, D, DC, MC, V.*

$–$$
B&B/INN
★   🏠 **Hilo Honu Inn.** A charming old Craftsman home lovingly restored by a friendly and hospitable couple from North Carolina, the Hilo Honu offers quite a bit of variety. The Honu's Nest provides fantastic views of the sunrise over Hilo Bay from the comforts of a large, comfy bed. The larger Bali Hai Suite has a sitting room and a window seat that looks out on tree ferns, orchids, and anthuriums. Upstairs, the entire second floor is the Samurai Suite, furnished with traditional tatami mats and beautiful antiques imported from Japan. Breakfast is delicious and usually includes a variety of homemade baked goods. **Pros:** beautifully restored home, spectacular Hilo Bay views, delicious breakfast, free Wi-Fi. **Cons:** only one room and two suites, not walking distance to downtown Hilo. ⊠ *465 Haili St., Hilo* ☎ *808/935–4325* ⊕ *www.hilohonu.com* ⇨ *1 room, 2 suites* ⚲ *In-room: no phone, refrigerator, DVD, Wi-Fi. In-hotel: Wi-Fi, parking (free), no-smoking rooms* ▭ *AE, DC, MC, V.*

$$$–$$$$
B&B/INN
★   🏠 **Palms Cliff House Inn.** This handsome Victorian-style mansion, 15 mi north of Hilo, is perched on the sea cliffs 100 feet above the crashing surf

of Pohakumano Bay. Individually decorated rooms have private lānai. Suites include double hot tubs (the one in Room 8 is by the window with a stunning view of the coast), but there's also a communal hot tub in the garden. A husband-and-wife team serves breakfast with pride on the veranda overlooking the cliffs; meals generally include fresh-baked muffins, locally grown fruit, a warm egg or meat dish (they always ask about food allergies or dietary restrictions ahead of time), and, of course, fantastic local coffee. **Pros:** stunning views, terrific breakfast, comfortable rooms with every amenity. **Cons:** service is erratic, remote location means you have to drive to restaurants. ⊠ *28-3514 Māmalahoa Hwy., Honomū* ☎ *808/963–6076 or 866/963–6076* ⊕ *www.palmscliffhouse. com* ➫ *4 rooms, 4 suites* ⌂ *In-room: no a/c (some), safe, refrigerator, DVD, Internet. In-hotel: laundry service, parking (free), no kids under 12, no-smoking rooms* ▭ *AE, D, DC, MC, V.*

$$
B&B/INN
★

🏨 **Shipman House Bed & Breakfast Inn.** You'll have a choice between three rooms in the "castle"—the turreted main house dating from 1899—or two rooms in a separate cottage. The B&B is on 5½ verdant acres on Reed's Island; the house is furnished with antique koa and period pieces, some dating from the days when Queen Liliʻuokalani came to tea. On Wednesday night, an authentic hula school practices Hawaiʻi's ancient dances in the house. Barbara (part of the Shipman family) and her husband Gary are friendly hosts with a vast knowledge of the area and the rest of the island; they're also excellent cooks, which means you should try absolutely everything at breakfast. **Pros:** great home cooking, historic home, friendly and knowledgeable local hosts. **Cons:** chock-full of antiques, not a great spot for kids. ⊠ *131 Kaʻiulani St., Hilo* ☎ *808/934–8002 or 800/627–8447* ⊕ *www.hilo-hawaii.com* ➫ *3 rooms, 2 cottage rooms* ⌂ *In-room: no a/c, no phone, refrigerator, no TV, Wi-Fi. In-hotel: Wi-Fi, parking (free), no kids 13 and under, no-smoking rooms* ▭ *AE, MC, V.*

HĀMĀKUA COAST

¢
HOTEL

🏨 **Hotel Honokaʻa Club.** This bargain hotel is 45 minutes from Hilo and close to Waipiʻo Valley. Rustic rooms range from lower-level dormitory-style units—bring your own sleeping bag—to upper-story rooms with private baths, ocean views, and a complimentary light Continental breakfast. **Pros:** historic hotel in historic town, close to Waipiʻo Valley, low prices. **Cons:** funky old hotel in need of an update, somewhat remote location. ⊠ *45-3480 Māmane St., Box 247, Honokaʻa* ☎ *808/775–0678 or 800/808–0678* ⊕ *www.hotelhonokaa.com* ➫ *5 rooms, 2 dorm-style rooms* ⌂ *In-room: no a/c, no phone, no TV (some), Wi-Fi. In-hotel: Wi-Fi, parking (free), no-smoking rooms* ▭ *MC, V.*

$$
B&B/INN
Fodor's Choice
★

🏨 **Waianuhea.** Waianuhea defines Hawaiian country elegance. Fully self-contained and run off solar power, this gorgeous country home sits in a forested area on the Hāmākua Coast. The four guest rooms and large suite have tasteful color schemes and lavish furnishings, complete with extra pillows, fluffy down comforters, and soaking tubs, and there is contemporary artwork throughout. The large common room with its stunning ocean views and lava-rock fireplace is a big attraction, especially at the wine tasting and hors d'oeuvres hour each evening. **Pros:**

Waianuhea

eco-friendly hotel, hot and healthy breakfast, beautiful views. **Cons:** very remote location, unreliable phone and Internet access. ✉ *45-3503 Kahana Dr., Honokaʻa* ✉ *Box 185, Honokaʻa 96727* ☎ *888/775–2577 or 808/775–1118* ⊕ *www.waianuhea.com* 🛏 *5 rooms* 🛏 *In-room: no a/c, safe (some), DVD, Wi-Fi. In-hotel: Wi-Fi, parking (free), no-smoking rooms* ⊟ *AE, D, MC, V.*

\$–\$\$
B&B/INN

🛏 **Waipiʻo Wayside.** Nestled amid the avocado, mango, orchid, and kukui trees of a plantation estate, this serene inn provides a retreat close to the Waipiʻo Valley. Each room has its own character with, for example, rare Chinese antiques or patchwork quilts. A sprawling garden has an orchid-covered deck and a little gazebo has hammocks to help you indulge your lazy side. Many of the rooms have ocean views and some also have skylights. The owner whips up an organic, hot breakfast including fresh mango, pineapple, and orange smoothies. **Pros:** close to Waipio, authentic Hawaiian feel, hammocks with views. **Cons:** remote location, no TV in rooms. ✉ *Waipiʻo Valley Rd., Hwy. 240, Honokaʻa* ☎ *808/775–0275 or 800/833–8849* ⊕ *www.waipiowayside.com* 🛏 *5 rooms* 🛏 *In-room: no a/c (some), no phone, no TV, Wi-Fi. In-hotel: Wi-Fi, parking (free), no-smoking rooms* ⊟ *MC, V* � ❍ *CP.*

4

BIG ISLAND ESSENTIALS

TRANSPORTATION

AIR TRAVEL

You can fly direct to Hilo International Airport and Kona International Airport from other islands; there are also a number of direct flights here from the mainland. If you're willing to change planes on Oʻahu or Maui, you can get to the Big Island from anywhere.

AIRPORTS AND CARRIERS

Hawaiian Airlines, go! Airlines, IslandAir, Mokulele Airlines, and PW Express offer regular service between the islands. In addition to offering very competitive rates and online specials, all have free frequent-flier programs which will entitle you to rewards and upgrades the more you fly. Be sure to compare prices offered by all of the interisland carriers. If you are somewhat flexible with your dates and times for island-hopping, you should have no problem getting a very affordable round-trip ticket.

In addition to its regular service between the Big Island and Maui, Mokulele Airlines also provides charter service from the Kona airport to Maui, Molokaʻi and Lānaʻi. Paragon Air offers 24-hour private charter service to and from the Hilo, Kamuela, and Kona airports. *See Travel Smart for airline contact information.*

The Big Island has two main airports: Hilo International Airport and Kona International Airport. If you're staying on the west side of the island, fly into Kona. If you're staying on the eastern side, in Hilo or near Volcano, fly into Hilo. Waimea-Kohala Airport, near Waimea, is a small airstrip used by charter planes companies.

Information Kona International Airport (KOA) (✉ *73-200 Kupipi St., Kailua-Kona* ☎ *808/329–3423*). **Hilo International Airport (ITO)** (✉ *General Lyman*

Field ☎ *808/934–5838 visitor information).* **Waimea-Kohala Airport (MUE)** (☎ *808/838–8701).*

TO AND
FROM KONA
AIRPORT

Kona International Airport is about 7 mi (a 10-minute drive) from Kailua-Kona. The Keauhou resort area stretches another 6 mi to the south beyond Kailua. It takes about 30 to 45 minutes by car to reach the upscale resorts along the North Kona-Kohala Coast. If you're staying in the Waimea area, expect an hour's drive north from Kona.

Limousine service with a chauffeur who serves as a personal guide is $100 or more an hour, with a two-hour minimum. A few have all the extras—bar, televisions, and narrated tours.

If you're staying in Kailua or at the Keauhou resort area south of the airport, check with your hotel to see if shuttle service is available. There's no regularly scheduled shuttle service from Kona, although private service is offered by the Kohala Coast resorts, and by a local shuttle company. The rates for both shuttles depend on the distance, but are less than taxi fare. Check-in for the resort shuttles is at the Kohala Coast Resort Association counters at the Aloha and Hawaiian airlines arrival areas. SpeediShuttle offers transportation between the airport and hotels, resorts, and condominium complexes from Waimea to Keauhou. There's an online reservation and fare quote system for information and bookings.

Taxi fares start at about $25 for transport to King Kamehameha's Kona Beach Hotel and are slightly more expensive for other Kailua-Kona hotels and condos. Taxi fares to Kohala Coast resorts range $50 to $70. Several taxis offer guided tours.

Information **Aloha Taxi** (☎ *808/325–5448).* **D&E Taxi** (☎ *808/329–4279).* **Luana Limousine** (☎ *808/326–5466).* **Paradise Taxi** (☎ *808/329–1234).* **SpeediShuttle** (☎ *877/242–5777* ⊕ *www.speedishuttle.com).*

TO AND FROM
HILO AIRPORT

Hilo International Airport is 2 mi from the hotels along Hilo's Banyan Drive. If you have chosen a B&B closer to Hawai'i Volcanoes National Park, plan on a 40-minute drive. If you're staying in the Waimea area, expect an hour's drive. Only Arnott's Lodge and the Hawai'i Naniloa Hotel provide airport shuttles. If you're not renting a car, you'll need to take a taxi. The approximate taxi rate is $3 flip, plus 30¢ every 1/8 mi, with surcharges for waiting time at 30¢ per minute and $1 per bag. Cab fares to locations around the island are estimated as follows: Banyan Drive hotels $11, Hilo town $12, Hilo Pier $13, Volcano $75, Kea'au $22, Pahoa $50, Honoka'a $105, Kamuela/Waimea $148, Waikoloa $188, and Kailua town $240. Limousine service starts at $100 an hour, with a two-hour minimum.

Information **Hilo Harry's Taxi** (☎ *808/935–7091).* **Percy's Taxi** (☎ *808/969–7060).*

BUS TRAVEL

Travelers can take advantage of the Hawai'i County Mass Transit Agency's free Hele-On Bus, which covers several routes throughout the island. A one-way journey between Hilo and Kona will take about four hours. There's regular service in and around downtown Hilo, Kailua-Kona, Waimea, North and South Kohala, Honoka'a, and Pāhoa. There is a charge of $1 per piece for bicycles and any luggage that can't fit under a seat. Visitors staying in Hilo can take advantage of the Transit Agency's Shared Ride Taxi program which provides door-to-door transportation in the area. It's $2 for a one-way fare or $30 for a book of 15 coupons.

Information Hele-On Bus (☎ *808/961–8744* ⊕ *www.hawaii-county.com/mass_transit/transit_main.htm*).

CAR TRAVEL
Technically, the Big Island is the only Hawaiian island you can completely circle by car, and driving is the best way to enjoy the sightseeing opportunities its miles of scenic roadway afford. Asking for directions will almost always produce a helpful explanation from the locals, but you should be prepared for an island term or two. Remember that Hawai'i residents refer to places as being either *mauka* (toward the mountains) or *makai* (toward the ocean) instead of using compass directions.

Hawai'i has a strict seat belt law. Those riding in the front seat must wear a seat belt and children under the age of 18 must be belted in the backseats as well. The fine for not wearing a seat belt is $92. Jaywalking is very common in the islands so pay careful attention to the roads, especially while driving in downtown Hilo, Kailua-Kona, and the smaller towns around the island. You can count on having to pay more at the pump for gasoline that you would on the U.S. mainland.

Although there are several rental companies, cars can be scarce during holiday weekends, special events (especially the Ironman Triathlon in October), and during peak seasons from mid-December through mid-March. It's best to book well in advance.

CAR RENTAL Alamo, Avis, Budget, Dollar, Enterprise, Hertz, National, and Thrifty have offices on the Big Island, and all but Enterprise and Thrifty have locations at both Kona and Hilo airports. Ask about additional fees for picking up a car at one location and dropping it off at the other. Companies charge up to $50 for the convenience, but if you arrange it ahead of time they often waive the fee.

To get the best rate on a rental car, book it in conjunction with an inter-island flight on Hawaiian or Aloha Airlines, or ask your travel agent to check out room-and-car packages. Drivers must be 25 years or older.

Most agencies make you sign an agreement that you won't drive on Saddle Road between Hilo and Waimea. This is a holdover from when it was actually dangerous. Now it's paved and not bumpy, although it still has no lighting, gas stations, or emergency phones. If you're thinking about stargazing, take the road up to Mauna Kea off Saddle Road for the clearest views. Alamo, Budget, Dollar, and Harper Rentals let you do this in their four-wheel-drive vehicles. *See Hawai'i Travel Smart for car rental contact information.*

CONTACTS AND RESOURCES

EMERGENCIES

Dial **911** in an emergency to reach the police, fire department, or an ambulance. Call one of the hospitals listed for a doctor or dentist close to you. The Volcano Update Hotline provides 24-hour recorded information.

Emergency Services Police (✉ *349 Kapiolani St., Hilo* ☏ *808/935–3311* ✉ *74-5221 Queen K. Hwy., Kealakekua* ☏ *808/326–4646*). **Poison Control Center** (☏ *800/222–1222*). **Volcano Update Hotline** (☏ *808/985–6000*).

Hospitals Hilo Medical Center (✉ *1190 Waiānuenue Ave., Hilo* ☏ *808/974–4700*). **Kona Community Hospital** (✉ *79-1019 Haukapila St., Kealakekua* ☏ *808/322–9311*). **Kona-Kohala Medical Associates** (✉ *75–137 Hualālai Rd., Kailua-Kona* ☏ *808/329–1346*). **North Hawai'i Community Hospital** (✉ *67-1125 Māmalahoa Hwy., Waimea* ☏ *808/885–4444*).

MEDIA

Bookstores Basically Books (✉ *160 Kamehameha Ave., Hilo* ☏ *808/961–0144* or *800/903–6277* ⊕ *www.basicallybooks.com*). **Borders Books & Music** (✉ *75-1000 Henry St., Kailua-Kona* ☏ *808/331–1668* ✉ *301 Maka'ala, Hilo* ☏ *808/933–1410*).

VISITOR INFORMATION

Information Big Island Visitors Bureau (✉ *250 Keawe St., Hilo* ☏ *808/961–5797* ✉ *65-1158 Mamalahoa Hwy., 27B, Kamuela* ☏ *808/886–1655* ⊕ *www.bigisland. org*). **Hilo Downtown Improvement Association** (✉ *329 Kamehameha Ave., Hilo* ☏ *808/935-8850* ⊕ *www.downtownhilo.com*). **Destination Kona Coast** (✉ *Box 2850, Kailua-Kona 96745* ☏ *808/329–6748* ⊕ *www.destinationkonacoast.com*). **Hawai'i Visitors and Convention Bureau** (⊕ *www.gohawaii.com*). **Kohala Coast Resort Association** (✉ *68-1310 Mauna Lani Dr., Kohala Coast 96743* ☏ *800/318–3637* or *808/885–6414* ⊕ *www.kohalacoastresorts.com*). **KonaWeb** (⊕ *www.konaweb.com*). **Weather** (☏ *808/961–5582*).

Kaua'i

WORD OF MOUTH

"We love Kaua'i, for the hiking, snorkeling, and a bunch of other reasons. It is true that it is more low key and less developed, which is why we love it."

—StephCar

WELCOME TO KAUA'I

TOP REASONS TO GO

★ **Nāpali Coast:** On foot, by boat, or by air—explore what is unarguably one of the most beautiful stretches of coastline in all Hawai'i.

★ **Kalalau Trail:** Hawai'i's ultimate adventure hike will test your endurance but reward you with lush tropical vegetation, white-sand beaches, and unforgettable views.

★ **Kayaking:** Kaua'i is a mecca for kayakers, with four rivers plus the spectacular coastline to explore.

★ **Waimea Canyon:** Dramatic, colorful rock formations and frequent rainbows make this natural wonder one of Kaua'i's most stunning features.

★ **Birds:** Birds thrive on Kaua'i, especially at the Kīlauea Point National Wildlife Refuge.

1 North Shore. Dreamy beaches, green mountains, breathtaking scenery, and abundant rain, waterfalls, and rainbows characterize the North Shore, which includes the towns of Kīlauea, Princeville, and Hanalei.

2 East Side. This is Kaua'i's commercial and residential hub, dominated by the island's largest town, Kapa'a. The airport, harbor, and government offices are found in the county seat of Līhu'e.

3 South Shore. Peaceful landscapes, sunny weather, and beaches that rank among the best in the world make the South Shore the resort capital of Kaua'i. The Po'ipū resort area is here along with the main towns of Kōloa, Lāwa'i, and Kalāheo.

Haena

Kalalau Trail

NĀPALI COAST

Kalalau Lookout

Koke'e State Park

550

WAIMEA CANYON

WEST SIDE
4

552

550

Kaulakahi Channel

50

Kekaha

Waimea

TO NI'IHAU

50

Hanapepe

Eleele

540

Hanapepe Bay

0   8 mi

0   8 km

GETTING ORIENTED

Despite its small size—550 square mi—Kauaʻi has four distinct regions, each with its own unique characteristics. The windward coast, which catches the prevailing trade winds, consists of the North Shore and East Side, while the drier leeward coast encompasses the South Shore and West Side. One main road nearly encircles the island, except for a 15-mi stretch of sheer cliffs called Nāpali Coast. The center of the island—Mt. Waiʻaleʻale, completely inaccessible by car and viewable only from above due to nearly year-round cloud cover—is the wettest spot on earth, getting about 460 inches of rain per year.

5

4 **West Side.** Dry, sunny, and sleepy, the West Side includes the historic towns of Hanapēpē, Waimea, and Kekaha. This area is ideal for outdoor adventurers because it's the entryway to the Waimea Canyon and Kōkeʻe State Park, and the departure point for most Nāpali Coast boat trips.

KAUA'I PLANNER

When You Arrive

All commercial flights land at Līhu'e Airport, about 3 mi east of Līhu'e town. A rental car is the best way to get to your hotel, though taxis and some hotel shuttles are available. From the airport it will take you about 15 to 25 minutes to drive to Wailua or Kapa'a, 30 to 40 minutes to reach Po'ipū, and 45 minutes to an hour to get to Princeville or Hanalei.

Timing Is Everything

If you're a beach lover, keep in mind that big surf can make many North Shore beaches unswimmable during winter months, while the South Shore gets its large swells in summer. If you want to see the humpback whales, February is the best month, though they arrive as early as December and a few may still be around in early April. In winter, Nāpali Coast boat tours can be rerouted due to high seas, the Kalalau Trail can become very wet and muddy or, at times, impassable, and sea kayaking is not an option. If you have your heart set on visiting Kaua'i's famed coast you may want to visit in the drier, warmer months (May–September).

Renting a Car

Unless you plan to stay strictly at a resort or do all of your sightseeing as part of guided tours, you'll need a rental car. There's bus service on the island, but they tend to be slow and don't go everywhere.

You most likely won't need a four-wheel-drive vehicle anywhere on the island, so save yourself the money. And while convertibles look fun, the frequent, intermittent rain showers and intense tropical sun make hardtops a better (and cheaper) choice.

■ TIP→ Reserve your vehicle in advance, especially during the Christmas holidays. This will not only ensure that you get a car, but also that you get the best rates. Kaua'i has some of the highest gas prices in the Islands. ⇨ *See Kaua'i Essentials for more information on renting a car and driving.*

■ TIP→ On Kaua'i, the directions *mauka* (toward the mountains) and *makai* (toward the ocean) are often used. Locals tend to refer to highways by name rather than by number.

Dining and Lodging on Kaua'i

Hawai'i is a melting pot of cultures, and nowhere is this more apparent than in its cuisine. From lū'au and "plate lunch" to sushi and steak, there's no shortage of interesting flavors and presentations.

Whether you're looking for a quick snack or a multicourse meal, ⇨ *go to Where to Eat to find the best eating experiences* the island has to offer. Jump in, and enjoy!

Choosing vacation lodging is a tough decision, but fret not—our expert writers and editors have done most of the legwork.

Looking for a tropical forest retreat, a big resort, or a private vacation rental? ⇨ *Where to Stay will give you all the details you need to book a place that suits your style.* Quick tips: Reserve your room far in advance and be sure to ask about discounts and special packages (hotel Web sites often have Internet-only deals).

Island Hopping

If you have a week or more on Kaua'i and you've never visited Pearl Harbor, the *Arizona* Memorial and USS *Missouri,* you may want to consider taking a day trip to O'ahu. Catch the first flight out and head straight to the *Arizona* Memorial, or you may risk long lines and an hours-long wait.

If you want to travel to Maui to experience the Road to Hāna or to the Big Island to see Volcanoes National Park, there are few convenient nonstop flights; most layover in Honolulu, so you'll have to plan an overnight.

Island Driving Times

It might not seem as if driving from the North Shore to the West Side, say, would take very much time, as Kaua'i is smaller in size than O'ahu, Maui, and certainly the Big Island. But it will take longer than you'd think from glancing at a map, and Kaua'i roads are subject to some pretty heavy traffic, especially going through Kapa'a and Līhu'e. Here are average driving times that will help you plan your excursions, starting from Ha'ena in the northwest and working clockwise around the island to Waimea in the southwest. During heavy visitor times—holidays and summer—or if there should happen to be a car accident, these times can see significant increases.

Ha'ena to Hanalei	15 minutes
Hanalei to Princeville	10 minutes
Princeville to Kīlauea	12 minutes
Kīlauea to Anahola	15 minutes
Anahola to Kapa'a	10 minutes
Kapa'a to Līhu'e	20 minutes
Līhu'e to Po'ipū	25 minutes
Po'ipū to Kalaheo	20 minutes
Kalaheo to Hanapepe	10 minutes
Hanapepe to Waimea	10 minutes

Seeing Nāpali

Let's put this in perspective: Even if you had only one day on Kaua'i, we'd still recommend heading to Nāpali Coast on Kaua'i's northwest side. Once you're there, you'll soon realize why no road traverses this series of cliffs that are lined up like dominos. That leaves three ways to experience the coastline—by air, by water, or on foot. We recommend all three, in this order: air, water, foot. Each one gets progressively more sensory.

Nāpali Coast runs 15 mi from Kē'ē Beach, one of Kaua'i's more popular snorkel sports, on the east side to Polihale State Park, the longest stretch of beach in the state, on the west side of the island.

If you can't squeeze in all three visits—air, water, and foot—or you can't afford all three, we recommend the helicopter tour for those strapped for time and the hiking for those with a limited budget. The boat tours are great for family fun.

Whatever way you choose to visit Nāpali, you might want to keep this awe-inspiring fact in mind: At one time, thousands of Hawaiians lived self-sufficiently in these valleys.

5

Updated by
Michael Levine

Even a nickname like "the Garden Island" fails to do justice to Kaua'i's beauty. Verdant trees grow canopies over the island's few roads; brooding mountains are framed by long, sandy beaches, coral reefs, and sheer sea cliffs. For years, Kaua'i managed to resist the rampant growth occurring elsewhere in the state. Its reputation for rain deterred tourists, and devastating hurricanes in 1982 and 1992 discouraged development.

Currently, a proliferation of new construction offers irrefutable proof that Kaua'i has been discovered, but life here remains simple, and the locals are determined to keep it that way. At 540 square mi Kaua'i is the fourth-largest island, and its population remains low at 63,000.

GEOLOGY

Kaua'i is the oldest and northernmost of the main Hawaiian Islands. Five million years of wind and rain have worked their magic, sculpting fluted sea cliffs and whittling away at the cinder cones and caldera that prove its volcanic origin. Foremost among these is Wai'ale'ale, one of the wettest spots on Earth. Its 460-inch annual rainfall feeds the mighty Wailua River, the only navigable waterway in Hawai'i. The vast Alaka'i Swamp soaks up rain like a sponge, releasing it slowly into the watershed that gives Kaua'i its emerald sheen.

FLORA AND FAUNA

Kaua'i offers some of the best birding in the state, due in part to the absence of the mongoose. Many *nēnē* (endangered Hawaiian state bird) reared in captivity have been successfully released here, along with an endangered forest bird called the *puai'ohi*. The island is also home to a large colony of migratory nesting seabirds, and has two refuges protecting endangered Hawaiian water birds. Kaua'i's most noticeable fowl, however, is the wild chicken. A cross between jungle fowl (*moa*) brought by the Polynesians, and domestic chickens and fighting cocks that escaped during the last two hurricanes, they are everywhere, and the roosters crow when they feel like it, not just at dawn. Consider yourself warned.

HISTORY

Kaua'i's residents have had a reputation for independence since ancient times. Called "the separate kingdom," Kaua'i alone resisted King Kamehameha's charge to unite the Hawaiian Islands. In fact, it was only by kidnapping Kaua'i's king, Kaumuali'i, and forcing him to marry Kamehameha's widow that the Garden Island was joined to the rest of Hawai'i. That spirit lives on today as Kaua'i residents resist the lure of tourism dollars captivating the rest of the islands. Local building rules maintain that no structure may be taller than a coconut tree, and Kaua'i's capital city, Līhu'e, is still more small town than city.

DID YOU KNOW?

You'll find a welcome respite at gorgeous and secluded Kalalau Beach when you reach the end of the arduous 11-mile Kalalau Trail.

LEGENDS AND MYTHOLOGY: THE MENEHUNE

Although all of the islands have a few stories about the *Menehune*—magical little people who accomplished great big feats—Kaua'i is believed to be their home base. The Menehune Fishpond, above Nāwilwili Harbor, is a prime example of their work. The story goes that the large pond (initially 25 mi in diameter) was built in one night by thousands of Menehune passing stones from hand to hand. A spy disrupted their work in the middle of the night, leaving two gaps that are still visible today (drive to the pond on Hulemalu Road, or kayak up Huleia Stream).

EXPLORING KAUA'I

The main road tracing Kaua'i's perimeter takes you past much more scenery than would seem possible on one small island. Chiseled mountains, thundering waterfalls, misty hillsides, dreamy beaches, lush vegetation, and quaint small towns compose the physical landscape. And there's plenty to do, as well as see: plantation villages, a historic lighthouse, wildlife refuges, a fern grotto, a colorful canyon, and deep rivers are all easily explored. Oh, one other thing: there is no road that goes all the way around the island. The island's renowned Nāpali Coast on the northwest side precludes car travel of any kind—4WD or otherwise.

■TIP➔While exploring the island, try to take advantage of the many roadside scenic overlooks to pull off and take in the constantly changing view. And don't try to pack too much into one day. Kaua'i is small, but travel is slow. The island's sights are divided into four geographic areas, in clockwise order: the North Shore, the East Side, the South Shore, and the West Side.

THE NORTH SHORE

The North Shore of Kaua'i includes the environs of Kīlauea, Princeville, Hanalei, and Hā'ena. Traveling north from the airport on Route 56, known locally as Kuhio Highway, the coastal highway crosses the Wailua River and the busy towns of Wailua and Kapa'a before emerging into a decidedly rural and scenic landscape, with expansive views of the island's rugged interior mountains. As the two-lane highway turns west and narrows, it winds through spectacular scenery and passes the posh resort community of Princeville before dropping down into Hanalei Valley. Here it narrows further and becomes a federally recognized scenic roadway (Route 560), replete with one-lane bridges (the local etiquette is for all the cars on one side to cross before yielding to those on the other side), hairpin turns, and heart-stopping coastal vistas. The road ends at Kē'ē, where the ethereal rain forests and fluted sea cliffs of Nāpali Coast Wilderness State Park begin.

In winter, Kaua'i's North Shore receives more rainfall than other areas of the island. Don't let this deter you from visiting. The clouds drift over the mountains of Nāmolokama, creating a mysterious mood and then, in a blink, disappear, rewarding you with mountains laced with a dozen waterfalls or more.

TOP ATTRACTIONS

Hanalei. Crossing the historic one-lane bridge into Hanalei reveals Old World Hawai'i, including working taro farms, poi making, and evenings of throwing horseshoes at Black Pot Beach Park—found unmarked (as most everything is on Kaua'i) at the east end of Hanalei Bay Beach Park. Although the recent real estate boom on Kaua'i has attracted mainland millionaires to build estate homes on the few remaining parcels of land in Hanalei, there's still plenty to see and do. It's *the* gathering place on the North Shore. Restaurants, shops, and people-watching here are among the best on the island, and you won't find a single brand name, chain, or big-box store around—unless you count surf brands like Quiksilver and Billabong. The beach and river offer swimming, snorkeling, boogie boarding, surfing, and kayaking. Those hanging around at sunset often congregate at the Hanalei Pavilion where a husband-and-wife slack-key-guitar-playing duo makes impromptu appearances. There's an old rumor, since quashed by the local newspaper, The *Garden Island,* which says Hanalei was the inspiration for the song *Puff the Magic Dragon* performed by the 1960s singing sensation Peter, Paul & Mary. Even with the newspaper's exposé, Hawai'i Movie Tours caps off their daylong visit of famous Kaua'i movie sites on the Hanalei Pier with a guide pointing out the shape of the dragon carved into the mountains encircling the town. ✉ *Rte. 560, 3 mi north of Princeville Shopping Center.*

Hanalei Valley Overlook. Dramatic mountains and a patchwork of neat taro farms bisected by the wide Hanalei River make this one of Hawai'i's loveliest sights. The fertile Hanalei Valley has been planted in taro since perhaps AD 700, save for a century-long foray into rice that ended in 1960. (The historic Haraguchi Rice Mill is all that remains of the era.) Many taro farmers lease land within the 900-acre Hanalei National Wildlife Refuge, helping to provide wetland habitat for four species of endangered Hawaiian water birds. ✉ *Rte. 56, across from Foodland, Princeville.*

Fodor'sChoice
★ **Kīlauea Point National Wildlife Refuge and Kīlauea Lighthouse.** A beacon for sea traffic since it was built in 1913, this National Historic Landmark has the largest clamshell lens of any lighthouse in the world. It's within a national wildlife refuge, where thousands of seabirds soar on the trade winds and nest on the steep ocean cliffs. Endangered nēnē geese, red-footed boobies, Laysan albatross, wedge-tailed shearwaters, white- and red-tailed tropicbirds, great frigatebirds, Pacific golden plovers (all identifiable by educational signboards) along with native plants, dolphins, humpback whales, huge winter surf, and gorgeous views of the North Shore add to the drama of this special place, making it well worth the modest entry fee. The gift shop has a great selection of books about the island's natural history and an array of unique merchandise, with all proceeds benefiting education and preservation efforts. ✉ *Kīlauea Lighthouse Rd., Kīlauea* ☎ *808/828–0168* ⊕ *www.fws.gov/ kilaueapoint* ⊠ *$5* ☉ *Daily 10–4.*

Moloa'a Sunrise Fruit Stand. Don't let the name fool you; they don't open at sunrise. (More like 8 AM, so come here after you watch the sunrise elsewhere.) And it's not just a fruit stand. Breakfast is light—bagels, granola, smoothies and, of course, coffee (even espresso, cappuccino,

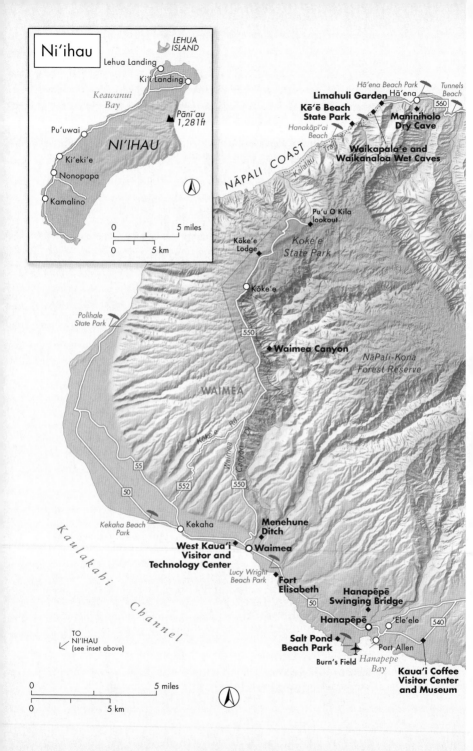

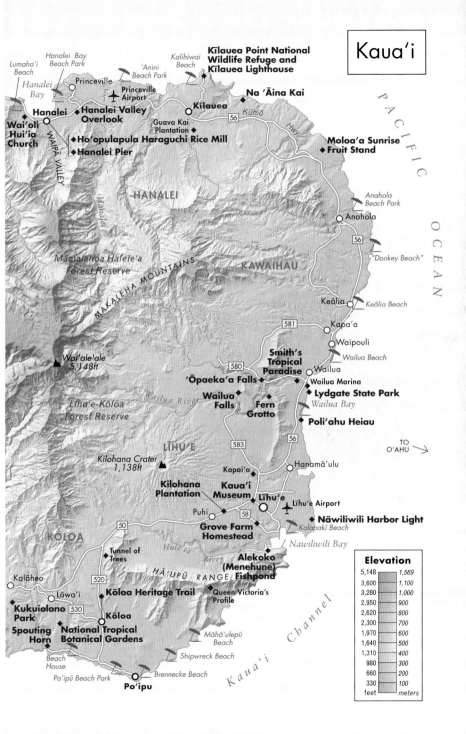

Kaua'i

Lumaha'i Beach
Hanalei Bay Beach Park
'Anini Beach Park
Kalihiwai Beach
Kīlauea Point National Wildlife Refuge and Kīlauea Lighthouse
Na 'Āina Kai

Princeville
Princeville Airport
Kīlauea

PACIFIC

Hanalei
Wai'oli Hui'ia Church
Hanalei Valley Overlook
Ho'opulapula Haraguchi Rice Mill
Hanalei Pier
Guava Kai Plantation

Moloa'a Sunrise Fruit Stand

Hanalei Bay

WAIPĀ VALLEY

Hanalei River

HANALEI

Māmalahoa Hālele'a Forest Reserve

Anahola Beach Park
Anahola

KAWAIHAU

OCEAN

MAKALEHA MOUNTAINS

56
"Donkey Beach"

Wai'ale'ale 5,148ft

Keālia
Keālia Beach

Līhu'e-Kōloa Forest Reserve

581
Kapa'a
Waipouli
Wailua Beach

Smith's Tropical Paradise

'Ōpaeka'a Falls
580
Wailua

Wailua River

Wailua Falls
Fern Grotto

Wailua Marina
Lydgate State Park
Wailua Bay

Poli'ahu Heiau

LIHU'E

56

TO O'AHU

Kilohana Crater 1,138ft

583
Kapai'a

Hanamā'ulu

Kilohana Plantation
Kaua'i Museum
Līhu'e

Puhi

Līhu'e Airport

58
Nāwiliwili Harbor Light
Kalapakī Beach

Grove Farm Homestead

KŌLOA

50

Hule'ia River

Nawiliwili Bay

Tunnel of Trees

HĀ'UPU RANGE

Alekoko (Menehune) Fishpond

Kalāheo
520
Lāwa'i
Kōloa Heritage Trail
Queen Victoria's Profile

530

Kukuiolono Park
Kōloa

Kaua'i Channel

Spouting Horn
National Tropical Botanical Gardens

Māhā'ulepū Beach

Shipwreck Beach

Beach House

Po'ipū Beach Park
Brennecke Beach
Po'ipu

Elevation

feet	meters
5,148	1,569
3,600	1,100
3,280	1,000
2,950	900
2,620	800
2,300	700
1,970	600
1,640	500
1,310	400
980	300
660	200
330	100
feet	meters

and latte) and tropical-style fresh juices (pineapple, carrot, watermelon, guava, even sugarcane). This is also a great stop to pick up sandwiches to go, although then you wouldn't enjoy the friendliness of Meow, the resident cat. Select local produce is always available, although not the variety you can find at the island's farmers' markets. What makes this fruit stand stand out is the fresh, natural ingredients like multigrain and spelt breads and nori as a wheat-free bread alternative. ⊠*Just past mile marker 16 makai on Rte. 56* ☎*808/822–1441* ⊙*Mon.–Sat. 8–4:30, Sun. 10:30–4:30.*

☕ ★ **Na 'Āina Kai.** One small sign along the highway is all that promotes this one-time private garden gone awry. Ed and Joyce Doty's love for plants and art now spans 240 acres, includes 13 different gardens, lagoons, a hardwood plantation, canyon, Japanese Tea House, Poinciana maze, waterfall, and a sandy beach. Throughout are more than 70 bronze sculptures, reputedly one of the nation's largest collections. Now a nonprofit organization, the latest project is a children's garden with a 16-foot-tall Jack and the Beanstalk bronze sculpture, gecko maze, tree house, kid-size train, and, of course, a tropical jungle. In a residential neighborhood and hoping to maintain good neighborly relations, the garden limits tours (guided only). Tour lengths vary widely, from 1½ to 5 hours. Reservations strongly recommended. ⊠*Rte. 56 north of mile marker 21, turn makai on Wailapa Rd. and follow signs* ☎*808/828–0525* ⊕*www.naainakai. org* ⊠ *Fees range from $30 for 1½-hr stroll to $75 for 5-hr hiking tour* ⊙*Tours: Tues.–Thurs. at 9 and 1, Fri. at 9 only.*

WORTH NOTING

Kīlauea. A former plantation town, Kīlauea town maintains its rural flavor in the midst of unrelenting gentrification encroaching all around it. Especially noteworthy are its historic lava-rock buildings, including **Christ Memorial Episcopal Church** on Kolo Street and the Kong Lung Company on Keneke Street, now an expensive shop. ⊠*Rte. 56, mile marker 23.*

Limahuli Garden. Narrow Limahuli Valley, with its fluted mountain peaks and ancient stone taro terraces, creates an unparalled setting for this botanical garden and nature preserve. Dedicated to protecting native plants and unusual varieties of taro, it represents the principles of conservation and stewardship held by its founder, Charles "Chipper" Wichman. Limahuli's priomordial beauty and strong mana (spiritual power) eclipse the extensive botanical collection. It's one of the most gorgeous spots on Kaua'i and the crown jewel of the National Tropical Botanical Garden, which Wichman now heads. Call ahead to reserve a guided tour, or tour on your own. Be prepared for walking a somewhat steep hillside. ⊠*Rte. 560, Hā'ena* ☎*808/826–1053* ⊕*www.ntbg. org* ⊠*Self-guided tour $15, guided tour $25 (reservations required)* ⊙*Tues.–Sat. 9:30–4.*

Maniniholo Dry Cave. According to legend, Maniniholo was the head fisherman of the Menehune—the possibly real, possibly mythical first inhabitants of the island. As they were preparing to leave Kaua'i and return home (wherever that was), Maniniholo called some of his workers to Hā'ena to collect food from the reef. They gathered so much that they couldn't carry it all, and left some near the ocean cliffs, with plans to retrieve it the following day. It all disappeared during the night, however, and Maniniholo realized that imps living in the rock fissures were the culprits. He and his men dug into the cliff to find and destroy the imps, leaving behind the cave that now bears his name. Across the highway from Maniniholo Dry Cave is **Hā'ena State Park.** ⊠ *Rte. 560, Hā'ena.*

Waikapala'e and Waikanaloa Wet Caves. Said to have been dug by Pele, goddess of fire, these watering holes used to be clear, clean, and great for swimming. Now stagnant, they're nevertheless a photogenic example of the many haunting natural landmarks of Kaua'i's North Shore. Waikanaloa is visible right beside the highway. Across the road from a small parking area, a five-minute uphill walk leads to Waikapala'e. ⊠ *Western end of Rte. 560.*

Wai'oli Hui'ia Church. Designated a National Historic Landmark, this little church—affiliated with the United Church of Christ—doesn't go unnoticed right alongside Route 560 in downtown Hanalei, and its doors are usually wide open (from 9 to 5, give or take) inviting inquisitive visitors in for a look around. Like the Wai'oli Mission House next door, it's an exquisite representation of New England architecture meets Hawaiian thatched buildings. During the 1992 visit of Hurricane 'Iniki, which brought sustained winds of 160 MPH and wind gusts up to 220 MPH, this little church was lifted off its foundation but, thankfully, lovingly restored. Services are held at 10 AM on Sunday with many hymns sung in Hawaiian. ⊠ *Located at mile marker 3 on Rte. 560, 5-5393A Kuhio Hwy.* ☎ *808/826–6253.*

THE EAST SIDE

The East Side encompasses Līhu'e, Wailua, and Kapa'a; it's also known as the "Coconut Coast," as there was once a coconut plantation where today's aptly named Coconut Marketplace is located. A small grove still exists on both sides of the highway. *Mauka* (toward the mountain), a fenced herd of goats keep the grass tended; on the *makai* (toward the ocean) side, you can walk through the grove, although it's best not to walk directly under the trees—locals joke that falling coconuts are the island's most dangerous plant life. Līhu'e is the county seat and the whole East Side is the island's center of commerce, so early morning and late afternoon drive times (or rush hour) can get congested. (Because there's only one main road, if there's a serious traffic accident the entire roadway may be closed, with no way around. Not to worry; it's a rarity.)

The road from the airport leads to the middle of Līhu'e. To the left and right are fast-food restaurants, Wal-Mart, Kmart, Borders Books and Music—most recently a Home Depot, Costco, and Starbucks, too—and a variety of county and state buildings. The avid golfer will like the three golf courses in Līhu'e—all within a mile or so of each other.

Turn to the right out of the airport for the road to Wailua. A bridge—under which the very culturally significant Wailua River gently flows—marks the beginning of town. Wailua is comprised of a few restaurants and shops, a few mid-range resorts along the coastline, and a housing

community *mauka*. It quickly blends into Kapa'a; there's no real demar-
cation. Kapa'a houses two of the biggest grocery stores on the island,
side by side: Foodland and Safeway. It also offers plenty of dining
options (for breakfast, lunch, and dinner) and gift shopping. Old Town
Kapa'a was once a plantation town, which is no surprise—most of the
larger towns on Kaua'i once were—however, this one didn't disappear
with the sugar mill and pineapple cannery. Old Town Kapa'a is made
up of a collection of wooden-front shops, some built by plantation
workers and still run by their progeny today.

TOP ATTRACTIONS

Kaua'i Museum. Maintaining a stately presence on Rice Street, the historic museum building is easy to find. It features a permanent display,
"The Story of Kaua'i," which provides a competent overview of the
Garden Island and Ni'ihau, tracing the islands' geology, mythology, and
cultural history. Local artists are represented in changing exhibits in the
second-floor Mezzanine Gallery. The gift shop alone is worth a visit,
with a fine collection of authentic Ni'ihau shell lei, feather hatband lei,
hand-turned wooden bowls, reference books, and other quality arts,
crafts, and gifts, many of them locally made. ⊠ *4428 Rice St., Līhu'e*
☎ *808/245–6931* ☜ *$7* ⊙ *Weekdays 9–4, Sat. 10–4.*

☺ **Lydgate State Park.** The park, named for the Reverend J.M. Lydgate,
founder of the Līhu'e English Union Church, has a large children-
designed and community-built playground, pavilion, and picnic area. It
also houses the remains of an ancient site where commoners who broke
a royal tabu could seek refuge from punishment. It's part of an extensive complex of sacred archaeological sites that runs from Wai'ale'ale
to the sea, underscoring the significance of this region to the ancient
Hawaiians. In recent years the community expanded the playground
to include a bridge of mazes, tunnels, and slides. It's a short walk or
drive south of the main park, off Nehe Drive. ⊠ *South of Wailua River
turn makai off Rte. 56 onto Leho Dr. and makai onto Nalu Rd.* ☜ *Free*
⊙ *Daily dawn–dusk.*

★ **'Ōpaeka'a Falls.** The mighty Wailua River produces many dramatic
waterfalls, and 'Ōpaeka'a (pronounced oh-pie-kah-ah) is one of the
best. It plunges hundreds of feet to the pool below and can be easily
viewed from a scenic overlook with ample parking. 'Ōpaeka'a means
"rolling shrimp," which refers to tasty native crustaceans that were once
so abundant they could be seen tumbling in the falls. ■TIP➔ Just before
reaching the parking area for the waterfalls, turn left into a scenic pullout
for great views of the Wailua River valley and its march to the sea. ⊠ *From
Rte. 56, turn mauka onto Kuamo'o Rd., drive 1½ mi to Wailua.*

Poli'ahu Heiau. Storyboards near this ancient *heiau* (sacred site) recount
the significance of the many sacred structures found along the Wailua
River. It's unknown exactly how the ancient Hawaiians used Poli'ahu
Heiau—one of the largest pre-Christian temples on the island—but legend says it was built by the Menehune because of the unusual stonework
found in its walled enclosures. From this site, drive downhill toward
the ocean to pōhaku hānau, a two-piece birthing stone said to confer
special blessings on all children born there, and pōhaku piko, whose

Continued on page 454

HAWAI'I'S PLANTS 101

Hawai'i is a bounty of rainbow-colored flowers and plants. The evening air is scented with their fragrance. Just look at the front yard of almost any home, travel any road, or visit any local park and you'll see a spectacular array of colored blossoms and leaves. What most visitors don't know is that the plants they are seeing are not native to Hawai'i; rather, they were introduced during the last two centuries as ornamental plants, or for timber, shade, or fruit.

Hawai'i boasts nearly every climate on the planet, excluding the two most extreme: arctic tundra and arid desert. The Islands have wine-growing regions, cactus-speckled ranchlands, icy mountaintops, and the rainiest forests on earth.

Plants introduced from around the world thrive here. The lush lowland valleys along the windward coasts are predominantly populated by non-native trees including yellow- and red-fruited **guava**, silvery-leafed **kukui**, and orange-flowered **tulip trees**.

The colorful **plumeria flower**, very fragrant and commonly used in lei making, and the giant multicolored **hibiscus flower** are both used by many women as hair adornments, and are two of the most common plants found around homes and hotels. The umbrella-like **monkeypod tree** from Central America provides shade in many of Hawai'i's parks including Kapiolani Park in Honolulu. Hawai'i's largest tree, found in Lahaina, Maui, is a giant **banyan tree.** Its canopy and massive support roots cover about two-thirds of an acre. The native **o'hia tree**, with its brilliant red brush-like flowers, and the **hapu'u**, a giant tree fern, are common in Hawai'i's forests and are also used ornamentally in gardens and around homes.

Bougainvillea	Guava	Monkeypod
Banyan	Ohia Lehua *	Tulip Tree
Plumeria	Pandanus	Hibiscus
Anthurium	Kukui Tree	Hapu'u

*endemic to Hawai'i

5

IN FOCUS HAWAI'I'S PLANTS 101

DID YOU KNOW?

Over 2,200 plant species are found in the Hawaiian Islands, but only about 1,000 are native. Of these, 282 are so rare, they are endangered. Hawai'i's endemic plants evolved from ancestral seeds arriving on the islands over thousands of years as baggage on birds, floating on ocean currents, or drifting on winds from continents thousands of miles away. Once here, these plants evolved in isolation creating many new species known nowhere else in the world.

crevices were a repository for umbilical cords left by parents seeking a clue to their child's destiny, which reportedly was foretold by how his cord fared in the rock. Some Hawaiians feel these sacred stones shouldn't be viewed as "tourist attractions," so always treat them with respect. Never stand or sit on the rocks, or leave any offerings. ⊠*Rte. 580, Kuamo'o Rd., Wailua.*

Wailua Falls. You may recognize this impressive cascade from the opening sequences of the *Fantasy Island* television series. Kaua'i has plenty of noteworthy waterfalls, but this one is especially picturesque, easy to find, and easy to photograph. ⊠*End of Rte. 583, Ma'alo Rd., in Kapai'a 4 mi from Rte. 56.*

WORTH NOTING

Alekoko (Menehune) Fishpond. No one knows just who built this intricate aquaculture structure in the Hule'ia River. Legend attributes it to the Menehune, a possibly real, possibly mythical ancient race of people known for their small stature, industrious nature, and superb stone-working skills. Volcanic rock was cut and fit together into massive walls 4 feet thick and 5 feet high, forming an enclosure for raising mullet and other freshwater fish that has endured for centuries. ⊠*Hulemalu Rd., Niumalu.*

Fern Grotto. The Fern Grotto has a long history on Kaua'i. For some reason, visitors seem to like it. It's really nothing more than a yawning lava tube swathed in lush fishtail ferns 3 mi up the Wailua River. Though it was significantly damaged after Hurricane 'Iniki and again after heavy rains in 2006, the greenery has completely recovered—plant life grows like a baseball slugger on steroids in Kaua'i's year-round sun and rain. Smith's Motor Boat Services is the only way to legally see the grotto. You can access the entrance with a kayak, but if boats are there, you may not be allowed to land. ⊠*Depart from Wailua Marina on mauka side of Rte. 56, just south of Wailua River* ≦*$20* ⊙*Daily departures 9:30–3:30* ☎*808/821–6892.*

♺ **Kilohana Plantation.** This estate dates back to 1896, when plantation manager Albert Spencer Wilcox first developed it as a working cattle ranch. His nephew, Gaylord Parke Wilcox, took over in 1936, building Kaua'i's first mansion. Today the 16,000-square-foot, Tudor-style home houses specialty shops, art galleries, and Gaylord's, a pretty restaurant with courtyard seating. Nearly half the original furnishings remain, and the gardens and orchards were replanted according to the original plans. You can tour the grounds for free; children enjoy visiting the farm animals. Horse-drawn carriage rides are available, or you can tour the old Grove Farm Plantation in a sugarcane wagon pulled by Clydesdales. A train runs 2.½ mi through 104 acres of lands representing the agricultural story of Kauai—then and now. ⊠*3-2087 Kaumuali'i Hwy., Rte. 50, Līhu'e* ☎*808/245–5608* ⊙*Mon.–Sat. 9:30–9:30, Sun. 9:30–5.*

Līhu'e. The commercial and political center of Kaua'i County, which includes the islands of Kaua'i and Ni'ihau, Līhu'e is home to the island's major airport, harbor, and hospital. This is where you can find the state and county offices that issue camping and hiking permits and the same fast-food eateries and big-box stores that blight the mainland.

The county is seeking help in reviving the downtown; for now, once your business is done, there's little reason to linger in lackluster Līhu'e. ⊠*Rtes. 56 and 50 96766.*

NEED A BREAK? Stop in at **Lotus Root** (⊠ *4-1384 Kuhio Hwy., Kapa'a* ☎ *808/823–6658*), an offshoot of the wildly popular vegan restaurant Blossoming Lotus, for a healthy and yummy snack. The juice bar and bakery serves pizza by the slice, breakfast burritos, and the outta-this-world Cloud Nine, a juice concoction made with papaya, macadamia nut, dates, coconut milk, and vanilla rooibos tea.

THE SOUTH SHORE

As you follow the main road south from Līhu'e, the landscape becomes lush and densely vegetated before giving way to drier conditions that characterize Po'ipū, the South Side's major resort area. Po'ipū owes much of its popularity to a steady supply of sunshine and a string of sandy beaches, although the beaches are smaller and more covelike than those on the West Side. With its extensive selection of accommodations, services, and activities, the South Shore attracts more visitors than any other region on Kaua'i. It's also attracting developers with big plans for the onetime sugar fields that are nestled in this region and enveloped by mountains. There are few roads in and out, and local residents are concerned about increased traffic and noise and dust pollution as a result of the construction. If you're planning to stay on the South Side, be sure to ask if your hotel, condo, or vacation rental will be impacted by the ongoing development during your visit.

Both Po'ipū and nearby Kōloa (site of Kaua'i's first sugar mill) can be reached via Route 520 (Maluhia Road) from the Līhu'e area. Route 520 is known locally as Tree Tunnel Road due to the stand of eucalyptus trees lining the road that were planted at the turn of the 20th century by Walter Duncan McBryde, a Scotsman who began cattle ranching on Kaua'i's South Shore. The canopy of trees was ripped to literal shreds twice—in 1982 during Hurricane 'Ewa and again in 1992 during Hurricane 'Iniki. And, true to Kaua'i, both times the trees grew back into an impressive tunnel. It's a distinctive way to announce, "You are now on vacation," for there's a definite feel of leisure in the air here. There's still plenty to do—snorkel, bike, walk, horseback ride, take an ATV tour, surf, scuba dive, shop, and dine—everything you'd want on a tropical vacation. From the west, Route 530 (Kōloa Road) slips into downtown Kōloa, a string of fun shops and restaurants, at an intersection with the only gas station on the South Shore.

TOP ATTRACTIONS

Kōloa. Hawai'i's lucrative foray into sugar was born in this sleepy town, where the first sugar was milled back in 1830. You can still see the mill's old stone smokestack. Little else remains, save for the charming plantation-style buildings that have kept Kōloa from becoming a tacky tourist trap for Po'ipū-bound visitors. The original small-town character has been preserved by converting historic structures along the main street into boutiques, restaurants, and shops. Placards describe the original tenants and life in the old mill town. Look for Kōloa Fish

Market, which offers *poke* (chopped, pickled raw tuna or other fish) and sashimi takeout, and Progressive Expressions, a popular local surf shop. ⊠*Rte. 520.*

National Tropical Botanical Gardens *(NTBG).* Tucked away in Lāwa'i Valley, these gardens include lands and a cottage once used by Hawai'i's Queen Emma for a summer retreat. Visitors can take a self-guided tour of the rambling 252-acre **McBryde Gardens** to see and learn about plants collected from throughout the tropics. The 100-acre **Allerton Gardens,** which can be visited only on a guided tour, artfully display statues and water features that were originally developed as part of a private estate. A secluded cove known as Lāwa'i Kai can be reached through Allerton Gardens (only on tour, with no time for romping around in the sand); the beach is otherwise largely inaccessible to the public. Reservations are required for tours of Allerton Gardens, but not for the self-guided tours of McBryde Gardens. The visitor center has a high-quality gift shop with botany-theme merchandise.

Besides harboring and propagating rare and endangered plants from Hawai'i and elsewhere, NTBG functions as a scientific research and education center. The organization also operates gardens in Limahuli, on Kaua'i's north shore, and in Hāna, on Maui's east shore. ⊠*Lāwa'i Rd., across from Spouting Horn parking lot, Po'ipū* ☎*808/742–2623* ⊕*www.ntbg.org* ⊠*Self-guided tour (McBryde) $20, guided tour (Allerton) $40* ☉*McBryde Gardens: Daily 9:30–4. Allerton Gardens tours (by reservation): Daily at 9:30, 10:30, 11:30, 12:30, 1:30, and 2:30.*

Spouting Horn. If the conditions are right, you can see a natural blowhole in the reef behaving like Old Faithful, shooting salt water high into the air. It's most dramatic during big summer swells, which force large quantities of water through an ancient lava tube with great force. ■TIP➜**Stay on the paved walkways as rocks can be slippery and wave action unpredictable.** Vendors hawk inexpensive souvenirs and other items in the parking lot. You may find good deals on shell jewelry, but ask for a certificate of authenticity to ensure it's a genuine Ni'ihau shell lei before paying the higher price that these intricate creations command. ⊠*At end of Lāwa'i Rd., Po'ipū.*

> **WORD OF MOUTH**
>
> "After packing, we decided to go to Spouting Horn nearby. As we left we noticed more storm clouds in the distance. When we got to Spouting Horn it was "spouting" tremendously! What a show (probably due to the distant storms)!" —CajunStorm

WORTH NOTING

Po'ipū. Po'ipū has emerged as Kaua'i's top visitor destination, thanks to its generally sunny weather and a string of golden-sand beaches dotted with oceanfront lodgings, including the Sheraton Kaua'i Resort and a half dozen condominium projects. More and more homes in the area are converting to private vacation rentals and B&Bs. (This trend across the island has created a shortage of affordable housing for residents.) Beaches are user-friendly, with protected waters for *keiki* (children) and novice snorkelers, lifeguards, clean restrooms, covered pavilions, and a sweet coastal promenade ideal for leisurely strolls. Some experts even rank Po'ipū Beach Park number one in the nation. That may be a bit of an overstatement, although it certainly does warrant high accolades. ■TIP➔In summertime, don't be surprised to see a monk-seal mom and her pup on the beach here; the seals seem to like this beach as much as the visitors. ⊠*Rte. 520.*

NEED A BREAK?

Stop in at Brennecke's Beach Broiler (⊠*2100 Ho'ōne Rd., Po'ipū* ☎*808/742–7588*), a longtime fixture on the beach in Po'ipū. After a day of sun, this is a perfect spot to chill out with a mango margarita or "world famous" mai tai, paired with a yummy pūpū platter.

THE WEST SIDE

Exploring the West Side is akin to visiting an entirely different world. The landscape is dramatic and colorful: a patchwork of green, blue, black, and orange. The weather is hot and dry, the beaches are long, and the sand is dark. Ni'ihau, a private island where only Hawaiians may live, can be glimpsed offshore. This is rural Kaua'i, where sugar is making its last stand and taro is still cultivated in the fertile river valleys. The lifestyle is slow, easy, and traditional, with many folks fishing and hunting to supplement their diets. Here and there modern industry has intruded into this pastoral scene: huge generators turn oil into electricity at Port Allen; scientists cultivate experimental crops of genetically engineered plants in Kekaha; the Navy launches rockets at Mānā to test the "Star Wars" missile defense system; and NASA mans a tracking station in the wilds of Koke'e. It's a region of contrasts that simply shouldn't be missed.

Heading west from Līhu'e or Po'ipū, you pass through a string of tiny towns, plantation camps, and historical sites, each with a story to tell of centuries past. There's Hanapēpē, whose coastal salt ponds have been harvested since ancient times; Kaumakani, where the sugar industry still clings to life; Fort Elisabeth, from which an enterprising Russian tried to take over the island in the early 1800s; and Waimea, where Captain Cook made his first landing in the Islands, forever changing the face of Hawai'i.

From Waimea town you can head up into the mountains, skirting the rim of magnificent Waimea Canyon and climbing higher still until you reach the cool, often-misty forests of Kōke'e State Park. From the vantage point at the top of this gemlike island, 3,200 to 4,200 feet above sea level, you can gaze into the deep verdant valleys of the North Shore and Nāpali Coast. This is where the "real" Kaua'i can still be found: the native plants, insects, and birds that are found nowhere else on Earth.

TOP ATTRACTIONS

Hanapēpē. In the 1980s Hanapēpē was fast becoming a ghost town, its farm-based economy mirroring the decline of agriculture. Today it's a burgeoning art colony, with galleries, craft studios, and a lively art-theme street fair on Friday nights. The main street has a new vibrancy enhanced by the restoration of several historic buildings. The emergence of Kaua'i Coffee as a major West Side crop and expanded activities at

5

SUNSHINE MARKETS

If you want to rub elbows with the locals and purchase fresh produce and flowers at very reasonable prices, head for **Sunshine Markets** (☎ 808/241–4946 ⊕ www.kauai.gov), also known as Kaua'i's farmers' markets. These busy markets are held weekly, usually in the afternoon, at locations all around the island. They're good fun, and they support small, neighborhood farmers. Arrive a little early, bring dollar bills to speed up transactions and plastic shopping bags to carry your produce, and be prepared for some pushy shoppers. Farmers are usually happy to educate visitors about unfamiliar fruits and veggies, especially when the crowd thins.

North Shore Sunshine Markets (✉ Waipa, mauka of Rte. 560 north of Hanalei after mile marker 3 ⊙ Tues. 2 PM ✉ Kīlauea Neighborhood Center, on Keneke St. in Kīlauea ⊙ Thurs. 4:30 PM ✉ Hanalei Community Center ⊙ Sat. 9:30 AM).

East Side Sunshine Markets (✉ Vidinha Stadium, Līhu'e, ½ mi south of airport on Rte. 51 ⊙ Fri. 3 PM ✉ Wailua Homesteads Park, Wailua, turn mauka on Kuamo'o Rd., drive ½ mi, turn right on Rte. 581/Olohena Rd., drive ½ mi ⊙ Tues. 3 PM ✉ Kapa'a, turn mauka on Rte. 581/Olohena Rd for 1 block ⊙ Wed. 3 PM).

South Shore Sunshine Markets ✉ Ballpark, Kōloa, north of intersection of Kōloa Road and Rte. 520 ⊙ Mon. noon.

Port Allen, now the main departure point for tour boats, also gave the town's economy a boost. ✉ Rte. 50.

NEED A BREAK? There's only one place in **Kōke'e State Park** to buy food and hot drinks, and that's the dining room of rustic **Kōke'e Lodge** (✉ Kōke'e State Park, 3600 Kōke'e Rd., mile marker 15 ☎ 808/335–6061 ⊙ No dinner). They're known for their corn bread—of all things. Peruse the gift shop for T-shirts, postcards, or campy Kōke'e memorabilia.

Fodor's Choice ★ Waimea Canyon. Carved over countless centuries by the mighty Waimea River and the forces of wind and rain, this dramatic gorge is aptly nicknamed the "Grand Canyon of the Pacific." Hiking and hunting trails wind through the canyon, which is 3,600 feet deep, 2 mi wide, and 10 mi long. The cliff sides have been sharply eroded, exposing swatches of colorful soil. The deep red, brown, and green hues are constantly changing in the sun, and frequent rainbows and waterfalls enhance the natural beauty. This is one of Kaua'i's prettiest spots, and it's worth stopping at both the **Pu'u ka Pele** and **Pu'u hinahina** lookouts to savor the views. Clean public restrooms and plenty of parking are at both lookouts.

WORTH NOTING

NEED A BREAK? It's not ice cream on Kaua'i if it's not Lappert's. Guava, mac nut, pineapple, mango, coconut, banana—Lappert's is the ice-cream capital of Kaua'i. Warning: Even at the factory store in Hanapēpē, the prices are no bargain. But, hey, you gotta try it. **Lappert's Ice Cream** (✉ On Hwy. 50 mauka, Hanapēpē ☎ 808/335–6121).

One of the most visited sites on Kauai is Waimea Canyon. Make sure to stop at Pu'u ka Pele and Pu'u hinahina lookouts.

Kaua'i Coffee Visitor Center and Museum. Two restored camp houses, dating from the days when sugar was the main agricultural crop on the Islands, have been converted into a museum, visitor center, and gift shop. About 3,400 acres of McBryde sugar land have become Hawai'i's largest coffee plantation. You can walk among the trees, view old grinders and roasters, watch a video to learn how coffee is processed, sample various estate roasts, and check out the gift store. New to the grounds is a self-guided tour through a small coffee grove with informative signage; allow approximately 15 minutes to complete it. From 'Ele'ele, take Highway 50 in the direction of Waimea Canyon and veer right onto Highway 540, west of Kalāheo. The center is 2½ mi from the Highway 50 turnoff. ⊠ *870 Halawili Rd., 'Ele'ele* ☎ *808/335–0813* ⊕ *www.kauaicoffee.com* ⊠ *Free* ☉ *Daily 9–5.*

Kukuiolono Park. Translated as "Light of the God Lono," Kukuiolono has serene Japanese gardens, a display of significant Hawaiian stones, and spectacular panoramic views. This quiet hilltop park is one of Kaua'i's most scenic areas and an ideal picnic spot. There's also a small golf course. ⊠ *Pāpālina Rd., Kalāheo* ☎ *808/332–9151* ⊠ *Free* ☉ *Daily 6:30–6:30.*

Waimea. Most recently Waimea was named to the national "Dozen Distinctive Destinations 2006" list, selected from 93 entries representing 39 states. This serene, pretty town has played a major role in Hawaiian history since 1778, when Captain James Cook became the first European to set foot on the Hawaiian Islands. Waimea was also the place where Kaua'i's King Kaumuali'i acquiesced to King Kamehameha's unification drive in 1810, averting a bloody war. The town hosted the first Christian

KAUA'I SIGHTSEEING TOURS

Aloha Kaua'i Tours. You get *way* off the beaten track on these 4WD van excursions. Choose from several options, including the half-day Backroads Tour covering mostly haulcane roads behind the locked gates of Grove Farm Plantation; and the half-day Rainforest Tour, which follows the Wailua River to its source, Mt. Wai'ale'ale. The expert guides are some of the best on the island. Rates are $70 and $80 for adults, respectively. ⊠ *Check in at Kilohana Plantation on Rte. 50 in Puhi, Līhu'e* ☎ *808/245–6400 or 800/452–1113* ⊕ *www.alohakauaitours.com.*

Hawai'i Movie Tours. Hawai'i Movie Tours' minibuses with in-van TV monitors let you see the actual scenes of films while visiting the real locations used for the filming of *Jurassic Park, Raiders of the Lost Ark, South Pacific, Blue Hawaii, Gilligan's Island,* and other Hollywood hits. The standard coastal tour is $119. We recommend this tour primarily for serious movie buffs. The four-wheel-drive Off Road Tour is $131 and takes you to film locations on private lands and rugged backcountry areas that are otherwise not easily visited. This tour is more suited for younger folk, as many of the sites are recognizable from the multiple *Jurassic Park* filmings on the island. ⊠ *4-885 Kūhiō Hwy., Kapa'a* ☎ *808/822–1192 or 800/628–8432* ⊕ *www.hawaiimovietour.com.*

Plantation Lifestyles Walking Tour. To see a rapidly vanishing lifestyle that once dominated life in Hawai'i, take the fascinating and unique Plantation Lifestyles Walking Tour through the residential area of a real mill camp in Waimea. Reservations are needed for the complimentary two-hour volunteer-led tour that also stops at other historical sites in Waimea and begins at 9:30 every Monday morning at the West Kaua'i Visitor Center. ☎ *808/337–1005*

Roberts Hawai'i Tours. The Wailua River–Waimea Canyon Tour gives a good overview of half the island including, Fort Elisabeth, 'Ōpaeka'a Falls, and Alekoko (Menehune) Fishpond. Guests are transported in air-conditioned, 17-passenger minivans. The $74.50 trip includes a boat ride up the Wailua River to the Fern Grotto, and a visit to the lookouts above Waimea Canyon. ☎ *808/245–9101 or 800/831–5541* ⊕ *www.robertshawaii.com.*

missionaries, who hauled in massive timbers and limestone blocks to build the sturdy Waimea Christian Hawaiian and Foreign Church in 1846. It's one of many lovely historic buildings preserved by residents who take great pride in their heritage and history. The town itself has the look of the Old West and the feel of Old Hawai'i, with a lifestyle that's decidedly laid-back. Waimea beaches are sunny and sandy, but near-shore waters are often murky with runoff from the Waimea River. It's an ideal place for a refreshment break while sightseeing on the West Side. ⊠ *Rte. 50.*

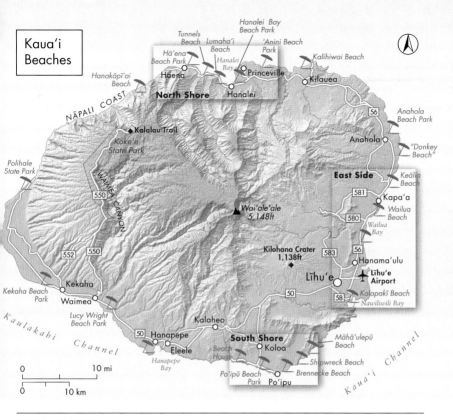

BEACHES

With more sandy beaches per mile of coastline than any other Hawaiian Island, Kaua'i could be nicknamed the Sandy Island just as easily as it's called the Garden Island. Totaling more than 50 mi, Kaua'i's beaches make up 44% of the island's shoreline—almost twice that of O'ahu, second on this list. The reason for this is, of course, Kaua'i's age. As the eldest sibling of the inhabited Hawaiian Islands, Kaua'i has had the most time to allow water and wind erosion to break down rock and coral into sand. But not all Kaua'i's beaches are the same. If you've seen one, you certainly haven't seen them all. Each beach is unique unto itself, for that day, that hour. Conditions, scenery, and intrigue can change throughout the day and certainly throughout the year, transforming, say, a tranquil lakelike ocean setting in summer into monstrous waves drawing internationally ranked surfers from around the world in winter.

There are sandy beaches, rocky beaches, wide beaches, narrow beaches, skinny beaches, and alcoves. Generally speaking, surf kicks up on the North Shore in winter and the South Shore in summer, although summer's southern swells aren't nearly as frequent or big as the northern winter swells that attract world-class surfers. Kaua'i's longest and

Be sure to set aside time to catch a sunset over Napali Coast from Kē'ē Beach on Kauai's North Shore.

widest beaches are found on the North Shore and West Side and are popular with beachgoers, although during winter's rains, everyone heads to the dry West Side. The East Side beaches tend to be narrower and have onshore winds less popular with sunbathers, although fishermen abound. Smaller coves are characteristic of the South Shore and attract all kinds of water lovers year-round, including monk seals.

In Hawai'i, all beaches are public, but their accessibility varies greatly. On Kaua'i, some require an easy ½-mi stroll, some require a four-wheel-drive vehicle, others require boulder-hopping, and one takes an entire day of serious hiking. And then there are those "drive-in" beaches onto which you can literally pull up and park your car. Kaua'i is not Disneyland, so don't expect much signage to help you along the way. One of the top-ranked beaches in all the world—Hanalei—doesn't have a single sign in town directing you to the beach. Furthermore, the majority of Kaua'i's beaches are remote, offering no services. ■ TIP→ If you want the convenience of restrooms, picnic tables, and the like, stick to county beach parks.

THE NORTH SHORE

If you've ever dreamed of Hawai'i—and who hasn't—you've dreamed of Kaua'i's North Shore. *Lush, tropical,* and *abundant* are just a few words to describe this rugged and dramatic area. And the views to the sea aren't the only attraction—the inland views of velvety green valley folds and carved mountain peaks will take your breath away. Rain is the reason for all the greenery on the North Shore, and winter is the rainy season. Not to worry, though; it rarely rains *everywhere* on the

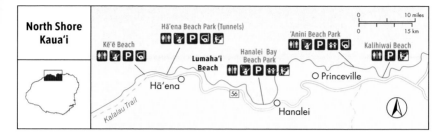

island at one time. ■TIP→The rule of thumb is to head south or west when it rains in the north.

The waves on the North Shore can be big—and we mean huge—in winter, drawing crowds to witness nature's spectacle. By contrast, in summer the waters can be completely serene. The beaches below are listed in order—west to east—from Hanakāpī'ai to Kalihiwai. Try one-stop shopping at Ching Young Village in Hanalei, which has several stores that will fill your trunk with goodies such as snorkel gear, surf and bodyboards, beach chairs, umbrellas, snacks, and coolers.

Kē'ē Beach. Highway 560 on the North Shore literally dead-ends at this beach, which is also the trailhead for the famous Kalalau Trail and the site of an ancient *heiau* dedicated to hula. The beach is protected—except during high surf—by an offshore reef creating a small sandy-bottom lagoon and making it a popular snorkeling destination. If there's a current, it's usually found on the western edge of the beach as the incoming tide ebbs back out to sea. Makana (a prominent peak also known as Bali Hai after the blockbuster musical *South Pacific*) is so artfully arranged, you'll definitely want to capture the memory, so don't forget your camera. The popularity of this beach makes parking difficult. Start extra early or, better yet, arrive at the end of the day, in time to witness otherworldly sunsets sidelighting Nāpali Coast. ⊠*End of Rte. 560, 7 mi west of Hanalei* ☞*Toilets, showers, parking lot.*

★ **Hā'ena Beach Park (Tunnels).** This is a drive-up beach park popular with campers year-round. The wide bay here—named Mākua and commonly known as Tunnels—is bordered by two large reef systems creating quite favorable waves for surfing during peak winter conditions. In July and August this same beach is usually transformed into lakelike conditions, and snorkelers enjoy the variety of fish life found in a hook-shaped reef made up of underwater lava tubes, on the east end of the bay. It's not unusual to find a couple of food vendors parked here selling sandwiches and drinks out of their converted bread vans. ⊠*Near end of Rte. 560, across from lava-tube sea caves, after stream crossing* ☞*Lifeguard, toilets, showers, food concession, picnic tables, grills/firepits, parking lot, camping.*

☺ **Hanalei Bay Beach Park.** This 2-mi, crescent beach surrounds a spacious
★ bay that is quintessential Hawai'i. After gazing out to sea and realizing you have truly arrived in paradise, look landward. The site of the mountains, ribboned with waterfalls, will take your breath away. In winter Hanalei Bay boasts some of the biggest onshore surf breaks in the state,

attracting world-class surfers. Luckily, the beach is wide enough to have safe real estate for your beach towel even in winter. In summer the bay is transformed—calm waters lap the beach, sailboats moor in the bay, and outrigger canoe paddlers ply the sea. Pack the cooler, haul out

WORD OF MOUTH

"One of my fondest memories is of floating in the water at Tunnel's Beach and not knowing which vista to gaze at first."   —turnit_on

the beach umbrellas, and don't forget the beach toys, because Hanalei Bay is definitely worth scheduling for an entire day, maybe two. ⊠ *In Hanalei, turn makai at Aku Rd. and drive 1 block to Weli Weli Rd. Parking areas are on makai side of Weli Weli Rd.* ☞ *Lifeguard, toilets, showers, picnic tables, grills/firepits, parking lot, camping.*

ⓒ   **'Anini Beach Park.** A great family park, 'Anini is unique in that it features one of the longest and widest fringing reefs in all Hawai'i, creating a shallow lagoon that is good for snorkeling and quite safe in all but the highest of winter surf. The reef follows the shoreline for some 2 mi and extends 1,600 feet offshore at its widest point. 'Anini is inarguably the windsurfing mecca on Kaua'i, even for beginners, and it's also attracting the newest athletes of wave riding: kiteboarders. ■ TIP➜ **Try the Sara Special at the lone food vendor here—'Anini Beach Lunch Shak, which is really a lunch wagon.** ⊠ *Turn makai off Rte. 56 onto Kalihiwai Rd., on Hanalei side of Kalihiwai Bridge; follow road left to reach 'Anini Rd. and beach* ☞ *Toilets, showers, food concession, picnic tables, grills/firepits, parking lot, camping.*

Kalihiwai Beach. A winding road leads down a cliff face to this picture-perfect beach. A jewel of the North Shore, Kalihiwai Beach is on par with Hanalei, just without the waterfall-ribbon backdrop. It's another one of those drive-up beaches, so it's very accessible. Most people park on the sand under the grove of ironwood trees. Families set up camp for the day at the west end of the beach, near the stream, where young kids like to splash and older kids like to boogie board. On the eastern edge of the beach, from which the road descends, there's a locals' favorite surf spot during winter's high surf. The onshore break can be dangerous during this time. During the calmer months of summer, Kalihiwai Beach is a good choice for beginning board riders and swimmers. ⊠ *Turn makai off Rte. 56 onto Kalihiwai Rd., on Kīlauea side of Kalihiwai Bridge* ☞ *Toilets, parking lot.*

THE EAST SIDE

The East Side of the island is considered the "windward" side, a term you'll often hear in weather forecasts. It simply means the side of the island receiving onshore winds. The wind helps break down rock into sand, so there are plenty of beaches here. Unfortunately, only a few of those beaches are protected, so many are not ideal for beginning ocean-goers, though they are perfect for long sunrise ambles. On super-windy days, kiteboarders sail along the east shore, sometimes jumping waves and performing acrobatic maneuvers in the air.

BEST SWIMMING SPOTS

You don't have to head to the beach to go swimming, and we're not talking chlorinated swimming pools, either. (There are enough beaches and swimming holes around Kaua'i that you should never have to set foot in chlorine.) But there's a difference between swimming in the ocean at the beach and swimming in these spots. These tend to be more remote, and—as the term *swimming hole* implies, they are enclosed. That doesn't mean they're safer than swimming in the ocean. Never dive—hidden boulders abound. Wear protective footwear—those boulders can have sharp edges. Stay away during or just after heavy rains and high surf—always exercise caution.

Queen's Bath. Listen to us when we tell you not to attempt this in winter. This is one of those places where rogue waves like to roam; unfortunately, so do people. Several have drowned here during North Shore swells, so always check ocean conditions. In summer, this is an experience unlike many others around Kaua'i, as the winter surf recedes, revealing a lava shelf with two good-size holes for swimming—sometimes even snorkeling. Turtles cruise in and out, too, via an underwater entry. The trail down is short but steep; then there's a section of lava rock scrambling before you get to the swimming holes. Access is in tony Princeville, amid private residences, so be sure to park only in the designated spot. ⊠ *In Princeville from Ka Haku Rd., turn makai on Punahele and right on Kapi'olani.*

Keāhua Forestry Arboretum. Not the deepest of swimming holes, this is, however, an excellent choice for families. The cascading stream makes for a fun spot for kids to splash. Stay away during heavy rains, as flash flooding does occur. ⊠ *In Wailua, take Kuamo'o Rd. mauka 6½ mi.*

Kipu Falls. This is a swimming hole extraordinaire. In addition to swimming, the more adventurous will enjoy leaping off the 25-foot waterfall or entering the water via a swinging rope. Just remember to be extremely careful. Although this is on private property, the owners do not seem to mind. A dirt trail approximately ½ mi in length leads to the falls. From Highway 50, at mile marker 3, turn *makai* onto Kipu Road. Take the first right to stay on Kipu Road and drive ½ mi, park on the side of the road, and follow the dirt trail to the falls. *96766*

Uluwehi Falls. If you paddle up the Wailua River for a couple of miles and hike a mile or so inland, you'll discover the 120-foot Uluwehi Falls, more commonly known as Secret Falls, with a big swimming area. Now, you could do this on your own—if you're familiar with the river and the trail; however, we recommend hiring one of the many Wailua River kayak guides, so you don't get lost. *96753*

The beaches below are listed in order from Keālia in the north to Kalapakī in the south. Snorkel and other beach gear is available at Seasport Divers, Snorkel Bob's, and Play Dirty, among others.

Keālia Beach. A half-mile long and adjacent to the highway heading north out of Kapa'a, Keālia Beach attracts body boarders and surfers year-round (possibly because the local high school is just up the hill). Keālia is not generally a great beach for swimming or snorkeling. The waters are usually rough and the waves crumbly because of an onshore

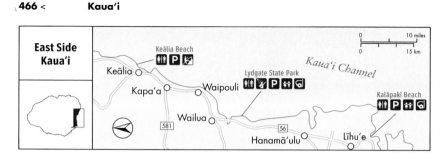

break (no protecting reef) and northeasterly trade winds. A scenic look-out on the southern end, accessed off the highway, is a superb location for saluting the morning sunrise or spotting whales during winter. A level trail follows the coastline north and is one of the most scenic coastal trails on the island for walking, running, and biking. ⊠ *At mile marker 10 on Rte. 56* ↷ *Lifeguard, toilets, parking lot.*

Wailua Beach. Some say the first Polynesians to land in Hawai'i landed at Wailua Beach. True or not, Wailua Beach and the immediate surrounding area is quite historical. The greatest concentration of archaeological remains on Kaua'i are found on the *mauka* side of the highway within the Wailua State Park complex; they are marked with historical signage, making a self-guided tour easy. Surfers, body boarders, and bodysurfers alike enjoy this beach year-round thanks to its dependable waves (usually on the north end); however, thanks to Hawai'i's dependable northeast trade winds, these waves are not the "cleanest" for surf aficionados. Many families spend the day under the Wailua Bridge at the river mouth, even hauling out their portable grills and tables to go with their beach chairs. During summer months, outrigger canoe races are often held on the river, which happens to be the largest in all Hawai'i. Numerous tour outfitters offer kayaking and hiking expeditions up the river. There are even water-skiing boats for hire and, more popular, twice-hourly tour boats running to the Fern Grotto, an amphitheater-shaped cave with perfect acoustics and, as the name implies, ferns growing everywhere, even from the ceiling of the cave. The great news about Wailua Beach is that it's almost impossible to miss; however, parking can be a challenge. ⊠ *Best parking for north end of beach is on Papaloa Rd. behind Shell station. For southern end of beach, best parking is in Wailua River State Park; to get there, turn mauka on Kuamo'o Rd. and left into park, then walk along river and under bridge* ↷ *Toilets, showers, parking lot.*

↺ **Lydgate State Park.** This is hands-down the best family beach park on Kaua'i. The waters off the beach are protected by a hand-built break-water creating two boulder-enclosed saltwater pools for safe swimming and snorkeling just about year-round. The smaller of the two is perfect for keiki. Behind the beach is Kamalani Playground, designed by the children of Kaua'i and built by the community. Children of all ages— that includes you—enjoy the swings, lava-tube slides, tree house, and more. Picnic tables abound in the park, and a large covered pavilion is available by permit for celebrations. Recently, Kamalani Bridge was built, again by the community and again based on the children's design, as a second playground south of the original. (The two are united by a walking path that will someday go all the way to Anahola Beach Park.) ✉ *Just south of Wailua River, turn makai off Rte. 56 onto Lehu Dr. and left onto Nalu Rd.* ☞ *Lifeguard, toilets, showers, picnic tables, grills/firepits, playground, parking lot.*

🐚 **Kalapakī Beach.** Five minutes south of the airport in Līhuʻe, you'll find this wide, sandy-bottom beach fronting the Kauaʻi Marriott. One of the big attractions is that this beach is almost always safe from rip currents and undertow because it's around the backside of a peninsula, in its own cove. There are tons of activities here, including all the usual water sports—beginning and intermediate surfing, body boarding, bodysurfing, and swimming—plus, there are two outrigger canoe clubs paddling in the bay and the Nāwiliwili Yacht Club's boats sailing around the harbor. Kalapakī is the only place on Kauaʻi where sailboats—in this case Hobie Cats—are available for rent (at Kauaʻi Beach Boys, which fronts the beach next to Duke's Canoe Club restaurant). Visitors can also rent snorkel gear, surfboards, body boards, and kayaks from Kauaʻi Beach Boys. A volleyball court on the beach is often used by a loosely organized group of local players; visitors are always welcome. ■ TIP➔ Families prefer the stream end of the beach, whereas those seeking more solitude will prefer the cliff side of the beach. Duke's Canoe Club restaurant is one of only a couple of restaurants on the island actually on a beach; the restaurant's lower level is casual, even welcoming beach attire and sandy feet, perfect for lunch or an afternoon cocktail. ✉ *Off Wapaʻa Rd., which runs from Līhuʻe to Nāwiliwili* ☞ *Toilets, food concession, picnic tables, grills/firepits, playground, parking lot.*

THE SOUTH SHORE

The South Shore's primary access road is Highway 520, a tree-lined, two-lane, windy road. As you drive along it, there's a sense of tunneling down a rabbit hole into another world, à la Alice. And the South Shore is certainly a wonderland. On average, it rains only 30 inches per year, so if you're looking for fun in the sun, this is a good place to start. The beaches with their powdery-fine sand are consistently good year-round, except during high surf, which, if it hits at all, will be in summer. If you want solitude, this isn't it; if you want excitement—this is the place for you.

The beaches are listed from Keoniloa west to Waiʻohai.

Keoniloa Beach (Shipwreck Beach). Few—except the public relations specialists at the Hyatt Regency Kauai Resort and Spa, which backs the beach—refer to this beach by anything other than its common name: Shipwreck Beach. Its Hawaiian name means "long beach." Both give it meaning. It is a long stretch of crescent beach punctuated by cliffs on both ends—and, yes, a ship once wrecked here. With its onshore break, the waters off Shipwreck are best for body boarding and bodysurfing; however, the beach itself is plenty big for sunbathing, sand castle–building, Frisbee, and other beach-related fun. Fishermen pole fish from shore and off the cliff and sometimes pick opihi (limpets) off

the rocks lining the foot of the cliffs. The eastern edge of the beach is the start of an interpretive dune walk (complimentary) held by the hotel staff every other Monday; check with the concierge for dates and times. ⊠ *Continue on Po'ipū Rd. past Hyatt Regency, turn makai on 'Ainako Rd.* ☞ *Parking lot.*

Brennecke Beach. There's little beach here on the eastern end of Po'ipū Beach Park, but Brennecke Beach is synonymous on the island with board- and bodysurfing, thanks to its shallow sandbar and reliable shore break. Because the beach is small and often congested, surfboards are prohibited near shore. The water on the rocky eastern edge of the beach is a good place to see the endangered green sea turtles noshing on plants growing on the rocks. ⊠ *Turn makai off Po'ipū Rd. onto Ho'owili Rd., then left onto Ho'ōne Rd.; beach is at intersection with Kuai Rd.* ☞ *Food concession, parking lot.*

🕭
Fodor'sChoice
★

Po'ipū Beach Park. The most popular beach on the South Shore, and perhaps on all of Kaua'i, is Po'ipū Beach Park. The snorkeling's good, the body boarding's good, the surfing's good, the swimming's good, and the fact that the sun is almost always shining is good, too. The beach can be crowded at times, especially on weekends and holidays, but that just makes people-watching that much more fun. You'll see keiki experiencing the ocean for the first time, snorkelers trying to walk with their flippers on, 'ukulele players, birthday party revelers, young and old, visitors and locals. Even the endangered Hawaiian monk seal may make an appearance. ⊠ *From Po'ipū Rd., turn right on Ho'ōne Rd.* ☞ *Lifeguard, toilets, showers, food, picnic tables, grills/firepits, playground, parking lot.*

Wai'ohai Beach. The first hotel built in Po'ipū in 1962 overlooked this beach, adjacent to Po'ipū Beach Park. Actually, there's little to distinguish where one starts and the other begins other than a crescent reef at the eastern end of Wai'ohai Beach. That crescent, however, is important. It creates a small, protected bay—good for snorkeling and beginning surfers. If you're a beginner, this is the spot. Don't forget: we always recommend lessons for beginners. Stop in Nukumoi Surf Shop next to Brennecke's Restaurant if you don't see any instructors lurking around the beach. However, when a summer swell kicks up, the near-shore conditions become dangerous; offshore, there's a splendid surf break for experienced surfers. The beach itself is narrow and, like its neighbor, gets very crowded in summer. ⊠ *From Po'ipū Rd., turn right on Ho'ōne Rd.* ☞ *Parking lot.*

CLOSE UP

Seal Spotting on the South Shore

When strolling on one of Kaua'i's lovely beaches, don't be surprised if you find yourself in the rare company of Hawaiian monk seals. These are among the most endangered of all marine mammals, with perhaps fewer than 1,500 remaining. They primarily inhabit the northwestern Hawaiian islands, although more are showing their sweet faces on the main Hawaiian islands, especially on Kaua'i. They're fond of hauling out on the beach for a long snooze in the sun, especially after a night of gorging themselves on fish. They need this time to rest and digest, safe from predators.

During the past several summers, female seals have birthed young in the calm waters of Kaua'i's Po'ipū Beach, where they have stayed to nurse their pups for up to six weeks. It seems the seals enjoy this particular beach for the same reasons we do: it's shallow and partially protected.

If you're lucky enough to see a monk seal, keep your distance and let it be. Although they may haul out near people, they still want and need their space. Stay several hundred feet away, and forget photos unless you've got a zoom lens. It's illegal to do anything that causes a monk seal to change its behavior, with penalties that include big fines and even jail time. In the water, seals may appear to want to play. It's their curious nature. Don't try to play with them. They are wild animals—mammals, in fact, with teeth. If you have concerns about the health or safety of a seal, or just want more information, contact the **Kaua'i Monk Seal Watch Program** (☎ *808/246–2860* ⊕ *www.kauaimonkseal.com*).

5

Beach House Beach. Don't pack the beach umbrella, beach mats, and cooler for this one. Just your snorkel gear. The beach, named after its neighbor the Beach House restaurant and on the road to Spouting Horn, is a small slip of sand during low tide and a rocky shoreline during high; however, it is conveniently located by the road's edge, and its rocky coastline and somewhat rocky bottom make it great for snorkeling. (As a rule, sandy-bottom beaches are not great for snorkeling. The rocks create safe hiding places and grow the food that fish and other marine life like to eat.) A sidewalk along the coastline on the restaurant side of the beach makes a great vantage point from which to peer into the water and look for the Hawaiian green sea turtle. It's also a gathering spot to watch the sun set. ■TIP➔**Make reservations for dinner at the Beach House days in advance and time it around sunset.** ⊠ *From Po'ipū Rd., turn onto Lāwa'i Rd; park on street near restaurant or in public parking lot across from beach* ⚲ *Toilets, showers, food, parking lot.*

THE WEST SIDE

Whereas Kaua'i's North Shore is characterized by the color green, the West Side's coloring is red. When you look more closely, you'll see that the red is dirt, which happens to have high iron content. With little vegetation on the West Side, the red dirt is everywhere—in the air, in a thin layer on the car, even in the river. In fact, the only river on the

West Side is named Waimea, which means "reddish water." The West Side of the island receives hardly enough rainfall year-round to water a cactus, and because it's also the leeward side, there are hardly any tropical breezes. That translates to sunny and hot with long, languorous, and practically deserted beaches. You'd think the leeward waters—untouched by wind—would be calm, but there's no offshore reef system, so the waters are not as inviting as one would like.

Salt Pond Beach Park. A great family spot, Salt Pond Beach Park features a naturally made, shallow swimming pond behind a curling finger of rock where keiki splash and snorkel. This pool is generally safe except during a large south swell, which usually occurs in summer, if at all. The center and western edge of the beach is popular with body boarders and bodysurfers. On a cultural note, the flat stretch of land to the east of the beach is the last spot in Hawai'i where ponds are used to harvest salt in the dry heat of summer. The beach park is popular with locals and can get crowded on weekends and holidays. ✉*From Rte. 50 in Hanapēpē, turn makai onto Lele Rd., Rte. 543* ☞*Lifeguard, toilets, showers, picnic tables, grills/firepits, parking lot, camping.*

Lucy Wright Beach Park. Named in honor of the first native Hawaiian schoolteacher, this beach is on the western banks of the Waimea River. It is also where Captain James Cook first came ashore in the Hawaiian Islands in 1778. If that's not interesting enough, the sand here is not the white, powdery kind you see along the South Shore. It's not even sandy like that on the East Side. It's a combination of pulverized, black lava rock and lighter-color reef. In a way, it looks like a mix of salt and pepper. Unfortunately, the intrigue of the beach doesn't extend to the waters, which are murky—thanks to river runoff—and choppy—thanks to an onshore break. So, it's not the best for water activities. The remains from the Waimea State Recreation Pier, built in 1864, are a popular pole-fishing location. ✉*From Rte. 50 in Waimea, turn makai on Moana Rd.* ☞*Toilets, picnic tables, parking lot.*

Fodor'sChoice **Polihale State Park.** The longest stretch of beach in Hawai'i starts in
★ Kekaha and ends about 15 mi away at the start of Nāpali Coast. At the Nāpali end of the beach is the 5-mi-long, 140-acre Polihale State Park. In addition to being long, this beach is 300 feet wide in places and backed by sand dunes 50 to 100 feet tall. Polihale is a remote beach accessed via a 5-mi haul cane road (four-wheel drive preferred but not required) at the end of Route 50 in Kekaha. ■TIP➔ Be sure to start the day with a full tank of gas and a cooler filled with food and drink. Many locals wheel their four-wheel-drive vehicles up and over the sand dunes right onto the beach, but don't try this in a rental car. You're sure to get stuck and found in violation of your rental car agreement.

On days of high surf, only experts surf the waves. In general, the water here is extremely rough and not recommended for recreation; however, there's one small fringing reef, called Queen's Pond, where swimming is usually safe. Neighboring Polihale Beach is the Pacific Missile Range Facility (PMRF), operated by the U.S. Navy. Since September 11, 2001, access to the beaches fronting PMRF is restricted. ✉*Drive to end of Rte. 50 and continue on dirt road; several access points along way* ☞*Toilets, showers, picnic tables, grills/firepits, parking lot, camping.*

WATER SPORTS AND TOURS

BOAT TOURS

Fodor'sChoice
★

Deciding to see Nāpali Coast by boat is the easy decision. Choosing the outfitter to go with is the tough decision. There are numerous boat tour operators to choose from, and, quite frankly, they all do a good job. Before you even think about this company or that, answer these three questions: What kind of boat? Where am I staying? Morning or afternoon? Once you settle on these three, you can easily zero in on the tour outfitter.

First, the boat. The most important thing is to match you and your group's personality with the personality of the boat. If you like thrills and adventure, the rubber, inflatable rafts—often called Zodiacs, which Jacques Cousteau made famous and which the U.S. Coast Guard uses—will entice you. They're fast, sure to leave you drenched, and can get quite bouncy. If you prefer a smoother, more leisurely ride, then the large catamarans are the way to go. The next boat choice is size. Both the rafts and catamarans come in small and large. Again, think smaller: more adventurous; larger: more leisurely. ■ TIP→ Do not choose a smaller boat because you think there will be fewer people. There might be fewer people, but you'll be jammed together sitting atop strangers. If you prefer privacy over socializing, go with a larger boat, so you can have more room to spread out. One advantage to smaller boats, however, is that—depending on ocean conditions—some may slip into a sea cave or two. If that sounds interesting to you, call the outfitter and ask their policy on entering sea caves. Some won't no matter the conditions, because they consider the caves sacred or because they don't want to cause any environmental damage.

There are three points where boats leave from around the island (Hanalei, Port Allen, and Waimea), and all head to the same spot: Nāpali Coast. Here's the inside skinny on which is the best—because they'll all say they're the best. It's really pretty easy. If you're staying on the North Shore, choose to depart out of the North Shore. If you're staying anywhere else, depart out of the West Side. It's that easy. Sure, the North Shore is closer to Nāpali Coast, but you'll pay more for less overall time. The West Side boat operators may spend more time getting to Nāpali Coast, but they'll spend about the same amount of time along Nāpali, plus you'll pay less. Finally, you'll also have to decide whether you want to go on the morning tour, which includes a deli lunch and a stop for snorkeling, or the afternoon tour, which does not stop to snorkel but does include a sunset over the ocean. The 5½-hour morning tour with snorkeling is more popular with families and those who love dolphins. You don't have to be an expert snorkeler or even have any prior experience, but if it is your first time, note that although there will be some snorkeling instruction, there might not be much. Hawaiian spinner dolphins are so prolific in the mornings that some tour companies guarantee you'll see them, although you can't get in the water and swim with them. The 3½-hour afternoon tour is more popular with nonsnorklers—obviously—and photographers interested in capturing the setting sunlight on the coast.

5

CATAMARAN TOURS

Fodor's Choice
★

Blue Dolphin Charters. This company operates 63-foot and 65-foot sailing (rarely raised and always motoring) catamarans designed with three decks of spacious seating with great visibility. ■ TIP➜ **The lower deck is best for shade seekers.** Upgrades from snorkeling to scuba diving—no need for certification—are available and run $35, but the diving is really best for beginners or people who need a refresher course. On Tuesday and Friday a tour of Nāpali Coast includes a detour across the channel to Ni'ihau for snorkeling and diving. Blue Dolphin likes to say they have the best mai tais "off the island," and truth is, they probably do. Morning snorkel tours of Nāpali include a deli lunch, and afternoon sunset sightseeing tours include a meal of kalua pork, teriyaki chicken, Caesar salad, and chocolate-chip cookies. Prices for adults range from $129 to $175. Two-hour whale-watching/sunset tours offered during winter, run $50. ⊠*In Port Allen Marina Center. Turn makai onto Rte. 541 off Rte. 50, at 'Ele'ele.* ☎*808/335–5553 or 877/511–1311* ⊕*www.kauaiboats.com.*

Fodor's Choice
★

Capt. Andy's Sailing Adventures. Departing from Port Allen and running two 55-foot sailing catamarans, Capt. Andy's runs the same five-hour snorkeling and four-hour sunset tours along Nāpali Coast as everyone else, though we're not crazy about the boat's layout, which has most of the seating inside the cabin. What they do that no one else does is embark out of Kukui'ula Harbor in Po'ipū for a two-hour sunset sail along the South Shore—with live Hawaiian music—every Wednesday, Friday, and Sunday evening. ■ TIP➜ **If the winds and swells are up on the North Shore, this is usually a good choice—especially if you're prone to seasickness.** Note: If you have reservations for the shorter tour, you will check in at their Kukui'ula Harbor office. Prices for adults range from $105 to $139. ⊠*In Port Allen Marina Center. Turn makai onto Rte. 541 off Rte. 50 at 'Ele'ele* ☎*808/335–6833 or 800/535–0830* ⊕*www.napali.com.*

Captain Sundown. If you're staying on the North Shore, it's really pretty simple. Captain Sundown is the choice. Get this: Captain Bob has been cruising Nāpali Coast for 35 years—six days a week, sometimes twice a day. (And right alongside Captain Bob is his son Captain Larry.) To say he knows the area is a bit of an understatement. Here's the other good thing about this tour: they take only 15 passengers. Now, you'll definitely pay more, but it's worth it. You don't check in too early—around 8 AM—and there's no rushing down the coastline. The morning snorkeling cruise is a leisurely six hours. The views of the waterfall-laced mountains behind Hanalei and Haena start immediately—themselves breathtaking—but then it's around Ke'e Beach and the magic of Nāpali Coast. All the while, the captains are trolling for fish, and if they catch any, guests get to reel 'em in. Afternoon sunset sails (seasonal) run three hours and check in around 3 PM. BYOB. Prices range from $138 to $162. ⊠*Meet in Hanalei at Tahiti Nui parking lot* ☎*808/826–5585* ⊕*www.captainsundown.com.*

Catamaran Kahanu. This Hawaiian-owned-and-operated company has been in business since 1985 and runs a 40-foot power catamaran with 18-passenger seating. Their five-hour tour includes snorkeling at

Get out on the water and see the Napali Coast in style on a luxe cruising yacht.

Nuʻalolo Kai. The boat is smaller than most and may feel a tad crowded, but the tour feels more personal, with a laid-back, ʻohana style. Salt water runs through the veins of this father-and-son team—Captains Lani and Kamua. Guests can learn the ancient cultural practice of weaving on board. There's no alcohol allowed. Price: $135. ⊠ From Rte. 50, turn left on Rte. 541 at ʻEleʻele, proceed just past Port Allen Marina Center, turn right at sign; check-in booth on left ☎808/645–6176 or 888/213–7711 ⊕www.catamarankahanu.com.

HoloHolo Charters. Choose between a 50-foot sailing (wind contingent and always motoring) catamaran trip to Nāpali Coast, and a 65-foot powered catamaran trip to the island of Niʻihau. Both boats have large cabins and little outside seating. Originators of the Niʻihau tour, HoloHolo Charters built their 65-foot powered catamaran with a wide beam to reduce side-to-side motion, and twin 425 HP turbo diesel engines specifically for the 17-mi channel crossing to Niʻihau. ■TIP→ They're the only outfitter running daily Niʻihau tours. Prices range from $99 to $179. ⊠ Check in at Port Allen Marina Center. Turn makai onto Rte. 541 off Rte. 50, at ʻEleʻele ☎808/335–0815 or 800/848–6130 ⊕www.holoholocharters.com.

RIVER BOAT TOURS TO FERN GROTTO

This 2-mi, upriver trip culminates at a yawning lava tube that is covered with enormous fishtail ferns. During the boat ride, guitar and ʻukulele players regale you with Hawaiian melodies and tell the history of the river. It's a kitschy bit of Hawaiiana, worth the little money ($20) and short time required. Flat-bottom, 150-passenger riverboats (that rarely fill up) depart from Wailua Marina at the mouth of the Wailua River.

■ TIP→ It's extremely rare, but occasionally after heavy rains the tour doesn't leave from the grotto; if you're traveling in winter, ask beforehand. Round-trip excursions take 1½ hours, including time to walk around the grotto and environs. Tours run every half hour from 9 to 3 daily. Reservations are not required. Contact **Smith's Motor Boat Services** (☎808/821–6892 ⊕*www.smithskauai.com* 96753) for more information.

ZODIAC TOURS

Captain Andy's Rafting Expeditions. This outfit used to be known as Captain Zodiac and first started running Nāpali in 1974. Departing out of Port Allen, this tour is much like the other raft tours—offering both snorkeling and beach landing excursions. Their rafts are on the smaller side—24 feet with a maximum of 15 passengers—and all seating is on the rubber hulls, so hang on. They operate three different rafts, so there's a good chance of availability. Price is $139, including snorkeling at Nu'alolo Kai. ⊠*In Port Allen Marina Center. Turn makai onto Rte. 541 off Rte. 50 at 'Ele'ele* ☎808/335–6833 *or 800/535–0830* ⊕*www.napali.com.*

Fodor's Choice ★ **Nāpali Explorer.** Owned by a couple of women, these tours operate out of two locations: Waimea, a tad closer to Nāpali Coast than most of the West Side catamaran tours, and, after numerous years away, now back in Hanalei again. Departing out of the West Side, the company runs two different sizes of inflatable rubber rafts: a 48-foot, 40-passenger craft with an onboard toilet, freshwater shower, shade canopy, and seating in the stern (which is surprisingly smooth and comfortable) and bow (which is where the fun is); and a 26-foot, 18-passenger craft for the all-out fun and thrills of a white-knuckle ride in the bow. Departing out of Hanalei, the *Ocean Adventurer* is a 38-foot, 28-passenger rigid-hull inflatable. The tours stop at various snorkel spots; in summer the smaller vessel ties up onshore at Nu'alolo Kai for a tour of the ancient fishing village. Rates range from $95 to $135, and charters are available. ⊠*Follow Rte. 50 west to Waimea; office mauka after crossing river. In Hanalei, meet at river mouth, at end of Weke Rd., Waimea and Hanalei* ☎808/338–9999 *or 877/335–9909* ⊕*www.napali-explorer.com.*

Fodor's Choice ★ **Z-Tourz.** What we like about Z-Tourz is that they are the only boat company to make snorkeling their priority. As such, they focus on the South Shore's abundant offshore reefs, stopping at two locations. If you want to see Nāpali, this boat is not for you; if you want to snorkel with the myriad of Hawai'i's tropical reef fish and turtles (pretty much guaranteed), it is. They run two three-hour tours daily on a 26-foot rigid-hull inflatable (think Zodiac) with a maximum of 16 passengers. Rate is $94. Check in at the company's Koloa office and they will take you to the boat by van. ⊠*3417 E. Po'ipū Rd. in Koloa* ☎808/742–7422 *or 888/998–6879* ⊕*www.ztourz.com.*

BOOGIE BOARDING AND BODYSURFING

The most natural form of wave riding is bodysurfing, a popular sport on Kaua'i because there are many shore breaks around the island. Wave riders of this style stand waist deep in the water, facing shore, and swim madly as a wave picks them up and breaks. It's great fun and requires no special skills and absolutely no equipment other than a swimsuit. The next step up is boogie boarding, also called body boarding. In this case, wave riders lie with their upper body on a foam board about half the length of a traditional surfboard and kick as the wave propels them toward shore. Again, this is easy to pick up, and there are many places around Kaua'i to practice. The locals wear short-finned flippers to help them catch waves, although they are not necessary for and even hamper beginners. It's worth spending a few minutes watching these experts as they spin, twirl, and flip—that's right—while they slip down the face of the wave. Of course, all beach safety precautions apply, and just because you see wave riders of any kind in the water doesn't mean it's safe. Any snorkeling gear outfitter also rents body boards.

BEST SPOTS

Some of our favorite bodysurfing and body boarding beaches are **Brennecke, Wailua, Keālia, Kalihiwai,** and **Hanalei.** *For directions, see Beaches, earlier in this chapter.*

DEEP-SEA FISHING

Simply step aboard and cast your line for mahimahi, 'ahi, ono, and marlin. That's about how soon the fishing—mostly trolling with lures—begins on Kaua'i. The water gets deep quickly here, so there's less cruising time to fishing grounds. Of course, your captain may elect to cruise to a hot location where he's had good luck lately.

There are oodles of charter fishermen around; most depart from Nāwiliwili Harbor in Līhu'e, and most use lures instead of live bait. Inquire about each boat's "fish policy," that is, what happens to the fish if any are caught. Some boats keep all; others will give you enough for a meal or two. On shared charters, ask about the maximum passenger count and about the fishing rotation; you'll want to make sure everyone gets a fair shot at reeling in the big one. Another option is to book a private charter. Shared and private charters run four, six, and eight hours in length.

BOATS AND CHARTERS

Captain Don's Sport Fishing & Ocean Adventure. Captain Don is flexible—he'll stop to snorkel or whale-watch if that's what the group (four to six) wants. Saltwater fly-fishermen (bring your own gear) are welcome. He'll even fish for bait and let you keep part of whatever you catch. The *June Louise* is a 34-foot twin diesel. Half-day rates start at $135 for shared, $575 for private charters. ⊠ *Nāwiliwili Harbor 96766* ☎ *808/639–3012* ⊕ *www.captaindonsfishing.com.*

Hana Pa'a. The advantage with Hana Pa'a is that they take fewer people (minimum two, maximum six), but you pay for it. Rates start at $325 for shared, $600 for private charters. Their fish policy is flexible and their boat is roomy. The *Maka Hou II* is a 38-foot Bertram. ⊠ *Nāwiliwili Harbor 96766* ☎ *808/823–6031 or 866/776–3474* ⊕ *www.fishkauai.com.*

Explore Kaua'i Sportfishing. If you're staying on the West Side, you'll be glad to know that Nāpali Explorer (of the longtime rafting tour business) is now running fishing trips out of Port Allen under the name Explore Kaua'i Sportfishing. They offer shared and exclusive charters of four, six, and eight hours in a 41-foot Concord called *Happy Times.* Their shared tours max out at six fishermen, and a portion of the catch is shared with all. They also use this boat for specialty charters—that is, film crews, surveys, burials, and even Ni'ihau fishing. Rates start at $145 per person. ☒ *Check in at Port Allen Small Boat Harbor* ☎ *808/338–9999 or 877/335–9909* ⊕ *www.napali-explorer.com.*

KAYAKING

★ Kaua'i is the only Hawaiian island with navigable rivers. As the oldest inhabited island in the chain, Kaua'i has had more time for wind and water erosion to deepen and widen cracks into streams and streams into rivers. Because this is a small island, the rivers aren't long, and there are no rapids; that makes them perfectly safe for kayakers of all levels, even beginners.

For more advanced paddlers, there aren't many places in the world more beautiful for sea kayaking than Nāpali Coast. If this is your draw to Kaua'i, plan your vacation for the summer months, when the seas are at their calmest. ■ TIP➔ **Tour and kayak-rental reservations are recommended at least two weeks in advance during peak summer and holiday seasons.** In general, tours and rentals are available year-round, Monday through Saturday. Pack a swimsuit, sunscreen, a hat, bug repellent, water shoes (sport sandals, aqua socks, old tennis shoes), and motion sickness medication if you're planning on sea kayaking.

RIVER KAYAKING

Tour outfitters operate on the Hulē'ia, Wailua, and Hanalei rivers with guided tours that combine hiking to waterfalls, as in the case of the first two, and snorkeling, as is the case of the third. Another option is renting kayaks and heading out on your own. Each has its advantages and disadvantages, but it boils down as follows:

If you want to swim at the base of a remote 100-foot waterfall, sign up for a five-hour kayak (4 mi round-trip) and hiking (2 mi round-trip) tour of the **Wailua River.** It includes a dramatic waterfall that is best accessed with the aid of a guide, so you don't get lost. ■ TIP➔ **Remember—it's dangerous to swim under waterfalls no matter how good a water massage may sound. Rocks and logs are known to plunge down, especially after heavy rains.**

If you want to kayak on your own, choose the **Hanalei River.** It's most scenic from the kayak itself—there are no trails to hike to hidden waterfalls. And better yet, a rental company is right on the river—no hauling kayaks on top of your car.

If you're not sure of your kayaking abilities, head to the **Hulē'ia River;** 3½-hour tours include easy paddling upriver, a nature walk through a rain forest with a cascading waterfall, a rope swing for playing Tarzan and Jane, and a ride back downriver—into the wind—on a motorized, double-hull canoe.

As for the kayaks themselves, most companies use the two-person sit-on-top style that is quite buoyant—no Eskimo rolls required. The only possible danger comes in the form of communication. The kayaks seat two people, which means you can share the work (good) with a spouse, child, parent, friend, or guide (the potential danger part). On the river, the two-person kayaks are known as "divorce boats." Counseling is not included in the tour price.

SEA KAYAKING

In its second year and second issue, *National Geographic Adventure* ranked kayaking Nāpali Coast second on its list of America's Best 100 Adventures, right behind rafting the Colorado River through the Grand Canyon. That pretty much says it all. It's the adventure of a lifetime in one day, involving eight hours of paddling. Although it's good to have some kayaking experience, feel comfortable on the water, and be reasonably fit, it doesn't require the preparation, stamina, or fortitude of, say, climbing Mt. Everest. Tours run May through September, ocean conditions permitting. In the winter months sea-kayaking tours operate on the South Shore—beautiful, but not Nāpali.

EQUIPMENT AND TOURS

Kayak Kaua'i. Based in Hanalei, this company offers guided tours on the Hanalei and Wailua rivers, and along Nāpali Coast. They have a great shop right on the Hanalei River for kayak rentals and camping gear. The guided Hanalei River Kayak and Snorkel Tour starts at the shop and heads downriver, so there's not much to see of the scenic river valley. (For that, rent a kayak on your own.) Instead, this three-hour tour paddles down to the river mouth, where the river meets the sea. Then, it's a short paddle around a point to snorkel at either Pu'u Poa Beach or, ocean conditions permitting, a bit farther at Hideaways Beach. This is a great choice if you want to try your paddle at a bit of ocean kayaking.

A second location in Kapa'a is the base for Wailua River guided tours and kayak rentals. It's not right on the river, however, so shuttling is involved. For rentals, the company provides the hauling gear necessary for your rental car. Guided tours range from $60 for the Hanalei River to $205 for the Nāpali Coast. Kayak rentals range from $29 for a single to $75 for a triple. ⊠*Hanalei: 1 mi past Hanalei bridge, on makai side* ⊠*Kapa'a: south end of Coconut Marketplace* ☎*808/826–9844 or 800/437–3507.*

Kayak Wailua. We can't quite figure out how this family-run business offers pretty much the same Wailua River kayaking tour as everyone else—except for lunch and beverages, which are BYO—for half the price, but they do. They say it's because they don't discount and don't offer commission to activities and concierge desks. Their 4½-hour kayak, hike, and waterfall swim costs $39.95, and their 3-hour kayak-to-a-swimming-hole costs $34.95. We say fork over the extra $5 for the longer tour and hike to the beautiful 150-foot Secret Falls. ⊠*In Wailua next to Wailua Shell Food Mart* ☎*808/822–3388* ⊕*www.kayakwailua.com.*

Nāpali Kayak. A couple of longtime guides for Kayak Kaua'i ventured out on their own a few years back to create this company that focuses solely on sea kayaking—Nāpali Coast in summer, as the name implies, and the South Shore in winter (during peak times only). These guys are highly experienced and still highly enthusiastic about their livelihood. So much so, that REI Adventures hired them to run their multiday, multisport tours. Now, that's a feather in their cap, we'd say. Prices start at $200. You can also rent kayaks; price range from $30 to $70. ⊠ *5-5075 Kūhiō Hwy., next to Postcards Café* 🕾 *808/826–6900 or 866/977–6900* ⊕ *www.napalikayak.com.*

↻ **Outfitters Kaua'i.** This well-established tour outfitter operates year-round river-kayak tours on the Hulē'ia and Wailua rivers, as well as sea-kayaking tours along Nāpali Coast in summer and the South Side in winter. Outfitters Kaua'i's specialty, however, is the **Kipu Safari.** This all-day adventure starts with kayaking up the Hulē'ia River and includes a rope swing over a swimming hole, a wagon ride through a working cattle ranch, a picnic lunch by a private waterfall, hiking, and a "zip" across the river (strap on a harness, clip into a cable, and zip across the river). It ends with a ride on a motorized double-hull canoe. It's a great tour for the family, because no one ever gets bored. The Kipu Safari costs $175; other guided tours range from $98 to $175. ⊠ *2827-A Po'ipū Rd., Po'ipū* 🕾 *808/742–9667 or 888/742–9886* ⊕ *www.outfitterskauai.com.*

Wailua Kayak & Canoe. This is the only purveyor of kayak rentals on the Wailua River, which means no hauling your kayak on top of your car (a definite plus). Rates are $45 for a single; $75 for a double. ⊠ *Across from Wailua Beach, turn mauka at Kuamo'o Rd. and take first left, 169 Wailua Rd., Kapa'a* 🕾 *808/821–1188.*

KITEBOARDING

Several years ago, the latest wave-riding craze to hit the islands was kiteboarding, and the sport is still going strong. As the name implies, there's a kite and a board involved. The board you strap on your feet; the kite is attached to a harness around your waist. Steering is accomplished with a rod that's attached to the harness and the kite. Depending on conditions and the desires of the kiteboarder, the kite is played out some 30 to 100 feet in the air. The result is a cross between waterskiing—without the boat—and windsurfing. Speeds are fast and aerobatic maneuvers are involved. Unfortunately, neither lessons nor rental gear are available for the sport on Kaua'i (Maui is a better bet), so if you aren't a seasoned kiteboarder already you'll have to be content with watching the pros—who can put on a pretty spectacular show. The most popular year-round spots for kiteboarding are **Kapa'a Beach Park** and **'Anini Beach Park.**

■ TIP➔ Many visitors come to Kaua'i dreaming of parasailing. If that's you, make a stop at Maui or the Big Island. There's no parasailing on Kaua'i.

SCUBA DIVING

The majority of scuba diving on Kaua'i occurs on the South Side. Boat and shore dives are available, although boat sites surpass the shore sites for a couple of reasons. First, they're deeper and exhibit the complete symbiotic relationship of a reef system, and second, the visibility is better a little farther offshore.

The dive operators below offer a full range of services, including certification dives, referral dives, boat dives, shore dives, night dives, and drift dives. ■TIP➔As for certification, we recommend completing your confined-water training and classroom testing before arriving on the island. That way, you'll spend less time training and more time diving.

BEST SPOTS

The best and safest scuba-diving sites are accessed by boat on the South Shore of the island, right off the shores of Po'ipū. The captain selects the actual site based on ocean conditions of the day. Beginners may prefer shore dives, which are best at **Kōloa Landing** on the South Shore year-round and **Mākua (Tunnels) Beach** on the North Shore in the calm summer months. Keep in mind, though, that you'll have to haul your gear a ways down the beach.

For the advanced diver, the island of Ni'ihau—across an open ocean channel in deep and crystal-clear waters—beckons and rewards, usually with some big fish. Seasport Divers, Fathom Five, and Bubbles Below venture the 17 mi across the channel in summer when the crossing is smoothest. Divers can expect deep dives, walls, and strong currents at Ni'ihau, where conditions can change rapidly. To make the long journey worthwhile, three dives and Nitrox are included.

EQUIPMENT, LESSONS AND TOURS

Bubbles Below. Marine ecology is the emphasis here aboard the 36-foot Kai Manu custom-built Radon. This company discovered some pristine dive sites on the West Side of the island where white-tip reef sharks are common—and other divers are not. Thanks to the addition of a 32-foot powered catamaran—the six-passenger *Dive Rocket*—they also run Ni'ihau, Nāpali, and North Shore dives year-round (depending on ocean conditions, of course). A bonus on these tours is the Grinds pizza served between dives. Open-water certification dives, check-out dives, and intro shore dives are available upon request. There's a charge of $120 for a standard two-tank boat dive and up to $25 extra for rental gear. ⊠*Port Allen Small Boat Harbor; turn makai onto Rte. 541 from Rte. 50 in 'Ele'ele* ☎*808/332–7333 or 866/524–6268* ⊕*www.bubbles belowkauai.com.*

Sacred Seas Scuba. This company specializes in shore diving only, typically at Kōloa Landing (year-round) and Tunnels (summers). They're not only geared toward beginning divers—for whom they provide a very thorough and gentle certification program as well as the Discover Scuba program—but also offer night dives and scooter (think James Bond) dives. Certified divers can participate in turtle surveys for the National Marine Fisheries. Their main emphasis is a detailed review of marine biology, such as pointing out rare dragon eel and harlequin shrimp tucked away in pockets of coral. ■TIP➔ Hands down, we recommend Sacred Seas Scuba for beginners, certification, and refresher dives. One reason is that their instructor-to-student ratio never exceeds 1:4—that's true of all their dive groups. Rates, which include gear rental for certified divers, are $79 for a one-tank dive and $119 for a two-tank dive. Beginners can get certified for $450. ⊠*2440 Ho'onani Rd., Suite 7, Koloa* ☎*808/635–7327 or 877/441–3483* ⊕*www.sacredseasscuba.com.*

Seasport Divers. Rated highly by readers of *Scuba Diving* magazine, Seasport Divers' 48-foot *Anela Kai* tops the chart for dive boat luxury. But owner Marvin Otsuji didn't stop with that. In 2006, he added a second boat—a 34-foot catamaran—that's outfitted for diving, but we like it as an all-around charter. The company does a brisk business, which means they won't cancel at the last minute because of a lack of reservations, like some other companies, and although they may book up to 12 people per boat, they provide two dive masters per group of six (certified) divers. ■TIP➜ They offer advanced-only trips in the morning and beginner/refresher groups in the afternoon. They also run a good-size dive shop for purchases and rentals, as well as a classroom for certification. Ni'ihau trips are available in summer. All trips leave from Kukui'ula Harbor in Po'ipū. Rates start at $125 for a two-tank boat dive; rental gear is $25 extra. ⊠ *Check-in office on Po'ipū Rd. just north of Lāwa'i Rd. turnoff to Spouting Horn. Look for yellow submarine in parking lot, 2827 Po'ipū Rd., Po'ipū* ☎ *808/742–9303 or 800/685–5889* ⊕ *www.seasportdivers.com.*

SNORKELING

Generally speaking, the calmest water and best snorkeling can be found on Kaua'i's North Shore in summer and South Shore in winter. The East Side, known as the windward side, has year-round, prevalent northeast trade winds that make snorkeling unpredictable, although there are some good pockets. The best snorkeling on the West Side is accessible only by boat.

A word on feeding fish: don't. As Captain Ted with HoloHolo Charters says, fish have survived and populated reefs for much longer than we have been donning goggles and staring at them. They will continue to do so without our intervention. Besides, fish food messes up the reef and—one thing always leads to another—can eliminate a once-pristine reef environment. As for gear, if you're snorkeling with one of the Nāpali boat tour outfitters, they'll provide it. However, depending on the company, it might not be the latest or greatest. If you have your own, bring it. On the other hand, if you're going out with SeaFun or Z-Tourz, not to worry. Their gear is top-notch. If you need to rent, hit one of the "snorkel-and-surf" shops such as Snorkel Bob's in Kōloa and Kapa'a, Play Dirty in Kapa'a, Nukumoi in Po'ipū and Waimea, or Seasport in Pōipū and Kapa'a, or shop Wal-Mart or Kmart if you want to drag it home. Typically, though, rental gear will be better quality than that found at Wal-Mart or Kmart. ■TIP➜ If you wear glasses, you can rent prescription masks at the rental shops—just don't expect them to match your prescription exactly.

BEST SPOTS

Just because we say these are good places to snorkel doesn't mean that the exact moment you arrive, the fish will flock—they are wild, after all. The beaches here are listed in clockwise fashion starting on the North Shore.

Although it can get quite crowded, **Ke'e Beach** (⊠ *At end of Rte. 560)* is quite often a good snorkeling destination. Just be sure to come during the off-hours, say early in the morning or later in the afternoon.

If you get up close with a Hawaiian Monk Seal, consider yourself lucky—they're endangered.

■ TIP→ Snorkeling here in winter can be hazardous. Summer is the best and safest time, although you should never swim beyond the reef.

The search for **Tunnels (Mākua)** (⊠*At Hā'ena Beach Park, near end of Rte. 560, across from lava-tube sea caves, after stream crossing*) is as tricky as the snorkeling. Park at Hā'ena Beach Park and walk east—away from Nāpali Coast—until you see a sand channel entrance in the water, almost at the point. Once you get here, the reward is fantastic. The name of this beach comes from the many underwater lava tubes, which always attract marine life. The shore is mostly beach rock interrupted by three sand channels. You'll want to enter and exit at one of these channels (or risk stepping on a sea urchin or scraping your stomach on the reef). Follow the sand channel to a drop-off; the snorkeling along here is always full of nice surprises. Expect a current running east to west. Snorkeling here in winter can be hazardous; summer is the best and safest time for snorkeling.

☽ **Lydgate Beach Park** (⊠*Just south of Wailua River, turn makai off Rte. 56 onto Lehu Dr. and left onto Nalu Rd.*) is the absolute safest place to snorkel on Kaua'i. With its lava-rock wall creating a protected swimming pool, this is the perfect spot for beginners, young and old. The fish are so tame here it's almost like swimming in a saltwater aquarium.

You'll generally find good year-round snorkeling at **Po'ipū Beach Park** (⊠*From Po'ipū Rd., turn right on Ho'ōne Rd.*), except during summer's south swells (which are not nearly as frequent as winter's north swells). The best snorkeling fronts the Marriott Waiohai Beach Club. Stay inside the crescent created by the sandbar and rocky point. The current runs east to west.

Don't pack the beach umbrella, beach mats, or cooler for snorkeling at **Beach House (Lāwa'i Beach)** (⊠ *Makai side of Lāwa'i Rd.; park on road in front of Lāwa'i Beach Resort*). Just bring your snorkeling gear. The beach—named after its neighbor the Beach House restaurant (yum)—is on the road to Spouting Horn. It's a small slip of sand during low tide and a rocky shoreline during high tide. However, it's right by the road's edge, and its rocky coastline and somewhat rocky bottom make it great for snorkeling. Enter and exit in the sand channel (not over the rocky reef) that lines up with the Lāwa'i Beach Resort's center atrium. Stay within the rocky points anchoring each end of the beach. The current runs east to west.

★ **Nu'alolo Kai** was once an ancient Hawaiian fishpond and is now home to the best snorkeling along Nāpali Coast (and perhaps on all of Kaua'i). The only way to access it is by boat, and only a few Nāpali snorkeling tour operators are permitted to do so. We recommend Nāpali Explorer and Kaua'i Sea Tours *(see Boat Tours).*

FodorśChoice
★
With little river runoff and hardly any boat traffic, the waters off the island of **Ni'ihau** are some of the clearest in all Hawai'i, and that's good for snorkeling. Like Nu'alolo Kai, the only way to snorkel here is to sign on with one of the two tour boats venturing across a sometimes rough open ocean channel: Blue Dolphin Charters and HoloHolo *(see Boat Tours).*

TOURS

☾ **SeaFun Kaua'i.** This guided snorkeling tour, for beginners and intermediates alike, is led by a marine expert, so not only is there excellent "how-to" instruction, but the guide actually gets in the water with you and identifies marine life. You're guaranteed to spot tons of critters you'd never see on your own. This is a land-based operation and the only one of its kind on Kaua'i. (Don't think those snorkeling cruises are guided snorkeling tours—they rarely are. A member of the boat's crew serves as lifeguard, not a marine life *guide*.) A half-day tour includes all your snorkeling gear—and a wet suit to keep you warm—and stops at two snorkeling locations, chosen based on ocean conditions. The cost is $80. ⊠ *Check in at Kilohana Plantation in Puhi, next to Kaua'i Community College* ☎ *808/245–6400 or 800/452–1113* ⊕ *www.aloha kauaitours.com.*

SURFING

Good old stand-up surfing is alive and well on Kaua'i, especially in winter's high surf season on the North Shore. If you're new to the sport, we highly recommend taking a lesson. Not only will this ensure you're up and riding waves in no time, but instructors will provide the right board for your experience and size, help you time a wave, and give you a push to get your momentum going. ■ TIP➔ **You don't need to be in top physical shape to take a lesson. Because your instructor helps push you into the wave, you won't wear yourself out paddling.** If you're experienced and want to hit the waves on your own, most surf shops rent boards for all levels, from beginners to advanced.

BEST SPOTS

Perennial-favorite beginning surf spots include **Po'ipū Beach** (the area fronting the Marriott Waiohai Beach Club); **Hanalei Bay** (the area next to the Hanalei Pier); and the stream end of **Kalapakī Beach.** More advanced surfers move down the beach in Hanalei to an area fronting a grove of pine trees known as **Pine Trees.** When the trade winds die, the north ends of **Wailua** and **Keālia** beaches are teeming with surfers. Breaks off **Po'ipū** and **Beach House/Lāwa'i Beach** attract intermediates year-round. During high surf, the break on the cliff side of **Kalihiwai** is for experts only.

LESSONS

Blue Seas Surf School. Surfer and instructor Charlie Smith specializes in beginners (especially children) and will go anywhere on the island to find just the right surf. His soft-top, long boards are very stable, making it easier to stand up. Rates start at $75 for a 1½-hour lesson. (Transportation provided, if needed.) ⊠ *Meet at beach; location varies depending on surf conditions* ☎ *808/634–6979* ⊕ *www.blueseassurfing school.com.*

Margo Oberg Surfing School. Seven-time world surfing champion Margo Oberg runs a surf school that meets on the beach in front of the Sheraton Kaua'i in Po'ipū. Lessons are $65 for two hours, though Margo herself rarely teaches anymore. ⊠ *Po'ipū Beach 96756* ☎ *808/332–6100* ⊕ *www.surfonkauai.com.*

Titus Kinimaka Hawaiian School of Surfing. Famed as a pioneer of big-wave surfing, this Hawaiian believes in giving back to his sport. Beginning, intermediate, and "extreme" lessons, including tow-in, are available. Unfortunately, Titus himself no longer offers lessons. Rates are $55 for a 90-minute group lesson and $120 for a 90-minute private lesson. ⊠ *Meets at Quiksilver store in Hanalei* ☎ *808/652–1116.*

EQUIPMENT

Progressive Expressions. ⊠ *On Kōloa Rd. in Old Kōloa Town* ☎ *808/742–6041.*

Tamba Surf Company. ⊠ *Mauka on north end of Hwy. 56, 4-1543 Kūhiō Hwy., Kapa'a* ☎ *808/823–6942.*

Hanalei Surf Company. ⊠ *Mauka at Hanalei Center, 5-5161 Kūhiō Hwy., Hanalei* ☎ *808/826–9000.*

WHALE-WATCHING

Every winter North Pacific humpback whales swim some 3,000 mi over 30 days, give or take a few, from Alaska to Hawai'i. Whales arrive as early as November and sometimes stay through April, though they seem to be most populous in February and March. They come to Hawai'i to breed, calve, and nurse their young.

Of course, nothing beats seeing a whale up close. During the season, any boat on the water is looking for whales; they're hard to avoid, whether the tour is labeled "whale-watching" or not. Several boat operators add two-hour afternoon whale-watching tours during the season that run on the South Shore (not Nāpali). Operators include **Blue Dolphin,**

Captain Andy's Sailing Adventures, Catamaran Kahanu, HoloHolo, and Nāpali Explorer *(⇨ see Boat Tours).*

WINDSURFING

Windsurfing on Kaua'i isn't nearly as popular as it is on Maui but 'Anini Beach Park is the place if you're going to windsurf or play the spectator. Rentals and lessons are available from **Windsurf Kaua'i** (☎ *808/828–6838).* Lessons run $85 for three hours, equipment included; rentals run $25 per hour. The instructor will meet you on 'Anini Beach.

GOLF, HIKING, AND OUTDOOR ACTIVITIES

AERIAL TOURS

Fodor'sChoice
★

From the air, the Garden Island blossoms with views you cannot see by land, on foot, or from the sea. In an hour you can see waterfalls, craters, and other places that are inaccessible even by hiking trails (some say that 70% or more of the island is inaccessible). The majority of flights depart from the Līhu'e airport and follow a clockwise pattern around the island. ■TIP→If you plan to take an aerial tour, it's a good idea to fly when you first arrive, rather than saving it for the end of your trip. It will help you visualize what's where on the island and it may help you decide what you want to see from a closer vantage point during your stay. Many companies advertise a low-price 30- or 40-minute tour, which they rarely fly, so don't expect to book a flight at the advertised rate. The most popular flight is 60 minutes long.

Blue Hawaiian Helicopters. The newest helicopter company to the island is not new to Hawai'i, having flown for 20 years on Maui and the Big Island. They are the only company on Kaua'i flying the latest in helicopter technology, the $1.8 million Eco-Star. It has 23% more interior space for its six passengers, has unparalleled viewing, and offers a few extra safety features none of the other helicopters on the island has. As the name implies, the helicopter is a bit more environmentally friendly, with a 50% noise-reduction rate. Their flights run a tad shorter than others (approximately 50 minutes instead of the 55 to 65 minutes that others tout), although the flight feels very complete. The rate is $274. A DVD of your actual tour is available for an additional $25. ⊠*Harbor Mall in Nawiliwili, Līhu'e* ☎*808/245–5800 or 800/745–2583* ⊕*www.bluehawaiian.com.*

Fodor'sChoice
★

Inter-Island Helicopters. This company flies four-seater Hughes 500 helicopters *with the doors off.* It can get chilly at higher elevations, so bring a sweater and wear long pants. They offer a spectacular tour that includes landing by a waterfall for a picnic and swim. Tours depart from Hanapēpē's Port Allen Airport. Prices range from $260 to $355 per person. ⊠*From Rte. 50, turn makai onto Rte. 543 in Hanapēpē* ☎*808/335–5009 or 800/656–5009* ⊕*www.interislandhelicopters.com.*

Safari Helicopters. This company flies the "Super" ASTAR helicopter, which offers floor-to-ceiling windows on its doors, four roof windows, and Bose X-Generation headphones. Two-way microphones allow passengers to converse with the pilot. The price is $221; a DVD is $30 extra. ⊠ *3225 Akahi St., Līhuʻe* ☎ *808/246–0136 or 800/326–3356* ⊕ *www.safariair.com.*

Sunshine Helicopter Tours. The majority of this company's pilots were born and raised in Hawaiʻi, making them excellent tour guides. Prices start at $239. ⊠ *3222 Kūhiō Hwy., Līhuʻe* ☎ *808/245–8881 or 888/245–4354* ⊕ *www.helicopters-hawaii.com.*

ATV TOURS

Although all the beaches on the island are public, much of the interior land—once sugar and pineapple plantations—is privately owned. This is really a shame, because the valleys and mountains that make up the vast interior of the island easily rival the beaches in sheer beauty. The good news is some tour operators have agreements with landowners making exploration possible, albeit a bit bumpy, and unless you have back troubles, that's half the fun.

Kauaʻi ATV Tours. This is *the* thing to do when it rains on Kauaʻi. Consider it an extreme mud bath. Kauaʻi ATV in Kōloa is the originator of the island's all-terrain-vehicle tours. Their $125 three-hour jaunt takes you through a private sugar plantation and historic cane-haul tunnel. The $155 four-hour tour visits secluded waterfalls and includes a picnic lunch. The more popular longer excursion includes a hike through a bamboo forest and a swim in a freshwater pool at the base of the falls—to rinse off all that mud. You must be 16 or older to operate your own ATV, but Kauaʻi ATV also offers its four-passenger "Ohana Bug" and two-passenger "Mud Bugs" to accommodate families with kids ages five and older. ⊠ *5330 Kōloa Rd., Kōloa* ☎ *808/742–2734 or 877/707–7088* ⊕ *www.kauaiatv.com.*

Kipu Ranch Adventures. This 3,000-acre property extends from the Huleia River to the top of Mt. Haupu. *Jurassic Park, Indiana Jones,* and *Mighty Joe Young* were filmed here, and you'll see the locations for all of them on the $125 three-hour Ranch Tour. The $150 four-hour Waterfall Tour includes a visit to two waterfalls and a picnic lunch. Kipu Ranch was once a sugar plantation, but today it is a working cattle ranch, so you'll be in the company of bovines as well as pheasants, wild boars, and peacocks. ⊠ *235 Kipu Rd., Līhuʻe* ☎ *808/246–9288* ⊕ *www.kiputours.com.*

BIKING

Kauaʻi is a labyrinth of cane-haul roads, which are fun for exploring on two wheels. The challenge is finding the roads where biking is allowed and then not getting lost in the maze. Maybe that explains why Kauaʻi is not a hub for the sport . . . yet. Still, there are some epic rides for those who are interested—both the adrenaline-rushing and the mellower beach cruiser kinds. If you want to grind out some mileage, the main highway skirting the coastal areas is perfectly safe, though there are only a few designated bike lanes. It's hilly, but you can find that keeping your eyes on the road and not the scenery is the biggest challenge. You can rent bikes (with helmets) from the activities desks of certain hotels, but these are not the best quality. You're better off renting from either Kaua'i Cycle in Kapa'a or Outfitters Kaua'i in Po'ipū.

Nāwiliwili to Anahola Bike/Pedestrian Path. For the cruiser, this path follows the coastline on Kaua'i's East Side. Eventually, it will run some 20 mi and offer scenic views, picnic pavilions, and restroom facilities along the way—all in compliance with the Americans with Disabilities Act. For now, the easiest way to access those completed sections of the path is from Keālia Beach. Park here and head north into rural lands with spectacular coastline vistas or head south into Kapa'a for a more interactive experience. ✉ *Trailhead: 1 mi north of Kapa'a; park at north end of Keālia Beach.*

Wailua Forest Management Road. For the novice mountain biker, this is an easy ride, and it's also easy to find. From Route 56 in Wailua, turn mauka on Kuamo'o Road and continue 6 mi to the picnic area, known as Keāhua Arboretum; park here. The potholed four-wheel-drive road includes some stream crossings—■ TIP➜ stay away during heavy rains, because the streams flood—and continues for 2 mi to a T-stop, where you should turn right. Stay on the road for about 3 mi until you reach a gate; this is the spot where the gates in the movie *Jurassic Park* were filmed, though it looks nothing like the movie. Go around the gate and down the road for another mile to a confluence of streams at the base of Mt. Wai'ale'ale. Be sure to bring your camera.

Waimea Canyon Road. For those wanting a road workout, climb this road, also known as Route 550. After a 3,000-foot climb, the road tops out at mile 12 adjacent to Waimea Canyon, which will pop in and out of view on your right as you ascend. From here it continues several miles (mostly level) past the Kōke'e Museum and ends at the Kalalau Lookout. It's paved the entire way, uphill 100%, and curvy. ■ TIP➜ There's not much of a shoulder—sometimes none—so be extra cautious. The road gets busier as the day wears on, so you may want to consider a sunrise ride. ✉ *Road turns mauka off Rte. 50 just after grocery store in downtown Waimea.*

EQUIPMENT AND TOURS

Kaua'i Cycle. This reliable, full-service bike shop rents, sells, and repairs bikes. Mountain bikes and road bikes are available for $25 to $60 per day and $125 to $195 per week with directions to trails. The Nāwiliwili to Anahola Bike/Pedestrian Path is right out their back door. ✉ *Across from Taco Bell, 934 Kūhiō Hwy., Kapa'a* ☎ *808/821–2115* ⊕ *www. bikehawaii.com/kauaicycle.*

Outfitters Kaua'i. Hybrid "comfort" and mountain bikes (both full suspension and hardtails), as well as road bikes, are available at this shop in Po'ipū. You can ride right out the door to tour Po'ipū, or get information on how to do a self-guided tour of Kōeʻe State Park and Waimea Canyon. The company also leads sunrise coasting tours (under the name **Bicycle Downhill**) from Waimea Canyon to the island's West Side beaches. Rentals cost $25 to $45 per day. Tours cost $98. ⊠*2827-A Poʻipū Rd., Poʻipū Follow Poʻipū Rd. south from Kōloa town; shop is on right before turnoff to Spouting Horn* ☎*808/742–9667 or 888/742–9887* ⊕*www.outfitterskauai.com.*

Pedal ʻn' Paddle. This company rents old-fashioned, single-speed beach cruisers and hybrid road bikes for $12 to $20 per day; $50 to $80 per week. In the heart of Hanalei, this is a great way to cruise the town; the more ambitious cyclist can head to the end of the road. Be careful, though, because there are no bike lanes on the twisting and turning road to Keʻe. ⊠*Ching Young Village, Rte. 560, Hanalei* ☎*808/826–9069* ⊕*www.pedalnpaddle.com.*

GOLF

For golfers, the Garden Island might as well be known as the Robert Trent Jones Jr. Isle. Four of the island's nine courses, including Poʻipū Bay—home of the PGA Grand Slam of Golf—are the work of Jones, who maintains a home at Princeville. Combine these four courses with those from Jack Nicklaus, Robin Nelson, and local legend Toyo Shirai, and you'll see that golf sets Kauaʻi apart from the other islands as much as the Pacific Ocean does. ■**TIP**➔ Afternoon tee times can save you big bucks.

Kauaʻi Lagoons Golf Club. With the pending development of the Kauaʻi Lagoons Resort, the golf club is getting a face-lift. That means Jack is back. Nicklaus is redesigning the back nine of his award-winning Kiele Course, originally opened in 1989. During this process, the club is down to 18 holes and pairing the front nine of Kiele with the back nine of its sister course, Mokihana—characterized by its "links" design. When the back nine of Kiele is complete, the front nine will close for its "facelift." Construction on Kiele is expected to continue through 2010; then, the plan is to upgrade the Mokihana Course. ⊠*3351 Hoʻolaulea Way, Līhuʻe* ☎*808/241–6000* ⊕*www.golfbc.com* ⌒*Kiele Course: 18 holes. 6674 yds. Par 72. Green fee: $195. Mokihana Course: 18 holes. 6578 yds. Par 72. Green fee: $130. Nine holes from each course open during redesign. Green fee: $175* ⌒*Facilities: Driving range, putting green, golf carts, rental clubs, lessons, restaurant, bar.*

Kiahuna Plantation Golf Course. A meandering creek, lava outcrops, and thickets of trees give Kiahuna its character. Robert Trent Jones Jr. (1983) was given a smallish piece of land just inland at Poʻipū, and defends par with smaller targets, awkward stances, and optical illusions. In 2003 a group of homeowners bought the club and brought Jones back to renovate the course, adding tees and revamping bunkers. The pro here boasts his course has the best putting greens on the island. The course's only downside is the dust screens—due to the recent development in Poʻipū. Expect them to come down in late 2008. This is the only course on Kauaʻi with a complete set of junior's tee boxes. ⊠*2545 Kiahuna Plantation Dr., Kōloa* ☎*808/742–9595* ⊕*www.kiahunagolf.com* ⌒*18* *holes. 6230 yds. Par 70. Green fee: $99* ☞*Facilities: Driving range, putting green, rental clubs, lessons, pro shop, restaurant, bar.*

Kukuiolono Golf Course. Local legend Toyo Shirai designed this fun, funky 9-holer where holes play across rolling, forested hills that afford views of the distant Pacific. Though Shirai has an eye for a good golf hole, Kukuiolono is out of the way and a bit rough, and probably not for everyone. But at $9 for the day, it's a deal—bring cash, though, as they don't accept credit cards. No tee times. ⊠ *854 Pu'u Rd., Kalāheo* ☎ *808/332–9151* ⚐ *9 holes. 3173 yds. Par 36. Green fee: $9* ☞ *Facilities: Driving range, putting green, golf carts, pull carts, rental clubs.*

FodorśChoice
★

Po'ipū Bay Golf Course. Po'ipū Bay has been called the Pebble Beach of Hawai'i, and comparisons are apt. Like Pebble Beach, Po'ipū is a links course built on headlands, not true links land. And as at Monterey Bay, there's wildlife galore. It's not unusual for golfers to see monk seals sunning on the beach below, sea turtles bobbing outside the shore break, and humpback whales leaping offshore. ⊠ *2250 Ainako St., Kōloa* ☎ *808/742–8711 or 800/858–6300* ⊕ *www.poipubaygolf.com* ⚐ *18 holes. 6612 yds. Par 72. Green fee: $200* ☞ *Facilities: Driving range, putting green, rental clubs, golf carts, golf academy/lessons, restaurant, bar.*

FodorśChoice
★

Princeville Resort. Robert Trent Jones Jr. built two memorable courses overlooking Hanalei Bay, the 27-hole Princeville Makai Course (1971) and the Prince Course (1990). The three Makai nines—Woods, Lake, Ocean—offer varying degrees of each element, plus lush mountain views above. Three quick snapshots: the par-3 seventh on the Ocean nine drops 100 feet from tee to green, with blue Hanalei Bay just beyond. The Ocean's par-3 eighth plays across a small bay where dolphins often leap. On the Woods' par-3 eighth, two large lava rocks in Jones's infamous Zen Bunker really are quite blissful, until you plant a tee shot behind one of them. The Prince was ranked by *Golf Digest* as Hawaii's number-one golf course on their 2006 list of America's Top 100 Greatest Courses. It's certifiably rated Hawai'i's second toughest (behind O'ahu's Ko'olau). This is jungle golf, with holes running through dense forest and over tangled ravines, out onto headlands for breathtaking ocean views, then back into the jungle. At this writing, the Makai Course was closed for renovations (golf course and clubhouse) and is expected to reopen in Fall 2009. **Makai Golf Course:** ⊠ *4080 Lei O Papa Rd., Princeville* ☎ *808/826–3580* ⊕ *www.princeville.com* ⚐ *27 holes. 6886 yds. Par 72. Green fee: $175* ☞ *Facilities: Driving range, putting green, rental clubs, golf carts, pro shop, golf academy/ lessons, snack bar.* **Prince Golf Course:** ⊠ *5-3900 Kūhiō Hwy., Princeville* ☎ *808/826–5001* ⊕ *www.princeville.com* ⚐ *18 holes. 6960 yds. Par 72. Green fee: $200* ☞ *Facilities: Driving range, putting green, rental clubs, golf carts, pro shop, golf academy/lessons, restaurant, bar.*

Wailua Municipal Golf Course. Voted by *Golf Digest* as one of Hawaii's 15-best golf courses, this seaside course was first built as a nine-hole golf course in the 1930s. The second nine holes were added in 1961. Course designer Toyo Shirai created a course that is fun but not punishing. Not only is this an affordable game with minimal water hazards, but it is challenging enough to have been chosen to host three USGA Amateur Public Links Championships. The trade winds blow steadily on the east side of the island and make the game all the more challenging. An ocean view and affordability make this one of the most popular courses on the island. Tee times accepted up to seven days in advance. *18 holes. Par 72. Green fee: $32 weekdays, $44 weekends. Half price after 2 PM. Cart rental: $18. Cash or traveler's checks only. ☞ Facilities: Driving range, rental clubs, golf carts, pro shop, lessons, snack bar ✉ 5350 Kūhiō Hwy., five min north of airport, Līhu'e ☎ 808/241–6666.*

HIKING

The best way to experience the 'aina—the land—on Kaua'i is to step off the beach and hike into the remote interior. You can find waterfalls so tall you'll strain your neck looking, pools of crystal-cool water for swimming, tropical forests teeming with plant life, and ocean vistas that will make you wish you could stay forever. ■ TIP➜ **For your safety wear sturdy shoes—preferably water-resistant ones.** All hiking trails on Kaua'i are free, so far. There's a rumor that the Waimea Canyon and Kōke'e state parks will someday charge an admission fee. Whatever it may be, it will be worth it.

Kalalau Trail. Of all the hikes on the island, Kalalau Trail is by far the most famous and in many regards the most strenuous. A moderate hiker can handle the 2-mi trek to Hanakapi'ai Beach, and for the seasoned outdoorsman, the additional 2 mi up to the falls is manageable. But be prepared to rock-hop along a creek and ford waters that can get waist high during the rain. Round-trip to Hanakapi'ai Falls is 8 mi. This steep and often muddy trail is best approached with a walking stick. The narrow trail will deliver one startling ocean view after another along a path that is alternately shady and sunny. The entire Kalalau Trail is 11 mi each way and requires a permit past the first 2 mi *(see Nāpali Coast, Emerald Queen of Kaua'i feature in this chaper for more information).* Wear tennis shoes or hiking sandals, and bring drinking water since the creeks on the trail are not potable. Snacks are always encouraged on a strenuous hike such as this one. ✉ *Drive north past Hanalei to end of road. Trailhead is directly across from Ke'e Beach.*

Shipwreck Shoreline Trail. This trail offers the novice hiker an accessible way to appreciate the rugged southern coast of Kaua'i. A cross-country course wends its way along the water, high above the ocean, through a lava field and past a sacred *heiau.* Walk all the way to Maha'ulepu, 2 mi north for a two-hour round-trip. ✉ *Drive north on Po'ipū Rd., turn right at Po'ipū Bay Golf Course sign. The street name is Ainako but is hard to see. Drive down to beach and park in lot.*

Sleeping Giant Trail. An easy and easily accessible trail practically in the heart of Kapa'a, the Sleeping Giant Trail—or simply "Sleeping Giant"—gains 1,000 feet over 2 mi. We prefer an early-morning—say, sunrise—hike, with sparkling blue-water vistas, up the east-side trailhead. At the top you can see a grassy grove with a picnic table; don't stop here. Continue carefully along the narrow trail toward the Giant's nose and chin. From here there are 360-degree views of the island. ✉ *In Wailua,* *turn mauka off Rte. 56 onto Haleilio Rd.; proceed 1 mi to small parking area on right.*

Waimea Canyon and Kōke'e State Parks. This park contains a 50-mi network of hiking trails of varying difficulty that take you through acres of native forests, across the highest-elevation swamp in the world, to the river at the base of the canyon, and onto pinnacles of land sticking their necks out over Nāpali Coast. All hikers should register at Kōke'e Natural History Museum, where you can find trail maps, current trail information, and specific directions. All mileage mentioned here is one-way.

The **Kukui Trail** descends 2½ mi and 2,200 feet into Waimea Canyon to the edge of the Waimea River—it's a steep climb. The **Awa'awapuhi Trail,** with 1,600 feet of elevation gains and losses over 3¼ mi, feels more gentle than the Kukui Trail, but it offers its own huffing-and-puffing sections in its descent along a spiny ridge to a perch overlooking the ocean.

The 3½-mi **Alaka'i Swamp Trail** is accessed via the **Pihea Trail** or a four-wheel-drive road. There's one strenuous valley section, but otherwise it's a pretty level trail—once you access it. This trail is a bird-watcher's delight and includes a painterly view of Wainiha and Hanalei valleys at the trail's end. The trail traverses the purported highest-elevation swamp in the world on a boardwalk so as not to disturb the fragile plant- and wildlife.

The **Canyon Trail** offers much in its short trek: spectacular vistas of the canyon and the only dependable waterfall in Waimea Canyon. The easy 2-mi hike can be cut in half if you have a four-wheel-drive vehicle. If you were outfitted with a headlamp, this would be a great hike at sunset as the sun's light sets the canyon walls ablaze in color. ⊠ *Kōke'e Natural History Museum: Kōke'e Rd., Rte. 550* ☏ *808/335–9975 for trail conditions.*

EQUIPMENT AND TOURS

Kaua'i Nature Tours. Father and son scientists started this hiking tour business. As such, their emphasis is on education and the environment. If you're interested in flora, fauna, volcanology, geology, oceanography, and the like, this is the company for you. They offer daylong hikes along coastal areas, beaches, and in the mountains. Hikes range from easy to strenuous and rates range from $110 to $140. ⊠ *Meets at designated spots around island. Provides transportation* ☏ *808/742–8305 or 888/233–8365* ⊕ *www.kauainaturetours.com.*

HORSEBACK RIDING

Most of the horseback riding tours on Kaua'i are primarily walking tours with very little trotting and no cantering or galloping, so no experience is required. Zip. Zilch. Nada. If you're interested, most of the stables offer private lessons. The most popular tours are the ones including a picnic lunch by the water. Your only dilemma may be deciding what kind of water you want—waterfalls or ocean. You may want to make your decision based on where you're staying. The "waterfall picnic" tours are on the wetter North Shore, and the "beach picnic" tours take place on the South Shore.

CJM Country Stables. Just past the Hyatt in Poʻipū, CJM Stables offers a three-hour picnic ride with noshing on the beach, as well as their more popular two-hour trail ride. The landscape here is rugged and beautiful, featuring sand dunes and limestone bluffs. CJM sponsors seasonal rodeo events that are free and open to the public. Prices range from $98 to $125. ✉ *1½ mi from Hyatt Regency Kauaʻi off Poʻipū Rd., Kōloa* ☎ *808/742–6096* ⊕ *www.cjmstables.com.*

Esprit de Corps. If you ride, this is the company for you. Esprit de Corps has three- to eight-hour rides and allows some trotting and cantering based on the rider's experience and comfort with the horse. What's also nice is the maximum group size: six. There are also pony parties and half-day horse camps for kids (usually summers). Weddings on horseback can be arranged, and custom rides for less experienced and younger riders (as young as two) are available, as well as private lessons for chilgen as young as 6. Trail ride rates range from $130 to $390. ✉ *End of Kualapa Pl., Kapaʻa* ☎ *808/822–4688* ⊕ *www.kauai horses.com.*

Fodor'sChoice **Princeville Ranch Stables.** A longtime *kamaʻāina* (resident) family operates
★ Princeville Ranch. They originated the waterfall picnic tours, which run three or four hours and include a short but steep hike down to Kalihiwai Falls, a dramatic three-tier waterfall, for swimming and picnicking. Princeville also has shorter, straight riding tours and private rides, and if they're moving cattle while you're visiting, you can sign up for a cattle drive. Prices range from $125 to $135. ✉ *West of Princeville Airport mauka between mile markers 27 and 28, Princeville* ☎ *808/826–6777* ⊕ *www.princevilleranch.com.*

MOUNTAIN TUBING

Kauaʻi Backcountry Adventures. Very popular with all ages, this laid-back adventure can book up two weeks in advance in busy summer months. Here's how it works: you recline in an inner tube and float down fern-lined irrigation ditches that were built more than a century ago—the engineering is impressive—to divert water from Mt. Waiʻaleʻale to sugar and pineapple fields around the island. Simple as that. They'll even give you a headlamp so you can see as you float through a couple of stretches of covered tunnels. The scenery from the island's interior at the base of Mt. Waiʻaleʻale on Līhuʻe Plantation land is superb. Ages five and up are welcome. The tour takes about three hours and includes a picnic lunch and a swim in a swimming hole. You'll definitely want to pack water-friendly shoes (or rent some from the outfitter), sunscreen, a hat, bug repellent, and a beach towel. Tours cost $99 per person and are offered morning and afternoon, daily. ✉ *3-4131 Kūhiō Hwy., across from gas station, Hanamāʻulu* ☎ *808/245–2506 or 888/270–0555* ⊕ *www.kauaibackcountry.com.*

Continued on page 500

NĀPALI COAST:
EMERALD QUEEN
OF KAUA'I

If you're coming to Kaua'i, Nāpali ("cliffs" in Hawaiian) is a major must-see. More than 5 million years old, these sea cliffs rise thousands of feet above the Pacific, and every shade of green is represented in the vegetation that blankets their lush peaks and folds. At their base, there are caves, secluded beaches, and waterfalls to explore.

The big question is how to explore this gorgeous stretch of coastline. You can't drive to it, through it, or around it. You can't see Nāpali from a scenic lookout. You can't even take a mule ride to it. The only way to experience its magic is from the sky, the ocean, or the trail.

FROM THE SKY

If you've booked a helicopter tour of Nāpali, you might start wondering what you've gotten yourself into on the way to the airport. Will it feel like being on a small airplane? Will there be turbulence? Will it be worth all the money you just plunked down?

Your concerns will be assuaged on the helipad, once you see the faces of those who have just returned from their journey: Everyone looks totally blissed out. And now it's your turn.

Climb on board, strap on your headphones, and the next thing you know the helicopter gently lifts up, hovers for a moment, and floats away like a spider on the wind—no roaring engines, no rumbling down a runway. If you've chosen a flight with music, you'll feel as if you're inside your very own IMAX movie.

Pinch yourself if you must, because this is the real thing. Your pilot shares history, legend, and lore. If you miss something, speak up: pilots love to show off their island knowledge. You may snap a few pictures (not too many or you'll miss the eyes-on experience!), nudge a friend or spouse and point at a whale breeching in the ocean, but mostly you stare, mouth agape. There is simply no other way to take in the immensity and greatness of Nāpali but from the air.

⇨ *See Chapter 5 for helicopter-tour information.*

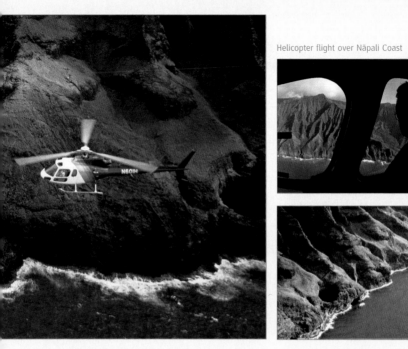

Helicopter flight over Nāpali Coast

GOOD TO KNOW

Helicopter companies depart from the north, east, and west shores. Our advice? Choose your departure location based on its proximity to where you're staying.

If you want more adventure—and air—choose one of the helicopter companies that flies with the doors off.

Some companies offer flights without music. Know the experience you want ahead of time. Some even sell a DVD of your flight, so you don't have to worry about taking pictures.

Wintertime rain grounds some flights; plan your trip early in your stay in case the flight gets rescheduled.

IS THIS FOR ME?

Taking a helicopter trip is the most expensive way to see Nāpali—as much as $280 for an hour-long tour.

Claustrophobic? Choose a boat tour or hike. It's a tight squeeze in the helicopter, especially in one of the middle seats.

Short on time? Taking a helicopter tour is a great way to see the island.

WHAT YOU MIGHT SEE

■ Nu'alolo Kai (an ancient Hawaiian fishing village) with its fringed reef

■ The 300-foot Hanakāpī'ai Falls

■ A massive sea arch formed in the rock by erosion

■ The 11-mile Kalalau Trail threading its way along the coast

■ The amazing striations of a'a and pāhoehoe lava flows that helped push Kaua'i above the sea

FROM THE OCEAN

Nāpali from the ocean is two treats in one: spend a good part of the day on (or in) the water, and gaze up at majestic green sea cliffs rising thousands of feet above your head.

There are three ways to see it: a mellow pleasure-cruise catamaran allows you to kick back and sip a mai tai; an adventurous raft (Zodiac) tour will take you inside sea caves under waterfalls, and give you the option of snorkeling; and a daylong outing in a kayak is a real workout, but then you can say you paddled 16 miles of coastline.

Any way you travel, you'll breathe ocean air, feel spray on your face, and see pods of spinner dolphins, green sea turtles, flying fish, and, if you're lucky, a rare Hawaiian monk seal.

Nāpali stretches from Ke'e Beach in the north to Polihale beach on the West Side. If your departure point is Ke'e, your journey will start in the lush Hanakāpī'ai Valley. Within a few minutes, you'll see caves and waterfalls galore. About halfway down the coast just after the Kalalau Trail ends, you'll come to an immense arch—formed where the sea eroded the less dense basaltic rock—and a thundering 50-foot waterfall. And as the island curves near Nu'alolo State Park, you'll begin to notice less vegetation and more rocky outcroppings.

⇨ *See Chapter 5 for more boat-tour information.*

(left and top right) Kayaking on Nāpali Coast
(bottom right) Dolphin on Nāpali Coast

GOOD TO KNOW

If you want to snorkel, choose a morning rather than an afternoon tour—preferably during a summer visit—when seas are calmer.

If you're on a budget, choose a non-snorkeling tour.

If you want to see whales, take any tour, but be sure to plan your vacation for December through March.

If you're staying on the North Shore or East Side, embark from the North Shore. If you're staying on the South Shore, it might not be worth your time to drive to the north, so head to the West Side.

IS THIS FOR ME?

Boat tours are several hours long, so if you have only a short time on Kaua'i, a helicopter tour is a better alternative.

Even on a small boat, you won't get the individual attention and exclusivity of a helicopter tour.

Prone to seasickness? A large boat can be surprisingly rocky, so be prepared.

WHAT YOU MIGHT SEE

■ Hawai'i's state fish—the humuhumunukunukuapuaa—otherwise known as the Christmas wrasse

■ Waiahuakua Sea Cave, with a waterfall coming through its roof

■ Tons of marine life, including dolphins, green sea turtles, flying fish, and humpback whales, especially in February and March

■ Waterfalls—especially if your trip is after a heavy rain

FROM THE TRAIL

If you want to be one with Nāpali—feeling the soft red earth beneath your feet, picnicking on the beaches, and touching the lush vegetation—hiking the Kalalau Trail is the way to do it.

Most people hike only the first 2 miles of the 11-mile trail and turn around on Hanakāpīʻai Trail. This 4-mile round-trip hike takes three to four hours. It starts at sea level and doesn't waste any time gaining elevation. (Take heart—the uphill lasts only a mile and tops out at 400 feet; then it's downhill all the way.) At the half-mile point, the trail curves west and the folds of Nāpali Coast unfurl.

Along the way you'll share the trail with feral goats and wild pigs. Some of the vegetation is native; much is introduced.

After the 1-mile mark the trail begins its drop into Hanakāpīʻai. You'll pass a couple of streams of water trickling across the trail, and maybe some banana, ginger, the native uluhe fern, and the Hawaiian ti plant. Finally the trail swings around the eastern ridge of Hanakāpīʻai for your first glimpse of the valley and then switchbacks down the mountain. You'll have to boulder-hop across the stream to reach the beach. If you like, you can take a 4-mile, round-trip fairly strenuous side trip from this point to the gorgeous Hanakāpīʻai Falls.

⇨ *See Chapter 5 for more Kalalau Trail hiking information.*

(left) Awaawapuhi mountain biker on razor-edge ridge
(top right) Feral goats in Kalalau Valley
(bottom right) Nāpali Coast

GOOD TO KNOW

Wear comfortable, amphibious shoes. Unless your feet require extra support, wear a self-bailing sort of shoe (for stream crossings) that doesn't mind mud. Don't wear heavy, waterproof hiking boots.

During winter the trail is often muddy, so be extra careful; sometimes it's completely inaccessible.

Don't hike after heavy rain—flash floods are common.

If you plan to hike the entire 11-mile trail (most people do the shorter hike described at left) you'll need a permit to go past Hanakāpī'ai.

IS THIS FOR ME?

Of all the ways to see Nāpali (with the exception of kayaking the coast), this is the most active. You need to be in decent shape to hit the trail.

If you're vacationing in winter, this hike might not be an option due to flooding—whereas you can take a helicopter or boat trip year-round.

WHAT YOU MIGHT SEE

■ Big dramatic surf right below your feet

■ Amazing vistas of the cool blue Pacific

■ The spectacular Hanakāpī'ai Falls; if you have a permit don't miss Hanakoa Falls, less than ½ mile off the trail

■ Wildlife, including goats and pigs

■ Zany-looking ōhi'a trees, with aerial roots and long, skinny serrated leaves known as hala. Early Hawaiians used them to make mats, baskets, and canoe sails.

LEPTOSPIROSIS

The sparkling waters of those babbling brooks trickling around the island can be life-threatening, and we're not talking about the dangers of drowning, although they, too, exist. Leptospirosis is a bacterial disease that is transmitted from animals to humans. It can survive for long periods of time in fresh water and mud contaminated by the urine of infected animals, such as mice, rats, and goats. The bacteria enter the body through the eyes, ears, nose, mouth, and broken skin. To avoid infection, do not drink untreated water from the island's streams; do not wade in waters above the chest or submerge skin with cuts and abrasions in island streams or rivers. Symptoms are often mild and resemble the flu—fever, diarrhea, chills, nausea, headache, vomiting, and body pains. Symptoms may occur two to 20 days after exposure. If you think you have these symptoms, see a doctor right away.

SKYDIVING

Skydive Kauai. Ten thousand feet over Kaua'i and falling at a rate of 120 MPH is probably as thrilling as it gets while airborne. First, there's the 25-minute plane ride to altitude in a Cessna 182, then the exhilaration of the first step into sky, the sensation of sailing weightless in the air over Kaua'i, and finally the peaceful buoyancy beneath the canopy of your parachute. A tandem free fall rates among the most unforgettable experiences of a lifetime. Wed that to the aerial view over Kaua'i and you've got a winning marriage. Tandem dive: $229. ⊠*Salt Pond Beach Park, Port Allen Airport 96716* ☏*808/335–5859* ⊕*skydivekauai.com.*

TENNIS

If you're interested in booking some court time on Kaua'i, there are public tennis courts in Waimea, Kekaha, Hanapēpē, Kōloa, Kalaheo, Līhu'e, Wailua Homesteads, Wailua Houselots, and Kapa'a New Park. For specific directions or more information, call the **County of Kaua'i Parks and Recreation Office** (☏*808/241–4463*). Many hotels and resorts have tennis courts on property; even if you're not staying there, you can still rent court time. Rates range from $10 to $15 per person per hour. On the South Shore, try the **Grand Hyatt Kaua'i** (☏*808/742–1234*) and **Kiahuna Swim and Tennis Club** (☏*808/742–9533*). On the North Shore try the **Princeville Tennis Center** (☏*808/826–1230*).

ZIPLINE TOURS

The latest adventure on Kaua'i is "zipping" or "ziplining." It's so new that the vernacular is still catching up with it, but regardless of what you call it, chances are you'll scream like a rock star fan while trying it. Strap on a harness, clip onto a cable running from one side of a river or valley to the other, and zip across. The step off is the scariest part. ■TIP➔Pack knee-length shorts or pants, athletic shoes, and courage for this adventure.

Fodor'sChoice **Outfitters Kaua'i.** This company offers a half-day, multisport adventure of
★ ziplining and rope-swinging with hiking in between. Four ziplines soar
over a Swiss Family Robinson–like jungle setting. Plus, you'll trek over
suspension bridges and elevated walkways, winding up at Kīpū Falls for
a swim. The price is $125. Outfitters Kaua'i also has a zipline stream
crossing as part of their Kipu Safari tour *(see Kayaking).* ⊠2827-A
Po'ipū Rd., Po'ipū ☎808/742–9667 *or* 888/742–9887 ⊕*www.outfitters
kauai.com.*

Princeville Ranch Adventures. The North Shore's answer to ziplining is an
eight-zipline course with a bit of hiking, waterfall crossing, and swimming thrown in for a half-day adventure. This is as close as it gets to
flying; just watch out for the albatross. Prices start at $125 for the Zip
Express and $145 for the Zip and Dip. ⊠ *West of Princeville Airport on
Rte. 56, between mile markers 27 and 28, Princeville* ☎808/826–7669
or 888/955–7669 ⊕*www.adventureskauai.com.*

SHOPPING

There aren't a lot of shops and spas on Kaua'i, but what you can find
here is a handful of places very much worth checking out for the quality
of their selection of items sold and services rendered.

Along with one major shopping mall, a few shopping centers, and a
growing number of big-box retailers, Kaua'i has some delightful mom-
and-pop shops and specialty boutiques with lots of character.

The Garden Island also has a large and talented community of artisans
and fine artists, with galleries all around the island showcasing their
creations. You can find many island-made arts and crafts in the small
shops, and it's worthwhile to stop in at crafts fairs and outdoor markets
to look for bargains and mingle with island residents.

If you're looking for a special memento of your trip that is unique to
Kaua'i County, check out the distinctive Ni'ihau shell lei. The tiny shells
are collected from beaches on Kaua'i and Ni'ihau, pierced, and strung
into beautiful necklaces, chokers, and earrings. It's a time-consuming
and exacting craft, and these items are much in demand, so don't be
taken aback by the high price tags. Those made by Ni'ihau residents will
have certificates of authenticity and are worth collecting. You often can
find cheaper versions made by non-Hawaiians at crafts fairs.

Stores are typically open daily from 9 or 10 AM to 5 PM, although some
stay open until 9 PM, especially those near resorts. Don't be surprised
if the posted hours don't match the actual hours of operation at the
smaller shops, where owners may be fairly casual about keeping to a
regular schedule.

THE NORTH SHORE

SHOPPING CENTERS

Ching Young Village. Despite a face-lift, this popular shopping center
looks a bit worn, but that doesn't deter business. The town's only grocery store, **Big Save,** is here along with a number of other shops useful

to locals and visitors. These include **Hanalei Music's Strings and Things,** where you can buy Hawaiian sheet music, compact discs, handmade instruments, and knitting supplies, as well as rent DVDs; **Village Variety,** which has a bit of everything; **Savage Pearls,** a fine jewelry store that specializes in Tahitian pearls and gifts; **Hot Rocket,** a teen-oriented surf-wear shop; **Hanalei Surf Company Back Door,** for beachwear and gear; **Hula Moon Gifts of Kaua'i,** which offers an assortment of island-themed treasures; **Village Snack & Bakery,** which sells excellent chocolate cake and coconut-cream pie; and several restaurants. A few steps away are **Evolve Love Artists Gallery,** a good place to find high-quality work by local artisans, and **On the Road to Hanalei,** a neat boutique with gifts, clothing, jewelry, housewares, and collectibles from Indonesia. ⊠ *Makai, after mile marker 2, 5-1590 Kūhiō Hwy., Hanalei* ☎ *808/826–7222* ⊕ *www.chingyoungvillage.com*

Hanalei Center. Listed on the Historic Register, the old Hanalei school has been refurbished and rented out to boutiques and restaurants. You can dig through '40s and '50s vintage memorabilia in the **Yellow Fish Trading Company,** search for that unusual gift at **Sand People.** Buy beach gear at the classic **Hanalei Surf Company,** casual island wear at **Hula Beach Clothing,** or women's clothing at **Tropical Tantrum.** For the kids, pick up something at **Rainbow Ducks Toys & Clothing.** For a little exercise, catch a class at the **Hanalei Yoga studio** in the two-story modern addition to the center, which also houses **Papaya's,** a well-stocked health-food store. ⊠ *Mauka, after mile marker 2, 5-5161 Kūhiō Hwy., Hanalei* ☎ *808/826–7677.*

Princeville Shopping Center. **Foodland,** a full-service grocery store, and **Island Ace Hardware** are the big draws at this small center. This is the last stop for gas and banking on the North Shore. You'll also find two restaurants, a sandal shop, a mail service center, a post office, an ice-cream shop, a kiosk with a good collection of Hawaiian and contemporary artists called **Paradise Music,** and **Magic Dragon Toy & Art Supply Co.,** a tiny but interesting toy-and-hobby shop. ⊠ *Makai, mile marker 28, 5-4280 Kūhiō Hwy., Princeville* ☎ *No phone.*

SHOPS

Kong Lung Co. Sometimes called the Gump's of Kaua'i, this gift store sells elegant clothing, exotic glassware, ethnic books, gifts, and artwork—all very lovely and expensive. The shop is housed in a beautiful 1892 stone structure right in the heart of Kīlauea. It's the showpiece of the pretty little Kong Lung Center, whose shops feature distinctive jewelry, handmade soaps and candles, hammocks, plants, excellent pizza and baked goods, artwork, and consignment clothing, among other items. Next door is the farmers' market, a good place to buy natural and gourmet foods, wines, and sandwiches. ⊠ *2490 Keneke St., Kīlauea* ☎ *808/828–1822.*

THE EAST SIDE: KAPA'A AND WAILUA

SHOPPING CENTERS

Coconut Marketplace. This visitor-oriented complex is on the busy Coconut Coast near resort hotels and condominiums. Sixty shops sell everything from snacks and slippers (as locals call flip-flop sandals) to scrimshaw. There are also restaurants open from breakfast to evening and a free Wednesday evening Polynesian show at 5. ✉ *4-484 Kūhiō Hwy., Kapa'a* ☎ *808/822–3641.*

Kaua'i Village Shopping Center. The buildings of this Kapa'a shopping village are in the style of a 19th-century plantation town. **ABC Discount Store** sells sundries; **Safeway** carries groceries and alcoholic beverages; **Longs Drugs** has a pharmacy, health and beauty products, and a good selection of Hawaiian merchandise; **Papaya's** has health foods; and other shops sell jewelry, gift items, children's clothes and toys, and art. Restaurants include Chinese, Mexican, and Vietnamese options, and there's also a **Jamba Juice,** a **Starbucks,** and an ice cream parlor. ✉ *4-831 Kūhiō Hwy., Kapa'a* ☎ *808/245–4700.*

Kinipopo Shopping Village. Kinipopo is a tiny little center on Kūhiō Highway. **Korean Barbeque** fronts the highway, as does **Goldsmith's Gallery,** which sells handcrafted Hawaiian-style gold jewelry. Worth a stop is **Tin Can Mailman,** with its eclectic collection of used books, stamps and coins, rare prints, vintage maps, and collectibles. ✉ *4-356 Kūhiō Hwy., Kapa'a* ☎ *No phone.*

Waipouli Town Center. **Foodland** is the focus of this small retail plaza, one of three shopping centers anchored by grocery stores in Kapa'a. You can also find a **Blockbuster** video outlet, **McDonald's, Pizza Hut, Fun Factory** video arcade, and a coffee shop, along with a local-style restaurant and a bar. ✉ *4-901 Kūhiō Hwy., Kapa'a* ☎ *808/822–9311.*

SHOPS AND GALLERIES

★ **Bambulei.** Two 1930s-style plantation homes have been transformed into a boutique featuring vintage and contemporary clothing, antiques, jewelry, and accessories. ✉ *4-369 Kūhiō Hwy., Wailua* ☎ *808/823–8641.*

Jim Saylor Jewelers. Jim Saylor has been designing beautiful keepsakes for more than two decades on Kaua'i. Gems from around the world, including black pearls and diamonds, appear in his unusual settings. ✉ *1318 Kūhiō Hwy., Kapa'a* ☎ *808/822–3591.*

Kaua'i Products Fair. Open weekends, this outdoor market features fresh produce, tropical plants and flowers, aloha wear, and collectibles along with craftspeople, artisans, and wellness practitioners who will give you a massage right on the spot. ✉ *Outside on north side of Kapa'a, mauka side of Kuhio Hwy.* ☎ *808/246–0988.*

Kela's Glass Gallery. The colorful vases, bowls, and other fragile items sold in this distinctive gallery are definitely worth viewing if you appreciate quality handmade glass art. It's expensive, but if something catches your eye, they'll happily pack it for safe transport home. ✉ *4-1354 Kūhiō Hwy., Kapa'a* ☎ *808/822–4527.*

Deja Vu Surf Outlet. This mom-and-pop operation has a great assortment of surfwear and clothes for outdoor fanatics, including tank tops, visors,

5

swimwear, and Kaua'i-style T-shirts at low prices. ⊠*4-1419 Kūhiō Hwy., Kapa'a* ☎*808/822–4401.*

Vicky's Fabric Shop. This small shop is packed full of tropical prints, silks, slinky rayons, soft cottons, and other fine fabrics, making it a must-stop for any seamstress. If you're seeking something that's truly one-of-a-kind, check out the selection of purses, aloha wear, and other quality handsewn items. ⊠*4-1326 Kūhiō Hwy., Kapa'a* ☎*808/822–1746.*

THE EAST SIDE: LĪHU'E

SHOPPING CENTERS

Kilohana Plantation. This 16,000-square-foot Tudor mansion contains art galleries, a jewelry store, and Gaylord's restaurant. The restored outbuildings house a craft shop and a Hawaiian-style clothing shop. The house itself is filled with antiques from its original owner and is worth a look. Horse-drawn carriage rides are available, with knowledgeable guides reciting the history of sugar on Kaua'i. ⊠*3-2087 Kaumuali'i Hwy., 1 mi west of Līhu'e* ☎*808/245–5608.*

Kukui Grove Center. This is Kaua'i's only true mall. Besides **Sears Roebuck** and **Kmart,** anchor tenants are **Longs Drugs, Macy's,** and **Star Market. Borders Books & Music,** and its coffee shop, is one of the island's most popular stores. **Starbucks** opened its first outlet on Kaua'i here. The mall's stores offer women's clothing, surf wear, art, toys, athletic shoes, jewelry, and locally made crafts. Restaurants range from fast food and sandwiches to Mexican and Chinese. The center stage often has entertainment. ⊠*3-2600 Kaumuali'i Hwy., west of Līhu'e* ☎*808/245–7784.*

SHOPS AND GALLERIES

Hilo Hattie, The Store of Hawai'i, Fashion Factory. This is the big name in aloha wear for tourists throughout the islands. You can visit the only store on Kaua'i, a mile from Līhu'e Airport, to pick up cool, comfortable aloha shirts and mu'umu'u in bright floral prints, as well as other souvenirs. While here, check out the line of Hawai'i-inspired home furnishings. ⊠*3252 Kūhiō Hwy., Līhu'e* ☎*808/245–3404* ⊕*www.hilohattie.com.*

Fodor'sChoice
★ **Kapaia Stitchery.** Hawaiian quilts made by hand and machine, a beautiful selection of fabrics, quilting kits, and fabric arts fill this cute little red plantation-style structure. The staff is friendly and helpful, even though a steady stream of customers keeps them busy. ⊠*Kūhiō Hwy., ½ mi north of Līhu'e* ☎*808/245–2281.*

Kaua'i Fruit and Flower Company. At this shop near Līhu'e you can buy fresh sugarloaf pineapple, ginger, coconuts, local jams, jellies, and honey, plus Kaua'i-grown papayas, bananas, and mangos in season. Stop by on your way to the airport (although it's hard to make a left turn back onto Kūhiō Highway) to buy fruit that's been inspected and approved for shipment to the mainland. ⊠*3-4684 Kūhiō Hwy., Līhu'e* ☎*808/245–1814 or 800/943–3108.*

★ **Kaua'i Museum.** The gift shop at the museum sells some fascinating books, maps, and prints, as well as lovely feather lei hatbands, Ni'ihau shell jewelry, handwoven *lau hala* hats, and other good-quality local crafts at reasonable prices. ✉*4428 Rice St., Līhu'e* ☎*808/246–2470.*

Kaua'i Products Store. Every seed lei, every finely crafted koa-wood box, every pair of tropical-flower earrings, indeed every item in this boutique is handcrafted on Kaua'i. Other gift options include koa-oil lamps, pottery, hand-painted silk clothing, sculpture, and homemade fudge. Although some of the merchandise isn't all that appealing, it's nice to support local talent when you can. ✉*Kukui Grove Center, 3-2600 Kaumuali'i Hwy., Līhu'e* ☎*808/246–6753.*

Kilohana Clothing Company. This store in the guest cottage by Gaylord's restaurant offers vintage Hawaiian clothing as well as contemporary styles using traditional Hawaiian designs. The store also features a wide selection of home products in vintage fabrics. ✉*Kilohana Plantation, 3-2087 Kaumuali'i Hwy., Līhu'e* ☎*808/246–6911.*

THE SOUTH AND WEST SIDE

SHOPPING CENTERS

'Ele'ele Shopping Center. Kaua'i's West Side has a scattering of stores, including those at this no-frills strip-mall shopping center. It's a good place to rub elbows with local folk or to grab a quick bite to eat at the casual **Grinds Cafe** or **Tois Thai Kitchen.** ✉*Rte. 50 near Hanapēpē, 'Ele'ele* ☎*808/246–0634.*

Po'ipū Shopping Village. Convenient to nearby hotels and condos on the South Shore, the two dozen shops here sell resort wear, gifts, souvenirs, and art. The upscale **Black Pearl Kaua'i** and **Na Hoku** shops are particularly appealing jewelry stores. There's a couple of art galleries and several fun clothing stores, including **Making Waves** and **Blue Ginger.** Also worth a visit are **Sand Kids** and **Whaler's General Store.** Restaurants include **Keoki's Paradise, Roy's, Po'ipū Tropical Burgers,** and **Puka Dog Hawaiian Style Hot Dogs.** A Tahitian dance troupe performs in the open-air courtyard Tuesday and Thursday at 5 PM. ✉*2360 Kiahuna Plantation Dr., Po'ipū Beach* ☎*808/742–2831.*

Waimea Canyon Plaza. As Kekaha's retail hub and the last stop for supplies before heading up to Waimea Canyon, this tiny, tidy complex of shops is surprisingly busy. Look for local foods, souvenirs, and island-made gifts for all ages. ✉*Kōke'e Rd. at Rte. 50, Kekaha* ☎*No phone.*

SHOPS AND GALLERIES

Kaua'i Coffee Visitor Center and Museum. Kaua'i produces more coffee than any other island in the state. The local product can be purchased from grocery stores or here at the source, where a sampling of the nearly one dozen coffees is available. Be sure to try some of the estate-roasted varieties. ✉*870 Halawili Rd., off Rte. 50, west of Kalāheo* ☎*808/335–0813 or 800/545–8605.*

Kaua'i Tropicals. You can have this company ship heliconia, anthuriums, ginger, and other tropicals in 5-foot-long boxes directly from its flower farm in Kalāheo. It accepts phone-in orders only. ✉*Kalāheo 96741* ☎*808/742–9989 or 800/303–4385.*

Fodor'sChoice **Kebanu Gallery.** A stunning collection of original wood sculptures,
★ whimsical ceramics, beaded jewelry, colorful glassware, and other creations—many of them by Hawai'i artists—makes this contemporary
shop a pleasure to visit. ⊠ *Old Kōloa Town, 3440 Po'ipū Rd., Kōloa*
☎ *808/742–2727.*

Paradise Sportswear. This is the retail outlet of the folks who invented
Kaua'i's popular "red dirt" shirts, which are dyed and printed with the
characteristic local soil. Ask the salesperson to tell you the charming
story behind these shirts. Sizes from infants up to 5X are available.
⊠ *4350 Waialo Rd., Kalaheo* ☎ *808/335–5670.*

SPAS

Though most spas on Kaua'i are associated with resorts, none are
restricted to guests only. And there's much by way of healing and wellness to be found on Kaua'i beyond the traditional spa—or even the day
spa. More and more retreat facilities are offering what some would call
alternative healing therapies. Others would say there's nothing alternative about them; you can decide for yourself.

Alexander Day Spa & Salon at the Kaua'i Marriott. This sister spa of Alexander Simson's Beverly Hills spa focuses on body care rather than exercise,
so don't expect any fitness equipment or exercise classes. Tucked away in
the back corner of the Marriott, the spa has the same ambience of stilted
formality as the rest of the resort, but it is otherwise a sunny, pleasant
facility. Massages are available in treatment rooms and on the beach,
although the beach locale isn't as private as you might imagine. The spa
offers a couple of unusual treatments not found elsewhere: oxygen inha-
lation therapy and Thai massage. Wedding-day and custom spa packages
can be arranged. The spa's therapists also offer massages in poolside
cabanas at Marriott's Waiohai Beach Club in Po'ipū, but there are no facilities (showers, steam, and so forth). ⊠ *Kaua'i Marriott Resort & Beach
Club, 3610 Rice St., Līhu'e* ☎ *808/246–4918* ⊕ *www.alexanderspa.com*
⫷ *$65–$170 massage. Facilities: Hair salon. Services: Body treatments—including masks, scrubs, and wraps—facials, hair styling, steam
treatment, makeup, manicures, massages, pedicures, waxing.*

Fodor'sChoice **ANARA Spa.** This luxurious facility is far and away the best on Kaua'i,
★ setting a standard that no other spa has been able to meet. It has all the
equipment and services you expect from a top resort spa, along with
a pleasant, professional staff. Best of all, it has indoor and outdoor
areas that capitalize on the tropical locale and balmy weather, further
distinguishing it from other resort spas. Its 46,500 square feet of space
includes the new Garden Treatment Village (opening in 2007), an open-
air courtyard with private thatched-roof huts, each featuring a relaxation
area, misters, and open-air shower in a tropical setting. At the Kupono
Café, you can relax and enjoy a healthful breakfast, lunch, or smoothie.
Ancient Hawaiian remedies and local ingredients are featured in many
of the treatments, such as a red-dirt clay wrap, coconut-mango facial,
and a body brush scrub that polishes your skin with a mix of ground
coffee, orange peel, and vanilla bean. The open-air lava-rock showers

are wonderful, introducing many guests to the delightful island practice of showering outdoors. The spa, which includes a full-service salon, adjoins the Hyatt's legendary swimming pool. ⊠*Hyatt Regency Kaua'i Resort and Spa, 1571 Po'ipū Rd., Po'ipū* ☎808/240–6440 ⊕*www. anaraspa.com* ☞*$155 and up massage. Facilities: Hair salon, outdoor hot tubs, sauna, steam room. Gym with cardiovascular machines, free weights, weight-training equipment. Services: Body scrubs and wraps, facials, manicures, massage, pedicures. Classes and programs: Aerobics, aquaerobics, body sculpting, fitness analysis, flexibility training, personal training, Pilates, step aerobics, weight training, yoga.*

Angeline's Mu'olaulani Wellness Center. It doesn't get more authentic than this. In the mid-1980s Aunty Angeline Locey opened her Anahola home to offer traditional Hawaiian healing practices. Now her son and granddaughter carry on the tradition. There's a two-hour treatment ($150) that starts with a steam, followed by a sea-salt-and-clay body scrub and a two-person massage. The real treat, however, is relaxing on Aunty's open-air garden deck. Hot-stone lomi is also available. Aunty's mission is to promote a healthy body image; as such, au naturel is the accepted way here, so if you're nudity-shy, this may not be the place for you. On second thought, Aunty would say it most definitely is; *Mu'olaulani* translates to "a place for young buds to bloom." ⊠*Directions provided upon reservation, Anahola* ☎808/822–3235 ⊕ *www. angelineslomikauai.com* ☞*Facilities: Steam room. Services: Body scrubs and massage.*

Hanalei Day Spa. As you travel beyond tony Princeville, life slows down. The single-lane bridges may be one reason. Another is the Hanalei Day Spa, an open-air, thatched-roof, Hawaiian-style hut nestled just off the beach on the grounds of Hanalei Colony Resort in Hā'ena. With a location like this, the spa itself can be no-frills—and it is. Services include facials, waxing, wraps, scrubs, and the like, though its specialty is massage: ayurveda, Zen shiatsu, Swedish, and even a baby massage (and lesson for mom, to boot). On Tuesday and Thursday, owner Darci Frankel teaches yoga, a discipline she started as a young child living in south Florida. That practice led her to start the Ayurveda Center of Hawai'i, operating out of the spa and offering an ancient Indian cleansing and rejuvenation program known as Pancha Karma. Think multiday wellness retreat. ⊠*Hanalei Colony Resort, Rte. 560, 6 mi past Hanalei* ☎808/826–6621 ⊕*www.hanaleidayspa.com* ☞*$90–$195 massage. Services: Body scrubs and wraps, facials, massage, waxing. Classes and programs: Pancha Karma, yoga.*

★ **A Hideaway Spa.** This is the only full-service day spa on the laid-back West Side. It's in one of the restored plantation cottages that make up the guest quarters at Waimea Plantation Cottages, creating a cozy and comfortable setting you won't find elsewhere. The overall feel is relaxed, casual, and friendly, as you'd expect in this quiet country town. The staff is informal, yet thoroughly professional. Try the kava kava ginger wrap followed by the lomi *'ili'ili*—hot stone massage. Ooh la la. ⊠*Waimea Plantation Cottages, 9400 Kaumuali'i Hwy., Waimea* ☎808/338–0005 ⊕*www.waimea-plantation.com* ☞*$50–$170 massage. Facilities: Outdoor hot tub, steam room. Services: Acupuncture,* *body scrubs and wraps, facials, hydrotherapy, massage. Classes and programs: Yoga.*

Princeville Health Club & Spa. Inspiring views of mountains, sea, and sky provide a lovely distraction in the gym area of this spa, which is well equipped but small and often overly air-conditioned. The treatment area is functional but lacks charm and personality. Luckily the gorgeous setting helps make up for it. This is the only facility of this kind on the North Shore, so it's well used, and the generally well-heeled clientele pay attention to their gym attire. It's in the clubhouse at the Prince Golf Course, several miles from the Princeville Hotel. A room in the hotel or round of golf at a Princeville course entitles you to reduced admission to the spa; otherwise it's $20 for a day pass. ⊠ *Prince Golf Course clubhouse, 53-900 Kūhiō Hwy., Princeville* ☎ *808/826–5030* ⊕ *www.princeville.com* ☞ *$115–$145 massage. Gym with cardiovascular machines, free weights, weight-training equipment. Services: Body scrubs and wraps, facials, massage. Classes and programs: Aerobics, aquaerobics, personal training, Pilates, step aerobics, tai chi, yoga.*

Qi Center. Technically, the Qi Center of Kaua'i is not a spa. It does, however, concern itself with healing, and because its technique is so gentle, it is, in a sense, pampering. More than that, it can be life changing—even life saving. Hong Liu, a qigong grand master of the highest degree opened the center in 2005 as part of his lifelong goal to share qigong with the West. The essence of qigong centers on building, increasing, and directing energy: physical, mental, and spiritual. Master Liu does not suggest qigong as an alternative to Western medicine but as an adjunct. The center in Līhu'e conducts all levels of qigong training as well as "humanitarian" (i.e., free) events for the community on such topics as asthma, allergies, and heart and senior health. ⊠ *3343 Kanakolu St., Līhu'e* ☎ *808/639–4300.*

ENTERTAINMENT AND NIGHTLIFE

Kaua'i has never been known for its nightlife. It's a rural island, where folks tend to retire early, and the streets are dark and deserted well before midnight. The island does have its nightspots, though, and the after-dark entertainment scene may not be expanding, but it is consistently present in areas frequented by tourists.

Most of the island's dinner and lū'au shows are held at hotels and resorts. Hotel lounges are a good source of live music, often with no cover charge, as are a few bars and restaurants around the island.

Check the local newspaper, *The Garden Island,* for listings of weekly happenings, or tune in to community radio station KKCR—found at 90.9, 91.9, and 92.7 on the FM dial, depending on where you are—at 5:30 PM for the arts and entertainment calendar. Free publications such as *Kaua'i Gold, This Week on Kaua'i,* and *Kaua'i Beach Press* also list entertainment events. You can pick them up at Līhu'e Airport near the baggage claim area, as well as at numerous retail areas on the island.

ENTERTAINMENT

Although lūʻau remain a primary source of evening fun for families on vacation, there are a handful of other possibilities. There are no traditional dinner cruises, but some boat tours do offer an evening buffet with music along Nāpali coast. A few times a year, Women in Theater (WIT), a local women's theater group, performs dinner shows at the Hukilau Lānai in Wailua. You can always count on a performance of *South Pacific* at the Hilton, and the Kauaʻi Community College Performing Arts Center draws well-known artists.

Kauaʻi Community College Performing Arts Center. This is the main venue for island entertainment, hosting a concert music series, visiting musicians, dramatic productions, and special events such as the International Film Festival. ⊠ *3-1901 Kaumualiʻi Hwy., Līhuʻe* ☎ *808/245–8270.*

DINNER SHOW

South Pacific Dinner Show. It seems a fitting tribute to see the play that put Kauaʻi on the map. Rodgers and Hammerstein's *South Pacific* has been playing at the Hilton Kauaʻi Beach Resort to rave reviews since 2002. The full musical production, accompanied by a cocktail reception and buffet, features local Kauaʻi talent. ⊠ *Grand Ballroom, Hilton Kauaʻi Beach Resort, Kauaʻi Beach Dr., Līhuʻe* ☎ *808/346–6500* ⊕ *www.southpacifickauai.com* 🍴 *$85* ⊘ *Wed. dinner and cocktails at 5:30, show at 6:45.*

LŪʻAU

Although the commercial lūʻau experience is a far cry from the backyard lūʻau thrown by local residents to celebrate a wedding, graduation, or baby's first birthday, they're nonetheless entertaining and a good introduction to the Hawaiian food that isn't widely sold in restaurants. Besides the feast, there's often an exciting dinner show with Polynesian-style music and dancing. It all makes for a fun evening that's suitable for couples, families, and groups, and the informal setting is conducive to meeting other people. Every lūʻau is different, reflecting the cuisine and tenor of the host facility, so compare prices, menus, and entertainment before making your reservation. Most lūʻau on Kauaʻi are offered only on a limited number of nights each week, so plan ahead to get the lūʻau you want. We tend to prefer those *not* held on resort properties, because they feel a bit more authentic. The lūʻau shows listed below are our favorites.

Grand Hyatt Kauaʻi Lūʻau. What used to be called Drums of Paradise has a new name and a new dance troupe but still offers a traditional lūʻau buffet and an exceptional performance. This oceanfront lūʻau comes with a view of the majestic Keoneloa Bay. ⊠ *Grand Hyatt Kauaʻi Resort and Spa, 1571 Poʻipū Rd., Poʻipū* ☎ *808/240–6456* 🍴 *$94* ⊘ *Thurs. and Sun. at 5.*

Lūʻau Kilohana. This lūʻau—on a former sugar plantation manager's estate—has a twist: all guests arrive at the feast by horse-drawn carriage (reservations are staggered to prevent lines). Families especially seem to enjoy the food and fun here. Even though sugar plantations are a decidedly Western affair, this lūʻau feels more authentic than those on a portable stage on resort grounds. The evening's theme is the history of sugar on the islands. Tahitian drumming and fire dancing add zest to the whole affair. ⊠*3-2087 Kaumuali'i St., Līhu'e* ☎*808/245–9593* ⊆*$95* ☽*Tues. and Fri. carriage rides begin at 5, dinner at 6, show at 8.*

Pa'ina o Hanalei. A conch shell is blown in the traditional way to signal the start of this gourmet lū'au feast held on the shore of Hanalei Bay. It's lavish, as one might expect from the Princeville Hotel, with a buffet line that's heavy on upscale, Pacific Rim cuisine and light on traditional lū'au fare. The event includes entertainment that celebrates the songs and dances of the South Pacific. *Please note: At this writing, the lū'au, like the rest of Princeville Resort, was closed for renovations and scheduled to reopen mid-2009.* ⊠*Princeville Resort, 5520 Ka Haku Rd., Princeville* ☎*808/826–2788* ⊆*$99* ☽*Mon. and Thurs. at 6.*

Fodor'sChoice
★
Smith's Tropical Paradise Lū'au. A 30-acre tropical garden provides the lovely setting for this popular lū'au, which begins with the traditional blowing of the conch shell and *imu* (pig roast) ceremony, followed by cocktails, an island feast, and an international show in the amphitheater overlooking a torch-lighted lagoon. It's fairly authentic and a better deal than the pricier resort events. ⊠*174 Wailua Rd., Kapa'a* ☎*808/821–6895* ⊆*$75* ☽*Mon., Wed., and Fri. 5–9:15.*

MUSIC

Check the local papers for outdoor reggae and Hawaiian-music shows, or one of the numbers listed below for more formal performances.

Hanalei Slack Key Concerts. Relax to the instrumental musical art form created by Hawaiian *paniolo* (cowboys) in the early 1800s. Shows are held at the Hanalei Family Community Center, which is *mauka* down a dirt access road across from St. Williams Catholic Church (Malolo Road) and then left down another dirt road. Look for a thatched-roof *hale* (house), several little green plantation-style buildings, and the brown double-yurt community center around the gravel parking lot. ⊠*Hanalei Family Community Center, Hanalei* ☎*808/826–1469* ⊕*www.hawaiianslackkeyguitar.com* ⊆*$20* ☽*Fri. at 4, Sun. at 3.*

Kaua'i Concert Association. This group offers a seasonal program at the Kaua'i Community College Performing Arts Center. A range of big-name artists, from Ricky Lee Jones to Taj Mahal, have been known to show up on Kaua'i for planned or impromptu performances. ⊠*3-1901 Kaumuali'i Hwy., Līhu'e* ☎*808/245–7464.*

BARS AND CLUBS

Nightclubs that stay open until the wee hours are rare on Kaua'i, and the bar scene is pretty limited. The major resorts generally host their own live entertainment and happy hours. All bars and clubs that serve alcohol must close at 2 AM, except those with a cabaret license, which allows them to close at 4 AM.

THE NORTH SHORE

Hanalei Gourmet. The sleepy North Shore stays awake—until 9:30, that is—each evening in this small, convivial setting inside Hanalei's restored old school building. The emphasis here is on local live jazz,

Kaua'i: Undercover Movie Star

Though Kaua'i has played itself in the movies (you may remember Nicolas Cage frantically shouting "Is it Kapa'a or Kapa'a-a?" into a pay phone in *Honeymoon in Vegas* (1992), most of its screen time has been as a stunt double for a number of tropical paradises. The island's remote valleys and waterfalls portrayed Venezuelan jungle in Kevin Costner's *Dragonfly* (2002) and a Costa Rican dinosaur preserve in Steven Spielberg's *Jurassic Park* (1993). Spielberg was no stranger to Kaua'i, having filmed Harrison Ford's escape via seaplane from Menehune Fishpond in *Raiders of the Lost Ark* (1981). The fluted cliffs and gorges of Kaua'i's rugged Nāpali Coast play the misunderstood beast's island home in *King Kong* (1976), and a jungle dweller of another sort, in *George of the Jungle* (1997), frolicked on Kaua'i. Harrison Ford returned to the island for 10 weeks during the filming of *Six Days, Seven Nights* (1998), a romantic adventure set in French Polynesia. Most recently, Ben Stiller, Jack Black, and Robert Downey Jr. filmed much of the raunchy war comedy *Tropic Thunder* (2008) on the Garden Island.

But these are all relatively contemporary movies. What's truly remarkable is that Hollywood discovered Kaua'i in 1933 with the making of *White Heat*, which was set on a sugar plantation and—like another more memorable movie filmed on Kaua'i—dealt with interracial love stories. In 1950, Esther Williams and Rita Moreno arrived to film *Pagan Love Song,* a forgettable musical. Then, it was off to the races, as Kaua'i saw no fewer than a dozen movies filmed on island in the 1950s, not all of them Oscar contenders. Rita Hayworth starred in *Miss Sadie Thompson* (1953) and no one you'd recognize starred in the tantalizing *She Gods of Shark Reef* (1956).

The movie that is still immortalized on the island in the names of restaurants, real estate offices, a hotel, and even a sushi item is *South Pacific* (1957). (You guessed it, right?) That mythical place called Bali Hai is never far away on Kaua'i. There's even an off-off-off-Broadway musical version of the movie performed today—some 50 years later—at the Kaua'i Beach Resort in Līhu'e.

In the 1960s Elvis Presley filmed *Blue Hawaii* (1961) and *Girls! Girls! Girls!* (1962) on the island. A local movie tour likes to point out the stain on a hotel carpet where Elvis's jelly doughnut fell.

Kaua'i has welcomed a long list of Hollywood's A-List: John Wayne in *Donovan's Reef* (1963); Jack Lemmon in *The Wackiest Ship in the Army* (1961); Richard Chamberlain in *The Thorn Birds* (1983); Gene Hackman in *Uncommon Valor* (1983); Danny DeVito and Billy Crystal in *Throw Momma From the Train* (1987); and Dustin Hoffman, Morgan Freeman, Renee Russo, and Cuba Gooding Jr. in *Outbreak* (1995).

Yet the movie scene isn't the only screen on which Kaua'i has starred. A long list of TV shows, TV pilots, and made-for-TV movies make the list as well, including *Gilligan's Island, Fantasy Island, Starsky & Hutch, Baywatch-Hawai'i*—even reality TV shows *The Bachelor* and *The Amazing Race 3.*

For the record, just because a movie was filmed here, doesn't mean the entire movie was filmed on Kaua'i. Take *Honeymoon in Vegas*—just one scene.

5

rock, and folk music. ⌧*5-5161 Kūhiō Hwy., Hanalei Center, Hanalei* ☏*808/826–2524.*

★ **Princeville Resort Living Room Lounge.** Every night from 7:30 to 10:30 this spacious lounge overlooking Hanalei Bay offers music with an ocean view. Musical selections range from contemporary to jazz to traditional Hawaiian. *Please note: At this writing, the lounge, like the rest of Princeville Resort, was closed for renovations and scheduled to reopen mid-2009.* ⌧*Princeville Resort, 5520 Ka Haku Rd., Princeville* ☏*808/826–9644.*

Tahiti Nui. This venerable and decidedly funky institution in sleepy Hanalei no longer offers its famous lū'au, ever since owner and founder Auntie Louise Marston died. Its fun-loving new owner, a Kiwi from New Zealand, is doing his best to keep the place hopping with nightly entertainment: Hawaiian music Tuesday and Thursday; karaoke on Monday and Thursday; and rock and roll Sunday, Wednesday, and Saturday. ⌧*5-5134 Kūhiō Hwy., Hanalei* ☏*808/826–6277* ⊕*www.thenui.com.*

THE EAST SIDE

Duke's Barefoot Bar. This is one of the liveliest bars on Kalapakī Beach. Contemporary Hawaiian music is performed in the beachside bar on Friday, and upstairs a traditional Hawaiian trio plays nightly for diners. The bar closes at midnight most nights. ⌧*Kalapakī Beach, Līhu'e* ☏*808/246–9599.*

Hukilau Lānai. This open-air bar and restaurant is on the property of the Kaua'i Coast Resort but operates independently. Trade winds trickle through the modest little bar, which looks out into a coconut grove. If the mood takes you, go on a short walk to the sea, or recline in big, comfortable chairs while listening to mellow jazz or Hawaiian slack-key guitar. Live music plays Sunday, Tuesday, and Friday, though the bar is open every day but Monday. Freshly infused tropical martinis—perhaps locally grown lychee and pineapple or a Big Island vanilla bean infusion—are house favorites. ⌧*520 Aleka Loop Kūhiō Hwy., Wailua* ☏*808/822–0600.*

Rob's Good Times Grill. Let loose at this sports bar, which also houses Kaua'i's hottest DJs spinning Thursday through Saturday from 9 PM to 2 AM. Wednesday you can kick up your heels with country line dancing from 7:30 PM to 11. Sunday, Monday, and Tuesday evenings are open mike for karaoke enthusiasts. ⌧*4303 Rice St., Līhu'e* ☏*808/246–0311.*

Tradewinds—A South Seas Bar. This salty mariner's den is surprisingly located within the cliché confines of a cheesy mall. Tradewinds has a tattered palm-frond roof and a tropical theme reminiscent of Jimmy Buffett, but you aren't likely to hear Buffett tunes here. In fact, you're more likely to meet Ernest Hemingway types. From karaoke to dart league competitions to live music, this little bar busts at the seams with local flavor. It's open daily from 10 AM to 2 AM. ⌧*Coconut Marketplace, Kūhiō Hwy., Kapa'a* ☏*808/822–1621.*

THE SOUTH SHORE AND WEST SIDE

Keoki's Paradise. A young, energetic crowd makes this a lively spot on Thursday, Friday, and Saturday nights, with live music from 7 to 9. After 9 PM, when the dining room clears out, there's a bit of a bar scene for singles. The bar closes at midnight. ⊠*Po'ipū Shopping Village, 2360 Kiahuna Plantation Dr., Po'ipū* ☎*808/742–7534.*

The Point at Sheraton Kaua'i. This is *the* place to be on the South Shore to celebrate sunset with a drink; the ocean view is unsurpassed. Starting at 8 PM on Friday, Saturday, and Monday, there's live entertainment until 12:30 AM, including salsa dancing and a DJ on Saturday, and swing dancing on Monday. ⊠*Sheraton Kaua'i Resort, 2440 Ho'onani Rd., Po'ipū* ☎*808/742–1661*

Waimea Brewing Company. Sip one of the award-winning beers in an airy plantation-style house in a 100-year-old coconut grove on the property of the Waimea Plantation Cottages. Home-brewed beer, outdoor seating, and a wraparound lānai make this brewery/eatery an authentic West Side experience. No promises, but there is usually live music on Tuesday, Wednesday, and Thursday. ⊠*9400 Kaumuali'i Hwy., Waimea* ☎*808/338–9733.*

WHERE TO EAT

In Kauai, if you're lucky enough to win an invitation to a potluck, baby lū'au, or beach party, don't think twice—just accept. The best grinds (food) are homemade, and so you'll eat until you're full, then rest, eat some more, and make a plate to take home, too.

But even if you can't score a spot at one of these parties, don't despair. Great local-style food is easy to come by at countless low-key places around the island, and as an extra bonus these eats are often inexpensive, and portions are generous. Expect plenty of meat—usually deep-fried or marinated in a teriyaki sauce and grilled *pulehu*-style—over an open fire—and starches. Rice is standard, even for breakfast, and often served alongside potato-macaroni salad, another island specialty. Another local favorite is *poke,* made from chunks of raw tuna or octopus seasoned with sesame oil, soy sauce, onions, and pickled seaweed. It's a great pūpū (appetizer) when paired with a cold beer.

Kaua'i's cultural diversity is apparent in its restaurants, which offer authentic Vietnamese, Chinese, Korean, Japanese, Thai, Mexican, Italian, and Hawaiian specialties. Less specialized restaurants cater to the tourist crowd, serving standard American fare—burgers, pizza, sandwiches, surf-and-turf combos, and so on. Kapa'a offers the best selection of restaurants, with options for a variety of tastes and budgets; most fast-food joints are in Līhu'e.

Parents will be relieved to encounter a tolerant attitude toward children, even if they're noisy. Men can leave their jackets and ties at home; attire tends toward informal, but if you want to dress up, you can. Reservations are accepted in most places and required at some of the top restaurants. ■TIP→One cautionary note: most restaurants stop serving dinner at 8 or 9 PM, so plan to eat early.

WHAT IT COSTS					
	¢	$	$$	$$$	$$$$
RESTAURANTS	under $10	$10–$17	$18–$26	$27–$35	over $35

Prices are for one main course at dinner.

THE NORTH SHORE

$$–$$$
MEDITERRANEAN
Fodor'sChoice
★

✕**Bar Acuda.** This tapas bar is a welcome addition to the Hanalei dining scene, rocketing right to top place in the categories of tastiness, creativity, and pizzazz. Owner-chef Jim Moffat's brief menu changes weekly: you might find sea bass, polenta, fried fish cakes, grilled veggies, a fresh mozzarella salad, and sausages with onions, all served with fresh bread. The small servings are intended to be shared, tapas-style. The food is consistently remarkable, with subtly intense sauces that further elevate the outstanding cuisine. It's super casual, but chic, with a nice porch for outdoor dining and the service is discreet, but thorough. ⊠*Hanalei Center, 5-5161 Kūhiō Hwy., Hanalei* ☎*808/826–7081* ▭*MC, V* ⊘*Closed Sun. and Mon.*

$$
JAPANESE

✕**Bouchon.** This second-story restaurant and sushi bar, known until recently as Sushi Blues, has a nice ambience, with copper tabletops, lovely views of mountains streaked with waterfalls, and photos of international jazz greats lining the staircase. Regular entertainment, a full bar, and a sake menu add to its appeal. Choose from steaks, seafood dishes, and specialty sushi items such as the Las Vegas Roll, which is filled with tuna, yellowtail, and avocado and fried in a tempura batter. ⊠*Ching Young Village, 5-5190 Kūhiō Hwy., Hanalei* ☎*808/826–9701* ▭*AE, D, DC, MC, V.*

$$$
AMERICAN

✕**Cafe Hanalei and Terrace.** You're in for a very romantic evening here: the view from the Princeville Resort overlooking Hanalei Bay is mesmerizing, and the food and service are superb. In all but the rainiest weather you'll want to be seated outside on the terrace. The Sunday brunch ($53 or $60 with champagne) and daily breakfast buffet are enormous feasts, as is the Friday night seafood buffet ($60). Japanese specialties, fresh-fish specials, and Kaua'i coffee rack of lamb are excellent choices for dinner. If you're on a budget, come for lunch when you can enjoy the fabulous views and a leisurely, relaxing meal—try the Cobb salad—for less than you'd spend at dinner. The pastry chef deserves praise for delicious, innovative desserts. Save room for the decadent Tower of Passion, a chocolate tower filled with passion-fruit mousse. *Please note: At this writing, Cafe Hanalei, like the rest of Princeville Resort, was closed for renovations and scheduled to reopen mid-2009.* ⊠*Princeville Resort, 5520 Ka Haku Rd., Princeville* ☎*808/826–2760* ▭*AE, D, DC, MC, V.*

$–$$
AMERICAN

✕**Hanalei Gourmet.** This spot in Hanalei's restored old schoolhouse offers dolphin-safe tuna, low-sodium meats, fresh-baked breads, and homemade desserts as well as a casual atmosphere where both families and the sports-watching crowds can feel equally comfortable. Early birds can order coffee and toast or a hearty breakfast. Lunch and dinner menus feature sandwiches, burgers, filling salads, and nightly specials of fresh local fish. They also will prepare a picnic and give it to you in an insulated backpack. A full bar and frequent live entertainment keep things hopping even after the kitchen closes. ✉ *5-5161 Kūhiō Hwy., Hanalei* ☎ *808/826–2524* ⊕ *www.hanaleigourmet.com* ◻ *D, DC, MC, V.*

$$
AMERICAN

✕ **Kīlauea Bakery and Pau Hana Pizza.** This bakery has garnered tons of well-deserved good press for its starter of Hawaiian sourdough made with guava as well as its specialty pizzas topped with such yummy ingredients as smoked ono (a Hawaiian fish), Gorgonzola-rosemary sauce, barbecued chicken, goat cheese, and roasted onions. Open from 6:30 AM, the bakery serves coffee drinks, delicious fresh pastries, bagels, and breads in the morning. Late risers beware: breads and pastries sell out quickly on weekends. Pizza, soup, and salads can be ordered for lunch or dinner. If you want to hang out or do the coffee shop bit in Kīlauea, this is the place. A pretty courtyard with covered tables is a pleasant place to linger. ✉ *Kong Lung Center, 2490 Keneke St., Kīlauea* ☎ *808/828–2020* ◻ *MC, V.*

$$$–$$$$
ITALIAN
Fodor'sChoice
★

✕ **La Cascata.** Terra-cotta floors, hand-painted murals, and trompe-l'oeil paintings give La Cascata a Tuscan-villa flair that makes it ideal for cozy, romantic dining. Picture windows offer dazzling views of Hanalei Bay, though you'll have to come before sunset to enjoy them. Local ingredients figure prominently on a fairly standard menu of pasta, fresh seafood, and meats prepared with competence and creativity. Savor *brodetto di pesce* ('iprawns, snapper, scallops, and clams with a lobster *bourdelaise* sauce served over linguine) or black-pepper-crusted duck breast with a sweet-potato mash and *griotte cherry gastrique*. The traditional tiramisu is exquisite, and the signature baby cake is a very adult confection. The service is professional and efficient. This is one of two excellent—though pricey—restaurants at the luxurious Princeville Resort. *Please note: At this writing, the lū'au, like the rest of Princeville Resort, was closed for renovations and scheduled to reopen mid-2009.* ✉ *Princeville Resort, 5520 Ka Haku Rd., Princeville* ☎ *808/826–2761* ⬧ *Reservations essential* ◻ *AE, D, DC, MC, V* ☉ *No lunch.*

$$$
AMERICAN

✕ **Postcards Café.** With its postcard artwork, beamed ceilings, and light interiors, this plantation-cottage restaurant has a menu consisting mostly of organic, additive-free vegetarian foods and fish. But don't get the wrong idea—this isn't simple cooking: specials might include carrot-ginger soup, taro fritters, or fresh fish served with peppered pineapple-sage sauce. Desserts are made without refined sugar. Try the chocolate silk pie made with barley malt chocolate, pure vanilla, and creamy tofu with a crust of graham crackers, sun-dried cherries, and crushed cashews. This is probably your best bet for dinner in Hanalei town. ✉ *5-5075A Kūhiō Hwy., Hanalei* ☎ *808/826–1191* ⊕ *www.postcards cafe.com* ◻ *AE, MC, V* ☉ *No lunch.*

THE EAST SIDE: KAPA'A AND WAILUA

$$
STEAK

✕ **Bull Shed.** The A-frame exterior of this popular restaurant imparts a distinctly rustic feel. Inside, light-color walls and a full wall of glass highlight an ocean view that is one of the best on Kaua'i. Come early

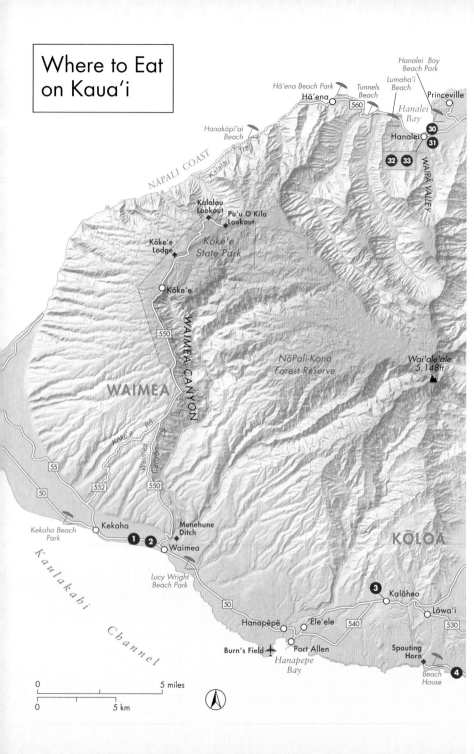

Where to Eat on Kaua'i

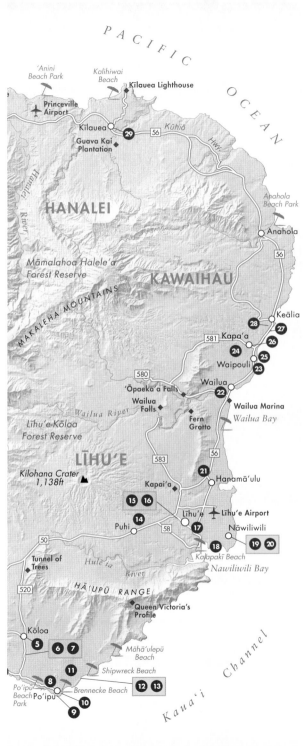

for a window seat, where you can watch surf crashing on the rocks while you study the menu. The food is simple and basic—think white bread and iceberg lettuce—but they know how to do surf and turf. You can try both in one of several combo dinner platters or order fresh island fish and thick steaks individually. The restaurant is best known for its prime rib and Australian rack of lamb. Longtime visitors love this place, which hasn't changed much in 20 years. Arrive by 5:30 for early-bird specials and your best shot at a window seat. ⊠ *796 Kūhiō Hwy., Kapaʻa* ☎ *808/822–3791 or 808/822–1655* ▤ *AE, D, DC, MC, V* ⊗ *No lunch.*

$ ✕ **Caffé Coco.** A restored plantation cottage set back off the highway and
AMERICAN   surrounded by tropical foliage is the setting for this island café. You'll know it by its bright lime-green storefront. An attached black-light art gallery and a vintage apparel shop called Bambulei make this a fun stop for any meal. Outdoor seating in the vine-covered garden is pleasant during nice weather, although on calm nights, it can get buggy. Acoustic music is offered regularly, attracting a laid-back local crowd. Pot stickers filled with tofu and mango sweet and sour sauce, ʻahi wraps, Greek and organic salads, fresh fish and soups, and a daily list of specials are complemented by wonderful desserts. Allow plenty of time, because the tiny kitchen can't turn out meals quickly. ⊠ *4-369 Kūhiō Hwy., Wailua* ☎ *808/822–7990* ▤ *MC, V* ⊗ *Closed Mon.*

¢–$ ✕ **Eggbert's.** If you're big on breakfasts, try Eggbert's, which serves
AMERICAN   breakfast items until 3 PM daily. In the Coconut Marketplace, this
☺   family-friendly restaurant, with a sunny soft-yellow interior, lots of windows, and lānai seating, is a great spot for omelets, banana pancakes, and eggs Benedict. Lunch selections include sandwiches, burgers, stir-fry, and fresh fish. Take-out orders are also available. ⊠ *Coconut Marketplace, 4-484 Kūhiō Hwy., Kapaʻa* ☎ *808/822–3787* ▤ *MC, V* ⊗ *No dinner.*

$–$$ ✕ **Kauaʻi Pasta.** If you don't mind a no-frills atmosphere in exchange for
ITALIAN   five-star food, this is the place. The husband of the husband-and-wife team that runs Kauaʻi Pasta left his executive chef position at Roy's to open a catering business. He leased a kitchen that happened to have a small dining area, and rather than let it go to waste, they open for dinner every evening except Monday. Specials, written on the whiteboard at the entrance, are always satisfying and delicious. The locals have this place figured out; they show up in droves. The food's fabulous, and the price is right. The Līhuʻe branch also serves lunch. ⊠ *4-939B Kūhiō Hwy., Kapaʻa* ☎ *808/822–7447* ▤ *MC, V* ⛅ *BYOB* ⊗ *Closed Mon.*

$$–$$$ ✕ **Lemongrass Grill.** The inside of Kapaʻa's Lemongrass Grill may remind
JAPANESE   you of a Pacific Rim–themed rustic tavern, with its stained wood interior, numerous paintings and carvings, and food that is as fresh as it can get. There's something for everybody here: salads, poultry, steaks and ribs, vegetarian fare, and of course, a wide selection of seafood, all with an island flair. Specials include a heaping seafood platter featuring lobster tails, scallops, shrimp scampi, the fish of the day, and an assortment of vegetables—they say it's "for two" but could easily feed three or four. Service is laid back, but friendly. ⊠ *4-885 Kūhiō Hwy., Kapaʻa* ☎ *808/821–2888* ▤ *AE, D, MC, V* ⊗ *No lunch.*

$$ ✕ **Mema Thai Chinese Cuisine.** Refined and intimate, Mema Thai serves its
THAI dishes on crisp white linens accented by tabletop orchid sprays. Menu
items such as broccoli with oyster sauce and cashew chicken reveal
Chinese origins, but the emphasis is on Thai dishes. A host of curries—
red, green, yellow, and house—made with coconut milk and kaffir-lime
leaves run from mild to mouth searing. The traditional green-papaya
salad adds a cool touch for the palate. ⊠ *Wailua Shopping Plaza, 369
Kūhiō Hwy., Kapa'a* ☎ *808/823–0899* ⊟ *AE, D, DC, MC, V* ⊗ *No
lunch weekends.*

$$–$$$ ✕ **Restaurant Kintaro.** If you want to eat someplace that's a favorite with
JAPANESE locals, visit Kintaro's. But be prepared to wait, because ever since the
island's visitors discovered this restaurant, the dining room and sushi
bar are always jammed. The recent surge in popularity hasn't affected
the food, but it has diminished the service. Try the Bali Hai, a roll of eel
and smoked salmon, baked and topped with wasabi mayonnaise. For
an "all-in-one-dish" meal, consider the *Nabemono*, a single pot filled
with a healthful variety of seafood and vegetables. *Teppanyaki* dinners
are meat, seafood, and vegetables flash-cooked on tabletop grills in
an entertaining display. Tatami-mat seating is available behind shoji
screens that provide privacy for groups. ⊠ *4-370 Kūhiō Hwy., Wailua*
☎ *808/822–3341* ⊟ *AE, D, DC, MC, V* ⊗ *Closed Sun. No lunch.*

$$ ✕ **Wailua Marina Restaurant.** Offering the island's only river view, this
AMERICAN marina restaurant—an island fixture for almost 40 years—is a good
spot to stop after a boat ride up the Wailua River to the Fern Grotto.
With more than 40 selections, the menu is a mix of comfort food and
more sophisticated dishes; portions are gigantic. The chef is fond of
stuffing: you'll find stuffed baked pork chops, stuffed chicken baked
in plum sauce, and 'ahi stuffed with crab. The steamed mullet is a
classic island dish. ⊠ *Wailua River State Park, Wailua Rd., Wailua*
☎ *808/822–4311* ⊟ *AE, D, DC, MC, V* ⊗ *Closed Mon.*

THE EAST SIDE: LĪHU'E

$$–$$$ ✕ **Café Portofino.** The menu at this authentic northern Italian restau-
ITALIAN rant is as inspired as the views of Kalapakī Bay and the Hā'upu range.
Fodor'sChoice Owner Giuseppe Avocadi's flawless dishes have garnered a host of culi-
★ nary awards and raves from dining critics. The fresh 'ahi carpaccio is a
signature dish, and pasta, scampi, and veal are enhanced by sauces that
soar like Avocadi's imagination. Linger over coffee and ice-cream–filled
profiteroles or traditional tiramisu while enjoying harp music. Excellent
service and a soothing, dignified ambience complete the delightful dining experience, making this one of your best bets for a quality meal in
Līhu'e. ⊠ *Kaua'i Marriott Resort & Beach Club, 3610 Rice St., Līhu'e*
☎ *808/245–2121* ⊟ *AE, D, DC, MC, V* ⊗ *No lunch.*

¢ ✕ **Dani's Restaurant.** Kaua'i residents frequent this big, sparsely furnished
HAWAIIAN eatery near the Līhu'e Fire Station for hearty, local-style food at breakfast and lunch. Dani's is a good place to try lū'au food without commercial lū'au prices. You can order Hawaiian-style *laulau* (pork and
taro leaves wrapped in ti leaves and steamed) or kālua pig, slow roasted
in an underground oven. Other island-style dishes include Japanese-
prepared *tonkatsu* (pork cutlet) and teriyaki beef, and there's always the

all-American New York steak. Omelets are whipped up with fish cake, kālua pig, or seafood; everything is served with rice. ✉ *4201 Rice St., Līhu'e* ☎ *808/245–4991* ▤ *MC, V* ⊗ *Closed Sun. No dinner.*

$$$
SEAFOOD
✕ **Duke's Canoe Club.** Surfing legend Duke Kahanamoku is immortalized at this casual bi-level restaurant set on Kalapakī Bay. Guests can admire surfboards, photos, and other memorabilia marking the Duke's long tenure as a waterman. It's an interesting collection, and an indoor garden and waterfall add to the pleasing ambience. Downstairs you'll find simple fare ranging from fish tacos and stir-fried cashew chicken to hamburgers, served 11 AM to 10:30 PM. At dinner, upstairs, fresh fish prepared in a variety of styles is the best choice. Duke's claims to have the biggest salad bar on the island, though given the lack of competition that isn't saying much. A happy-hour drink and appetizer is a less expensive way to enjoy the moonrises and ocean views here—though it can get pretty crowded. The Barefoot Bar is a hot spot for after-dinner drinks, too. ✉ *Kaua'i Marriott Resort & Beach Club, 3610 Rice St., Līhu'e* ☎ *808/246–9599* ▤ *AE, D, DC, MC, V.*

$$$–$$$$
ECLECTIC
✕ **Gaylord's.** In what was at one time Kaua'i's most expensive plantation estate, Gaylord's pays tribute to the elegant dining rooms of 1930s high society. Tables with candlelight sit on a cobblestone patio surrounding a fountain and overlooking a wide lawn. The innovative menu features classic American cooking with an island twist. Try wonton-wrapped prawns with a wasabi plum sauce, Australian venison, blackened prime rib, or fresh-fish specials. Lunches are a mix of salads, sandwiches, and pasta, enjoyed in a leisurely fashion. The lavish Sunday brunch may include such specialties as sweet-potato hash and Cajun 'ahi in addition to the standard omelets and pancakes. Before or after dining you can wander around the estate grounds or take a horse-drawn carriage ride. ✉ *Kilohana Plantation, 3-2087 Kaumuali'i Rd., Līhu'e* ☎ *808/245–9593* ▤ *AE, D, DC, MC, V.*

¢–$
HAWAIIAN
✕ **Hamura Saimin.** Folks just love this funky old plantation-style diner. Locals and tourists stream in and out all day long, and neighbor islanders stop in on their way to the airport to pick up take-out orders for friends and family back home. *Saimin* is the big draw, and each day the Hiraoka family dishes up about 1,000 bowls of steaming broth and homemade noodles, topped with a variety of garnishes. The barbecued chicken and meat sticks adopt a smoky flavor during grilling. The landmark eatery is also famous for its *liliko'i* (passion fruit) chiffon pie. ■ TIP➔ As one of the few island eateries open until midnight on Friday and Saturday (10 PM Monday through Thursday), it's favored by night owls. ✉ *2956 Kress St., Līhu'e* ☎ *808/245–3271* ▤ *No credit cards.*

¢–$
JAPANESE
✕ **Hanamā'ulu Restaurant, Tea House, Sushi Bar, and Robatayaki.** Business is brisk at this landmark Kaua'i eatery. The food is a mix of Japanese, Chinese, and local-style cooking, served up in hearty portions. The ginger chicken and fried shrimp are wildly popular, as are the fresh sashimi and sushi. Other choices include tempura, chicken *katsu* (Japanese-style fried chicken), beef broccoli, and *robatayaki* (grilled seafood and meat). The main dining room is rather unattractive, but the private rooms in back look out on the Japanese garden and fishponds and feature traditional seating on tatami mats at low tables. These tearooms

can be reserved and are favored for family events and celebrations. ✉ *1-4291 Kūhiō Hwy., Rte. 56, Hanamā'ulu* ☎ *808/245–2511* ▭ *MC, V* ☽ *Closed Mon.*

$$

AMERICAN

✕ **JJ's Broiler.** This spacious, low-key restaurant offers hearty American fare, including burgers and 2-pound buckets of steamer clams bathed in white wine, garlic, and herbs. On sunny afternoons, ask for a table on the lānai overlooking Kalapakī Bay and try one of the generous salads. The house specialty is Slavonic steak, a broiled sliced tenderloin dipped in a buttery wine sauce. ✉ *Anchor Cove, 3146 Rice St., Nāwiliwili* ☎ *808/246–4422* ▭ *D, MC, V.*

$

AMERICAN

✕ **Līhu'e Barbecue Inn.** Few Kaua'i restaurants are more beloved than this family-owned eatery, a mainstay of island dining since 1940. The menu runs from traditional American to Asian. Try the baby back ribs, seared ahi and garlic shrimp, or classic surf and turf; or choose a full Japanese dinner from the other side of the menu. If you can't make up your mind, strike a compromise with the inn's tri-sampler. Opt for the fruit cup—fresh, not canned—instead of soup or salad, and save room for a hefty slice of homemade cream pie, available in all sorts of flavors. ✉ *2982 Kress St., Līhu'e* ☎ *808/245–2921* ▭ *MC, V.*

THE SOUTH SHORE AND WEST SIDE

$$–$$$

AMERICAN

Fodor's Choice

★

✕ **Beach House.** This restaurant partners a dreamy ocean view with impressive cuisine. Few Kaua'i experiences are more delightful than sitting at one of the outside tables and savoring a delectable meal while the sun sinks into the glassy blue Pacific. It's the epitome of tropical dining, and no other restaurant on Kaua'i can offer anything quite like it. Chef Todd Barrett's menu changes often, but the food is consistently creative and delicious. A few trademark dishes appear regularly, such as mint-coriander lamb rack, fire-roasted sashimi-grade 'ahi, and lemongrass and kaffir-lime sea scallops. Seared macadamia-nut-crusted mahimahi, a dish ubiquitous on island menus, gets a refreshing new twist when served with a liliko'i-lemongrass beurre blanc. Save room for the signature molten chocolate desire, a decadent finale at this pleasing and deservedly popular restaurant. ✉ *5022 Lāwa'i Rd., Kōloa* ☎ *808/742–1424* ⌁ *Reservations essential* ▭ *AE, DC, MC, V* ☽ *No lunch.*

$$–$$$

STEAK

✕ **Brennecke's Beach Broiler.** Brennecke's is decidedly casual and fun, with a busy bar, windows overlooking the beach, and a cheery blue-and-white interior. It specializes in big portions in a wide range of offerings including New York steaks, crab legs, shrimp, and the fresh catch of the day. Can't decide? Then, create your own combination meal. This place is especially good for happy hour (3 PM to 5 PM), as the drink and pūpū menus are tomes. The standard surf and turf is not remarkable in any way, but the ocean view is nice. There's a take-out deli downstairs. ✉ *2100 Ho'ōne Rd., Po'ipū* ☎ *808/742–7588* ▭ *AE, D, DC, MC, V.*

$$

ITALIAN

✕ **Casa di Amici.** Tucked away in a quiet neighborhood above Po'ipū Beach, this "House of Friends" has live classical piano music on weekends and an outside deck open to sweeping ocean views. Entrées from the internationally eclectic menu include a saffron-vanilla paella risotto made with black tiger prawns, fresh fish, chicken breast, and homemade Italian sausage. For dessert, take the plunge with a baked Hawai'i: a chocolate-macadamia-nut brownie topped with coconut and passion-fruit sorbet and flambéed Italian meringue. The food and setting are pleasant, but service can be maddeningly slow, especially when you're really hungry. ⊠*2301 Nalo Rd., Po'ipū* ☎*808/742–1555* ☰*AE, D, DC, MC, V* ⊘*No lunch.*

$$$–$$$$
ITALIAN
Fodor's Choice
★

✕**Dondero's.** The inlaid marble floors, ornate tile work, and Italianate murals that compose the elegant interior at this restaurant compete with a stunning ocean view. And in addition to the beautiful setting, Dondero's offers outstanding food, a remarkable wine list, and impeccable service, making this Kaua'i's best restaurant. Chef Vincent Pecoraro combines old-world techniques with new energy to create menu selections as enticing as the surroundings. Pistachio-crusted rack of lamb with a root-vegetable fritter and pancetta mashed sweet potatoes, and lobster piccata on a bed of fettuccine with sundried tomatoes and a truffle cream sauce thrill the palate and delight the eye. Order a light, traditional tiramisu or chocolate crème brûlée with fresh raspberries so you can linger over coffee. The waitstaff deserves special praise for its thoughtful, discrete service. ⊠*Grand Hyatt Kaua'i Resort and Spa, 1571 Po'ipū Rd., Kōloa* ☎*808/240–6456* ☰*AE, D, DC, MC, V* ⊘*No lunch.*

$–$$
STEAK

✕**Kalāheo Steak House.** Prime rib, tender top sirloin, Kalāheo shrimp, Alaskan king crab legs, and Portuguese bean soup are competently prepared and served up in hearty portions at this cozy, country-ranch-house-style restaurant. Weathered wood furnishings and artifacts pay tribute to Hawai'i's *paniolo*, who can still be found in these parts. Wines range from $19 to $45 a bottle. ⊠*4444 Pāpālina Rd., Kalāheo* ☎*808/332–7217* ☰*AE, D, MC, V* ⚠*Reservations not accepted* ⊘*No lunch.*

$$
SEAFOOD

✕**Keoki's Paradise.** Built to resemble a dockside boathouse, this active, boisterous place fills up quickly, especially on live-music nights (Sunday, Monday, and Wednesday to Friday). Seafood appetizers span the tide from sashimi to Thai shrimp sticks, crab cakes, and scallops crusted in *panko* (Japanese-style bread crumbs). The day's fresh catch is available in half a dozen styles and sauces. And there's a sampling of beef, chicken, and pork-rib entrées for the committed carnivore. A lighter menu is available at the bar for lunch and dinner. ⊠*Po'ipū Shopping Village, 2360 Kiahuna Plantation Dr., Kōloa* ☎*808/742–7534* ☰*AE, D, DC, MC, V.*

$$–$$$
ITALIAN

✕**Plantation Gardens.** A historic plantation manager's home has been converted to a restaurant that serves seafood and kiawe-grilled meats with a Pacific Rim and Italian influence. You'll walk through a tropical setting of torch-lighted orchid gardens and lotus-studded koi ponds to a cozy, European-style dining room with cherry wood floors and veranda dining. The menu is based on fresh, local foods: fish right off the boat, herbs and produce picked from the plantation's gardens, fruit delivered by neighborhood farmers. The result is Italian cuisine with an island flair—seafood *laulau* (seafood wrapped in ti leaves and steamed) served with mango chutney—served alongside traditional classics such as rosemary-skewered pork tenderloin and pan-roasted scallops. Definitely save room for dessert: the *liliko'i* (passionfruit) cheesecake is a

Continued on page 527

LŪ'AU: A TASTE OF HAWAI'I

The best place to sample Hawaiian food is at a backyard lū'au. Aunties and uncles are cooking, the pig is from a cousin's farm, and the fish is from a brother's boat.

But invitations to those occasions are rare. So your choice is most likely between a commercial lū'au and a restaurant that serves Hawaiian food.

Most commercial lū'au will offer you some of the authentic diet; they're also about umbrella drinks, laughs, spectacle, and fun. Expect to spend a leisurely evening and no small amount of cash.

For greater authenticity, folksy experiences, and rock-bottom prices, visit a Hawaiian restaurant (most are in simple, anonymous storefronts in residential neighborhoods). Locals will be happy to help you negotiate the menu.

In either case, much of what is known today as Hawaiian food would be as foreign to a 16th-century Hawaiian as risotto or chow mien. The pre-contact diet was simple and healthy–mainly raw and steamed seafood and vegetables. Early Hawaiians used earth ovens and heated stones to cook seafood, taro, sweet potatoes, and breadfruit and seasoned their food with sea salt and ground kukui nuts. Seaweed, fern shoots, sweet potato vines, coconut, banana, sugarcane, and select greens and roots rounded out the diet.

Successive waves of immigrants added their favorites to the ti leaf–lined table. So it is that foods as disparate as salt salmon and chicken long rice are now Hawaiian— even though there is no salmon in Hawaiian waters and long rice (cellophane noodles) is Chinese.

AT THE LŪʻAU: KĀLUA PORK

The heart of any lūʻau is the *imu*, the earth oven in which a whole pig is roasted. The preparation of an imu is a bonding affair for most families, who tackle it only once a year or so, for a baby's first birthday or at Thanksgiving, when many Islanders prefer to imu their turkeys. Commercial lūʻau operations have it down to a science, however.

THE ART OF THE STONE
The key to a proper imu is the *pohaku*, the stones. Imu cook by means of long, slow, moist heat released by special stones that can withstand a hot fire without exploding. Many Hawaiian families treasure their imu stones, keeping them in a pile in the backyard and passing them on through generations.

PIT COOKING
The imu makers first dig a pit about the size of a refrigerator, then lay down *kiawe* (mesquite) wood and stones, and build a white-hot fire that is allowed to burn itself out. The ashes are raked away, and the hot stones covered with banana and ti leaves. Well-wrapped in ti or banana leaves and a net of chicken wire, the pig is lowered onto the leaf-covered stones. *Laulau* (leaf-wrapped bundles of meats, fish, and taro leaves) may also be placed inside. Leaves—ti, banana, even ginger—cover the pig followed by wet burlap sacks (to create steam). The whole is topped with a canvas tarp and left to steam overnight.

OPENING THE IMU
This is the moment everyone waits for: The imu is unwrapped like a giant present and the imu keepers gingerly wrestle out the steaming pig. When it's unwrapped, the meat falls moist and smoky-flavored from the bone, looking and tasting just like Southern-style pulled pork, but without the barbecue sauce.

WHICH LŪʻAU?
The Feast at Lele. Top-notch value and price, great wine list.

Old Lahaina Lūʻau. Intimate and the most traditional; a perennial sell-out.

Wailea Beach Marriott Honuaʻula Lūʻau. Imu ceremony and buffet.

MEA 'AI 'ONO.
GOOD THINGS TO EAT.

LAULAU

Steamed meats, fish, and taro leaf in ti-leaf bundles: fork-tender, a medley of flavors; the taro resembles spinach.

Laulau

LOMI LOMI SALMON

Salt salmon in a piquant salad or relish with onions, tomatoes.

POI (DON'T CALL IT LIBRARY PASTE.)

Poi, a paste made of pounded taro root, is an acquired taste, but give it a try.

Consider: The Hawaiian Adam is descended from *kalo* (taro). Young taro plants are called "keiki"–children. Poi is the first food after mother's milk for many Islanders. 'Ai, the word for food, is synonymous with poi in many contexts.

Lomi Lomi Salmon

Not only that, we like it. "There is no meat that doesn't taste good with poi," the old Hawaiians said.

But you have to know how to eat it: with something rich or powerfully flavored. "It is salt that makes the poi go in," is another adage. When you're served poi, try it with a mouthful of smoky kālua pork or salty lomi lomi salmon. Its slightly sour blandness cleanses the palate. And if you don't like it, smile and say something polite. (And slide that bowl over to a local.)

Poi

E HELE MAI 'AI! COME AND EAT!

Hawaiian restaurants tend to be inconveniently located in well-worn storefronts with little or no parking, outfitted with battered tables and clattering Melmac dishes, open odd (and usually limited) hours and days, and often so crowded you have to wait. But they personify aloha, invariably run by local families who welcome tourists who take the trouble to find them.

Many are cash-only operations and combination plates are a standard feature: one or two entrées, a side such as chicken long rice, choice of poi or steamed rice and—if the place is really old-style—a tiny portion of coarse Hawaiian salt and some raw onions for relish.

Most serve some foods that aren't, strictly speaking, Hawaiian, but are beloved of

kama'āina, such as salt meat with watercress (preserved meat in a tasty broth), or *akubone* (skipjack tuna fried in a tangy vinegar sauce).

Our two favorites: **Aloha Mixed Plate** and **A.K.'s Café**.

MENU GUIDE

Much of the Hawaiian language encountered during a stay in the Islands will appear on restaurant menus and lists of lū'au fare. Here's a quick primer.

'ahi: *yellowfin tuna.*

aku: *skipjack, bonito tuna.*

'ama'ama: *mullet; it's hard to get but tasty.*

bento: *a box lunch.*

chicken lū'au: *a stew made from chicken, taro leaves, and coconut milk.*

haupia: *a light, pudding-like sweet made from coconut.*

imu: *the underground ovens in which pigs are roasted for lū'au.*

kālua: *to bake underground.*

kaukau: *food. The word comes from Chinese but is used in the Islands.*

kimchee: *Korean dish of pickled cabbage made with garlic and hot peppers.*

Kona coffee: *coffee grown in the Kona district of the Big Island.*

laulau: *literally, a bundle. Laulau are morsels of pork, chicken, butterfish, or other ingredients wrapped with young taro leaves and then bundled in ti leaves for steaming.*

liliko'i: *passion fruit, a tart, seedy yellow fruit that makes delicious desserts, juice, and jellies.*

lomi lomi: *to rub or massage; also a massage. Lomi lomi salmon is fish that has been rubbed with onions and herbs; commonly served with minced onions and tomatoes.*

lū'au: *a Hawaiian feast; also the leaf of the taro plant used in preparing such a feast.*

lū'au leaves: *cooked taro tops with a taste similar to spinach.*

mahimahi: *mild-flavored dolphinfish, not the marine mammal.*

mai tai: *potent rum drink with orange and lime juice, from the Tahitian word for "good."*

malasada: *a Portuguese deep-fried doughnut without a hole, dipped in sugar.*

manapua: *dough wrapped around diced pork or other fillings.*

manō: *shark.*

niu: *coconut.*

'ōkolehao: *a liqueur distilled from the ti root.*

onaga: *pink or red snapper.*

ono: *a long, slender mackerel-like fish; also called wahoo.*

'ono: *delicious; also hungry.*

'opihi: *a tiny shellfish, or mollusk, found on rocks; also called limpets.*

pāpio: *a young ulua or jack fish.*

pohā: *Cape gooseberry. Tasting a bit like honey, the pohā berry is often used in jams and desserts.*

poi: *a paste made from pounded taro root, a staple of the Hawaiian diet.*

poke: *chopped, pickled raw tuna or other fish, tossed with herbs and seasonings.*

pūpū: *Hawaiian hors d'oeuvre.*

saimin: *long thin noodles and vegetables in broth, often garnished with small pieces of fish cake, scrambled egg, luncheon meat, and green onion.*

sashimi: *raw fish thinly sliced and usually eaten with soy sauce.*

tī leaves: *a member of the agave family. The fragrant leaves are used to wrap food while cooking and removed before eating.*

uku: *deep-sea snapper.*

ulua: *a member of the jack family that also includes pompano and amberjack. Also called crevalle, jack fish, and jack crevalle.*

dream. In short, the food is excellent and the setting charming. ⊠*Kiahuna Plantation, 2253 Po'ipū Rd., Kōloa* ☎*808/742–2216* ▭*AE, DC, MC, V* ⊗*No lunch.*

$$$–$$$$
MODERN
HAWAIIAN

✕**Roy's Po'ipū Bar & Grill.** Hawai'i's culinary superstar, Roy Yamaguchi, is fond of sharing his signature Hawaiian fusion cuisine by cloning the successful Honolulu restaurant where he got his start. You'll find one of these copycat eateries on Kaua'i's South Side in a shopping-center locale that feels too small and ordinary for the exotic food. The menu changes daily, and the hardworking kitchen staff dreams up 12 to 15 (or more) specials each night—an impressive feat. Though the food reflects the imaginative pairings and high-quality ingredients of the original Roy's and the presentation is spectacular, the atmosphere is a little different. As with most restaurant branches, it just doesn't have the heart and soul of the original. The visitors who fill this celebrity restaurant each night don't seem to mind, but those looking for authenticity may prefer the Beach House, a little way down the road. ⊠*Po'ipū Shopping Village, 2360 Kiahuna Plantation Dr., Kōloa* ☎*808/742–5000* ▭*AE, D, DC, MC, V* ⊗*No lunch.*

$$–$$$
SEAFOOD

✕**Shells Steak and Seafood.** Chandeliers made from shells light the dining room and give this restaurant its name. The menu is upscale surf and turf, with prime cuts of steak and fresh fish enhanced by tropical spices and sauces. Shells is one of three signature restaurants in the Sheraton's Oceanfront Galleria. Each of these restaurants has been designed to embrace the view of the Pacific Ocean from sunrise to starlight. ⊠*Sheraton Kaua'i Resort, 2440 Ho'onani Rd., Po'ipū Beach, Kōloa* ☎*808/742–1661* ▭*AE, D, DC, MC, V* ⊗*No lunch.*

$$$–$$$$
SEAFOOD

✕**Tidepools.** The Grand Hyatt Kaua'i is notable for its excellent restaurants, which differ widely in their settings and cuisine. This one is definitely the most tropical and campy, sure to appeal to folks seeking a bit of island-style romance and adventure. Private grass-thatch huts seem to float on a koi-filled pond beneath starry skies while torches flicker in the lushly landscaped grounds nearby. The equally distinctive food has an island flavor that comes from the chef's advocacy of Hawai'i Regional Cuisine and extensive use of Kaua'i-grown products. You won't go wrong ordering the fresh-fish specials or one of the signature dishes, such as wok-seared soy-, sake-, and ginger-marinated 'ahi; grilled mahimahi; or pan-seared beef tenderloin. Start with Tidepools' pūpū platter for two—with a lobster cake, peppered beef fillet, and 'ahi sashimi—to wake up your taste buds. If you're still hungry at the end of the meal, the ginger crème brûlée is sure to satisfy. ⊠*Grand Hyatt Kaua'i Resort and Spa, 1571 Po'ipū Rd., Kōloa* ☎*808/742–1234 Ext. 4260* ▭*AE, D, DC, MC, V* ⊗*No lunch.*

$
AMERICAN

✕**Tomkats Grille.** Tropical ponds, a waterfall, a large bar area, and a porch overlooking an inner courtyard give this grill a casual island vibe. Try the blackened "katch of the day" with tropical salsa, or the homemade chili and burger. Wash it down with a glass of wine or one of 35 ales, stouts, ports, and lagers. Plenty of Tomkats' Nibblers—such as buffalo wings and sautéed shrimp—enliven happy hour from 3 to 6 PM. ⊠*Old Kōloa Town, 5402 Kōloa Rd., Kōloa* ☎*808/742–8887* ▭*MC, V.*

$$ **×Waimea Brewing Company.** Housed within the Waimea Plantation Cot-
AMERICAN tages, this brewpub-restaurant is spacious, with hardwood floors and
open-air decks. Dine indoors amid rattan furnishings or at a bar deco-
rated with petroglyphs and colored with Kaua'i red dirt. Kalua pork
enchiladas, hamburgers, beef short ribs, and fresh fish are highlights.
Entrées are reasonably priced. It's a good place to stop while traveling to
or from Waimea Canyon, and the microbrews are worth a try. ⊠*9400
Kaumuali'i Hwy., Waimea* ☎*808/338–9733* ▭*AE, D, MC, V.*

$$ **×Wrangler's Steakhouse.** Denim-cover seating, decorative saddles, and a
STEAK stagecoach in a loft helped to transform the historic Ako General Store
in Waimea into a West Side steak house. You can eat under the stars
on the deck out back or inside the old-fashioned, wood-panel dining
room. The 16-ounce New York steak comes sizzling, and the rib eye
is served with capers. Those with smaller appetites might consider the
vegetable tempura or the 'ahi served on penne pasta. Local folks love
the special lunch: soup, rice, beef teriyaki, and shrimp tempura served in
a three-tier *kaukau* tin, or lunch pail, just like the ones sugar-plantation
workers once carried. A gift shop has local crafts (and sometimes a
craftsperson doing demonstrations). ⊠*9852 Kaumuali'i Hwy., Waimea*
☎*808/338–1218* ▭*AE, MC, V* ☙*Closed Sun.*

WHERE TO STAY

The Garden Island has lodgings for every taste, from swanky resorts
to rustic cabins, and from family-friendly condos to romantic bed-and-
breakfasts. When choosing a place to stay, location is an important
consideration—Kaua'i may look small, but it takes more time than you
might think to get around. If at all possible, stay close to your desired
activities. Prices are highest near the ocean and in resort communities
such as Princeville and Po'ipū.

As a rule, resorts offer a full roster of amenities and large, well-appointed rooms. They are all oceanfront properties that lean toward the luxurious. If you want to golf, play tennis, or hang at a spa, stay at a resort.
You'll also be more likely to find activities for children at resorts, including camps that allow parents a little time off. The island's hotels tend
to be smaller and older, with fewer on-site amenities.

Individual condominium units are equipped with all the comforts of
home, but each property offers different services, so inquire if you want
tennis courts, golf, and on-site restaurants. They're ideal for families,
couples traveling together, and longer stays.

Vacation rentals run the gamut from fabulous luxury estates to scruffy
little dives. It's buyer-beware in this unregulated sector of the visitor
industry, so choose carefully. Many homes are in rural areas far from
beaches, or in crowded neighborhoods that may be a bit too local-style
for some tastes. Condos and vacation rentals typically require a minimum stay of three nights to a week, along with a cleaning fee.

The island's bed-and-breakfasts allow you to meet local residents and
experience the aloha spirit more directly. They tend to be among the
more expensive types of lodging, though, and don't assume you get a

lavish breakfast unless it's a featured attraction. You'll usually get a very comfortable room in a private house along with a morning meal; some properties have stand-alone units on-site.

If you need help choosing a property, **Bed & Breakfast Kaua'i** (☎ *800/822–1176* ☒ *503/826–0087* ⊕ *www.bnbkauai.com*) may prove helpful. Liz Hey, a longtime island resident, maintains a network of more than three dozen cottages, condos, and B&Bs that consider all lifestyles and budgets. Most large real estate companies also maintain a roster of vacation rentals.

WHAT IT COSTS					
	¢	$	$$	$$$	$$$$
HOTELS	under $100	$100–$180	$181–$260	$261–$340	over $340

Hotel prices are for two people in a standard double room in high season. Condo price categories reflect studio and one-bedroom rates.

THE NORTH SHORE

The North Shore is mountainous and wet, which accounts for its rugged, lush landscape. Posh resorts and condominiums await you at Princeville, a community with dreamy views, excellent golf courses, and lovely sunsets. It maintains the lion's share of North Shore accommodations—primarily luxury hotel rooms and condos built on a plateau overlooking the sea. Hanalei, a bayside town in a broad valley, has a smattering of hotel rooms and numerous vacation rentals, many within walking distance of the beach. Prices tend to be high in this resort area. If you want to do extensive sightseeing on other parts of the island, be prepared for a long drive—one that's very dark at night.

$$$
RESORT
☵ **Hanalei Bay Resort.** This condominium resort has a lovely location overlooking Hanalei Bay and Nāpali Coast. Three-story buildings angle down the cliffs, making for some steep walking paths. Units are extremely spacious, with high, sloping ceilings and large private lānai. Rattan furniture and island art add a casual feeling to rooms. Studios have small kitchenettes not meant for serious cooking. The larger units have full kitchens. The resort's upper-level pool is one of the nicest on the island, with authentic lava-rock waterfalls, an open-air hot tub, and a kid-friendly sand "beach." The tennis courts are on-site, and you have golf privileges at Princeville Resort. **Pros:** beautiful views, tennis courts on property, tropical pool. **Cons:** steep walkways, no beach. ✉ *5380 Honoiki Rd., Princeville* ☎ *808/826–6522 or 800/827–4427* ☒ *808/826–6680* ⊕ *www.hanaleibayresort.com* ↻ *134 units* ⌂ *In-room: safe, kitchen, refrigerator. In-hotel: tennis courts, pools, beachfront, children's programs (ages 5–12), laundry facilities* ☰ *AE, D, DC, MC, V.*

$$$
HOTEL
☵ **Hanalei Colony Resort.** This 5-acre property, the only true beachfront resort on Kaua'i's North Shore, is a laid-back, go-barefoot kind of place sandwiched between towering mountains and the sea. Its charm is in its simplicity. There are no phones, TVs, or stereos in the rooms. Each of the two-bedroom units can sleep a family of four. The units are well

WHERE TO STAY IN KAUA'I

	Property Name	Worth Noting	Pools	Beach	Golf Course	Tennis Courts	Gym	Spa	Children's Programs	Rooms	Restaurants	Other	Location
	The North Side												
23	Hanalei Bay Resort	Great views	2	yes	priv.	8		mass.	5–12	134	1	kitchens	Princeville
25	Hanalei Colony Resort	Go-barefoot kind of place	1	yes						48		no a/c	Hā'ena
24	Westin Princeville Ocean Resort	New/great activities	2	yes	no		yes	yes	5–12	173	1		Princeville
	The East Side												
15	Aloha Beach Resort Kaua'i	Beach cottages available	2			1	yes			250	1		Kapa'a
19	Aston Kaua'i Beach at Maka'iwa	Popular nightly lū'au	1	yes		3				311	1		Kapa'a
12	Garden Island Inn	Beach across the street								24		no a/c	Lihu'e
22	Hotel Coral Reef	Good location, low price		yes			yes			26		no a/c	Kapa'a
13	Kaua'i Marriott Resort & Beach Club	26,000-sq-ft pool	1	yes	yes	7	yes	yes	5–12	599	2	shops	Lihu'e
17	Aston Islander on the Beach	Plantation-style design	1	yes						200			Kapa'a
21	Aloha Cottages	Oceanfront								2		no a/c	Kapa'a
20	Best Western Plantation Hale Suites	Beach across the street	3							110		kitchens	Kapa'a
16	Kapa'a Sands	Hawai'i-owned and operated	1	yes						20		no a/c	Kapa'a
18	Kaua'i Coast Resort at the Beachboy	Uncrowded beach	1	yes		1	yes	yes		108	1	kitchens	Kapa'a
14	Rosewood Bed and Breakfast	Located on a plantation								7		no a/c	Kapa'a

The South Shore

❸ ★	Grand Hyatt Kaua'i Resort and Spa	5 acres of swimming lagoons	1	yes	yes	4	yes	yes	5–12	602	6	shops	Kōloa
❽	Sheraton Kaua'i Resort	Ocean wing right on water	2	yes		3	yes	mass.	5–12	413	4		Kōloa
⓫	Hideaway Cove	Quiet								7		kitchens	Po'ipū
❻	Outrigger Kiahuna Plantation	Popular with families	1	yes	yes	6				333	1	no a/c	Kōloa
❺	Po'ipū Kapili	Delux PH suites available	1			2				60		no A/C	Kōloa
❾	Po'ipū Plantation Resort	Full breakfast								12		3-night minimum	Po'ipū
❿	Po'ipū Shores	Excellent whale-watching	1							39		no a/c	Kōloa
❼	Suite Paradise Po'ipū Kai	Short walk to beach	6			9				130	1	no a/c	Kōloa
❹	Whalers Cove	Rocky beach	1	yes						30		no a/c	Kōloa

The West Side

❷ ★	Waimea Plantation Cottages	Good for large groups	1	yes				yes		48	1	no a/c	Waimea
❶	Kōke'e Lodge	Rustic wilderness cabins								12	1	no a/c	Kekaha

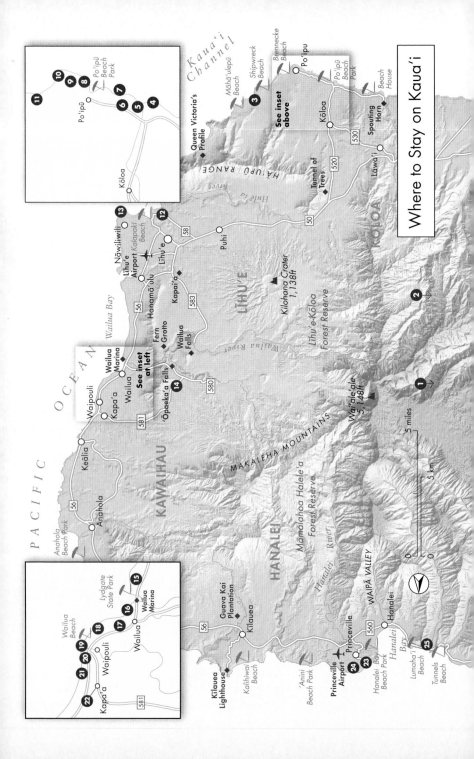

Where to Stay on Kaua'i

PACIFIC OCEAN

Kaua'i Channel

Inset (top left – Po'ipū area)
⓫ ⓾ ❾ ❽ ❼ ❻ ❺ ❹
Po'ipū
Po'ipū Beach Park
Kōloa

Main map labels
Queen Victoria's Profile
Māhā'ulepū Beach
Shipwreck Beach
Brennecke Beach
Po'ipū
Po'ipū Beach Park
Beach House
❸
See inset above
Kōloa
530
Spouting Horn
Lāwa'i
520
Tunnel of Trees
HA'UPU RANGE
Hāʻula River
KŌLOA
50
Kilohana Crater 1,138ft
LĪHU'E
Līhu'e Forest Reserve

Nāwiliwili
Kalapakī Beach
Līhu'e Airport
Līhu'e
⓭
⓬
58
Puhi
583
Hanamā'ulu
Kapa'a'a
Fern Grotto
Wailua Falls
Wailua River
580
'Ōpaeka'a Falls
⓮
Wai'ale'ale 5,148ft

Wailua Marina
See inset at left
Waipouli
Kapa'a
Wailua
581
Keālia
Anahola
Anahola Beach Park
56
KAWAIHAU

MAKALEHA MOUNTAINS

Māmalahoa Halele'a Forest Reserve

HANALEI
Hanalei River
WAIPĀ VALLEY

Guava Kai Plantation
Kīlauea Lighthouse
Kīlauea
Kalihiwai Beach
'Anini Beach Park
56
Princeville Airport
Princeville
560
⓬❹ ⓬❸
Hanalei Bay
Hanalei Bay Beach Park
Hanalei
Lumaha'i Beach
Tunnels Beach
⓬❺

Inset (bottom left – Wailua/Kapa'a area)
Lydgate State Park
Wailua Beach
Wailua Marina
Wailua
⓭❺
⓭❻
⓭❼
⓭❽
⓭❾
⓬⓿
⓬❶
⓬❷
Waipouli
Kapa'a
581

5 miles
5 km

maintained, with Hawaiian-style furnishings, full kitchens, and lānai. Amenities, such as cocktail receptions and cultural activities, vary from season to season. There's an art gallery with coffee bar on-site. **Pros:** oceanfront setting, private, quiet, seventh night free. **Cons:** remote location, damp climate. ✉ *5-7130 Kūhiō Hwy., Hāʻena* ☎ *808/826–6235 or 800/628–3004* 🖶 *808/826–9893* ⊕ *www.hcr.com* ⤳ *48 units* ♿ *In-room: no a/c, no phone, kitchens, no TV. In-hotel: pool, beachfront, laundry facilities* ▭ *AE, MC, V.*

$$$$
RESORT

🏨 **Princeville Resort.** *At this writing, this renowned property—built into the cliffs above Hanalei Bay—was undergoing major renovations, due to be completed in fall 2009. When it reopens, it will be rebranded a prestigious St. Regis property. Call or check the Web site for the latest information.* ✉ *5520 Ka Haku Rd., Princeville* ☎ *808/826–9644 or 888/488–3535* 🖶 *808/826–1166* ⊕ *www.stregisprinceville.com.* ⤳ *201 rooms, 51 suites* ♿ *In-room: refrigerator. In-hotel: 4 restaurants, room service, bars, golf courses, tennis courts, pool, gym, spa, beachfront, children's programs (ages 5–12), laundry service* ▭ *AE, D, DC, MC, V.*

$$$$
RESORT

🏨 **Westin Princeville Ocean Resort Villas.** Spread out over 18.5 acres some 200 feet above Kauaʻi's Anini Beach in tony Princeville, the Westin Princeville Ocean Resort Villas marries the comforts of condominium living with the top-notch service and amenities of a luxurious hotel resort. From the tapa-inspired art in each villa's living room to the wood cutouts of Hawaiʻi's state plant, taro, the look of the place is decidedly that of a Hawaiian plantation. The "hang-loose" attitude for which Hawaiʻi is so famous definitely prevails here in the best possible way. Friendly employees sport nametags with their favorite "passion," such as shopping, sleeping, watching TV, or eating, which makes for fun conversation. **Pros:** on-site mini-market, extensive on-site activities, first-rate kids' program, regular shuttle to nearby attractions in Princeville. **Cons:** path to nearby beach is a six- to seven-minute walk and a bit steep for youngsters, whirlpool tub barely fits one adult. ✉ *3939 Wyllie Rd., Princeville* ☎ *808/826–2404 or 808/826–4793* ⊕ *www.westinprinceville.com* ⤳ *173 studio units, 173 1-bedroom units* ♿ *In-room: safe, kitchen, refrigerator, DVD, Ethernet, Wi-Fi. In-hotel: restaurant, 2 bars, 2 pools, gym, laundry service, concierge, parking (free), no-smoking rooms.* ▭ *AE, D, DC, MC, V.*

THE EAST SIDE

KAPAʻA AND WAILUA

The East Side, or Coconut Coast, is a good centralized home base if you want to see and do it all. Since Kapaʻa is the island's major population center, this area has a lived-in, real-world feel. It has a number of smaller, older properties that are modestly priced but still comfortable, as well as private vacation rentals in the hills behind town that may be too rural and far from the beach for most visitors. This is also where you can find some of the best deals on accommodations and a wider choice of inexpensive restaurants and shops than in the resort areas. The beaches here are so-so for swimming but nice for sunbathing, walking, and watching the sun and moon rise.

Līhu'e is not the most desirable place to stay on Kaua'i, in terms of scenic beauty, although it does have its advantages, including easy access to the airport. It's located smack-dab in the middle of the island, too, giving you good access to sights and activities on all parts of the island. Restaurants and shops are also plentiful, and there's lovely Kalapakī Bay for beachgoers.

$$$
RESORT

Aloha Beach Resort Kaua'i. Nestled between Wailua Bay and the Wailua River, this low-key, low-rise resort is an easy, convenient place to stay. Families will enjoy being within walking distance of Lydgate Beach Park. It's also close to shops and low-cost restaurants. Rooms are in two wings and have beach, mountain, or ocean views. The resort also offers one-bedroom beach cottages with kitchenettes. **Pros:** excellent cultural program, walk to beach and park, convenient locale. **Cons:** exiting hotel parking lot onto highway can be difficult, restaurant meals are average. ⊠ *3-5920 Kūhiō Hwy., Kapa'a* ☎ *808/823–6000 or 888/823–5111* 🖷 *808/823–6666* ⊕ *www. abrkauai.com* 🛏 *216 rooms, 10 suites, 24 beach cottages* 🖐 *In-room: safe, kitchen (some), dial-up. In-hotel: restaurant, tennis court, pools, gym* 🖃 *AE, D, DC, MC, V.*

$
RENTAL

Aloha Cottages. Owners Charlie and Susan Hoerner restored a three-bedroom plantation home on Kapa'a's Baby Beach to reflect the charm of yesteryear with the conveniences of today. Think plank flooring, gingerbread, and stained glass alongside a Wolf stove, Bosch dishwasher, and granite countertops. The orientation is due east; you won't have to leave your bed—or living room or lānai—to watch the sunrise, the whales breach, or the full moon rise. In addition to the main house, there's a cozy bungalow in back that's perfect for honeymooners and couples on good speaking terms. Rent both (weekly rentals only) to sleep a total of eight. The location, view, and home don't get much better than this. Credit cards are accepted via PayPal only. **Pros:** comfortable, homelike ambience, good for large groups, safe children's beach. **Cons:** located on heavily used stretch of shoreline. ⊠ *1041 Moana Kai Rd., Kapa'a* ☎ *808/823–0933 or 877/915–1015* ⊕ *www.alohacottages. com* 🛏 *2 cottages* 🖐 *In-room: no a/c, kitchen* 🖃 *MC, V.*

$$
RENTAL

Best Western Plantation Hale Suites. These attractive plantation-style one-bedroom units have well-equipped kitchenettes and garden lānai. Rooms are clean and pretty, with white-rattan furnishings and pastel colors. You couldn't ask for a more convenient location for dining, shopping, and sightseeing: it's across from Waipouli Beach and near Coconut Marketplace. Request a unit away from noisy Kūhiō Highway. **Pros:** bright, spacious units, three pools, walking distance to shops, restaurant, beach. **Cons:** traffic noise in mountain-view units, coral reef makes ocean swimming challenging. ⊠ *484 Kūhiō Hwy., Kapa'a* ☎ *808/822–4941 or 800/775–4253* ⊕ *www.plantation-hale.*

com ↻110 units ♿In-room: safe, kitchen, Wi-Fi. In-hotel: pools, laundry facilities ☰AE, D, DC, MC, V.

$ ⊺ **Hotel Coral Reef.** Coral Reef has been in business since the 1960s and
HOTEL is something of a beachfront landmark. It went through a major renovation in 2007, and now the accommodations are on a par with the prime location. Besides remodeling the rooms, the owners added a large pool that looks onto the ocean. The two two-room units are good for families. **Pros:** nice pool, sauna, oceanfront setting, convenient location. **Cons:** exiting property onto highway can be difficult, coral reef makes ocean swimming marginal, no resort amenities. ⊠1516 Kūhiō Hwy., Kapa'a ☎808/822–4481 or 800/843–4659 ⊕www.hotelcoralreef.com ↻24 suites ♿In-room: safe, refrigerator (some). In-hotel: pool, gym, beachfront, laundry facilities ☰MC, V.

$ ⊺ **Kapa'a Sands.** An old rock etched with kanji, Japanese characters,
RENTAL reminds you that the site of this condominium gem was formerly occupied by a Shinto temple. Two-bedroom rentals—equipped with full kitchens and private lānai—are a fair deal. Studios feature pull-down Murphy beds to create more daytime space. Ask for an oceanfront room to get the breeze. **Pros:** discounts for extended stays, walking distance to shops, restaurants, and beach, turtle and monk seal sightings common. **Cons:** no frills lodging, traffic noise in mountain-facing units. ⊠380 Papaloa Rd., Kapa'a ☎808/822–4901 or 800/222–4901 🖨808/822–1556 ⊕www.kapaasands.com ↻20 units ♿In-room: no a/c, kitchen, VCR. In-hotel: pool, beachfront ☰MC, V.

$$–$$$ ⊺ **Kaua'i Coast Resort at the Beachboy.** Fronting an uncrowded stretch of
RENTAL beach, this three-story primarily time-share resort is convenient and a bit more upscale than nearby properties. The fully furnished one- and two-bedroom condo units, each with a private lānai and well-equipped kitchen, are housed in three buildings. They are decorated in rich woods, tropical prints, and Hawaiian-quilt designs. The 8-acre property looks out on the ocean and offers a heated pool with waterscapes, a day spa, a children's pool, a good restaurant, and an oceanside hot tub. It's in the Coconut Marketplace, so it's within walking distance of shops, restaurants, and a movie theater. **Pros:** lovely pool, excellent restaurant, convenient. **Cons:** difficult to access highway from hotel, coral reef makes ocean swimming marginal. ⊠520 Aleka Loop, Kapa'a ☎808/822–3441 or 877/977–4355 ⊕www.shellhospitality.com ↻108 units ♿In-room: safe, kitchen, refrigerator, dial-up. In-hotel: restaurant, tennis court, pool, gym, spa, beachfront ☰AE, D, DC, MC, V.

$$–$$$ ⊺ **Aston Islander on the Beach.** A Hawai'i-plantation style design gives
HOTEL this 6-acre beachfront property a pleasant, low-key feeling. Rooms are spread over eight three-story buildings, with lānai that look out on lovely green lawns. Rooms have showers but not tubs. A free-form pool sits next to a golden-sand beach, and you can take the lounge chairs to the ocean's edge. **Pros:** convenient location, kids eat and stay free, online rate deals. **Cons:** accessing highway from parking lot can be difficult, coral reef makes ocean swimming marginal. ⊠440 Aleka Loop, Kapa'a ☎808/822–7417 or 877/997–6667 ⊕www.astonhotels.com ↻198 rooms, 2 suites ♿In-room: safe, refrigerator, Wi-Fi. In-hotel: bar, pool, beachfront, laundry facilities ☰AE, D, DC, MC, V.

$$$
HOTEL

Aston Kaua'i Beach at Maka'iwa. Formerly known as the Kaua'i Coconut Beach Resort, this popular oceanfront hotel was bought and refurbished by Courtyard by Marriott in 2005 and then sold to ResortQuest in 2006. The bright, spacious rooms face the ocean or pool and have been outfitted with modern amenities, including free wireless high-speed Internet access. Each oceanfront room has a large lānai. The 11-acre site has always been desirable, nestled as it is among ancient coconut groves and close to a coastal bike and walking path, shops, restaurants, the ocean, and the airport. Both new owners wisely kept the best of the old resort, including its sunset torch-lighting ceremony. **Pros:** convenient location, online room deals, pleasant grounds. **Cons:** accessing highway from parking lot can be difficult, coral reef makes ocean swimming marginal. *650 Aleka Loop, Kapa'a 808/822–3455 or 877/997–6667 www.astonhotels.com 311 rooms In-room: safe, Wi-Fi. In-hotel: restaurant, tennis courts, pool, beachfront, no-smoking rooms AE, D, DC, MC, V.*

Location, location, location. The Coconut Coast is the only resort area on Kaua'i where you can actually walk to the beach, restaurants, and stores from your condo. It's not only convenient, but comparatively cheap. You pay less for lodging, meals, services, merchandise, and gas here—all because the reefy coastline isn't as ideal as the sandy-bottom bays that front the fancy resorts found elsewhere. We think the shoreline is just fine. There are pockets in the reef to swim in, and the coast is very scenic and uncrowded. It's a good choice for families because the prices are right and there's plenty to keep everyone happy and occupied.

$
B&B/INN

Rosewood Bed and Breakfast. This charming bed-and-breakfast on a macadamia-nut plantation estate offers four separate styles of accommodations, including a two-bedroom Victorian cottage, a little one-bedroom grass-thatch cottage, a bunkhouse with three rooms and a shared bath, and the traditional main plantation home with two rooms, each with private bath. The bunkhouse and thatched cottage feature outside hot-cold private shower areas hidden from view by a riot of tropically scented foliage. **Pros:** varied accommodations, good breakfast, attractive grounds. **Cons:** some traffic noise, no beach. *872 Kamalu Rd., Kapa'a 808/822–5216 808/822–5478 www.rosewoodkauai. com 3 cottages, 3 rooms in bunkhouse, 2 rooms in main house In-room: no a/c, no phone, kitchen. In-hotel: no-smoking rooms No credit cards.*

LĪHU'E

$
B&B/INN

Garden Island Inn. Bargain hunters love this three-story inn near Kalapakī Bay and Anchor Cove shopping center. You can walk across the street and enjoy the majesty of Kalapakī Beach or check out the facilities and restaurants of the Marriott. It's clean and simple, and the innkeepers are friendly, sharing fruit and beach gear. **Pros:** walk to beach, restaurants, and shops, good for families, extended stays, and budget travel. **Cons:** some traffic noise, near a busy harbor, limited grounds, no pool. *3445 Wilcox Rd., Kalapakī Beach, Līhu'e 808/245–7227 or 800/648–0154 808/245–7603 www.garden islandinn.com 21 rooms, 2 suites, 2 condos In-room: no a/c* *(some), kitchen (some), refrigerator, Wi-Fi. In-hotel: no elevator, no-smoking rooms* ⊟*AE, DC, MC, V.*

$$–$$$
RESORT
☺

‣ **Kaua'i Marriott Resort & Beach Club.** An elaborate tropical garden, waterfalls right off the lobby, Greek statues and columns, and an enormous 26,000-square-foot swimming pool characterize the grand—and grandiose—scale of this resort on Kalapakī Bay, which looks out at the dramatic Hā'upu mountains. This resort has it all—fine dining, shopping, a spa, golf, tennis, and water activities of all kinds. Rooms have tropical decor, and most have expansive ocean views. It's comfortable and convenient, though the airport noise can be a turnoff. Many of the rooms have been converted to time-shares, too. **Pros:** oceanfront setting, good restaurants, convenient location. **Cons:** airport noise, ocean water is sometimes polluted after heavy rains, parking inconvenient. ⊠*3610 Rice St., Kalapakī Beach, Līhu'e* ☎*808/245–5050 or 800/220–2925* ⊠*808/245–5148* ⊕*www.marriotthotels.com* ⟋*356 rooms, 11 suites, 232 time-share units* ☆*In-room: refrigerator. In-hotel: 2 restaurants, room service, golf courses, tennis courts, pool, gym, spa, beachfront, children's programs (ages 5–12), airport shuttle* ⊟*AE, D, DC, MC, V.*

5

THE SOUTH SHORE

Sun-seekers usually head south to the condo-studded shores of Po'ipū, where three- and four-story complexes line the coast and the surf is generally ideal for swimming. As the island's primary resort community, Po'ipū has the bulk of the island's accommodations, and more condos than hotels, with prices in the moderate to expensive range. Although it accommodates many visitors, its extensive, colorful landscaping and low-rise buildings save it from feeling dense and overcrowded, and it has a delightful coastal promenade perfect for sunset strolls. Surprisingly, the South Shore doesn't have as many shops and restaurants as one might expect for such a popular resort region, but there are still ample choices. ■ TIP➔ The area's beaches are among the best on the island for families, with sandy shores, shallow waters, and grassy lawns adjacent to the sand.

$$$$
RESORT
☺
Fodor'sChoice
★

‣ **Grand Hyatt Kaua'i Resort and Spa.** Dramatically handsome, this classic Hawaiian low-rise is built into the cliffs overlooking an unspoiled coastline. It's open, elegant, and very island-style, making it our favorite of the megaresorts. It has four very good restaurants, including Dondero's, the best on Kaua'i. Spacious rooms, two-thirds with ocean views, have a plantation theme with bamboo and wicker furnishings and island art. Five acres of meandering fresh- and saltwater-swimming lagoons—a big hit with kids—are beautifully set amid landscaped grounds. While adults enjoy treatments at the first-rate ANARA Spa, kids can check out Camp Hyatt. **Pros:** fabulous pool, excellent restaurants, Hawaiian ambience. **Cons:** no swimming beach, small, dreary balconies. ⊠*1571 Po'ipū Rd., Kōloa* ☎*808/742–1234 or 800/633–7313* ⊠*808/742–1557* ⊕*www.kauai.hyatt.com* ⟋*565 rooms, 37 suites* ☆*In-room: safe, refrigerator, Ethernet. In-hotel: 6 restaurants, room service, bars, golf course, tennis courts, pool, gym, spa, beachfront, children's programs (ages 5–12)* ⊟*AE, D, DC, MC, V.*

$$ 🏠 **Hideaway Cove.** On a residential street ending in a cul-de-sac, Hide-
RENTAL away Cove is very quiet, even though it's one block from the ocean's
edge in the heart of Po'ipū. What were once two homes have been con-
verted to seven complete vacation homes. Owner Herb Lee appointed
each with resort-quality furniture and furnishings—even original art-
work. The two-bedroom Seabreeze villa comes with a hot tub on the
lānai. The three-bedroom Oceanview villa connects via an internal stair-
case with the two-bedroom Aloha villa to provide a large five-bedroom
home with two complete living areas—perfect for two families traveling
together. Rates drop with a seven-night stay, effectively making the sev-
enth night free. **Pros:** high-quality furnishings, private lānai, hot tub or
Jacuzzi in each unit. **Cons:** not on the ocean, high cleaning fee. ⊠*2307
Nalo Rd., Po'ipū* ☎*808/635–8785 or 866/849–2426* ⊕*www.hide
awaycove.com* ➟*9 units* &*In-room: kitchen, DVD, VCR. In-hotel:
laundry facilities* ⊟*AE, D, MC, V.*

$$$ 🏠 **Outrigger Kiahuna Plantation.** Kaua'i's largest condo project is lacklus-
RENTAL ter, though the location is excellent. Forty-two plantation-style, low-
rise buildings arc around a large, grassy field leading to the beach. The
individually decorated one- and two-bedroom units vary in style, but
all are clean, have lānai, and get lots of ocean breezes. This is a popular
destination for families who take advantage of the swimmable beach
and lawn for picnics and games. **Pros:** great sunset and ocean views are
bonuses in some units. **Cons:** not the best place to stay if you're looking
for a romantic getaway. ⊠*2253 Po'ipū Rd., Kōloa* ☎*808/742–6411
or 800/688–7444* 🖶*808/742–1698* ⊕*www.outrigger.com* ➟*333 units*
&*In-room: no a/c, kitchen, VCR, Ethernet. In-hotel: restaurant, golf
course, tennis courts, pool, beachfront* ⊟*AE, DC, MC, V.*

$$–$$$ 🏠 **Po'ipū Kapili.** Spacious one- and two-bedroom condo units are minutes
RENTAL from Po'ipū's restaurants and beaches. White-frame exteriors and dou-
ble-pitched roofs complement the tropical landscaping. Interiors include
full kitchens and entertainment centers. There are garden and across-
the-street ocean views to choose from. Three deluxe 2,600-square-foot
penthouse suites have enormous lānai, private elevators, and cathedral
ceilings. You can mingle at a weekly coffee hour held beside the ocean-
view pool or grab a good read from the resort library. Fresh seasonings
are ready to be picked from the herb garden, and there's a barbecue
poolside. In winter you can whale-watch as you cook. A five-night
minimum stay is required. **Pros:** units are roomy, good guest services,
property is small. **Cons:** units are ocean-view but not oceanfront, a
bit pricier than other condos in the area. ⊠*2221 Kapili Rd., Kōloa*
☎*808/742–6449 or 800/443–7714* 🖶*808/742–9162* ⊕*www.poipu
kapili.com* ➟*60 units* &*In-room: no a/c, kitchen, VCR, Ethernet. In-
hotel: tennis courts, pool, laundry facilities, no elevator* ⊟*MC, V.*

$ 🏠 **Po'ipū Plantation Resort.** Plumeria, ti, and other tropical foliage create
RENTAL a lush landscape for this resort, which has one B&B-style plantation
home and nine one- and two-bedroom cottage apartments. All cottage
units have wood floors and full kitchens and are decorated in light, airy
shades. The 1930s plantation home has two rooms with private baths
and two suites. A full complimentary breakfast is served daily for those
staying in the main house. A minimum three-night stay is required, but

Grand Hyatt Kaua'i Resort and Spa

Grand Hyatt Kaua'i Resort and Spa

Waimea Plantation Cottages

rates decrease with the length of stay. **Pros:** hot tub, attractively furnished, full breakfast at B&B. **Cons:** three-night minimum, no Internet in room. ✉ *1792 Pe'e Rd., Po'ipū* ☎ *808/742–6757 or 800/634–0263* 🖶 *808/742–8681* ⊕ *www.poipubeach.com* ⇄ *3 rooms, 9 cottages* △ *In-room: kitchen (some), VCR. In-hotel: laundry facilities, public Wi-Fi, no elevator* ⊟ *D, MC, V.*

$$$
RENTAL
📺 **Po'ipū Shores.** Sitting on a rocky point above pounding surf, this is a perfect spot for whale- or turtle-watching. Weddings are staged on a little lawn beside the ocean, and a sandy swimming beach is a 10-minute walk away. There are three low-rise buildings, with a pool in front of the middle one. Condo units are individually owned and decorated. All have large windows, and many of them have bedrooms on the ocean side; each unit either shares a sundeck or has a lānai. **Pros:** every unit faces the water, oceanfront pool, wildlife viewing. **Cons:** units vary widely in style, no resort amenities. ✉ *1775 Pe'e Rd., Kōloa* ☎ *808/742–7700 or 800/367–5004* 🖶 *808/742–9720* ⊕ *www.castle resorts.com* ⇄ *39 units* △ *In-room: no a/c, kitchen, Wi-Fi. In-hotel: pool, laundry facilities* ⊟ *AE, MC, V.*

$$–$$$
RESORT
📺 **Sheraton Kaua'i Resort.** The ocean wing accommodations here are so close to the water you can practically feel the spray of the surf as it hits the rocks below. Beachfront rooms have muted sand and eggshell colors, which complement the soothing atmosphere of this quiet, calm resort. Brighter palettes enliven the garden rooms. Dining rooms, king beds, and balconies differentiate the suites. Hawaiian artisans stage crafts demonstrations under a banyan tree in the central courtyard. The dining Galleria was designed so that all restaurants take advantage of the endless ocean horizon. **Pros:** ocean-view pool, quiet, nice dining views. **Cons:** rather staid ambience. ✉ *2440 Ho'onani Rd., Po'ipū Beach, Kōloa* ☎ *808/742–1661 or 888/488–3535* 🖶 *808/742–9777* ⊕ *www.sheraton-kauai.com* ⇄ *399 rooms, 14 suites* △ *In-room: safe, refrigerator, Wi-Fi. In-hotel: 4 restaurants, room service, bar, tennis courts, pools, gym, beachfront, children's programs (ages 5–12), laundry facilities* ⊟ *AE, D, DC, MC, V.*

$$
RENTAL
📺 **Suite Paradise Po'ipū Kai.** Condominiums, many with cathedral ceilings and all with big windows overlooking the lawns, give this property the feeling of a spacious, quiet retreat inside and out. Large furnished lānai have views to the ocean and across the 110-acre grounds. All the condos are furnished with modern kitchens. Some units are two-level; some have sleeping lofts. Three- to four-bedroom units are also available. A two-night minimum stay is required. Walking paths connect to both Brennecke and Shipwreck beaches. **Pros:** close to nice beaches, full kitchens, good rates for the location. **Cons:** units aren't especially spacious, beaches not ideal for swimming. ✉ *1941 Po'ipū Rd., Kōloa* ☎ *808/742–6464 or 800/367–8020* 🖶 *808/742–9121* ⊕ *www.suite-paradise.com* ⇄ *130 units* △ *In-room: no a/c (some), safe, kitchen, VCR, dial-up. In-hotel: restaurant, tennis courts, pools* ⊟ *AE, D, DC, MC, V.*

$$$$
RENTAL
📺 **Whalers Cove.** Perched about as close to the water's edge as they can get, these two-bedroom condos are the most luxurious on the South Shore. The rocky beach is good for snorkeling, and a short drive or brisk walk will get you to a sandy stretch. A handsome koa-bedecked

reception area offers services for the plush units. Two barbecue areas, big picture windows, spacious living rooms, lānai, and modern kitchens with washer-dryers make this a home away from home. **Pros:** extremely luxurious, outstanding setting, fully equipped units. **Cons:** beach not ideal for swimming, no stores or restaurants within easy walking distance. ⊠ *2640 Pu'uholo Rd., Kōloa* ☎ *808/742–7571 or 800/225–2683* 🖶 *808/742–9121* ⊕ *www.whalers-cove.com* 🛏 *39 units* ᗡ *In-room: no a/c, kitchen (some), VCR, dial-up. In-hotel: pool, beachfront, laundry facilities* ▭ *AE, MC, V.*

THE WEST SIDE

If you want to do a lot of hiking or immerse yourself in the island's history, find a room in Waimea (though this is not a resort area so be aware that the pickings are slim). There's one resort that's unlike any other resort in the Islands, and a few spartan cabins are rented in nearby Kōke'e State Park. As a result, you won't find many restaurants and shops, but you will encounter dark skies, quiet days, miles of largely deserted beach, and a rural environment that speaks to the area's deep roots in cattle ranching and sugar.

¢   🏔 **Kōke'e Lodge.** If you're an outdoors enthusiast, you can appreciate

B&B/INN Kaua'i's mountain wilderness from the 12 rustic cabins that make up this lodge. They are austere, to say the least, but more comfortable than a tent, and the mountain setting is grand. Wood-burning stoves ward off the chill and dampness (wood is a few dollars extra). If you aren't partial to dormitory-style sleeping, request the cabins with two bedrooms; both styles sleep six and have kitchenettes. The lodge restaurant serves a light breakfast and lunch between 9 and 5 daily. **Pros:** outstanding setting, more refined than camping, cooking facilities. **Cons:** austere, no restaurants for dinner, remote. ⊠ *3600 Kōke'e Rd., at mile marker 15, Waimea* 🖂 *Box 367, Waimea 96796* ☎ *808/335–6061* ⊕ *www. kokeelodgekauai.com* 🛏 *12 cabins* ᗡ *In-room: no a/c, no phone, kitchen (some), no TV. In-hotel: restaurant* ▭ *D, DC, MC, V.*

$$ 🏔 **Waimea Plantation Cottages.** History buffs will adore these recon-

RENTAL structed sugar-plantation cottages, which offer a vacation experience

Fodor'sChoice unique in all Hawai'i. The one- to five-bedroom cottages are tucked

★ among coconut trees along a lovely stretch of coastline on the sunny West Side. (Note that swimming waters here are sometimes murky, depending on weather conditions.) ■TIP➜It's a great property for family reunions or other large gatherings. These cozy little homes, replete with porches, feature plantation-era furnishings, modern kitchens, and cable TV. Barbecues, hammocks, porch swings, a gift shop, a spa, and a museum are on the property. **Pros:** unique, homey lodging, quiet and low-key. **Cons:** not a white-sand beach, rooms are not luxurious. ⊠ *9400 Kaumuali'i Hwy., Box 367, Waimea* ☎ *808/338–1625 or 800/992–4632* 🖶 *808/338–2338* ⊕ *www.waimea-plantation.com* 🛏 *57 cottages* ᗡ *In-room: no a/c, kitchen (some), dial-up (some). In-hotel: restaurant, bar, pool, spa, beachfront, no elevator, public Internet* ▭ *AE, D, DC, MC, V.*

5

KAUA'I ESSENTIALS

TRANSPORTATION

AIR TRAVEL

Regular air service from Honolulu, and a few direct flights from Maui, the Big Island, and select West Coast cities make for convenient, if not quick, travel to the Garden Island.

CARRIERS Hawai'i-based carriers go! Airlines, and Hawaiian Airlines offer regular round-trip flights from Honolulu and Neighbor Islands to Līhu'e Airport. Rates vary widely from $63 to $170 one-way. It's generally a 20- to 40-minute flight, depending on where you start. Hawaiian airlines also provide a few direct flights from select West Coast cities, as do United Airlines and American Airlines.

AIRPORTS The Līhu'e Airport is 3 mi east of the town of Līhu'e. All commercial and cargo flights use this modern airport. It has just two baggage-claim areas, each with a visitor information center. There's a heliport that serves tour helicopters nearby.

Used only by a tour helicopter company and a few private planes, the Princeville Airport is a tiny strip on the North Shore, set within rolling ranches and sugarcane fields. It's a five-minute drive from the Princeville Resort and condo development, and a 10-minute drive from the shops and accommodations of Hanalei.

Contacts Līhu'e Airport (☎ 888/246–1448). **Princeville Airport** (☎ 808/826–3040). **Go! Airlines** ☎ 888/434-5946 ⊕ www.iflygo.com. **Jawaiian Airlines** ☎ 800/367-5320 ⊕ www.hawaiianair.com

GROUND TRANSPOR- TATION Līhu'e Airport is a five-minute drive from Līhu'e. If you're staying in Wailua or Kapa'a, your driving time from Līhu'e is 15 to 25 minutes; to Princeville and Hanalei it's about 45 to 60 minutes.

To the south, it's a 30- or 40-minute drive from Līhu'e to Po'ipū, the major resort area. To Waimea, the drive takes a little more than an hour; to the mountains of Kōke'e, allow a good two hours driving time from Līhu'e.

Check with your hotel or condo to see if there's free shuttle service from the airport. Marriott Kaua'i and Radisson Kaua'i Beach Resort provide airport shuttles to and from the Līhu'e Airport. In addition, travelers who've booked a tour with Kaua'i Island Tours, Roberts Hawa'i, or Polynesian Adventure Tours will be picked up at the airport.

If you're not renting a car and your hotel doesn't provide a shuttle, you'll need to take a taxi or limousine. Taxi fares around the island are $2.50 at the meter drop plus $2.50 per mile. That means a taxicab from Līhu'e Airport to Līhu'e town runs $8 to $10 and to Po'ipū about $40, excluding tip. Akiko's Taxi offers its services from the east side of the island. Po'ipū Taxi will take you to Līhu'e and Po'ipū. Scotty Taxi provides quick service around the airport and Līhu'e. City Cab and North Shore Cab will collect you at the airport if you call ahead to make arrangements. There are three limousine companies that service Līhu'e Airport: Any Time Shuttle, Custom Limousine, and Kaua'i Limousine.

Contacts Akiko's Taxi (☎ *808/822–7588*). **Any Time Shuttle** (☎ *808/927–1120*). **City Cab** (☎ *808/245–3227 or 808/639–7932*). **Custom Limousine** (☎ *808/246–6318*). **Kaua'i Limousine** (☎ *808/245–4855*). **North Shore Cab Company** (☎ *808/826–4118 or 808/639–7829*). **Po'ipū Taxi** (☎ *808/639–2042 or 808/639–2044*). **Scotty Taxi** (☎ *808/245–7888 or 808/639–9807*).

CAR TRAVEL

CAR RENTAL Unless you plan to stay strictly at a resort or do all of your sightseeing as part of guided tours, you'll need a rental car. You can take the bus, but it's a slow mode of travel that won't take you everywhere you might want to go. You can easily walk to the rental-car counters, directly across the street from the baggage claim at Līhu'e Airport. They'll shuttle you to their nearby lot to pick up your car. All the major companies have offices at the Līhu'e Airport. Several companies operate small reservation desks at major hotels, but spur-of-the-moment rentals will cost you more than prearranged ones.

CAR TRAVEL Although Kaua'i is relatively small, its sights stretch across the island and its narrow, often busy roads are not especially conducive to walking or bicycling. You may be able to walk to beaches, stores, and restaurants in your resort area, but major attractions are not usually within walking distance. The best way to experience all of Kaua'i's stunning beauty is to get in a car and explore.

It's easy to get around on Kaua'i, but be prepared for slow travel and high gas prices. A two-lane highway that widens to three lanes in several places nearly encircles the island. It's essentially one road, called Kūhiō Highway on its northwest course and Kaumuali'i Highway when it turns to the southwest. Līhu'e serves as the juncture point. Your rental-car company will supply you with a decent map, and others can be found in the free tourist magazines.

Traffic is a major source of irritation for residents, who encounter it at unpredictable times and the usual rush-hour periods. It's thickest between Līhu'e and the South Side, and all around Kapa'a. Residents know the tight spots, so don't worry, they'll let you into the line of traffic or stop so you can make your left turn. Be sure to acknowledge them with a wave and repeat the kindness when you can. Aggressive driving is not appreciated. And if you're gawking at the sights and holding up traffic, pull over and let cars go by.

■ TIP➔**Although Kaua'i looks like paradise, it does have crime. Lock your car whenever you park and never leave valuables in your rental car, even for a short time. Pay attention to parking signs and speed limits. And be sure to buckle up, as seat-belt citations carry hefty fines.**

CONTACTS AND RESOURCES

EMERGENCIES

To reach the police, ambulance, or fire department in case of any emergency, dial **911**.

Kaua'i's Wilcox Memorial Hospital in Līhu'e has X-ray facilities, physical therapy, a pharmacy, and an emergency room. It's linked to Kaua'i Medical Clinic (KMC), with physicians trained in many different specialties, and clinics all around the island. Major emergency cases are airlifted to O'ahu. West Kaua'i Medical Center serves the area from Po'ipū to Kekaha.

Most pharmacies close around 5 PM, though Longs Drugs, Safeway, and Wal-Mart stay open a few hours later.

DOCTORS **Kaua'i Medical Clinic** (⊠ *3-3420-B Kūhiō Hwy., Līhu'e* ☎ *808/245–1500, 808/245–2471 pharmacy, 808/245–1831 24-hr on-call physicians, 808/338–9431 after-hours emergencies* ⊠ *North Shore Clinic, Kīlauea and Oka Rds., Kīlauea* ☎ *808/828–1418* ⊠ *4392 Waialo Rd., 'Ele'ele* ☎ *808/335–0499* ⊠ *5371 Kōloa Rd., Kōloa* ☎ *808/742–1621* ⊠ *4-1105 Kūhiō Hwy., Kapa'a* ☎ *808/822–3431*).

HOSPITALS **West Kaua'i Medical Center** (⊠ *4643 Waimea Canyon Dr., Waimea* ☎ *808/338–9431*). **Wilcox Memorial Hospital** (⊠ *3420 Kūhiō Hwy., Līhu'e* ☎ *808/245–1010, emergency room, 808/245–1100 main number*).

PHARMACIES **Longs Drugs** (⊠ *Kukui Grove Center, Rte. 50, Līhu'e* ☎ *808/245–8871*). **Safeway Food and Drug** (⊠ *Kaua'i Village Shopping Center, 4-831 Kūhiō Hwy., Kapa'a* ☎ *808/822–2191*). **Shoreview Pharmacy** (⊠ *4-1177 Kūhiō Hwy., Suite 113, Kapa'a* ☎ *808/822–1447*). **Westside Pharmacy** (⊠ *1-3845 Kaumuali'i Hwy., Hanapēpē* ☎ *808/335–5342*).

VISITOR INFORMATION

The Kaua'i Visitors Bureau has an office at 4334 Rice Street, Līhu'e's main thoroughfare, near the Kaua'i Museum.

You'll find plenty of kiosk-type activity centers that can help you book tours, schedule activities, and rent recreational gear, convertibles, mopeds, and motorcycles all over the island. Beware, some of them are linked to time-share projects, and you may have to sit through a sales pitch to get those great deals.

Po'ipū Beach Resort Association is the central source of information about the South Side. You can make online reservations find out about activities and attractions, and request maps and brochures.

The many free visitor magazines are also helpful, offering maps, descriptions of activities, discount coupons, sightseeing and shopping tips, and other tidbits of advice and information.

Information Kaua'i Visitors Bureau (⊠ *4334 Rice St., Suite 101, Līhu'e* ☎ *808/245–3971 or 800/262–1400* 🖷 *808/246–9235* ⊕ *www.kauaidiscovery.com*). **Po'ipū Beach Resort Association** (📭 *Box 730, Kōloa 96756* ☎ *808/742–7444 or 888/744–0888* 🖷 *808/742–7887* ⊕ *www.poipu-beach.org*).

Moloka'i

WORD OF MOUTH

"My wife and I did the day trip from Lahaina to Moloka'i, and things are soooo different there. People are few and far between, and the pace very slow. I never could get over all those beautiful tropical beaches with only a few people. Be prepared to create most of your own nightlife."

—kanunu

WELCOME TO MOLOKA'I

TOP REASONS TO GO

★ **Kalaupapa Peninsula:** Hike or take a mule ride down the world's tallest sea cliffs to a fascinating, historic community that once housed patients suffering from leprosy.

★ **Hike to a waterfall in Hālawa:** A fascinating guided hike through private property takes you past ancient ruins, restored taro patches, and a sparkling cascade.

★ **Deep-sea fishing:** Sport fish are plentiful in these waters, as are gorgeous views of several islands. Fishing is one of the island's great adventures.

★ **Get close to nature:** Deep valleys, sheer cliffs, and the untamed ocean are the main attractions on Moloka'i.

★ **Pāpōhaku Beach:** This 3-mi stretch of golden sand is one of the most sensational beaches in all of Hawai'i. Sunsets and barbecues are perfect here.

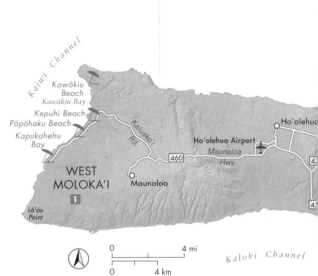

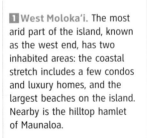

1 West Moloka'i. The most arid part of the island, known as the west end, has two inhabited areas: the coastal stretch includes a few condos and luxury homes, and the largest beaches on the island. Nearby is the hilltop hamlet of Maunaloa.

2 Central Moloka'i. The island's only true town, Kaunakakai, with its mile-long wharf, is here. Nearly all the island's eateries and stores are in or close to Kaunakakai. Highway 470 crosses the center of the island, rising to the top of the sea cliffs and the Kalaupapa overlook. At the base of the cliffs is Kalaupapa National Historic Park, a top attraction.

PACIFIC OCEAN

Kalaupapa Airfield
KALAUPAPA PENINSULA
Kalaupapa
Kalaupapa National Historic Park
Hālawa Beach
Hālawa
Moa'ula Falls
Kualapu'u
CENTRAL MOLOKA'I
2
Kamakou Preserve
3 EAST MOLOKA'I
450
Waialua
Waialua Beach Park
Kaunakakai
Pauwalu
Kamiloloa Heights
Kawela
One Ali'i Beach Park
Kamehameha V Hwy.
Pūko'o
Kalua'aha
'Ualapu'e
Pailolo Channel

6

3 **East Moloka'i.** The scenic drive around this undeveloped area, also called the east end, passes through the green pastures of Pu'u O Hoku Ranch and climaxes with a descent into Hālawa Valley. As you continue east, the road becomes increasingly narrow and the island ever more lush.

GETTING ORIENTED

Shaped like a long bone, Moloka'i is only about 10 mi wide on average, and four times that long. The north shore thrusts up from the sea to form the tallest sea-cliffs on Earth, while the south shore slides almost flat into the water, then fans out to form the largest shallow-water reef system in the United States. Surprisingly, the highest point on Moloka'i rises only to about 4,000 feet.

MOLOKA'I PLANNER

What You Won't Find on Moloka'i

Moloka'i is a great place to be outdoors. And that's a good thing, because with only about 8,000 residents Moloka'i has very little of what you would call "indoors." There are no tall buildings, no traffic lights, no streetlights, no stores bearing the names of national chains, and nothing at all like a resort. Among the Hawaiian Islands, Moloka'i has distinguished itself as the one least interested in attracting tourists. At night the whole island grows dark, creating a velvety blackness and a wonderful, rare thing called silence.

Will It Rain?

Moloka'i's weather mimics that of the other islands: mid- to low 80s year-round, slightly rainier in winter. Because the island's accommodations are clustered at low elevation or along the leeward coast, warm weather is a dependable constant for visitors (only 15 to 20 inches of rain fall each year on the coastal plain). As you travel up the mountainside, the weather changes with bursts of forest-building downpours.

Timing Is Everything

If you're keen to explore Moloka'i's beaches, coral beds, or fishponds, summer is your best bet for nonstop calm seas and sunny skies. For a taste of Hawaiian culture, plan your visit around a festival. In January, islanders and visitors compete in ancient Hawaiian games at the Ka Moloka'i Makahiki Festival. The Moloka'i Ka Hula Piko, an annual daylong event in May, draws premiere hula troupes, musicians, and storytellers. Long-distance canoe races from Moloka'i to O'ahu are in late September and early October. Although never crowded, the island is busier during these events—book accommodations and transportation six months in advance.

Dining and Lodging On Moloka'i

Moloka'i appeals most to travelers who appreciate genuine Hawaiian ambience rather than swanky digs. Most hotel and condominium properties range from adequate to funky. Visitors who want to lollygag on the beach should choose one of the condos or home rentals in West Moloka'i. Locals tend to choose Hotel Moloka'i, located seaside just 2 mi from Kaunakakai. Travelers who want to immerse themselves in the spirit of the island should seek out a condo or cottage, the closer to East Moloka'i the better.

Dining on Moloka'i is more a matter of eating. There are no fancy restaurants, just pleasant low-key places to eat out. Try the Hotel Moloka'i dining room for a selection of fresh, local-style food. Other options include plate lunch, pizza, coffee-shop-style sandwiches, and make-it-yourself health food fixings.

Cell Phones and Internet

There are many locations on the island where cell phone reception is difficult, if not impossible, to obtain. Your best bet for finding service is in Kaunakakai. There is in-room, high-speed Internet access at the Hotel Moloka'i.

Updated by
Joana Varawa

Moloka'i is generally thought of as the last bit of "real" Hawai'i. Tourism has been held at bay by the island's unique history and the deep pride of the island's predominantly native Hawaiian population, despite the fact that the longest white-sand beach in Hawai'i can be found along its western shore.

With sandy beaches to the west, sheer sea cliffs to the north, and a rainy, lush eastern coast, Moloka'i offers a bit of everything, including a peek at what the islands were like 50 years ago. No one is in much of a hurry, and a favorite expression is "Slow down, you're on Moloka'i."

Only 38 mi long and 10 mi wide at its widest point, Moloka'i is the fifth-largest island in the Hawaiian archipelago. Eight thousand residents call Moloka'i home, nearly 60% of whom are Hawaiian.

GEOLOGY

Roughly 1.5 million years ago two large volcanoes—Kamakou in the east and Maunaloa in the west—broke the surface of the Pacific Ocean and created the island of Moloka'i. Shortly thereafter a third and much smaller caldera, Kauhako, popped up to form the Makanalua Peninsula on the north side. After hundreds of thousands of years of rain, surf, and wind, an enormous landslide on the north end sent much of the mountain into the sea, leaving behind the sheer sea cliffs that make Moloka'i's north shore so spectacularly beautiful.

HISTORY

Moloka'i is named in chants as the child of the moon goddess Hina. For centuries, the island was occupied by natives who took advantage of the excellent reef fishing and ideal conditions for growing taro. When leprosy broke out in the Hawaiian Islands in the 1840s, the Makanalua Peninsula, surrounded on three sides by the Pacific and accessible only by a steep, switchback trail, was selected as the place to exile people suffering from the disease. The first patients were thrown into the sea to swim ashore as best they could, and left with no facilities, shelter, or supplies. In 1873 a missionary named Father Damien, who is expected to soon be canonized, arrived and began to serve the peninsula's suffering inhabitants. Though leprosy, now known as Hansen's disease, is no longer contagious and can be remitted, the buildings and infrastructure created by those who were exiled here still exists, and some longtime residents have chosen to stay in their homes. Visitors are welcome but must book a tour operated by Damien Tours of Kalaupapa. No one is allowed to wander unescorted, and no one may take photographs without the written permission of the resident.

THE BIRTHPLACE OF HULA

Tradition has it that centuries ago La'ila'i came to Moloka'i and lived on Pu'u Nana at Ka'ana. She brought the art of hula and taught it to the people, who kept it secret for her descendents, making sure the sacred dances were performed only at Ka'ana. Five generations later Laka was born into the family and learned hula from an older sister. She chose to share the art and traveled throughout the Islands teaching the dance, though she did so without her family's consent. The yearly Ka Hula Piko Festival, held on Moloka'i in May, celebrates the birth of hula at Ka'ana.

EXPLORING MOLOKA'I

The first thing to do on Moloka'i is to drive everywhere. It's a feat you can accomplish comfortably in two days. Depending on where you stay, spend one day exploring the west end and the other day exploring the east end. Basically you have one 40-mi west–east highway (two lanes, no stoplights) with three side trips: the little west-end town of Maunaloa; the Highway 470 drive (just a few miles) to the top of the north shore and the overlook of Kalaupapa Peninsula; and the short stretch of shops in Kaunakakai town. After you learn the general lay of the land, you can return to the places that interest you most. ■TIP→ Directions on the island are often given as mauka (toward the mountains) and makai (toward the ocean).

WEST MOLOKA'I

The remote beaches and rolling pastures on Moloka'i's west end are presided over by Maunaloa, a dormant volcano, and a sleepy little former plantation town of the same name. Pāpōhaku, the Hawaiian Islands' second-longest white sand beach, is here, as is the 53,000-acre Moloka'i Ranch, which is currently shuttered due to a land dispute.

TOP ATTRACTIONS

★ **Maunaloa.** This quiet, small town was built in 1923 to house the workers on the island's pineapple plantation. Although the fields of golden fruit are long gone, some of the old dwellings have been restored, anchoring the west end of Moloka'i. You'll find a kite shop, a gallery with local and imported art and jewelry, and an eclectic general store on the short main street. This is the last place to buy supplies before heading out to explore the beaches of the west end. ⌧ *Western end of Maunaloa Hwy., Rte. 460.*

Fodor'sChoice **Pāpōhaku Beach.** The most splendid stretch of golden-white sand ★ on Moloka'i, Pāpōhaku is also the island's largest beach—it stretches 3 mi along the western shore. Even on busier days you're likely to see only a handful of other people. If

MOLOKA'I VIBES

Moloka'i is one of the last places in Hawai'i where most of the residents are living an authentic rural lifestyle and wish to retain it. Many oppose developing the island for visitors or outsiders, so you won't find much to cater to your needs, but if you take time and talk to the locals you will find them hospitable and friendly. Some may even invite you home with them. It's a safe place, but don't interrupt private parties on the beach or trespass on private property. Consider yourself a guest in someone's house, rather than a customer.

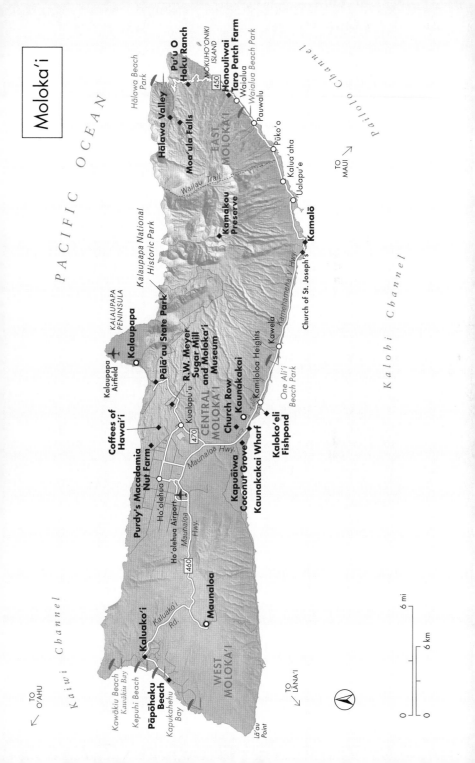

the waves are high, swimming is dangerous. ⊠*Kaluako'i Rd., 2 mi beyond the deserted Kaluako'i Hotel and Golf Club.*

WORTH NOTING

Kaluako'i Hotel and Golf Club. This late-1960s resort passed through several owners, and is now closed and forlorn. The last owner, Moloka'i Ranch, has given up resort operations and is no longer maintaining the property. The abandoned golf course and landscaping is dying, and the buildings are boarded up. Some very nice condos are still operating nearby, however, and the white sand beach along the coast (Kepuhi Beach) is still worth a visit. ⊠*Kaluako'i Rd., Maunaloa.*

CENTRAL MOLOKA'I

Most residents live centrally, near the island's one and only true town, Kaunakakai. It's just about the only place on the island to get food and supplies. It *is* Moloka'i. Go into the shops along and around Ala Mālama Street. Buy stuff. Talk with people. Take your time and you'll really enjoy being a visitor. Also in this area, on the north side, is Coffees of Hawai'i, a 500-acre coffee plantation, and the Kalaupapa National Historic Park, one of the island's most notable sights.

TOP ATTRACTIONS

Coffees of Hawai'i. Visit the headquarters of a 500-acre Moloka'i coffee plantation, where you can enjoy a mule-pulled wagon tour then stay for lunch. The espresso bar serves freshly made sandwiches, *liliko'i* (passion fruit) cheesecake, and java in artful ways. Their "moca mamma" is a special Moloka'i treat. This is the place to pick up additions to your picnic lunch if you're headed to Kalaupapa. The gift shop offers a wide range of Moloka'i handicrafts, memorabilia, and, of course, coffee. Call in advance to ask about various tours (fee) of the plantation. ⊠*630 Farrington Hwy., off Rte. 470, Kualapu'u* ☎*877/322–3276 or 808/567–9490* ⊕*www.coffeesofhawaii.com* ☉*Café and gift shop weekdays 7–5, Sat. 8–4, Sun. 8–2.*

Kalaupapa. *See photo feature, A Tale of Tragedy and Triumph.*

★ **Kaunakakai.** Central Moloka'i's main town looks like a fading 1940s movie set. Along the one-block main drag is a cultural grab bag of restaurants and shops. Many people are friendly and willing to supply directions. The preferred dress is shorts and a tank top, and no one wears anything fancier than a cotton skirt or aloha shirt. ⊠*Rte. 460, about 3 blocks north of Kaunakakai Wharf.*

NEED A BREAK?
Stop for some of Dave's Hawaiian Ice Cream at the **Kamo'i Snack-n-Go** (⊠ *28 Kamo'i St., Kaunakakai* ☎*808/553–3742*). Sit on one of the benches in front for a Moloka'i rest stop. Snacks, crack seed, cold drinks, and water are also available.

Fodor'sChoice **Moloka'i Mule Ride.** Mount a friendly, well-trained mule and wind along
★ a 3-mi, 26-switchback trail to reach the town of Kalaupapa, which was once home to patients with leprosy who were exiled to this remote spot. The path was built in 1886 as a supply route for the settlement below. Once in Kalaupapa, you will take a guided tour of the town. A

light picnic lunch is provided. The trail is very steep, down some of the highest sea cliffs in the world. ■TIP→ Only those in good shape should attempt the ride, as two hours each way on a mule can take its toll. The entire event takes seven hours. Make reservations ahead of time, as spots are limited. The same outfit can arrange for you to hike down or fly in, or some combination of a hike in and fly out. No one is allowed in the park or on the trail without booking a tour. *See A Tale of Tragedy & Triumph photo feature, below, for more information.* ⌂*100 Kala'e Hwy., Rte. 470, Kualapu'u* ☏*808/567–6088 or 800/567–7550* ⊕*www.muleride.com* ✉*$165* ⊙*Mon.–Sat. 8–3.*

WORD OF MOUTH

"I've done both the mule ride and flown in. The mule ride isn't as dangerous as it may appear as the animals are smart, well trained and very experienced. The plane ride made me more nervous as the runway isn't very long. However, the plane would be quicker and you won't get a saddle sore!"

—offlady

★ **Pālā'au State Park.** One of the island's few formal recreation areas, this cool retreat covers 233 acres at a 1,000-foot elevation. A short path through an ironwood forest leads to **Kalaupapa Lookout,** a magnificent overlook with views of the town of Kalaupapa and the 1,664-foot-high sea cliffs protecting it. Informative plaques have facts about leprosy, Father Damien, and the colony. The park is also the site of **Kauleonānāhoa** (the phallus of Nānāhoa)—women in old Hawai'i would come to the rock to enhance their fertility, and it is said some still do. It is a sacred site, so be respectful and don't deface the boulders. The park is well maintained, with trails, camping facilities, restrooms, and picnic tables. ⌂*Take Rte. 460 west from Kaunakakai and then head mauka (toward the mountains) on Rte. 470, which ends at park* ☏*No phone* ✉*Free* ⊙*Daily dawn–dusk.*

Purdy's Macadamia Nut Farm. Moloka'i's only working macadamia-nut farm is open for educational tours hosted by the knowledgeable and entertaining owner. A family business on Hawaiian homestead land in Ho'olehua, the farm takes up 1.5 acres with a flourishing grove of some 50 trees more than 70 years old. Taste a delicious nut right out of its shell or home roasted, and dip it into macadamia-blossom honey; then buy some at the shop on the way out. Look for Purdy's sign behind Moloka'i High School. ⌂*Lihipali Ave., Ho'olehua* ☏*808/567–6601* ⊕*www.molokai-aloha.com/macnuts* ✉*Free* ⊙*Weekdays 9:30–3:30, Sat. 10–2, Sun. and holidays by appointment.*

R. W. Meyer Sugar Mill and Moloka'i Museum. Built in 1877, this three-room mill has been reconstructed as a testament to Moloka'i's agricultural history. Some of the equipment may still be in working order, including a mule-driven cane crusher, redwood evaporating pans, some copper clarifiers, and a steam engine. A small museum with changing exhibits on the island's early history and a gift shop are on-site as well. The facility serves as a campus for Elderhostel educational programs. ⌂*Rte. 470, 2 mi southwest of Pālā'au State Park, Kala'e* ☏*808/567–6436* ✉*$3.50* ⊙*Mon.–Sat. 10–2.*

DID YOU KNOW?

Taro, grown in engineered ponds called loʻi, is a Hawaiian food staple; the pounded root is used to make poi. The Taro plant is revered as an ancestor of the Hawaiian people.

WORTH NOTING

Church Row. Standing together along the highway are several houses of worship with primarily native Hawaiian congregations. Notice the unadorned, boxlike style of architecture so similar to missionary homes. ⊠ *Mauka (toward the mountains) side of Rte. 460, 5½ mi southwest of airport.*

Kapuāiwa Coconut Grove. At first glance this looks like a sea of coconut trees. Close-up you can see that the tall, stately palms are planted in long rows leading down to the sea. This is a remnant of one of the last surviving royal groves planted for Prince Lot, who ruled Hawai'i as King Kamehameha V from 1863 until his death in 1872. The park, which once boasted over 1,000 trees, is now closed for renovations but you can park on the side of the road and walk in to the beach. Watch for falling coconuts. ⊠ *Makai (toward the ocean) of Rte. 460, 5½ mi south of airport.*

Kaunakakai Wharf. Docks, once bustling with barges exporting pineapples, now host visiting boats, the ferry from Lahaina, and the weekly barge from O'ahu. The wharf is also the starting point for excursions, including fishing, sailing, snorkeling, whale-watching, and scuba diving. ⊠ *Rte. 450 at Ala Mālama St.; drive makai (toward the ocean) on Kaunakakai Pl., which dead-ends at wharf.*

> ### BE PREPARED
>
> Since Moloka'i is not oriented to the visitor industry you won't find much around to cater to your needs. Pick up a disposable cooler in Kaunakakai town, then visit the local markets and fill it with road supplies. Don't forget water, sunscreen, and mosquito repellent.

EAST MOLOKA'I

On the beautifully undeveloped east end of Moloka'i, you can find ancient fishponds, a magnificent coastline, splendid ocean views, and a fertile valley that's been inhabited for 14 centuries. The eastern uplands are flanked by Mt. Kamakou, the island's highest point at 4,961 feet and home to the Nature Conservancy's Kamakou Preserve. Mist hangs over waterfall-filled valleys, and ancient lava cliffs jut out into the sea.

TOP ATTRACTIONS

Fodor'sChoice ★ **Hālawa Valley.** As far back as AD 650 a busy community lived in this valley, the oldest recorded habitation on Moloka'i. Hawaiians lived in a perfectly sustainable relationship with the valley's resources, growing taro and fishing until the 1960s, when cultural changes plus an enormous flood wiped out the taro patches and forced the old-timers to abandon their traditional lifestyle. Now a new generation of Hawaiians has returned and begun the challenging work of restoring the taro fields. Much of this work involves rerouting stream water to flow through carefully engineered level ponds called *lo'i*. The taro plants with their big dancing leaves grow in the submerged mud of the *lo'i*, where the water is always cool and flowing. Hawaiians believe that the taro plant is their ancestor and revere it both as sustenance and as a spiritual necessity. The Hālawa Valley Cooperative leads hikes through the valley, which is home to two sacrificial temples, many historic sites, and

Continued on page 561

Father Damien's Church, St. Philomena

KALAUPAPA PENINSULA: TRAGEDY & TRIUMPH

For those who crave drama, there is no better destination than Moloka'i's Kalaupapa Peninsula—but it wasn't always so. For 100 years this remote strip of land was "the loneliest place on earth," a feared place of exile for those suffering from leprosy (now known as Hansen's Disease).

The world's tallest sea cliffs, rain-chiseled valleys, and tiny islets dropped like exclamation points along the coast emphasize the passionate history of the Kalaupapa Peninsula. Today, it's impossible to visit this stunning National Historic Park and view the evidence of human ignorance and heroism without responding. You'll be tugged by emotions—awe and disbelief for starters. But you'll also glimpse humorous facets of everyday life in a small town. Whatever your experience here may be, chances are you'll return home feeling that the journey to present-day Kalaupapa is one you'll never forget.

THE SETTLEMENT'S EARLY DAYS

Father Damien with patients outside St. Philomena church.

IN 1865, PRESSURED BY FOREIGN RESIDENTS, the Hawaiian Kingdom passed "An Act to Prevent the Spread of Leprosy." Anyone showing symptoms of the disease was to be permanently exiled to Kalawao, the north end of Kalaupapa Peninsula—a spot walled in on three sides by nearly impassable cliffs. The peninsula had been home to a fishing community for 900 years, but those inhabitants were evicted and the entire peninsula declared settlement land.

The first 12 patients were arrested and sent to Kalawao in 1866. People of all ages and many nationalities followed, taken from their homes and dumped on the isolated shore. Officials thought the patients could become self-sufficient, fishing and farming sweet potatoes in the stream-fed valleys. That was not the case. Settlement conditions were deplorable.

Father Damien, a Belgian missionary, was one of four priests who volunteered to serve the leprosy settlement at Kalawao on a rotating basis. There were 600 patients at the time. His turn came in 1873; when it was up, he refused to leave. He is credited with turning the settlement from a merciless exile to a place where hope could be heard in the voices of his recruited choir. He organized the building of the St. Philomena church, nearly 300 houses, and a home for boys. A vocal advocate for his adopted community, he pestered the church for supplies, administered medicine, and oversaw the nearly daily funerals. Sixteen years after his arrival, in 1889, he died from the effects of leprosy, having contracted the disease during his service. Known around the world for his sacrifice, Father Damien was beatified by the Catholic Church in 1995, and is expected to be canonized as early as 2010.

Mother Marianne heard of the mission while working at a hospital in Syracuse, New York. Along with six other Franciscan Sisters, she volunteered to work with those with leprosy in the Islands. They sailed to the desolate Kalaupapa Peninsula in November of 1888. Like the Father, the Sisters were considered saints for their tireless work. Mother Marianne stayed at Kalaupapa until her death in 1918; she was beatified by the Catholic Church in 2005.

VISITING KALAUPAPA TODAY

Kalaupapa Peninsula

FROZEN IN TIME, Kalaupapa's one-horse town has bittersweet charm. Signs posted here and there remind residents when the bank will be open (once monthly), where to pick up lost sunglasses, and what's happening at the tiny town bar. The town has the nostalgic, almost naive ambience expected from a place almost wholly segregated from modern life.

About 30 former patients remain at Kalaupapa (by choice, as the disease is controlled by drugs and the patients are no longer carriers), but many travel frequently to other parts of the world and all are over the age of 60. Richard Marks, the town sheriff and owner of Damien Tours, will likely retire soon, as will the elderly postmistress. They haven't, however, lost their chutzpah. Having survived a lifetime of prejudice and misunderstanding, Kalaupapa's residents aren't willing to be pushed around any longer—several recently made the journey to Honolulu to ask for the removal of a "rude and insensitive" superintendent.

To get a feel for what their lives were like, visit the National Park Service Web site (⊕ www.nps.gov/kala/docs/start.htm) or buy one of several heartbreaking memoirs at the park's library-turned-bookstore.

THE TRUTH ABOUT HANSEN'S DISEASE

■ A cure for leprosy has been available since 1941. Multi-drug therapy, a rapid cure, has been available since 1981.

■ With treatment, none of the disabilities traditionally associated with leprosy need occur.

■ Most people have a natural immunity to leprosy. Only 5% of the world's population is even susceptible to the disease.

■ There are still about 500,000 new cases of leprosy each year; at least two-thirds are in India.

■ All new cases of leprosy are treated on an outpatient basis.

■ The term "leper" is offensive and should not be used. It is appropriate to say "a person is affected by leprosy" or "by Hansen's Disease."

GETTING HERE

The Kalaupapa Trail and Peninsula are all part of Kalaupapa National Historic Park (☎ 808/567–6802 ⊕ www.nps. gov/kala/), which is open every day but Sunday for tours only. Keep in mind, there are no public facilities (except an occasional restroom) anywhere in the park. Pack your own food and water, as well as light rain gear, sunscreen, and bug repellent.

TO HIKE OR TO RIDE?
There are two ways to get down the Kalaupapa Trail: in your hiking boots, or on a mule.

Hiking: Hiking allows you to travel at your own pace and stop frequently for photos—not an option on the mule ride. The hike takes about 1 hour down and 1½ hours up. You must book a tour in order to access the trail. **Damien Tours** ☎ 808/567–6171.

Kalaupapa Beach & Peninsula

THE KALAUPAPA TRAIL
Unless you fly (flights are available through Pacific Wings [☎ 808/873–0877 or 888/575–4546 ⊕ www.pacificwings. com]), the only way into Kalaupapa National Historic Park is on a dizzying switchback trail. The switchbacks are numbered—26 in all—and descend 1,700 feet to sea level in just under 3 mi. The steep trail is more of a staircase, and most of the trail is shaded. Keep in mind, however, that footing is uneven and there is little to keep you from pitching over the side. If you don't mind heights, you can stare straight down to the ocean for most of the way. *Access Kalaupapa Trail off Hwy. 470 near the Kalaupapa Overlook. There is ample parking near end of Hwy. 470.*

Mule-Skinning: You'll be amazed as your mule trots up to the edge of the switchback, swivels on two legs, and completes a sharp-angled turn—26 times. The guides tell you the mules can do this in their sleep, but that doesn't take the fear out of the first few switchbacks. Make reservations well in advance. **Moloka'i Mule Ride** ☎ 808/567–6088 or 808/567–7550 ⊕ www.muleride.com.

IMPORTANT INFORMATION
Daily tours are offered Monday through Saturday through Damien Tours or Moloka'i Mule Ride. Be sure to reserve in advance. Visitors ages 16 and under are not allowed at Kalaupapa, and photographing patients without their written permission is forbidden.

the 3-mi trail to Moa'ula Falls, a 250-foot cascade. The $75 fee ($45 for children 7–11; under 6 free with paying adult) goes to support the restoration work. ⊠*Eastern end of Rte. 450* ☎*808/553–9803* ⊕*www. gomolokai.com.*

Honouliwai Taro Patch Farm. Although they are not reviving an entire valley and lifestyle like the folks in Hālawa, Jim and Lee Callahan are reviving taro cultivation on their small farm watered by a year-round spring. The owners provide 1½-hour tours so visitors can experience all phases of taro farming, from planting to eating. Lee was raised in Thailand, so she uses a traditional Southeast Asian farm device—a plow-pulling water buffalo named Bigfoot. Tours are available every day, but you must call for an appointment and directions when you are on the island. ⊠*East of mile marker 20, Rte. 450; call for directions* ☎*808/558–8922* ⊕*www. angelfire.com/film/chiangmai/index.html* ☜*$20.*

★ **Kaloko'eli Fishpond.** With its narrow rock walls arching out from the shoreline, Kaloko'eli is typical of the numerous fishponds that define southern Moloka'i. Many of them were built around the 13th century under the direction of powerful chiefs. This early type of aquaculture, particular to Hawai'i, exemplifies the ingenuity of precontact Hawaiians. One or more openings were left in the wall, where gates called *makaha* were installed. These gates allowed seawater and tiny fish to enter the enclosed pond but kept larger predators out. The tiny fish would then grow too big to get out. At one time there were 62 fishponds around Moloka'i's coast. ⊠*Rte. 450, about 6 mi east of Kaunakakai.*

OFF THE BEATEN PATH

★ **Kamakou Preserve.** Tucked away on the slopes of Mt. Kamakou, Moloka'i's highest peak, the 2,774-acre preserve is a dazzling wonderland full of wet 'ōhi'a (hardwood trees of the myrtle family, with red blossoms called *lehua* flowers) forests, rare bogs, and native trees and wildlife. Guided hikes, limited to eight people, are held one Saturday each month; reserve well in advance. You can visit the park without a tour, but you need a good four-wheel-drive vehicle (which is hard to find on the island), and the Nature Conservancy requests that you sign in at the office and get directions first. ⊠*The Nature Conservancy, 23 Pueo Pl., Kualapu'u* ☎*808/553–5236* ⊕*www.nature.org* ☜*Free; donation for guided hike, $10 members, $25 nonmembers, includes 1-yr membership.*

WORTH NOTING

Kamalō. A natural harbor used by small cargo ships during the 19th century and a favorite fishing spot for locals, this is also the site of the **Church of St. Joseph's,** a tiny white church built by Father Damien of the Kalaupapa colony in the 1880s. The door may be locked but, if not, slip inside and sign the guest book. The congregation keeps the church in beautiful condition. ⊠*Rte. 450, about 11 mi east of Kaunakakai, makai (toward the ocean).*

NEED A BREAK?

The best place to grab a snack or picnic supplies is **Mana'e Goods & Grinds** (⊠*Rte. 450, 16 mi east of Kaunakakai, Puko'o* ☎*808/558–8498 or 808/558–8186*). It's the only place on the east end where you can find essentials such as ice and bread, and not-so-essentials such as burgers and shakes. Try a refreshing smoothie while here.

Pu'u O Hoku Ranch. A 14,000-acre private spread in the highlands of East Moloka'i, Pu'u O Hoku was developed in the 1930s by wealthy industrialist Paul Fagan. Route 450 cuts right through this rural gem with its pastures and grazing horses and cattle. As you drive slowly along, enjoy the splendid views of Maui and Lāna'i. The small island off the coast is Mokuho'oniki, a favorite spot among visiting humpback whales, where the military practiced bombing techniques during World War II. The ranch offers two guest cottages and a retreat facility for groups. If you love seclusion you will love it here. ⊠ *Rte. 450 about 25 mi east of Kaunakakai* ☎ *808/558–8109* ⊕ *www.puuohoku.com.*

GUIDED TOURS

Moloka'i Off-Road Tours and Taxi. Visit Hālawa Valley, Kalaupapa Lookout, Maunaloa town, and other points of interest in the comfort of an air-conditioned van on four- or six-hour tours. Pat and Alex Pua'a, your personal guides, will even help you mail a coconut back home. Tours start at $98 per person, two-person minimum, and usually begin at 10 AM. Charters and four-wheel-drive tours are also available. ☎ *808/553–3369.*

BEACHES

Moloka'i's unique geography gives the island plenty of drama and spectacle along the shorelines but not so many places for seaside basking and bathing. The long north shore consists mostly of towering cliffs that plunge directly into the sea and is inaccessible except by boat, and even then only in summer. Much of the south shore is enclosed by a huge reef that stands as far as a mile offshore and blunts the action of the waves. Within this reef you will find a thin strip of sand, but the water here is flat, shallow, and at times clouded with silt. This reef area is best suited to wading, pole fishing, kayaking, or learning how to windsurf.

The big, fat, sandy beaches lie along the west end. The largest of these—one of the largest in the Islands—is Pāpōhaku Beach, which fronts a grassy park shaded by a grove of *kiawe* (mesquite) trees. These stretches of west-end sand are generally unpopulated. ■ TIP→ The solitude can be a delight, but it should also be a caution; the sea here can be treacherous. At the east end, where the road hugs the sinuous shoreline, you encounter a number of pocket-size beaches in rocky coves, good for snorkeling. Don't venture too far out however, or you may find yourself caught in dangerous currents. The road ends at Hālawa Valley with its unique double bay, which is not recommended for swimming.

If you need beach gear, head to Moloka'i Fish and Dive at the west end of Kaunakakai's only commercial strip or rent kayaks from Moloka'i Outdoors at Kaunakakai Wharf.

All of Hawai'i's beaches are free and public. Camping, by permit (fee varies), is permitted at Pāpōhaku and One Ali'i beach parks. None of the beaches on Moloka'i have telephones or lifeguards, and they're all under the jurisdiction of the **Department of Parks, Land and Natural Resources** ✑ *Box 1055, 90 Ainoa St., Kaunakakai 96748* ☎ *808/553–3204* ⊕ *www.hawaiistateparks.org.*

WEST MOLOKA'I

Moloka'i's west end looks across a wide channel to the island of O'ahu. This crescent of coastline holds the island's best sandy beaches as well as the most arid and sunny weather. This side of the island is largely uninhabited and few signs of development mark the coast besides a few condos, the Kaluako'i Resort (now closed), and a handful of ocean-view homes. Remember: all beaches are public property, even those that front developments, and most have public access roads. Beaches below are listed from north to south.

Kawākiu Beach. Seclusion is the reason to come to this remote beach, accessible only through a gate (that is sometimes locked) by four-wheel drive or a 45-minute walk. The white-sand beach is beautiful. △**Rocks and undertow can make swimming extremely dangerous at times, so use caution.** ⊠*Past Ke Nani Kai condos on Kaluako'i Rd., look for dirt road off to right. Park here and hike in or, with 4WD, drive along dirt road to beach* ☞ *No facilities.*

Kepuhi Beach. Kaluako'i Hotel is closed, but it does have this half mile of ivory white sand. The beach shines beautifully against the turquoise sea, black outcroppings of lava, and magenta bougainvillea flowers of the resort's landscaping. When the sea is perfectly calm, lava ridges in the water make good snorkeling spots. With any surf at all, however, the water around these rocky places churns and foams, wiping out visibility and making it difficult to avoid being slammed into the jagged rocks. ⊠*Kaluako'i Rd., at Kaluako'i Hotel and Golf Club (which is now closed)* ☞ *Toilets, showers.*

Fodor's Choice **Pāpōhaku Beach.** One of the most sensational beaches in Hawai'i, ★ Pāpōhaku is a 3-mi-long strip of light golden sand, the longest of its kind on the island. ■**TIP**➜ **Some places are too rocky for swimming, so look carefully before entering the water and go in only when the waves are small (generally in summer).** There's so much sand here that Honolulu once purchased barge loads in order to replenish Waīkīkī Beach. A shady beach park just inland is the site of the Ka Hula Piko Festival of Hawaiian Music and Dance, held each year in May. The park is also a great sunset-facing spot for a rustic afternoon barbecue. Camping is allowed with a permit, available from the Department of Parks, Land and Natural Resources in Kaunakakai. ⊠*Kaluako'i Rd.; 2 mi south of Kaluako'i Hotel and Golf Club (which is now closed)* ☞ *Toilets, showers, picnic tables, grills/firepits.*

Kapukahehu Bay. Locals like to surf just out from this bay in a break called Dixie's or Dixie Maru. The

> ## BEACH SAFETY
>
> Unlike protected shorelines such as Kā'anapali on Maui, the coasts of Moloka'i are exposed to rough sea channels and dangerous rip currents. The ocean tends to be calmer in the morning and in summer. No matter what the time, however, always study the sea before entering. Unless the water is placid and the wave action minimal, it's best to simply stay on shore. Don't underestimate the power of the ocean. Protect yourself with sunblock. Cool breezes make it easy to underestimate the power of the sun as well.

DID YOU KNOW?

Long, sandy, and golden, Pāpōhaku Beach on the west end is one of Hawai'i's most spectacular for sunning and sunsets. The ocean is generally calmer in summer and in the morning.

sandy protected cove is usually completely deserted on weekdays but can fill up when the surf is up. The water in the cove is clear and shallow with plenty of well-worn rocky areas. These conditions make for excellent snorkeling, swimming, and boogie boarding on calm days. ⊠ *Drive about 3½ mi south of Pāpōhaku Beach to end of Kaluako'i Rd.; beach-access sign points to parking* ☞ *No facilities.*

CENTRAL MOLOKA'I

The south shore is mostly a huge, reef-walled expanse of flat saltwater edged with a thin strip of gritty sand and stones, mangrove swamps, and the amazing system of fishponds constructed by the chiefs of ancient Moloka'i. From this shore you can look out across glassy water to see people standing on top of the sea—actually, way out on top of the reef—casting fishing lines into the distant waves. This is not a great area for beaches, but is interesting in its own right.

One Ali'i Beach Park. Clear, close views of Maui and Lāna'i across the Pailolo Channel dominate One Ali'i Beach Park (*One* is pronounced *o-nay*, not *won*), the only well-maintained beach park on the island's south-central shore. Moloka'i folks gather here for family reunions and community celebrations; the park's tightly trimmed expanse of lawn could almost accommodate the entire island population. Swimming within the reef is perfectly safe, but don't expect to catch any waves. Nearby is the restored One Ali'i fishpond. ⊠ *Rte. 450, east of Hotel Moloka'i* ☞ *Toilets, showers, picnic tables.*

EAST MOLOKA'I

The east end unfolds as a coastal drive with turnouts for tiny cove beaches—good places for snorkeling, shore-fishing, or scuba exploring. Rocky little Mokuho'oniki Island marks the eastern point of the island and serves as a playground for humpback whales in winter. The road loops around the east end, then descends and ends at Hālawa Valley.

Waialua Beach Park. This arched strip of golden sand, a roadside pull-off near mile marker 20, also goes by the name Twenty Mile Beach. The water here, protected by the flanks of the little bay, is often so clear and shallow (sometimes too shallow) that even from land you can watch fish swimming among the coral heads. ■ **TIP→ This is the most popular snorkeling spot on the island, a pleasant place to stop on the drive around the east end.** ⊠ *Drive east on Rte. 450 to mile marker 20* ☞ *No facilities.*

Hālawa Beach Park. The vigorous water that gouged the steep, spectacular Hālawa Valley also carved out two bays side by side. Coarse sand and river rock has built up against the sea along the wide valley mouth, creating some protected pool areas that are good for wading or floating around. Most people come here just to hang out and absorb the beauty of this remote valley. All of the property in the valley is private, so do not wander without a guide. Sometimes you'll see people surfing, but it's not wise to entrust your safety to the turbulent open sea along this coast. ⊠ *Drive east on Rte. 450 to dead-end* ☞ *Toilets.*

WATER SPORTS AND TOURS

Moloka'i's shoreline topography limits opportunities for water sports. The north shore is all sea cliffs; the south shore is largely encased by a huge, taming reef. ⚠**Open-sea access at west-end and east-end beaches should be used with caution because seas are rough, especially in winter.** Generally speaking, there's no one around—certainly not lifeguards—if you get into trouble. For this reason alone, guided excursions are recommended. At least be sure to ask for advice from outfitters or residents. Two kinds of water activities predominate: kayaking within the reef area, and open-sea excursions on charter boats, most of which tie up at Kaunakakai Wharf.

BOOGIE BOARDING AND BODYSURFING

You rarely see people boogie boarding or bodysurfing on Moloka'i, and the only surfing is for advanced wave riders. The best spots for boogie boarding, when conditions are safe (occasional summer mornings), are the west-end beaches. Another option is to seek out waves at the east end around mile marker 20.

DEEP-SEA FISHING

For Moloka'i people, as in days of yore, the ocean is more of a larder than a playground. It's common to see residents fishing along the shoreline or atop South Shore Reef, using poles or lines. If you'd like to try your hand at this form of local industry, you can rent or buy fishing equipment and ask for advice at **Moloka'i Fish and Dive** (✉ *61 Ala Mālama St., Kaunakakai* ☎ *808/553–5926* ⊕ *molokaifishanddive. com*).

Deep-sea fishing by charter boat is a great Moloka'i adventure. The sea channels here, though often rough and windy, provide gorgeous views of several islands. The big sport fish are plentiful in these waters, especially mahimahi, small marlin, and various kinds of tuna. Generally speaking, boat captains will customize the outing to your interests, share a lot of information about the island, and let you keep some or all of your catch. That's Moloka'i style—personal and friendly.

BOATS AND CHARTERS

Alyce C. The six-passenger, 31-foot cruiser runs excellent sportfishing excursions in the capable hands of Captain Joe. The cost for the boat is $550 for a full-day trip, $500 for six to seven hours, and $450 for four to five hours. Shared charters are available for six passengers maximum. Gear is provided. It's a rare day when you don't snag at least one memorable fish. ✉ *Kaunakakai Wharf, Kaunakakai* ☎ *808/558–8377* ⊕ *www.alycecsportfishing.com.*

Fun Hogs Sportfishing. Trim and speedy, the 27-foot flybridge sportfishing boat named *Ahi* offers half-day ($428), six-hour ($535), and full-day ($642) sportfishing excursions. Skipper Mike Holmes also provides one-way or round-trip journeys to Lāna'i, as well as (in winter only) sunset cruises. ✉ *Kaunakakai Wharf, Kaunakakai* ☎ *808/567–6789.*

Moloka'i Action Adventures. Walter Naki's Moloka'i roots go back forever, and he knows the island intimately. What's more, he has traveled (and fished) all over the globe, and he's a great talker. He will create customized fishing and hunting expeditions and gladly share his wealth of experience. He will also take you to remote beaches for a day of swimming. If you want to explore the north side under the great sea cliffs, this is the way to go. His 21-foot *Boston Whaler* is usually seen at the mouth of Hālawa Valley, in the east end. ☎808/558–8184.

KAYAKING

Moloka'i's south shore is enclosed by the largest reef system in the United States—an area of shallow, protected sea that stretches over 30 mi. This reef gives inexperienced kayakers an unusually safe, calm environment for shoreline exploring. ⚠Outside the reef, Moloka'i waters are often rough and treacherous. Kayakers out here should be strong, experienced, and cautious.

BEST SPOTS

The **South Shore Reef** area is superb for flat-water kayaking any day of the year. It's best to rent a kayak from Moloka'i Outdoors in Kaunakakai and slide into the water from Kaunakakai Wharf, on either side. Get out in the morning before the wind picks up and paddle east, exploring the ancient Hawaiian fishponds. When you turn around to return, you'll usually get a push home by the wind, which blows strong and westerly along this shore in the afternoon.

Independent kayakers who are confident about testing their skills in rougher seas can launch at the west end of the island from **Hale O Lono Harbor** (at the end of a long, bumpy, private dirt road from Maunaloa town). At the east end of the island, enter the water near mile marker 20 or beyond and explore in the direction of Mokuho'oniki Island. ⚠Kayaking anywhere outside the South Shore Reef is safe only on calm days in summer.

EQUIPMENT, LESSONS, AND TOURS

Moloka'i Fish and Dive. At the west end of Kaunakakai's commercial strip, this all-around outfitter provides guided kayak excursions inside the South Shore Reef. One excursion paddles through a dense mangrove forest and explores a huge, hidden ancient fishpond. A bonus of going with guides: if the wind starts blowing hard, they tow you back with their boat. The fee is $89 for the half-day trip. Check at the store (61 Ala Mālama Street) for numerous other outdoor activities. ✉*61 Ala Mālama St., Kaunakakai* ☎*808/553–5926* ⊕*molokaifishanddive.com.*

Moloka'i Outdoors. This is the place to rent a kayak for exploring on your own. Kayaks rent for $26–$39 per day (weekly rates offered), and extra paddles are available. ✉*Kaunakakai Wharf, Kaunakakai* ☎*808/553–4227 or 877/553–4477* ⊕*www.molokai-outdoors.com.*

SAILING

Moloka'i is a place of strong predictable winds that make for good and sometimes rowdy sailing. The island views in every direction are stunning. Kaunakakai Wharf is the home base for all of the island's charter sailboats.

SCUBA DIVING

Moloka'i Fish and Dive is the only PADI-certified purveyor of scuba gear, training, and dive trips on Moloka'i. Shoreline access for divers is extremely limited, even nonexistent in winter. Boat diving is the way to go. Without guidance, visiting divers can easily find themselves in risky situations with wicked currents. Proper guidance, though, opens an undersea world rarely seen.

Moloka'i Fish and Dive. Owners Tim and Susan Forsberg can fill you in on how to find dive sites, rent you the gear, or hook you up with one of their PADI-certified dive guides to take you to the island's best underwater spots. Their 32-foot dive boat, the *Ama Lua,* is certified for 18 passengers and can take eight divers and gear. Two tank dives lasting about five hours cost $155 with gear, $135 if you bring your own. They know the best blue holes and underwater-cave systems, and they can take you swimming with hammerhead sharks. ⊠ *61 Ala Mālama St., Kaunakakai* ☎ *808/553–5926* ⊕ *molokaifishanddive.com.*

SNORKELING

During the times when swimming is safe—mainly in summer—just about every beach on Moloka'i offers good snorkeling along the lava outcroppings in the island's clean and pristine waters. Certain spots inside the South Shore Reef are also worth checking out.

BEST SPOTS

Kepuhi Beach. In winter, the sea here is deadly. But in summer, this ½-mi-long west-end beach offers plenty of rocky nooks that swirl with sea life. The presence of outdoor showers is a bonus. Take Kaluako'i Road all the way to the west end. Park at Kaluako'i Resort (it's closed) and walk to the beach.

Waialua Beach Park. A thin curve of sand rims a sheltered little bay loaded with coral heads and aquatic life. The water here is shallow—sometimes so shallow that you bump into the underwater landscape—and it's crystal clear. To find this spot, head to the east end on Route 450, and pull off near mile marker 20. When the sea is calm, you'll find several other good snorkeling spots along this stretch of road.

EQUIPMENT AND TOURS

Rent snorkel sets from either Moloka'i Outdoors or Moloka'i Fish and Dive in Kaunakakai. Rental fees are nominal—$6 to $10 a day. All the charter boats carry snorkel gear and include dive stops.

Fun Hog Sportfishing. Mike Holmes, captain of the 27-foot powerboat *Ahi,* knows the island waters intimately, likes to have fun, and is willing to arrange any type of excursion—for example, one dedicated entirely to snorkeling. His 2½-hour snorkel trips leave early in the morning and explore rarely seen fish and turtle posts outside the reef west of the wharf. Bring your own food and drinks; the trips cost $65 per person. ⊠*Kaunakakai Wharf, Kaunakakai* ☎*808/567–6789.*

Moloka'i Fish and Dive. Climb aboard their 27-foot cabin cruiser or 31-foot twin hull Power Cat for a snorkel trip to Moloka'i's pristine barrier reef. Trips cost $69 per person and include equipment, water, and soft drinks. ⊠*61 Ala Mālama St., Kaunakakai* ☎*808/553–5926.*

> ### ACTIVITY SPECIALISTS
>
> There are basically two activity vendors on the island who book everything: **Moloka'i Fish and Dive** (⊠*61 Ala Mālama St., Kaunakakai* ☎*808/553–5926* ⊕*molokaifish anddive.com*) and **Moloka'i Outdoors** (⊠*Kaunakakai Wharf Kaunakakai* ☎*808/553–4227 or 877/ 553–4477* ⊕*www.molokai-out doors.com*). Be sure to book well in advance because not all activities are offered daily.

WHALE-WATCHING

Maui gets all the credit for the local wintering humpback-whale population. Most people don't realize that the big cetaceans also come to Moloka'i. Mokuho'oniki Island at the east end serves as a whale playground, and the whales pass back and forth along the south shore. This being Moloka'i, whale-watching here will never involve floating amid a group of boats all ogling the same whale.

BOATS AND CHARTERS

Alyce C. Although this six-passenger sportfishing boat is usually busy hooking mahimahi and marlin, the captain gladly takes three-hour excursions to admire the humpback whales. The price is $75 per person, depending on the number of passengers in the group. ⊠*Kaunakakai Wharf, Kaunakakai* ☎*808/558–8377* ⊕*www.alycecsportfishing.com.*

Ama Lua. This 32-foot dive boat, certified for up to 18 passengers, is respectful of whales' privacy and the laws that protect them. A 2½-hour whale-watching trip is $70 per person; they depart from Kaunakakai Wharf at 7 ᴀᴍ during whale season, roughly from December to April. Call Moloka'i Fish and Dive for reservations or information. ⊠*91 Ala Mālama St., Kaunakakai* ☎*808/553–5926 or 808/552–0184* ⊕*molokaifishanddive.com.*

Fun Hogs Sportfishing. The *Ahi*, a flybridge sportfishing boat, takes 2½-hour whale-watching trips in the morning from December to April. The cost is $70 per person. Bring your own snacks and drinks. You can print your ticket on-line ahead of time and arrive ready to go. ⊠*Kaunakakai Wharf, Kaunakakai* ☎*808/567–6789* ⊕*www. molokaifishing.com.*

6

Bikers on Moloka'i can explore the North Shore sea cliffs overlooking the Kalaupapa Peninsula.

GOLF, HIKING, AND OUTDOOR ACTIVITIES

BIKING

Street biking on this island is a dream for pedalers who like to eat up the miles. Moloka'i's few roads are long, straight, and extremely rural. You can really stretch out and go for it—no traffic lights and most of the time no traffic. If you don't happen to be one of those athletes who always travels with your own customized cycling tool, you can rent something from **Moloka'i Bicycle** (⊠ *80 Mohala St., Kaunakakai* ☎ *808/553–3931*) in Kaunakakai.

GOLF

Ironwood Hills Golf Course. Like the other nine-hole plantation-era courses with which it shares lineage, Ironwood Hills is not for everyone. It helps if you like to play laid-back golf with locals and can handle occasionally rugged conditions. On the plus side, most holes here offer lovely views of the ocean. Fairways are *kukuya* grass and run through pine, ironwood, and eucalyptus trees. Carts are rented, but there's not always someone there to rent you a cart—in which case, there's a wooden box for your green fee (honor system), and happy walking. ⊠ *Kala'e Hwy. Kualapu'u* ⃗ *9 holes. 3088 yds. Par 35. Green fee: $20* ☞ *Facilities: Putting green, golf carts, pull carts.*

HIKING

Rural and rugged, Moloka'i is an excellent place for hiking. Roads and developments are few, so the outdoors is always beckoning. The island is steep, so hikes often combine spectacular views with hearty physical exertion. Because the island is small, you can traverse quite a bit of it on foot and come away with the feeling of really knowing the place. And you won't see many other people around. Just remember that much of what may look like deserted land is private property, so be careful not to trespass without permission or an authorized guide.

BEST SPOTS

Kalaupapa Trail. You can make a day of hiking down to Kalaupapa Peninsula and back by means of a 3-mi, 26-switchback trail. The trail is nearly vertical, traversing the face of some of the highest sea cliffs in the world. Only those in excellent condition should attempt this hike. You must book with Damien Tours to access the trail and see the peninsula. *See A Tale of Tragedy & Triumph earlier in this chapter.*

★ **Kamakou Preserve.** Four-wheel drive is essential for this half-day (minimum) journey into the Moloka'i highlands. The Nature Conservancy of Hawai'i manages the 2,774-acre Kamakou Preserve, one of the last stands of Hawai'i's native plants and birds. A long, rough dirt road, which begins not far from Kaunakakai town, leads to the preserve. The road is not marked, so you must check in with the **Nature Conservancy's Moloka'i office** (⊠ *At Moloka'i Industrial Park about 3 mi west of Kaunakakai, 23 Pueo Pl.* ☎ *808/553–5236* ⊕ *www.nature.org*), for directions. Let them know that you plan to visit the preserve, and pick up the informative 24-page brochure with trail maps.

On your way up to the preserve, be sure to stop at Waikolu Overlook, which gives a view into a precipitous north-shore canyon. Once inside the preserve, various trails are clearly marked. The trail of choice—and you can drive right to it—is the 1.5-mi boardwalk trail through Pēpē'ōpae Bog, an ecological treasure. Organic deposits here date back at least 10,000 years, and the plants are undisturbed natives. This is the landscape of prediscovery Hawai'i and can be a mean trek. ■ TIP➔ **Wear long pants and bring rain gear. Your shoes ought to provide good traction on the slippery, narrow boardwalk and muddy trails.**

Kawela Cul-de-Sacs. Just east of Kaunakakai, three streets—Kawela One, Two, and Three—jut up the mountainside from the Kamehameha V Highway. These roads end in cul-de-sacs that are also informal trailheads. Rough dirt roads work their way from here to the top of the mountain. The lower slopes are dry, rocky, steep, and austere. (It's good to start in the cool of the early morning.) A hiker in good condition can get all the way up into the high forest in two or three hours. There's no park ranger and no water fountain. These are not for the casual stroller. But you will be well rewarded.

GOING WITH A GUIDE

Fodor's Choice
★ **Hālawa Valley Cultural Waterfall Hike.** Hālawa is a gorgeous, steep-walled valley carved by two rivers and rich in history. Site of the earliest Polynesian settlement on Moloka'i, Hālawa sustained island culture with

6

its ingeniously designed *lo'i,* or taro fields. In the 1960s, because of changing cultural conditions and a great flood, the valley became derelict. Now Hawaiian families are restoring the *lo'i* and taking visitors on guided walks through the valley, which includes two of Moloka'i's *luakini heiau* (sacred temples). Half-day visits, starting at 9:30 AM or 2 PM cost $75 (less for children) and support the work of restoration. Call ahead to book your visit. Bring water, food, and insect repellent, and wear shoes that are stable and can get wet. ☎*808/553–9803* ⊕*www. gomolokai.com* ✉*$75.*

Historical Hikes of West Moloka'i. This company has six guided hikes, ranging from two to six hours. The outings focus on Moloka'i's cultural past, and take you to sites such as an ancient quarry, an early fishing village, or high sea cliffs where Hawaiian chiefs played games during the traditional *Makahiki* (harvest festival) season. Backpacks are provided, as is lunch on intermediate and advanced hikes. Guides Lawrence and Catherine Aki are knowledgeable and passionate about Hawaiian culture. ☎*808/552–0184, 808/553–5926, or 800/274–9303* ⊕*www. gomolokai.com* ✉*$45–$125.*

SHOPPING

Moloka'i has one main commercial area: Ala Mālama Street in Kaunakakai. There are no department stores or shopping malls, and the clothing available is typical island wear. A handful of family-run businesses line the main drag of Maunaloa, a rural former plantation town. Most stores in Kaunakakai are open Monday through Saturday between 9 and 6. In Maunaloa most shops close by 4 in the afternoon and all day Sunday.

ARTS AND CRAFTS

Big Wind Kite Factory and Plantation Gallery. The factory has custom-made appliquéd kites you can fly or display. Designs range from hula girls to tropical fish. Also in stock are kite-making kits, paper kites, minikites, and wind socks. Ask to go on the factory tour, or take a free kite-flying lesson. The gallery is adjacent to and part of the kite shop and carries locally made crafts, Hawaiian books and CDs, Asian import jewelry and fabrics, and an elegant line of women's linen clothing. ✉*120 Maunaloa Hwy., Maunaloa* ☎*808/552–2364.*

Moloka'i Artists & Crafters Guild. A small shop above the American Savings Bank downtown, the guild has locally made folk art like dolls, clay flowers, hula skirts, aloha-print visors, and children's wear. They also carry original art by Moloka'i artists and Giclée prints, jewelry, locally produced music, and Father Damien keepsakes. ✉*40 Ala Mālama St., Suite 201, Kaunakakai* ☎*808/553–8018.*

CLOTHING AND SHOES

Imports Gift Shop. Both fancy and casual island-style wear is sold here, across from Kanemitsu Bakery. ✉*82 Ala Mālama St., Kaunakakai* ☎*808/553–5734.*

Moloka'i Island Creations. Try this shop for exclusive swimwear, beach cover-ups, sun hats, and tank tops. ⊠ *61 Ala Mālama St., Kaunakakai* ☏ *808/553–5926.*

Moloka'i Surf. This surf shop is known for its wide selection of Moloka'i T-shirts and sportswear. They also sell boogie boards. ⊠ *130 Kamehameha V Hwy., Kaunakakai* ☏ *808/553–5093.*

FOOD

Friendly Market Center. The best-stocked supermarket on the island has a slogan—"Your family store on Moloka'i"—that is truly credible. Hats, T-shirts, and sun-and-surf essentials keep company with fresh produce, meat, groceries, liquor, and sundries. Locals say the food is fresher here than at the other major supermarket. It's open weekdays 8:30 AM to 8:30 PM and Saturday 8:30 AM to 6:30 PM. ⊠ *90 Ala Mālama St., Kaunakakai* ☏ *808/553–5595.*

Maunaloa General Store. Victuals and travel essentials, like meat, produce, dry goods, and drinks—and even fresh doughnuts on Sunday morning—are available here. It's convenient for guests staying at the nearby condos and for those wishing to picnic at one of the west-end beaches. It's open Monday through Saturday 8 AM to 6 PM. ⊠ *200 Maunaloa Hwy., Maunaloa* ☏ *808/552–2346.*

Misaki's Inc. In business since 1922, Misaki's has authentic island allure. Pick up housewares and beverages here, as well as your food staples, Monday through Saturday 8:30 AM to 8:30 PM, and Sunday 9 AM to noon. ⊠ *78 Ala Mālama St., Kaunakakai* ☏ *808/553–5505.*

Moloka'i Wines 'n' Spirits. Don't let the name fool you; along with a surprisingly good selection of fine wines and liquors, the store also carries cheeses and snacks. It's open Sunday through Thursday 9 AM to 8 PM, Friday and Saturday until 9. ⊠ *77 Ala Mālama St., Kaunakakai* ☏ *808/553–5009.*

JEWELRY

Imports Gift Shop. You'll find a small collection of 14-karat-gold chains, rings, earrings, and bracelets, plus a jumble of Hawaiian quilts, pillows, books, and postcards here. The shop also carries stunning Hawaiian heirloom jewelry, a unique style of gold jewelry inspired by popular Victorian pieces, that has been crafted in Hawai'i since the late 1800s. It's made to order. ⊠ *82 Ala Mālama St., Kaunakakai* ☏ *808/553–5734.*

Moloka'i Island Creations. This store features its own unique line of jewelry, including sea opal, coral, and silver, as well as other gifts and resort wear. ⊠ *61 Ala Mālama St., Kaunakakai* ☏ *808/553–5926.*

SPORTING GOODS

Moloka'i Bicycle. This bike shop rents and sells mountain and road bikes as well as jogging strollers, kids' trailers, helmets, and racks. It supplies maps and information on biking and hiking and will drop off and pick up equipment for a fee nearly anywhere on the island. Call or stop by Wednesday from 3 PM to 6 PM or Saturday from 9 AM to 2 PM to arrange what you need. ⊠ *80 Mohala St., Kaunakakai* ☏ *808/553–3931 or 800/709–2453* ⊕ *www.bikehawaii.com/molokaibicycle.*

6

Moloka'i Fish and Dive. This is *the* source for your sporting needs, from snorkel rentals to free and friendly advice. This is also a good place to pick up original-design Moloka'i T-shirts, water sandals, books, and gifts. ⊠*61 Ala Mālama St., Kaunakakai* ☎*808/553–5926* ⊕*molokaifishanddive.com.*

ENTERTAINMENT AND NIGHTLIFE

Local nightlife consists mainly of gathering with friends and family, sipping a few cold ones, strumming 'ukulele and guitars, singing old songs, and talking story. Still, there are a few ways to kick up your heels. Pick up a copy of the weekly *Moloka'i Dispatch* and see if there's a concert, church supper, or dance. The bar at the Hotel Moloka'i is always a good place to drink. It has live music by island performers every night, and Moloka'i may be the best place to hear authentic, old-time, nonprofessional Hawaiian music. Don't be afraid to get up and dance should the music move you. The "Aloha Friday" weekly gathering here, from 4 to 6 PM, features Na Ohana Aloha, a group of accomplished *kupuna* (old-timers) with guitars and 'ukulele. This scheduled, feel-good event is a peak experience for any Moloka'i trip. The group also performs on Sunday afternoons at Coffees of Hawai'i. The Paddlers Inn in Kaunakakai has live music on Wednesday, Friday, and Saturday nights. It's informal and can get lively, especially on weekends when it's open until 1 AM. For something truly casual, stop in at Kanimitsu Bakery on Ala Mālama Street in Kaunakakai for their nightly hot bread sale (Tuesday through Sunday, until 10 PM or they sell out of bread); it's fresh from the ovens. You'll meet everyone in town and can take some hot bread home to your condo for a late-night treat.

WHERE TO EAT

During a week's stay, you might easily hit all the dining spots worth a visit and then return to your favorites for a second round. The dining scene is fun because it's a microcosm of Hawai'i's diverse cultures. You can find locally grown vegetarian foods, spicy Filipino cuisine, and Hawaiian fish with a Japanese influence—such as *'ahi* or *aku* (types of tuna), mullet, and moonfish grilled, sautéed, or mixed with seaweed and eaten raw as *poke* (marinated raw fish). Most eating establishments are on Ala Mālama Street in Kaunakakai, with pizza, pasta, and ribs all within a block or two. If you're heading to East or West Moloka'i for the day, be sure to stock up on provisions before you go as there is no place to eat in these areas. You can buy a disposable cooler and groceries at the Friendly Market Center in Kaunakakai. A more limited selection of snacks and groceries is also available in Maunaloa at the Maunaloa General Store.

WHAT IT COSTS				
	¢	$	$$	$$$	$$$$
RESTAURANTS	under $10	$10–$17	$18–$26	$27–$35	over $35

Restaurant prices are for a main course at dinner.

CENTRAL MOLOKA'I

$$
HAWAIIAN

✕**Hula Shores.** This is *the* place to hang out on Moloka'i. Locals relax at the bar listening to live music every night, or they come in for theme-night dinners. Service is brisk and friendly, the food is good, and the atmosphere casual. Prime rib specials on Friday and Saturday nights draw a crowd. Try the *kālua* pork and cabbage or the hibachi chicken. Every Friday from 4 to 6 PM Moloka'i's *kūpuna* (old-timers) bring their instruments here for a lively Hawaiian jam session, a wonderful experience of grassroots aloha spirit. ⊠*Hotel Moloka'i, 1300 Kamehameha V Hwy., Kaunakakai* ☎*808/553–5347* ⊟*AE, DC, MC, V.*

¢
CAFÉ
Fodor's Choice
★

✕**Kanemitsu Bakery and Restaurant.** Stop for morning coffee with fresh-baked bread or a taste of *lavosh*, a pricey flat bread flavored with sesame, taro, Maui onion, Parmesan cheese, or jalapeño. Or try the round Moloka'i bread—a sweet, pan-style white loaf that makes excellent cinnamon toast. Be prepared to wait, and settle down into Moloka'i time. ⊠*79 Ala Mālama St., Kaunakakai* ☎*808/553–5855* ⊟*No credit cards* ⊙*Closed Tues.*

$
HAWAIIAN

✕**Kualapu'u Cookhouse.** The only restaurant in rural Kualapu'u and a local favorite, this laid-back diner is a classic refurbished green-and-white plantation house. Inside, paintings of hula dancers and island scenes enhance the simple furnishings. Typical fare is a plate of chicken or pork *katsu* served with rice. Try their mahi burger or chicken stir-fry with fresh vegetables. It's across the street from the Kualapu'u Market. ⊠*Farrington Hwy., 1 block west of Rte. 470, Kualapu'u* ☎*808/567–9655* ⊟*No credit cards* ⊙*Closed Sun. No dinner Mon.*

¢
HAWAIIAN

✕**Moloka'i Drive Inn.** Fast food Moloka'i-style is served at a walk-up counter. Hot dogs, fries, and sundaes are on the menu, but residents usually choose the foods they grew up on, such as *saimin* (thin noodles and vegetables in broth), plate lunches, shave ice (snow cone), and the beloved *loco moco* (rice topped with a hamburger and a fried egg, covered in gravy). ⊠*15 Kamoi St., Kaunakakai* ☎*808/553–5655* ⊟*No credit cards.*

$
AMERICAN

✕**Moloka'i Pizza Cafe.** Cheerful and busy, Moloka'i Pizza is a popular gathering spot for families. Pizza, sandwiches, salads, pasta, and fresh fish are simply prepared and served without fuss. Eat in or take out. Kids keep busy on a few little coin-operated rides and their art decorates the walls. ⊠*Kaunakakai Pl. at Wharf Rd., Kaunakakai* ☎*808/553–3288* ⊟*No credit cards.*

¢
VEGETARIAN

✕**Outpost Natural Foods.** Outpost is Moloka'i's only health-food store. It's a good place to pick up local produce, a few organic items, and a selection of ingredients for a healthful picnic lunch. ⊠*70 Makaena*

St., Kaunakakai ☎*808/553–3377* ═*AE, D, MC, V* ⊙*Closed Sat. No dinner.*

¢ ✕**Oviedo's.** Don't let the sagging front door fool you. This modest and
PHILIPPINE spotless lunch counter specializes in delicious *adobos* (stews) with traditional Filipino spices and sauces. Try the tripe, pork, or beef *adobo*
for a taste of tradition. Locals say that Oviedo's makes the best crispy
roast pork in the state. You can eat in at one of the four tables or take
out. ✉*145 Puali St., Kaunakakai* ☎*808/553–5014* ═*No credit cards*
⊙*Closed Sun.*

¢ ✕**Paddlers Inn.** Roomy and comfortable, this restaurant with an exten-
ECLECTIC sive menu is right in Kaunakakai town but on the ocean side of Kamehameha V Highway. There are three eating areas—standard restaurant
seating, a shady cool bar, and an open-air courtyard where you can
sit at a counter eating *poke* (raw, marinated cubes of fish) and drinking beer while getting cooled with spray—on hot days—from an overhead misting system. The food is a blend of island-style and standard
American fare (fresh poke every day; a prime rib special every Friday
night). It's a popular hangout for the younger set and has live entertainment every Wednesday and Friday. ✉*10 Mohala St., Kaunakakai*
☎*808/553–5256* ═*MC, V.*

¢ ✕**Sundown Deli.** This clean little rose-color deli focuses on freshly made
DELI takeout food. Sandwiches come on a half dozen types of bread, and
the Portuguese bean soup and chowders are rich and filling. ✉*145
Ala Mālama St., Kaunakakai* ☎*808/553–3713* ═*No credit cards*
⊙*Closed Sun. No dinner.*

WHERE TO STAY

The coastline along Moloka'i's west end has ocean-view condominium
units and luxury homes available as vacation rentals. If you are familiar with the high-end Lodge at Moloka'i Ranch, please note that it is
currently closed and future plans for the property remain unknown.
Central Moloka'i offers seaside condominiums and the icon of the
island—Hotel Moloka'i. The only lodgings on the east end are some
guest cottages in magical settings and the ranch house at Pu'u O Hoku.
The **Moloka'i Visitors Association** (☎*800/800–6367*) has a brochure with
an up-to-date listing of vacation rentals operated by their members.

Moloka'i Vacation Properties (☎*800/367–2984 or 808/553–8334* ⊕*www.
molokai-vacation-rental.net*) handles upgraded condo rentals that
include initial bathroom amenities, cleaning supplies, maps, and complimentary coffee. The company can act as an informal concierge during
your stay. There is a three-night minimum on all properties.

Note: Maui County has regulations concerning vacation rentals; to
avoid disappointment, always contact the property manager or the
owner and ask if the accommodation has the proper permits and is in
compliance with local ordinances.

6

WHAT IT COSTS					
	¢	$	$$	$$$	$$$$
HOTELS	under $100	$100–$180	$181–$260	$261–$340	over $340

Hotel prices are for two people in a double room in high season, including tax and service. Condo price categories reflect studio and one-bedroom rates. Prices do not include 11.41% tax.

WEST MOLOKA'I

If you are considering renting a condo unit fronting the Kaula Koi golf course, keep in mind that the course has been abandoned, and at this writing, presents a bit of a dismal view.

$ **Ke Nani Kai.** These pleasant one- and two-bedroom condo units have
RENTAL ocean views and nicely maintained tropical landscaping. Furnished lānai have flower-laden trellises and the spacious interiors are decorated with rattans and pastels. Each unit has a washer-dryer unit and a fully equipped kitchen. The beach is across the road. **Pros:** located on island's secluded west end; Internet; uncrowded pool. **Cons:** amenities vary as each unit is individually owned; far from commercial center; golf course units overlook abandoned course. ⊠ *Kaluako'i Rd., Maunaloa* ☎ *808/553–8334 or 800/367–2984* ⊕ *www.molokai-vacation-rental. net* ✍ *120 units* ⚗ *In-room: no a/c, kitchen, Internet. In-hotel: tennis courts, pool, laundry facilities* ☐ *AE, MC, V.*

$–$$ **Paniolo Hale.** Perched high on a ridge overlooking a favored local
RENTAL surfing spot, Paniolo Hale is Moloka'i's best condominium property. Architecturally elegant studios and one- or two-bedroom units all have beautiful screened lānai, well-equipped kitchens, and washers and dryers; some have spectacular ocean views. Rooms are tidy and simple and many are beautifully furnished with ample lounging areas. The property boasts mature tropical landscaping and a private serene setting. **Pros:** close to beach; quiet surroundings;, perfect if you are an expert surfer. **Cons:** amenities vary; far from shopping; golf course units front abandoned course; three-night minimum. ⊠ *Lio Pl., Kaunakakai* ☎ *808/553–8334 or 800/367–2984* ⊕ *www.molokai-vacation-rental. net* ✍ *77 units* ⚗ *In-room: kitchen. In-hotel: pool* ☐ *AE, MC, V.*

CENTRAL MOLOKA'I

$–$$ **Hotel Moloka'i.** Staff members are helpful and friendly at this local
HOTEL favorite, where the two-story, semi-A-frame buildings are arranged in a landscaped tropical setting. Some units overlook the reef and distant Lana'i. The rooms were renovated in late 2007 and are bright and comfortably furnished. The airy Hula Shores restaurant overlooks the ocean and serves breakfast, lunch, dinner, and libations—with local entertainment nightly. Ask about deals in conjunction with airlines and rental-car companies when you make your reservation. There is an activities desk in the lobby. **Pros:** five minutes to shopping and town; some kitchenettes; authentic Hawaiian entertainment. **Cons:** no-frills; can be difficult to secure a reservation on weekends; lower-priced rooms

are small and plain. ⊠*Kamehameha V Hwy., Box 1020, Kaunakakai* ☏*808/553–5347 or 800/535–0085* ⊕*www.hotelmolokai.com* ⏎*40 rooms* ⏷*In-room: no a/c, Internet. In-hotel: restaurant, room service, pool, laundry facilities, public Internet* ▭*AE, D, MC, V.*

$$
RENTAL 🏨 **Moloka'i Shores.** Some of the units in this oceanfront, three-story condominium complex have a view of the water. One-bedroom, one-bath units or two-bedroom, two-bath units all have full kitchens and furnished lānai, which look out on 4 acres of lawn. There's a great view of Lāna'i in the distance and a chance to see whales in season. **Pros:** convenient location; some units upgraded; near water. **Cons:** uninspiring basic accommodations; fussy cancellation policy ⊠*1000 Kamehameha V Hwy., Kaunakakai* ☏*808/553–5954 or 800/535–0085* ⊕*www.marcresorts.com* ⏎*100 units* ⏷*In-room: no a/c, kitchen. In-hotel: pool, laundry facilities* ▭*AE, D, MC, V.*

$
RENTAL 🏨 **Wavecrest.** This oceanfront condominium complex is convenient if you want to explore the east side of the island—it's 13 mi east of Kaunakakai. Individually decorated one- and two-bedroom units have full kitchens. Each has a furnished lānai, some with views of Maui and Lāna'i. Be sure to ask for an updated unit when you reserve. The 5-acre oceanfront property has access to a beautiful reef, excellent snorkeling and kayaking, and an oceanfront pool with covered barbecue. **Pros:** convenient location for divers; good value; nicely maintained grounds. **Cons:** amenities vary as each unit is individually owned; far from shopping; overlooks channel and can get windy. ⊠*Rte. 450 near mile marker 13* ⏷*Moloka'i Vacation Rentals, Box 1979, Kaunakakai 96748* ☏*800/367–2984 or 808/553–8334* ⊕*www.molokai-vacation-rental.net* ⏎*126 units* ⏷*In-room: no a/c, kitchen. In-hotel: tennis courts, pool, beachfront* ▭*AE, MC, V.*

6

EAST MOLOKA'I

$
RENTAL 🏨 **Pu'u O Hoku Ranch.** At the east end of Moloka'i, near mile marker 25, lie these three ocean-view accommodations, on 14,000 isolated acres of pastures and forest. This is a remote and serene location for people who want to get away or meet in a retreat atmosphere. One country cottage has two bedrooms, basic wicker furnishings, and *lau hala* (natural fiber) woven matting on the floors. An airy four-bedroom cottage has a small deck and a somewhat Balinese air. For large groups—family reunions, for example—the Ranch has a lodge with 11 rooms, 9 bathrooms, and a large kitchen. The full lodge goes for $1,250 nightly (rooms

are not available on an individual basis). **Pros:** ideal for large groups; authentic working organic ranch; great hiking. **Cons:** on remote east end of island; rooms in the main lodge cannot be individually rented; road to property is narrow and winding. ✉ *Rte. 450, Kaunakakai* ☎ *808/558-8109* ⊕ *www.puuohoku.com* ⟶ *1 2-bedroom cottage, 1 4-bedroom cottage, 11 rooms in lodge* ⚬ *In-room: no a/c, kitchen. In-hotel: pool* ═ *MC, V.*

MOLOKA'I ESSENTIALS

TRANSPORTATION

AIR TRAVEL

If you're flying in from the mainland United States or one of the neighbor islands, you must first make a stop in Honolulu. From there, it's a 25-minute trip to Moloka'i.

AIRPORTS Moloka'i's transportation hub is Ho'olehua Airport, a tiny airstrip 8 mi west of Kaunakakai and about 18 mi east of Maunaloa. An even smaller airstrip serves the little community of Kalaupapa on the north shore.

Information Ho'olehua Airport (☎ *808/567-6140*). **Kalaupapa Airfield** (☎ *808/ 567-6331*).

CARRIERS Three commercial airlines provide daily flights between Moloka'i and O'ahu in turboprop aircraft. If you fly into the airstrip at Kalaupapa, you must book a ground tour with Damien Tours before you depart. Island Air and go! Airlines fly from Honolulu to Ho'olehua and Pacific Wings flies from Honolulu to Kalaupapa, and from Ho'olehua to Kalaupapa.

Contacts Damien Tours (☎ *808/567-6171*). **go! Airlines** (☎ *888/435/9462* ⊕ *www.iflygo.com*). **Island Air** (☎ *800/652-6541* ⊕ *www.islandair.com*). **Pacific Wings** (☎ *808/873-0877 or 888/575-4546* ⊕ *www.pacificwings.com*).

GROUND From Ho'olehua Airport, it takes about 10 minutes to reach Kaunakakai TRANSPOR- and 25 minutes to reach the west end of the island by car. There's no TATION public bus.

A taxi will cost about $28 from the airport to Kaunakakai with Hele Mai Taxi.

Shuttle service for two passengers costs about $18 from Ho'olehua Airport to Kaunakakai. For shuttle service, call Moloka'i Off-Road Tours and Taxi or Moloka'i Outdoors. Keep in mind, however, that it's difficult to visit the island without a rental car.

Contacts Hele Mai Taxi (☎ *808/336-0967 or 808/553-5700*). **Moloka'i Off-Road Tours and Taxi** (☎ *808/553-3369*). **Moloka'i Outdoors** (☎ *808/553-4477 or 877/553-4477* ⊕ *www.molokai-outdoors.com*).

CAR TRAVEL

If you want to explore Moloka'i from one end to the other, you must rent a car. With just a few main roads to choose from, it's a snap to drive around here.

The gas stations are in Kaunakakai. When you park your car, be sure to lock it—thefts do occur. All front-seat occupants and back-seat passengers under the age of 18 must wear seat belts; violators risk a $92 fine. Children under eight must ride in a federally approved child passenger-restraint device, easily leased at the rental agency. Ask your rental agent for a free *Moloka'i Drive Guide.*

CAR RENTAL   Alamo maintains a counter at Ho'olehua Airport. Expect to pay $40 to $50 per day for a standard compact and $50 to $60 for a midsize car. Rates are seasonal and may run higher during the peak winter months. ■**TIP→** Make arrangements in advance because there may not be cars available when you walk in. If you're flying on a commercial airliner, see whether fly-drive package deals are available—you might luck out and find a less-expensive rate. Hotels and outfitters might also offer packages.

Locally owned Island Kine Rent-a-Car offers airport or hotel pickup and sticks to one rate year-round for vehicles in a broad spectrum from two- and four-wheel drives to 11-passenger vans. Be sure to check the vehicle before departing the agency; there is a $75 surcharge for taking a four-wheel-drive vehicle off-road.

Major Agency Alamo (☎877/222-9075 ⊕www.alamo.com).

Local Agency Island Kine Rent-a-Car (☎808/553-5242 or 866/527-7368 ⊕www.molokai-car-rental.com).

FERRY TRAVEL

The Moloka'i Ferry crosses the channel every day between Lahaina (Maui) and Kaunakakai, making it easy for West Maui visitors to put Moloka'i on their itineraries. Keep in mind that the ferry is an older vessel that has had some mechanical difficulties in the past, and the crossing can be very rough in strong trade-wind weather, especially on the return trip. The 1½-hour trip takes passengers but not cars, so arrange ahead of time for a car rental or tour at the arrival point.

Contact Moloka'i Ferry (☎808/661-3392 or 800/275-6969 ⊕www.molokai ferry.com).

CONTACTS AND RESOURCES

EMERGENCIES

Round-the-clock medical attention is available at Moloka'i General Hospital. Severe cases or emergencies are often airlifted to Honolulu.

Emergency Services Ambulance and general emergencies (☎911). **Coast Guard** (☎808/552-6458 on O'ahu). **Fire** (☎808/553-5601 in Kaunakakai, 808/567-6525 at Ho'olehua Airport). **Police** (☎808/553-5355).

Hospital Moloka'i General Hospital (✉ *280A Puali St., Kaunakakai* ☎ *808/ 553-5331*).

VISITOR INFORMATION

There's tourist information in kiosks and stands at the airport in Ho'olehua or at the Moloka'i Visitors Association. The association has a brochure that lists a number of activity vendors, accommodations, and places to eat. Call them for a copy before you leave home; they are very helpful and can also advise you about specific locations and sites. Be sure to book all activities well in advance because not every activity is available every day. Plan ahead and you will have a happier visit.

Information Maui Visitors Bureau (📞 *On Maui: 1727 Wili Pa Loop, Wailuku 96793* ☎ *808/244-3530* ⊕ *www.visitmaui.com*). **Moloka'i Visitors Association** (✉ *12 Kamo'i St., Suite 200, Kaunakakai 96748* ☎ *808/553-3876 or 800/800-6367* ⊕ *molokai-hawaii.com*).

Lāna'i

WORD OF MOUTH

"The island is full of charm—away from any type of commercial-ism. If you need to relax this is your place. The beaches on Lāna'i are wonderful. If you end up on the northwest side of the island you can have a pristine couple of miles of beach for yourself. Quite a feeling you won't get anywhere else."

—ARIC

WELCOME TO LĀNA'I

TOP REASONS TO GO

★ **Seclusion and Serenity:** Lāna'i is small: local motion is slow motion. Get into the spirit and go home rested instead of exhausted.

★ **Garden of the Gods:** Walk amid the eerie red-rock spires that ancient Hawaiians believed to be a sacred spot. The ocean views are magnificent, too; sunset is a good time to visit.

★ **A Dive at Cathedrals:** Explore underwater pinnacle formations and mysterious caverns lighted by shimmering rays of light.

★ **Dole Park:** Hang out in the shade of the Cook pines in Lāna'i City and talk story with the locals for a taste of old-time Hawai'i.

★ **Hit the water at Hulopo'e Beach:** This beach may have it all; good swimming, a shady park for perfect picnicking, great reefs for snorkeling, and sometimes plenty of spinner dolphins.

Polihua Beach

◆ Ka'ena Pt.

◆ Garden of the Gods

Polihua Rd.

0   2 mi

0   2 km

Kaumalapa'u

Kaumalapa'u Harbor

440   Lāna'i Airport

1 **Lāna'i City and Upcountry.** Lāna'i City is really a tiny plantation village. Locals hold conversations in front of Dole Park shops and from their pickups on the road, and kids ride bikes in colorful impromptu parades while cars wait for them. Cool and serene, Upcountry is graced by Lāna'i City, towering Cook pine trees, and misty mountain vistas.

2 **Mānele Bay.** The more developed beach side of the island, Mānele Bay and harbor is where it's happening: swimming, picnicking, off-island excursions, and boating are all concentrated in this very accessible area.

Shipwreck
Beach

**WINDWARD
LĀNA'I**

3

Keōmuku
Beach

Four Seasons Resort
Lodge at Kō'ele

Halepalaoa

Lāna'i City

Mt. Lāna'ihale
▲ 3,370 ft

UPCOUNTRY

1

Lōpā
Beach

Naha
Beach

Four Seasons
Resort Lāna'i
at Mānele Bay

2

Mānele Bay

Hulopo'e
Beach

3 **Windward Lāna'i.** This area is the long white-sand beach at the base of Lāna'ihale. Now uninhabited, it was once occupied by thriving Hawaiian fishing villages and a sugarcane plantation.

GETTING ORIENTED

Unlike the other Hawaiian islands with their tropical splendors, Lāna'i looks like a desert: kiawe trees right out of Africa, red-dirt roads that glow molten at sunset, and a deep blue sea that literally leads to Tahiti. Lāna'ihale (house of Lāna'i), the mountain that bisects the island, is carved into deep canyons by rain and wind on the windward side, and the drier leeward side slopes gently to the sea, where waves pound against surf-carved cliffs.

7

LĀNA'I PLANNER

Navigating Without Signs

Lāna'i has no traffic, no traffic lights, and only three paved roads. Bring along a good topographical map, study it, and keep in mind your directions. Stop from time to time and refind landmarks and gauge your progress. Distance is better measured in the condition of the road than in miles. Watch out for other jeep drivers who also don't know where they are. Never drive to the edge of lava cliffs, as rock can give way under you. ■ TIP→ Directions on the island are often given as mauka (toward the mountains) and makai (toward the ocean).

Renting a Car

Renting a four-wheel-drive vehicle is expensive but almost essential to get beyond the resorts. There are only 30 mi of paved road on the island. The rest of your driving takes place on bumpy, muddy, secondary roads, which generally aren't marked. Make reservations far in advance, because Lāna'i's fleet of vehicles is limited. If you're staying at the island's hotels, a convenient shuttle bus can take you from the beach to Upcountry.

Timing Is Everything

Whales are seen off Lāna'i's shores from December through April. A Pineapple Festival on the July 4 Saturday in Dole Park features local food, Hawaiian entertainment, a pineapple-eating and -cooking contest, and fireworks. Buddhists hold their annual outdoor Obon Festival honoring departed ancestors with joyous dancing, food booths, and taiko drumming in early July. Lāna'i celebrates the statewide Aloha Festivals in mid-October with a hometown parade, car contests, more food, and more music. Beware hunting season weekends—from mid-February through mid-May, and mid-July through mid-October.

Dining and Lodging On Lāna'i

Although Lāna'i has a somewhat wide range of choices for dining, from simple plate-lunch local eateries to fancy upscale gourmet resort restaurants, the range of lodgings is limited. Essentially there are only three options to choose from: the two Four Seasons Resorts Lāna'i (at Mānele Bay and Upcountry at the Lodge at Kō'ele), and the older Hotel Lāna'i. Camping at Hulopo'e Bay is another option for stays of three nights or less but is not practical for most travelers.

Will It Rain?

As higher mountains on Maui capture the trade-wind clouds, Lāna'i receives little rainfall and has a desert ecology. It's always warmer at the beach and can get cool or even cold (by Hawaiian standards) Upcountry. Consider the wind direction when planning your day. If it's blowing a gale on the windward beaches, head for the beach at Hulopo'e or check out Garden of the Gods. Overcast days, when the wind stops or comes lightly from the southwest, are common in whale season. Try a whale-watching trip or the windward beaches.

By Joana
Varawa

With no traffic or traffic lights and miles of open space, Lāna'i seems lost in time, and that can be a good thing. Small (141 square mi) and sparsely populated, it is the smallest inhabited Hawaiian Island and has just 3,500 residents, most of them living Upcountry.

Though it may seem a world away, Lāna'i is separated from Maui and Moloka'i by two narrow channels, and is easily accessed by boat from either island. The two resorts on the island are run by the Four Seasons. If you yearn for a beach with amenities, a luxury resort, and golf course, the Four Seasons Resort Lāna'i at Mānele Bay beckons from the shoreline. Upcountry, the luxurious Four Seasons Resort Lodge at Kō'ele provides cooler pleasures. This leaves the rest of the 100,000-acre island open to explore.

FLORA AND FAUNA
Lāna'i bucks the "tropical" trend of the other Hawaiian Islands with African kiawe trees, Cook pines, and eucalyptus in place of palm trees, and deep blue sea where you might expect shallow turquoise bays. Abandoned pineapple fields are overgrown with drought-resistant grasses, Christmas berry, and lantana; native plants, *a'ali'i* and *'ilima*, are found in uncultivated areas. Axis deer from India dominate the ridges, and wild turkeys lumber around the resorts. Whales can be seen December through April and a family of resident spinner dolphins drops in regularly at Hulopo'e Bay.

ON LĀNA'I TODAY
Despite its fancy resorts, Lāna'i still has that sleepy old Hawai'i feel. Residents are a mix of just about everything—Hawaiian/Chinese/German/Portuguese/Filipino/Japanese/French/Puerto Rican/English/Norwegian, you name it. The plantation was divided into ethnic camps, which helped retain cultural cuisines. Potluck dinners feature sashimi, Portuguese bean soup, *laulau* (morsels of pork, chicken, butterfish, or other ingredients wrapped with young taro shoots in tī leaves), potato salad, teriyaki steak, chicken *hekka* (a gingery Japanese chicken stir-fry), and Jell-O. The local language is pidgin, a mix of words as complicated and rich as the food. In recent years, David Murdock's plan to pay for the resorts by selling expensive homes next to them has met with opposition from locals.

THE GHOSTS OF LĀNA'I
Lāna'i has a reputation for being haunted (at one time by "cannibal spirits") and evidence abounds: a mysterious purple *lehua* (an evergreen tree that normally produces red flowers) at Keahialoa; the crying of a ghost chicken at Kamoa; Pohaku O, a rock that calls at twilight; and remote spots where cars mysteriously stall, and lights are seen at night. Tradition has it that Pu'u Pehe (an offshore sea stack) was a child who spoke from the womb, demanding *awa* root. A later story claims it is the grave of a woman drowned in a cave at the nearby cliffs. Hawaiians

believe that places have *mana* (spiritual power), and Lāna'i is far from an exception.

EXPLORING LĀNA'I

Lāna'i has an ideal climate year-round, hot and sunny at the sea and a few delicious degrees cooler Upcountry. In Lāna'i City, the nights and mornings can be almost chilly when a mystic fog or harsh trade winds settle in. Winter months are known for *slightly* rougher weather—periodic rain showers and higher surf.

You can easily explore Lāna'i City and the island's two resorts without a car; just hop on the hourly shuttle. To access the rest of this untamed island, you'll need to rent a four-wheel-drive vehicle. Take a map, be sure you have a full tank, and bring a snack and plenty of water. Ask the rental agency or your hotel's concierge about road conditions before you set out. If the roads are impassable (as they often are after heavy rains) you may be able to negotiate a refund for your rental car. The main road on Lāna'i, Route 440, refers to both Kaumalapau Highway and Mānele Road.

LĀNA'I CITY, GARDEN OF THE GODS, AND MĀNELE BAY

Pineapples once blanketed the Pālāwai, the great basin south of Lāna'i City. Before that it was a vast dryland forest; now most of it is fenced-in pasture or a game-bird reserve, and can only be viewed from the Mānele Road. Although it looks like a volcanic crater, it isn't. Some say that the name Pālāwai is descriptive of the mist that sometimes fills the basin at dawn and looks like a huge shining lake.

The area northwest of Lāna'i City is wild; the Garden of the Gods is one of its highlights.

TOP ATTRACTIONS

Fodor'sChoice
★ **Garden of the Gods.** This preternatural plateau is scattered with boulders of different sizes, shapes, and colors, the products of a million years of wind erosion. Time your visit for sunset, when the rocks begin to glow—from rich red to purple—and the fiery globe sinks to the horizon. Magnificent views of the Pacific Ocean, Moloka'i, and, on clear days, O'ahu provide the perfect backdrop for photographs.

> **WORD OF MOUTH**
>
> "On Lāna'i, we found the dirt road to the Garden of the Gods, with further journey on to the isolated Polihua Beach, to be quite scenic and the most extreme legal off-roading experience in Hawai'i."   —JohnD

The ancient Hawaiians shunned Lāna'i for hundreds of years, believing the island was the inviolable home of spirits. Standing beside the oxide-red rock spires of this strange, raw landscape, you might be tempted to believe the same. This lunar savanna still has a decidedly eerie edge, but the shadows disappearing on the horizon are those of mouflon sheep and axis deer, not the fearsome spirits of lore. According to tradition, Kawelo, a Hawaiian priest, kept a perpetual fire burning on an altar

You need a four-wheel-drive to explore the eroded rocks of the Garden of the Gods.

at the Garden of the Gods, in sight of the island of Moloka'i. As long as the fire burned, prosperity was assured for the people of Lāna'i. Kawelo was killed by a rival priest on Moloka'i and the fire went out. Keahikawelo, the fire of kawelo, is the presumed site of the altar. ⊠ 6 *mi north of Lāna'i City ✢ From Stables at Kō'ele, follow dirt road through pasture, turn right at crossroad marked by carved boulder, head through abandoned fields and ironwood forest to open red-dirt area marked by a carved boulder.*

Ka Lokahi o Ka Mālamalama Church. This picturesque church was built in 1938 to provide services for Lāna'i's growing population—for many people, the only other Hawaiian church, in coastal Keōmuku, was too far away. A classic structure of preplantation days, the church had to be moved from its original Lāna'i Ranch location when the Lodge at Kō'ele was built. Sunday services are still held, in Hawaiian and English; visitors are welcome, but are requested to attend quietly. ✢ *Left of entrance to Four Seasons Resort Lodge at Kō'ele.*

Kānepu'u Preserve. Kānepu'u is the largest example in Hawai'i of a rare native dryland forest characterized by Hawaiian sandalwood, olive, and ebony trees. Thanks to landowners Castle & Cooke Resorts, the 590-acre remnant forest is protected from the axis deer and mouflon sheep that graze on the landscape beyond its fence. More than 45 native plant species, including *na'u*, the endangered Hawaiian gardenia, can be seen here. A short self-guided loop trail, with eight signs illustrated by local artist Wendell Kaho'ohalahala, reveals this ecosystem's beauty and the challenges it faces. ⊠ *Polihua Rd., 4.8 mi north of Lāna'i City.*

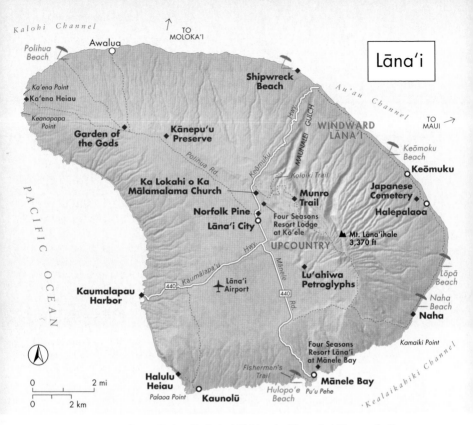

Kaumalapau Harbor. Built in 1926 by the Hawaiian Pineapple Company, which later became Dole, this is Lāna'i's principal commercial seaport. The cliffs that flank the western shore are as much as 1,000 feet tall. Water activities aren't allowed here, but it's a dramatic sunset spot. The harbor is closed to visitors on barge days: Wednesday, Thursday, and Friday. ⊠ *Western terminus of Hwy. 440 (Kaumalapau Hwy.)* ⊕ *From Lāna'i City turn right and follow Kaumalapau Hwy. west as far as it goes.*

Lāna'i City. This tidy plantation town, built in 1924 by Jim Dole, is home to old-time residents, recently arrived resort workers, and second-home owners, and is slowly changing from a quiet rural village to a busy little town. A simple grid of roads here is lined with stately Cook pines, and all the basic services a person might need. The pace is slow and the people are friendly. **Dole Park**, in the center of Lāna'i City, is surrounded by small shops and restaurants, and is a favorite spot among locals for sitting, strolling, and talking story. Visit the **Lāna'i Arts & Cultural Center** to get a glimpse of this island's creative abundance. ⊠ *339 7th Ave.*

Lu'ahiwa Petroglyphs. On a steep slope overlooking the Pālāwai Basin are 34 boulders with carvings. Drawn in a mixture of styles dating to the late 1700s and early 1800s, the simple stick figures depict animals, people, and mythic beings. A nearby *heiau*, or temple, no longer visible, was used to summon the rains and was dedicated to the god Kāne. Do not draw on or deface the carvings, and do not add to the collection. ✛ *From Lāna'i City turn left on Hwy. 440 (Mānele Rd.) and continue to first dirt road on your left. Follow dirt road along fields 1.2 mi; do not go left uphill but continue straight and when you see boulders on hillside, park and walk up to petroglyphs.*

Mānele Bay. The site of a Hawaiian village dating from AD 900, Mānele Bay is flanked by lava cliffs hundreds of feet high. Though included in a Marine Life Conservation District, it's the island's only public boat harbor and was the location of most postcontact shipping until Kaumalapau Harbor was built in 1926. The ferries to and from Maui and Ma'alea pull in here. Public restrooms, a small café, water, and picnic tables make it a busy pit stop—you can watch the boating activity as you rest and refuel.

Just offshore to the west is **Pu'u Pehe.** Often called Sweetheart Rock, the isolated 80-foot-high islet carries a sad Hawaiian legend that is probably not true. The rock is said to be named after Pehe, a woman so beautiful that her husband, afraid that others would steal her away, kept her hidden in a sea cave. One day, while Pehe was alone, the surf surged into the cave and she drowned. Her grief-stricken husband buried her on the summit of this rock and then jumped to his own death. A more authentic, if less romantic, story is that the enclosure on the summit is a shrine to birds, built by bird-catchers. Archaeological investigation has revealed that the enclosure was not a burial place. ✛ *From Lāna'i City follow Hwy. 440 (Mānele Rd.) 9 mi south to bottom of hill and look for large sign marking harbor on your left.*

WORTH NOTING

Halulu Heiau. The well-preserved remains of an impressive *heiau* (temple) at Kaunolū village, which was actively used by Lāna'i's earliest residents, attest to this spot's sacred history. As late as 1810, this hilltop temple was considered a place of refuge, where those who had broken *kapu* (taboos) were forgiven and where women and children could find safety in times of war. If you explore the area, be respectful; take nothing with you and leave nothing behind. This place is hard to find, so get someone to mark a map for you. The road is alternately rocky, sandy, and soft at the bottom. ✛ *From Lāna'i City follow Hwy. 440 (Kaumalapau Hwy.) west toward Kaumalapau Harbor. Pass airport, then look for carved boulder on hill on your left. Turn left on dirt road, follow it 3 mi to another carved boulder, turn right then head downhill.*

Kaunolū. Close to the island's highest cliffs, Kaunolū was once a prosperous fishing village. This important archaeological site includes a major *heiau* (temple), terraces, stone floors, and house platforms. The impressive 90-foot drop to the ocean through a gap in the lava rock is called **Kahekili's Leap.** Warriors would make the dangerous jump into the shallow 12 feet of water below to show their courage. The road is very rocky then gets sandy at the bottom. ✛ *From Lāna'i City follow Hwy. 440 (Kaumalapau Hwy.) west past the airport turnoff; at carved boulder on your left on hill, turn left onto an unmarked dirt road;*

continue 3 mi until you reach the second carved boulder and then go right (makai [toward the ocean]) 3 mi to village.

Lāna'i Culture & Heritage Center. This small, carefully arranged, historical museum features artifacts and photographs from Lāna'i's varied and rich history. Plantation-era clothing and tools, precious feather lei, stone adzes and poi pounders, ranch memorabilia, old maps, and family portraits combine to give you a good idea of the history of the island and its people. Postcards, maps, books, and pamphlets for sale. The friendly staff can orient you to the island's historical sites and provide directions. ⊠*730 Lāna'i Ave., Lāna'i City* ☎*808/565–7177* ⊕*www.lanaichc.org.*

Norfolk pine. More than 160 feet high, this majestic pine tree was planted here, at the former site of the manager's house, in 1875. Almost 30 years later, George Munro, then the ranch manager, would observe how, in foggy weather, water collected on its foliage, forming a natural rain. This fog drip led Munro to supervise the planting of Cook pines along the ridge of Lāna'ihale and throughout the town in order to add to the island's water supply. ⊠*Entrance of Four Seasons Resort Lodge at Kō'ele, 1 Keōmuku Hwy., Lāna'i City.*

WINDWARD LĀNA'I

The eastern section of Lāna'i is wild and untouched. An inaccessible *heiau,* or temple, is the only trace of human habitation, with the exception of rocks and boulders marking old shrines, and trails. Four-wheel drive is a must to explore this side of the isle, and be prepared for hot, rough conditions. Hawaiians request that you not stack or disturb rocks. Pack a picnic lunch and bring plenty of drinking water.

TOP ATTRACTIONS

★ **Munro Trail.** This 12.8-mi jeep trail along a fern- and pine-clad narrow ridge was named after George Munro, manager of the Lāna'i Ranch Co., who began a reforestation program in the 1950s to restore the island's much-needed watershed. The trail climbs **Lāna'ihale** (House of Lāna'i), which, at 3,370 feet, is the island's highest point; on clear days you'll be treated to a panorama of canyons and almost all of the Hawaiian Islands. ■**TIP**➔ The one-way road gets very muddy, and trade winds can be strong. A sheer drop-off in some sections requires an attentive driver. Keep an eye out for hikers along the way. You can also hike the Munro Trail *(see Golf, Hiking & Outdoor Activities later in this chapter),* though it's a difficult trek: it's steep, the ground is uneven, and there's no water. ⊹*From Four Seasons Resort Lodge at Kō'ele head north on Hwy. 440 (Keōmuku Hwy.) for 1¼ mi, then turn right onto Cemetery Rd. and continue straight, passing cemetery on right.*

★ **Shipwreck Beach.** The rusting World War II tanker off this 8-mi stretch of sand adds just the right touch to an already photogenic beach. Maui is visible in the distance, and Moloka'i lies just across beautiful but unrelenting Kalohi Channel. Strong trade winds have propelled innocent vessels onto the reef since at least 1824, when the first shipwreck was recorded. Some believe that the unknown Navy oiler you see stranded today, however, was intentionally scuttled. To see petroglyphs of warriors and dogs decorating dark-red boulders, follow the painted rocks and signs at the end of the road south about 200 yards. ■TIP➜ The water is unsafe for swimming; stick to beachcombing. ✛ *Take Hwy. 440 (Keōmuku Hwy.) to its eastern terminus, then turn left on dirt road and continue north for 2 mi.*

WORTH NOTING

Halepalaoa. Named for the whale bones that once washed ashore

WORD OF MOUTH

"Lāna'i is one funky-looking island. There are places like the Garden of the Gods, where it looks like you are on another planet. We also drove the Munro Trail, which takes you up to the highest part of the island. Spectacular scenery."

—Alex

here, Halepalaoa, or house of whale ivory, was the site of the wharf used by the short-lived Maunalei Sugar Company to ship cane in 1899. Some say the sugar company failed because the sacred stones of nearby **Kahe'a Heiau** were used for the construction of the cane railroad. Angry gods turned the drinking water salty, forcing the sugar company to close after just two years in 1901. The remains of the *heiau* (temple), once an important place of worship for the people of Lāna'i, are now difficult to find through the *kiawe* (mesquite) overgrowth. There's good public beach access here with clear shallow water for swimming, but no facilities. ✛ *Take Hwy. 440 (Keōmuku Hwy.) to its eastern terminus, then turn right on dirt road and continue south for 5½ mi.*

Japanese Cemetery. In 1899 sugar came to this side of Lāna'i. A plantation took up about 2,400 acres and seemed a profitable proposition, but that same year, disease wiped out the labor force. This authentic Buddhist shrine commemorates the Japanese workers who died. ⊠ *Take Hwy. 440 (Keōmuku Hwy.) to its eastern terminus, then turn right on dirt road and continue south for 6½ mi.*

Keōmuku. There's an eerie beauty about Keōmuku, with its faded memories and forgotten homesteads. During the late 19th century, this busy Lāna'i community of some 900 to 2,000 residents served as the headquarters of Maunalei Sugar Company. After the company failed, the land was used for ranching, but by 1954 the area lay abandoned. Its church, **Ka Lanakila O Ka Mālamalama,** was built in 1903. It has been partially restored by volunteers, and visitors often leave some small token, a shell or faded lei, as an offering. ✛ *Take Hwy. 440 (Keōmuku Hwy.) to its eastern terminus, then turn right on dirt road and continue south for 5 mi.*

Naha. An ancient rock-walled fishpond—visible at low tide—lies here, where the sandy shoreline ends and the cliffs begin their rise along the island's shores. The beach is a frequent resource for local fisherfolk. ■TIP➜ Treacherous currents make this a dangerous place for swimming. ✛ *Take Hwy. 440 (Keōmuku Hwy.) to its eastern terminus, then turn right on dirt road and continue south for 11 mi. The shoreline dirt road ends here.*

The calm crescent of Hulopo'e Beach is perfect for swimming, snorkeling, or just relaxing.

BEACHES

Lāna'i offers miles of secluded white-sand beaches on its windward side, plus the moderately developed Hulopo'e Beach, which is adjacent to the Four Seasons Resort Lāna'i at Mānele Bay. Hulopo'e is accessible by car or hotel shuttle bus; to reach the windward beaches you'll need a four-wheel-drive vehicle. Offshore reef, rocks, and coral make swimming on the windward side problematic, but it's fun to splash around in the shallow water. Driving on the beach itself is illegal and can be dangerous. Beaches in this chapter are listed alphabetically.

FodorśChoice

★

Hulopo'e Beach. A short stroll from the Four Seasons Resort Lāna'i at Mānele Bay, Hulopo'e is considered one of the best beaches in Hawai'i. The sparkling crescent of this Marine Life Conservation District beckons with calm waters safe for swimming almost year-round, great snorkeling reefs, tide pools, and, sometimes, spinner dolphins. A shady, grassy beach park is perfect for picnics. If the shore break is pounding, or if you see surfers riding big waves, stay out of the water. In the afternoons, watch Lāna'i High School students heave outrigger canoes down the steep shore break and race one another just offshore. ⊹ *From Lāna'i City turn left on Hwy. 440 (Mānele Rd.) and go 9 mi south to bottom of hill; turn right, road dead-ends at beach's parking lot* ⌀ *Toilets, showers, picnic tables, grills, parking lot.*

Lōpā Beach. A popular surfing spot for locals, Lōpā is also an ancient fishpond. With majestic views of West Maui and Kaho'olawe, this remote, white-sand beach is a great place for a picnic. ⚠ **Don't let the sight of surfers fool you: the channel's currents are too strong for swimming.**

⊠*East side of Lāna'i* ⊹ *Take Hwy. 440 (Keōmuku Hwy.) to its eastern terminus, then turn right on dirt road and continue south for 7 mi* ☞ *No facilities.*

★ **Polihua Beach.** This often-deserted beach gets a star for beauty with its long, wide stretch of white sand and clear views of Moloka'i. However, the dirt road to get here can be bad with deep, sandy places (when it rains it's impassable), and frequent high winds whip up sand and waves. ■TIP→ In addition, strong currents and a sudden drop in the ocean floor make swimming dangerous. On the more positive side, the northern end of the beach ends at a rocky lava cliff with some inter-

THE COASTAL ROAD

Road conditions can change overnight and become impassable due to rain in the uplands. Car-rental agencies should be able to give you updates before you hit the road. Many of the spur roads leading to the windward beaches from the coastal dirt road cross private property and are closed off by chains. Look for open spur roads with recent tire marks (a fairly good sign that they are safe to drive on). It's best to park on firm ground and walk in to avoid getting your car mired in the sand.

esting tide pools. Polihua is named after the sea turtles that lay their eggs in the sand. (Do not drive on the beach and endanger their nests.) Curiously, wild bees sometimes gather around your car for water at this beach. To get rid of them, put out water some place away from the car and wait a bit. ⊠ *Windward Lāna'i, 11 mi north of Lāna'i City* ⊹ *Turn right on marked dirt road past Garden of the Gods* ☞ *No facilities.*

Shipwreck Beach. Beachcombers come to this fairly accessible beach for shells and washed-up treasures; photographers for great shots of Moloka'i, just across the 9-mi-wide Kalohi Channel; and walkers for the long stretch of sand. It may still be possible to find glass-ball fishing floats but more common is waterborne debris from the Moloka'i channel. Kaiolohia, its Hawaiian name, is a favorite local diving spot. ■TIP→ An offshore reef and rocks in the water mean that it's not for swimmers, though you can play in the shallow water on the shoreline. ⊠ *North shore* ⊹ *Take Hwy. 440 (Keōmuku Hwy.) to its eastern terminus, then turn left on dirt road and continue north for 3 mi* ☞ *No facilities.*

WATER SPORTS AND TOURS

DEEP-SEA FISHING

Some of the best sportfishing grounds in Maui County are off the southwest shoreline of Lāna'i. Pry your eyes open and go deep-sea fishing in the early morning, with departures at 6 or 6:30 AM from Mānele Harbor. Console yourself with the knowledge that Maui fishers have to leave an hour earlier to get to the same prime locations. Peak seasons are spring and summer, although good catches have been landed year-round. Mahimahi, *ono* (a mackerel-like fish; the word means "delicious" in Hawaiian), *'ahi* tuna, and marlin are prized catches and preferred eating.

BOATS AND CHARTERS

Fish-N-Tips. This roomy 36-foot Twin-Vee with tuna tower will get you and your family to the fishing grounds in comfort, and Captain Jason will do everything except reel in the big one for you. Plan on trolling along the south coast for *ono* (a mackerel-like fish) and around the point at Kaunolū for mahimahi or marlin. A trip to the offshore buoy often yields skipjack tuna or big *'ahi* (yellowfin tuna), and the captain and crew are always open to a bit of bottom fishing. Fishing gear, sodas, and water are included. A four-hour charter (six-passenger maximum) is $850; each additional hour costs $150. Guests can keep up to a third of all fish caught. Shared charters on Sunday are $200 per person. Book with the concierge at your resort or call directly. ☎808/565–7676.

KAYAKING

Lāna'i's southeast coast offers leisurely paddling and miles of scenic coastline with deserted beaches to haul up on inside the windward reef. Curious sea turtles and friendly manta rays may tag along your kayak for company. When the wind comes from the southwest, the windward coast is tranquil. Kayaking along the leeward cliffs is more demanding with rougher seas and strong currents. No kayaking is permitted in the Marine Conservation District at Hulopo'e Bay.

Early mornings tend to be calmer. The wind picks up as the day advances. Expect strong currents along all of the coasts. Experience on the water is advised, and knowing how to swim is essential. There is one other glitch: there are no kayak rentals on the island, so you need to book a tour or bring your own.

TOURS

Trilogy Oceansports Lāna'i. Join Trilogy's experienced ocean kayak guide for a full morning of kayaking inside the reef of Lāna'i's unspoiled coastline. This six-hour adventure costs $170 for adults and $85 for *keiki*, or kids (ages three to five). Lunch, sodas, bottled water, and snacks are served. Reservations are required at least 24 hours in advance. Book with your hotel concierge or online. ☎888/628–4800 ⊕*www.sailtrilogy.com.*

RAFTING

If you're looking to get out on the water without fishing, Trilogy Oceansports Lāna'i offers comfortable marine mammal tours on a 32-foot, hard-bottom inflatable raft.

TOURS

Trilogy Oceansports Lāna'i. Trilogy offers a 1½-hour marine mammal watch on the *Manele Kai*, a 32-foot, jet-drive, hard-bottom inflatable raft. Cruise the coast and search for protected whales, dolphins, and monk seals. Sodas and bottled water provided. Cost is $80 for adults, $40 for *keiki* (kids) under 15. You can book trips through your hotel concierge, but try online first, where discounts are often available. ☎888/628–4800 ⊕*www.scubalanai.com.*

SCUBA DIVING

When you have a dive site such as Cathedrals—with eerie pinnacle formations and luminous caverns—it's no wonder that scuba-diving buffs consider exploring the waters off Lāna'i akin to having a religious experience.

BEST SPOTS

Just outside of Hulopo'oe Bay, the boat dive site **Cathedrals** was named the best cavern dive site in the Pacific by *Skin Diver* magazine. Shimmering light makes the many openings in the caves look like stained-glass windows. A current generally keeps the water crystal clear, even if it's turbid outside. In these unearthly chambers, large *ulua* and small reef shark add to the adventure. **Sergeant Major Reef,** off Kamaiki Point, is named for big schools of yellow- and black-striped *manini* (sergeant major fish) that turn the rocks silvery as they feed. The site is made up of three parallel lava ridges, a cave, and an archway, with rippled sand valleys between the ridges. Depths range 15 to 50 feet.

EQUIPMENT, LESSONS, AND TOURS

Trilogy Oceansports Lāna'i. Serious divers should go for Trilogy's two-tank dive; location depends on the weather. You must be certified, so don't forget your documentation. The $213 fee includes a light breakfast of cinnamon rolls and coffee. Equipment, wet suits, accessories are included. Beginners (minimum age 12) can try a one-tank introductory dive for $101. You'll wade into Hulopo'e Bay with an instructor at your side; actual dive time is 20 to 30 minutes. Certified divers can choose a 35- to 40-minute wade-in dive at Hulopo'e, also for $101. ☎888/628–4800 ⊕*www.scubalanai.com.*

SNORKELING

Snorkeling is the easiest ocean sport available on the island, requiring nothing but a snorkel, mask, fins, and good sense. Borrow equipment from your hotel or purchase some in Lāna'i City if you didn't bring your own. Wait to enter the water until you are sure no big sets of waves are coming; and observe the activity of locals on the beach. If little kids are playing in the shore break, it's usually safe to enter. ■ TIP→ To get into the water safely, always swim in past the breakers, and in the comparative calm put on your fins, then mask and snorkel.

BEST SPOTS

Hulopo'e Beach is an outstanding snorkeling destination. The bay is a State of Hawai'i Marine Conservation District and no spearfishing or diving is allowed. Schools of *manini* (sergeant major fish) feeding on the coral coat the rocks with flashing silver, and you can view *kala* (unicorn fish), *uhu* (parrot fish), and *papio* (small trevally) in all their rainbow colors. As you wade in from the sandy beach, the best snorkeling is toward the left. Beware of rocks and surging waves. When the resident spinner dolphins are in the bay, it's courteous to watch them from the shore. If swimmers and snorkelers go out, the dolphins may leave and be deprived of their necessary resting place. Another wade-in snorkel spot is just beyond the break wall at **Mānele Small Boat Harbor.** Enter over the rocks, just past the boat ramp. ■TIP→ It's dangerous to enter if waves are breaking.

EQUIPMENT, LESSONS, AND TOURS

Trilogy Oceansports Lāna'i. A 4½-hour blue-water snorkeling and adventure catamaran trip explores Lāna'i's pristine coastline with Trilogy's experienced captain and crew. The trip includes lessons, equipment, and deluxe lunch served onboard. Tours are offered Monday, Wednesday, Friday, and Saturday; cost is $181 for adults and $90 for kids 15 and under. You can book trips through your hotel concierge, but try online first, where discounts are often available. ☎888/628–4800 ⊕*www. sailtrilogy.com.*

SURFING

Surfing on Lāna'i can be truly enjoyable. Quality, not quantity, characterizes this isle's few breaks. Be considerate of the locals and they will be considerate of you—surfing takes the place of megaplex theaters and pool halls here, serving as one of the island's few recreational luxuries.

BEST SPOTS

Don't try to hang 10 at **Hulopo'e Bay** without watching the conditions for a while. When it "goes off," it's a tricky left-handed shore break that requires some skill. Huge summer south swells are for experts only. The southeast-facing breaks at **Lōpā Beach** are inviting for beginners. Give them a try in summer, when the swells roll in nice and easy.

EQUIPMENT AND LESSONS

Lāna'i Surf School. Nick and his wife Alex offer the only surf instruction on the island. Sign up for their "4X4 Safari"—a four-hour adventure that includes hard- or soft-top boards, snacks, and transportation to "secret spots." Nick, who was born on Lāna'i, is a former Hawai'i State Surfing Champion. Group lessons are $175 per person (minimum of two); private lessons are $200. Experienced riders can rent short- or long-boards overnight for $58 with a $125 deposit; stand-up paddles are available for an additional $25. ☎808/306–9837 ⊕*www.lanai surfsafari.com.*

GOLF, HIKING, AND OUTDOOR ACTIVITIES

BIKING

Many of the same red-dirt roads that invite hikers are excellent for biking, offering easy flat terrain and long clear views. There's only one hitch: you may have to bring your own bike, as there are no rentals or tours available for nonresort guests.

BEST SPOTS

A favorite biking route is along the fairly flat red-dirt road northward from Lāna'i City through the old pineapple fields to Garden of the Gods. Start your trip on Keōmuku Highway in town. Take a left just before the Lodge at Kō'ele's tennis courts, and then a right where the road ends at the fenced pasture, and continue on to the north end and the start of Polihua and Awalua dirt roads. If you're really hardy you could bike down to Polihua Beach and back, but it would be a serious all-day trip. In wet weather these roads turn to mud and are not advisable. Go in the early morning or late afternoon because the sun gets hot in the middle of the day. Take plenty of water, spare parts, and snacks.

For the exceptionally fit, it's possible to bike from town down the Keōmuku Highway to the windward beaches and back, or to bike the Munro Trail *(see Hiking)*. Experienced bikers also bike up and down the Mānele Highway from Mānele Bay to town.

CAMPING

Camping isn't encouraged outside Lāna'i's one official campground at Hulopo'e: the island is privately owned; islanders are keen on privacy; and, unless you know about local conditions, camping on the beach can be hazardous.

★ **Castle & Cooke Resorts Campground.** The inviting, grassy campground at Hulopo'e Beach has shade trees, clean restrooms, barbecue grills, beachside showers, and a big grass lawn, perfect for Frisbee. All of that *and* it happens to be a stone's throw from one of the best beaches in the state. (Camping on the beach itself is reserved for residents only.) Buy charcoal in Lāna'i City, as well as basic camping supplies and food. Cutting firewood is not allowed. It is possible to walk from Mānele Harbor to the campground. Call in advance; it's $20 for a permit, plus a $5 fee per person per night (three-night limit). ☎ *808/565–3273 for permits and advance reservations.*

GOLF

Lāna'i has two resort courses that offer very different environments and challenges. They are so diverse that it's hard to believe they're on the same island, let alone just 20 minutes apart by resort shuttle.

The Challenge at Mānele. Designed by Jack Nicklaus (1993), this course sits right over the water of Hulopo'e Bay. Built on lava outcroppings, the course features three holes on cliffs that use the Pacific Ocean as a water hazard. The five-tee concept challenges the best golfers—tee shots over natural gorges and ravines must be precise. This unspoiled natural terrain is a stunning backdrop, and every hole offers ocean views. ⊠ *Four Seasons Resort Lāna'i at Mānele Bay, Challenge Dr., Lāna'i City* ☎ *808/565–2222* ⊕ *www.fourseasons.com/manelebay/golf* ⚐ *18 holes. 6310 yds. Par 72, slope 126. Green fee: hotel guests $210, nonguests $225* ⚐ *Facilities: Driving range, putting green, golf carts, rental clubs, pro shop, lessons, restaurant, bar.*

The Experience at Kō'ele. This challenging Greg Norman (1991) layout begins at an elevation of 2,000 feet. The front nine moves dramatically through ravines wooded with pine, koa, and eucalyptus trees; seven lakes and streams with cascading waterfalls dot the course. No other course in Hawai'i offers a more incredible combination of highland

terrain, inspired landscape architecture, and range of play challenges.
✉ *Four Seasons Resort Lodge at Kō'ele, 1 Keōmuku Hwy., Lāna'i
City* ☎808/565–4653 ⊕*www.fourseasons.com/koele/golf* ⚑ *18 holes.
6310 yds. Par 72, slope 134. Green fee: hotel guests $210, nonguests
$225* ☞ *Facilities: Driving range, putting green, golf carts, rental clubs,
pro shop, lessons, restaurant, bar.*

HIKING

Only 30 mi of Lāna'i's roads are paved. But red-dirt roads and trails,
ideal for hiking, will take you to sweeping overlooks, isolated beaches,
and shady forests. Don't be afraid to leave the road to follow deer
trails, but make sure to keep your landmarks in clear sight so you can
always retrace your steps. Or take a self-guided walk through Kāne
Pu'u, Hawai'i's largest native dryland forest. You can explore the Munro Trail over Lāna'ihale with views of plunging canyons, or hike along
an old, coastal fisherman trail or across Koloiki Ridge. Wear hiking
shoes, a hat, and sunscreen, and carry plenty of water.

BEST SPOTS

Koloiki Ridge. This marked, moderate trail starts behind the Lodge at
Kō'ele and takes you along the cool and shady Munro Trail to overlook
the windward side, with impressive views of Maui, Moloka'i, Maunalei
Valley, and Naio Gulch. The average time for the 5-mi round-trip is two
hours. Bring snacks and water, and take your time. A map is available
at Four Seasons Resort Lodge at Kō'ele.

Lāna'i Fisherman Trail. Local fishermen still use the Lāna'i Fisherman Trail
to get to their favorite fishing spots. The trail takes about 1½ hours to
hike and follows the rocky shoreline below the Four Seasons Resort at
Lāna'i Mānele Bay, along cliffs bordering the golf course. Caves and
tide pools beckon beneath you, but be careful climbing down. The
marked trail entrance begins at the west end of Hulopo'e Beach. Keep
your eyes open for spinner dolphins cavorting offshore and the silvery
flash of fish feeding in the pools below you. The condition of the trail
varies with weather and frequency of maintenance and can be slippery
and rocky. Wear shoes, not flip-flops.

Munro Trail. This is the real thing: a strenuous 12.8-mi trek that begins
behind the Four Seasons Resort Lodge at Kō'ele and follows the ridge of
Lāna'ihale through the rain forest. The island's most demanding hike, it
has an elevation gain of 1,400 feet and leads to a lookout at the island's
highest point, Lāna'ihale. It's also a narrow dirt road; watch out for
careening jeeps. The trail is named after George Munro, who supervised
the planting of Cook pine trees and eucalyptus windbreaks. Mules used
to wend their way up the mountain carrying the pine seedlings. Unless
you arrange for someone to pick you up at the trail's end, you have
a long boring hike back through the Pālāwai Basin to return to your
starting point. The top is often cloud-shrouded and can be windy and
muddy, so check conditions before you start.

Pu'u Pehe Trail. Beginning to the left (facing the ocean) of Hulopo'e
Beach, this trail travels a short distance around the coastline, and then
climbs up a sharp, rocky rise. At the top, you're level with the offshore

stack of Pu'u Pehe and can overlook miles of coastline in both directions. The trail is not difficult, but it's hot and steep. Be aware of nesting endangered seabirds and don't approach their nests. ⚠ **Never approach the edge, as the cliff can easily give way.** The hiking is best in the early morning or late afternoon, and it's a perfect place to look for whales in season (December–April). Wear shoes; this is not a hike for sandals or slip-ons.

HORSEBACK RIDING

Stables at Kō'ele. The subtle beauty of the high country slowly reveals itself to horseback riders on the backcountry Paniolo rides. Two-hour adventures traverse leafy trails with scenic overlooks. Well-trained horses take riders of all skill levels (under 225 pounds, nine years and older). Prices start at $95 for a two-hour group ride and go to $160 for a two-hour private ride. Lessons are also available. Book rides at the Four Seasons Resort Lodge at Kō'ele. ☎*808/565–4424.*

SPORTING CLAYS AND ARCHERY

★ **Lāna'i Pine Sporting Clays and Archery Range.** Outstanding rustic terrain, challenging targets, and a well-stocked pro shop make this sporting-clays course top-flight in the expert's eyes. Sharpshooters can complete the meandering 14-station course, with the help of a golf cart, in 1½ hours. There are group tournaments, and even kids can enjoy skilled instruction at the archery range and compressed-air rifle gallery. The $50 archery introduction includes an amusing "pineapple challenge"—contestants are given five arrows with which to hit a paper pineapple target. The winner takes home a crystal pineapple as a nostalgic souvenir of the old Dole Plantation days. Guns and ammunition are provided with the lessons. Prices range from $80 to $150 depending on amount of ammunition and activity. ✉*Just past Cemetery Rd. on windward side of island, first left at sign on Hwy. 440 (Keōmuku Hwy.)* ☎*808/559–4600.*

SHOPPING

A miniforest of Cook pine trees in the center of Lāna'i City surrounded by small shops and restaurants, Dole Park is the closest thing to a mall on Lāna'i. Except for the high-end resort boutiques and pro shops, it provides the island's only shopping. A morning or afternoon stroll around the park offers an eclectic selection of gifts and clothing, plus a chance to chat with residents. Friendly general stores are reminiscent of the 1920s, and new galleries and a boutique have original art and fashions for men, women, and children. The shops close Sunday and after 5 PM, except for the general stores, which are open a bit later.

ARTS AND CRAFTS

Dis 'n Dat. This tiny, jungle-green shop packs in thousands of art, gift, and jewelry items in a minuscule space enlivened by a glittering crystal ceiling. Fanciful garden ornaments, serene Buddhas, and Asian antiques add to the charm. ⊠*418 8th St., Lānaʻi City* ☎*808/565–9170* ⊕*www. disndatshop.com.*

Gifts with Aloha. Casual resort wear is sold alongside a great collection of Hawaiiana books and the work of local artists, including ceramic ware, *raku* (Japanese-style lead-glazed pottery), fine handblown glass, and watercolor prints. Look for a complete selection of Hawaiian music CDs and Lānaʻi-designed Stone Shack shirts. ⊠*363 7th St., Lānaʻi City* ☎*808/565–6589* ⊕*www.giftswithaloha.com.*

CLOTHING

Lānaʻi Beach Walk. This small shop is crammed with a wide variety of styles and colors of the now indispensable "crocs," as well as colorful resort clothing, logo tee shirts, swimwear, and classy skirts and dresses. Tropical knickknacks and souvenirs complete the inventory. ⊠*850 Fraser Ave., Lānaʻi City* ☎*808/565–9249.*

Local Gentry. This tiny, classy store has clothing for every need, from casual men's and women's beachwear to evening resort wear, shoes, jewelry, and hats. A selection of Lānaʻi logo-wear is also available. Proprietor Jenna Gentry Majkus will mail your purchases for the cost of the postage, and can put you on her e-mail list for future fashion offerings. ⊠*363 7th St., Lānaʻi City* ☎*808/565–9130.*

FOOD

Pine Isle Market. This is one of Lānaʻi City's two markets, stocking everything from beach toys to cosmetics to canned vegetables. Staff is friendly and it's a great place to buy fresh fish. Look at the photos of famous local fish and fishermen opposite the beer case. Closed Sunday and during lunch hours from noon to 1:30 PM, Monday through Thursday. ⊠*356 8th St., Lānaʻi City* ☎*808/565–6488.*

Richard's. Castle & Cooke Resorts has taken over this store from Richard Tamashiro, who founded it in 1946. Along with groceries, Richard's has camping gear, common household items, a good array of fine wines, and a few gourmet food items. ⊠*434 8th St., Lānaʻi City* ☎*808/565–3780.*

Sergio's Oriental Store. Sergio's, the closest thing to a mini Costco on Lānaʻi, has Filipino sweets and pastries; case-loads of sodas, water, and juices; family-size containers of condiments; and frozen fish and meat. Open 8 to 8 daily. ⊠*831-D Houston St., Lānaʻi City* ☎*808/ 565–6900.*

GALLERIES

Jordanne Fine Art Studio. Take a piece of historic Lānaʻi home: Jordanne Weinstein's affordable, whimsical portraits of rural island life and gold-leaf pineapple paintings make terrific souvenirs. Greeting cards and small prints complete the offerings. Stop into her bright studio just off of Dole Park, where she paints on-site. ⊠*850 Fraser Ave., Lānaʻi City* ☎*808/563–0088* ⊕*www.jordannefineart.com.*

Lānaʻi Art Center. Local artists practice and display their crafts at this dynamic center. Workshops in the pottery, photography, woodworking, and painting studios welcome visitors, and individual instruction may be arranged. The center's gift shop sells original art and unique

Lāna'i handicrafts. The art center sponsors occasional concerts and cultural events. Check with them for the schedule or visit the Web site. It's closed Sunday. ⊠*339 7th St., Lāna'i City* ☎*808/565–7503* ⊕*www.lanaiart.org.*

Mike Carroll Gallery. The dreamy, soft-focus oil paintings of resident painter Mike Carroll are showcased along with wood bowls and koa 'ukulele by Warren Osako, and fish-print paper tapestries by Joana Varawa. Local photographer Ron Gingerich, island artists Cheryl McElfresh and Billy O'Connell, and jeweler Susan Hunter are also featured. ⊠*443 7th St., Lāna'i City* ☎*808/565–7122* ⊕*www.mikecarrollgallery.com.*

GENERAL STORES

International Food and Clothing Center. You may not find everything the name implies, but this old-fashioned emporium does stock items for your everyday needs, from fishing gear to beer. It's a good place for last-minute camping supplies. It's closed Saturday. ⊠*833 'Ilima Ave., Lāna'i City* ☎*808/565–6433.*

Lāna'i City Service. In addition to being Lāna'i's only gas station, auto-parts store, and car-rental operation, this outfit sells Hawaiian gift items, sundries, hot dogs and *manapua* (steamed buns with pork filling), T-shirts, beer, sodas, and bottled water in the **Plantation Store.** Open 6:30 AM to 8:30 PM daily for gas and sundries; auto-parts store open weekdays 7 AM to 4 PM. It's closed from noon to 1 PM. ⊠*1036 Lāna'i Ave., Lāna'i City* ☎*808/565–7227.*

SPAS

If you're looking for rejuvenation, the whole island could be considered a spa, though the only spa facilities are at the Mānele Bay hotel or the Lodge at Kō'ele. For a quick polish in Lāna'i City, try one of the following spots. **Island Images** (☎*808/565–7870*) offers hair care for men and women, pedicures, manicures, waxing, and threading. **Nita's In Style** (☎*808/565–8082*) features hair-care services for men, women, and children.

Lodge at Kō'ele's Banyan Suite Spa. Located on the mezzanine of the Great Hall, this simple, serene spa offers a varied menu of massage treatments, including the new hot-shell treatment, Hawaiian Lomi Lomi, sports massage, and the Hehi Lani Royal Foot Treatment. Relax after your massage with herbal tea on the adjacent balcony, which offers great sunset views, or return to your room in a fluffy spa robe. Two tables accommodate couples and all massages are private. Open to non–resort guests with advance reservations. Massage services can also be enjoyed in the privacy of your room. ⊠*Four Seasons Resort Lodge at Kō'ele, 1 Keōmuku Hwy., Lāna'i City* ☎*808/565–7300* ⊕*www.fourseasons. com/koele/spa* ☞*$150 50-min massage. Gym with: cardiovascular machines, free weights. Services: aromatherapy, hot-rock massage, guided stretching, reflexology.*

The Spa at Mānele. State-of-the-art pampering enlists a panoply of oils and unguents that would have pleased Cleopatra. The Spa After Hours Experience relaxes you with private services including a neck

Continued on page 608

MORE THAN A FOLK DANCE

Hula has been called "the heartbeat of the Hawaiian people" and also "the world's best-known, most misunderstood dance." Both are true. Hula isn't just dance. It is storytelling. No words, no hula.

Chanter Edith McKinzie calls it "an extension of a piece of poetry." In its adornments, implements, and customs, hula integrates every important Hawaiian cultural practice: poetry, history, genealogy, craft, plant cultivation, martial arts, religion, protocol. So when 19th century Christian missionaries sought to eradicate a practice they considered depraved, they threatened more than just a folk dance.

With public performance outlawed and private hula practice discouraged, hula went underground for a generation, to rural villages. The fragile verbal link by which culture was transmitted from teacher to student hung by a thread. Even increasing literacy did not help because hula's practitioners were a secretive and protected circle.

As if that weren't bad enough, vaudeville, Broadway, and Hollywood got hold of the hula, giving it the glitz treatment in an unbroken line from "Oh, How She Could Wicky Wacky Woo" to "Rock-A-Hula Baby." Hula became shorthand for paradise: fragrant flowers, lazy hours. Ironically, this development assured that hundreds of Hawaiians could make a living performing and teaching hula. Many danced 'auana (modern form) in performance; but taught kahiko (traditional), quietly, at home or in hula schools.

Today, 30 years after the cultural revival known as the Hawaiian Renaissance, language immersion programs have assured a new generation of proficient—and even eloquent—chanters, songwriters, and translators. Visitors can see more, and more authentic, traditional hula than at any other time in the last 200 years.

Like the culture of which it is the beating heart, hula has survived.

Lei *po'o*. Head lei. In kahiko, greenery only. In 'auana, flowers.

Face emotes appropriate expression. Dancer should not be a smiling automaton.

Shoulders remain relaxed and still, never hunched, even with arms raised. No bouncing.

Eyes always follow leading hand.

Lei. Hula is rarely performed without a shoulder lei.

Arms and hands remain loose, relaxed, below shoulder level—except as required by interpretive movements.

Traditional hula skirt is loose fabric, smocked and gathered at the waist.

Hip is canted over weight-bearing foot.

Knees are always slightly bent, accentuating hip sway.

Kupe'e. Ankle bracelet of flowers, shells, or—traditionally—noise-making dog teeth.

In kahiko, feet are flat. In 'auana, they may be more arched, but not tiptoes or bouncing.

BASIC MOTIONS

Speak or Sing

Moon or Sun

Grass Shack or House

Mountains or Heights

Love or Caress

At backyard parties, hula is performed in bare feet and street clothes, but in performance, adornments play a key role, as do rhythm-keeping implements.

In hula kahiko (traditional style), the usual dress is multiple layers of stiff fabric (often with a pellom lining, which most closely resembles *kapa*, the paperlike bark cloth of the Hawaiians). These wrap tightly around the bosom but flare below the waist to form a skirt. In pre-contact times, dancers wore only kapa skirts. Monarchy-period hula is performed in voluminous Mother Hubbard mu'umu'u or high-necked muslin blouses and gathered skirts. Men wear loincloths or, for monarchy period, white or gingham shirts and black pants—sometimes with red sashes.

In hula 'auana (modern), dress for women can range from grass skirts and strapless tops to contemporary tea-length dresses. Men generally wear aloha shirts, but sometimes grass skirts over pants or even everyday gear. (One group at a recent competition wore wetsuits to do a surfing song!)

SURPRISING HULA FACTS

■ Grass skirts are not traditional; workers from Kiribati (the Gilbert Islands) brought this custom to Hawai'i.

■ In olden-day Hawai'i, *mele* (songs) for hula were composed for every occasion—name songs for babies, dirges for funerals, welcome songs for visitors, celebrations of favorite pursuits.

■ Hula *ma'i* is a traditional hula form in praise of a noble's genitals; the power of the *ali'i* (royalty) to procreate gave *mana* (spiritual power) to the entire culture.

■ Hula students in old Hawai'i adhered to high standards: scrupulous cleanliness, no sex, daily cleansing rituals, certain food prohibitions, and no contact with the dead. They were fined if they broke the rules.

■ Traditional hula is accompanied by percussion instruments such as drums, rattles, and sticks.

■ Laka is the goddess of hula. Although many legends deal with the origins of hula, one says that Laka created it on the island of Moloka'i. The goddess was said to have traveled around the islands to teach hula.

■ Today there are halau hula (hula schools) around the United States and the world. Check out www.mele.com for some of them.

WHERE TO WATCH

■ Check out local publications for listings of hula performances. The two Four Seasons resorts may have them, as may the library in Lāna'i City.

and shoulder massage and a 50-minute treatment of your choice. Then melt down in the sauna or steam room, finish off with a scalp massage and light *pūpū* (snacks), and ooze out to your room. The *Ali'i* banana-coconut scrub and pineapple-citrus polish treatments have inspired their own cosmetic line. Massages in private *hale* (houses) in the courtyard gardens are available for singles or couples. A tropical fantasy mural, granite stone floors, eucalyptus steam rooms, and private cabanas set the scene for indulgence. ⊠*Four Seasons Resort Lāna'i at Mānele Bay, 1 Mānele Rd., Lāna'i City* ☎*808/565–2000* ⊕*www. fourseasons.com/manelebay/spa* ☞*$145 50-min massage; $340 per person 2-hr Spa After Hours Experience (2-person minimum). Gym with: cardiovascular equipment, free weights. Services: aromatherapy, body wraps, facials, hair salon, hair care, mani/pedicures, reflexology, waxing. Classes and programs: aquaerobics, guided hikes, hula classes, personal training, tai chi, yoga.*

ENTERTAINMENT AND NIGHTLIFE

Lāna'i is certainly not known for its nightlife. Fewer than a handful of places stay open past 9 PM. At the resorts, excellent piano music or light live entertainment makes for a quiet, romantic evening. Another romantic alternative is star-watching from the beaches or watching the full moon rise in all its glory.

Four Seasons Resort Lāna'i at Mānele Bay. Hale Aheahe (House of Gentle Breezes), the classy open-air lounge with upscale *pūpū* (snacks) and complete bar, offers musical entertainment nightly from 5:30 to 9:30. Local musicians invite you to try your hula skills, and darts, pool, and shuffleboard are riotous fun. ☎*808/565–2000.*

Four Seasons Resort Lodge at Kō'ele. The cozy cocktail bar stays open until 11 PM. The lodge also features quiet piano music in its Great Hall every evening from 7 to 10, as well as special performances by well-known Hawaiian entertainers and local hula dancers. Sit fireside and enjoy a late-night cocktail and plan your next day's activities. ☎*808/565–4000.*

Hotel Lāna'i. A visit to the small, lively bar here is an opportunity to visit with locals and find out more about the island. Enjoy entertainment by Lāna'i musicians in the big green tent Saturday and Sunday nights. Last call is at 9:30. ☎*808/565–7211.*

Lāna'i Theater and Playhouse. This 153-seat, 1930s landmark theater was closed at this writing; call to check, however. ⊠*465 7th St., Lāna'i City* ☎*808/565–7500.*

SUNSET CRUISES

Trilogy Oceansports Lāna'i. On Tuesday, Thursday, and Saturday, Trilogy offers a Sunset Sail on a large catamaran, departing at either 3:45 (April–September) or 4:45 (October–March). This trip is perfect if you want to get out on the ocean and experience a relaxing time on the water. The two-hour sail includes hot and cold appetizers, soft drinks, and filtered water. You are encouraged to bring your own beer and wine and the crew will keep it cold for you. The sunset sail costs $106 for adults; $53 for children 15 and under. You can book trips through your hotel concierge, but try online first, where discounts are often available. ☎888/628–4800 ⊕*www.scubalanai.com.*

WHERE TO EAT

Lāna'i's own version of Hawai'i Regional Cuisine (modern Hawaiian food) draws on the fresh bounty provided by local hunters and fishermen, combined with the skills of well-trained chefs. The upscale menus at the Lodge at Kō'ele and the Four Seasons Resort at Lāna'i Mānele Bay encompass European-inspired cuisine as well as innovative preparations of 'ahi, wild deer, and boar. Lāna'i City's eclectic ethnic fare runs from construction-worker-size local plate lunches to pizza and pesto pasta. ■TIP→ Keep in mind that Lāna'i "City" is really just a small town; restaurants sometimes choose to close the kitchen early.

WHAT IT COSTS

	¢	$	$$	$$$	$$$$
RESTAURANTS	under $10	$10–$17	$18–$26	$27–$35	Over $35

Prices are for a main course at dinner.

MĀNELE BAY

$$
AMERICAN

✕**The Challenge at Mānele Clubhouse.** This terraced restaurant has a stunning view of the legendary Pu'u Pehe offshore island, which only enhances its imaginative fare. Tuck into a Hulopo'e Bay prawn BLT, or the crispy battered fish-and-chips with Meyer lemon tartar sauce. The fish tacos are splendid and specialty drinks add to the informal fun. ⊠*Four Seasons Resort Lāna'i at Mānele Bay, 1 Mānele Bay Rd., Lāna'i City* ☎*808/565–2230* ⊟*AE, DC, MC, V* ⊗*No dinner.*

$$$$
PACIFIC RIM

✕**Four Seasons Hulopo'e Court.** Hulopo'e Court offers dinner and an extensive breakfast buffet in airy comfort. Retractable awnings shade the terrace, which overlooks the wide sweep of the bay. Inside, comfy upholstered chairs, cream walls, wood paneling, and modernized Hawaiian decor create an almost equally inviting backdrop. At breakfast, fresh-baked pastries and made-to-order omelets ensure your day will start well. For dinner, the selection of fresh local fish includes the catch of the day, miso-marinated mahimahi, and crispy whole Pacific snapper with stir-fry vegetables. Meat-eaters can try the grilled beef fillet or Kurobuta pork loin with bok choy and kimchi fried rice; both are local favorites. The chocolate cake is near perfect and their coffee is excellent. ⊠*Four Seasons Resort Lāna'i at Mānele Bay, 1 Mānele Bay Rd., Lāna'i City* ☎*808/565–2290* ⌚*Reservations essential* ⊟*AE, DC, MC, V* ⊗*No lunch.*

$$$$
ITALIAN

✕**'Ihilani.** The fine dining room at the Four Seasons Resort Lāna'i at Mānele Bay shimmers with crystal chandeliers and gleaming silver in a serene setting illuminated by floor-to-ceiling etched-glass doors. Executive chef Oliver Beckert offers an upscale version of Italian comfort food designed around classic meat and fish dishes. Homemade spinach gnocchi with marinara sauce, and *onaga* (red snapper) served alla puttanesca with artichoke puree and a spicy tomato and caper sauce, are good choices. Slow-braised osso buco with risotto Milanese, or chicken marsala with creamy goat cheese polenta will satisfy the most discriminating palates. Service is nonintrusive but attentive. ⊠ *Four Seasons Resort Lāna'i at Mānele Bay, 1 Mānele Bay Rd., Lāna'i City* ☎ *808/565–2296* ⚓ *Reservations essential* ⊟ *AE, DC, MC, V* ⊘ *No lunch.*

> ## FOOD WITH A VIEW
>
> Don't miss lunch at the Challenge at Mānele clubhouse, overlooking Hulopo'e Bay. The view is spectacular. Palm trees frame a vista of the white-sand beach with the rocky headland of Pu'u Pehe (Sweetheart Rock) punctuating the luminous sky. You may also be rewarded with a perfect view of a visiting family of spinner dolphins resting in the transparent waters below.

$$$$
SEAFOOD
✕ **The Ocean Grill Bar & Restaurant.** Poolside at the Four Seasons Resort Lāna'i at Mānele Bay, the Ocean Grill offers informal lunch and dinner in a splendid setting. The big umbrellas are cool and cheerful, and bamboo-inspired upholstered chairs in yellow and green are deliciously comfortable. If you're a coffee drinker, a Kona Cappuccino Freeze by the pool is a must. Favorite lunch items include the *kālua* (pit-roasted) pork and cheese quesadilla, or the 'ahi tuna salade niçoise with fresh island greens. The dinner menu includes a combination of small and large plates that lean toward the healthy side. Try the wok-fried buckwheat noodles with plump tiger shrimp or lemongrass steamed *onaga* (red snapper) served with a refreshing carrot-miso vinaigrette. The view of Hulopo'e Bay is stunning and the service is Four Seasons' brand of cool aloha. ⊠ *Four Seasons Resort Lāna'i at Mānele Bay, 1 Mānele Bay Rd., Lāna'i City* ☎ *808/565–2092* ⊟ *AE, DC, MC, V.*

LĀNA'I CITY AND UPCOUNTRY

$
HAWAIIAN
✕ **Blue Ginger Café.** Owners Joe and Georgia Abilay have made this cheery place into a Lāna'i City institution with consistent, albeit simple, food. Locally inspired paintings and photos line the walls inside, while the town passes the outdoor tables in parade. For breakfast, try the Portuguese sausage omelet with rice or fresh pastries. Lunch selections range from burgers and pizza to Hawaiian staples such as saimin noodles or *musubi* (fried Spam wrapped in rice and seaweed). Try a shrimp stir-fry for dinner. ⊠ *409 7th St., Lāna'i City* ☎ *808/565–6363* ⊟ *No credit cards.*

$$$$
HAWAIIAN
Fodor's Choice
★
✕ **The Dining Room.** Reflecting the lodge's country-manor elegance, this peaceful and romantic octagonal restaurant is one of the best in the state. Terra-cotta walls and soft peach lighting flatter everyone and intimate tables are well spaced to allow for private conversations. Expanding on Hawaiian regional cuisine, the changing menu includes lava rock seared venison prepared table-side, succulent crispy *onaga* (red snapper) with Kona crab and leek fondue, and oven roasted Colorado lamb crusted with Provencale herbs and served with roasted baby artichokes. Start with a Big Island lobster savory crepe or a salad of organic island

greens with Meyer lemon vinaigrette, and finish with a warm raspberry soufflé (ordered in advance). A master sommelier provides exclusive wine pairings and the service is flawless. ⊠ *Four Seasons Resort Lodge at Kō'ele, 1 Keōmuku Hwy., Lāna'i City* ✆ *Box 631380, Lāna'i City 96763* ☎ *808/565–4580* ⚓ *Reservations essential* ▭ *AE, DC, MC, V* ⊘ *No lunch.*

$$ ✕ **The Experience at Ko'ele Clubhouse.** The clubhouse overlooks the emer-
AMERICAN ald greens of the golf course, making this a pleasant spot for casual fare. Sit inside and watch sports on the TV, or on the terrace to enjoy the antics of lumbering wild turkey families. The grilled fresh-catch sandwich is accompanied by fries; the succulent hamburgers are the best on the island. Salads and sandwiches, beer and wine, soft drinks, and some not very inspiring desserts complete the menu. ⊠ *Four Seasons Resort Lodge at Kō'ele, 1 Keōmuku Hwy., Lāna'i City* ☎ *808/565–4605* ▭ *AE, DC, MC, V* ⊘ *No dinner.*

¢ ✕ **565 Café.** Named after the oldest telephone prefix on Lāna'i, this is
HAWAIIAN a convenient stop for anything from pizza to a Pālāwai chicken-breast sandwich on fresh-baked focaccia. Make a quick stop for plate lunches or try a picnic *pūpū* (appetizer) platter of chicken *katsu* (Japanese-style breaded and fried chicken) to take along for the ride. If you need a helium balloon for a party, you can find that here, too. The patio and outdoor tables are kid-friendly, and an outdoor Saturday afternoon flea market adds to the quirkiness. ⊠ *408 8th St., Lāna'i City* ☎ *808/565–6622* ▭ *D, MC, V* ⊘ *Closed Sun.*

$$$$ ✕ **Lāna'i City Grille.** Simple white walls, local art, ceiling fans, and unob-
AMERICAN trusive service provide the setting for a menu designed and supervised by celebrity chef Beverly Gannon. Try the pecan-crusted catch of the day, or the always-popular rotisserie chicken. The pan-seared Lāna'i-caught venison has not traveled far from the wild. Although the menu is a bit on the heavy side for Hawai'i, the Grille is a pleasant alternative to the Four Seasons, and a lively gathering place for friends and family. ⊠ *Hotel Lāna'i, 828 Lāna'i Ave., Lāna'i City* ☎ *808/565–4700* ⚓ *Reservations essential* ▭ *AE, MC, V.*

¢ ✕ **Lāna'i Coffee.** A block off Dole Park, this café offers a nice spot to sit
CAFÉ outside, sip cappuccinos, and watch the slow-pace life of the town slip by. Bagels with lox, deli sandwiches, and pastries add to the caloric content, while blended espresso shakes and gourmet ice cream complete the old-world illusion. Local kids pile in after school. Caffeine-inspired specialty items make good gifts and souvenirs. ⊠ *604 'Ilima St., Lāna'i City* ☎ *808/565–6962* ⊘ *Closed Sun.*

$$ ✕ **Pele's Other Garden.** This colorful little eatery is a deli and bistro all
ITALIAN in one. For lunch, deli sandwiches or daily hot specials satisfy hearty appetites. At night the restaurant turns into an intimate tablecloth-dining bistro, complete with soft jazz music. A nice wine list enhances an Italian-inspired menu. Start with bruschetta, then choose from a selection of pasta dishes or pizzas. Designer beers and a mini sports bar add to the liveliness. ⊠ *811 Houston St., at 8th St., Lāna'i City* ☎ *808/565–9628 or 888/764–3354* ⊕ *www.pelesothergarden.com* ▭ *AE, DC, MC, V.*

7

$$$$
AMERICAN

✕**The Terrace.** Floor-to-ceiling glass doors open onto formal gardens and lovely vistas of the mist-clad mountains. Breakfast, lunch, and dinner are served in an informal atmosphere with attentive service. Try poached eggs on crab cakes to start the day and a grilled beef fillet with Parmesan whipped potatoes to finish it. The soothing sounds of the grand piano in the Great Hall in the evening complete the ambience. ✉ *Four Seasons Resort Lodge at Kō'ele, 1 Keōmuku Hwy., Lāna'i City* ☎ *808/565–4580* ▤ *AE, DC, MC, V.*

WHERE TO STAY

Though Lāna'i has few properties, it does have a range of price options. Four Seasons manages both the Lodge at Kō'ele and Four Seasons Resort Lāna'i at Mānele Bay. Although the room rates are different, guests can partake of all the resort amenities at both properties. If you're on a budget, consider the Hotel Lāna'i.

House rentals give you a feel for everyday life on the island; ⊕ *www. gohawaii.com* has information. In hunting seasons, from mid-February through mid-May, and from mid-July through mid-October, most private properties are booked way in advance. **Note:** Maui County has regulations concerning vacation rentals; to avoid disappointment, always contact the property manager or owner and ask if the accommodation has the proper permits and is in compliance with local laws. You can also log onto the Maui County Web site (⊕ *www.co.maui.hi.us*), click on "Planning Department," and search for updated information on legal rentals.

WHAT IT COSTS					
	¢	$	$$	$$$	$$$$
HOTELS	under $100	$100–$180	$181–$260	$261–$340	over $340

Hotel prices are for two people in a double room in high season, including tax and service. Condo price categories reflect studio and one-bedroom rates. Prices do not include 11.41% tax.

$$$$
RESORT
♻
Fodor's Choice
★

⊡ **Four Seasons Resort Lāna'i at Mānele Bay.** This ornate resort overlooking Hulopo'e Bay combines Mediterranean and Asian architectural elements: elaborate life-size paintings of Chinese court officials, gold brocade warrior robes, and artifacts decorate the open-air lobbies. Courtyard gardens separate two-story guest-room buildings. Ground-floor rooms are best—many open right up onto a lawn overlooking Hulopo'e Beach—though spectacular coastline vantages are had just about anywhere on the property. Adults can indulge in Evian spritzers and massage by the pool while *keiki* (children) hunt for crabs and play 'ukulele. At night, everyone can meet for shuffleboard and darts in Hale Ahe Ahe, the swank game room. A shuttle runs from the resort to other destinations on Lāna'i every half hour during high season, and every hour during low season. **Pros:** fitness center with ocean views and daily classes; teens have their own center; friendly pool bar. **Cons:** 20 minutes to town for shopping and restaurants; must rely on

Four Seasons Resort Lāna'i at Mānele Bay

Four Seasons Resort Lodge at Kō'ele

shuttle or rental car to leave property; ambience may seem stiff and formal to some. ⌂*Box 631380, 1 Mānele Bay Rd., Lāna'i City 96763* ☎*808/565–2000 or 800/321–4666* ⊕*www.fourseasons.com/manele baya* ✉*215 rooms, 21 suites* ♿*In-room: safe, refrigerator, DVD, Internet. In-hotel: 4 restaurants, room service, bars, golf course, tennis courts, pool, gym, spa, children's programs (ages 5–12), laundry service, public Internet, no-smoking rooms* ⊟*AE, DC, MC, V.*

WORD OF MOUTH

"We went for our honeymoon and planned to do 2 days at each resort. We started at the Lodge and loved it so much we stayed there. We liked how cozy it was and loved the grounds. Each morning we took the shuttle to Mānele and then returned each afternoon when we needed to get out of the sun for a little croquet and wild turkey watching at the Lodge. Since it is so easy to take the shuttle back and forth, you can't go wrong either way!"   —ginabee

$$$$
RESORT
Fodor's Choice
★

⌂ Four Seasons Resort Lodge at Kō'ele. In the highlands edging Lāna'i City, this grand country estate exudes luxury and quiet romance. Secluded by old pines, 1.5 mi of paths meander through formal gardens with a huge reflecting pond, a wedding gazebo, and an orchid greenhouse. Afternoon tea is served in front of the immense stone fireplaces beneath the high-beamed ceilings of the magnificent Great Hall for a fee of $29. The music room lounge is a relaxing haven after a day on the lodge's golf course or sporting-clays range. A long veranda, furnished with wicker lounge chairs, looks out over rolling green pastures toward spectacular sunsets. **Pros:** beautiful surroundings; impeccable service; walking distance to shops and restaurants in Lāna'i City. **Cons:** doesn't feel like Hawai'i; can get chilly at 1,700-foot elevation (especially in winter); not much to do in rainy weather. ⌂*Box 631380, 1 Keōmuku Hwy., Lāna'i City 96763* ☎*808/565–4000 or 800/321–4666* ⊕*www.fourseasons.com/koele* ✉*94 rooms, 8 suites* ♿*In-room: safe, refrigerator, Internet. In-hotel: 4 restaurants, room service, bar, golf course, tennis courts, pool, gym, bicycles, children's programs (ages 5–12), laundry service, no-smoking rooms* ⊟*AE, DC, MC, V.*

$–$$
HOTEL

⌂ Hotel Lāna'i. Built in 1923 to house visiting pineapple executives, this 10-room inn was once the only accommodation on the island. The South Pacific–style rooms, with country quilts, white walls, ceiling fans, and bamboo shades make it seem like you're staying in someone's guest room. The two end rooms offer great views with porches overlooking the pine trees and Lāna'i City. The restaurant, the Lāna'i City Grille, has an intimate and well-stocked bar. A self-serve Continental breakfast with fresh-baked breads is served in the foyer and is included in the rate. **Pros:** friendly service; walking distance to town. **Cons:** rooms are a bit stark; noisy at times; no room phones; no activities. ✉*828 Lāna'i Ave., Lāna'i City* ☎*808/565–7211 or 800/795–7211* ⊕*www.hotellanai.com* ✉*10 rooms, 1 cottage* ♿*In-room: no a/c, no phone, no TV (some). In-hotel: restaurant, no-smoking rooms* ⊟*AE, MC, V.*

LĀNA'I ESSENTIALS

TRANSPORTATION

AIR TRAVEL

Island Air is the only commercial airline serving Lāna'i City. Nonstop flights from O'ahu's Honolulu International Airport begin at $44 one-way, depending on availability. Traveling from other islands requires a stop in Honolulu.

The airport has a federal agricultural inspection station, so guests departing to the mainland can check luggage directly.

Information Island Air (☎ *800/652–6541* ⊕ *www.islandair.com*). **Lāna'i Airport** (☎ *808/565–6757*).

GROUND TRANSPOR- TATION Lāna'i Airport is a 10-minute drive from Lāna'i City. If you're staying at the Hotel Lāna'i, the Four Seasons Resort Lodge at Kō'ele, or the Four Seasons Resort Lāna'i at Mānele Bay, you'll be met by a shuttle, which serves as transportation between the resorts and Lāna'i City. The one-time $36 per person fee buys you unlimited use of the shuttle for the length of your stay. See the resort receptionist at the airport. Dollar will arrange to pick you up if you're renting a jeep or minivan. Cost is $5 per person round-trip, and one person in your party rides for free. Call from the red courtesy phone at the airport.

CAR TRAVEL

There are only 30 mi of paved road on the island. Keōmuku Highway starts just past the Lodge at Kō'ele and runs north to Shipwreck Beach. Mānele Road (Highway 440) runs south down to Mānele Bay and Hulopo'e Beach. Kaumalapau Highway (also Highway 440) heads west to Kaumalapau Harbor. The rest of your driving takes place on bumpy, muddy, secondary roads, which generally aren't marked.

You'll never find yourself in a traffic jam, but it's easy to get lost on the unmarked dirt roads. Before heading out, ask for a map at your hotel desk. Always remember *mauka* (toward the mountains) and *makai* (toward the ocean) for basic directions. If you're traveling on dirt roads, take water. People still drive slowly, wave, and pull over to give each other lots of room. The only gas station on the island is in Lāna'i City, at Lāna'i City Service (open 7 to 7 daily).

CAR RENTAL Renting a four-wheel-drive vehicle is expensive but almost essential if you'd like to explore beyond the resorts and Lāna'i City. Make reservations far in advance of your trip, because Lāna'i's fleet of vehicles is limited. Lāna'i City Service, a subsidiary of Dollar Rent A Car, is open daily 7 to 7. Jeep Wranglers go for $139 a day, and minivans are $129 a day.

Information Lāna'i City Service (✉ *Lāna'i Ave. at 11th St. 96763* ☎ *808/565–7227 or 800/533–7808*).

FERRY TRAVEL

Expeditions' ferries cross the channel seven times daily, departing from Lahaina and Mā'alaea on Maui, to Mānele Bay Harbor on Lāna'i. Expeditions also arranges golf and land tours for passengers. The crossing takes 45 minutes from Lahaina, and 75 minutes from Mā'alaea, and costs $30 each way. Be warned: passage can be rough, especially in winter. On the flip side, you might see whales along the way during the season. Go early for smoother water.

Information Expeditions (☎ *808/661–3756 or 800/695–2624* ⊕ *www.go-lanai. com*).

TO AND FROM
THE HARBOR

If you are staying at the Four Seasons Resort Lāna'i at Mānele Bay or the Lodge at Kō'ele, transportation from the harbor is almost effortless; the resort staff accompanies you on the boat, and shuttles stand ready to deliver you and your belongings to either resort. If you aren't staying with the Four Seasons, it's pretty much the same drill—the bus drivers will herd you onto the appropriate bus and take you into town for $10 per person. Advance reservations aren't necessary (or even possible), but be prepared for a little confusion on the dock.

Information Lāna'i City Service (⊠ *Lāna'i Ave. at 11th St.96763* ☎ *808/565–7227 or 800/533–7808*).

SHUTTLE TRAVEL

A shuttle transports hotel guests between the Hotel Lāna'i, the Four Seasons Resort Lodge at Kō'ele, the Four Seasons Resort Lāna'i at Mānele Bay, and the airport. A $36 fee added to the room fee covers all transportation during the length of stay.

CONTACTS AND RESOURCES

EMERGENCIES

In an emergency, dial **911** to reach an ambulance, the police, or the fire department. The Lāna'i Family Clinic, part of the Straub Clinic & Hospital, is the island's health-care center. It's open weekdays from 8 to 5 and closed on weekends. There is no pharmacy so be sure to bring needed medications.

Information Straub Clinic & Hospital (⊠ *628 7th St., Lāna'i City* ☎ *808/565–6423 clinic, 808/565–6411 hospital*).

VISITOR INFORMATION

Lāna'i Visitor's Bureau is open between 8AM and 4PM and is your best bet for general information and maps. The Lāna'i Culture & Heritage Center in the old Dole Administration Building also has information and maps. The Maui Visitors Bureau also has some information on the island.

Information Lāna'i Visitor's Bureau (⊠ *431 7th St., Suite A, Lāna'i City* ☎ *808/565–7600* ⊕ *www.visitlanai.net*). **Maui Visitors Bureau** (☎ *808/244–3530* ⊕ *www.visitmaui.com*).

HAWAIIAN VOCABULARY

Although an understanding of Hawaiian is by no means required on a trip to the Aloha State, a *malihini*, or newcomer, will find plenty of opportunities to pick up a few of the local words and phrases. Traditional names and expressions are widely used in the Islands. You're likely to read or hear at least a few words each day of your stay.

With a basic understanding and some uninhibited practice, anyone can have enough command of the local tongue to ask for directions and to order from a restaurant menu. One visitor announced she would not leave until she could pronounce the name of the state fish, the *humuhumunukunukuāpua'a*.

Simplifying the learning process is the fact that the Hawaiian language contains only eight consonants—H, K, L, M, N, P, W, and the silent *'okina*, or glottal stop, written '—plus one or more of the five vowels. All syllables, and therefore all words, end in a vowel. Each vowel, with the exception of a few diphthongized double vowels such as *au* (pronounced "ow") or *ai* (pronounced "eye"), is pronounced separately. Thus *'Iolani* is four syllables (ee-oh-la-nee), not three (yo-la-nee). Although some Hawaiian words have only vowels, most also contain some consonants, but consonants are never doubled.

Pronunciation is simple. Pronounce *A* "ah" as father; *E* "ay" as in weigh; *I* "ee" as in marine; *O* "oh" as in no; *U* "oo" as in true.

Consonants mirror their English equivalents, with the exception of *W*. When the letter begins any syllable other than the first one in a word, it is usually pronounced as a *V*. *'Awa*, the Polynesian drink, is pronounced "ava," *'ewa* is pronounced "eva."

Almost all long Hawaiian words are combinations of shorter words; they are not difficult to pronounce if you segment them. *Kalaniana'ole*, the highway running east from Honolulu, is easily understood as *Kalani ana 'ole*. Apply the standard pronunciation rules—the stress falls on the next-to-last syllable of most two- or three-syllable Hawaiian words—and Kalaniana'ole Highway is as easy to say as Main Street.

Now about that fish. Try *humu-humu nuku-nuku āpu a'a.*

The other unusual element in Hawaiian language is the *kahakō*, or macron, written as a short line [ˉ] placed over a vowel. Like the accent [ˊ] in Spanish, the kahakō puts emphasis on a syllable that would normally not be stressed. The most familiar example is probably *Waikīkī*. With no macrons, the stress would fall on the middle syllable; with only one macron, on the last syllable, the stress would fall on the first and last syllables. Some words become plural with the addition of a macron, often on a syllable that would have been stressed anyway. No Hawaiian word becomes plural with the addition of an *S*, since that letter does not exist in the language.

What follows is a glossary of some of the most commonly used Hawaiian words. Hawaiian residents appreciate visitors who at least try to pick up the local language.

'a'ā: rough, crumbling lava, contrasting with *pāhoehoe*, which is smooth.

'ae: yes.

aikane: friend.

āina: land.

akamai: smart, clever, possessing savoir faire.

akua: god.

ala: a road, path, or trail.

ali'i: a Hawaiian chief, a member of the chiefly class.

aloha: love, affection, kindness; also a salutation meaning both greetings and farewell.

'ānuenue: rainbow.

'a'ole: no.

'apōpō: tomorrow.

'auwai: a ditch.

auwē: alas, woe is me!

'ehu: a red-haired Hawaiian.

'ewa: in the direction of 'Ewa plantation, west of Honolulu.

hala: the pandanus tree, whose leaves (*lau hala*) are used to make baskets and plaited mats.

hālau: school.

hale: a house.

hale pule: church, house of worship.

ha mea iki or **ha mea 'ole:** you're welcome.

hana: to work.

haole: ghost. Since the first foreigners were Caucasian, *haole* now means a Caucasian person.

hapa: a part, sometimes a half; often used as a short form of *hapa haole,* to mean a person who is part-Caucasian.

hau'oli: to rejoice. *Hau'oli Makahiki Hou* means Happy New Year. *Hau'oli lā hānau* means Happy Birthday.

heiau: an outdoor stone platform; an ancient Hawaiian place of worship.

holo: to run.

holoholo: to go for a walk, ride, or sail.

holokū: a long Hawaiian dress, somewhat fitted, with a yoke and a train. Influenced by European fashion, it was worn at court, and at least one local translates the word as "expensive mu'umu'u."

holomū: a post–World War II cross between a *holokū* and a mu'umu'u, less fitted than the former but less voluminous than the latter, and having no train.

honi: to kiss; a kiss. A phrase that some tourists may find useful, quoted from a popular hula, is *Honi Ka'ua Wikiwiki:* Kiss me quick!

honu: turtle.

ho'omalimali: flattery, a deceptive "line," bunk, baloney, hooey.

huhū: angry.

hui: a group, club, or assembly. A church may refer to its congregation as a *hui* and a social club may be called a *hui.*

hukilau: a seine; a communal fishing party in which everyone helps to drive the fish into a huge net, pull it in, and divide the catch.

hula: the dance of Hawai'i.

iki: little.

ipo: sweetheart.

ka: the. This is the definite article for most singular words; for plural nouns, the definite article is usually *nā*. Since there is no *S* in Hawaiian, the article may be your only clue that a noun is plural.

kahuna: a priest, doctor, or other trained person of old Hawai'i, endowed with special professional skills that often included prophecy or other supernatural powers; the plural form is kāhuna.

kai: the sea, salt water.

kalo: the taro plant from whose root *poi* (paste) is made.

kamā'aina: literally, a child of the soil; it refers to people who were born in the Islands or have lived there for a long time.

kanaka: originally a man or humanity, it is now used to denote a male Hawaiian or part-Hawaiian, but is occasionally taken as a slur when used by non-Hawaiians. *Kanaka maoli,* originally a full-blooded Hawaiian person, is used by some native Hawaiian rights activists to embrace part-Hawaiians as well.

kāne: a man, a husband. If you see this word on a door, it's the men's room. If you see *kane* on a door, it's probably a misspelling; that is the Hawaiian name for the skin fungus tinea.

kapa: also called by its Tahitian name, *tapa,* a cloth made of beaten bark and usually dyed and stamped with a repeat design.

kapakahi: crooked, cockeyed, uneven. You've got your hat on *kapakahi.*

kapu: keep out, prohibited. This is the Hawaiian version of the more widely known Tongan word *tabu* (taboo).

kapuna: grandparent; elder.

kēia lā: today.

keiki: a child; *keikikāne* is a boy, *keiki-wahine* a girl.

kona: the leeward side of the Islands, the direction (south) from which the *kona* wind and *kona* rain come.

kula: upland.

kuleana: a homestead or small plot of ground on which a family has been installed for some generations without necessarily owning it. By extension, *kuleana* is used to denote any area or department in which one has a special interest or prerogative. You'll hear it used this way: If you want to hire a surfboard, see Moki; that's his *kuleana*.

lā: sun.

lamalama: to fish with a torch.

lānai: a porch, a balcony, an outdoor living room. Almost every house in Hawai'i has one. Don't confuse this two-syllable word with the three-syllable name of the island, Lāna'i.

lani: heaven, the sky.

lau hala: the leaf of the *hala*, or pandanus tree, widely used in handicrafts.

lei: a garland of flowers.

limu: sun.

lolo: stupid.

luna: a plantation overseer or foreman.

mahalo: thank you.

makai: toward the ocean.

malihini: a newcomer to the Islands.

mana: the spiritual power that the Hawaiian believed inhabited all things and creatures.

manō: shark.

manuwahi: free, gratis.

mauka: toward the mountains.

mauna: mountain.

mele: a Hawaiian song or chant, often of epic proportions.

Mele Kalikimaka: Merry Christmas (a transliteration from the English phrase).

Menehune: a Hawaiian pixie. The *Menehune* were a legendary race of little people who accomplished prodigious work, such as building fishponds and temples in the course of a single night.

moana: the ocean.

mu'umu'u: the voluminous dress in which the missionaries enveloped Hawaiian women. Now made in bright printed cottons and silks, it is an indispensable garment. Culturally sensitive locals have embraced the Hawaiian spelling but often shorten the spoken word to "mu'u." Most English dictionaries include the spelling "muumuu."

nani: beautiful.

nui: big.

ohana: family.

'ono: delicious.

pāhoehoe: smooth, unbroken, satiny lava.

Pākē: Chinese. This *Pākē* carver makes beautiful things.

palapala: document, printed matter.

pali: a cliff, precipice.

pānini: prickly pear cactus.

paniolo: a Hawaiian cowboy, a rough transliteration of *español,* the language of the Islands' earliest cowboys.

pau: finished, done.

pilikia: trouble. The Hawaiian word is much more widely used here than its English equivalent.

puka: a hole.

pupule: crazy, like the celebrated Princess Pupule. This word has replaced its English equivalent in local usage.

pu'u: volcanic cinder cone.

waha: mouth.

wahine: a female, a woman, a wife, and a sign on the ladies' room door; the plural form is *wāhine.*

wai: freshwater, as opposed to salt water, which is *kai.*

wailele: waterfall.

wikiwiki: to hurry, hurry up (since this is a reduplication of *wiki,* quick, neither W is pronounced as a V).

Note: Pidgin is the unofficial language of Hawai'i. It is a Creole language, with its own grammar, evolved from the mixture of English, Hawaiian, Japanese, Portuguese, and other languages spoken in 19th-century Hawai'i, and it is heard everywhere.

Travel Smart Hawaii

WORD OF MOUTH

"Condos in Hawai'i are a great value—you can cook your own meals when you want and they usually come with washers and dryers so you can pack lightly and wash. Doing more than 2 islands in 2-3 weeks in my opinion would be too hectic and would not allow enough time to really see each island plus have time to relax."

—montereybob

GETTING HERE & AROUND

■ AIR TRAVEL

Flying time to Hawai'i is about 10 hours from New York, 8 hours from Chicago, and 5 hours from Los Angeles.

Hawai'i is a major destination link for flights traveling between the U.S. mainland and Asia, Australia, New Zealand, and the South Pacific. Although the Neighbor Island airports are smaller and more casual than Honolulu International, during peak times they can also be quite busy. Allot extra travel time to all airports during morning and afternoon rush-hour traffic periods.

Plan to arrive at the airport 60 to 90 minutes before departure for interisland flights.

Plants and plant products are subject to regulation by the Department of Agriculture, both on entering and leaving Hawai'i. Upon leaving the Islands, you'll have to have your bags X-rayed and tagged at one of the airport's agricultural inspection stations before you proceed to check-in. Pineapples and coconuts with the packer's agricultural inspection stamp pass freely; papayas must be treated, inspected, and stamped. All other fruits are banned for export to the U.S. mainland. Flowers pass except for gardenia, rose leaves, jade vine, and mauna loa. Also banned are insects, snails, soil, cotton, cacti, sugarcane, and all berry plants.

You'll have to leave dogs and other pets at home. A 120-day quarantine is imposed to keep out rabies, which is nonexistent in Hawai'i. If specific pre- and post-arrival requirements are met, animals may qualify for a 30-day or five-day-or-less quarantine.

Airline Security Issues Transportation Security Administration (⊕ *www.tsa.gov*) has answers for almost every question that might come up.

Air Travel Resources in Hawai'i State of Hawaii Airports Division Offices (☎ *808/836–6417* ⊕ *www.hawaii.gov/dot/airports*).

AIRPORTS

All of Hawai'i's major islands have their own airports, but Honolulu's International Airport is the main stopover for most domestic and international flights. From Honolulu, there are flights to the Neighbor Islands almost every half-hour from early morning until evening. In addition, some carriers now offer non-stop service directly from the mainland to Maui, Kaua'i, and the Big Island on a limited basis. No matter the island, all of Hawai'i's airports are "open-air," meaning you can enjoy those trade-wind breezes up until the moment you step on the plane.

HONOLULU/O'AHU AIRPORT

Hawai'i's major airport is Honolulu International, on O'ahu, 20 minutes (9 mi) west of Waikīkī. When traveling interisland from Honolulu, you will depart from either the interisland terminal or the commuter-airline terminal, located in two separate structures adjacent to the main overseas terminal building. A free bus service, the Wiki Wiki Shuttle, operates between terminals.

Information Honolulu International Airport (HNL) (☎ *808/836–6413* ⊕ *www.hawaii.gov/dot/airports*).

MAUI AIRPORTS

Maui has two major airports. Kahului Airport handles major airlines and interisland flights; it's the only airport on Maui that has direct service from the mainland. If you're arriving from another island and you're staying in the West Maui, you can avoid the hour drive from the Kahului Airport by flying into Kapalua–West Maui Airport, which is served by go! Express, Hawaiian Air, Mokulele Airlines, and Pacific Wings. The tiny town of Hāna in East Maui also has an airstrip, served by PW Express and charter flights from Kahului and Kapalua. Flying here from one of the other airports is a great option if you want to avoid the long and winding drive to Hāna.

Information Kahului Airport (OGG) (☎808/872-3893). **Kapalua–West Maui Airport (JHM)** (☎808/669-0623). **Hāna Airport (HNM)** (☎808/248-8208).

MOLOKA'I & LĀNA'I AIRPORTS

Moloka'i's Ho'olehua Airport is small and centrally located, as is Lāna'i Airport. Both rural airports handle a limited number of flights per day. Visitors coming from the mainland to these islands must first stop in Maui or O'ahu and change to an interisland flight.

Information Lāna'i: **Lāna'i Airport (LNY)** (☎808/565-6757). Moloka'i: **Ho'olehua Airport (MKK)** (☎808/567-6361).

BIG ISLAND AIRPORTS

Those flying to the Big Island of Hawai'i regularly land at one of two fields. Kona International Airport at Keāhole, on the west side, best serves Kailua-Kona, Keauhou, and the Kohala Coast. Hilo International Airport is more appropriate for those going to the east side. Waimea-Kohala Airport, called Kamuela Airport by residents, is used primarily for commuting among the Islands.

Information Hilo International Airport (ITO) (☎808/934-5838). **Kona International Airport at Keāhole (KOA)** (☎808/329-3423). **Waimea-Kohala Airport (MUE)** (☎808/887-8126).

KAUA'I

On Kaua'i, visitors fly into Līhu'e Airport, on the east side of the island.

Information Līhu'e Airport (LIH) (☎808/246-1448).

FLIGHTS

America West, American and United fly into O'ahu, Maui, Kaua'i, and the Big Island. Alaska flies into O'ahu and Kaua'i. Delta and Northwest serve O'ahu (Honolulu), Maui, and the Big Island. Continental flies into Honolulu.

go! Airlines, Hawaiian Airlines, Mokulele Airlines and PW Express offer regular service between the islands. In addition to offering very competitive rates and online specials, all have frequent-flier programs, which will entitle you to rewards and upgrades the more you fly. Be sure to compare prices offered by all of the interisland carriers. If you are somewhat flexible with your dates and times for island-hopping, you should have no problem getting a very affordable round-trip ticket.

There are three companies that provide charter flights between the Islands. Mokulele Airlines services O'ahu, Maui, and Moloka'i. Pacific Wings serves O'ahu, Lāna'i, Maui, Moloka'i, and the Big Island. Services include premiere (same-day departures on short notice), premium (24-hour notice), group, and cargo/courier. The company also has a frequent-flier program. Paragon Air offers 24-hour private charter service from any airport in Hawai'i. In business since 1980, the company prides itself on its perfect safety record. Should you want to explore Kaluapapa or other sites on Moloka'i and Maui from the air and ground, you can book tours through Paragon that depart from either the Kahului or Kapalua–West Maui airport.

Airline Contacts American Airlines (☎800/433-7300 ⊕www.aa.com). **Continental Airlines** (☎800/523-3273 ⊕www.continental.com). **Delta Airlines** (☎800/221-1212 ⊕www.delta.com). **United Airlines** (☎800/864-8331 ⊕www.united.com).

Interisland Flights go! Airlines/go! Express (☎888/434-5946 ⊕www.iflygo.com). **Hawaiian Airlines** (☎800/367-5320 ⊕www.hawaiianair.com). **Mokulele Airlines** (☎866/260-7070 ⊕www.mokuleleairlines.com). **PW Express** (☎888/866-5022 ⊕www.flypwx.com).

∎ BOAT TRAVEL

There is daily ferry service between Lahaina or Maʻalaea Harbor, Maui, and Mānele Bay, Lānaʻi, with Expeditions Lānaʻi Ferry. The 9-mi crossing costs $60 round-trip, per person, and takes 45 minutes or so, depending on ocean conditions (which can make this trip a rough one). Molokaʻi Ferry offers twice daily ferry service between Lahaina, Maui, and Kaunakakai, Molokaʻi. Travel time is about 90 minutes each way and the one-way fare is $66.40 per person (including taxes and fees); a book of six one-way tickets costs $307.10 (including taxes and fees). Reservations are recommended for both ferries.

At this writing, Hawaii Superferry, a high-speed interisland ferry with routes between Honolulu and Kahului, Maui, has been suspended. Consult the Superferry Web site or go to www.gohawaii.com.

Information Expeditions Lānaʻi Ferry (☏ 800/695–2624 ⊕ www.go-lanai.com). **Hawaiʻi Superferry** (⊕ www.hawaiisuper ferry.com). **Molokai Ferry** (☏ 866/307–6524 ⊕ www.molokaiferry.com).

∎ CAR TRAVEL

Technically, the Big Island of Hawaiʻi is the only island you can completely circle by car, but each island offers plenty of sightseeing from its miles of roadways. Oʻahu can be circled except for the roadless west-shore area around Kaʻena Point. Elsewhere, major highways follow the shoreline and traverse the island at two points. Rush-hour traffic (6:30 to 8:30 AM and 3:30 to 6 PM) can be frustrating around Honolulu and the outlying areas, as many thoroughfares allow no left turns due to contra-flow lanes. Traffic on Maui can be very bad branching out from Kahului to and from Pāʻia, Kīhei, and Lahaina. Drive here during peak hours and you'll know why local residents are calling for restrictions on development. Parking along many streets is curtailed during these times, and towing is strictly practiced. Read curbside parking signs before leaving your vehicle, even at a meter.

On Kauai, the 15-mi stretch of the Na Pali coast is the only part of the island that's not accessible by car. Otherwise, one main road can get you from Barking Sands Beach on the west coast to Haʻena on the north coast.

Although Molokaʻi and Lānaʻi have fewer roadways, car rental is still worthwhile and will allow plenty of interesting sightseeing. A four-wheel-drive vehicle is best on these islands.

Asking for directions will almost always produce a helpful explanation from the locals, but you should be prepared for an island term or two. Instead of using compass directions, remember that Hawaiʻi residents refer to places as being either *mauka* (toward the mountains) or *makai* (toward the ocean) from one another. Other directions depend on your location: in Honolulu, for example, people say to "go Diamond Head," which means toward that famous landmark, or to "go ʻewa," meaning in the opposite direction. A shop on the mauka–Diamond Head corner of a street is on the mountain side of the street on the corner closest to Diamond Head. It all makes perfect sense once you get the lay of the land.

RENTAL CARS

If you plan to do lots of sightseeing, it's best to rent a car. Even if all you want to do is relax at your resort, you may want to hop in the car to check out a popular restaurant. All of the big national rental car agencies have locations throughout Hawaiʻi, but Dollar is the only company that has offices on all of the major Hawaiian Islands. There also are several local rental car companies so be sure to compare prices before you book. While in the islands, you can rent anything from an econobox to a Ferrari. On the Big Island, Lānaʻi, and Molokaʻi, four-wheel-drive vehicles are recommended for exploring off the beaten path. Rates are usually better if you reserve though a rental agency's Web site. It's wise to make reservations far in advance and make sure that a confirmed reservation guarantees you a car, especially if visiting during peak seasons or for major conventions or sporting events. It's not uncommon to find several car categories sold out during major events on some of the smaller islands.

Rates begin at about $25 to $35 a day for an economy car with air-conditioning, automatic transmission, and unlimited mileage, depending on your pickup location. This does not include the airport concession fee, general excise tax, rental vehicle surcharge, or vehicle license fee. When you reserve a car, ask about cancellation penalties and drop-off charges should you plan to pick up the car in one location and return it to another.

In Hawai'i you must be 21 years of age to rent a car and you must have a valid driver's license and a major credit card. Those under 25 will pay a daily surcharge of $15 to $25. Your unexpired mainland driver's license is valid for rental for up to 90 days. Request car seats and extras such as GPS when you make your reservation. Hawai'i's Child Restraint Law requires that all children three years and younger be in an approved child safety seat in the backseat of a vehicle. Children ages 4 to 7 must be seated in a rear booster seat or child restraint such as a lap and shoulder belt. Car seats and boosters range from $5 to $8 per day. Since many island roads are two lanes, be sure to allow plenty of time to return your vehicle so that you can make your flight. Traffic can be bad during morning and afternoon rush hour. Give yourself about 3½ hours before departure time to return your vehicle.

ROAD CONDITIONS

It's difficult to get lost in most of Hawai'i. Roads and streets, although they may challenge the visitor's tongue, are well marked; just watch out for the many one-way streets in Waikīkī. Keep an eye open for the Hawai'i Visitors and Convention Bureau's red-caped King Kamehameha signs, which mark major attractions and scenic spots. Ask for a map at the car-rental counter. Free publications containing good-quality road maps can be found on all Islands.

Many of Hawai'i's roads are two-lane highways with limited shoulders—and yes, even in paradise, there is traffic, especially during the morning and afternoon rush hour. In rural areas, it's not unusual for gas stations to close early. If you see that your tank is getting low, don't take any chances; fill up when you see a station. In Hawai'i, turning right on a red light is legal, except where noted. Use caution during heavy downpours, especially if you see signs warning of falling rocks. If you're enjoying views from the road or need to study a map, pull over to the side. Remember the aloha spirit when you are driving; allow other cars to merge, don't honk (it's considered extremely rude in the Islands), leave a comfortable distance between your car and the car ahead of you; use your headlights, especially during sunrise and sunset, and use your turn signals.

ROADSIDE EMERGENCIES

If you find yourself in an emergency or accident while driving on any of the islands, pull over if you can. If you have a cell phone with you, call the roadside assistance number on your rental car contract or AAA Help. If you find that your car has been broken into or stolen, report it immediately to your rental car company and they can assist you. If it's an emergency and someone is hurt, call 911 immediately and stay there until medical personnel arrive.

Emergency Services AAA Help (☎ *800/222–4357*).

RULES OF THE ROAD

Be sure to buckle up. Hawai'i has a strictly enforced seat-belt law for front-seat passengers. Always strap children under age four into approved child-safety seats. Children 18 and under, riding in the

Car Rental Resources

Automobile Associations

U.S.: American Automobile Association	315/797–5000	www.aaa.com;
National Automobile Club	650/294–7000	www.thenac.com

Local Agencies

AA Aloha Cars-R-Us	800/655–7989	www.hawaiicarrental.com
Advantage Rent-A-Car (O'ahu)	800/777–5500	www.tradewindsudrive.com
Adventure Lāna'i EcoCentre (Lāna'i)	808/565–7373	www.adventurelanai.com
Aloha Campters (Maui)	808/281–8020	www.alohacampers.com
GB Adventures (Big Island)	877/864–8361	www.gb-adventures.com
Discount Hawaii Car Rentals	888/292–3307	www.discounthawaiicarrental.com
Harper Car and Truck Rental (Big Island)	800/852–9993	www.harpershawaii.com
Hawaiian Discount Car Rentals	800/591–8605	www.hawaiidrive-o.com
Imua Camper Company (Big Island)		www.imua-tour.com
Island Kine Auto Rental (Moloka'i)	866/527–7368	www.molokai-car-rental.com
JN Car and Truck Rentals (O'ahu)	800/475–7522, 808/831–2724	www.jnautomotive.com

Major Agencies

Alamo	800/462–5266	www.alamo.com
Avis	800/331–1212	www.avis.com
Budget	800/527–0700	www.budget.com
Dollar	800/800–4000	www.dollar.com
Enterprise	800/261–7331	www.enterprise.com
Hertz	800/654–3131	www.hertz.com
National Car Rental	800/227–7368	www.nationalcar.com
Thrifty	800/847–4389	www.dollar.com

backseat, are also required by state law to use seat belts. The highway speed limit is usually 55 MPH. In-town traffic moves from 25 to 40 MPH. Jaywalking is very common, so be particularly watchful for pedestrians, especially in congested areas such as Waikīkī. Unauthorized use of a parking space reserved for persons with disabilities can net you a $150 fine.

ESSENTIALS

∎ ACCOMMODATIONS

Hawai'i truly offers something for everyone. Are you looking for a luxurious ocean-front resort loaded with amenities, an intimate two-room B&B tucked away in a lush rain forest, a house with a pool and incredible views for your extended family, a condominium just steps from the 18th hole, or even a campsite at a national park? You can find all of these and more throughout the islands.

Most hotels and other lodgings require you to give your credit-card details before they will confirm your reservation. If you don't feel comfortable e-mailing this information, ask if you can fax it (some places even prefer faxes). However you book, get confirmation in writing and have a copy of it handy when you check in. Be sure you understand the hotel's cancellation policy. Some places allow you to cancel without any kind of penalty—even if you prepaid to secure a discounted rate—if you cancel at least 24 hours in advance. Others require you to cancel a week in advance or penalize you the cost of one night. Small inns and B&Bs are most likely to require you to cancel far in advance. Most hotels allow children under a certain age to stay in their parents' room at no extra charge, but others charge for them as extra adults; find out the cutoff age for discounts.

∎TIP→Assume that hotels operate on the European Plan (EP, no meals) unless we specify that they use the Breakfast Plan (BP, with full breakfast), Continental Plan (CP, Continental breakfast), Full American Plan (FAP, all meals), Modified American Plan (MAP, breakfast and dinner) or are all-inclusive (AI, all meals and most activities).

For price-category information, see Where to Eat and Where to Stay sections in each chapter.

BED & BREAKFASTS

For many travelers, nothing compares to the personal service and guest interaction offered at bed-and-breakfasts. There are hundreds of B&Bs throughout the islands that offer charming accommodations and breakfasts with everything from tropical fruits and juices, Kona coffee, French toast with macadamia nuts and liliko'i syrup, and even the local favorites of rice and *poi*. Many B&Bs invite their guests to enjoy complimentary wine tastings and activities such as lei making and basket weaving. Each island's Web site also features a listing of member B&Bs that are individually owned.

Contacts Bed & Breakfast.com (☎512/322–2710 or 800/462–2632 ⊕www. bedandbreakfast.com) also sends out an online newsletter. **Bed & Breakfast Inns Online** (☎310/280–4363 or 800/215–7365 ⊕www.bbonline.com). **Better Bed and Breakfasts** (⊕www.betterbedandbreakfasts. com). **BnB Finder.com** (☎212/432–7693 or 888/547–8226 ⊕www.bnbfinder. com). **Hawai'i's Best Bed & Breakfasts** (☎808/263–3100 or 800/262–9912 ⊕www. bestbnb.com).

CONDOMINIUM AND HOUSE RENTALS

Vacation rentals are perfect for couples, families, and friends traveling together who like the convenience of staying at a home away from home. Properties managed by individual owners can be found on online vacation rental listing directories such as CyberRentals and Vacation Rentals By Owners, as well as on the visitors bureau Web site for each island. There also are several island-based management companies with vacation rentals.

Compare companies, as some offer Internet specials and free night stays when booking. Policies vary, but most require a minimum stay, usually greater during peak travel seasons.

Contacts CyberRentals (⊕ *www.cyberrentals. com*). **Vacation Rentals By Owner** (⊕ *www. vrbo.com*).

HOME EXCHANGES

With a direct home exchange you stay in someone else's home while they stay in yours. The exchange clubs listed below feature dozens of Hawai'i homes available for exchange. Many of the homes are on the beach or have ocean views.

Exchange Clubs Home Exchange.com (☎ *800/877–8723* ⊕ *www.homeexchange. com*); $99.95 for a 1-year online listing. **HomeLink International** (☎ *800/638–3841* ⊕ *www.homelink.org*); $110 yearly for Web-only membership; $170 includes Web access and two catalogs. **Intervac U.S.A.** (☎ *800/756–4663* ⊕ *www.intervacusa.com*); $65 for Web-only membership.

HOSTELS

Hostels offer bare-bones lodging at low, low prices—often in shared dorm rooms with shared baths—to people of all ages, though the primary market is young travelers. Many hostels provide shared cooking facilities. In some hostels you aren't allowed to be in your room during the day, and there may be a curfew at night. Nevertheless, hostels provide a sense of community, with public rooms where travelers often gather to share stories. Most Hawai'i hostels cater to a lively international crowd of backpackers, hikers, surfers, and windsurfers; those seeking intimacy or privacy should seek out a B&B. Hostelling International, a network of more than 4,000 properties in 60 countries, lists two O'ahu member hostels. Membership, which costs $28 per year for adults, allows you to stay in affiliated hostels at member rates. Prices at these two Hostelling International member hostels are about $20 to $64 per night. Other hostels of note in the islands include Camp Slogett in Kōke'e State Park, a lodge, cottage, campground, and hostel owned by the YWCA of Kaua'i; Banana Bungalow Maui Hostel; and Arnott's Lodge and Hiking Adventures in Hilo on the Big

Island. Hostels.com has on online listing of several other hostels on O'ahu, Maui, Kaua'i, and the Big Island.

Information Arnott's Lodge and Hiking Adventures (☎ *808/969–7097* ⊕ *www. arnottslodge.com*). **Banana Bungalow Maui Hostel** (☎ *800/846–7835* ⊕ *www.mauihostel. com*). **Hostelling International—USA** (☎ *301/495–1240* ⊕ *www.hiusa.org*). **Hostels. com** (⊕ *www.hostels.com*). **YWCA of Kauai** (☎ *808/245–5959* ⊕ *www.campingkauai.com*).

HOTELS

All hotels listed have private bath unless otherwise noted.

■ COMMUNICATIONS

INTERNET

If you've brought your laptop with you to the Islands, you should have no problem connecting to the Internet. Most of the major hotels and resorts offer high-speed access in rooms and/or lobbies. You should check with your hotel in advance to confirm that access is wireless; if not, ask whether in-room cables are provided. In some cases there will be an hourly or daily charge billed to your room. If you're staying at a small inn or B&B without Internet access, ask the proprietor for the nearest café or coffee shop with wireless access.

Visitors can also access the Internet at any Hawai'i State Public Library. You can reserve a computer for 60 minutes once a week, via phone or walk-in. You'll need to sign up for a library card, which costs $10 for a three-month period.

Contacts Cybercafes (⊕ *www.cybercafes. com*) lists more than 4,000 Internet cafés worldwide. **Hawai'i State Public Library System** (⊕ *www.librarieshawaii.org*).

■ EATING OUT

Whether it's a romantic candlelit dinner for two along the ocean or a hole-in-the-wall serving traditional Hawaiian fare like *kālua* pig, poi, *lomi* salmon, chicken long rice, and *pipikaula*, you'll find this and more throughout the islands. When it comes to eating, Hawai'i has something for every taste bud and every budget. With chefs using abundant locally grown fruits and vegetables, vegetarians often have many exciting choices for their meals. And because Hawai'i is popular destination for families, restaurants almost always have a kids' menu. When you're booking your accommodations or making a reservation at a hotel dining establishment, ask if they have free or reduced-price meals for children.

MEALS AND MEALTIMES

Food in Hawai'i is a reflection of the state's diverse cultural makeup and tropical location. Fresh seafood, organic fruits and vegetables, free-range poultry and meat, and locally grown products are the hallmarks of Hawai'i regional cuisine. Its preparations are drawn from across the Pacific Rim, including Japan, the Philippines, Korea, and Thailand—and now, "Hawaiian food" is a cuisine in its own right. (Visit any restaurant run by Alan Wong, OnJin Kim, Beverly Gannon, Peter Merriman, Amy Ferguson, Roy Yamaguchi, or D.K. Kodama for proof of that.) Even more exciting, there are dozens of up-and-coming new chefs who are stretching the culinary boundaries by creating innovative fusions for visitors and residents alike.

Breakfast is usually served from 6 or 7 AM to 9:30 or 10 AM. Enjoy tropical fresh fruit and juices; banana, mango, or coconut breads; Kona coffee; and specialties like island-style French toast made with Portuguese sweet bread or *mochi* waffles made with sweet rice flour. ■TIP➔Take note that in many restaurants, if you order a regular coffee, you'll get coffee with milk and sugar.

Lunch typically runs from 11:30 AM to around 1:30 or 2 PM, and will include salads, sandwiches, and lighter fare. The "plate lunch" is a favorite of many local residents, and usually consists of grilled teriyaki chicken, beef, or fish, served with two scoops of white rice and two side salads, with a big ladle of gravy over the meat and rice. The phrase "broke da mouth," often used to describe these plates, refers not only to their size, but also to their tastiness.

Dinner is usually served from 5 to 9 PM and, depending on the restaurant, can be a simple or lavish affair. Stick to the chef specials if you can because they usually represent the best of the season. *Poke* (marinated raw tuna) is a local hallmark and can often be found on *pūpū* menus.

Meals in resort areas are pricey but often excellent. The restaurants we list are the cream of the crop in each price category.

Unless otherwise noted, the restaurants listed in this guide are open daily for lunch and dinner.

PAYING

For guidelines on tipping see Tipping below.

For price-category information, see the Where to Eat and Where to Stay sections in each chapter.

RESERVATIONS AND DRESS

Hawai'i is decidedly casual. Aloha shirts and shorts or long pants for men and island-style dresses or casual resort wear for women are standard attire for evenings in most hotel restaurants and local eateries. T-shirts and shorts will do the trick for breakfast and lunch.

Regardless of where you are, it's a good idea to make a reservation if you can. In some places, it's expected. We only mention reservations specifically when they are essential (there's no other way you'll ever get a table) or when they are not accepted. For popular restaurants, book as far ahead as you can (often 30 days), and reconfirm as soon as you arrive. (Large parties should always call ahead to check the reservations policy.) We mention dress only when men are required to wear a jacket or a jacket and tie.

WINES, BEER, AND SPIRITS

Hawai'i has a new generation of microbreweries, including on-site microbreweries at many restaurants. The drinking age in Hawai'i is 21 years of age, and a photo ID must be presented to purchase alcoholic beverages. Bars are open until 2 AM; venues with a cabaret license can stay open until 4 AM. No matter what you might see in the local parks, drinking alcohol in public parks or on the beaches is illegal. It's also illegal to have open containers of alcohol in motor vehicles.

▌HEALTH

Hawai'i is known as the Health State. The life expectancy here is 79 years, the longest in the nation. Balmy weather makes it easy to remain active year-round, and the low-stress aloha attitude certainly contributes to general well-being. When visiting the Islands, however, there are a few health issues to keep in mind.

The Hawai'i State Department of Health recommends that you drink 16 ounces of water per hour to avoid dehydration when hiking or spending time in the sun. Use sunblock, wear UV-reflective sunglasses, and protect your head with a visor or hat for shade. If you're not acclimated to warm, humid weather you should allow plenty of time for rest stops and refreshments. When visiting freshwater streams, be aware of the tropical disease leptospirosis, which is spread by animal urine and carried into streams and mud. Symptoms include fever, headache, nausea, and red eyes. If left untreated it can cause liver and kidney damage, respiratory failure, internal bleeding, and even death. To avoid this, don't swim or wade in freshwater streams or ponds if you have open sores and don't drink from any freshwater streams or ponds.

On the Islands, fog is a rare occurrence, but there can often be "vog," an airborne haze of gases released from volcanic vents on the Big Island. During certain weather conditions such as "Kona Winds," the vog can settle over the Islands and wreak havoc with respiratory and other health conditions, especially asthma or emphysema. If susceptible, stay indoors and get emergency assistance if needed.

The Islands have their share of bugs and insects that enjoy the tropical climate as much as visitors do. Most are harmless but annoying. When planning to spend time outdoors in hiking areas, wear long-sleeve clothing and pants and use mosquito repellent containing deet. In very damp places you may encounter the dreaded local centipede. On the Islands they usually come in two colors, brown and blue, and they range from the size of a worm to an 8-inch cigar. Their sting is very painful, and the reaction is similar to bee- and wasp-sting reactions. When camping, shake out your sleeping bag before climbing in, and check your shoes in the morning, as the centipedes like cozy places. If planning on hiking or traveling in remote areas, always carry a first-aid kit and appropriate medications for sting reactions.

▌HOURS OF OPERATION

Even people in paradise have to work. Generally local business hours are weekdays 8 to 5. Banks are usually open Monday through Thursday 8:30 to 3 and until 6 on Friday. Some banks have Saturday-morning hours. Grocery and department stores, as well as shopping malls and boutiques, are open seven days a week.

WORD OF MOUTH

Was the service stellar or not up to snuff? Did the food give you shivers of delight or leave you cold? Did the prices and portions make you happy or sad? Rate restaurants and write your own reviews in Travel Ratings or start a discussion about your favorite places in Travel Talk on ⊕www.fodors.com. Your comments might even appear in our books. Yes, you, too, can be a correspondent!

FOR INTERNATIONAL TRAVELERS

CURRENCY

The dollar is the basic unit of U.S. currency. It has 100 cents. Coins are the penny (1¢); the nickel (5¢), dime (10¢), quarter (25¢), half-dollar (50¢), and the very rare golden $1 coin and even rarer silver $1. Bills are denominated $1, $5, $10, $20, $50, and $100, all mostly green and identical in size; designs and background tints vary. You may come across a $2 bill, but the chances are slim.

CUSTOMS

Information U.S. Customs and Border Protection (⊕ www.cbp.gov).

DRIVING

Gas costs in Hawai'i range from $3 to $4 a gallon. Driving in the United States is on the right. Speed limits are posted in miles per hour, between 25 MPH to 55 MPH in the Islands. Watch for lower limits near schools (usually 20 MPH). Honolulu's freeways have special lanes, marked with a diamond, for high-occupancy vehicles (HOV)—cars carrying two people or more. Hawai'i has a strict seat-belt law. Passengers in the front seats must be belted. Children under the age of 3 must be in approved safety seats in the backseat and those aged 4 to 7 must be in a rear booster seat or child restraint such as a lap and shoulder belt. Morning (between 6:30 and 9:30 AM) and afternoon (between 3:30 and 6:30 PM) rush-hour traffic around major cities on most of the Islands can be bad, so use caution. In rural areas, it's not unusual for gas stations to close early. If you see that your tank is getting low, don't take any chances; fill up when you see a station.

If your car breaks down, pull onto the shoulder and wait for help, or have your passengers wait while you walk to an emergency phone. If you have a cell phone with you, call the roadside assistance number on your rental car agreement.

ELECTRICITY

The U.S. standard is AC, 110 volts/60 cycles. Plugs have two flat pins set parallel to each other.

EMBASSIES

Contacts Australia(☎ 202/797-3000 ⊕ www. austemb.org). **Canada** (☎ 202/682-1740 ⊕ www.canadianembassy.org). **United Kingdom** (☎ 202/588-7800 ⊕ www.britainusa. com).

Australia Australian Consulate (✉ 1000 Bishop St., Honolulu ☎ 808/524-5050).

Canada Canadian Consulate (✉ 1000 Bishop St., Honolulu ☎ 808/524-5050).

New Zealand New Zealand Consulate (✉ 900 Richards St., Room 414, Honolulu ☎ 808/543-7900).

United Kingdom British Consulate (✉ 1000 Bishop St., Honolulu ☎ 808/524-5050).

EMERGENCIES

For police, fire, or ambulance, dial 911 (0 in rural areas).

HOLIDAYS

New Year's Day (Jan. 1); Martin Luther King Day (3rd Mon. in Jan.); Presidents' Day (3rd Mon. in Feb.); Memorial Day (last Mon. in May); Independence Day (July 4); Labor Day (1st Mon. in Sept.); Columbus Day (2nd Mon. in Oct.); Thanksgiving Day (4th Thurs. in Nov.); Christmas Eve and Christmas Day (Dec. 24 and 25); and New Year's Eve (Dec. 31).

MAIL

You can buy stamps and aerograms and send letters and parcels in post offices. Stamp-dispensing machines can occasionally be found in airports, bus and train stations, office buildings, drugstores, and convenience stores. U.S. mailboxes are stout, dark blue steel bins; pickup schedules are posted inside the bin (pull down the handle to see them). Parcels weighing more than a pound must be mailed at a post office or at a private mailing center. Within the United States a first-class letter weighing 1 ounce or less costs 42¢; each additional ounce costs 24¢. Postcards cost 27¢. Postcards or 1-ounce airmail letters to most countries cost 94¢; postcards or 1-ounce letters to Canada or Mexico cost 72¢. To receive mail on the road, have it sent c/o General Delivery at your destination's main post office (use the correct five-digit zip code). You must pick up mail in person within 30 days, with a driver's license or passport for identification.

Contacts DHL (☎ 800/225–5345 ⊕ www. dhl.com). **Federal Express** (☎ 800/463–3339 ⊕ www.fedex.com). **Mail Boxes, Etc./The UPS Store** (☎ 800/789–4623 ⊕ www.mbe.com). **United States Postal Service** (⊕ www.usps. com).

PASSPORTS & VISAS

Visitor visas aren't necessary for citizens of Australia, Canada, the United Kingdom, or most citizens of European Union countries coming for tourism and staying for fewer than 90 days. If you require a visa, the cost is $100, and waiting time can be substantial, depending on where you live. Apply for a visa at the U.S. consulate in your place of residence; check the U.S. State Department's special Visa Web site for further information.

Visa Information Destination USA (⊕ www. unitedstatesvisas.gov).

PHONES

Numbers consist of a three-digit area code and a seven-digit local number. The area code for all calls in Hawai'i is 808. For local calls to businesses on the island where you are staying, you only need to dial the seven-digit number (not the 808 area code). If you are calling businesses on other neighboring islands, you will need to use "1-808" followed by the number. Calls to numbers prefixed by "800," "888," "866," and "877" are toll-free and require that you first dial a "1". For calls to numbers prefixed by "900" you must pay—usually dearly. For international calls, dial "011" followed by the country code and the local number. For help, dial "0" and ask for an overseas operator. Most phone books list country codes and U.S. area codes. The country code for Australia is 61, for New Zealand 64, for the United Kingdom 44. Calling Canada is the same as calling within the United States, whose country code, by the way, is 1. For operator assistance, dial "0." For directory assistance, call 555–1212 or occasionally 411 (free at many public phones). You can reverse long-distance charges by calling "collect"; dial "0" instead of "1" before the 10-digit number. Instructions are generally posted on pay phones. Usually you insert coins in a slot (usually 25¢–50¢ for local calls) and wait for a steady tone before dialing. On long-distance calls the operator tells you how much to insert; prepaid phone cards, widely available in various denominations, can be used from any phone. Follow the directions to activate the card (there's usually an access number, then an activation code), then dial your number.

CELL PHONES

The United States has several GSM (Global System for Mobile Communications) networks, so multiband mobiles from most countries (except for Japan) work here. Unfortunately, it's almost impossible to buy a pay-as-you-go mobile SIM card in the U.S.—which allows you to avoid roaming charges—without also buying a phone. That said, cell phones with pay-as-you-go plans are available for well under $100. AT&T, T-Mobile, and Virgin Mobile offer affordable, pay-as-you-go service.

Many self-serve gas stations stay open around-the-clock, with full-service stations usually open from around 7 AM until 9 PM. U.S. post offices are open weekdays 8:30 AM to 4:30 PM and Saturday 8:30 to noon. On O'ahu, the Ala Moana post office branch is the only branch, other than the main Honolulu International Airport facility, that stays open until 4 PM on Saturday.

Most museums generally open their doors between 9 AM and 10 AM and stay open until 5 PM Tuesday through Saturday. Many museums operate with afternoon hours only on Sunday and close on Monday. Visitor-attraction hours vary throughout the state, but most sights are open daily with the exception of major holidays such as Christmas. Check local newspapers upon arrival for attraction hours and schedules if visiting over holiday periods. The local dailies carry a listing of "What's Open/What's Not" for those time periods.

Stores in resort areas sometimes open as early as 8, while shopping-center opening hours open at 9:30 or 10 on weekdays and Saturday, a bit later on Sunday. Bigger malls stay open until 9 PM weekdays and Saturday and close between 5 and 6 PM on Sunday. Boutiques in resort areas may stay open as late as 11.

▮ MONEY

Prices throughout this guide are given for adults. Substantially reduced fees are almost always available for children, students, and senior citizens.

ATMS AND BANKS

Automatic teller machines for easy access to cash are everywhere on the Islands. ATMs can be found in shopping centers, small convenience and grocery stores, and inside hotels and resorts, as well as outside most bank branches. For a directory of locations, call ☎800/424–7787 for the MasterCard/Cirrus/Maestro network or ☎800/843–7587 for the Visa/Plus network.

CREDIT CARDS

Throughout this guide, the following abbreviations are used: **AE**, American Express; **D**, Discover; **DC**, Diners Club; **MC**, MasterCard; and **V**, Visa. It's a good idea to inform your credit-card company before you travel, especially if you're going abroad and don't travel internationally very often. Otherwise, the credit-card company might put a hold on your card owing to unusual activity—not a good thing halfway through your trip. Record all your credit-card numbers—as well as the phone numbers to call if your cards are lost or stolen—in a safe place, so you're prepared should something go wrong. Both MasterCard and Visa have general numbers you can call if your card is lost, but you're better off calling the number of your issuing bank, since MasterCard and Visa usually just transfer you to your bank; your bank's number is usually printed on your card.

Reporting Lost Cards American Express (☎800/992–3404 in U.S. ⊕ www.american express.com). **Diners Club** (☎800/234–6377 in U.S. ⊕ www.dinersclub.com). **Discover** (☎800/347–2683 in U.S. ⊕ www.discover card.com). **MasterCard** (☎800/622–7747 in U.S. ⊕ www.mastercard.com). **Visa** (☎800/847–2911 in U.S. ⊕ www.visa.com).

▮ PACKING

Hawai'i is casual: sandals, bathing suits, and comfortable, informal clothing are the norm. In summer synthetic slacks and shirts, although easy to care for, can be uncomfortably warm. Only a few upscale restaurants require a jacket for dinner. The aloha shirt is accepted dress in Hawai'i for business and most social occasions. Shorts are standard daytime attire, along with a T-shirt or polo shirt. There's no need to buy expensive sandals on the mainland—here you can get flip-flops for a couple of dollars and off-brand sandals for $20. Golfers should remember that many courses have dress codes requiring a collared shirt; call courses you're interested in for details. If you're not prepared, you can pick up appropriate clothing at resort pro shops. If you're visiting in winter or planning to visit a high-altitude area, bring a sweater or light- to medium-weight jacket. A polar fleece pullover is ideal.

One of the most important thing to tuck into your suitcase is sunscreen. Hats and sunglasses offer important sun protection, too. All major hotels in Hawai'i provide beach towels.

You might also want to pack a light raincoat or folding umbrella, as morning rain-showers are not uncommon. And on each of the island's windward coasts, it can be rainy, especially during the winter months. If you're planning on doing any exploration in rain forests or national parks, bring along a sturdy pair of hiking boots.

Contacts Accuweather.com (⊕ *www.accu weather.com*).

▌ SAFETY

Hawai'i is generally a safe tourist destination, but it's still wise to follow common sense safety precautions. Hotel and visitor-center staff can provide information should you decide to head out on your own to more remote areas. Rental cars are magnets for break-ins, so don't leave any valuables in the car, not even in a locked trunk. Avoid poorly lighted areas, beach parks, and isolated areas after dark as a precaution.

When hiking, stay on marked trails, no matter how alluring the temptation might be to stray. Weather conditions can cause landscapes to become muddy, slippery, and tenuous, so staying on marked trails will lessen the possibility of a fall or getting lost.

Ocean safety is of the utmost importance when visiting an island destination. Don't swim alone, and follow the international signage posted at beaches that alerts swimmers to strong currents, man-of-war jellyfish, sharp coral, high surf,

sharks, and dangerous shore breaks. At coastal lookouts along cliff tops, heed the signs indicating that waves can climb over the ledges. Check with lifeguards at each beach for current conditions, and if the red flags are up, indicating swimming and surfing are not allowed, don't go in. Waters that look calm on the surface can harbor strong currents and undertows, and not a few people who were just wading have been dragged out to sea.

Be wary of those hawking "too good to be true" prices on everything from car rentals to attractions. Many of these offers are just a lure to get you in the door for time-share presentations. When handed a flier, read the fine print before you make your decision to participate.

Women traveling alone are generally safe on the Islands, but always follow the safety precautions you would use in any major destination. When booking hotels, request rooms closest to the elevator, and always keep your hotel-room door and balcony doors locked. Stay away from isolated areas after dark; camping and hiking solo are not advised. If you stay out late visiting nightclubs and bars, use caution when exiting nightspots and returning to your lodging.

▌**TIP**➔Distribute your cash, credit cards, IDs, and other valuables between a deep front pocket, an inside jacket or vest pocket, and a hidden money pouch. Don't reach for the money pouch once you're in public.

▌ TAXES

There's a 4.16% state sales tax on all purchases, including food. A hotel room tax of 7.25%, combined with the sales tax, equals an 11.41% rate added onto your hotel bill. A $3-per-day road tax is also assessed on each rental vehicle.

▌ TIME

Hawai'i is on Hawaiian Standard Time, five hours behind New York, two hours behind Los Angeles, and 10 hours behind London.

When the U.S. mainland is on daylight saving time, Hawai'i is not, so add an extra hour of time difference between the Islands and U.S. mainland destinations. You may also find that things generally move more slowly here. That has nothing to do with your watch—it's just the laid-back way called Hawaiian time.

Time Zones Timeanddate.com (⊕ *www.time anddate.com/worldclock*).

TIPPING GUIDELINES FOR HAWAI'I	
Bartender	$1 to $5 per round of drinks, depending on the number of drinks
Bellhop	$1 to $5 per bag, depending on the level of the hotel and whether you have bulky items like golf clubs, surfboards, etc.
Hotel Concierge	$5 or more, depending on the service
Hotel Doorman	$1 to $5 if s/he helps you get a cab or helps with bags, golf clubs, etc.
Hotel Maid	$2 to $5 a day, depending on the level of the hotel (either daily or at the end of your stay, in cash)
Hotel Room-Service Waiter	$1 to $2 per delivery, even if a service charge has been added
Porter/Skycap at Airport	$1 to $3 per bag
Spa Personnel	15% to 20% of the cost of your service
Taxi Driver	15% to 20%, but round up the fare to the next dollar amount
Tour Guide	10% of the cost of the tour
Valet Parking Attendant	$2 to $5, each time your car is brought to you
Waiter	15% to 20%, with 20% being the norm at high-end restaurants; nothing additional if a service charge is added to the bill

▌TIPPING

As this is a major vacation destination and many of the people who work in the service industry rely on tips to supplement their wages, tipping is not only common, but expected.

▌TOURS

Globus has seven Hawai'i itineraries ranging from 7 to 13 days, including an escorted cruise on Norwegian Cruise Lines' *Pride of America*. Perillo Tours offers a 7-day two-islander tour to O'ahu and Maui and a 10-day three-islander tour to O'ahu, Maui and Kaua'i. Tauck Travel and Trafalgar offer several land-based Hawai'i itineraries with plenty of free time to explore the islands. Tauck offers 7- and 11-night multi-island tours, including a "Magical Hawai'i" trip for families. Trafalgar has 7-, 9-, 10-, and 12-night multi-island tours. If you want to stay in the islands longer, YMT Vacations has a 15-day, four-island (O'ahu, Maui, Kaua'i, and the Big Island) tour.

EscortedHawaiiTours.com, owned and operated by Atlas Cruises & Tours, sells more than a dozen Hawai'i trips ranging from 7 to 12 nights, operated by various guided tour companies including Globus, Tauck, and Trafalgar.

Recommended Companies Atlas Cruises & Tours (☎ *800/942–3301* ⊕ *www.Escorted HawaiiTours.com*). **Globus** (☎ *866/755–8581* ⊕ *www.globusjourneys.com*). **Perillo Tours** (☎ *800/431–1515* ⊕ *www.perillotours.com*). **Tauck Travel** (☎ *800/788–7885* ⊕ *www.tauck. com*). **Trafalgar** (☎ *866/544–4434* ⊕ *www. trafalgar.com*). **YMT Vacations** (☎ *800/922– 9000* ⊕ *www.ymtvacations.com*).

SPECIAL-INTEREST TOURS
BIRD-WATCHING

There are more than 150 species of birds that live in the Hawaiian Islands. Field Guides has a three-island (O'ahu, Kaua'i, and the Big Island), 11-day guided bird-watching trip that focuses on endemic land birds and specialty seabirds. The trip is held in the spring when bird activity is at its peak. The trip costs about $4,375 per person and includes accommodations, meals, ground transportation, interisland air, an eight-hour pelagic boat trip, and guided bird-watching excursions. Travelers must make their own travel arrangements to and from their gateway city.

Victor Emanuel Nature Tours offers two eight-night birding trips to the islands: *Kaua'i and Hawai'i in March* and *Fall Hawai'i* to O'ahu, Kaua'i, and the Big Island. The guide for both tours is Bob Sundstrom, a skilled birder with a special interest in bird song, who has been leading birding tours in Hawai'i and other destinations since 1989. The tour costs about $4,000 per person, including accommodations, meals, interisland air, ground transportation, and guided excursions. Travelers must purchase their own tickets to and from their gateway city.

Contacts Field Guides (☎ 800/728–4953 ⊕ www.fieldguides.com). **Victor Emanuel Nature Tours** (☎ 800/328–8368 ⊕ www. ventbird.com).

CULTURE
Elderhostel offers several guided Hawai'i tours for older adults that provide fascinating in-depth looks into the culture, history, and beauty of the Islands. The nonprofit educational travel organization has been leading all-inclusive learning adventures around the world since 1975. For all Elderhostel programs, travelers must purchase their own airfare if coming from outside of Hawai'i. Below are a few typical trips; the Web site shows more options.

Presented in association with Volcano Arts Center, Moloka'i Museum & Cultural Center, and Hawai'i Pacific University, *Islands of Life in the Pacific* is a 15-night, five-island, Elderhostel tour. Travelers start their tour on the Big Island where they explore Hawai'i Volcanoes National Park, Pu'uhonua O Hōnaunau, and Kaloko-Honokōhau National Historic Park. While on Maui, visitors will explore 'Īao Valley and Hana, hike into the crater of Haleakala, discover the charms of upcountry Maui and the towns of Olinda, Makawao, and Pā'ia, and enjoy lectures on the geology, history, and culture of the island. Following a ferry ride to Moloka'i, participants will get a tour of the Moloka'i Museum and Sugar Mill and journey into the awe-inspiring Kalaupapa National Historic Park. They'll enjoy two nights on Kaua'i with visits to Waimea Canyon and Kōke'e State Park; Kīlauea Point National Wildlife Refuge and Kīlauea Lighthouse, where thousands of endangered birds make their home; and the charming town of Hanalei, the setting for the movie *South Pacific*. The trip ends on O'ahu with visits to the USS *Arizona* and the National Memorial Cemetery of the Pacific at Punchbowl Crater. Prices for the tour start at around $4,200 per person and include accommodations, meals, ground transportation, interisland air, and ferry transportation between the islands and all activities.

Elderhostel offers a number of other multi-island tours, including: *Tall Ship Sail Training: Sailing the Hawaiian Islands,* an six-night sailing adventure through the Hawaiian Islands aboard a 96-foot three-masted schooner; the 11-night *Paradise Adventure From Mountains To Sea* tour, whose participants will do everything from river kayaking and hiking to surfing; the nine-night *Oahu's North Shore and Kona: Marine Studies and Snorkeling* tour, on which travelers can immerse themselves in Hawai'i's fascinating marine life; and the Oahu and Big Island *Hawaiian Water Adventure: An Intergenerational Marine Exploration* tour for children ages 10 to 13 accompanied by an adult.

Contact Elderhostel (☎ 800/454–5768 ⊕ www.elderhostel.org).

HIKING
Hawaii Three Island Hiker is a seven-night hiking tour to Kaua'i, the Big Island, and Maui offered by The World Outdoors. Included in the price of about

$3,700 per person are accommodations, meals, interisland air between the three islands, shuttle transportation, support vehicle, professional guides, T-shirt, and water bottle. The trip is rated moderately easy to moderate. The World Outdoors has been organizing and leading adventure trips around the world for more than 20 years.

Contacts The World Outdoors
(☎ 800/488–8483 ⊕ www.theworldoutdoors. com).

▌ VISITOR INFORMATION

Before you go, contact the Hawai'i Visitors & Convention Bureau (HVCB), ⊕ www.gohawaii.com, for general information on each island. You can request via phone or online, "Islands of Aloha," a free visitors guide with information on accommodations, transportation, sports and activities, dining, arts and entertainment, and culture. The HVCB Web site has a calendar section that allows you to see what local events are in place during the time of your stay.

Contact Hawai'i Visitors & Convention Bureau (☎ 808/923–1811, 800/464–2924 for brochures ⊕ www.gohawaii.com).

You might also want to check out ⊕ www. ehawaii.gov, the state's official Web site, for information on camping, fishing licenses and other visitor services. Each island has its own Web site as well: ⊕ www.bigisland. org (Big Island Visitors Bureau); ⊕ www. visitmaui.com (Maui County Visitors Bureau); ⊕ www.visit-oahu.com (O'ahu Visitors Bureau); ⊕ www.kauaidiscovery.

com (Kaua'i Visitors Bureau); ⊕ www.visit lanai.net (Lāna'i Visitors Bureau); and ⊕ www.molokai-hawaii.com (Moloka'i Visitors Association).

Visit ⊕ www.honoluluweekly.com for a weekly guide to the arts, entertainment, and dining in Honolulu; ⊕ www.hono lulu.gov, from the City and County of Honolulu with calendar of events for Blaisdell arena and concert hall and the Royal Hawaiian Band; ⊕ www.hawaii museums.org, the Web site from the Hawai'i Museums Association. Be sure to check out ⊕ www.nps.gov for information on the eight parks managed by the National Park Service.

The Hawai'i Ecotourism Site, ⊕ www. alternative-hawaii.com, provides listings of everything from eco-culture events on the islands to Hawai'i Heritage tour guides, and the Hawai'i Ecotourism Association, ⊕ www.hawaiiecotourism. org, has an online directory of more than 100 member companies offering tours and activities. The Hawai'i Department of Land and Natural Resources, ⊕ www. hawaii.gov/dlnr/, has information on hiking, fishing and camping permits and licenses; on-line brochures on hiking safety and mountain and ocean preservation; as well as details on volunteer programs.

INDEX

Photo Credits

1-2, Douglas Peebles/eStock Photo. 5, J.D. Heaton/Age fotostock. Chapter 1: Experience Hawaii: 8-9, SuperStock/Age fotostock. 10, J.D. Heaton/Picture Finders/Age fotostock. 11 (left), SuperStock/Age fotostock. 11 (right), Big Island Visitors Bureau. 12 (left), Danita Delimont/Alamy. 12 (top center), Oahu Visitors Bureau. 12 (bottom center), David Schrichre/Photo Resource Hawaii. 12 (top right), Andre Nantel/Shutterstock. 12 (bottom right), Deborah Davis/Alamy. 13 (top left), Stephen Frink Collection/Alamy. 13 (top center), Photo Resource Hawaii/Alamy. 13 (bottom center), Lee Foster/Alamy. 13 (right), Robert Coello/Kauai Visitors Bureau. 14, Molokai Ranch. 15, Douglas Peebles/Age fotostock. 16 SuperStock/Age fotostock. 17 (left), Walter Bibikow/viestiphoto.com. 17 (right), Photodisc. 20, Walter Bibikow/viestiphoto.com. 21 (left), Corbis. 21 (right), Walter Bibikow/viestiphoto.com. 23, Oahu Visitors Bureau. 24, Luca Tettoni/ viestiphoto.com. 27, Scott West/viestiphoto.com. 27, SuperStock/Age fotostock. Chapter 2: Oahu: 29, Polynesian Cultural Center. 30 (top), Ken Ross/www.viestiphoto.com. 30 (bottom left), Michael S. Nolan/Age fotostock. 30 (bottom right), SuperStock/Age fotostock. 31, Oahu Visitors Bureau. 41, J.D. Heaton/ Picture Finders/Age fotostock. 42, Oahu Visitors Bureau. 43 (left and center), Walter Bibikow/viestiphoto.com. 43 (right), Douglas Peebles/Age fotostock. 44, Stuart Westmorland/Age fotostock. 45 (left), The Royal Hawaiian. 45 (center), Atlantide S.N.C./Age fotostock. 45 (right), Liane Cary/Age fotostock. 55, U.S. National Archives. 57 (top), Corbis. 57 (bottom), NPS/USS Arizona Memorial Photo Collection. 58, Army Signal Corps Collection in the U.S. National Archives. 58 (inset), USS Missouri Memorial Association. 59, USS Bowfin Submarine Museum & Park. 67-69, ASP Tostee. 70, Carol Cunningham/cunninghamphotos.com. 81, SuperStock/Age fotostock. 87, Photo Resource Hawaii/Alamy. 104, Photo Resource Hawaii/Alamy. 117, Ann Cecil/Photo Resource Hawaii/Alamy. 148 (top and bottom), Halekulani. 157 (top and bottom), The Kahala. 160 (top and bottom), Turtle Bay Resort. Chapter 3: Maui: 165, Michael S. Nolan/Age fotostock. 166 (top), Chris Hammond/www.viestiphoto.com. 166 (bottom), Walter Bibikow/www.viestiphoto.com. 167 (top), Walter Bibikow/www.viestiphoto.com. 167 (bottom), Douglas Peebles/Age fotostock.